enible Home

Published by
Starcott Media Services
6906 Royalgreen Drive
Cincinnati, Ohio 45244-4004

Printed in the United States of America
Second Edition
Copyright © 1996, 1997 by James T. Dulley
All rights reserved
9, 8, 7, 6, 5, 4, 3, 2

ISBN 0-9625583-8-9

We recommend care and adherence to standard construction safety procedures. Wear adequate protective clothing and safety gear (approved safety
eyeglasses, work gloves, breathing filter mask) when working with power
and hand tools, and with building and insulation materials. If you have
questions about proper safety procedures or protective clothing to wear,
contact your local health department, Occupational Safety and Health
Administration or Environmental Protection Agency. Neither the author
nor the publisher takes responsibility for accidents that may occur during the
building or use of any of the projects or products described in this book.

Introduction

Today, people are interested in lowering their housing costs and are concerned about conserving the earth's precious resources to protect the environment for future generations. By improving your home's efficiency, making wise informed purchases, and doing some repair and project yourself, you can save a substantial amount of money each year. Using much of the information in this book, I have cut my utility bills in my own home by more than 70% from the previous owner's utility bills while improving my comfort. I do more than 90% of the repair and home improvement projects myself.

My syndicated column, **_enible Home_**, appears each week in more than 350 newspapers from coast to coast. Each column offers a different Update Bulletin which provides more comprehensive information on the weekly topic.

I have selected 81 Update Bulletins and the related newspaper columns which include many do-it-yourself projects and information on new money-saving and efficient products. The actual savings you realize from making any of these improvements or by installing various products depend on the efficiency of your current systems and your local utility rates. Always do a payback analysis before investing your time and money in a project or a product.

Before attempting any of the do-it-yourself projects, read the Update Bulletin completely. Always wear adequate protective clothing and glasses. When these projects effect any mechanical systems in your house (furnace, air conditioner, water heater, etc.), contact a contractor or technician familiar with your specific model. Some models are unique and require specific clearances and adjustments when making improvements. Be sure to check your local building and fire codes.

Proper handling of materials is essential on any home improvement project. Some materials, such as asbestos or fiberglass, require special precautions. If you think a material contains asbestos, **do not** handle it. Contact a contractor experienced with handling asbestos. Do not dust, sweep, or vacuum particles suspected of containing asbestos. This will disturb tiny asbestos fibers and may make them airborne. The fibers are so small that they cannot be seen and can pass through normal vacuum cleaner filters and get back into the air. The dust should be removed by wet-mopping procedures or by trained asbestos contractors using specially-designed "HEPA" vacuum cleaners.

Some possible asbestos-containing materials include cement pipes, wallboard and siding; asphalt and vinyl floor tile; ceiling tiles and lay-in panels; all types of insulation; and roofing felt and shingles. Special precautions should be taken during removal of the exposed or damaged asbestos-containing material. Do not disturb any material you think may contain asbestos unless you have to. Removal of the material is usually the last alternative.

This book is divided into seven general topic areas with many related Update Bulletins and columns in each. The chapter topic refers to the subject of the first question of each column and its corresponding Update Bulletin.

Model numbers provided are the most current as of this printing. Actual model numbers may vary with specific colors or styles. If any of the model numbers have changed, a retail dealer or the manufacturer can provide you with the new model number based on the old one shown.

If you would like to receive a _free_ current topics listing of the 200 Update Bulletins available (handling fee of $2.00 per bulletin ordered), write to Starcott Media Services at the address on the preceding page. Please include a self-addressed stamped envelope with your request for the listing.

Table of Contents

Chapter   **Pages**

I. Heating & Cooling · 1 - 60

superefficient gas furnaces, ductless (mini-split) air conditioners, central air conditioners, electric radiant heat, high-efficiency gas and electric heat pumps, warm water floor radiant heating systems, zone heat, window/room air conditioners, high-efficiency gas and oil boilers, computerized smart thermostats, direct-vent gas space heaters, Finnish and soapstone fireplaces, high-efficiency gas fireplaces, air conditioner covers, air conditioner maintenance

II. Indoor Environment · 61 - 100

whole-house air cleaners, room air cleaners, ceiling paddle fans, whole-house ventilation fans, water testing and purifier/filters, water softeners and scale reducers, heat recovery ventilators, quiet bath fans, room humidifiers, do-it-yourself formaldehyde gas tests

III. Windows & Doors · 101 - 152

room humidifiers, high-efficiency vinyl replacement windows, interior plastic storm windows, do-it-yourself storm windows, wood windows, fiberglass and wood doors, window film/sunblock screen/see-thru shade, do-it-yourself roman shades, do-it-yourself window shutter/bookcase, rolling window shutters, glass block windows, retractable window awnings

IV. Water Heating · 153 - 176

tankless/instantaneous water heaters, heat pump water heaters, gas water heaters, electric water heaters, low-flow showerhead, kits, faucet and toilet tank water savers, improvements to water heaters, troubleshooting guide for water heaters

V. Appliances · 177 - 224

allergy-safe vacuum cleaners, central vacuum cleaners, clothes washers, clothes dryers, clothes dryer vents, whole-house surge suppressors, electric ranges, professional gas ranges, microwave ovens, high-efficiency refrigerator/freezers, dishwashers, small appliances/bread makers

VI. Construction · 225 - 272

ceramic-filled paints, solar desiccant dehumidifier, reflective attic foils, ridge vents, stress-skin panel houses, foam/concrete blocks and panels, superinsulation construction, roofing materials, siding materials, soundproof wall designs, non-settling wall insulation, door thresholds, exterior door vestibules, wind and sun shelter for patio door

VII. Miscellaneous · 273 - 320

compact fluorescent bulbs and kits, outdoor security lighting, low voltage outdoor lights, electric/rechargeable lawn mowers, water saving toilet devices, dams and flappers, home security systems, gas, electric and wood pellet barbecue grills, ozonator pool purifiers, smart house automated systems, whirlpools and soft tubs, automatic drip lawn watering systems, automobile natural gas conversions, pet doors

Q: Does it make economic sense to replace my noisy old gas furnace (it still works) with a new "super" model? Will a super furnace reduce chilly drafts and clean the air better for my allergies?

A: The answer to all your questions is "Yes". Older gas furnaces operate at about 60 percent efficiency. Installing a new super furnace at 95 percent efficiency can cut the typical family's utility bills by up to $400 per year.

Several new models use "smart" ECM blower motors. If a carpet should slide over a register, the motor senses greater resistance and speeds up to compensate. It checks every five seconds. Also, efficient ECM motors use two-thirds less electricity than standard motors, for an additional $100 savings per year.

Central air conditioners operate more efficiently with a new super furnace blower and comfort is improved. Some new furnaces are designed smaller to provide extra space for larger, high efficiency air conditioner coils. Most of the design changes for the new furnace models target improvements in comfort and indoor air quality - two-stage (low/high) output burners, variable-speed blowers, more sophisticated temperature controls, quieter operation, and cleaner indoor air.

The highest efficiency super furnaces use a two-stage burner. On low fire, the burner uses about 40 percent less gas than on high fire. The blower also runs slower and much quieter on low fire. These typically cost about $400 more than a single-stage burner model.

Other than on the coldest days, the furnace runs on low fire. At this lower heat output, it stays on longer. This maintains steady room temperatures (only 1 degree swing) and eliminates chilly drafts from a high blower speed.

For someone with allergies, this is a plus. By keeping the furnace running longer, the central air cleaner has more time to remove allergens from the air. The gentle air circulation also reduces stuffiness and dryness.

Super furnaces use condensing heat exchangers. Sealed combustion designs use outdoor combustion air to minimize drafts and the possibility of carbon monoxide poisoning. By capturing nearly all the heat, the cool flue gases are blown outdoors (induced vent fan) through a small plastic pipe.

Since no chimney is needed, these furnaces are ideal for converting from costly electric heat to gas. Even if natural gas is not available, heating with bottled gas may be less expensive than using electric heat. Bottled gas conversion kits are available for all super furnaces.

Q: My daughter takes long showers and often forgets to switch off the bathroom vent fan when she is finished. How long should she let the fan run and does it draw out much air?

A: It is important to run the vent fan to remove excess moisture, but running it too long wastes electricity and heated air. A typical vent fan will exhaust all the air in a bathroom in about five minutes. Running it for about five minutes after you are finished showering is usually adequate.

If your daughter continues to leave it on, install a timer switch available at most home centers). Adjust it to shut the fan off after ten minutes. This allows five minutes while showering and five minutes for venting.

- Primary heat exchanger
- Low/high two-stage burners
- Secondary condensing heat exchanger
- Efficient vent fan motor
- Flue exhaust through small plastic pipe
- Variable-speed blower motor

The most efficient furnaces use two-stage burners and variable-speed blowers. The efficiency ratings only take into account the gas usage. All of the furnaces listed with *"variable-speed"* blowers use ECM motors. These motors use only $1/3$ as much electricity as standard motors, for an additional savings. Future efficiency ratings of furnaces will probably take the electricity usage into account too.

The effective efficiency of two-stage low/high output burners is also higher than the ratings indicate. Since they operate on low output the majority of the time, room temperatures stay very constant. This allows you to set your furnace thermostat a little lower without sacrificing comfort. This provides another 3% to 5% savings. Models that use *"sealed combustion air"* are more efficient. These draw the combustion air from outdoors. The gas burns in a sealed chamber which is totally isolated from your house air. These minimize drafts inside your house and insure adequate combustion air. Where *"combustion air"* is not listed, the furnaces draw the air from indoors. Replacing your old furnace with a sealed combustion model requires an extra air inlet pipe to be installed.

Annual Savings from Installing a New Higher Efficiency Furnace							
Furnace Efficiency	Approximate Annual Operating Cost						
60%	$400	$500	$600	$700	$800	$900	$1,000
65%	$365	$460	$550	$640	$735	$825	$915
70%	$340	$425	$510	$595	$675	$760	$845
75%	$315	$395	$470	$550	$630	$710	$785
80%	$295	$365	$440	$515	$585	$660	$735
85%	$275	$345	$410	$485	$550	$620	$685
90%	$255	$320	$385	$450	$515	$580	$640
95%	$240	$305	$365	$425	$485	$545	$605

To use this chart: Estimate the approx. efficiency of your current furnace. If it is more than 10 years old, the efficiency is likely to be about 60%. Then locate your current annual operating costs (use your natural gas bills less water heating and cooking). Use this chart to estimate how much you can save with a more efficient furnace.

Example: If your current furnace is 60% AFUE, and your annual operating cost is $700, the cost to operate a new 90% AFUE furnace will be about $450, an annual savings of about $250.

Manufacturers of Super-Efficient Gas Furnaces

AMANA REFRIGERATION, Amana, IA 52204 - (800) 843-0304 (319) 622-5511

model - "Air Command 95"   efficiency - 95.0%
capacities - 6 models: 45,000 to 150,000 Btuh   dimensions - 48 in. high x 10.5 to 18.5 in. x 28 in.
configurations - Upflow
burner - Single-stage   blower - Single-speed
warranty - Heat exchanger: 25-year warranty, coil: 20-year warranty, parts: 2-year limited warranty

AMERICAN STANDARD, 1 Centennial Plaza, Piscataway, NJ 08855 - (800) 821-7700 (908) 980-3000

model - "The Freedom 90"   efficiency - 91.0% to 92.0%
capacities - 11 models: 38,000 to 111,000 Btuh   dimensions - 40 in. high x 17.5 to 24.5 in. x 28 in.
configurations - Upflow, downflow, left and right side horizontal
burner - Single-stage   blower - Single- or variable-speed
combustion air - Sealed on single-speed blower model, not on variable-speed model
warranty - Limited lifetime

ARCOAIRE/COMFORTMAKER, P.O.Box 3005, Lavergne, TN 37086 - (800) 547-331 (615) 793-0450

model - "Enviro Plus 90"   efficiency - 90.0% to 92.0%
capacities - 8 models: 45,000 to 112,625 Btuh   dimensions - 48 in. high x 19.1 to 26.3 in. x 28.5 in.
configurations - Upflow
burner - Single-stage   blower - Single-speed
warranty - Limited lifetime parts-only on heat exchanger to original owner, other parts 5-year

ARMSTRONG/JOHNSON AIREASE, 421 Monroe St., Bellevue, OH 44811 - (419) 483-4840

model - "Ultra SX 90"

efficiency - 90.0%

capacities - 14 models: 45,000 to 112,000 Btuh

dimensions - 46 in. high x 17.5 to 26.5 in. x 28.7 in.

configurations - Upflow and counterflow

burner - Single-stage

blower - Single-speed

warranty - Limited lifetime on primary and secondary heat exchangers to original owner

BARD MANUFACTURING CO., P.O.Box 607, Bryan, OH 43506 - (419) 636-1194

model - "The Eternity DCH, DCC & DCL"

efficiency - 90.0% to 92.0%

capacities - 6 models: 36,000 to 115,000 Btuh

dimensions - 52 in. high x 19 to 26 in. x 29.2 in.(DCH & DCC); 35.5 in. high x 19 to 26 in. x 48.5 in. (DCL)

configurations - Upflow, counterflow and low-boy configurations

burner - Single-stage

blower - Single-speed

combustion air - Sealed

warranty - Limited lifetime on heat exchangers, 5-year limited all other parts

BRYANT, DAY & NIGHT, PAYNE, P.O. Box 70, Indianapolis, IN 46206 - (800) 468-7253 (317) 243-0851

model - "Plus 90i"

efficiency - Up to 96.6%

capacities - 4 models: 40,000 to 100,000 Btuh

dimensions - 40 in. high x 17.5 to 24.5 in. x 28 in.

configurations - Upflow, downflow, left and right side horizontal

burner - Two-stage

blower - Variable-speed

combustion air - Sealed

warranty - Limited lifetime on heat exchanger, 3-year limited parts ignitor, 5-year limited on other parts

CARRIER CORPORATION, P.O. Box 4808, Syracuse, NY 13221 - (800) 227-7437 (315) 432-6000

model - "Weathermaker Infinity"

efficiency - Up to 96.6%

capacities - 4 models: 40,000 to 100,000 Btuh

dimensions - 40 in. high x 17.5 to 24.5 in. x 28 in.

configurations - Upflow, downflow, left and right side horizontal

burner - Two-stage

blower - Variable-speed

combustion air - Sealed

warranty - Limited lifetime on heat exchangers, 5-year limited on motors and microprocessor

CENTURY/COMFORT-AIRE/HEAT CONTROLLER, PO Box 1089, Jackson, MI 49204 - (517) 787-2100

model - "Unicell 90"

efficiency - 92.0%

capacities - 12 models: 45,000 to 120,000 Btuh

dimensions - 46 in. high x 21 to 24 in. x 28.7 in.

configurations - Upflow and downflow

burner - Single-stage

blower - Single-speed

warranty - Limited lifetime

COLEMAN EVCON, P.O. Box 19014, Wichita, KS 67204 - (800) 426-5362 (316) 261-3211

model - "T.H.E. Gas Furnace"

efficiency - 90.0% to 91.5%

capacities - 5 models: 41,000 to 84,000 Btuh

dimensions - 46 in. high x 16.8 to 20 in. x 28 in.

configurations - Upflow

burner - Single-stage

blower - Single-speed

combustion air - Sealed

warranty - Limited lifetime

CONSOLIDATED INDUSTRIES CORP., PO Box 7800, Lafayette, IN 47903 - (317) 477-9500

model - "Quatro QF90"

efficiency - 90.0%

capacities - 10 models: 45,000 to 95,000 Btuh

dimensions - 46 in. high x 16.8 to 20 in. x 28.7 in.

configurations - Upflow, downflow, left and right side horizontal

burner - Single-stage

blower - Single-speed

combustion air - Sealed

warranty - Limited lifetime

THE DUCANE COMPANY, 800 Dutch Square Blvd., Columbia, SC 29210 - (803) 798-1600

model - "FPA Series"

efficiency - 94.0%

capacities - 4 models: 50,000 to 125,000 Btuh

dimensions - n/a

configurations - Horizontal configuration

burner - Single-stage

blower - Single-speed

combustion air - Sealed

warranty - Heat exchanger: 25-year warranty, parts: 1-year limited

GOODMAN MFG. CORP., 1501 Seamist, Houston, TX 77008 - (713) 861-2500

model - "GMN Series"
capacities - 4 models: 54,000 to 108,000 Btuh
configurations - Upflow and downflow
burner - Single-stage
warranty - Limited lifetime on heat exchanger, 5-year limited on parts

efficiency - 92.0%
dimensions - 46 in. high x 14 to 24.5 in. x 28 in.
blower - Single-speed   combustion air - Sealed

HEIL/TEMPSTAR, P.O.Box 3005, Lavergne, TN 37086 - (615) 793-0450

model - "DC90 Gas Furnace"
capacities - 4 models: 50,000 to 100,000 Btuh
configurations - Upflow and downflow
burner - Single-stage
warranty - Limited lifetime on heat exchanger, extended 5-year parts/labor warranty

efficiency - 90.0% to 92.0%
dimensions - 48 in. high x 19.2 to 26.7 in. x 28.5 in.
blower - Two-speed   combustion air - Sealed

LENNOX INDUSTRIES, P.O. Box 799900, Dallas, TX 75379 - (214) 497-5000

model - "Pulse 21"
capacities - 4 models: 55,000 to 95,000 Btuh
configurations - Upflow, downflow, left and right side horizontal
burner - Two-stage, pulse combustion
warranty - Limited lifetime on main heat exchanger and condenser coil, 5-year limited on electronics

efficiency - 94.5% to 96.2%
dimensions - 49 to 54.2 in. high x 21.2 to 26.5 in. x 26.1 in.
blower - Variable-speed   combustion air - Sealed

LUXAIRE/FRASER-JOHNSTON/YORK, P.O. Box 1592, York, PA 17405 - (717) 771-7890

model - "Luxaire" / "Stellar Plus Seriers"
capacities - 12 models: 38,000 to 133,000 Btuh
configurations - Upflow and downflow
burner - Single-stage
warranty - Limited lifetime on heat exchanger, 5-year limited on parts

efficiency - 92.6%
dimensions - 52 in. high x 12.2 to 26.2 in. x 28 in.
blower - Single-speed   combustion air - Sealed

NORDYNE, A NORTEK CO., 1801 Park 270 Dr., St. Louis, MO 63146 - (314) 878-6200

model - "Miller G3RC"
capacities - 5 models: 36,000 to 109,000 Btuh
configurations - Upflow
burner - Single-stage
warranty - Lifetime on primary heat exchanger, 6-year on parts

efficiency - 90.0%
dimensions - 45.7 in. high x 14.2 to 22.5 in. x 28 in.
blower - Single-speed   combustion air - Sealed

RHEEM/RUUD, P.O. Box 17010, Fort Smith, AR 72903 - (800) 848-7883 (501) 646-4311

model - "90 Plus"
capacities - 12 models: 45,000 to 120,000 Btuh
configurations - Upflow and downflow
burner - Single-stage
warranty - Limited lifetime, 5-year on controls

efficiency - 92.0+%
dimensions - 34 in. high x 17.5 to 24.5 in. x 28.7 in.
blower - Single-speed

THERMO PRODUCTS, PO Box 217, N. Judson, IN 46366 - (219) 896-2133

model - "Thermo Pride Lowboy"
capacities - 4 models: 50,400 to 125,000 Btuh
configurations - Upflow
burner - Single-stage
warranty - Limited lifetime to original owner, 5-year on parts

efficiency - 90.0% to 96.0%
dimensions - 38 to 46.5 in. high x 23 to 25 in. x 48 to 54.5 in.
blower - Single-speed   combustion air - Sealed

THE TRANE COMPANY, 6200 Troup Hwy., Tyler, TX 75711 - (903) 581-3568

model - "XV 90"
capacities - 3 models: 80,000 to 120,000 Btuh
configurations - Upflow, downflow, left and right side horizontal
burner - Two-stage
warranty - Limited lifetime

efficiency - 91.0% to 92.0%
dimensions - 48.7 to 53 in. high x 18 to 24 in. x 31 in.
blower - Variable-speed   combustion air - Sealed

Q: I want to add air-conditioning, but I cannot afford a central air system. I don't want noisy room air conditioners either. How efficient are the new quiet ductless mini-split models?

A: New ductless air conditioners are efficient and extremely quiet. These air conditioners are ideal for any home, especially ones without air ducts (hot water or electric baseboard heat) or for a room addition. Not having to install ducts lowers the total cost. Heat pump models are available too.

A mini-split ductless system is somewhat like a central air ducted system because the compressor is outdoors. Small quiet cooling blower units (only 8 inches deep) are mounted on the walls or ceilings in one to three rooms. Often, three indoor blower units are adequate to cool an entire house.

The chilled refrigerant from the single outdoor compressor flows through small tubing to the indoor units. Some models allow you to locate the indoor units up to 100 feet from the outdoor compressor.

To install the indoor unit, you only have to cut a 3-inch diameter hole in an outside wall. Refrigerant tubing and electric power come from the outdoor compressor unit, so you do not have to run wiring indoors.

Even if your house has a ducted hot-air furnace, a ductless cooling system has advantages over central air - zone cooling, hand-held remote control, cool air outlet high on wall, and cleaner air for people with allergies.

Zone cooling can lower your electric bills. With a ductless system, you can easily keep your higher-activity areas (workroom, play room, etc.) cooler than other rooms. Built-in computerized clock thermostats let you automatically raise and lower the temperature in each area.

Many ductless systems have hand-held remote controls (like a TV remote) to adjust the temperature, blower speeds, humidity control, louver directions, etc. from your easy chair or bed. There is also a

control keypad on the wall right beneath it.

Since the small indoor blowers are mounted high on a wall or a ceiling, the cool air naturally circulates evenly throughout your rooms. This reduces isolated cold spots. Some models also have a special low-humidity mode.

If you have allergies and want to keep your bedroom air allergen free, a ductless system allows you to isolate that room while keeping it cool. There is also a built-in blower filter to further clean the air.

Q: I know that I should close the damper in my fireplace chimney in the winter, but is it necessary to close it in the summer too? Since hot air rises, the hot outdoor air should not come down.

A: If you air-condition your home, you should close the fireplace chimney damper. Even though it is cooler indoors, the sun shining on the chimney makes it warm. This creates an upward draft and draws out cooled air.

If you do not air-condition and you rely on ventilation, leave the chimney damper open in the summer. A masonry chimney stays warm late into the evening. The natural draft helps draw air through your windows on a still day.

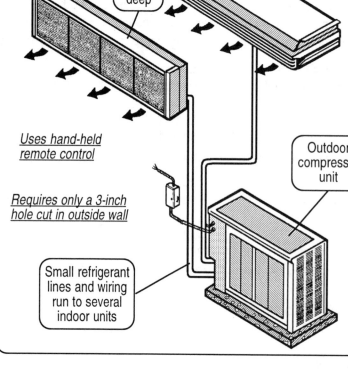

Wall-mounted indoor blower

Only 8" deep

Ceiling-mounted indoor blower

Uses hand-held remote control

Requires only a 3-inch hole cut in outside wall

Outdoor compressor unit

Small refrigerant lines and wiring run to several indoor units

The following pages list manufacturers of the most efficient ductless units along with specific information about each model. *"Model"* is usually a series of similar units of various sizes. *"Output"* refers to the cooling output range for a particular model. *"SEER"* is the seasonal **cooling** efficiency for the system. Where there are heat pump models, the output still refers to cooling. The actual heating output can vary slightly. *"HSPF"* refers to the **heating** efficiency. A higher HSPF and SEER indicate higher efficiency. Have a heating contractor determine the maximum heating and cooling needs of your home. A scroll compressor, in the outdoor unit, is especially quiet.

_ _

Manufacturers of Ductless Mini-Split Systems

BURNHAM CORP., PO Box 3079, Lancaster, PA 17604 - (717) 397-4701

COOLING MODELS

model - "B" series - wired wall mtd.	output - 8,700 to 27,600 Btuh	SEER - 9.0 to 11.2
model - "RAS" series - wireless wall mtd.	output - 8,700 to 17,200 Btuh	SEER - 10.2 to 11.3
model - "BCM" series - ceiling mtd., floor	output - 17,500 to 29,000 Btuh	SEER - 9.0 to 10.0

HEAT PUMPS

model - "RAS" series - wireless wall mtd.	output - 11,400 to 17,500 Btuh	SEER/HSPF - 10.0 to 10.1 / 6.5 to 6.8
model - "BCH" series - ceiling mtd., floor	output - 17,500 to 23,500 Btuh	SEER/HSPF - 9.5 to 10.0 / 6.8 to 7.3
compressor type - rotary		control - wired and wireless remote

features - The indoor and outdoor units can be placed up to 49 feet apart. The wireless remote has an automatic shift of fan speed, 24-hour timer, sensor dry and automatic operation, high sensitive IC-thermostat and 3 minute delay circuit to prevent fuse blowing. The air handlers are quiet and equipped with four-way deflectors to direct air in any angle.

CARRIER CORP., PO Box 4808, Syracuse, NY 13221 - (800) 227-7437

COOLING MODELS

model - "KB" series - wall mtd.	output - 9,700 to 23,200 Btuh	SEER - 10.2 to 11.0
model - "QKB" series - in-ceiling cassette	output - 19,000 to 35,000 Btuh	SEER - 10.0 to 10.5
model - "QAB" series - ceiling mtd., floor	output - 25,000 to 48,000 Btuh	SEER - 11.0 to 11.5

HEAT PUMPS

model - "QK" series - wall mtd.	output - 10,200 to 23,400 Btuh	SEER/HSPF - 10.2 to 11.0 / 7.0 to 7.3
model - "QAE" series - ceiling mtd.	output - 24,000 to 48,000 Btuh	SEER/HSPF - 10.2 to 11.0 / 6.8 to 7.3
model - "QKE" series - in-ceiling cassette	output - 18,000 to 34,400 Btuh	SEER/HSPF - 10.0 to 10.5 / 6.8
compressor type - reciprocating		control - wired and wireless remote

features - There is an automatic timer for start/stop, automatic air sweep louvers and an automatic restart function after power failure. The air filters are slide-in and there is a 3-speed fan motor. A fresh air intake accessory system is available and it is equipped with demand defrost.

ENVIRO MASTER INT'L., 5780 Success Dr., Rome, NY 13440 - (315) 336-3716

COOLING MODELS

model - "WCX" series - wall mtd.	output - 9,000 to 36,000 Btuh	SEER - 10.0
model - "CLC" series - ceiling mtd.	output - 9,000 to 48,000 Btuh	SEER - 10.0
model - "FCX & CCX" series - floor	output - 9,000 to 18,000 Btuh	SEER - 10.0

HEAT PUMPS

model - "America" series	output - 9,000 to 48,000 Btuh	SEER/HSPF - 10.0 to 11.0 / 6.8 to 7.6
compressor type - rotary - 9,000 - 12,000 Btuh, bristol inertia - 18,000+ Btuh		control - wired

features - Hydronic heat coils are available in 1 or 2 row configurations and electric supplemental heat options are also available. Fresh air intakes are provided on selected indoor units with manual and motorized damper options available. Included is a reverse cycle defrost.

FRIEDRICH, PO Box 1540, San Antonio, TX 78295 - (210) 225-2000

COOLING MODELS

model - "M" series - wall mtd.	output - 9,000 to 23,000 Btuh	SEER - 9.0 to 11.5
model - "C" series - in-ceiling cassette	output - 24,000 to 41,000 Btuh	SEER - 10.0 to 10.5
model - "S" series - ceiling mtd.	output - 24,600 to 42,000 Btuh	SEER - 10.0 to 10.2

FRIEDRICH - cont'd

HEAT PUMPS

model - "M" series - wall mtd.	output - 11,400 to 17,500 Btuh	SEER/HSPF - 10.0 to 10.1 / 7.3 to 7.4
model - "S" series - ceiling mtd.	output - 26,000 to 45,000 Btuh	SEER/HSPF - 10.0 to 10.5 / 7.6
compressor type - rotary - 9,000 - 12,000 Btuh, reciprocating - 18,000+ Btuh		control - wired and wireless remote

features - An LCD remote controller allows on/off timer and 24 hour programming. The self-diagnostic circuitry monitors the system for peak performance, plus does a filter check, self defrosts and has anti-ice control. It also comes with a battery back-up for power outages.

HEAT CONTROLLER, 1900 Wellworth, Jackson, MI 49204 - (517) 787-2100

COOLING MODELS

model - "SPHV" series - wall mtd., floor	output - 9,750 to 17,800 Btuh	SEER - 8.1 to 9.7

HEAT PUMPS

model - "WHV" series - thru-the-wall mtd.	output - 11,500 to 18,000 Btuh	SEER/HSPF - 8.5 to 9.7 / 7.0 to 7.5
compressor type - rotary		control - wired

features - The system can be mounted with a distance of up to 40 feet between the evaporator and condenser sections. The air outlet grille is adjustable and multi-directional allowing the air flow to be directed to where it is needed. The unit will operate on resistance heat and recycle automatically to the heat pump.

HITACHI AMERICA, 220 White Plains Rd., Terrytown, NY 10591 - (914) 631-0600

COOLING MODELS

model - "T" series - wall mtd.	output - 8,700 to 17,500 Btuh	SEER - 10.0 to 11.3
model - "S" series - in-ceiling cassette	output - 26,000 to 45,000 Btuh	SEER - 10.0
model - "S" series - ceiling mtd., floor	output - 26,000 to 45,000 Btuh	SEER - 10.0

HEAT PUMPS

model - "T" series - wall mtd.	output - 11,400 to 17,500 Btuh	SEER/HSPF - 10.0 to 10.2 / 7.3 to 7.4
model - "S" series - ceiling mtd.	output - 26,000 to 45,000 Btuh	SEER/HSPF - 10.0 / 7.3 to 7.5
model - "S" series - in-ceiling cassette	output - 26,000 to 45,000 Btuh	SEER/HSPF - 10.0 / 7.6
compressor type - rotary for "T" series, scroll for "S" series		control - wired and wireless remote

features - A full function LCD remote control panel allows automatic start/stop with cool, heat, and fan selection. It has a seven position automatic louver operation and temperature setpoint indicator. It is equipped with a sleep timer for automatic night setback. The units are precharged and can be up to 49 feet apart without additional charge - the maximum is 115 feet equivalent length.

KOLDWAVE/HEAT EXCHANGERS, 8100 N. Monticello, Skokie, IL 60076 - (708) 679-0300

COOLING MODELS

model - "Hi-lite" series - wall mtd.	output - 9,000 to 24,000 Btuh	SEER - 12.85

HEAT PUMPS

model - "RAS" series - wireless wall mtd.	output - 9,000 to 24,000 Btuh	SEER/HSPF - 12.85 / 7.5 to 7.6
compressor type - rotary for 9 to 12 Btuh, bristol inertia for 18+ Btuh		control - wired and wireless remote

features - The air filters are a metallic design which are easily pulled out and washable. A chilled water coil is available with the system. The thermostat includes indicator lights and rocker switches to control mode selection and the fan speed.

MITSUBISHI, PO Box 6007, Cypress, CA 90630 - (714) 220-4640

COOLING MODELS

model - "MS & PK" series - wall mtd.	output - 8,800 to 28,500 Btuh	SEER - 10.0 to 10.9
model - "PL" series - in-ceiling cassette	output - 18,400 to 42,000 Btuh	SEER - 10.0 to 10.4
model - "PC&MF" series - ceiling mtd., floor	output - 11,600 to 48,000 Btuh	SEER - 8.9 to 11.0

HEAT PUMPS

model - "MSH" series - wall mtd.	output - 8,800 to 14,200 Btuh	SEER/HSPF - 8.9 to 10.0 / 6.5 to 6.8
model - "PCH" series - ceiling mtd.	output - 24,000 to 42,000 Btuh	SEER/HSPF - 8.9 to 10.4 / 7.1 to 7.4
model - "PLH" series - in-ceiling cassette	output - 17,300 to 42,000 Btuh	SEER/HSPF - 10.0 to 10.3 / 7.0 to 7.4
compressor type - rotary		control - wired and wireless remote

features - A wireless LCD remote controller uses a unique control that allows the user to adjust the temperature to exactly the level desired simply by tapping a button. Piping can be extended up to 100 feet without charging - 164 feet when charging is used. The self diagnostics allow the unit to stop operating and indicates the location of the problem.

SANYO, 21350 Lassen St., Chatsworth, CA 91311 - (818) 998-7322

COOLING MODELS

model - "K" series - wall mtd.   output - 9,000 to 34,000 Btuh   SEER - 10.0
model - "T" series - ceiling mtd.   output - 11,500 to 45,000 Btuh   SEER - 10.0 to 10.7
model - "F" series - floor   output - 7,200 to 33,000 Btuh   SEER - 10.0 to 10.3

HEAT PUMPS

model - "K" series - wall mtd.   output - 8,800 to 20,600 Btuh   SEER/HSPF - 10.0 / 6.8
model - "T" series - ceiling mtd.   output - 24,000 to 43,000 Btuh   SEER/HSPF - 10.0 to 10.7 / 6.8 to 7.2
compressor type - rotary   control - wired and wireless remote

features - The LCD wireless remote control uses an infrared beam which can access all functions from as far away as 25 feet. The control has a 24-hour programmable timer with a night setback mode. A fresh air intake is available. The auto-louver mechanism oscillates the unique air discharge vanes up and down for even distribution.

TADIRAN ELECTRICAL APPLIANCES, 40 Seaview Blvd., Port Washington, NY 11050 - (516) 621-4179

COOLING MODELS

model - "Astro" series - wall mtd.   output - 9,800 to 24,000 Btuh   SEER - 10.0 to 10.9
model - "Galaxy" series - floor   output - 13,700 to 35,000 Btuh   SEER - 10.0 to 11.4

HEAT PUMPS

model - "Astro" series - wall mtd.   output - 5,200 to 20,000 Btuh   SEER/HSPF - 10.0 to 10.1 / 6.6 to 7.3
model - "Galaxy" series - floor   output - 6,700 to 31,000 Btuh   SEER/HSPF - 9.5 to 10.0 / 6.8 to 7.3
compressor type - rotary - 9,000 - 12,000 Btuh, bristol inertia - 18,000+ Btuh   control - wired and wireless remote

features - Five way air flow control provides comfortable air movement throughout the room. The unit is equipped with a 6-second restart after stop.

TOSHIBA AMERICA, 1010 Johnson Dr., Buffalo Grove, IL 60089 - (708) 541-9400

COOLING MODELS

model - "RAS & RAV" series - wall mtd.   output - 9,000 to 26,000 Btuh   SEER - 10.1 to 11.5
model - "RAV" series - ceiling mtd.   output - 26,000 Btuh   SEER - 10.1

HEAT PUMPS

model - "RAV" series - wall mtd.   output - 12,500 to 24,000 Btuh   SEER/HSPF - 10.0 to 12.0 / 6.8 to 7.1
model - "RAV" series - ceiling mtd.   output - 24,000 to 36,000 Btuh   SEER/HSPF - 10.0 / 6.8 to 7.1
compressor type - rotary- 9,000 -12,000 Btuh, scroll - 18,000+ Btuh   control - wired and wireless remote

features - The unit is equipped with a 24-hour programmable timer, 3 minute delay safety, and automatic fan speed controller. The louver automatically moves up and down to create a comfortable air flow throughout the room.

How Much You Save by Installing a New Ductless Mini-Split Air Conditioner

SEER	Approximate Annual Operating Cost - $							
6.0	200	300	400	500	600	700	800	900
7.0	175	260	345	430	515	600	690	780
8.0	150	225	300	375	450	525	605	685
9.0	135	200	270	335	400	465	540	610
10.0	120	180	240	300	360	420	485	550
11.0	110	165	220	275	330	385	440	500
12.0	100	150	200	250	300	350	405	455

To use this chart: Estimate the approximate SEER efficiency of your current air conditioner. Check with your contractor. Then locate your current annual operating costs. Look down in the same column across from the new efficiency for new operating cost.

Example: If your current air conditioner has a SEER of 6.0 and your annual operating cost is $500, the cost to operate a new 13.0 SEER air conditioner will be about $230, an annual savings of $270.

Q: My old central air conditioner still works, but I wonder if I should replace it with a super efficient one. How much can I expect to save on my electric bills? Are the new natural gas cooling units efficient and should I consider one?

A: Your old air conditioner (A/C) probably has a SEER (efficiency ratio) of about 6 or 7. A new super efficient electric unit has a SEER of 15. Installing one can cut your cooling costs by more than 50 percent. New natural gas central A/C units have an equivalent SEER as high as 27.

New super efficient electric A/C units use two-speed compressors and variable-speed indoor blowers. On the low, energy saving speed (runs at high speed only on the hottest days), each cycle run time is longer. Indoor temperature swings between on-off cycles are virtually eliminated.

The air gently circulates almost continuously and noise is reduced. With soft start, the initial burst of warm (cold in the winter) air from the ducts is eliminated. This is ideal for allergy sufferers because air cleaners are more effective and humidity levels, mold, mites, etc. are reduced.

The indoor blowers use special electrically commutated motors (ECM). These not only provide true variable-speed operation for better

comfort, but they use less than half as much electricity as standard blower motors.

The most efficient single-speed A/C units use scroll compressors. Scroll compressors have fewer moving parts than standard reciprocating piston compressors. Without pistons and valves, scroll compressors are quieter too.

Microprocessor comfort control

Two-speed condenser fan

Auxiliary gas heat for wintertime

Recuperator reclaims extra heat from engine

Low-maintenance one-cylinder natural gas engine

Computerized 17-speed engine control for comfort

Openings for air flow through condenser coils

Variable-speed indoor air blower for less temperature fluctuations

As scroll compressors wear over years of operation, they seal better and operate smoother than when they were new. Their basic design is reliable and they should continue to operate at high efficiency levels for many years.

If you have natural gas, there are gas-powered A/C units that use a no-compressor absorption process. These also heat your house in the winter.

Another super efficient gas central A/C and heating unit uses a compressor. With an equivalent SEER of 27, it can cut cooling costs by 75 percent. It looks just like a standard electric central A/C unit outdoors and is quieter.

A small natural gas-powered engine runs the compressor. Since an engine can run at any speed, it automatically fine tunes the cooling output (17 levels) to the cooling needs of your house continually, 24 hours per day.

In the winter, this year-round gas A/C unit heats your house at more than 100 percent efficiency. It combines the heat pump principal with the excess heat from running the engine. This cuts your heating costs by half.

Q: I am planning the addition of a sunroom to my house. I will use it for growing some plants and hopefully get some free solar heating in the winter from it. Should I get one with a slanted or vertical front?

A: Get one with a vertical or near vertical glass front. Although the slanted front designs are usually less expensive, they tend to overheat in the summer, even in northern climates.

If you plan to use your sunspace to help heat your house in the winter, include adequate solar mass. This is often accomplished with a heavy brick or concrete floor.

Manufacturers of Super Efficient Air Conditioners

AMANA REFRIGERATION, Amana, IA 52204 - (800) 843-0304 (319) 622-5511

model - "RCC" series   capacities - 18,600 to 59,500 Btuh*   SEER - 12.05
noise level - 78 dB   compressor type - reciprocating   speeds - single-speed
warranty - 10 year limited on compressor and coil, 1 year parts
features - The unit is offered with a low profile and is compact in size. The steel grille is vinyl-coated and surrounds the coil, the fan and the fan motor.

AQUA CAL, INC., 2737 24th St. N., St. Petersburg, FL 33713 - (813) 823-5642

model - "Southern Cooler"   capacities - 24,000 to 36,000 Btuh   SEER - 11.0 to 11.1
noise level - 77 dB   compressor type - scroll   speeds - single-speed
warranty - 10 year limited on compressor, coil and cabinet, 5 year parts
features - The unit is a unique triangular shape made of a durable, single-piece, high-impact polyethylene cabinet and base that is virtually indestructible. The corners are rounded making them safe around children. A two-speed motor operates quietly at energy-efficient low speed at low temperatures.

ARCOAIRE/COMFORTMAKER, PO Box 3005, Lavergne, TN 37086 - (800) 982-3081 (615) 793-0450

model - "Ultra High Efficiency"   capacities - 25,000 to 59,500 Btuh   SEER - 13.05
noise level - 78 dB   compressor type - scroll   speeds - single-speed
warranty - 10 year limited on compressor, 5 year parts
features - The unit has a two-speed fan with a totally-enclosed motor that reduces noise levels. The coil guard and grille shield are plastic-coated for extra protection.

ARMSTRONG/JOHNSON AIREASE, 421 Monroe St., Bellevue, OH 44811 - (419) 483-4840

model - "SCU13A" series   capacities - 24,000 to 58,000 Btuh   SEER - 13.1
noise level - 79 dB   compressor type - scroll   speeds - single-speed
warranty - 10 year limited on compressor , 2 year parts
features - The raised coil and cabinet stops debris from collecting in the coil and causing loss of airflow. Special scroll compressor mounts reduce vibration and lower the noise level. The corners on the unit are rounded to offer safety and a clean and attractive appearance.

BARD MANUFACTURING CO., PO Box 607, Bryan, OH 43506 - (419) 636-1194

model - "Twelve Plus UAC"   capacities - 24,000 to 60,000 Btuh   SEER - 12.0
noise level - 76 dB   compressor type - scroll   speeds - single-speed
warranty - 5 years on the entire system
features - The unit has special shock absorbing compressor mounts which lower the noise level and reduce vibration. A large 24 inch fan blade allows smoother airflow.

BRYANT, DAY & NIGHT, PAYNE, PO Box 70, Indianapolis, IN 46206 - (800) 468-7253 (317) 243-0851

model - "Two Speed Plus"   capacities - 36,000 to 60,000 Btuh   SEER - 13.7 to 16.2
noise level - 78 dB   compressor type - reciprocating   speeds - two-speed
warranty - 10 year limited on compressor, 2 year parts
features - The unit is available with a two-stage programmable thermostat that monitors the system. The Zone Perfect™ system lets you divide your home into four different zones so you may customize each zone to your specific needs.

model - "597" series   capacities - 24,000 to 60,000 Btuh   SEER - 12.0 to 14.0
noise level - 70 dB   compressor type - scroll   speeds - single-speed
warranty - 10 year limited on compressor and coil, 1 year parts
features - Equipped with the AeroQuiet System that consists of three design features: an advanced sound hood, Aerocoustic™ design and an energy-efficient fan and fan motor. The sound hood wraps around the compressor and the aerocoustic design allows smoother airflow through the wired dome top.

CARRIER CORP., PO Box 4808, Syracuse, NY 13221 - (800) 227-7437 (315) 432-6000

model - "Synergy 2000"   capacities - 36,000 to 60,000 Btuh   SEER - 13.5 to 16.6
noise level - 78 dB   compressor type - reciprocating   speeds - two-speed
warranty - 10 year limited on compressor, 1 year parts
features - The high-efficiency fan motor is two-speed for quiet performance and money savings. The compressor is surrounded by a special sound hood that buffers the compressor noise. A two-speed thermostat is available with a malfunction and speed indicator light. The thermostat maintains the temperature within 2.5° from your preferred set point. It runs on low speed about 80% of the time.

CENTURY/COMFORT-AIRE, PO Box 1089, Jackson, MI 49204 - (517) 787-2100

model - "Energy Knight" capacities - 19,500 to 56,000 Btuh SEER - 12.40 to 12.85
noise level - 76 dB compressor type - scroll speeds - single-speed
warranty - 5 year limited on the compressor, 1 year parts
features - A time delay and high and low pressure controls are available. The top grille is steel reinforced for extra strength. The upward air discharge minimizes air restriction and noise from the outdoor condenser fan motor.

COLEMAN EVCON, PO Box 19014, Wichita, KS 67204 - (800) 426-5362 (316) 261-3211

model - "Cooler 14" capacities - 18,000 to 60,000 Btuh SEER - 14.0
noise level - 83 dB compressor type - bristol inertia speeds - single-speed
warranty - 10 year limited on compressor, 1 year parts
features - The unit is equipped with a multi speed blower for maximum efficiency. The low pitched fan blades can move large quantities of air very quietly. The unit has a bell-mouth venturi design that lowers power consumption, reduces sound levels, and increases outdoor airflow.

GOODMAN MFG. CORP., 1501 Seamist, Houston, TX 77008 - (713) 861-2500

model - "CKQ" series capacities - 20,00 to 36,000 Btuh SEER - 14.0
noise level - 84 dB compressor type - bristol inertia speeds - two-speed
warranty - 5 years on the entire system
features - There is an elevated base pan that protects the unit from rust. The condenser fan motor is completely enclosed and permanently lubricated. The compressor is isolated from the fan system for extra sound reduction.

HEAT CONTROLLER, PO Box 1089, Jackson, MI 49204 - (517) 787-2100

model - "Energy Knight" capacities - 19,500 to 56,000 Btuh SEER - 12.40 to 12.85
noise level - 76 dB compressor type - scroll speeds - single-speed
warranty - 5 year limited on the compressor, 1 year parts
features - The upward air discharge minimizes air restriction and noise from the outdoor condenser fan motor. The air is also kept away from bushes and shrubs. Time delay and high and low pressure controls are available. The top grille is steel reinforced for extra strength.

HEIL/TEMPSTAR, PO Box 3005, Lavergne, TN 37086 - (615) 793-0450

model - "9600 Ultra High" capacities - 24,000 to 60,000 Btuh SEER - 13.05
noise level - 76 dB compressor type - scroll speeds - single-speed
warranty - 10 year limited on compressor, 5 year limited on coil, 1 year parts
features - A two-speed fan motor and the compressor sound blanket enclosure provide extra quiet operation. The wraparound condenser coil sends the exhaust air upward.

LENNOX INDUSTRIES, PO Box 799900, Dallas, TX 75379 - (214) 497-5000

model - "Power Saver" capacities - 36,000 to 60,000 Btuh SEER - 12.5 to 15.75
noise level - 76 dB compressor type - reciprocating speeds - two-speed
warranty - 10 year limited on the compressor, 5 year parts
features - The compressor compartment is insulated with thick fiberglass to reduce sound transmission. It is available with the Harmony II® zoning system that allows you to program up to four different zones in your house for your individual comfort levels. The Efficiency Plus™ controls and reduces indoor humidity levels.

LUXAIRE/FRASER-JOHNSTON, PO Box 1592, York, PA 17405 - (717) 771-7890

model - "HARB" series capacities - 24,000 to 60,000 Btuh SEER - 12.0
noise level - 78 dB compressor type - scroll speeds - single-speed
warranty - 5 years on the entire system
features - The system is equipped with a two-speed thermostat and condenser fan motor which operates at low speed during normal temperatures and at high speed only on the hottest days. The compressor is mounted on rubber isolators to reduce the outdoor noise to a minimum.

NORDYNE, A NORTEK CO., 1801 Park 270 Dr., St. Louis, MO 63146 - (314) 878-6200

model - "S1B" series capacities - 18,000 to 58,000 Btuh SEER - 14.0
noise level - 76 dB compressor type - reciprocating speeds - two-stage (three-speed)
warranty - 6 years on the entire system
features - It features a variable-speed blower with an efficient ECM motor. The two independent compressors (two-stage) are sized at 40% and 60% of full capacity. The unit therefore operate at 40%, 60% and 100% of capacity. There is an outdoor temperature sensor that determines which compressor (40% or 60%) starts first. Requires a two-stage indoor thermostat.

RHEEM/RUUD, PO Box 17010, Fort Smith, AR 72917 - (800) 848-7883 (501) 646-4311

model - "13 SEER" series | capacities - 18,000 to 60,000 Btuh | SEER - 13.0

noise level - 78 dB | compressor type - scroll | speeds - single-speed

warranty - 10 year limited on compressor, 5 year limited on coil, 1 year parts

features - A patented motor mount protects the fan motor from the elements for a longer life. The grille pattern allows the air to blow up and away from shrubbery and helps noise reduction. There is a one-piece painted drawn pan that elevates the coil off the pan and the pan off the pad helping to reduce rust or corrosion.

ROBUR CORP., 2300 Lynch Rd., Evansville, IN 47711 - (812) 424-1800

model - "AC and AY" series | cooling capacities - 36,000 to 60,000 Btuh | gas input - 58,000 to 125,000 Btuh

noise level - n/a | heating capacities - 110,000 to 165,000 Btuh | heating efficiency - 81% to 82%

warranty - 5 year limited | heating efficiency - 81% to 82% | * SEER (equiv.) - approx. 10

features - This system is a gas-fired absorption air conditioner that is CFC-free, using ammonia and water as the refrigerant system. It allows for zoning flexibility. *SEER equiv. depends on relative gas and electric rates in your area.

THERMO PRODUCTS, PO Box 217, N. Judson, IN 46366 - (219) 896-2133

model - "AC" series | capacities - 18,000 to 41,000 Btuh | SEER - 11.0 to 12.5

noise level - 76 dB | compressor type - scroll | speeds - single-speed

warranty - 10 year limited on compressor and coil, 5 year parts

features - The unit is equipped with a brownout delay relay to prevent the system from operating during a low voltage condition. It automatically shuts the system off and lets it safely restart when the voltage is interrupted. The evaporator coils are equipped with a thermal expansion valve that monitores and regulates the flow of refrigerant.

THE TRANE COMPANY, 6200 Troup Hwy., Tyler, TX 75707 - (903) 581-3568

model - "XL 1400" | capacities - 18,000 to 60,000 Btuh | SEER - 14.0 to 15.4

noise level - 76 dB | compressor type - reciprocating | speeds - single-speed

warranty - 10 year limited on compressor and coil, 2 year parts

features - The unit is equipped with a two speed fan motor for quiet and efficient operation. The compressor is wrapped in insulation to reduce the noise level. The top is protected with a solid weatherguard top to keep dirt leaves and other debris from clogging the unit.

YORK HEATING AND AIR CONDITIONING, PO Box 1592, York, PA 17403 - (717) 771-7890

model - "Stellar Ultra" | capacities - 12,000 to 60,000 Btuh | SEER - 16.7

noise level - 74 dB | compressor type - bristol inertia | speeds - two-stage (three-speed)

warranty - 10 year limited on compressor, 5 year parts

features - It features a variable-speed blower with an efficient ECM motor. The two independent compressors (two-stage) are sized at about 40% and 60% of full capacity. The unit therefore operate at 40%, 60% and 100% of capacity. Requires a two-stage indoor thermostat. The exact percentage split of capacity between stage one and stage two varies with the size of unit.

model - "Triathlon" | capacities - 18,000 to 60,000 Btuh | SEER - 15.0 to 27.0

noise level - n/a | compressor type - reciprocating | speeds - 17 -speed

warranty - 5 year limited on the engine, compressor and all other parts

features - This is a gas-powered heating and cooling unit and has a computer-controlled variable-speed (17 speeds) engine that runs at a slow , energy-saving speed for long periods of time. This helps pull humidity from the air allowing much greater comfort indoors. It is available with a 7-day programmable thermostat.

How Much You Save by Installing a New Efficient Central Air Conditioner							
SEER	*Approximate Annual Operating Cost - $*						
6.0	200	300	400	500	600	700	800	900
7.0	175	260	345	430	515	600	690	780
8.0	150	225	300	375	450	525	605	685
9.0	135	200	270	335	400	465	540	610
10.0	120	180	240	300	360	420	485	550
11.0	110	165	220	275	330	385	440	500
12.0	100	150	200	250	300	350	405	455
13.0	90	140	185	230	280	325	370	425
14.0	85	130	170	215	260	300	345	385
15.0	80	120	160	200	240	280	320	360
16.0	75	115	150	190	225	265	300	340
20.0	60	80	110	140	165	190	220	250
27.0	40	69	80	100	120	145	165	185

To use this chart: Estimate the approximate SEER efficiency of your current air conditioner. Locate your current annual operating costs. Look down in the same column across from the new efficiency for new operating cost.

Example: If your current air conditioner has a SEER of 6.0 and your annual operating cost is $500, the cost to operate a new 13.0 SEER air conditioner will be about $230, an annual savings of $270.

Q: How energy efficient and safe (around my children) are electric radiant wall picture heaters? I need a heater to produce warmth fast for my bathroom in the morning and the children's playroom.

A: Radiant wall picture heaters are energy efficient. They provide heat quickly, just like feeling the radiant warmth of the sun on a cold day. I use one on my basement wall across from my pool table for quick heat.

The surface temperature never exceeds 170 degrees, so they are safe around children. In case they get knocked off the wall, some models have tip-over automatic shut off switches. They plug into a standard 120-volt outlet.

These are called picture heaters because they look like a wall painting (one inch thick). Many are landscapes, sunsets or snow scenes. If you are artistic, order a less expensive blank heater and paint your own scene with acrylic paint. A decorative frame can be added without reducing efficiency.

Several sizes are available from about 2 ft. by 2 ft. (310 watts) to 2 ft. by 3 ft. (475 watts). It costs about 3 to 4 cents per hour to operate. "Under desk" floor models with a thermostat are ideal for chilly offices.

Radiant heat is naturally energy efficient. People feel as comfortable in a room at 64 degrees with radiant heat as in a room at 72 degrees with typical forced air heat. Radiant heaters create just enough warm air circulation for more constant floor to ceiling air temperatures.

Lowering the room temperature not only cuts heating bills, but it is more comfortable and healthier.

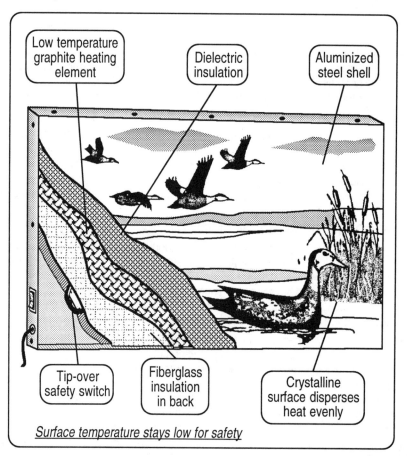

Low temperature graphite heating element

Dielectric insulation

Aluminized steel shell

Tip-over safety switch

Fiberglass insulation in back

Crystalline surface disperses heat evenly

Surface temperature stays low for safety

Since a radiant heater does not heat the air excessively as a forced air heater does, the air is not dried out. Also, radiant heaters are totally quiet and maintenance-free (no moving parts).

There are easy-to-install options for using radiant heat as the sole heat source for a large room or entire house. Narrow radiant cove heaters (3 ft. to 11 ft. in length) can be mounted on the wall near the ceiling.

Cove heaters provide the majority of their warmth as quick radiant heat. The long narrow housing (about 3 by 4 inches across) has slots to provide some of the heat as warm air circulation. These are ideal for zone heating a house because each room can have its own thermostat.

Flat (one-inch thick) radiant panels can be attached under a ceiling or recessed in it. Other options include electric heating wires, fiberglass cloth or plastic sheets with wires or graphite conductors embedded inside. For simple installation, some drywall is made with the wire already inside.

Q: I am building a house that will use passive solar heating. What is the best way to plan the rooms for the best natural heat circulation?

A: An open floor plan is best for passive solar heating. Adding a low-speed continuous air circulation blower motor to your existing central furnace also helps. These motors run efficiently at the low speed (about one-quarter of the high speed).

Finish the interior walls with large openings between rooms. For efficiency and a contemporary look, build curved walls and transitions between rooms. National Gypsum makes bendable drywall (called High Flex) for this purpose. It is one-quarter inch thick, so two layers are needed.

Radiant heaters warm you like the sun does. This allows you to keep your room air cooler and still be comfortable. The cooler you keep your house temperature, the lower your utility bills will be.

#642 Musical bears

For quick, efficient room heat, as in a bathroom, a wall picture heater is effective and safe. Several of the available scenes are shown on this page. If you are one and paint your own. Under-desk models have pressure sensitive tape plugged into a portable thermostat

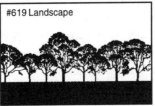
#619 Landscape

(full color) from Aztec artistic, order a blank radiant heaters are great for the office. SSHC's for mounting under a desk. These heaters can be and they operate on 120 volts.

Cove heaters (figure #1) are ideal for heating a larger area, up to 12 feet long. Most have an aluminum front cover with a special coating for quick heating when you first switch them on. They provide just enough heat (about 13%) from natural air flow from the top to gently circulate the room air. Radiant panel heaters can be mounted under the ceiling or recessed into it.

#628 Hanging basket

Floor heating systems use either cables or special sheeting (ESWA and Flexwatt). Sheeting is the easiest for retrofitting an old house. See page 16 for instructions for installing a floor warming system by Flexwatt Corp.

Drywall with heating cable embedded in it (Panelectric) makes installation simple. An electrician connects the lead wires from the drywall panels to the wall thermostat. There are several heat outputs for each panel size.

Installation of the multi-sized panels is as easy for an electrician to install as an electric light fixture - mounted on the surface, flush, placed in a suspended ceiling grid, or freely suspended. Painting, overspraying with water base acoustical material, or framing creates the desired aesthetic effect. Do not operate until dry.

Amperage Draw for a specific panel may be easily obtained by dividing the specific voltage (120, 208, 240 or 277 volts) into the panel output wattage. Hence an 800 watt 44RP panel, operating on 240 volts, would draw 3.3 amps.

Sizing for supplemental heat, approximately 3-4 watts per square foot of room area may be adequate: As the primary source of heat, with R-19 walls and R-30 ceiling, 5-7 watts per square foot is usually adequate.

Operating Characteristics

Surface Temperature: 180°-190°F (82.2°-87.8°C). Nominal, uniform across entire heating element surface. Rise Time to Operating Temperature: 4 minutes (maximum).

Radiant Output (Horizontal): 90% of input energy. All radiant energy from an Enerjoy® Panel is totally safe, low temperature.

Finish Fire Rating: Flame spread (E-84) less than 25.

Specifications for *SSHC, INC.*

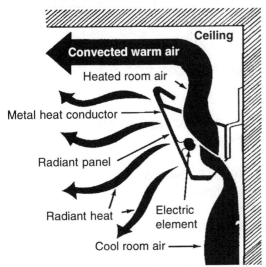

Ceiling

Convected warm air

Heated room air

Metal heat conductor

Radiant panel

Radiant heat

Electric element

Cool room air

figure #1 - Cove heater - 3" by 4" cross section

Specifications for QMark					
Model	Watts	Volts	Amps	Btu/hr	Length
RCC-4512	450	120	3.7	1536	34"
RCC-4524	450	240	1.9	1536	34"
RCC-6012	600	120	5.0	2048	47"
RCC-6024	600	240	2.5	2048	47"
RCC-7512	750	120	6.2	2560	59"
RCC-7524	750	240	3.1	2560	59"
RCC-9012	900	120	7.5	3072	71"
RCC-9024	900	240	3.7	3072	71"
RCC-10512	1050	120	8.8	3584	83"
RCC-10524	1050	240	4.4	3584	83"
RCC-12012	1200	120	10.0	4096	94"
RCC-12024	1200	240	5.0	4096	94"
RCC-15024	1500	240	6.2	5120	118 1/4"
RCC-18024	1800	240	7.5	6143	132"

Manufacturers of Radiant Heating Systems and Products

ALCATEL/ESWA, 1507 Park Ave., Perkasie, PA 18944 - (215) 453-9228

<u>type</u> - cable - used for floor heating - covered with ½" to 2" thick layer of concrete or mortar

<u>watts</u> - the length and gauge of cable depends on size of room to heat - 240 volts only

<u>controls</u> - manual control with a simple on-off switch or automatic wall-mounted thermostat

<u>type</u> - sheeting - metal foil sandwiched and sealed between strong flexible clear plastic sheets

<u>watts</u> - 9 watts/ft^2 for 16" OC (on centers) and 12 watts/ft^2 for 24" OC

<u>controls</u> - manual control with a simple on-off switch or automatic wall mounted thermostat

AZTEC, 70 Beauty Spot Rd., E., Bennettsville, SC 29512 - (803) 479-4006

<u>type</u> - picture (see page 14 for available scenes and construction, blank heaters also available)

<u>size</u> - 23½" x 23½" (310 watts) and 23½" x 35½" (475 watts)

<u>type</u> - under desk model - sets on floor with stand to tilt a slight angle from vertical

<u>size</u> - 15" x 22" (170 watts) and 17½" x 25½" (250 watts)

<u>controls</u> - 10 amp portable thermostat

ENERGOTECH, PO Box 214, Torrington, CT 06790 - (203) 673-7685

<u>type</u> - panel - all panels 2" - mounts under ceiling (240-volt panels up to 3300 watts are available

<u>size/watts</u> - 25½"x11½"/800w, 66¼"x6¼"/1000w, 37¾"x11½"/1200w, 66¼"x11½"/2000w

<u>controls</u> - optional built-in thermostat kit available

FLEXWATT CORP., 2380 Cranberry Hwy., W. Wareham, MA 02576 - (800) 992-4328 (508) 291-2000

<u>type</u> - floor heat sheeting - (see page #16) - graphite-based conductive ink sealed between transparent layers

<u>watts</u> - each one-foot panel is 10 watts   <u>size</u> - 12", 16" or 24" on center spacing

HEAT PRODUCTS, 1204 S. Marion St., Lake City, FL 32055 - (904) 752-5097

<u>type</u> - micro-thin ceiling cable - cables attached under ceiling and covered with thin texturized plaster-like coating

<u>controls</u> - wall mounted thermostat

PANELECTRIC HEATING SYSTEMS, Route 4, Irving, KY 40336 - (800) 228-9022 (606) 723-7731

<u>type</u> - cables embedded in ⅝" drywall panels - 208/240 volts only   <u>watts</u> - 245, 330, 450, 475, 600, 720

<u>size</u> - 4' x 6', 4' x 8', 4' x 10', 4' x 12' - various wattages available for each panel size

<u>controls</u> - wall mounted thermostat

QMARK, 470 Beauty Spot Rd., E., Bennettsville, SC 29512 - (803) 479-4006

<u>type</u> - cove - (see page #14 for specifications) - can be mounted within 2½" of drywall ceiling

<u>length/watts</u> - 34"/450 w, 47"/600 w, 59"/750w, 71"/900w, 83"/1050w, 94"/1200w, 118¼"/1500w, 132"/1800w

<u>controls</u> - optional thermostat kit available

<u>type</u> - sheeting - fiberglass cloth embedded with graphite dispersion - 100 ft. rolls or factory-cut pieces

<u>size</u> - 18 watts/lineal ft. for 16" OC and 28½ watts/lineal ft. for 24" OC

<u>controls</u> - optional thermostat kit available

RADIANT SYSTEMS, PO Box 40, Yutan, NE 68073 - (402) 625-2535

<u>type</u> - cove

<u>length/watts</u> - 34"/450 w, 47"/600 w, 59"/750w, 71"/900w, 83"/1050w, 94"/1200w, 118¼"/1500w, 132"/1800w

<u>controls</u> - optional built-in thermostat kit or wall thermostat available

SSHC, INC., PO Box 769, Old Saybrook, CT 06475 - (203) 388-3848

<u>type</u> - panel, under desk model

<u>size</u> - panels - 2'x2', 2'x4', 2'x6'   <u>watts</u> - 200, 300, 400, 610, 800, 820, 1000, 1220, 1640

<u>controls</u> - adjustable thermostat

SUN-EL CORP., PO Box 488, Latrobe, PA 15650 - (412) 537-3600

<u>type</u> - panel - all panels 2" - mounts under ceiling (240-volt panels up to 3300 watts are available

<u>size/watts</u> - 25½"x11½"/800w, 66¼"x6¼"/1000w, 37¾"x11½"/1200w, 66¼"x11½"/2000w

<u>controls</u> - optional built-in thermostat kit available

THERMAL ART HEATERS, 8828 Somerset, Paramount, CA 90723 - (800) 628-4328

<u>type</u> - picture (some painted scenes available - mfg. would prefer to sell unpainted ones)

<u>size</u> - 24" x 15" (100 watts), 24" x 31" (300 watts), 24" x 44" (450 watts)

THERMOPRO TECHNOLOGIES, PO Box 600505, N. Miami, FL 33160 - (305) 949-1706

<u>type</u> - cove - designed for 87% radiant heat and 13% convection heat - mount about one foot below ceiling

<u>length/watts</u> - 22"/225w, 34"/450w, 47"/600w, 59"/750w, 71"/900w, 83"/1050w, 94"/1200w, 118"/1500w, 142"/1800w

<u>controls</u> - thermostat kit and wall mounted thermostat available

Install the Floor Warming System - (Flexwatt Corp.)

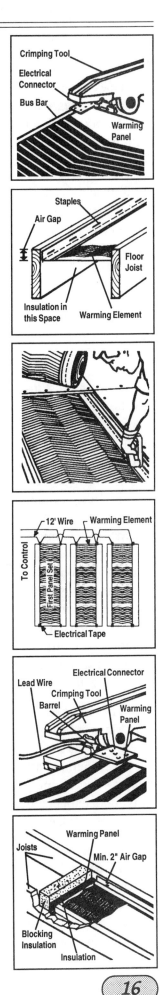

1. Cut Warming Material

Using your joist measurements, determine the number of warming panels per joist bay you will use. These units make up the panel sets you will install.

Cut each panel set approximately 12" less than the total joist bay length to allow for wiring. Cut only along the dotted lines in the clear section between warming panels.

2. Attach Connectors

Crimp a connector over each silver colored bus bar at one end of the panel sets. You will need two connectors per panel set.

To attach a connector to the warming material, simply center the flat portion evenly over one end of a bus bar and squeeze it flat, first with your fingers and then with the crimping tool. Make sure that the "teeth" of the connector bite into the bus bar. Refer to the drawing.

3. Attach Electrical Tape

Place dielectric ("electrical") tape over each of the bus bars without connectors at the opposite end of the warming panels.

4. Attach the Panel Sets to the Floor Joists

Install the warming material between the joists beneath the subfloor. You must maintain an air gap of at least 2" between the bottom of the subfloor and the panel sets.

Fold along the perforated edge of the warming material and staple to the inside of joists, maintaining the minimum 2" clearance. Staple as closely as possible to the fold line.

Note: You can also install the system from above prior to the placement of a new subfloor. Put insulation in place before stapling warming panels.

5. Wire the Panels Sets

After you have attached the panel sets to the joists, wire them in parallel according to the following drawing. All wiring must be done in accordance with the National Electrical Code and local regulations.

To attach wires to a connector, strip about ¼" from the end of the wire. Insert the end(s) into the barrel section of the electrical connector and squeeze tightly with the crimping tool as shown in the drawing.

6. Attach Insulators

After you have wired all the panel sets, put the clear plastic insulators over the connectors. You will need two insulator sets per panel set.

Simply place one half of an insulator over a connector and snap the other half into place by mating the pins and holes of each half. Squeeze them together with finger pressure.

Note: If the insulator does not close tightly, reposition it so that the connector is located between the ribs of the insulator and squeeze again.

7. Install Power Control

If a visual check of your installation is satisfactory, install your control system (clock timer, on-off switch of thermostat) according to the manufacturer's instructions. Always connect the white wire from the warming panels to the grounding conductor.

Complete the Installation

Insulate Beneath the Warming Material

Always install insulation beneath the warming material to direct the heat toward the floor being warmed. Install at least 3" of fiberglass batting or equivalent between the joists, beneath the panel sets. Gently place the insulation so that it is in contact with the panel sets.

Important: At the ends of each panel set, continue to add insulation, filling the joist space right up to the subfloor. This will contain all the warmth under your floor.

Q: My utility bills are skyrocketing. Does it make sense to replace my noisy old heat pump, even though it still works, with a new superefficient model? What comfort and efficiency features should I consider?

A: Replacing your heat pump with a new quiet electric model can lower your heating costs by 30% to 40%. New superefficient heat pumps can produce up to $3 worth of heat for each $1 on your electric bills. New designs are more reliable and quieter.

If you have natural gas, the newest innovation is a natural-gas powered heat pump (Triathlon by York). Depending on your relative gas and electric rates, it can cut your heating and cooling costs by as much as 75%. It uses a low-maintenance, one-cylinder quiet engine to drive the compressor. With 17 speeds, it automatically continuously adjusts the heat output to your needs.

The most efficient electric heat pumps use two-speed or two-stage compressors. These heat pumps vary the heat (and cooling) output into your house as the outdoor temperature and weather conditions change.

With a two-speed (one compressor) design, most of the time, the heat pump runs at the slow speed. This reduces the amount of electricity used. During very cold or hot weather, the compressor automatically shifts to the high speed.

A two-stage model has two separate compressors, one small and one large, inside the outdoor unit. In effect, it provides three speeds - small compressor only, large only, or both. Comfort is excellent.

Coupling any of the above designs with a new variable-speed indoor blower fine tunes the heat output. At the long-running slow speed

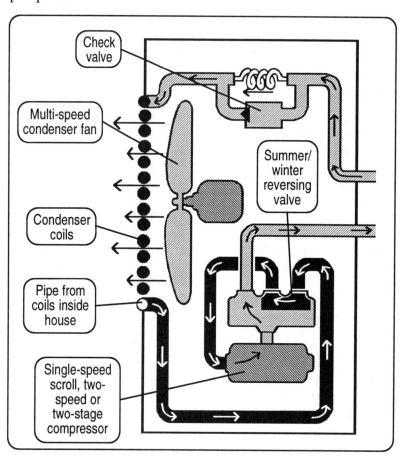

Check valve

Multi-speed condenser fan

Condenser coils

Pipe from coils inside house

Single-speed scroll, two-speed or two-stage compressor

Summer/ winter reversing valve

or stage one, it cycles on and off less often. This maintains a constant indoor temperature.

Many efficient single-speed heat pumps use a scroll compressor. Scroll compressors have few moving parts than a standard compressor. Without the pistons and hardware of standard compressors, scroll compressors are much quieter.

As these few scroll moving parts wear over years of operation,

they actually seal better and operate smoother than when they were new. The basic design is very reliable and they should continue to operate at high efficiency-levels as they age.

When you compare efficiencies of various electric heat pumps, use the Heating Season Performance Factor (HSPF) for heating, and Seasonal Energy Efficiency Ratio (SEER) for cooling. Also compare the type of compressor and speeds, which effect comfort and noise level. The most expensive model is not always the best choice for your specific house.

Q: I want to help reduce the greenhouse effect. About how much carbon dioxide (greenhouse gas) is produced per person each year?

A: The majority of carbon dioxide gas (CO_2) produced is from burning fossil fuels to produce energy. On average more than 40,000 pounds of CO_2 are released into the air per year for each person.

To run a typical average-efficiency refrigerator for one year, a coal-fired power plant produces more than 2,000 pounds of CO_2. Switching to a new high-efficiency refrigerator can reduce this amount by about 600 pounds.

A rule of thumb is that for each kilowatt-hour of electricity saved, about 2 pounds of CO_2 is eliminated from entering the atmosphere.

The chart on page 20 shows the savings by replacing an old heat pump with a new efficient model. You must calculate the summer and winter savings and combine them for the annual savings.

The key component in determining the efficiency of a heat pump is the type and number of speeds of the compressor. The most efficient compressor type is a multi-speed design. Both the heating and air-conditioning outputs vary depending on the instantaneous heating and cooling needs of your house. These designs also improve comfort and provide even room temperatures. A single-speed scroll compressor is the next most efficient design. Scroll compressors are also quieter than reciprocating compressors These specifications for each model are listed under *"compressor type"* and *"speeds"*.

Most manufacturers offer several model sizes - *"capacities"* - for which the ranges are shown. 12,000 Btu/hr is equal to one ton of cooling. *"SEER"* is the cooling efficiency and *"HSPF"* is the heating efficiency. These are the best comparisions of efficiencies among various models. The *"blower"* specifications refers to the number of speeds for the indoor blower. Multi- or variable-speeds provides greater comfort and energy savings. If you are installing a new heat pump for central air conditioning with a gas furnace for heating, your cooling blower speeds will be limited to the existing furnace air handler.

-- --

Manufacturers of Super-Efficient Heat Pumps

AMANA REFRIGERATION INC., Amana, IA 52204 - (800) 843-0304 (319) 622-5511

model -"PHA Series" — capacities - 25,600 to 58,000 Btuh
HSPF - 7.0 — SEER - 10.0
compressor type - reciprocating — speeds - single-speed
blower - single-speed
warranty - 10 year limited on compressor and coils, limited 1 year on all other parts.

ARCOAIRE/COMFORTMAKER, P.O.Box 3005, Lavergne, TN 37086 - (615) 793-0450

model - "The YF" — capacities - 18,000 to 60,000 Btuh
HSPF - 7.7 — SEER - 11+
compressor type - scroll — speeds - single-speed
blower - single-speed
warranty - 5 years on the compressor, limited 1 year on all other parts.

ARMSTRONG/JOHNSON AIR-EASE, 421 Monroe St., Bellevue, OH 44811 - (419) 483-4840

model - "The Concept 12" — capacities - 24,000 to 60,000 Btuh
HSPF - 7.6 — SEER - 12.0
compressor type - scroll — speeds - single-speed
blower - single-speed
warranty - 10 years on the compressor, all other parts 2 years.

BARD MANUFACTURING CO., P.O.Box 607, Bryan, OH 43506 - (419) 636-1194

model - "The Ten Plus" — capacities - 24,000 to 60,000 Btuh
HSPF - 8.0 — SEER - 10.0
compressor type - scroll — speeds - single-speed
blower - single-speed
warranty - 5 years on the compressor, 1 year on all other parts.

BRYANT, DAY & NIGHT, PAYNE, P.O. Box 70, Indianapolis, IN 46206 - (800) 468-7253

model - "Two Speed Plus" — capacities - 36,000 to 60,000 Btuh
HSPF - 8.8 — SEER - 15.8
compressor type - reciprocating — speeds - two-speed
blower - single or variable-speed
warranty - 10 years on the compressor and coil, 1 year on all other parts.
model - "697 Series" — capacities - 18,000 to 60,000 Btuh
HSPF - 8.3 — SEER - 13.0
compressor type - scroll — speeds - single-speed
blower - single or variable-speed
warranty - 10 years on the compressor and coil, 1 year on all other parts.

CARRIER CORP., P.O. Box 4808, Syracuse, NY 13221 - (800) 227-7437 (315) 432-6000

model - "Synergy 2000"
HSPF - 9.0
compressor type - reciprocating
blower - variable-speed
warranty - 10 years on the compressor, all other parts 1 year limited.

capacities - 36,000 to 60,000 Btuh
SEER - 16.0
speeds - two-speed

model - "Weathermaster 2000"
HSPF - 7.6
compressor type - scroll
blower - single-speed
warranty - 10 years on the compressor, all other parts 1 year limited.

capacities - 24,000 to 48,000 Btuh
SEER - 11.0
speeds - single-speed

CENTURY/HEAT CONTROLLER, PO Box 1089, Jackson, MI 49203 - (517) 787-2100

model - "Reverse-A-Matic"
HSPF - 8.8
compressor type - scroll
blower - single-speed
warranty - 5 years on the compressor, 1 year on all other parts.

capacities - 18,000 to 60,000 Btuh
SEER - 13.1
speeds - single-speed

GOODMAN MFG. CORP., 1501 Seamist, Houston, TX 77008 - (713) 861-2500

model -"CPJ Series"
HSPF - 8.0
compressor type - scroll
blower - variable-speed
warranty - 5 years on all parts.

capacities - 18,000 to 60,000 Btuh
SEER - 13.0
speeds - single-speed

HEIL/TEMPSTAR, P.O.Box 3005, Lavergne, TN 37086 - (615) 793-0450

model - "9000 Series"
HSPF - 8.0
compressor type - scroll
blower - variable-speed
warranty - 10 years on the compressor, 2 years on all other parts.

capacities - 18,000 to 36,000 Btuh
SEER - 12.0
speeds - single-speed

LENNOX INDUSTRIES, P.O. Box 799900, Dallas, TX 75379 - (214) 497-5000

model - "Power Saver"
HSPF - 8.75
compressor type - reciprocating
blower - single or variable-speed
warranty - 10 year limited on the compressor, 5 year limited on all other parts.

capacities - 36,000 to 58,000 Btuh
SEER - 16.0
speeds - two-speed

model - "HP26 Series"
HSPF - 8.7
compressor type - scroll
blower - single-speed
warranty - 10 year limited on the compressor, 5 year limited on all other parts.

capacities - 23,600 to 44,500 Btuh
SEER - 13.0
speeds - single-speed

LUXAIRE/FRASER-JOHNSTON, P.O. Box 1592, York, PA 17405 - (717) 771-7890

model - "EASH Series"
HSPF - 8.2
compressor type - scroll
blower - single-speed
warranty - 5 years on the compressor, all other parts 1 year.

capacities - 12,000 to 60,000 Btuh
SEER - 12.4
speeds - single-speed

NORDYNE, A NORTEK CO., PO Box 46911, St. Louis, MO 63146 - (314) 878-6200

model - "T1BE Series"
HSPF - 8.0
compressor type - reciprocating
blower - single-speed
warranty - 5 years on the compressor, all other parts 6 years.

capacities - 12,000 to 60,000 Btuh
SEER - 10.0
speeds - two-stage (three-speed)

features - It features a variable-speed blower with an efficient ECM motor. The two independent compressors (two-stage) are sized at 40% and 60% of full capacity. The unit therefore operate at 40%, 60% and 100% of capacity. There is an outdoor temperature sensor that determines which compressor (40% or 60%) starts first. Requires a two-stage indoor thermostat.

RHEEM/RUUD MFG., 5600 Old Greenwood Rd., Fort Smith, AR 72903 - (501) 646-4311

model - "Classic XIII/Achiever 13" - Rheem/Ruud
HSPF - 8.9
compressor type - scroll
blower - single-speed
warranty - 10 years on the compressor, 1 year on all other parts.

capacities - 12,600 to 54,500 Btuh
SEER - 13.1
speeds - single-speed

THE TRANE COMPANY, 6200 Troup Hwy., Tyler, TX 75707 - (903) 581-3568

model -"XL 1400"
HSPF - 8.5
compressor type - reciprocating
blower - two-speed
warranty - 10 years on compressor and coil, 2 years on all other parts.

capacities - 24,000 to 60,000 Btuh
SEER - 14.0
speeds - single-speed

model -"XE 1200"
HSPF - 8.0
compressor type - reciprocating
blower - single or variable-speed
warranty - 5 years on compressor and coil, 1 year on all other parts.

capacities - 18,000 to 60,000 Btuh
SEER - 12.0
speeds - single-speed

YORK HEATING & AIR CONDITIONING, P.O. Box 1592, York, PA 17403 - (717) 771-7890

model - "Stellar Plus"
HSPF - 8.2
compressor type - scroll
blower - variable-speed
warranty - 10 year on the compressor, 5 year on all other parts.

capacities - 12,000 to 60,000 Btuh
SEER - 12.0
speeds - single-speed

model - "Triathlon"
*HSPF (equiv.) - 20
compressor type - reciprocating
warranty - 5 year limited on the engine, compressor and all other parts.

capacities - 18,000 to 60,000 Btuh
*SEER (equiv.) - 15.0 to 27.0
speeds - 17 -speed

features - This is a gas-powered heating and cooling unit and has a computer-controlled variable-speed (17 speeds) engine that runs at a slow , energy-saving speed for long periods of time. This helps pull humidity from the air allowing much greater comfort indoors. It is available with a 7-day programmable thermostat. * HSPF and SEER equiv. depends on relative gas and electric rates in your area.

SEER or HSPF	Approximate Annual Operating Cost - $							
6.0	200	300	400	500	600	700	800	900
7.0	175	260	345	430	515	600	690	780
8.0	150	225	300	375	450	525	605	685
9.0	135	200	270	335	400	465	540	610
10.0	120	180	240	300	360	420	485	5520
11.0	110	165	220	275	330	385	440	500
12.0	100	150	200	250	300	350	405	455
13.0	90	140	185	230	275	325	370	415
14.0	85	130	170	215	260	300	345	385
15.0	80	120	160	200	240	280	320	360
16.0	75	115	150	190	225	265	300	340
20.0	60	80	110	140	165	190	220	250
27.0	40	69	80	100	120	145	165	185

Table title: **How Much You Save by Installing a New Efficient Heat Pump**

To use this chart: Estimate the approx. efficiency (HSPF or SEER) of your current heat pump. Check with your contractor. Then locate your current annual operating costs. Look down in the same column across from the new efficiency for new operating cost.

Example: If your current heat pump has a SEER of 6.0 and your annual operating cost is $500, the cost to operate a new 13.0 SEER heat pump will be about $230, an annual savings of $270.

Q: I am considering adding a "warm feet" water radiant floor heating system for a new room addition. How comfortable and efficient is it and can it be extended to other chilly rooms in my house?

A: "Warm feet" radiant floor heating systems are very energy efficient. They typically cut your gas or oil bills by 15 to 30 percent as compared to common forced air systems. They are simple to install in new construction and can be retrofitted to an existing house with conventional central heating and air conditioning systems.

If you're like me, when your feet are cold, you're cold all over, even in a warm room. By keeping the floor at about 75 degrees, it warms your body with radiant heat just like standing in the sun on a clear crisp day. Some complete radiant systems can be ordered with solar collectors included.

The comfort benefits of radiant floor heat are many - no blower noise, no drafts, less outdoor air leakage (reduces allergens indoors), constant floor to ceiling air temperature, less dust, mold etc. There are no floor air registers, so your furniture can be located anywhere in the room.

The "warm feet" feeling also allows you to set your central thermostat six to eight degrees lower and still be as comfortable. Individual room thermostats and automatic temperature zone controls can be installed to fine tune the temperature and the amount of heat going to various rooms.

Most radiant floor systems use a super efficient boiler. Thin flexible tubing for the warm water is usually attached in a serpentine pattern beneath the floors. It can be used in conjunction with existing baseboard systems or forced air systems by installing a heat exchanger in the blower.

To convert to a radiant system, there are many installation options. The simplest method is to staple the tubing to the underside of the flooring. Thin sheet aluminum pieces are sometimes attached to help diffuse heat more evenly. Install batt insulation under floor and tubes.

For a second-floor, the thin tubing can be laid on top of the floor. A one-inch-thick layer of special lightweight cement is spread over the entire floor. The cement not only holds and distributes heat well, but it seals air leaks and greatly reduces noise transmission through the floor and eliminates squeaks. Cover it with tile floor covering or carpeting

For new construction, like your addition built on a slab or over a basement, the tubing can be embedded in the concrete when it is poured. This provides very even, efficient heating. The tubing can be laid on top of the slab and covered with the cement layer.

Q: I am remodeling my bathroom and adding a large super efficient R-8 casement window. I am having trouble removing the old tile adhesive from the walls so I can paint them. What do you recommend?

A: Old tile adhesive can get rock-hard. You need a hammer and a scraper to get some of it off. Do not worry about gouging the wall surface. You'll have to skim coat the wall before painting.

Another method is to remove the old adhesive covered drywall and replace it with new drywall. It's not a lot more work and you will have access to the wall cavity. Fill gaps with insulation where it has settled.

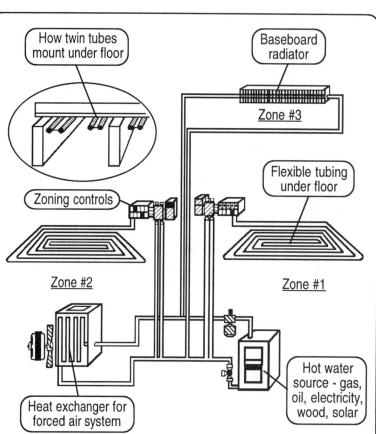

How twin tubes mount under floor

Baseboard radiator

Zone #3

Zoning controls

Flexible tubing under floor

Zone #2

Zone #1

Heat exchanger for forced air system

Hot water source - gas, oil, electricity, wood, solar

Manufacturers of Warm Water Radiant Floor Systems

BIO-THERMAL UNLIMITED, Box 191, Ellenville, NY 12428 - (800) 882-3628 (914) 647-6700
   type of tubing - bio-flex is made of elastomer with a braided synthetic fiber cord inside, bio-pex is made of cross- linked polyethylene and radiant roll is flexible dual elastomeric counterflow tubing
   diameter sizes - $3/8$", $1/2$" and $5/8$"   zoning available - no

HEATLINK USA, 89 54th St. S. W., Grand Rapids, MI 49548 - (800) 968-8905 (616) 532-4266
   type of tubing - pex pipe is made of cross-linked polyethylene
   diameter sizes - $1/4$", $3/8$", $1/2$", $5/8$", $3/4$" and 1"   zoning available - yes, up to ten zones

HEATWAY, 3131 W. Chestnut Expy, Springfield, MO 65802 - (800) 255-1996 (417) 864-6108
   type of tubing - entran 3 is made of synthetic rubber with an oxygen barrier, twintran is counterflow tubing
   diameter sizes - $3/8$", $1/2$", $3/4$" and 1"   zoning available - yes, individual room/zone
   special features - complete solar system available

INFLOOR HEATING SYSTEMS, PO Box 253, Hamel, MN 55340 - (612) 478-6477
   type of tubing - polybutylene, cross-linked polyethylene, oxygen barrier, and non-barrier tubing
   diameter sizes - $3/8$" and $1/2$"   zoning available - yes, individual room/zone

RADIANTEC, PO Box 1111, Lyndonville, VT 05851 - (800) 451-7593 (802) 626-8045
   type of tubing - polybutylene, polyethylene and partially cross-linked polyethylene
   diameter sizes - $7/8$" and $3/4$"   zoning available - no
   special features - complete solar system available

REHAU INC., P.O. Box 1706, Leesburg, VA 22075 - (800) 247-9445 (703) 777-5255
   type of tubing - cross-linked polyethylene
   diameter sizes - $1/2$", $3/4$" and 1"   zoning available - no

SIEGMUND INC., 14771-E New Myford Rd., Tustin, CA 92680 - (714) 731-5706
   type of tubing - tri-o-flex is made of polyethylene with an inner core of aluminum, duo flex is made of polyethylene
   diameter sizes - $3/8$", $1/2$", $3/4$" and 1"   zoning available - yes, individual room/zone
   special features - Modular sheets provide noise reduction, prevent heat loss, provide a moisture barrier, and serve as the base for easy installation of the heating pipe without the use of tools.

STADLER CORP., 3 Yankee Division Rd., Bedford, MA 01730 - (617) 275-3122
   type of tubing - pextron is made of cross-linked polyethylene with oxygen diffusion barrier
   diameter sizes - $1/2$", $3/4$" and 1"   zoning available - yes, individual room/zone
   special features - A climate panel system is available. The panels are 7" wide x 48" long and allow the tubing to snap into place and stay there. This unit can be screwed either above or below the subfloor.

THERMAL EASE, PO Box 11787, Bainbridge Island, WA 98110 - (206) 842-9552
   type of tubing - polybutylene, cross-linked polyethylene, oxyguard barrier cross-linked polyethylenel and oxyguard barrier polybutylene
   diameter sizes - $3/8$", $1/2$", $5/8$", $3/4$" and 1"   zoning available - yes

WIRSBO COMPANY, 5925 - 148th St. W., Apple Valley, MN 55124 - (612) 891-2000
   type of tubing - hepex is made of cross-linked polyethylene with an oxygen diffusion barrier, pex pipe is cross-linked polyethylene without the barrier
   diameter sizes - $3/8$", $1/2$" and $5/8$"   zoning available - yes, up to 10 zones

Floor Panel Temperatures in °F

chart #1 - Use this chart to predict how much heat you will get by heating the floor.

Predicting How Much Heat You Will Get by Heating the Floor

Floors that exceed 85°F in temperature are beginning to get uncomfortably warm. Excessive floor temperatures can result in athlete's foot and possible shrinkage of wooden floor products that were not dried properly. It is poor design practice if floor temperature exceeds 85°F on a routine basis, but it is acceptable if it happens infrequently.

It can be seen from _chart #1_ on page 22 that a floor temperature of 85°F will result in a Btu emission of 50 Btu/sq.ft./hour. Into a room at 65°F. (A mean effective temperature of 65°F is equivalent to a comfort level of about 70°F in a non radiantly heated area.)

A Btu output of only 18.75 Btu/sq. ft./hour will be adequate to heat a building with "good" insulating characteristics when it is -10°F outside.

18.75 Btu/sq. ft./hour	=	.25 Btu/hour/sq. ft./degree F	x	75 degrees F
(heat output)		(insulating value)		(temp. diff.)

Chart #1 shows that this Btu output can be achieved with floor temperatures well below 80°F. At these reasonable temperatures, there is no reason to be concerned about problems associated with excess floor temperatures. The floor will actually be slightly warmer during the summer and the underfloor heating system thus provides the benefits of temperature stability to the floor materials.

The heat output of an 85°F floor may not be adequate to heat poorly insulated structures when it is very cold without unreasonable high floor temperature. Such a building should either have its insulation upgraded or it should be provided with another supplemental heat source.

50 Btu/sq. ft./hour	=	2.0 Btu/hour/sq. ft./degree F	x	25 degrees F
				(temp. diff.)

Lightweight Cement Specifications

Effect of Floor Coverings

Floor coverings can have a major influence when designing a radiant floor heating system. For example, a floor covered with ceramic tile or wood flooring can put out three times the BTUs of a floor covered with a heavy carpet and pad.

Area Zone Control Will Heat

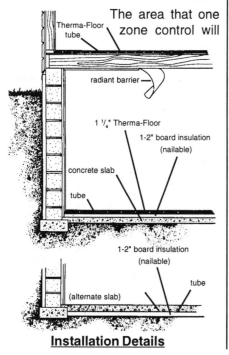

The area that one zone control will

Installation Details

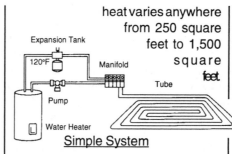

Simple System

heat varies anywhere from 250 square feet to 1,500 square feet.

The amount of heat loss, the type of floor coverings and the tube spacing all influence the size of the area.

Tubing Specifications

Tubing: Polybutylene, cross-linked polyethylene, oxygen barrier, and non-barrier tubing available, made to ASTM D 3309, ASTM F 876, DIN 4726.
Design rating: 100 psi (689 kPa) at 180°F (82°C).
Dimensions (inside): 3/8" (10 mm), 1/2" (15 mm), 3/4" (20 mm).
Lengths: Individual tube circuits up to 1,000' (300 m) long.

Therma-Floor Specifications

Function: Interior underlayment, not a wearing surface
Compressive Strength: Up to 2,500 psi (17,225 kPa)
Static Loading: Up to 2,000 psi (13,780

kPa)
'k' Factor: 4.96 BTU/sq. ft./hour/°F/inch thickness(56.54 kJ/m²)
Specific Heat: 224 BTU/lb.—°F @ 85°F(.52 kJ/Kg @ 29°C)
Weight: At 1 1/4" (32 mm), less than 12 lbs./sq. ft. (58.56 Kg/m²)
Dry Density: Typical density is 115 lbs./cu. ft. (1,840 Kg/m³)
Minimum Depth: 1 1/4" (32 mm)

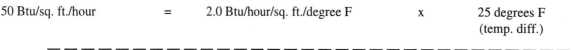

Conventional System

Thermal Resistance at 1 1/4" (32 mm): R-0.26

Zone Control Specifications

Pump: 115 VAC, 1.0 amp, 1/25 h.p.
Normal output: 90° to 140°F.
Maximum fluid temperature: 190°F.
Control circuit: 24VAC.

Under a Suspended Wood Floor Using Aluminum Heat Emission Plates.

1. Connect the loop to the supply manifold.
2. Snap the tubing into the heat emission plates, and following the tubing layout plan, staple the heat emission plates to the under side of the subfloor. Leave a small gap between each plate. Place two staples on each end between the tubing, and two in the center between the tubing.
3. During installation, it will become necessary to loop the tubing from one joist cavity 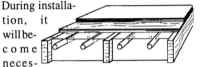 to another. This is achieved by looping the tubing below the joist dividing the two cavities. This presents problems if the underside of the floor is finished. It will then be necessary to either lower the ceiling to accommodate the thickness of the tubing, or drill a hole through the floor joist and run the tubing through the joist.
4. Connect the end of the loop to the return manifold. Complete the installation.
5. Pressure test the system in accordance with local building codes.
6. Install suitable insulation below the plates to limit downward loss.

— — — — — — — — —

Poured Floor Underlayment on a Suspended Wood Floor

1. Connect one end of the loop to the supply manifold.
2. Make sure the wood stapler head is securely fastened to the stapler and the stapler is loaded with 1 1/4" staples. Staple the tubing to the wood subfloor.
3. Staple the tubing as necessary along the straight runs to ensure it will stay in place (additional staples will be added later). At the 180° turns, secure one staple at the top of the arc and two staples, one on each side, 12" below the top of the arc.
4. Once the complete loop has been laid out, connect the end of the tubing to the return manifold.
5. Attach the walking stick to the stapler and fasten the tubing to the subfloor every two feet or as necessary to prevent it from dislodging and/or floating up into the pour. Complete the tubing installation.
6. Pressure test the system in accordance with local building codes.
7. Apply a suitable concrete mixture over the tubing.

Single Concrete Pour Over a Sand Bed Encasing the Tubing

1. Lay out the wire mesh or rebar over the base material.
2. Connect the loop to the supply manifold.
3. Secure the tubing to the wire mesh or rebar.
4. Secure the tubing every four feet along straight runs. At the 180° turns, tie the tubing once at the top of the arc and once on each side, 12" from the top of the arc, to prevent it from dislodging and/or floating up into the pour.
5. Once the complete loop has been laid out, connect the end of the loop to the return manifold. Complete the installation.
6. Pressure test the system in accordance with local building codes.
7. Apply sand over the tubing.
8. Apply a suitable concrete mixture over the sand.

— — — — — — — — —

On a Suspended Wood Floor Using Aluminum Heat Emission Plates

1. Mark the approximate location of the tubing on the subfloor.
2. Starting at the area furthest from the manifold, glue & nail a 1x6 furring strip to the subfloor along the exterior wall.
3. Using a heat emission plate as a guide, nail and glue another 1x6 furring strip parallel to the first. Be sure to leave a 1" space between furring strips for the groove of the heat emission plate.
4. Staple the heat emission plates to the furring strips on one side of the tubing only. This will allow the plates to expand as the subfloor or finish flooring is nailed down. Leave a small gap between plates.
5. Connect one end of the loop to the supply manifold.
6. Following the tubing layout pattern, snap the tubing into the heat emission plate.
7. Connect the other end of the loop to the return manifold. Complete the tubing installation.
8. Pressure test the system in accordance with local building codes.
9. Apply a suitable construction adhesive to the furring strips where exposed between the heat emission plates.
10. Apply a suitable subfloor or finish flooring over the tubing.
11. Install suitable insulation below the floor to limit downward loss.

Concrete or Poured Underlayment Over a Concrete Slab Using a Stapler System

1. Affix the high density insulation (1/2" minimum thickness) to the lower concrete slab by means of a suitable construction adhesive, fastener, or slurry coat of gypsum.
2. Connect the loop to the manifold.
3. Make sure the foam stapler head is securely fastened to the stapler and the stapler is loaded with 2 1/2" staples. Staple the tubing to the foam.
4. Staple the tubing every six feet on straight runs (additional staples will be added later). At the 180° turns secure two staples at the top of the arc, and two staples on each side, six inches below the top of the arc.
5. Once the complete loop has been laid out and secured to the foam, connect the loop to the return manifold.
6. Attach the walking stick to the stapler and fasten the tubing to the foam every two feet or as necessary to prevent it from dislodging and/or floating up into the pour. Complete the installation.
7. Pressure test the system in accordance with local building codes.
8. Apply concrete mixture over the tubing.

— — — — — — — — —

Single Concrete Pour Over Slab Insulation Using Copper Coated Wire Ties

1. Lay out the recommended high density insulation over the base material.
2. Lay out the wire mesh or rebar.
3. Connect one end of the loop to the supply manifold using only compression fittings.
4. Secure tubing to the wire mesh or rebar.
5. Tie the tubing to the wire mesh or rebar using copper coated wire ties and wire twister. Secure the tubing to the wire mesh or rebar every four feet along straight runs. At the 180° turns tie the tubing at the top of the arc and once on each side, 12" from the top of the arc, to prevent it from dislodging and/or floating up into the pour.
6. Once the complete loop has been laid out, connect the end of the loop to the return manifold. Complete the tubing installation.
7. Securely fasten, as necessary, the wire mesh or rebar to the insulation.
8. Pressure test the system in accordance with local building codes.
9. Apply concrete mixture over the tubing.

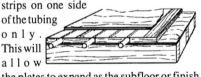

Q: We would like to add a zone control kit to our furnace to set different temperatures in various rooms. Can we also vary the temperature schedule in each room? How much will it cut my utility bills?

A: Adding a zone control kit to existing furnace ducts improves comfort and lowers your utility bills year-round. It wastes energy dollars to keep bedrooms toasty warm all day. A playroom temperature can be set higher after school when it is used or the living room can be set higher in the evening.

The savings and improved comfort from zoning are often greatest when air-conditioning in the summer. Almost every house has several rooms, typically on a second floor or on the west side, that never get cool enough. A zone control kit completely eliminates this problem and saves electricity too.

Zone control kits include several basic components - duct dampers, individual room clock thermostats and a central control unit. The thermostats can provide four programmable setback temperatures and times to fine tune each room or zone (group of rooms) for your family's schedule.

When a room gets to the proper temperature, the damper in the duct to that room closes a little to maintain the set temperature. If you are cooking in the kitchen or entertaining and creating an unusual amount of additional heat in one or two rooms, that duct damper closes to compensate for it.

Simple two zone systems are most common. One zone is for the bedrooms and the other zone for the rest of your house. More complex systems can provide thermostats and duct dampers for each room.

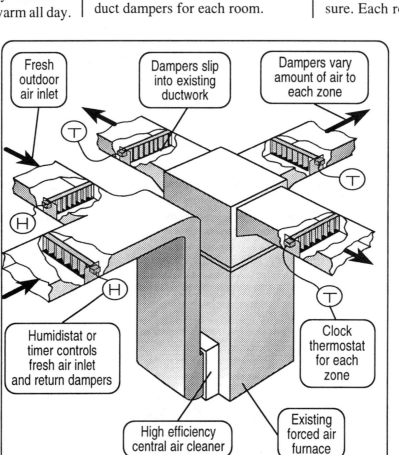

Fresh outdoor air inlet

Dampers slip into existing ductwork

Dampers vary amount of air to each zone

Humidistat or timer controls fresh air inlet and return dampers

High efficiency central air cleaner

Existing forced air furnace

Clock thermostat for each zone

Some systems allow you to change the temperature and setback schedule from your office. Just telephone the system and tell it that you will be several hours later than usual. Another option ducts fresh outdoor air into your return ducts. The zone system controls the timing and amount of fresh air added.

Round or rectangular duct dampers are available in many sizes to fit any duct in your house. To install a rectangular damper, use tin snips to cut a hole in the side of the duct. Slip in the damper and screw it in place. Circular dampers replace a short section of the duct.

Most duct dampers use mechanical louvers. A small servo motor controls the rotation of the louvers to vary the degree of closure. Each room thermostat is connected with safe low-voltage (24 volt) wires.

Another simple damper design uses inflatable "pillows" inside the duct. As these inflate, they control the size of the duct opening and the amount of heated or cooled air getting to each room.

Q: How do I determine which light bulbs to replace with new efficient compact fluorescent bulbs? The compact fluorescent bulbs are much more expensive than standard bulbs.

A: It is simple to determine the savings from replacing a standard bulb with a compact fluorescent bulb. Just multiply the wattage difference by your local electric rate to determine the savings per hour.

For seldom used lights, a compact fluorescent does not make economic sense. For example, if a closet light is on only five minutes per day, the savings would take 160 years to pay back the compact fluorescent's higher price.

Zone control systems cut your utility bills by allowing you to set back the temperatures for extended periods in certain rooms or zones (groups of rooms). Manufacturers of the most efficient zone control systems are listed below.

Comfort is also improved. You can schedule rooms to be comfortably heated (or cooled in the summer) when you are using them. A zone control system also allows you to balance the forced air system to eliminate excessively hot or cold rooms. Pages 27 and 28 show detailed descriptions of several typical systems, sample ductwork/zone layouts, and design considerations.

The illustration to the right shows a typical zone system with a fresh air inlet. This improves comfort and indoor air quality in an airtight, energy efficient house. The dampers controlling the outdoor air inlet damper and the existing return air duct damper are programmed to work together. All of the zone thermostats are connected to a central "brain" which controls the dampers for maximum efficiency and comfort.

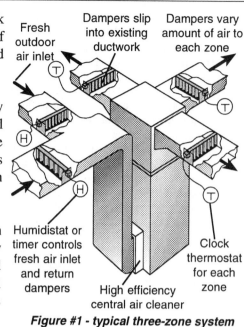

Figure #1 - typical three-zone system

Manufacturers of Zone Control Systems

ARZEL TECHNOLOGY, 26210 Emory Road., Cleveland, OH 44128 - (216) 831-6068
> model - "P400 Series"   zones available - two, three and four
> model - "P800 Series"   zones available - two, four, six and eight

CARRIER CORPORATION, PO Box 4808, Syracuse, NY 13221 - (315) 432-3803
> model - "Weathermaker Two Zone"   zones available - two with flexibility to add zones
> model - "Comfort Zone"   zones available - four

ENERZONE, 4103 Pecan Orchard, Parker, TX 75009 - (214) 424-9808
> model - "Ultra Zone"   zones available - two to eighteen
> type of damper - FlexDamper®, inflatable dampers available in round, rectangular or custom shapes

HONEYWELL INC., 1985 Douglas Dr. N., Golden Valley, MN 55422 - (800) 345-6770 ext. 703
> model - "W180 Zone Control"   zones available - up to twelve

RESEARCH PRODUCTS, PO Box 1467, Madison, WI 53701 - (800) 334-6011 (608) 257-8801
> model - "PerfectTemp"   zones available - two and three

TROLEX (TROL-A-TEMP), 57 Bushes Ln., Elmwood Park, NJ 07407 - (800) 828-8367 (201) 794-8004
> model - "Mastertrol MABS II"   zones available - two
> model - "Mastertrol MM2"   zones available - up to five
> model - "Mastertrol ABS XX"   zones available - two or three, expandable to thirty

VALERA CORP. (ENERSTAT CORP.), 800 Proctor Ave., Ogdensburg, NY 13669 - (613) 342-0570
> model - "System 2"   zones available - two
> model - "System 3 Plus 2"   zones available - up to five
> model - "System 10"   zones available - up to ten, expandable to eighteen

ZTECH, 9605 Oates Dr., Sacramento, CA 95827 - (916) 369-8130
> model - "ClimateZone"   zones available - two

Ductwork/Damper Layout and Design For Zone Control System (Honeywell Inc. & Trolex)

The most important factor in zoning any system is a properly designed duct system. In any system, be it new or retrofit, zone control can be installed as long as a few simple duct design rules are considered.

The first point to consider is that the majority of the time only one or two zones may be calling, especially in residential systems. It is important that a constant volume of air flow be maintained through the HVAC unit when only the one or two zones are calling. Therefore, the duct systems should be slightly oversized from what normally is installed. It is also important not to oversize the duct system too much as this can lower the pressure and velocity, of the airflow, when all zones are open.

These types of zone control systems have been used for over 25 years. Experience and hundreds of thousands of zone control installations have shown that the duct design comes down to two simple approaches.

figure #1

The first approach is for smaller systems, usually 5 tons (2,000 CFM) or less, and 3 zones or less. On the new and retrofit installations where the ducts can be sized to accommodate zone control, it is recommended that each zone truck be sized to handle about 60% to 70% of the total airflow. This is a median duct size to satisfy two extremes. The most common extreme is when only one zone is calling. That one zone duct that would be open would not be so small as to restrict enough air volume where it would cause a high static pressure, high velocity, or reduce the volume of airflow through the unit. Since all zone ducts are the same size, the airflow conditions should be the same no matter which zone is calling. On the other hand, when all 2 or 3 zones are calling, the duct system is not so large that when all zones' dampers are open, the air pressure and velocity are too low for adequate air circulation in the zones.

For example, the supply duct system is normally sized to maintain a 0.1" Static Pressure. On a 3 ton (1,200 CFM) system, the duct size is usually a 24" x 8". Taking a duct size that is 60% to 70% of the 24" x 8" duct would equal a 14" x 8" or 16" x 8" duct. In this example, by having either a 14" x 8" or 16" x 8" duct for each zone, it would be able to move a sufficient volume of air without reducing the airflow through the unit. It is also important to provide an adequate number of takeoffs per zone, in order to distribute the volume of air. On systems less than 3½ tons (1,400 CFM) a minimum of 5 to 6, 6" round takeoffs, or the equivalent thereof, is suggested. Systems of 4 tons (1,600 CFM) or more, would be 5 to 6, 8" round takeoffs or the equiva- lent thereof.

On systems that are over 5 tons (2,000 CFM), sizing the ductwork to handle 60% to 70% of the total airflow often becomes impractical. Also these systems are large enough in that they require more than 3 zones. These size systems should be adequately sized to handle the total airflow when all zones are open and use a Static Pressure Regulating Damper, Model SPRD, to by-pass any excess air when only a smaller number of zones are open on the system.

figure #2

Relieving Excess Air Pressure

In any new or retrofit zoning application, where a Mastertrol panel is not used, or when the duct system is undersized where any one zone cannot handle at least 60% to 70% of the total air flow, the excess air must then be by-passed. Trol-A-Temp has developed two methods of relieving the excess air. The first can be the use of a separate duct used as a dump or by-pass zone. This duct would be controlled by a Static Pressure Regulating Damper, Model SPRD. As a number of zone dampers close and only a small number of zones remain open, the SPRD will automatically open as the air pressure in the duct system increases. This air can them be by-passed into a hallway, false ceiling, basement, return air duct or other non-critical temperature area. As the zone dampers all begin to open, the air pressure in the duct system will then decrease. The reduction of air pressure in the duct system will automatically close the SPRD.

Another method of relieving excess is to undersize the damper to the duct, of some of the larger zones. For example, if a duct is 24" x 8", use a smaller 22" x 8" damper. This will allow a couple of inches of free area for air to continually by-pass into that zone, while another smaller zone may not be able to handle the majority of the air flow. Caution, however, must be used here in order to prevent too much by-pass air from overheating or over-cooling a particular zone.

Air-Conditioning And Coil Freeze Up

One of the most commonly asked questions in regards to zoning is, how do you avoid the air conditioning coil from freezing, if only one or two small zones are open, and a large majority of the zone dampers are closed? As stated previously, properly designing the duct system will help prevent coil freeze-up. However, on many retrofit systems where the duct system cannot be properly sized, it presents a problem. The use of a SPRD by-pass damper to relieve any excess air pressure when only one or two small zones are open is the best answer. This is important as the air flow across the air conditioning coil must not be reduced. As long as adequate air flow is maintained across the coil, freeze-up should not occur unless precipitated by other causes such as clogged air filters, or low refrigerant pressures or blocked supply ducts. To help prevent coil-freeze-up, it may be desirable to use an Anti Freeze-Up Control, Model AFUC. This control would act as a low limit to prevent the coil from freezing. Quite often with zoning, if there is a reduction of air flow when only a small zone calls, that small zone requires only a small amount of cooling and, therefore, the zone thermostat satisfies and shuts-off the cooling before the coil begins to freeze.

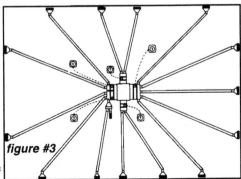

figure #3

Zone Control and System Performance

When zoning any system, it is important to realize that a constant air flow must be maintained across the air conditioning or heat pump coil. By properly designing the duct system, this is easily achieved. All fan motors are rated to maintain a specific volume of air, at a specific static pressure. Once this static pressure rating is overcome, the volume of air that the fan produces is reduced. The suggested duct sizing in this catalog will often remain well below the static pressure ratings of most of today's fan motors rated at 0.5" Static Pressure. By comparing our suggested duct sizing with a duct sizing chart or calculator, you will find when only one zone duct is open, a static pressure of .35". This is well below the .50" that the fan is rated for, and will not reduce the volume of air across the air conditioning or heat pump coil.

A quick check of the refrigeration pressures, on the compressor, would determine if the air volume changes as various zone dampers close down. Connect the gauges to the high and low side of the compressor, calling for cooling in all zones, so that all zone dampers are open. The refrigeration pressures should be in accordance with the manufacturer's specifications. Now begin to close down each zone, one by one, until only one zone is open and still calling for cooling. If the zone ducts are not equally sized, close off the larger zones first until the smallest zone is then open. After each zone damper closes, wait a few minutes to see if the refrigeration pressures change. If the pressures do not change, the air volume (CFM) is remaining constant and the air conditioner or heat pump is running at its peak efficiency. If the pressures change, indicating a reduction of air flow, then a by-pass zone is needed to relieve the excess air pressure.

figure #4

Air Velocity and Noise

When zoning any system, questions often arise regarding excessive air noise and velocity. Provided the duct system is properly designed and sized, these problems never occur. If these problems do occur, the solution is to by-pass the excessive air causing the noise. This may be done by adding the SPRD or by undersizing a particular damper to the zone duct or by taking a blade or two out of the larger zone dampers on the system.

Correcting Existing Systems

Zone control can provide better temperature control and reduce energy costs on many existing systems. Zone control will overcome most of the problems associated with undersized heating and cooling systems. In many residential and light commercial systems, do all zones call for conditioned air at the same time? Frequently it is only a small number of zones that call and, therefore, not all of the heating or cooling is required to condition only a couple of zones. In these instances, a 2½ or 3 ton air conditioning unit can be used instead of a 3½ or 4 ton unit.

figure #6

figure #5

Often with existing systems, zone control is a necessity in order to properly balance the building's temperature. While zone control can help to better balance the system, it is not the answer for undersized or poorly designed duct systems.

When looking at zoning an existing system, the supply duct system must be examined first. Here it must be determined if the ductwork is accessible to install a damper and if the ductwork is already split into individual zones or not. The perfect system for retrofit is when the ductwork is accessible and each zone is supplied by a separate trunk. In some of the existing homes, the ductwork may not be easily accessible and, therefore, the motorized registers or diffusers would be used to control the individual outlets. In many retrofit applications, it is necessary to use a by-pass zone or undersize the dampers to the ducts in larger zones in order to relieve the excess air when only one or two small zones call.

Zoning Heat Pumps

Heat pumps are becoming a very popular form of heating and cooling in many parts of the country. When heat pumps are used they are sized according to the cooling load, which almost always is less than the heating load. For example, usually a 3 ton heat pump may be installed where normally a 100,000 Btuh gas or oil furnace would have been used. That heat pump now provides only 36,000 Btus of heating, without including any backup heating. That 36,000 Btus is not enough to heat the whole house on some of the colder winter days; however, it may be enough to heat one or two zones, but not all of the zones. It is for this reason that all heat pumps should be zoned, because of their limited capacity. Even as the outdoor air temperature drops, the heat pump loses efficiency and no longer puts out the amount of Btus it was normally designed to. As this occurs, it is necessary for the heat pump to rely on a backup form of heating. However, if the heat pump is zoned, individual zones by themselves may require less than 36,000 Btus and even as the heat pump loses efficiency, it may still have enough Btu capacity to heat an individual zone or two without having to rely on the backup heating source. This allows the balance point of the backup heat to be lowered and the most efficient use of the heat pump to be utilized, especially when the backup heating is electric resistance.

Description of Zone Control Illustrations

figure #1 - 3-ZONE SPLIT LEVEL system in a typical split level house is shown with a damper and thermostat controlling the flow of air through the trunk duct to each zone. Installation requires a 3-Zone Mastertrol, 3 dampers, with thermostats.

figure #2 - ZONE CONTROL FOR A BI-LEVEL HOUSE is shown with one thermostat and damper controlling the upstairs living area zone, same for the bedroom zone, and same for downstairs recreation area. A three zone Mastertrol Panel, one 40 VA transformer, plus three dampers and thermostats is the only material required for the installation.

figure #3 - ROOM BY ROOM COMFORT CONTROL may be installed on most any new or existing heating-cooling system by controlling the flow of air at each outlet with automatic square to round transition dampers.

figure #4 - 2-ZONE RANCH HOUSE is shown with a thermostat in each zone controlling a corresponding zone damper. For a Mastertrol installation, the following material would be required: One 2-Zone Mastertrol Panel, 2 AOBD Dampers with thermostats, and one 40 VA Transformer.

figure #5 - A 4-ZONE SYSTEM for a professional office or home is shown with the air to each room or zone controlled by a damper and thermostat. Installation requires a 4-Zone Mastertrol, 4 dampers and thermostats, and one 40 VA transformer.

figure #6 - ROOM BY ROOM TEMPERATURE CONTROL is shown in this 5-zone radial system, which may be located either overhead or in slab.

Q: I need a new super-efficient room air conditioner that is very quiet and cools without drafts. What features should I look for and does it make sense to use one even if I have central air-conditioning?

A: New super-efficient window air conditioners have many unique energy-saving and comfort features. With the higher internal insulation levels, efficient motors, and airtight construction, they are also very quiet.

The highest-efficiency window air conditioners have an Energy Efficiency Ratio (EER) of 12.0. Small models cost less than 4 cents per hour to run and weigh only about 100 lb., so you can easily move them from window to window.

This is twice as efficient as some models made just five years ago. These models also provide better air distribution and temperature control, both important for energy savings and comfort. To realize the maximum savings, it is imperative that you select the proper-size model for your room.

One new model has motorized oscillating louvers to distribute the air evenly throughout your room. Switch them off to direct the cool air to just one location. This feature reduces drafts and noise by allowing you to choose a slower blower speed and still feel comfortable.

More blower speeds are better. A super-efficient model should have at least three speeds and some have five speeds. The low speed is extremely quiet. Manually adjustable four-way or six-way directional air flow louvers are effective. You can face each set in a different direction.

Another energy-saving and sound-reducing option switches the blower off when the compressor stops. This is especially useful at night in a bedroom when the cooling needs are lower. Although the air distribution is not as even as with a continuous blower, it is quieter and saves electricity.

Other models use special heat anticipator thermostats just like on your wall-mounted thermostat. This anticipates the room temperature changes and minimizes temperature swings.

Even if you have central air-conditioning, it makes sense to install a window unit in the most used room or perhaps a bedroom. This allows you to set your central thermostat higher and save 10% to 20%. A typical older three-ton central air conditioner can increase your electric bills by 46 cents (EER=7, $.09/kilowatt-hr.) for each hour the compressor is running.

Q: I recently installed an efficient insulated steel front door on my house. How can I install a deadbolt myself in a steel door? I have installed them in wood doors before.

A: You install the deadbolt in an insulated steel door the same way as in a wood door. Most insulated steel doors have a wood frame and wood reinforcement around the lockset holes. Foam insulation panels are either fitted inside or the foam is injected in under pressure.

You will have to use a hole saw made to cut sheet metal. A standard wood hole saw will not be effective. Since many steel doors have magnetic weatherstripping, carefully position the hole in the jamb so that the door contacts the weatherstripping when you close and lock it.

Super-quiet with insulation

High-efficiency compressor

Six-way or oscillating louvers

Condenser coils

Multi-speed blower

Easy to clean filter

Automatic thermostat

Energy saver blower switch

Even if you have central air-conditioning, it can make sense to also use a room air conditioner in your most used room. This allows you to set your central thermostat higher and save more electricity than it costs to run the small room air conditioner.

Page 31 lists the model numbers, Energy Efficiency Ratios (EER), and the cooling output capacities of the models. For your information, one ton of cooling is equal to 12,000 Btuh (Btu/hour).

I have only listed the super-efficient models with an EER of 10 or above. Many manufacturers are not listed because they are identical to other models. For example, Fedders owns Climatrol, Hampton Bay, Marta America, etc.

Several of General Electric's room air conditioners have the electrically-powered oscillating louvers. This feature helps to distribute the cool air throughout your room.

G.E. also offers a built-in timer to automatically turn the air conditioner on and off. This is convenient if you live alone and you want the air conditioner to come on right before you arrive home from work. You can also buy separate plug-in timers to accomplish the same thing.

It is extremely important to select the proper-cooling capacity window air conditioner for your needs. If you install one that is too large, it will not run long enough to adequately dehumidify the air. The room will cool down fast and the compressor will stop. You will end up with muggy cool air.

If the air conditioner is too small, it will not be able to cool your room on the hottest days. It will also be running nearly constantly and the noise may be bothersome.

The worksheet on page 32 (which uses figure #1 on this page) will help you to determine what cooling capacity you need. It is a little complicated, but worthwhile completing. If your calculations indicate a capacity that is not available from any of these manufacturers, select the next closest smaller size.

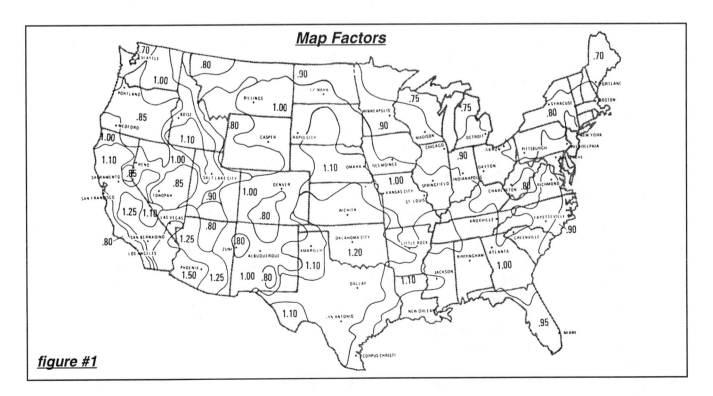

figure #1

AMANA, Amana, IA 52204 - (800) 843-0304 (319) 622-5511

model - "Q Zone" • "Compact"	cooling output - 6,900 • 9,800 Btuh	EER* - 10.0 • 10.2	wattage - 670 • 960
dehumidification - 2.0 • 2.6 pints/hour	fan speeds - 3 • 3	CFM - 180 • 290	weight - 68 • 114 lbs.
model - "Quiet Zone High Capacity"	cooling output - 13,800 Btuh	EER - 10.3	wattage - 1,315 watts
dehumidification - 3.7 pints/hour	fan speeds - 3	CFM - 380	weight - 150 lbs.

CARRIER CORP., PO Box 4808, Syracuse, NY 13221 - (800) 227-7437

model - "XCB and YCB Electronic"	cooling output - 12,000 Btuh	EER - 10.0	wattage - 1,200
dehumidification - 4.4 pints/hour	fan speeds - 3	CFM - 290	weight - 115 lbs.
model - "TC Siesta"	cooling output - 8,600 Btuh	EER - 10.0	wattage - 875
dehumidification - 2.1 pints/hour	fan speeds - 3	CFM - 240	weight - 63 lbs.

EMERSON, 3421 Route 22 E., Whitehouse, NJ 08888 - (800) 283-4599 (908) 725-0500

model - "Ultra Light" • "Compact Q"	cooling output - 5,000 • 6,000 Btuh	EER - 8.0 • 10.0	wattage - 625 • 600
dehumidification - 1.8 • 1.6 pints/hour	fan speeds - 2 • 3	CFM - 140 • 200	weight - 44 • 64 lbs.
model - "Modulaire"	cooling output - 12,000 Btuh	EER - 9.5	wattage - 1,260
dehumidification - 3.9 pints/hour	fan speeds - 3	CFM - 310	weight - 97 lbs.

FEDDERS NORTH AMERICA, 3421 Route 22 E., Whitehouse, NJ 08888 - (800) 283-4599 (908) 725-0500

model - "Air-Lite" • "Portable"	cooling output - 5,000 • 6,000 Btuh	EER - 8.0 • 10.0	wattage - 625 • 600
dehumidification - 1.6 pints/hour	fan speeds - 2 • 3	CFM - 140 • 200	weight - 44 • 64 lbs.
model - "Whisperer"	cooling output - 12,000 Btuh	EER - 9.5	wattage - 1,260
dehumidification - 3.9 pints/hour	fan speeds - 3	CFM - 310	weight - 97 lbs.

FRIEDRICH, PO Box 1540, San Antonio, TX 78295 - (210) 225-2000

model - "Quiet Electronic" • "Q Star"	cooling output - 10,200 • 7,100 Btuh	EER - 11.7 • 10.3	wattage - 870 • 690
dehumidification - 2.6 • 2.5 pints/hour	fan speeds - 4 • 3	CFM - 300 • 140	weight - 115 • 82 lbs.
model - "Slider/Casement"	cooling output - 10,000 Btuh	EER - 9.5	wattage - 1,050
dehumidification - 2.5 pints/hour	fan speeds - 2	CFM - 245	weight - 83 lbs.

FRIGIDAIRE, 6000 Perimeter Dr., Dublin, OH 43017 - (800) 451-7007 (614) 792-4100

model - "Quiet-One" • "Compact"	cooling output - 6,100 • 8,000 Btuh	EER - 10.0 • 9.5	wattage - 610 • 845
dehumidification - 1.4 • 2.0 pints/hour	fan speeds - 3 • 3	CFM - 190 • 250	weight - 60 • 64 lbs.
model - "Intermediate" • "Heavy Duty"	cooling output - 12,000 • 15,000 Btuh	EER - 9.5 • 10.4	wattage - 1,265 • 1,430
dehumidification - 3.4 • 3.0 pints/hour	fan speeds - 3 • 3	CFM - 270 • 500	weight - 106 • 138 lbs.

GENERAL ELECTRIC, Appliance Park, Louisville, KY 40225 - (800) 626-2000

model - "Premium" • "Deluxe"	cooling output - 10,000 • 5,800 Btuh	EER - 10.0 • 10.0	wattage - 1,000 • 580
dehumidification - 3.2 • 0.9 pints/hour	fan speeds - 3 • 2	CFM - 310 • 220	weight - 88 • 64 lbs.
model - "Value"	cooling output - 12,000 Btuh	EER - 9.1	wattage - 1,310
dehumidification - 3.6 pints/hour	fan speeds - 2	CFM - 330	weight - 93 lbs.

GIBSON, 6000 Perimeter Dr., Dublin, OH 43017 - (800) 458-1445

model - "Panorama" • "Compact"	cooling output - 6,100 • 5,450 Btuh	EER - 10.0 • 10.0	wattage - 610 • 545
dehumidification - 1.4 • 1.1 pints/hour	fan speeds - 3 • 3	CFM - 190 • 175	weight - 60 • 60 lbs.
model - "Intermediate" • "Heavy Duty"	cooling output - 12,000 • 15,000 Btuh	EER - 9.5 • 10.4	wattage - 1,265 • 1,430
dehumidification - 3.5 • 3.0 pints/hour	fan speeds - 3 • 3	CFM - 255 • 500	weight - 106 • 138 lbs.

PANASONIC, 50 Meadowland Parkway, Secaucus, NJ 07094 - (201) 348-7000

model - "3 in One" • "Deluxe "	cooling output - 7,800 • 10,000 Btuh	EER - 10.0 • 10.0	wattage - 780 • 1,000
dehumidification - 2.3 • 3.2 pints/hour	fan speeds - 2 • 3	CFM - 220 • 310	weight - 66 • 88 lbs.
model - "Compact "	cooling output - 7,000 Btuh	EER - 8.5	wattage - 820
dehumidification - 2.1 pints/hour	fan speeds - 2	CFM - 160	weight - 46 lbs.

SHARP, PO Box 650, Mahwah, NJ 07430 - (800) 237-4277 (201) 529-8703

model - "Comfort Touch" • "Mechanical"	cooling output - 8,500 • 14,000 Btuh	EER - 8.5 • 10.0	wattage - 850 • 1,380
dehumidification - 1.9 • 3.8 pints/hour	fan speeds - 3 • 3	CFM - 250 • 410	weight - 46 • 120 lbs.

WHIRLPOOL CORP., Benton Harbor, MI 49022 - (800) 253-1301

model - "Designerstyle" • "Value"	cooling output - 14,000 • 10,000 Btuh	EER - 10.2 • 9.0	wattage - 1,372 • 1,110
dehumidification - 3.5 • 2.8 pints/hour	fan speeds - 3 • 3	CFM - 475 • 268	weight - n/a

WHITE WESTINGHOUSE, PO Box 7181, Dublin, OH 43017 - (800) 245-0600 (614) 792-4000

model - "Mobilaire" • "Compact"	cooling output - 6,100 • 8,000 Btuh	EER - 10.0 • 9.5	wattage - 610 • 845
dehumidification - 1.4 • 2.0 pints/hour	fan speeds - 3	CFM - 190 • 250	weight - 60 • 67 lbs.
model - "Intermediate" • "Heavy Duty"	cooling output - 12,000 • 15,000 Btuh	EER - 9.5 • 10.4	wattage - 1,265 • 1,430
dehumidification - 3.4 pints/hour	fan speeds - 3	CFM - 270 • 500	weight - 106 • 138 lbs.

These are the highest EER efficiencies in this series. There are other Btuh/EER available.

Instructions for using Cooling Load Estimate Form for Room Air Conditioners

(FROM AHAM STANDARD RAC-1)

A. This cooling load estimate form is suitable for estimating the cooling load for comfort air-conditioning installations which do not require specific conditions of inside temperature and humidity.

B. The form is based on an outside design temperature of 95°F dry bulb and 75°F wet bulb. It can be used for areas in the continental United States having other outside design temperatures by applying a correction factor for the particular locality as determined from the map.

C. The form includes "day" factors for calculating cooling loads in rooms where daytime comfort is desired (such as living rooms, offices, etc.), as well as "night" factors for calculating cooling loads in rooms where only nighttime comfort is desired (such as bedrooms). "Night" factors should be used only for those applications where comfort air-conditioning is desired during the period from sunset to sunrise.

D. The numbers of the following paragraphs refer to the correspondingly numbered item on the form:

1. Multiply the square feet of window area for each exposure by the applicable factor. The window area is the area of the wall opening in which the window is installed. For windows shaded by inside shades or venetian blinds, use the factor for "Inside Shades." For windows shaded by outside awnings or by both outside awnings and inside shades (or venetian blinds), use the factor for "Outside Awnings." "Single Glass" includes all types of single-thickness windows, and "Double Glass" includes sealed air-space types, storm windows, and glass block. Transfer only one number, representing the largest cooling load, to the right hand column.

2. Multiply the total square feet of all windows in the room by the applicable factor.

3a. Multiply the total length (linear feet) of all walls exposed to the outside by the applicable factor. Doors should be considered as being part of the wall. Outside walls facing due north should be calculated separately from outside walls facing other directions. Walls which are permanently shaded by adjacent structures should be considered as being "North Exposure." Do not consider trees and shrubbery as providing permanent shading. An uninsulated frame wall or a masonry wall 8 inches or less in thickness is considered "Light Construction." An insulated frame wall or a masonry wall over 8 inches in thickness is considered "Heavy Construction."

3b. Multiply the total length (linear feet) of all inside walls between the space to be conditioned and any unconditioned spaces by the given factor. Do not include inside walls which separate other air-conditioned rooms.

4. Multiply the total square feet of roof or ceiling area by the factor given for the type of construction most nearly describing the particular application. (Use one line only.)

5. Multiply the total square feet of floor area by the factor given. Disregard this item if the floor is directly on the ground or over a basement.

6. Multiply the total width (linear feet) of any doors or arches which are continually open to an unconditioned space by the applicable factor.

NOTE — Where the width of the doors or arches is more than 5 feet, the actual load may exceed the calculated value. In such cases, both adjoining rooms should be considered as a single large room, and the room air conditioner unit or units should be selected according to a calculation made on this new basis.

7. Total the loads estimated for the foregoing 6 items.

8. Multiply the sub-total obtained in Item 7 by the proper correction factor, selected from the map, for the particular locality.

9. Multiply the number of people who normally occupy the space to be air conditioned by the factor given. Use a minimum of 2 people.

10. Determine the total number of watts for lights and electrical equipment, except the air conditioner itself, that will be in use when the room air conditioning is operating. Multiply the total wattage by the factor given.

11. Add the loads estimated in the foregoing items 8 through 10 to obtain the total estimated design cooling load in BTU/hr.

E. For best results, a room air conditioning unit or units with a cooling capacity rating (determined per AHAM RAC-1) close to the estimated load should be selected. In general, a greatly oversized unit which would operate intermittently will be much less satisfactory than one which is slightly undersized and which would operate more nearly continuously.

F. Intermittent loads such as kitchen and laundry equipment are not included in this form.

Cooling Load Estimate Form for Room Air Conditioners*

Customer _____ Address _____

Estimated By _____ Date _____ Space to be used for _____

Heat Gain From	Quantity	FACTORS				BTU/hr (Quantity × Factor)
		Night	Day			
			No Shades*	Inside Shades*	Outside Awnings*	(Area × Factor)
1. WINDOWS, heat gain from direct radiation of the sun. (Total all windows for each exposure, but transfer only one number, representing the largest cooling load, to the right hand column.)						
Northeast	sq ft	0	60	25	20	
East	sq ft	0	80	40	25	
Southeast	sq ft	0	75	30	20	Use only the largest load
South	sq ft	0	75	35	20	
Southwest	sq ft	0	110	45	30	
West	sq ft	0	150	65	45	
Northwest	sq ft	0	120	50	35	
North	sq ft	0	0	0	0	

*These factors are for single glass only. For glass block, multiply the above factors by 0.5; for double glass or storm windows, multiply the above factors by 0.8.

Heat Gain From	Quantity	Night	Day	BTU/hr
2. WINDOWS, heat gain by conduction (Total for all windows)				
Single glass	sq ft	14	14	
Double glass or glass block	sq ft	7	7	

3. WALLS (based on linear feet of wall)	Quantity	Night	Light Construction	Heavy Construction	BTU/hr
a. Outside walls North exposure	ft	20	30	20	
Other than North exposure	ft	20	60	30	
b. Inside walls (between conditioned and unconditioned spaces only)	ft	30	30		

Heat Gain From	Quantity	Night	Day	BTU/hr
4. ROOF OR CEILING (Use one only.)				
a. Roof, uninsulated	sq ft	5	19	
b. Roof, with 1 inch or more insulation	sq ft	3	8	
c. Ceiling, with occupied space above	sq ft	3	3	
d. Ceiling, insulated, with attic space above	sq ft	4	5	
e. Ceiling, uninsulated, with attic above	sq ft	7	12	
5. FLOOR (Disregard if floor is directly on ground or over basement.)	sq ft	3	3	
6. DOORS AND ARCHES CONTINUOUSLY OPEN TO UNCONDITIONED SPACE (linear feet of width)	ft	200	300	
7. SUB-TOTAL	XXXX	XXX	XXX	
8. GEOGRAPHICAL LOCATION MAP FACTOR		(Item 7) × _____ Factor From Map		
9. NUMBER OF PEOPLE	_____	600	600	
10. LIGHTS AND ELECTRICAL EQUIPMENT IN USE	watts	3	3	
11. TOTAL COOLING LOAD [BTU/hr to be used for selection of room air conditioner(s)]	XXX	XX	XXX	

*For more precise determination of heat load, consult ASHRAE Handbook of Fundamentals

Q: We plan to build a new house. Does it make sense to install a central hot water heat (boiler) system instead of a forced-air heating system? What are its advantages? We need central air-conditioning too.

A: A new central hot water heat boiler system often can heat a home less expensively than a forced-air system. Gas boilers have efficiencies as high as 94% and oil as high as 88%. If you are replacing an old boiler in your home, installing one of these boilers can cut your heating costs by 30%.

There are several simple methods to incorporate central air-conditioning with hot water heat. Since the air ducts are used for cooling only, you can locate them for maximum efficiency. Mini-split ductless air conditioners are also efficient and provide cooling in typically hard-to-cool rooms.

In addition to efficient heating, hot water heating systems provide comfort. Room temperatures remain constant without the repeated initial gusts of cold air followed by hot air as with a forced air system. Without blowers and ducts, hot water systems are quiet and dust free.

The small baseboard radiators heat your house in two ways. First, heat is radiated directly from the radiators to objects and people in the rooms. This feels warm, like standing in the sun in the winter. Room air naturally circulates up through the radiators and gently heats the air in the room.

The combination of radiant and warm air heat provides comfort without the "dry feel", typical of forced air heat. A boiler also provides a virtually limitless supply of hot water for morning showers.

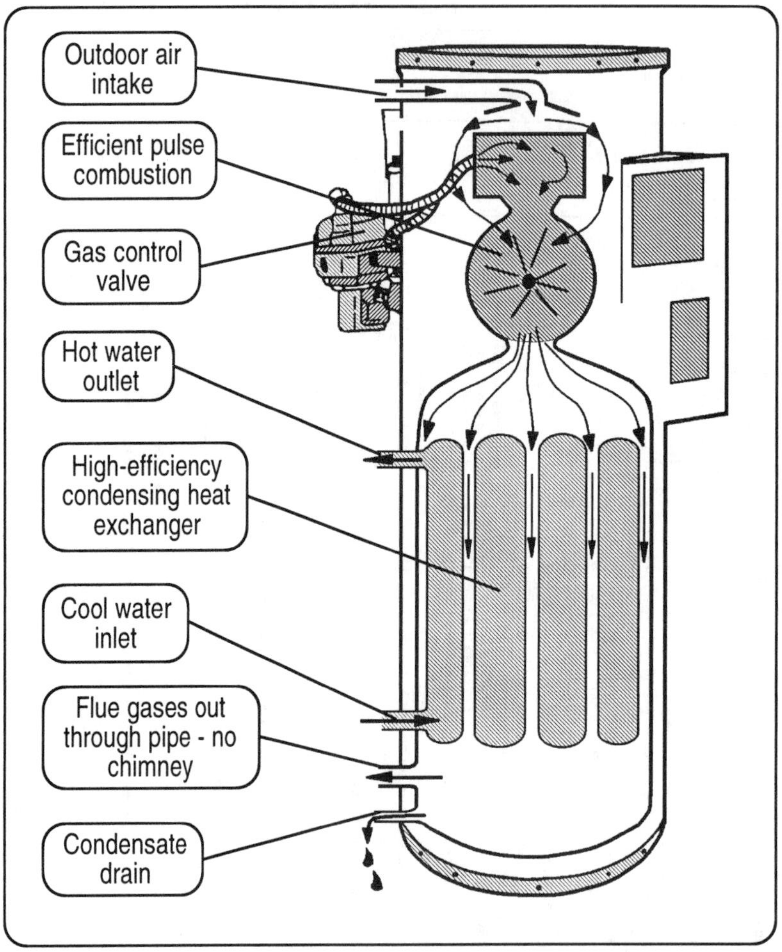

Diagram labels:
- Outdoor air intake
- Efficient pulse combustion
- Gas control valve
- Hot water outlet
- High-efficiency condensing heat exchanger
- Cool water inlet
- Flue gases out through pipe - no chimney
- Condensate drain

One efficient hot water heating technique uses pipes in the floor. The entire floor gets warm and radiates heat upward. This makes you feel very comfortable (warm feet), even in a cool room. By keeping the air temperature lower, your total heating bills are significantly lower.

The most energy-efficient boiler uses gas and a pulse technology. When your system calls for heat, a spark plug starts the highly efficient combustion in the boiler heat exchanger. Each "pulse" ignites the next pulse of gas.

A pulse boiler, along with other induced draft models, do not require a chimney. Exhaust gases are vented outdoors through a horizontal pipe. By avoiding the cost of a chimney, it's ideal for conversion from electric heat.

Zone heating (keeping different rooms at different temperatures throughout the day) is done with simple automatic water valves. Zoning can cut your annual heating costs by 20% or more and improve your comfort.

Q: I have good-quality thermal pane windows, but one of them has developed fog in between the glass panes. Is there any way to repair it?

A: There is no way to remove the fog from between the glass panes. The air gap is sealed at the factory with a special desiccant (drying) chemical inside. The entire double pane glass unit must be replaced.

Most good-quality thermal windows come with at least a 10-year warranty and they should last many years more than that. If you can't locate the contractor who installed them, you will probably have to pay for the labor costs yourself.

The manufacturers of the highest efficiency oil and gas boilers, along with product specifications, are shown on pages 34, 35, and 36. Most of these models have several heat outputs for each, so the model names are listed as "series". The names of other model series, their fuel type, and efficiencies are listed.

The number of heat capacities and the ranges are shown for each model series. For oil boilers, the heat capacity is shown as actual DOE heat output. For gas boilers, it is shown as heat input. You can determine the heat output for the gas models by multiplying the heat input by the efficiency (AFUE - annual fuel utilization efficiency).

The type of venting (draft) is important, especially if you are planning to replace an electric heating system or your current chimney is in poor condition. With induced exhaust draft, a small exhaust blower forces the fuel gases outdoors through a horizontal pipe. You need not build or repair your chimney. The dimensions shown help you to determine if you have space to fit one of these new boilers in your utility area.

Annual Savings from Installing a New Higher Effiency Boiler							
Boiler Efficiency	Approximate Annual Operating Cost - $						
60%	400	500	600	700	800	900	1000
65%	365	460	550	640	735	825	915
70%	340	425	510	595	675	760	845
75%	315	395	470	550	630	710	785
80%	295	365	440	515	585	660	735
85%	275	345	410	485	550	620	685
90%	255	320	385	450	515	580	640
95%	240	305	365	425	485	545	605

To use this chart: Estimate the approx. efficiency of your current boiler. If it is more than 10 years old, the efficiency is likely to be about 60%. Then locate your current annual operating costs (use your fuel oil bills or your natural gas bills less water heating and cooking). Use this chart to estimate how much you can save with a more efficient boiler.

Example: If your current boiler is 60% AFUE, and your annual operating cost is $700, the cost to operate a new 90% AFUE boiler will be about $450, and annual savings of about $250.

High-Efficiency Oil- and Gas-Fired Boilers

AXEMAN-ANDERSON, 300 E. Mountain Ave., S. Williamsport, PA 17701 - (717) 326-9114

model - "Olympia 1"　　　　　　　　fuel - oil　　　　　　efficiency - 88%
capacities - 2 models: 80,000 to 103,000 Btuh　　　draft - natural
dimensions - 20 in. x 15.5 in. x 21 in. high
other models - "NPO series" - oil - 84% to 85.9%

model - "Olympia 1"　　　　　　　　fuel - gas　　　　　efficiency - 85.3%
capacities - 2 models: 91,000 to 119,000 Btuh　　　draft - natural
dimensions - 20 in. x 15.5 in. x 21 in. high

BRYANT, DAY & NIGHT, PAYNE, PO Box 70, Indianapolis, IN 46206 - (800) 468-7253 (317) 243-0851

model - "238 series"　　　　　　　　fuel - oil　　　　　efficiency - 84.0% to 85.9%
capacities - 6 models: 92,000 to 239,000 Btuh　　　draft - natural
dimensions - 20 in. x 17.7 in. to 24.2 in. x 36 in. high

model - "237 series"　　　　　　　　fuel - gas　　　　efficiency - 82.9% to 84.5%
capacities - 4 models: 42,500 to 150,000 Btuh　　　draft - induced
dimensions - 23.2 in. x 11 to 27.2 in. x 29 in. high
other models - "235 series" - gas - 80.7% to 81.6%

BURNHAM CORP., PO Box 3079, Lancaster, PA 17604 - (717) 397-4701

model - "V1 series"　　　　　　　　fuel - oil　　　　　efficiency - 83.2% to 85.4%
capacities - 8 models: 73,000 to 248,000 Btuh　　　draft - natural
dimensions - 21 in. x 15.5 in. x 29 in. high

BURNHAM CORP. - cont'd

model - "XG2000A series"
capacities - 4 models: 62,000 to 164,000 Btuh
dimensions - 21 in. x 16 in. x 33 in. high
other models - "V7 series" - oil - 81.9% to 86.2%, "2A series" - gas - 80.6% to 82.6%

fuel - gas
efficiency - 83.3% to 84.8%
draft - induced

CARRIER CORP., PO Box 4808, Syracuse, NY 13221 - (800) 227-7437 (315) 432-6000

model - "61HW series"
capacities - 6 models: 92,000 to 239,000 Btuh
dimensions - 19.6 in. x 17.7 to 24.2 in. x 36 in. high
fuel - oil
efficiency - 84.0% to 85.9%
draft- natural

model - "61SW series"
capacities - 4 models: 42,500 to 150,000 Btuh
dimensions - 23.2 in. x 10.7 to 20.5 in. x 29 in. high
other models - "61CW & CS series" - gas - 80.4% to 81.5%
fuel - gas
efficiency - 82.9% to 84.5%
draft - induced

COLUMBIA BOILER CO., PO Box 1070, Pottstown, PA 19464 - (610) 323-2700

model - "WB series"
capacities - 6 models: 108,000 to 178,000 Btuh
dimensions - 22.6 in. x 24.6 in. x 37.4 in. high
other models - "EM series" - oil - 80.1% to 82.6%, "FT series" - oil - 81.3% to 83.4%
fuel - oil
efficiency - 84.0% to 85.0%
draft - induced

GLOWCORE, PO Box 360591, Cleveland, OH 44136 - (800) 676-4546 (216) 225-3134

model - "GB series"
capacities - 5 models: 40,000 to 160,000 Btuh
draft - induced - vents outdoors through horizontal small plastic pipe
dimensions - 18 to 21.1 in. x 11 in. x 44 to 50.1 in. high
fuel - gas
efficiency - 88.8% to 89.0%

H.B. SMITH CO., 57 Main St., Westfield, MA 01085 - (413) 562-9631

model - "8 series"
capacities - 8 models: 91,000 to 250,000 Btuh
dimensions - 18 in. x 34.7 in. x 33 to 47.2 in. high
other models - "BB14 series" - oil - 85%
fuel - oil
efficiency - 86%
draft - natural

model - "PDE series"
capacities - 4 models: 42,500 to 150,000 Btuh
dimensions - 13.3 to 20.1 in. x 30.8 in. x 40.2 in. high
other models - "G-100 series" - gas - 81%
fuel - gas
efficiency - 81.8% to 83.7%
draft - induced

HYDROTHERM, 260 N. Elm St., Westfield, MA 01085 - (413) 568-9571

model - "PB series"
capacities - 8 models: 91,000 to 250,000 Btuh
dimensions - 18 in. x 33 to 47.2 in. x 34.7 in. high
fuel - oil
efficiency - 84.3% to 86.2%
draft - natural

model - "A**B series"
capacities - 3 models: 52,000 to 150,000 Btuh
dimensions - 14 to 17 in. diameter x 30.2 to 47.2 in. high
fuel - gas
efficiency - 90.4% to 90.6%
draft - induced - condensing heat exchanger

model - "HI series"
capacities - 3 models: *85/50,000 to 165/100,000 Btuh
    *These models have two-stage burners - high/low output shown above
dimensions - 37 in. x 12.5 in. x 17.8 to 45.0 in. high
other models - "R series" - gas - 80.0% to 82.7%, "HY series" - gas - 82.0% to 82.8%
fuel - gas
efficiency - 82.3% to 83.5%
draft - induced

LENNOX, P.O. Box 799900, Dallas, TX 75379 - (214) 497-5000

model - "O-E series"
capacities - 6 models: 92,000 to 239,000 Btuh
dimensions - 19.6 in. x 17.7 to 24.2 in. x 36 in. high
fuel - oil
efficiency - 84.0% to 85.9%
draft - natural

model - "CXEB"
capacities - 6 models: 42,500 to 225,000 Btuh
dimensions - 11 to 27.2 in. x 23.2 in. x 29 in. high
other models - "CPWB series" - gas - 80.0% to 80.4%
fuel - gas
efficiency - 82.0% to 84.4%
draft - induced

LOCHINVAR CORP., 2005 Elm Hill Pike, Nashville, TN 37210 - (615) 889-8900

model - "PNN 0250"
capacities - 1 model - 250,000 Btuh
dimensions - 23 in. x 36 in. x 34 in. high
fuel - gas
efficiency - 88%
draft - induced

NEW YORKER BOILER CO., PO Box 295, Colmar, PA 18915 - (215) 822-0114

model - "FR series"
fuel - oil
efficiency - 85.0% to 86.1%

capacities - 6 models: 98,000 to 232,000 Btuh
draft - natural

dimensions - 18.1 in. x 24.5 in. x 31.7 in. high

other models - "S-AP series" - oil - 80.0% to 81.4%

PEERLESS HEATER CO., PO Box 388, Boyertown, PA 19512 - (610) 367-2153

model- "JOTW series"
fuel - oil
efficiency - 83.8% to 86.5%

capacities - 9 models: 91,000 to 338,000 Btuh
draft - induced

dimensions - 22 in. x 26.8 to 39.2 in. x 41 in. high

other models - oil - "WB series" - oil - 81.9% to 83.9%

model - "PDE series"
fuel - gas
efficiency - 84.0% to 84.8%

capacities - 3 models: 65,000 to 130,000 Btuh
draft - induced

dimensions - 30.8 in. x 13.3 to 20.1 in. x 40.2 in. high

other models - "WB series" - oil - 81.9% to 83.9%, "61 series" - gas - 80.3% to 81.7%

PENNCO INC., 237 Main St., Clarendon, PA 16313 - (814) 723-8371

model - "Keystone"
fuel - oil
efficiency - 84.0% to 86.4%

capacities - 9 models: 74,000 to 239,000 Btuh
draft - natural

dimensions - 17.7 to 24.2 in. x 19.6 in. x 36 in. high

model - "FSB series"
fuel - gas
efficiency - 82% to 84.4%

capacities - 6 models: 42,500 to 225,000 Btuh
draft - induced

dimensions - 11 to 27.2 in. x 23.2 in. x 29 in. high

other models - "15HW series" - gas - 80.7% to 81.5%, "16HS" - gas - 80.4% to 81.5%

RAYPAK, INC., 31111 Agoura Rd., Westlake Village, CA 91361 - (818) 889-1500

model - "H series"
fuel - gas
efficiency - 81.1% to 84.0%

capacities - 6 models: 30,000 to 180,000 Btuh
draft - natural

dimensions - 18 in. x 26.5 in. x 31.2 in. high

SLANT/FIN CORP., 100 Forest Dr., Greenvale, NY 11548 - (516) 484-2600

model - "Liberty"
fuel - oil
efficiency - 83.3% to 86.0%

capacities - 8 models: 91,000 to 329,000 Btuh
draft - natural

dimensions - 24.2 to 41.1 in. x 25 in. x 31.9 in. high

model - "Victory"
fuel - gas
efficiency - 82.5% to 84.8%

capacities - 6 models: 33,000 to 180,000 Btuh
draft - induced

dimensions - 19.7 in. x 14.6 in. x 28.4 in. high

other models - "Sentry" - gas - 83.1% to 84.4%

TELEDYNE LAARS, 20 Industrial Way, Rochester, NH 03867 - (800) 362-5678 (603) 335-3355

model - "Mini Como II"
fuel - gas
efficiency - 83.0% to 84.4%

capacities - 4 models: 50,000 to 125,000 Btuh
draft - natural

dimensions - 24 in. x 28 in. x 59.7 in. high

THERMO-DYNAMICS BOILER CO., PO Box 325, Schuykill Haven, PA 17972 - (717) 385-0731

model - "BY series"
fuel - oil
efficiency - 84.1% to 87.0%

capacities - 3 models: 91,000 to 150,000 Btuh
draft - natural

dimensions - 20.3 to 26.2 in. x 25.7 to 26.2 in. x 26.6 to 35.2 in. high

other models - "CWL-LE series" - oil - 84.1% to 86.0%, "S series" - oil - 84.3% to 86.0%

TRIANCO-HEATMAKER, INC., 111 York Ave., Randolph, MA 02368 - (617) 961-1660

model - "H series"
fuel - gas
efficiency - 84.0% to 87.0%

capacities - 3 models: 60,000 to 100,000 Btuh
draft - induced

dimensions - 21 in. x 29.5 in. x 66 in. high

VALLIANT, 2607 River Rd., Cinnaminson, NJ 08077 - (800) 225-1770

model - "GA92-CS"
fuel - gas
efficiency - 80.3% to 83.8%

capacities - 3 models: 60,000 to 100,000 Btuh
draft - induced

dimensions - 22.2 in. x 30.5 in. x 58 in. high

WEIL-MCLAIN, 500 Blaine St., Michigan City, IN 46360 - (219) 879-6561

model - "GV series"
fuel - gas
efficiency - 87.0% to 87.5%

capacities - 4 models: 61,000 to 153,000 Btuh
draft - induced

dimensions - 27.1 to 37.6 in. x 17.6 in. x 28.9 in. high

other models - "HEII series" - gas - 82.2% to 82.4%, "CG series" - gas - 81.4% to 83.0%

Q: Is it true that a new inexpensive "smart" thermostat can cut my heating costs by 10%. There are a lot of them on the market. Can I install one myself and how can I tell which one is best for my home?

A: Installing a new automatic smart wall thermostat can easily cut your heating and air conditioning bills by 10%. The new models are very easy to install and to program. I installed one in place of my standard thermostat in my own home in about fifteen minutes.

A new smart thermostat not only saves money, but it provides greater comfort for your family. Your house can be toasty warm when you go to bed. It automatically cools down over night while you sleep and then warms up again just before you awake in the morning.

These thermostats are so smart that they remember how long it took to heat up your house the previous morning. The thermostat starts your furnace just in time so it is warm when you awake, yet with the maximum savings.

If there are other times during the day when the temperature can be lower, the savings will be greater. For example, if everyone is gone for several hours during the day, program the thermostat to lower the temperature automatically. At times when you are active during the day, the temperature can be comfortably lower than when you relax in the evening.

When selecting a smart thermostat, consider your family's needs and activity schedule. Some models offer up to six different temperatures at six different times per 24-hour period. For many busy families, this flexibility allows for greater

Different schedule possible for each day of week

- Digital display
- Microprocessor brain inside
- Simple instructions
- Temperature/time adjustment
- Auto fan switch

savings without sacrificing any personal comfort.

Also, consider the number of different daily time/temperature schedules a smart thermostat accommodates. Some thermostats allow you to program a totally different schedule for each day of the week. This is convenient if you work just several days a week or have other regularly-scheduled activities away from your home.

Most smart thermostats, even if they allow for only one weekday schedule, also allow for a separate weekend schedule or even a different Saturday and a Sunday schedule.

The smart thermostat in my home has an instant override button not requiring reprogramming of the temperature schedule. If I leave to go to a Bengals football game for four hours, I can instantly set it back for only four hours. This is also a convenient feature if you stay home sick, for example. A battery-backup saves the program if there is a power outage.

Q: I have heard that saving $500 from energy-conservation improvements to my home is better than making $500 interest on a similar-size financial investment. Why is this true?

A: The return from making energy-saving improvements is better because it is after-tax money. For example, if you invest $1,000 in the stock market and make a return of $50, you have to pay tax on it. That may leave you with only $30 in your pocket.

If the same $1,000 energy-saving improvement yields $50 in savings, that is after-tax money. You get to keep all $50 in your pocket. The load and resultant wear and tear on your heating and cooling systems is also reduced.

Installing a new smart thermostat is one of the most cost-effective methods to lower both your heating and air-conditioning costs. Much of the following discussion is about wintertime temperature setbacks for furnaces. The same information applies for summertime temperature setups with central air conditioners.

In addition to cutting your monthly utility bills, your comfort will be improved and your furnace and air conditioner will last longer. If you have allergies and rely on a furnace-mounted air cleaner, the quality of the air inside your house will also be better.

The smart thermostats cycle your furnace or air conditioner on and off usually at 6 cycles per hour. The cycle length varies depending on how much heating or cooling your house needs at that time. This reduces the settling of particles and allows the air cleaner to remove them more effectively.

The chart on the following page lists the major manufacturers of smart thermostats, their model numbers, programming cycle flexibility, and number of different temperature settings available per 24-hour period. The model number preceded by "(HP)" indicate a heat pump application. The descriptions of the various programming cycles (7, 5+1+1, and 5+2) are listed at the bottom of page 39.

The 7-day cycle smart thermostats are a little more expensive than an equivalent 5+1+1 or 5+2. A 7-day model usually takes only slightly longer to program initially. A 5+1+1 is the most popular choice for most homeowners. This schedule flexibility (the same program for the five weekdays and a different program on Saturday and Sunday) is adequate for most families. I use a 7-day smart thermostat in my home since my schedule is not the same from Monday through Friday. Some manufacturers offer their 7-day model only in a more-expensive commercial model with multi-stage features you probably will not need.

As an example of a typical schedule, I have my thermostat programmed to come up to 68 degrees at 7:00 a.m.. At 10:00 a.m., it drops to 62 degrees. At 5:00 p.m., it comes back up to 66 degrees. At 11:30 p.m., it drops back to 60 degrees over night until 7:00 a.m. the next morning. I set different temperatures for the air-conditioning mode in the summer.

The amount of savings that you will realize depends on how many degrees you set back your thermostat, the length of time of the setback, and the severity of your climate. The chart on page 40 shows the savings for an eight-hour setback for 5 and 10 degrees. Select the city nearest you to determine the severity of the climate and then read off the savings. If you set back the thermostat for more or fewer hours each day, factor the savings up or down accordingly.

When you install a thermostat yourself, be very careful to wire it up properly. **TURN OFF THE ELECTRICITY TO THE FURNACE FIRST**. The color coding and terminal designations are not standardized among furnace or air conditioner manufacturers. Yellow does not always go to the "Y" terminal and the fan "G" is not always green. If you plan to install it yourself, consider buying the smart thermostat from a heating and cooling contractor. If you have problems with the installation or determining the proper wiring hookup, the contractor can give you some knowledgeable advice.

If you have a heat pump with backup auxiliary heat, you will need a special smart thermostat. This thermostat keeps the expensive backup heaters from kicking on when the thermostat setting switches up to a higher temperature. These heat pump thermostats have more sophisticated computerized brains and cost about $50-$75 more than one for a gas or oil furnace. Since there are about 7 wires to hook up properly, I would recommend having a heat pump smart thermostat professionally installed.

These heat pump thermostats remember how long it took to reheat your house over the past 48-hours of cycles. Based on this, it knows when to switch on the heat pump to reheat your house so it is at your desired temperature as the preset time. It also senses how fast your house is reheating.

If the rate is too slow with the heat pump alone, it will cycle the backup expensive auxiliary heat on and off to get the proper temperature increase. It will remember this and start the heat pump a little earlier next time so the backup heat will not be needed. During extremely cold weather, the backup heaters will have to come on anyway just to keep your house warm enough.

Manufacturers of Smart Setback Thermostats

CARRIER CORPORATION, P.O. Box 4808, Syracuse, NY 13221 - (800) 227-7437 (315) 432-6000

model - "Carrier" program cycle options - 7 no. temperature settings - 4

EMERSON ELECTRIC, 9797 Reavis Rd., St. Louis, MO 63123 - (314) 577-1300

model - "1F80" program cycle options - 5+2 no. temperature settings - 4
model - "1F90-51" program cycle options - 5+2 no. temperature settings - 4
model - "1F971" program cycle options - 7 no. temperature settings - 4

ENERSTAT, 800 Proctor Ave., Ogdensburg, NY 13669 - (800) 267-1909 (613) 342-0570

model - "Slimline" program cycle options - 7 no. temperature settings - 4
model - "Slimline" program cycle options - 5+2 no. temperature settings - 4
model - "ET52" program cycle options - 5+1+1 no. temperature settings - 4

HONEYWELL, 1985 Douglas N., Golden Valley, MN 55422V - (800) 328-5111 (612) 870-2682

model - "Chronotherm III" program cycle options - 7 no. temperature settings - 4
model - "Chronotherm III" program cycle options - 5+1+1 no. temperature settings - 4
model - "Honeywell 34" program cycle options - 5+1+1 no. temperature settings - 4
model - "Magic Stat" program cycle options - 7 no. temperature settings - 4
model - "Magic Stat" program cycle options - 5+2 no. temperature settings - 4

HUNTER FAN CO., 2500 Frisco Ave., Memphis, TN 38114 - (901) 743-1360

model - "Auto Temp" program cycle options - 5+1+1 no. temperature settings - 4
model - "Set 'n Save" program cycle options - 5+2 no. temperature settings - 4
model - "Set Save II Plus" program cycle options - 7 no. temperature settings - 4
model - "Auto Temp Plus" program cycle options - 7 no. temperature settings - 4

MAPLE CHASE (JAMESON), 2820 Thatcher Rd., Downers Grove, IL 60515 - (708) 963-1550

model - "09610 & 09620" program cycle options - 7 no. temperature settings - 4
model - "09600" program cycle options - 5+2 no. temperature settings - 4

LIGHTSTAT, PO Box 326, Canto, CT 06019 - (800) 292-2444 (203) 693-2444

model - "TGH1" temperature control range - 55° to 75°F setbacks - 10° or 15° from set point
model - "TGC1" temperature control range - 70° to 85°F setbacks - 15° or 25° from set point
model - "TMC" temperature control range - 40° to 90°F setbacks - heat - 60°F, cool - 85°F
description - When the room lights dim the thermostat sets back the heating or cooling temperature depending on the switch position. It has a light sensitivity control to compensate for windows and night security lights.

LUX PRODUCTS, 6000 I Commerce Pky, Mt. Laurel, NJ 08054 - (800) 421-1130

model - "TX1000" program cycle options - 5+1+1 no. temperature settings - 3
model - (HP)"T601052" program cycle options - 7 no. temperature settings - 3

SEARS, 3333 Beverly Rd., Hoffman Estates, IL 60179 - (800) 359-2000 (708) 286-2500

model - "Weekender" program cycle options - 5+2 no. temperature settings - 4

Description of Programming Cycle Options

7 - different programs for each day of the week

5+1+1 - same program for 5 consecutive days and individual programs
for each of the next two days

5+2 - same program for 5 consecutive days and one program for next two days

% of Heating/Cooling Energy You Could Save with Setback (average efficiency home)

City					City				
Albuquerque, NM	12%	24%	10%	16%	Los Angeles, CA	15%	30%	20%	27%
Atlanta, GA	15%	27%	12%	19%	Louisville, KY	13%	24%	11%	18%
Atlantic City, NJ	12%	23%	13%	20%	Madison, WI	10%	19%	13%	19%
Billings, MT	10%	20%	9%	16%	Memphis, TN	15%	26%	11%	17%
Birmingham, AL	15%	28%	12%	17%	Miami, FL	18%	30%	11%	17%
Boise, ID	11%	22%	8%	15%	Milwaukee, WI	10%	19%	13%	19%
Boston, MA	11%	22%	13%	20%	Minneapolis, MN	9%	18%	12%	20%
Buffalo, NY	10%	20%	14%	22%	New Orleans, LA	16%	30%	11%	17%
Burlington, VT	9%	18%	14%	22%	New York, NY	12%	23%	13%	20%
Charleston, SC	16%	29%	13%	19%	Oklahoma City, OK	14%	26%	11%	16%
Cheyenne, WY	10%	19%	12%	17%	Omaha, NE	11%	20%	12%	19%
Chicago, IL	11%	21%	13%	20%	Philadelphia, PA	11%	24%	13%	20%
Cincinnati, OH	12%	24%	12%	19%	Phoenix, AZ	16%	30%	7%	11%
Cleveland, OH	10%	21%	13%	21%	Pittsburgh, PA	11%	22%	13%	20%
Columbus, OH	11%	22%	12%	19%	Portland, ME	10%	19%	15%	21%
Corpus Christi ,TX	17%	30%	10%	15%	Portland, OR	13%	24%	11%	20%
Dallas, TX	15%	28%	9%	14%	Providence, RI	11%	21%	16%	24%
Denver, CO	11%	22%	10%	17%	Roanoke, VA	12%	24%	12%	19%
Des Moines, IA	11%	20%	12%	19%	Salt Lake City, UT	11%	21%	10%	16%
Detroit, MI	11%	21%	13%	22%	San Diego, CA	16%	30%	25%	33%
Dodge City, KS	12%	23%	9%	15%	San Francisco, CA	14%	26%	14%	19%
Greensboro, NC	14%	25%	12%	19%	Seattle, WA	12%	24%	16%	23%
Houston, TX	16%	30%	9%	14%	Sioux Falls, SD	10%	19%	11%	18%
Indianapolis, IN	11%	22%	12%	19%	Spokane, WA	11%	20%	10%	18%
Jackon, MS	16%	30%	11%	17%	Springfield, MA	11%	20%	13%	20%
Jacksonville, FL	17%	30%	11%	17%	St Louis, MO	12%	23%	11%	18%
Kansas City, MO	12%	23%	10%	16%	Syracuse, NY	11%	20%	13%	21%
Las Vegas, NV	15%	27%	7%	11%	Washington, DC	13%	25%	13%	20%
Little Rock, AR	15%	27%	10%	16%	Wilmington, DE	12%	23%	13%	20%

Explanation of the Above Savings Chart:

First number - % savings from single 8 hour per day, 10 degrees heating setback (70 to 60 degrees)

Second number - % savings from double 8 hour per day, 10 degrees heating setback

Third number - % savings from single 11 hour per day 5, degrees cooling setup (75 to 80 degrees)

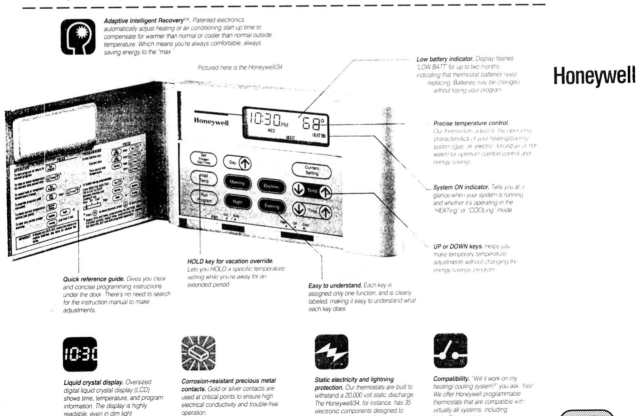

Adaptive Intelligent Recovery™. Patented electronics automatically adjust heating or air conditioning start up time to compensate for warmer than normal or cooler than normal outside temperature. Which means you're always comfortable, always saving energy to the "max."

Pictured here is the Honeywell/34

Low battery indicator. Display flashes "LOW BATT" for up to two months indicating that thermostat batteries need replacing. Batteries may be changed without losing your program.

Honeywell

Precise temperature control. Our thermostats adjust to the operating characteristics of your heating/cooling system (gas, oil, electric, forced air or hot water) for optimum comfort control and energy savings.

System ON indicator. Tells you at a glance when your system is running and whether it's operating in the "HEATing" or "COOLing" mode.

UP or DOWN keys. Helps you make temporary temperature adjustments without changing the energy-savings program.

Quick reference guide. Gives you clear and concise programming instructions under the door. There's no need to search for the instruction manual to make adjustments.

HOLD key for vacation override. Lets you HOLD a specific temperature setting while you're away for an extended period.

Easy to understand. Each key is assigned only one function, and is clearly labeled, making it easy to understand what each key does.

Liquid crystal display. Oversized digital liquid crystal display (LCD) shows time, temperature, and program information. The display is highly readable, even in dim light.

Corrosion-resistant precious metal contacts. Gold or silver contacts are used at critical points to ensure high electrical conductivity and trouble-free operation.

Static electricity and lightning protection. Our thermostats are built to withstand a 20,000 volt static discharge. The Honeywell/34, for instance, has 35 electronic components designed to protect your thermostat from static electricity and from lightning strikes.

Compatibility. "Will it work on my heating/ cooling system?" you ask. Yes! We offer Honeywell programmable thermostats that are compatible with virtually all systems, including high-efficiency ones.

Q: We have a good gas furnace, but our family room is still chilly. We are considering adding a small gas heater. What types of heaters are most efficient, quiet and safe since our children play in there?

A: Installing a small gas space heater is your most efficient option. Some new easy-to-install direct vent units are extremely quiet and have efficiencies up to 84 percent, probably higher than your furnace.

Even if someone does not have a chilly room, it may make sense to install a gas space heater in the most commonly used room. By keeping one or two rooms toasty warm, especially in the evening, the central furnace thermostat can be set lower for big savings.

In some new space heaters, the gas flame (using a thermocouple) produces enough electricity to power the internal electronic controls. If there is an electrical power outage and your furnace or heat pump stop, these space heaters stay on to keep pipes from freezing.

The safest, quietest and most efficient gas heaters use a direct vent, sealed combustion design. These draw in combustion air from outdoors and exhausts flue gases through one small double wall pipe. No chimney is needed, so installation on an outside wall is simple and inexpensive.

This type of sealed combustion is very safe. The combustion process is totally isolated from indoor air. Some high-efficiency models use electronic ignition to eliminate a wasteful pilot light.

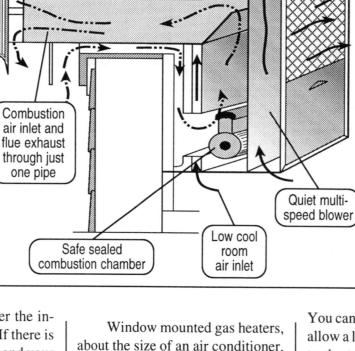

Optional humidifier tray and air filter — Heated air outlets — Combustion air inlet and flue exhaust through just one pipe — Safe sealed combustion chamber — Low cool room air inlet — Quiet multi-speed blower

Window mounted gas heaters, about the size of an air conditioner, are also safe and easy to move. They just need a gas line and common electric outlet.

If you select a model with a pilot light, choose one with a piezo-electric sparker. To start it initially, you just push a button, as on your barbecue grill. After that, a built-in or wall thermostat controls the cycling of the burner.

Most direct vent room heaters rely on the natural upward flow of room air through the heater. For better heat distribution, optional dual variable-speed blowers are most quiet and powerful. These are ideal for a chilly bedroom where low noise is imperative.

Other available options and accessories to consider are built-in air filters, thermostats and humidifier trays. Several tall direct vent wall furnaces use counterflow heat exchangers. These are efficient and the hot air blows out at floor level. This provides excellent heat distribution.

Q: I keep my house fairly humid because of respiratory problems. Our water comes from a well and the toilet tanks sweat. Should I run heated water to my toilet tanks?

A: Toilets are the greatest water consumer in most homes. You can install a tempering valve to allow a little hot water into the pipes to the toilets. This should be your last resort since it wastes energy.

First try a foam insulation toilet tank kit. Many plumbing supply outlets carry them. The foam is attached to the inside of the tanks walls. Another option is to install a new insulated toilet tank. Most toilet manufacturers have replacement insulated tanks available to fit your existing bowl.

Some new gas space heaters have efficiencies as high as 84%, higher than many furnaces. They are ideal for a chilly room, room addition or to zone heat your house.

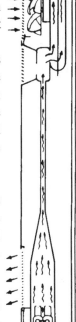

The manufacturers of space heaters are listed on detailed information about

the highest efficiency gas pages 43 and 44 along with their models.

"*Direct vent*" designs and easiest to install. Figure rect vent heater works. Both tion air and flue gases are one concentric double-walled there is no chimney or flue heat is needed.

are the most efficient #2 shows how a di- the outdoor combus- vented through only pipe. This is ideal if near the room where

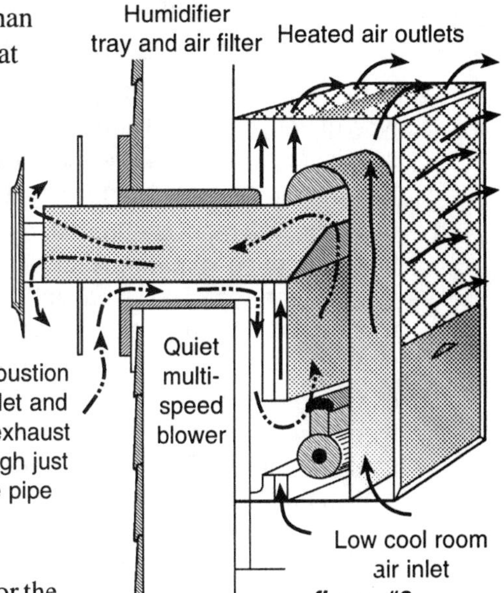

Most gas space heaters room air to flow through the output, all have optional your room. Some of the heat- can be heated.

rely on natural convection for the heat exchanger. For greater heat blower kits. These increase the distribution of heated air throughout ers also have double heated air outlet kits. By installing this, two rooms

Counterflow wall gas space heaters. A counterflow distribution. All counterflow the heated air outlet near the vertical flue) model. See trolled).

furnaces (see figure #1) are very efficient, but are larger than standard heat exchanger design forces heated air out at floor level for the best heat models therefore need a blower. Gravity models are also available with top. You can install either a direct vent or vented (needs a chimney or chart below for estimated gas operating costs (thermostatically con-

figure # 1

figure #2

Most models produce their own electricity to operate the thermostat and controls and they continue to operate during power outages. If you only use your gas heater occasionally, choose one with a piezo spark igniter for easy lighting. Some models offer humidifier trays and air filters to improve air quality.

Gas Cost ($) To Use Heater For 24 Hours (50% Burner On-Time)													
Gas Rate	Rated Heating Capacity For Space Heater - 1,000 Btu per hour (Btuh)												
¢/therm	10	15	20	25	30	35	40	45	50	55	60	65	70
30	0.36	0.54	0.72	.90	1.08	1.26	1.44	1.62	1.80	1.98	2.16	2.34	2.52
35	0.42	0.63	0.84	1.05	1.26	1.47	1.68	1.89	2.10	2.31	2.52	2.73	2.94
40	0.48	0.72	0.96	1.20	1.44	1.68	1.92	2.16	2.40	2.64	2.88	3.12	3.36
45	0.54	0.81	1.08	1.35	1.62	1.89	2.16	2.43	2.70	2.97	3.24	3.51	3.78
50	0.60	0.90	1.20	1.50	1.80	2.10	2.40	2.70	3.00	3.30	3.60	3.90	4.20
55	0.66	0.99	1.32	1.65	1.98	2.31	2.64	2.97	3.30	3.63	3.96	4.29	4.62
60	0.72	1.08	1.44	1.80	2.16	2.52	2.88	3.24	3.60	3.96	4.32	4.68	5.04
65	0.78	1.17	1.56	1.95	2.34	2.73	3.12	3.51	3.90	4.29	4.68	5.07	5.46
70	0.84	1.26	1.68	2.10	2.52	2.94	3.36	3.78	4.20	4.62	5.04	5.46	5.88
75	0.90	1.35	1.80	2.25	2.70	3.15	3.60	4.05	4.50	4.95	5.40	5.85	6.30

Manufacturers of High Efficiency Gas Space Heaters

DESA INTERNATIONAL, 2701 Industrial Dr., Bowling Green, KY 42102 - (502) 781-9600

capacities - 2 models - 20,000 to 30,000 Btuh   efficiency - 74%
type of venting - direct vent   blowers - optional automatic two-speed
special features - The unit includes a push button piezo pilot ignition, 100% safety pilot, an automatic built-in thermostat, cast iron burner with air shutter adjustment, and a complete vent kit.

capacities - 2 models - 25,000 to 40,000 Btuh   efficiency - 77%
type of venting - thru-the-window/direct vent   blowers - single-speed
special features - The Dynavent™ heater offers flexibility with installation. Its small size allows installation in a window or through an exterior wall. Depending on your application the gas connection can be made from the interior or exterior. An optional window kit is available.

capacities - 8 models - 35,000 to 65,000 Btuh   efficiency - 70%
type of venting - vented   blowers - optional single-speed or two-speed
special features - The controls are easy to use and top-mounted. Every model includes a built-in thermostat and a push button piezo pilot ignition. The units include a safety switch that shuts off both pilot light and burner if a venting problem should develop and a safety pilot that shuts off the gas valve if a fuel supply interruption occurs.

capacities - 1 models - 45,000 to 65,000 Btuh   efficiency - 76%
type of venting - vented floor   blowers - single-speed
special features - It is equipped with a piezo pilot ignition and an automatic wall thermostat. The pilot and main burner include automatic safety shut-off. It has an aluminized steel combustion chamber for rust protection. The floor grille has a temperature safety limit switch for your added protection.

EMPIRE COMFORT SYSTEMS, 918 Freburg Ave., Belleville, IL 62222 - (800) 851-3153

capacities - 4 models - 10,000 to 35,000 Btuh   efficiency - 70%
type of venting - direct vent   blowers - optional automatic two-speed
special features - Included is a push button piezo system and a wall thermostat that does not require electricity to operate. A vent kit is included to vent through an outside wall and is available with an optional vinyl siding kit. The pilot and main burners include an automatic shut-off for safety.

capacities - 2 models - 55,000 Btuh   efficiency - 76%
type of venting - direct vent counterflow wall furnace   blowers - optional automatic two-speed
special features - The front panels remove easily for cleaning and servicing. The blower circulates the warmth at floor level. An optional outlet kit is available for multi-room heating capacity.

capacities - 2 models - 55,000 Btuh   efficiency - 76%
type of venting - vented counterflow wall furnace   blowers - optional automatic two-speed
special features - These units have a push-button piezo ignition. It has a 24 volt wall thermostat and safety controls for automatic shut-off of the pilot and main burners.

LOUISVILLE TIN & STOVE CO., PO Box 2767, Louisville, KY 40201 - (502) 589-5380

capacities - 2 models - 15,000 to 33,000 Btuh   efficiency - 75%
type of venting - direct vent   blowers - two-speed
special features - A simple vent system is provided with each unit and the vent cap includes a safety screen to prevent entry by small animals. The blower is thermostatically controlled with a variable speed control switch and functions automatically as unit heats up and cools down.

capacities - 2 models - 40,000 to 62,500 Btuh   efficiency - 76%
type of venting - direct vent counterflow wall furnace   blowers - two-speed
special features - It is available with a manual spark ignitor and a wall thermostat is a standard option. It is equipped with a multi-port stainless steel burner, optional electronic ignition.

capacities - 3 models - 35,000 to 65,000 Btuh   efficiency - 76%
type of venting - vented counterflow wall furnace   blowers - two-speed
special features - There is a built-in safety pilot and pressure regulator. An optional register kit is available to send additional heat out the sides or into as many as three rooms, optional electronic ignition.

capacities - 3 models - 25,000 to 50,000 Btuh   efficiency - 75%
type of venting - top vent wall furnace   blowers - single-speed
special features - A vent spill safety device automatically shuts the unit off if the flue is blocked. It is available in single or dual wall designs. An optional night setback thermostat and fan for installation on top of furnace to increase circulation are available. A free standing kit is available so there is no need for cutting holes in the wall.

LOUISVILLE TIN & STOVE CO. - cont'd

capacities - 11 models - 20,000 to 70,000 Btuh

efficiency - 84%

type of venting - vented

blowers - variable-speed

special features - The top is multi-louvered to direct the warm air toward the room. The blower controls are located on the top and provides an infinite speed.

capacities - 1 models - 30,000 to 75,000 Btuh

efficiency - 75%

type of venting - vented floor

blowers - two-speed

special features - The safety limit control maintains the lowest grill temperature consistent with heating required. It also cycles unit off if the grill is blocked by a rug or furniture.

capacities - 1 models - 15,000 to 30,000 Btuh

efficiency - 72%

type of venting - mobile home direct vent

blowers - optional variable-speed

special features - It is available with a manual push button lighter. The slotted-port burner is designed for quiet ignition and is constructed of cast iron. The burner and control are easily removed for cleaning and service.

PERFECTION SCHWANK, PO Box 749, Waynesboro, GA 30830 - (706) 554-2101

capacities - 3 models - 12,000 to 30,000 Btuh

efficiency - 75%

type of venting - direct vent

blowers - optional automatic two-speed

special features - There is a choice of thermostats either mounted on the wall or on the heater casing. The units are equipped with a push button piezo ignitor.

capacities - 3 models - 40,000 to 57,000 Btuh

efficiency - 76%

type of venting - vented counterflow wall furnace

blowers - single-speed

special features - These units are available with hot surface direct ignition which is ignited at each cycle or a standing pilot. A stainless steel burner insures complete fuel combustion.

capacities - 3 models - 25,000 to 50,000 Btuh

efficiency - 75%

type of venting - top vent wall furnace

blowers - single-speed

special features - A rear register kit is available for thru-the wall installation to provide warmth for adjacent rooms.

capacities - 3 models - 35,000 to 70,000 Btuh

efficiency - 73%

type of venting - vented

blowers - single-speed /optional three-speed

special features - Special floor pads for protection to carpet and flooring is available.

RINNAI AMERICA, 1662 Lukken Industrial Dr., W., LaGrange, GA 30240 - (800) 621-9419

capacities - 2 models - 22,000 to 38,400 Btuh

efficiency - 84%

type of venting - direct vent

blowers - two-speed

special features - The "EnergySaver" includes a built-in thermostat, humidifier, automatic electronic ignition, special heat exchangers, and fan-forced venting. There is a built-in humidifier tray to increase the room humidity so you can run the heater at a lower setting. A top-mounted filter protects fans from dust and dirt and are easily removed for cleaning. The heat exchanger and the burner are manufactured of stainless steel.

WILLIAMS FURNACE, 225 Acacia St., Colton, CA 92324 - (800) 266-0993 (909) 825-0993

capacities - 3 models - 14,000 to 30,000 Btuh

efficiency - 73%

type of venting - direct vent

blowers - optional automatic two-speed

special features - All models have a piezo pilot ignition and a glass observation door. All models are available with a wall or a self-contained bulb thermostat. They have 100% safety shut-off as a standard feature. The face panels are available in new designer colors of red, white, and black.

capacities - 3 models - 35,000 Btuh

efficiency - 78%

type of venting - vented

blowers - two-speed

special features - A unique side relief draft hood uses cooler room air at the side of the furnace, rather than the front for venting. Since it uses the cooler air it reduces the heat loss up the vent.

capacities - 4 models - 25,000 to 65,000 Btuh

efficiency - 75%

type of venting - top vent wall furnace

blowers - two-speed

special features - It has a special airstream mounted vent safety shut-off system and is designed to eliminate pilot outage. An optional crossflow blower to mount inside face panel is available.

capacities - 2 models - 35,000 to 65,000 Btuh

efficiency - 75%

type of venting - vented

blowers - optional automatic single-speed

special features - Units have a built-in thermostat control and a built-in draft diverter to permit close-to-wall installation.

Q: When we lived in Sweden, we heated with just one large fireplace. We burned it for only 45 minutes, twice a day. How efficient are these fireplaces? Do they burn clean enough to meet U.S. requirements?

A: You are referring to true masonry (often called Finnish) fireplaces with super high heat capacity. In Scandinavia, with its high energy costs, 90 percent of the homes heat exclusively with a masonry fireplace. It provides even radiant warmth, like sitting in the sun on a cold day.

A true masonry fireplace is a beautiful work of art. The exterior is hand built from decorative tiles, brick, stone or stucco. The final appearance is limited only by your imagination and the skill of the mason.

The interior fire-burning section can be custom built or made from precast, color-coded, do-it-yourself kits. Many have optional gold-plated trim, built-in baking ovens, shelves, benches, cathedral arches, etc.

Inside a Finnish fireplace, the wood burns extremely hot, as high as 2000 degrees, for only 30 to 45 minutes. You need only build this intense, short duration fire twice each day for 24 hours of even heat. Many use over-fire air flow designs with the kindling on top for efficiency and easy lighting.

The heavy mass of the masonry fireplace absorbs this intense heat and slowly releases it into your home. The exterior never exceeds 150 degrees. Over the 11-hour period between fires in a Finnish fireplace, the combustion air intake is closed and sealed. This eliminates chilly drafts, common with a typical fireplace, in the rest of your home.

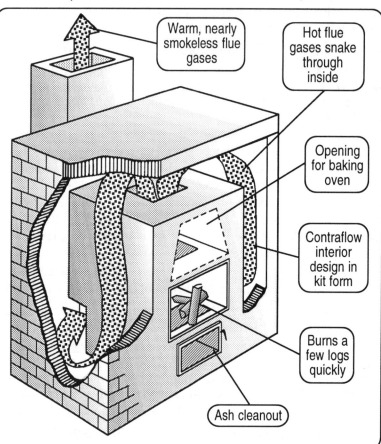

Warm, nearly smokeless flue gases

Hot flue gases snake through inside

Opening for baking oven

Contraflow interior design in kit form

Burns a few logs quickly

Ash cleanout

Finnish fireplaces are very energy efficient. With the super hot, short duration fire, the combustion efficiency is 90 percent or higher. These fireplaces produce very little smoke or pollution. At 2000 degrees in the firebox, nearly all of the particles and gases are completely burned.

A contraflow design is the most efficient. With this design, the flue gases flow up the center of the fireplace and back down internal side passages to the chimney. This forces the hot gases to snake through for more heat retention.

If your budget and floor space are limited, free-standing radiant soapstone wood-burning stoves are an efficient option. These stoves are built with several hundred pounds of soapstone panels on them.

Natural polished soapstone is very beautiful and has double the heat capacity of steel or cast iron. Soapstone stoves burn much hotter than typical metal stoves and retain the heat for even, comfortable warmth.

Q: Without changing the thermostat setting, the temperature in my house seems to vary excessively. What could be causing this and do thermostats wear out?

A: Thermostats are very reliable and generally do not wear out. First try cleaning it. Carefully, snap off the cover and clean off any dust with a fine brush. Just a fine layer of dust can insulate it and reduce sensitivity.

If you have remodeled your house or now keep some doors closed, the air flow patterns may have changed. This can create either stagnant air pockets or drafts across the thermostat. Both can affect its sensitivity. Reroute the low-voltage thermostat wire to a better location for mounting.

With high heat capacity of the materials in masonry (Finnish) fireplaces and soapstone wood-burning stoves, the fire's heat is absorbed and slowly radiated into your house. This allows you to make a short duration, very hot (clean burning) fire, yet still have continuous heat.

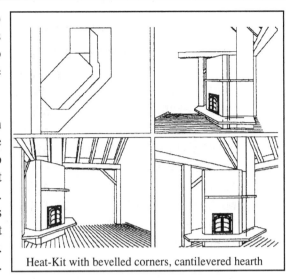

Manufacturers are listed on page 47. Most of the Finnish masonry fireplaces are available as internal kits. The final decorative exterior is usually built to your design by a local mason. Page 47 also shows the components of a typical kit. The illustration to the right shows how a kit can be built into a corner with a decorative hearth. Baking ovens are also available in most kits. Biofire also offers special, hand crafted, decorative exterior tiles. You should contact each of the manufacturers for detailed information on its models. You will need their input to design a system for your specific home.

Heat-Kit with bevelled corners, cantilevered hearth

Use the selector chart on page 48 when buying firewood. The higher moisture content woods will have to be seasoned longer before burning them. Higher energy content wood is usually a better buy. The bottom of the page shows typical burning instructions for a masonry fireplace.

Heating Instructions

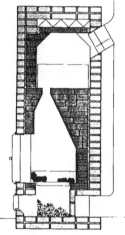

To ignite the fire, open the ashbox door, loading door, and the shut-off damper. Thereafter, during the gas combustion process, close the ashbox door and regulate primary air with the ashbox door draft slide. The ashbox door can also be latched slightly ajar during the first half of the burning cycle. Secondary combustion air is regulated through the main door draft slides. The fire should be concentrated and vigorous. The fire should not be poked or disturbed at this stage.

When gas combustion is largely completed and only a bed of live coals remains, the secondary draft slide in the main loading doors should be closed. When the coals have burned down considerably, they should be poked to mix the whole layer and get it to burn completely and evenly. Once this fire is out, wait at least three or four hours before a second loading to achieve more heat output and to keep thermal stresses within the system tolerable.

The dampers are cracked slightly open or designed with built in gas slots to allow carbon monoxide to escape up the chimney. When all the embers are dark, combustion is complete and no more carbon monoxide is being produced. Only at this stage can the dampers be completely closed.

Do not ever neglect a masonry heater while the fire is burning or while the damper is open.

Manufacturers of Finnish Fireplaces and Soapstone Stoves

AMERICAN ENERGY SYSTEMS, 20 Academy Lane, Hutchinson, MN 55350 - (612) 587-6565

BIOFIRE INC., 3220 Melbourne, Salt Lake City, UT 84106 - (801) 486-0266

CROSS-FIRE, 12159 Brawn Rd., Wainfleet, Ontario, Canada L0S 1V0 - (905) 899-2432

DWS, - ENVIROTECH, PO Box 323, Vashon Island, WA 98070 - (800) 325-3629 (206) 463-3722

★ **HEARTHSTONE,** PO Box 1069, Morrisville, VT 05661 - (802) 888-5232

KENT VALLEY MASONRY, 23631 SE 216 St., Maple Valley, WA 98038 - (206) 432-0134

LOPEZ QUARRIES, 111 Barbara Lane, Everett, WA 98203 - (206) 353-8963

MAINE WOOD HEAT CO., RFD 1, Box 640, Norridgewock, ME 04957 - (207) 696-5442

MASONRY STOVE BUILDERS, RR 5, Shawville, Quebec, Canada J0X 2Y0 - (613) 722-6261

MASTERCRAFT MASONRY, PO Box 73, Brush Prairie, WA 98606 - (206) 432-0134

TEMP-CAST ENVIROHEAT, PO Box 94059, Toronto, Ontario M4N 3R1 - (800) 561-8594

TULIKIVI, PO Box 200, Schuyler, VA 22969 - (804) 831-2228

VESTA, 373 Old Seven Mile Ridge Rd., Burnsville, NC 28714 - (800) 473-5240 (704) 675-5666

W. MOBERG DESIGN, 921 SW Morrison Ste. 440, Portland, OR 97205 - (503) 227-0547

★ **WOODSTOCK SOAPSTONE CO.,** Airpark Rd., Box 37H, W. Lebanon, NH 03784 - (603) 298-5955

* *Soapstone wood-burning stoves*

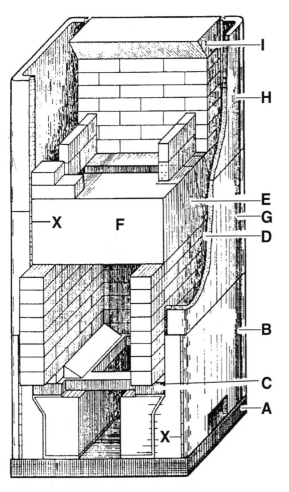

X = Expansion joint

Key	Part Name	Description
	Parts List - in Order of Installation	
A	Insulating Base Slab	simplifies layout insulating refractory, reduces heat transfer to foundation
B	Lower Channel Liners (2)	incorporates bottom manifold proprietary 1800F s.s.-fibre reinforced refractory precut flue & cleanout openings to your layout
C	Firebox Floor	gives correct firebrick layout cutout for grates
D	Firebox Angled Sidepiece (lower)	establishes correct fireback angle eliminates firebrick cutting
E	Firebox Angled Sidepiece (upper)	see above
F	Firebox Lintel/Throat	spans firebox opening insulating refractory facing stainless steel reinforced
G	Middle Channel Liners (2)	built-in expansion joints proprietary composite refractory allows thin-shell construction
H	Upper Channel Liners (2)	see above
I	Ceiling Transitions (2)	lightweight castable refractory gives correct ceiling shape for max. air/fuel mixing

HEAT KIT tm *Component Location*   Manufactured by **Masonry Stove Builders**

Dimensions

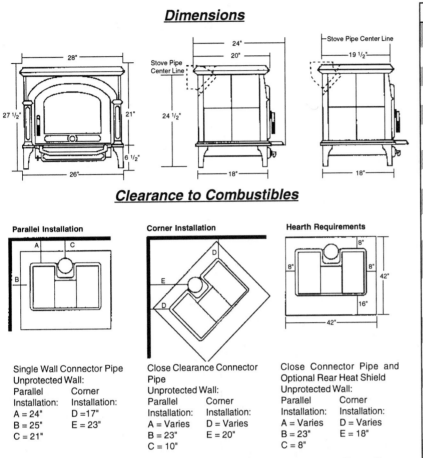

Clearance to Combustibles

Parallel Installation

Corner Installation

Hearth Requirements

Single Wall Connector Pipe
Unprotected Wall:

Parallel Installation:	Corner Installation:
A = 24"	D = 17"
B = 25"	E = 23"
C = 21"	

Close Clearance Connector Pipe
Unprotected Wall:

Parallel Installation:	Corner Installation:
A = Varies	D = Varies
B = 23"	E = 20"
C = 10"	

Close Connector Pipe and Optional Rear Heat Shield
Unprotected Wall:

Parallel Installation:	Corner Installation:
A = Varies	D = Varies
B = 23"	E = 18"
C = 8"	

*Tested with Metalbestos, Security, Simpson-Duravent and Ameritech Close Clearance Pipe connected to a listed Class "A" chimney or masonry chimney. Clearances to combustibles can be reduced to 12" through the use of approved wall protection as specified by NFPA 211. This applies to all types of installations (parellel, corner, single wall or close clearance connector pipe).

Specifications

Maximum heat output	55,000 BTU/hr. (cordwood)
Burn time	Up to 8 hours
Heat life	Up to 12 hours
Efficiency	71.40%
Particulate emissions	4.9 grams/hr.
Fire box capacity	2.0 cu. ft. 40 lbs. of wood
Maximum log length	19" logs
Stovepipe size	6" diameter
Self cleaning door glass	Infrared reflective ceramic glass
Recommended chimney	6" diameter metal or 8" x 8" chimney
Flue exit	Top or rear exit from recessed 45 degree flue collar
Stove control	Single manual air intake lever controls operation of entire stove
Actual weight Shipping weight	400 lbs. 435 lbs.
Optional equipment	Rear heat shield: Outside air adaptor kit
Soapstone finish	Polished grey soapstone
Castings finish	Black matte cast iron; Black, Brown, Almond, Navy, Colonial Blue, or Red Porcelain Enamel
Warranty	3 years

Specifications of the "Phoenix" Soapstone woodstove manufactured by **Hearth Stone**

Hardwood Fuel Values

Species	Energy Content (millions Btu/cord)	Moisture Content		Average Density lb/cord @ 20% moisture
		Heartwood	Sapwood	
White Oak	29.1	39	44	4400
Sugar Maple	27.0	39	42	4100
American Beech	27.4	35	42	4000
Red Oak	27.63	38	42	3900
Yellow Birch	26.6	43	42	3800
White Ash	25.7	32	31	3700
American Elm	23.8	49	48	3400
Red Maple	23.8	38	49	3400
White Birch	23.6	47	42	3400
Black Cherry	21.4	37	52	3300
Douglas Fir	20.6	27	53	2900
White Pine	15.8	35	55	2200
Eastern Hemlock	17.1	49	54	2200

Q: I'm tired of the mess when burning wood in my fireplace. Can I replace it easily with a new remote-controlled gas fireplace? Is a gas fireplace efficient and what features should I look for in one?

A: With new gas fireplaces, it is difficult to distinguish the gas log flames from real wood flames. Special burner materials and orifice patterns create the natural look. The rest of the fireplace front is identical to a wood-burning model in appearance. Some have 14-karat gold plated trim.

Even with the golden flame color, some gas fireplaces have efficiencies as high as 80%, probably more efficient than your furnace. Most designs have air circulation blowers and wall thermostat options. With a large 40,000 Btu/hr. heat output, a gas fireplace can easily heat a small house.

If you don't currently have a fireplace, there are easy-to-install "zero-clearance" gas fireplaces available. Zero clearance means that the firebox has multi-layer insulated sheet metal sides.

This allows you to build them into a wall, directly against the studs, without creating a fire hazard. These can vent flue gases horizontally through an outside wall so you need not necessarily build a chimney. If you install one in an existing fire-

place, you can vent it vertically up the chimney.

The convenience features of gas fireplaces also increase their efficiency. From your sofa, you can use a hand-held remote control (like a TV remote) to start the fire, control the blower speeds, and heat output. This avoids wasteful overheating and longer fires than are actually needed.

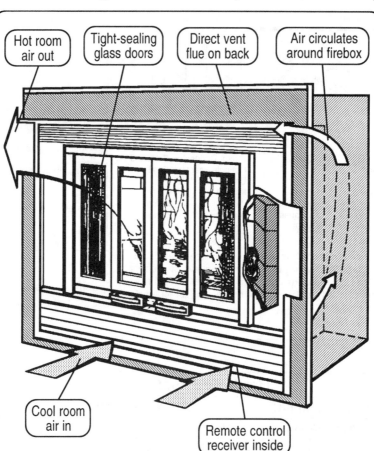

Hot room air out

Tight-sealing glass doors

Direct vent flue on back

Air circulates around firebox

Cool room air in

Remote control receiver inside

Optional wall thermostat available

Sealed direct vent designs are energy efficient and safe. Flue gases vent directly out the fireplace back to the outdoors. Through the same double-wall concentric pipe or a separate pipe, outdoor combustion air comes in.

This eliminates the loss of heated room air up the flue and chilly drafts inside your home. Since there is adequate outdoor air intake, the

chance of incomplete combustion and backdrafting fumes coming into your room is minimal.

Multi- or variable-speed room air circulation blowers improve comfort and energy savings. A wall-mounted thermostat connected to your gas fireplace, like a furnace thermostat, maintains a fairly even room temperature. It switches the burners up or down depending on the heating needs.

A few models have variable heat output burners. With three or four heat levels, you can maintain a constant room temperature. The burners are located forward and rear, so even on low, the flames look like wood flames.

Q: I recently bought a house and found that it had urea formaldehyde insulation installed eight years ago. Should I consider having it removed from the walls?

A: According to the U.S. Consumer Products Safety Commission, the majority of the formaldehyde outgassing occurs in the first year. After eight years, the level of formaldehyde gas in your house should not be higher than any other house with the insulation.

If you are still concerned, you can buy do-it-yourself formaldehyde gas test kits. Some kits have in-home analysis and others require lab analysis.

High-efficiency gas fireplaces have efficiencies as high as 80% (see *"efficiency"*), yet they provide an authentic-looking "real wood" flame. This is accomplished with special burner and log materials and burner design. The chart below shows the cost to operate various size gas fireplaces at various utility rates.

You can install a gas fireplace inside an existing masonry wood-burning fireplace or add a new one to a wall. Choose a "zero-clearance" design for the later. With these, you build the wood stud framing flush against the insulated fireplace cabinet without creating a fire hazard.

The manufacturers of high-efficiency gas fireplaces are shown on pages 51 and 52 along with specifications and suggested retail prices. Heat capacity for gas appliances is rated by the input heat content of the gas. Multiply the "heat capacity" by the efficiency to get the heat output. Where a range of heat capacities is shown, this indicates several different fireplace models.

Several manufacturers offer multi-stage burners with more than one heat output level (see *"special features"*). With most other gas fireplace models, the burners are either on or off, like your gas furnace.

The most convenient type of control is a hand-held remote control, like for your TV. You can control on-off, thermostat, and air circulation blower speeds (see *"special features"*). A wall mounted thermostat and on-off switch are also convenient features.

The source for combustion air and the type of venting are important for efficiency, comfort, and ease of installation. Bringing in outdoor combustion air stops drafts inside your home and blocks the loss of heated room air. Many of the fireplaces offer outdoor combustion air kits which are easily installed (see *"combustion air"*).

Direct venting means that the exhaust gases are vented outdoors through a horizontal pipe. This makes installation easier, especially when you are building a new fireplace on an outside wall. Often with direct venting, the inlet combustion air and outlet flue gases flow through a single concentric pipe.

A single or multi-speed blower increases the heat output of a fireplace and improves the distribution of heated air. Most fireplaces either have a blower installed or a blower kit option (see *"blower speeds"*).

One unique blower design (positive pressure - Alpine Fireplace Furnaces) mounts the blower outdoors behind the fireplace. Fresh outdoor air is blown in around the firebox heat exchangers and out into your room. This creates a very slight positive pressure inside your home. By opening a window a little in a room at the other end of your house, the heated air naturally flows there. This improves the heated air circulation throughout your entire home.

Heat Capacity 1,000 Btuh	Gas Cost to Operate Fireplace - cents per hour										
	Gas Rate - $/1,000 cubic feet										
	2.50	3.00	3.50	4.00	4.50	5.00	5.50	6.00	6.50	7.00	7.50
10	2.4	2.9	3.4	3.9	4.4	4.9	5.4	5.9	6.4	6.8	7.3
15	3.7	4.4	5.1	5.9	6.6	7.3	8.0	8.8	9.5	10.2	11.0
20	4.9	5.9	6.8	7.8	8.8	9.8	10.7	11.7	12.7	13.7	14.6
25	6.1	7.3	8.5	9.8	11.0	12.2	13.4	14.6	15.9	17.1	18.3
30	7.3	8.8	10.2	11.7	13.2	14.6	16.1	17.6	19.0	20.5	22.0
35	8.5	10.2	12.0	13.7	15.3	17.1	18.8	20.5	22.2	23.9	25.6
40	9.8	11.7	13.7	15.6	17.6	19.5	21.5	23.4	25.4	27.3	29.3
45	11.0	13.2	15.4	17.6	19.8	22.0	24.1	26.3	28.5	30.7	32.9
50	12.2	14.6	17.1	19.5	22.0	24.4	26.8	29.3	31.7	34.1	36.6

Manufacturers of High-Efficiency Gas Fireplaces and Inserts

ALPINE FIREPLACE FURNACES, 782 W. State St., Lehi, UT 84043 - (801) 768-8411

    heat capacity - 31,000 Btuh   efficiency - 70%

    blower speeds - Variable speeds

    combustion air - Outdoor - positive pressure - discussed on page 1

FIREPLACE MANUFACTURERS, 2701 S. Harbor Blvd., Santa Ana, CA 92704 - (800) 888-2050

    heat capacity - 15,000 to 42,000 Btuh   efficiency - ratings not available

    blower speeds - Variable speed and single speed

    combustion air - Direct vent and outdoor combustion air kit available

    special features - Hand-held and wall switch remote control

HEATILATOR, 1915 W. Sanders St., Mt. Pleasant, IA 52641 - (319) 385-9211

    heat capacity - 22,500 to 33,000 Btuh   efficiency - 60% to 70%

    blower speeds - Variable speeds

    combustion air - Direct vent and outdoor combustion air kit available

    special features - remote wall switch, many models and styles available

HEAT-N-GLO, 6665 West Hwy. 13, Savage, MN 55378 - (800) 669-4328 (612) 890-8367

    heat capacity - 20,000 to 48,000 Btuh   efficiency - 70%

    blower speeds - Variable speeds

    combustion air - Direct vent and outdoor combustion air kit available

    special features - Hand-held remote control, optional air filter

HUSSONG MFG. CO., PO Box 577, Lakefield, MN 56150 - (800) 253-4904 (507) 662-6641

    heat capacity - 22,000 to 34,000 Btuh   efficiency - 74%

    blower speeds - Variable speeds

    combustion air - Direct vent on 22,000 BTUH model, outdoor combustion air kits available on others

    special features - Remote wall switch, concentric inlet/outlet venting

JOHNSON GAS APPLIANCE, 520 E. Ave. NW, Cedar Rapids, IA 52405 - (319) 365-5267

    heat capacity - 14,000 to 31,500 Btuh   efficiency - 80%

    blower speeds - One or two speeds

    combustion air - Outdoor combustion air kits available

MARCO MFG. INC., 2520 Industry Way, Lynwood, CA 90262 - (800) 232-1221 (213) 564-3201

    heat capacity - 15,000 Btuh   efficiency - 74%

    blower speeds - Single speed

    combustion air - Outdoor combustion air kits available

MAJESTIC, 1000 E. Market St., Huntington, IN 46750 - (800) 525-1898 (219) 356-8000

    heat capacity - 14,000 to 50,000 Btuh   efficiency - 70%

    blower speeds - Variable speeds

    combustion air - Outdoor combustion air kit available

    special features - Hand-held and wall remote controls, automatic flue damper

MENDOTA HEARTH, 1890 Wooddale Dr., St. Paul, MN 55125 - (800) 825-2858 (612) 731-5367

    heat capacity - 33,000 to 38,000 Btuh   efficiency - 80%

    blower speeds - Variable speeds

    combustion air - Outdoor combustion air kits available

    special features - Hi/lo two burner heat control, gold-plated trim

ORVILLE PRODUCTS, PO Box 902, Orville, OH 44667 - (216) 683-4010

    heat capacity - 20,000 - 26,000 Btuh   efficiency - 75%

    blower speeds - Variable speeds

    combustion air - Direct vent with or without induced draft

    special features - Hand-held remote control, gold-plated trim option

Manufacturers of High-Efficiency Gas Fireplaces and Inserts - cont'd

RUEGG FIREPLACES, 216 Hwy 206, Ste. 12, Somerville, NJ 08876 - (908) 281-9555

heat capacity - n/a - radiant heat only   efficiency - ratings not available
blower speeds - Variable speeds
combustion air - Combined 10% outdoor and 90% indoor combustion air
special features - Gold-plated trim, glass slides up and is concealed when not in use

SUPERIOR, 4325 Artesia Ave., Fullerton, CA 92633 - (714) 521-7302

heat capacity - 21,000 to 45,000 Btuh   efficiency - 65%
blower speeds - Variable speeds
combustion air - Direct vent with or without induced draft blower, outdoor combustion air kits available
special features - Wall switch or hand-held remote control

TRAVIS INDUSTRIES, 10850 117th Pl. NE, Kirkland, WA 98033 - (206) 827-9505

heat capacity - 22,500 to 39,500 Btuh   efficiency - 80%
blower speeds - Two speeds
combustion air - Outdoor combustion air kits available
special features - Hand-held remote control, wall thermostat available, 24-karat gold plated trim

VALOR/FBD INC., 601 Hope St., Bowling Green, KY 42101 - (800) 654-8534

heat capacity - Variable - 10,000 to 22,000 Btuh   efficiency - 72%
blower speeds - No blower, radiant heat and natural convection
combustion air - Direct vent - concentric inlet/flue pipe
special features - Three heat settings, arch window option

VERMONT CASTINGS, PO Box 501, Bethel, VT 05032 - (800) 227-8683

heat capacity - 30,000 Btuh   efficiency - ratings not available
blower speeds - Variable speeds - also natural convection
combustion air - Not available
special features - Free-standing - cast iron construction

- -

Features of the Comfortec C60 Gas Fireplace Insert by Orville

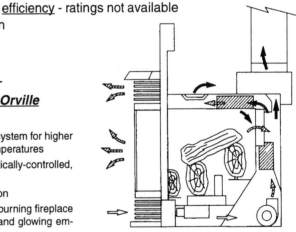

- Built in modulating thermostat allows you to set the control and the C60 will keep your room at the desired temperature.
- High-efficiency heat exchange system
- Up to 30,000 BTU thermostatically-controlled burner
- High temperature, radiating ceramic glass window, no need for a screen
- Heat by-pass damper control
- Certified to standards of safety and performance including a 100% safety shut-off gas valve and pressure regulator
- Aluminized steel used for the burn chamber
- for longer product life
- Unique venting and baffling system for higher efficiency and lower flue temperatures
- Maintenance free, thermostatically-controlled, variable speed fan system
- Easy-start piezo spark ignition
- The look of a geniune wood-burning fireplace with dancing yellow flames and glowing embers
- Five heat-resistant, ceramic fiber logs with the rough-sawn texture of real oak
- Uses standard 4" B-vent flue, or an approved chimney liner

The thermostatically-controlled variable speed fan system will push warm air to the cold corners of your room.

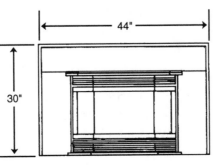

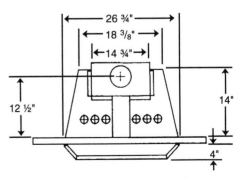

Q: My central air conditioner can not always keep my house cool enough and my summer electric bills are too high. Will shading the air conditioner help and what can I do myself to make it more efficient?

A: A simple annual do-it-yourself tune-up of your central air conditioner can cut your cooling costs by at least 10%. In addition, the cooling output will be greater for those sweltering summer days and your air conditioner will need fewer service calls and expensive repairs.

Shading the outdoor unit and house wall (especially a brick or stucco wall) near it also helps. By keeping the air surrounding the air conditioner cooler, it produces more cooling output with less electricity.

You can use landscaping or build a cover to shade your outdoor compressor unit and wall. Check with your cooling contractor for the proper clearance. Adequate air flow is essential for high efficiency.

One effective air conditioner cover design also provides storage for your garden tools, fertilizers, hoses, etc. The larger you make it, the more shade and cooling it provides. This design is basically a plywood storage bin built several feet back from the outdoor unit. Build it with a sloped roof (for shade) that extends up over the compressor unit and attaches to your house. The sloped roof gives added height for adequate clearance.

Make the frame for the storage bin/cover with any common lumber. You can cover it with plywood siding. Install a piano hinge and a top so you can secure it with a padlock.

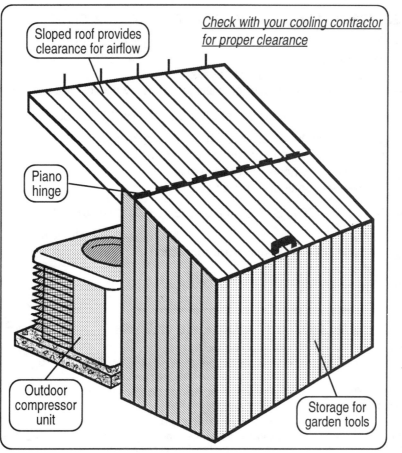

Sloped roof provides clearance for airflow

Piano hinge

Outdoor compressor unit

Check with your cooling contractor for proper clearance

Storage for garden tools

Before building the storage bin/cover, do a tune-up of the outdoor unit. Remove the screws and sheet metal housing. Clean out any debris (leaves, sticks, toys, etc.). Always turn off the main circuit breaker to it first.

Spray the dirt off the condenser coils with a garden hose. Water will not hurt the condenser coils, but try to avoid spraying the electric controls directly.

Carefully straighten any bent condenser coil fins with the tip of a sharp knife or a narrow screwdriver. You can buy an inexpensive plastic fin comb designed specifically for this purpose. Replace the sheet metal cover.

Make sure the screws on the small access panels are tight and that the panels are not bent, leaving gaps. Air is drawn in these gaps instead of over the coils resulting in higher electric bills and less cooling. Go indoors, remove the blower access panel, and vacuum those coils.

Q: I just installed a low-flow shower head with a push button "soap-up" valve. When I push it in to turn off the water, it still drips a little. What causes the dripping?

A: There is nothing wrong with the soap-up button on your shower head. The purpose of the push button valve on the shower head is to allow you to turn off the water while you lather up. When you are ready to rinse, you will not have to readjust the water temperature again.

The valve is designed to drip just a little to maintain the proper water temperature when you switch it back on. If it did not drip, you would get either an initial shot of very cold or hot water, usually hot.

Before you begin to build a storage bin/air conditioner cover, check with your heating and air-conditioning contractor, or with the manufacturer of your air conditioner, for the recommended clearance around the outdoor condenser unit.

It is <u>extremely</u> important to have adequate air flow through the condenser coils. These are the coils in the outdoor unit that transmit the heat to the outdoor air. If air flow is impeded, the air conditioner can not remove as much heat from your house as it should and it will have to run longer and waste electricity.

As long as you meet the clearance recommendations, you can size it for adequate storage capacity. Tilt the roof at an angle that is consistent with the slope of your roof. It will look better.

Required Materials for Storage Bin
lumber - 2x4 pressure treated
plywood - 5/8-inch or 3/4-inch exterior grade
#8 penny nails - cement coated or galvanized
#16 penny nails - cement coated or galvanized
angle supports
scrap wood
piano hinge
screws for piano hinge and for wooden handle
exterior paint
optional - stain
wood glue
wooden handle
latch
padlock

Do-It-Yourself Instructions for Storage Bin/Air Conditioner Cover

1) First construct a base box for the unit on the ground. You can use 2x4's (1,2). Nail them together to form the base box. Make sure the frame is square. Use #16 penny nails (3 1/2" long either cement coated or galvanized type. Since it will be setting on the ground, pressure treated lumber (CCA) is recommended. When handling or sawing pressure treated lumber, follow recommended safety procedures.

2) Cover the base box with a piece of 5/8-inch exterior grade plywood for the floor. It may be desirable to use pressure treated plywood (CCA) except the additional cost must be considered. Use #8 penny nails (2 1/2" long) either cement coated or galvanized type. If you are going to store a lot of heavy tools in the storage unit, you may wish to use 3/4-inch plywood. Drill several 1/2-inch diameter holes near the perimeter of the floor to allow for drainage of water due to rain.

3) Build the framing for the storage box using 2x4 lumber. First cut the soleplates (3) for the bottom members of the side walls. Then cut the uprights to form the sides. The back uprights (4) will all be the same length. The side uprights (5) will be longer as they get closer to the house wall (the angle will provide the correct pitch (slope) for the roof).

4) Attach the soleplates to the floor and install the upright framing. Support it at the back with a 2x4 (6). This will be the first roof frame member. Temporary diagonal wood bracing (light scrap wood) may be used to ensure the unit is true square, plumb, level and perpendicular. Remove bracing as permanent outer siding is installed.

5) Cut two long 2x4 rafters (7) which will reach from the back support (6) to the side of your house. You will have to notch one end of each long 2x4 so that it will fit over the members at point (8). The proper angle cut shall be made at the other end of the rafter as it meets and attaches to the house wall.

6) Attach these two long 2x4's to the upright framing making sure you have them sloped at the proper angle. Attach another 2x4 support (9) between them at the top. This is the location of the hinge for the storage compartment cover (door). Attach another support (10) between the uprights nearest the condenser unit. Attach support piece (12) to the house wall where the ends of the rafters (7) will be fastened.

7) Properly set intermediate rafters (11) between the uprights and the upper support (12). Securely nail into place.

8) Attach the plywood sheathing to side walls as shown in diagram. Galvanized nails will resist the dampness best. Do not run the sheathing all the way to the ground. Leave a gap of at least $3/4$-inch to allow moisture to escape. Thickness and type of wall sheathing to be used is a matter of home owner choice.

9) Use 2 pieces of plywood for the roof (preferable $5/8$-inch or $3/4$-inch exterior grade material). Size them so that the break is over support member (9). Nail the large roof piece over the condenser unit to the rafters. Then attach the smaller section of plywood with a piano hinge. That will be the cover (door) for the storage compartment. **Note:** If a standard width of plywood (4 foot) is to be used for the roof, the rough outside dimension of the storage compartment should be a maximum of 46 inches wide. This will allow for siding thicknesses and roof overhang at the side walls. If decorative rake moldings are desired, reduce rough width of storage compartment accordingly.

10) You should paint the completed unit both inside and out with several coats of good quality exterior paint. A lighter color will help keep it even cooler for your air conditioner. If you are storing valuable items, add a latch and padlock to the storage compartment door.

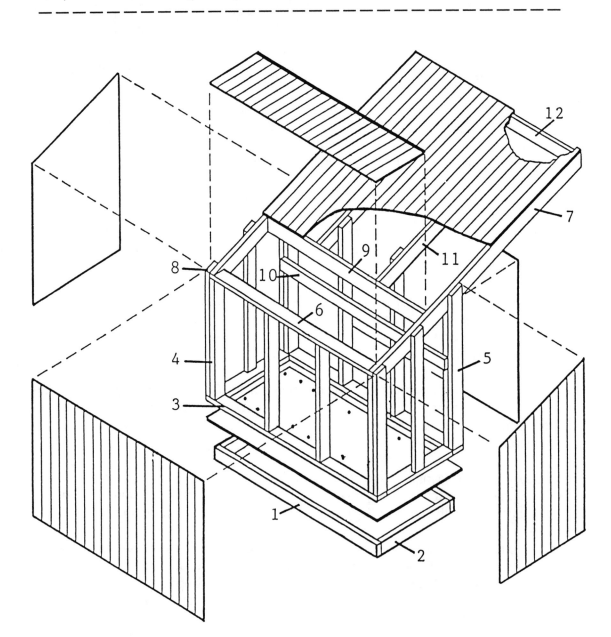

Do-It-Yourself Instructions for Open-End Air Conditioner Cover

1) Construct the unit so that all sides are equally wide. If you will be placing it around an already-in-place unit, you will want to prepare concrete corner pads on which the unit can rest. If the compressor unit is not yet in place, pour a square concrete slab with 3½x3½-inch notches in each corner to accommodate the 4x4 uprights. Also check the owner's manual that came with the air conditioner for any restrictions on blocking air intakes or exhaust.

2) Cut 4x4 uprights (1) to size and connect them at the top with four 1x6's (2) as shown in the diagram. Miter the corners of the 1x6's.

3) Construct each side panel by nailing 1x8 louvers (3) between two 1x4's (4). Angle the 1x8's to create a louver effect. Fit all three preassembled panels between the 4x4 uprights and secure them to the 4x4's.

4) Cut another series of 1x8 louvers (5) for the top of the enclosure. Position them carefully, then nail through the 1x6's, into the ends of the 1x8's.

5) Paint or stain the unit as desired. If you use pressure treated lumber, you can let it weather naturally. You should use a sealant on it.

6) If you have set the enclosure on concrete pads, drill a ½-inch hole into the center of each and a corresponding hole in the bottom of each upright. Dowel the two surfaces together with reinforcing rods. For units on notched slabs, drill holes through the 4x4's into the concrete slab. Again dowel with reinforcing rods.

Required Materials for Open-End Cover

lumber - 1x6, 1x8, 4x4
pressure treated
galavanized nails
wood glue
exterior paint
optional stain
optional wood sealant
reinforcing rods

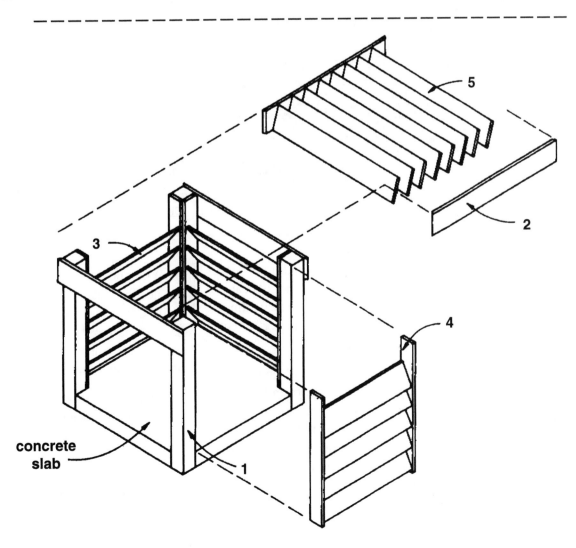

concrete slab

Q: Our central air conditioner does not always keep us cool and our electric bills are high, but we cannot afford a new one now. Are there add-on gadgets or simple maintenance to make it work better?

A: There are several simple add-on devices that increase the cooling output of your old central air conditioner (A/C) and reduce your electric bills. Doing a simple A/C tune-up yourself also helps.

One simple do-it-yourself add-on A/C device, Xzelaire, can cut your cooling costs by 10%. It is small and mounts on your wall next to your thermostat. Since it uses 24-volt power from the thermostat, it is safe to install yourself. Wiring it is simple. Thermostat wires are usually color-coded.

This device saves energy by running the blower for a few minutes after the compressor stops each cycle. This keeps room air circulating to harvest all the "coolth" from the cooling coil and metal ducts in your house.

Without this device, the electricity used to cool the ductwork at the start of each cycle is wasted inside the walls, basement, attic or utility room as the ducts warm up. Newer central A/C's have a similar device built-in.

Another type of device, called a desuperheater, uses the wasted ex-haust heat from your air conditioner's condenser to provide free water. This not only saves electricity for cooling and for heating water, but it can increase the maximum A/C cooling output on the hottest afternoons.

One desuperheater, HotTap, uses double wall copper tubing inside a block of insulation as the heat exchanger. The super hot refriger-ant from the air conditioner compressor flows through this heat exchanger. If you have a heat pump, it can heat your water more efficiently in the winter too.

The double-wall copper tubing seals the freon from the water, but it readily transmits the freon's heat. The unit mounts outdoors near the compressor and uses only 60 watts to operate the small circulation motor.

Adding a dehumidifying heat pipe kit in the A/C blower can increase comfort and efficiency. Whole-house dehumidifiers can also help with allergies.

To do your own A/C efficiency tune-up, switch the power off first. Remove the outdoor sheet metal cover and clean out any debris. If any condenser fins are bent over, carefully straighten them with the tip of a knife.

Go indoors and remove the sheet metal side on the indoor blower unit. This provides access to the evaporator coils. Clean them gently with your vacuum cleaner brush. Put a few drops of oil on the blower motor bearings.

Q: We are in the process of building our two-story house. Should I insulate the exterior wall area behind the heating ducts? How thick should the insulation be?

A: You should definitely insulate the heating ducts from the outside walls. Often, leaky and poorly insulated ducts are the leading energy waster in a house for both heating and air-conditioning.

Contact your heating contractor to determine where the ducts will be run and the depth of the ducts he plans to use. This will determine where to add the duct insulation and the maximum thickness that will fit.

Switch off electricity at fuse box first

Remove outdoor sheet metal housing

Spray off condenser coils

Compressor

Carefully straighten any bent coil fins

Trim back shrub for adequate air flow

You can make your central air conditioner more efficient and get greater maximum cooling output. If you have not had it professionally serviced in several years, have it checked. Also, see page 60 about how to do your own mini tune-up each year.

The Xzelaire Thermostat device is most effective in weather where the central A/C cycles on and off frequently.

Adding a whole-house

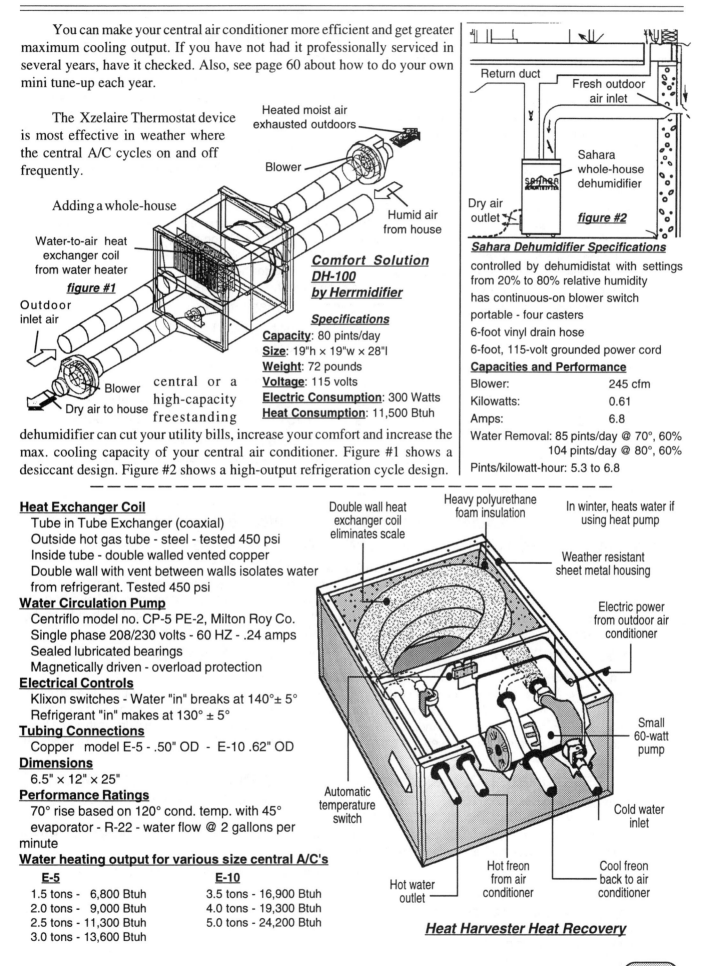

Heated moist air exhausted outdoors

Blower

Humid air from house

Water-to-air heat exchanger coil from water heater
figure #1

Outdoor inlet air

Blower
Dry air to house

central or a high-capacity freestanding

dehumidifier can cut your utility bills, increase your comfort and increase the max. cooling capacity of your central air conditioner. Figure #1 shows a desiccant design. Figure #2 shows a high-output refrigeration cycle design.

Return duct

Fresh outdoor air inlet

Sahara whole-house dehumidifier

Dry air outlet

figure #2

Comfort Solution DH-100 by Herrmidifier

Specifications
Capacity: 80 pints/day
Size: 19"h × 19"w × 28"l
Weight: 72 pounds
Voltage: 115 volts
Electric Consumption: 300 Watts
Heat Consumption: 11,500 Btuh

Sahara Dehumidifier Specifications
controlled by dehumidistat with settings from 20% to 80% relative humidity
has continuous-on blower switch
portable - four casters
6-foot vinyl drain hose
6-foot, 115-volt grounded power cord

Capacities and Performance
Blower:	245 cfm
Kilowatts:	0.61
Amps:	6.8

Water Removal: 85 pints/day @ 70°, 60%
104 pints/day @ 80°, 60%

Pints/kilowatt-hour: 5.3 to 6.8

Heat Exchanger Coil
Tube in Tube Exchanger (coaxial)
Outside hot gas tube - steel - tested 450 psi
Inside tube - double walled vented copper
Double wall with vent between walls isolates water from refrigerant. Tested 450 psi

Water Circulation Pump
Centriflo model no. CP-5 PE-2, Milton Roy Co.
Single phase 208/230 volts - 60 HZ - .24 amps
Sealed lubricated bearings
Magnetically driven - overload protection

Electrical Controls
Klixon switches - Water "in" breaks at 140°± 5°
Refrigerant "in" makes at 130° ± 5°

Tubing Connections
Copper   model E-5 - .50" OD - E-10 .62" OD

Dimensions
6.5" × 12" × 25"

Performance Ratings
70° rise based on 120° cond. temp. with 45° evaporator - R-22 - water flow @ 2 gallons per minute

Water heating output for various size central A/C's

E-5	E-10
1.5 tons - 6,800 Btuh	3.5 tons - 16,900 Btuh
2.0 tons - 9,000 Btuh	4.0 tons - 19,300 Btuh
2.5 tons - 11,300 Btuh	5.0 tons - 24,200 Btuh
3.0 tons - 13,600 Btuh	

Double wall heat exchanger coil eliminates scale

Heavy polyurethane foam insulation

In winter, heats water if using heat pump

Weather resistant sheet metal housing

Electric power from outdoor air conditioner

Small 60-watt pump

Cold water inlet

Cool freon back to air conditioner

Hot freon from air conditioner

Automatic temperature switch

Hot water outlet

Heat Harvester Heat Recovery

Manufacturers of Central A/C Comfort and Efficiency Improvement Devices

SDT USA, P.O. Box 12098, Santa Rosa, CA 95406 - (707) 577-8053

model - "Xzelaire" voltage - 24-volt thermostat circuit

general description - This Xzelaire power saver is an add-on accessory to central air-conditioning systems which are five to ten years old. It is installed at the wall thermostat and connected to the thermostat. Xzelaire senses when the thermostat shuts off the compressor and it keeps the circulating blower running for a short period after this. This recaptures some of the start-up energy from each on/off cycle.

ENERGY CONSERVATION, P.O. Box 520585, Longwood, FL 32752 - (800) 834-0400 (407) 829-4328

model - "HotTap" capacity range - 1.5 to 6 tons

general description - This desuperheater device draws heat from the air conditioner freon instead of having the heat exhausted as usual to the outdoor air from the condenser coils. You can feel this waste hot air blowing out from the outdoor A/C unit. It is mounted outdoors near the central A/C compressor unit. An insulated heat exchanger inside the unit transfers the heat from the freon to the water. It will require an air-conditioning technician to attach the freon pipes and the water pipes to and from the water heater. There are two models available depending on the cooling capacity of your central air conditioner.

HEAT HARVESTER, 9848 Monroe Dr., Dallas, TX 75220 - (214) 358-2500

model - "E-5" capacity range - 1.5 to 3 tons

model - "E-10" capacity range - 3.5 to 5 tons

general description - This operates in a fashion very similar to the Heat Harvester described above. The heat exchanger is encased in polyurethane rigid foam insulation. It has special temperature sensors to make sure that the freon is not overly cooled. One model is designed to handle most residential-size central A/C's.

HEAT PIPE TECHNOLOGY, P.O. Box 999, Alachua, FL 32615 - (800) 393-3464 (904) 462-3464

model - "Hot Plate" capacity range - any size

general description - This is a flat (only 2.5 in. high × 22.5 in. octagon) heat exchanger that you set your existing water heater on top of. The hot refrigerant from your central air conditioner transfers its heat to the water inside the water heater. No electricity or pumps are needed.

- -

Manufacturers of Whole-House Dehumidifying Devices

HERRMIDIFIER CO., P.O. Box 11148, Lancaster, PA 17605 - (717) 394-4021

model - "DH-1000" dehumidifying rate - 80 pints per day

general description - This design (called Comfort Solution) uses a slowly rotating desiccant (a material which attracts moisture) wheel. Humid room air flows over the dry portion of the wheel and moisture is drawn from the air to the wheel. Outdoor air, heated and dried by your water heater, flows over the other half of the wheel removing the moisture it just picked up. As the wheel rotates, it continually dries out the indoor air.

THERMA-STOR PRODUCTS, P.O. Box 8050A, Madison, WI 53708 - (800) 533-7533 (608) 222-5301

model - "Sahara" dehumidifying rate - 104 pints per day

general description - This is a whole-house dehumidifier that uses a refrigeration type of dehumidification cycle. It is two to three times as efficient as a standard dehumidifier because it uses the cool, dry exhaust air to precool the incoming humid air. It runs on standard 115 volts. It can be ducted to a window so that it draws in some fresh outdoor air to eliminate a stale, closed in feeling. The outdoor air is dehumidified and filtered before it blows out indoors.

HEAT PIPE TECHNOLOGY, P.O. Box 999, Alachua, FL 32615 - (800) 393-3464 (904) 462-3464

model no. - "DHP series" use with - 24,000 through 60,000 Btuh air conditioners

sizes - 43 w × 17 to 33 d × 3.5 h in. nominal air flow - 1,200; 1,600; and 2,000 cfm blower

general description - This is an add-on dehumidifying heat pipe that is used with your present air handler evaporator coil. (Note the height dimension is only 3.5 in.)

model no. - "Z-coil series" cooling/heating output - 36,000; 48,000; and 60,000 Btuh

sizes - 21 w × 22 to 32 d × 25 h in. nominal air flow - 1,200; 1,600; and 2,000 cfm blower

general description - This is an evaporator coil assembly to replace the existing coil in your air handler (furnace/air conditioner blower). The dehumidifying heat pipe heat exchanger is built into the new coil assembly. The entire evaporator coil is replaced.

Do-it Yourself Maintenance for Central A/C

1) Turn off circuit breaker to shut off all electric-ditioner. After you the thermostat lower to doesn't still have power or remove fuse ity to the air con-switch it off, set make sure it and comes on.

2) Check the outdoor compressor unit. It contains the condenser coils and a fan that dissipates heat from these coils. The coils and the fins can become clogged with dirt and debris.

3) Remove the sheet metal cover over the outdoor unit. It is usually held on by a few sheet metal screws. Wear work  gloves to protect your hands. Remove any large debris like leaves and twigs.

4) Spray off the condenser coils with your garden hose. Although the units are made to withstand rain, try not to spray the electric control unit directly.

5) Once you have cleaned the coils, carefully inspect the fins. Carefully straighten any bent fins using a thin knife. It is important for all of the fins to be open so as much air as possible flows through the coils. Your air conditioner service supply center should also have inexpensive plastic fins combs used to straighten the fins.

6) Check around the compressor for any signs of oil that may be leaking from the crankcase. If you notice a leak, call your serviceman immediately. If it runs low on oil, it will be permanently damaged.

7) Check the fan motor housing at the the shaft. Some motors and quire periodic oiling with a drops of SAE 10W oil. If you sure about your unit, contact the contractor who installed it. Replace the sheet metal cover. ends of fans re-f e w are un-

8) Go indoors to the blower section of the air conditioner. Replace the furnace filter if you have not done so recently. If you clean turers clean have an electronic air cleaner, the inserts per the manufac-instructions. Thereafter, or replace the filter every month or two.

9) Remove the inspection cover by the blower. Check the tension on the belt. It should flex about ½" in the center. If it is too loose, loosen the motor mounting bolt and slide the motor to tighten the belt.

10) Running the blower faster with air conditioning is sometimes better. and air-You speed eter of 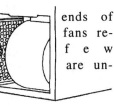 Check with your heating conditioning contractor. can adjust the blower by adjusting the diam-the motor drive pulley. If you screw the two sides of the pulley closer together, the blower speed is increased. If you separate them farther, the blower will slow down. A faster blower

speed provides greater cooling, but less dehumidification.

11) Gently using a brush and your vacuum cleaner, clean any dust and dirt off of the blower blades. This can really improve the air flow and the efficiency of the blower.

12) If there are oil locations on the motor and blower bearings, put several drops of SAE 10W oil on them. This should be done every year.

13) If you can get to the indoor evaporator coils that are at the top of blower chamber, carefully clean them off. They may have some heavy deposits from the condensation of the water vapor in the air. Check the condensate drain tube to make sure it is open.

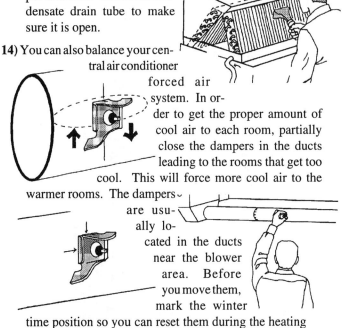

14) You can also balance your central air conditioner forced air system. In order to get the proper amount of cool air to each room, partially close the dampers in the ducts leading to the rooms that get too cool. This will force more cool air to the warmer rooms. The dampers are usually located in the ducts near the blower area. Before you move them, mark the winter time position so you can reset them during the heating season.

Do-it Yourself Maintenance for Window A/C

1) Unplug the window unit from the wall outlet.

2) Carefully snap off the front cover and remove the foam filter. Be careful because it can easily be torn. Wash it out per the manufacturer's instructions. Vacuum and clean the evaporator coils that are located behind the filter. You can use a mild detergent solution to clean them.

3) Depending on its design, remove the outdoor metal housing or slide the unit out of the housing. Wash off the condenser coils and straighten any bent fins. You can use a detergent solution on these too.

4) Clean off the fan blades for the condenser fan. These will be very dirty on the leading edge. Oil the fan motor bearings if required. Some bearings are permanently lubricated.

5) Check the evaporator coil drain to make sure it is open. Also check the tilt of the unit in the window so the water forming on the evaporator coils drains outdoors and not inside your wall or window opening. Replace the cover on the unit. Seal it in the window opening with adhesive-backed foam weatherstripping.

Q: My allergies are killing me and I need a whole-house air cleaner. What is the most effective and easy-to-install air cleaner that will not reduce the efficiency of my central air conditioner and furnace?

A: There are new designs of whole-house air cleaners (mount in forced-air furnace/air-conditioning blower) that can remove up to 99% of pollen, molds, cat dander, smoke, etc. from the air. I have allergies myself and I have tested many different air cleaner designs in my own heat pump.

Several easy-to-install air cleaners slip into the existing one-inch filter slot with no modifications. Installing one improves your air conditioner and furnace efficiency by keeping the dust off of the heat exchanger coils.

Residential air cleaner designs include - self-charging electrostatic, pleated media, electronic, and HEPA (high-efficiency particulate air). Self-charging air cleaners use a combination of materials. This creates a natural static charge to trap allergens and dust. They use no electricity.

You clean the filter element with a garden hose or in a bathtub. The water neutralized the static charge and the particles easily wash away. With regular cleaning, a self-charging air cleaner will last many years. One new slip-in self-charging

model, System 4, has a small built-in smoke detector (9-volt battery). Its smoke alarm alerts you as it automatically shuts off the furnace blower. It also alerts you when it's time to clean it.

Another slip-in design is available in kits so you can custom size it for your existing filter opening. These air cleaners have permanent

anti-microbial treated filter material to control bacteria and fungi growth. Self-charging electrostatic prefilters are also available for electronic air cleaners.

The most effective (and expensive) air cleaner uses thick HEPA (often used in hospitals) and carbon filters. It removes over 99.97% of particles down to 0.3 microns, odors, and harmful vapors. The air cleaner has its own blower and housing de-

signed to attach to your ducts for simple installation.

Electronic air cleaners are very effective, particularly for smaller smoke and dust particles. They use only as much electricity as a 40-watt light bulb. You can easily clean the filter elements in your dishwasher.

Disposable pleated media filters are more effective than simple fiberglass filters, but much less than a HEPA unit. Some cost less than $6 each.

The type of allergies you have determine which type of air cleaner is best for you. Molds and pollen are relatively large particles. Cigarette smoke and some dusts are a hundred times smaller.

Q: I just bought a five-year-old house and the windows have a slight bluish tint on sunny days. The seller told me that they were high-efficiency windows. Should they be bluish?

A: The sellers probably were telling you the truth. A bluish tint, when viewed from outdoors, is not uncommon with low-e (low-emissivity) glass. The low-e windows in my own home look this way on a sunny day.

A low-e coating, on the inside surface of double-pane windows, lets visible light through, but blocks heat loss. This type of glass is quickly becoming the standard replacement window glass.

Automatically shuts off blower during fire

Built-in smoke detector

Insulating vinyl frame

Plastic rods inside create static charge

Anti-microbial polypropylene filter material

Installing a good-quality in-duct air cleaner and filter can help reduce problems with allergies. I have allergies to mold, pollen, and cat dander myself. I have tried several types of air cleaners and they did help reduce my symptoms.

Figure #1 shows the sizes of various allergens and pollutants. The common allergens like mold, pollen, etc. are considered to be large particles. Smoke, dust, and grease are very small. Figure #2 show the size of several items measured in microns for your reference.

On pages 63 and 64, I have listed the manufacturers of the highest-quality and most effective air cleaners and replacement filters. The four basic types of units listed are HEPA, self-charging electrostatic, pleated media, and electronic. Also listed are efficiency, dust arrestance and features.

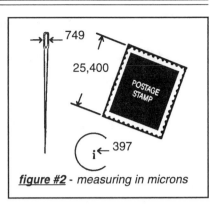

figure #2 - measuring in microns

"*Efficiency*" refers to a dust spot efficiency test. The higher the efficiency, the more effective an air cleaner is at removing all particles and allergens, especially the very small ones. The HEPA and electronic air cleaners are best for removing these very small particles. These are a good choice if you are allergic to smoke or dusts.

"*Dust arrestance*" refers to the percentage of all particles removed, by weight. This indicates the air cleaner's effectiveness at removing the larger particles since they weigh the most. For example, the self-charging electrostatic units are effective for larger allergen particles, but since they have a low efficiency, they do not remove the tiny smoke particles as well. Some of these have anti-microbial treated material to reduce the growth of bacteria, molds, and fungi. All self-charging units are cleaned in a bathtub or by spraying with a garden hose.

Most of the self-charging air cleaners are one inch thick, so they slip into the existing filter slot. Thicker pleated media air cleaners (you should replace filter element every year) are more effective than thin ones.

The Farr Company and the Purity Home Products units are the only one-inch thick pleated media listed. The thicker pleated media units require some duct modifications to fit in place. Pleated media units are a lower-cost, yet fairly effective alternative to electronic and HEPA units. All the electronic air cleaner units require duct modifications and electric wiring.

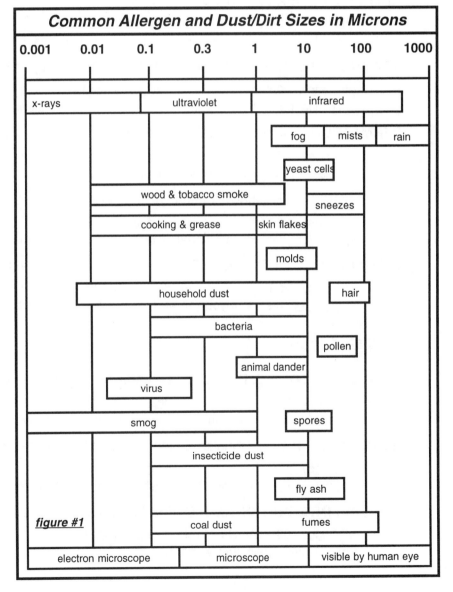

figure #1

Manufacturers of Whole-House Central Air Cleaners

HEPA - (high efficiency particulate air)

PURE AIR SYSTEMS, P.O. Box 418, Plainfield, IN 46168 - (800) 869-8025 (317) 839-9135

efficiency - 99.9%   dust arrestance - 99.9%
special features - has its own blower, thick charcoal filter removes odors

Self-Charging Electrostatic

ALL AMERICAN FILTERS, 1871 S. Dixie Hwy., Pampano Beach, FL 33060 - (305) 785-1926
efficiency - <20%   dust arrestance - 88%
special features - ten-year warranty, fire-resistant frame

DUST FREE, P.O. Box 519, Royse City, TX 75189 - (214) 635-9564

efficiency - <20%   dust arrestance - 93%
special features - five-year warranty, carbon filter option

HI-TECH FILTERS, 80 Myrtle St., North Quincy, MA 02171 - (800) 448-3249 (617) 328-7756

efficiency - <20%   dust arrestance - 83%
special features - 10-year warranty, coated aluminum rust-proof frame

NEWTRON, P.O. Box 27175, Cincinnati, OH 45227 - (800) 543-9149 (513) 561-7373

efficiency - <20%   dust arrestance - 86%
special features - built-in smoke alarm, anti-microbial material, cleaning signal

PERMATRON, 11400 Melrose St., Franklin Park, IL 60131 - (800) 882-8012 (708) 451-0999

efficiency - <20%   dust arrestance - 91%
special features - carbon filter coating, stainless steel option for corrosive air, electronic prefilter

POLYTRON, P.O. Box 5881, Beaumont, TX 77726 - (800) 842-7659 (409) 838-0540

efficiency - <20%   dust arrestance - 84%
special features - lifetime warranty, rust-free aluminum frame and galvanized steel grid

WEBB PRODUCTS, 11 Lincoln St., Kansas City, KS 66103 - (800) 875-3212 (913) 384-3221

efficiency - <20%   dust arrestance - 91%
special features - do-it-yourself kits to vary sizes, anti-microbial material, optional carbon filter

Pleated Media

FARR COMPANY, P.O. Box 92187, Los Angeles, CA 90009 - (310) 536-6300

efficiency - 20%   dust arrestance - 85%
special features - 1 inch thick, has wire filter supports for even filtering/air distribution

HONEYWELL, 1985 N. Douglas, Golden Valley, MN 55422 - (800) 328-5111 (612) 870-2682

efficiency - 30%   dust arrestance - 92%
special features - 4 inches thick, washable, same duct housing as electronic for easy upgrade

LAKE AIR INTERNATIONAL, P.O. Box 4150, Racine, WI 53404 - (800) 558-9436 (414) 632-1229

efficiency - 65% (7 inches thick) dust arrestance - 98%
special features - lifetime warranty

Pleated Media - continued

PURITY HOME PROD., P.O. Box 231, Baltimore, OH 43105 - (800) 444-2072 (614) 862-8115

efficiency - <20%   dust arrestance - 94%
special features - 1 inch thick, four-stages - 2 filters, 1 carbon, 1 adhesive layer to trap particles

RESEARCH PRODUCTS, P.O. Box 1467, Madison, WI 53701 - (608) 257-8801

efficiency - 65% (7 inches thick) dust arrestance - 98%
special features - lifetime warranty

TRION, P.O. Box 760, Sanford, NC 27331 - (800) 227-3917 (919) 775-2201

efficiency - 40%   dust arrestance - 98%
special features - carbon filter option

Electronic

CIMATEC, 8031Jarry East, Montreal, Canada H1J1H6 - (800) 565-5326

efficiency - 30%   dust arrestance - 90%
special features - only one-inch thick, 24-volt power, produces no ozone, less cleaning

HONEYWELL, see previous list

efficiency - 95%   dust arrestance - 98%
special features - small cells fit easily into dishwasher, test button on cover, remote output panel

LAKE AIR INTERNATIONAL, see previous list

efficiency - 95%   dust arrestance - 98%
special features - special durable power supply, less ozone levels, five-year warranty

TRION, see previous list

efficiency - 90%   dust arrestance - 98%
special features - special small size to minimize duct modifications, carbon filter option

WHITE-RODGERS, 9797 Reavis Rd., St. Louis, MO 63123 - (800) 876-8324 (314) 577-1300

efficiency - 87%   dust arrestance - 98%
special features - 3 sizes from 600 to 2,200 cfm, carbon filter option

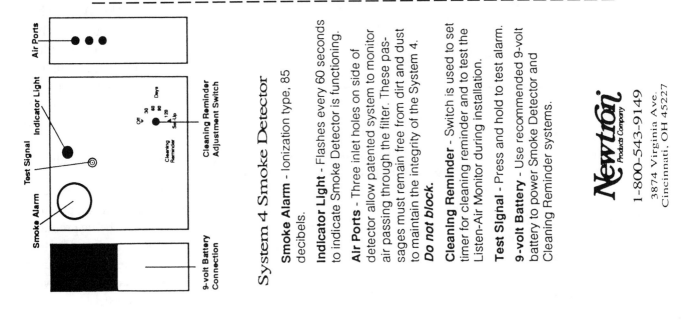

System 4 Smoke Detector

Smoke Alarm - Ionization type, 85 decibels.

Indicator Light - Flashes every 60 seconds to indicate Smoke Detector is functioning.

Air Ports - Three inlet holes on side of detector allow patented system to monitor air passing through the filter. These passages must remain free from dirt and dust to maintain the integrity of the System 4. *Do not block.*

Cleaning Reminder - Switch is used to set timer for cleaning reminder and to test the Listen-Air Monitor during installation.

Test Signal - Press and hold to test alarm.

9-volt Battery - Use recommended 9-volt battery to power Smoke Detector and Cleaning Reminder systems.

Newtron
Products Company
1-800-543-9149
3874 Virginia Ave.
Cincinnati, OH 45227

Q: For my allergies, does it make sense to run a small room air cleaner even though there is a filter on my furnace? What are the most effective types of room air cleaners and are they expensive to operate?

A: It does make sense to use a freestanding room air cleaner even if your furnace has a blower filter or built-in air cleaner. Running a large room air cleaner can be more effective than a central air cleaner because it runs continuously. A furnace unit cleans only when the furnace is running.

I have an electronic air cleaner on my furnace, but I also run a small HEPA (high efficiency particulate air) unit in my bedroom at night. This is effective for removal of mold and dust mite allergens. My air cleaner uses only about 100 watts (several cents per day) on the low quiet speed.

The most common types of room air cleaners are HEPA, electronic precipitator, pleated media, self-charging electrostatic, ionizer, and ozone. Each type of air cleaner is particularly effective for specific-size allergen particles, so don't just buy the cheapest one on sale.

HEPA and electrostatic precipitators are the most effective overall, especially for extremely small smoke particles. A HEPA (very dense and finely-packed filter material) air cleaner is 99% efficient at removing most tiny particles (dust, smoke, pollen, mold spores, etc.) from the air.

Super-high-efficiency HEPA filters are often used in hospital operating rooms and industrial "clean room" areas. Pleated media is a lower efficiency, more-loosely-packed type of HEPA filter and less expensive. Many have a replaceable carbon filter element to remove odors also.

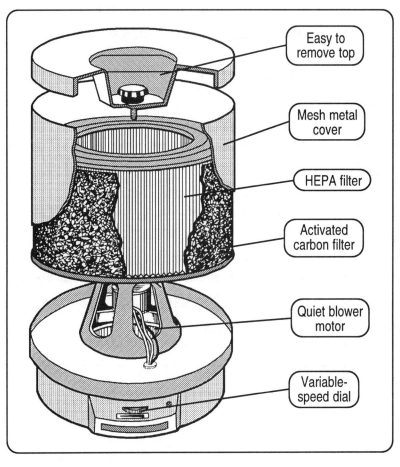

- Easy to remove top
- Mesh metal cover
- HEPA filter
- Activated carbon filter
- Quiet blower motor
- Variable-speed dial

Electronic precipitators electrically charge allergen particles as they pass through the air cleaner. These charged particles then stick to collector plates with the opposite charge in the air cleaner. Remove the filter cells and wash them in your dishwasher or bathtub, every month.

Self-charging electrostatic filters use a material that develops a static charge as air moves through it to trap the particles. They are most effective for larger allergens particles. Ionizers also cause particles to stick to walls and tables so they can be easily cleaned. Ozone actually reacts with and destroys the particles.

Select a room air cleaner with a high maximum air flow rate and several speeds, especially for a bedroom. You can turn it on high for several hours and then switch it to a low, quiet speed for sleeping. Also you should consider the weight, which can range from about 12 pounds to 43 pounds, for ease of moving from room to room.

Q: When I had my gas furnace and water heater serviced last year, the serviceman said that they were burning cleanly because there was a nice blue flame. Is this the best way to tell?

A: No. Although a clean burning (low carbon monoxide - CO) flame is blue, a blue flame does not insure that CO is not being produced. The shape and steadiness of the flame are also indicators of the combustion quality.

To be safe, your service technician should have test equipment to measure if CO gas is being produced in excessive concentrations. The testing device is inserted into the flue to measure the gases directly. Always request a flue gas test.

Room air cleaners can be more effective than furnace mounted air cleaners because you can operate these continuously. The energy usage on most models is less than 100 watts. You will most often operate them on the lower, more quiet speeds.

Before you select a room air cleaner, determine what type of contaminants that you want to remove from the air. These will most often be the types of particles that you are allergic to. Then use the data in figure #1 to determine the level of filtering quality that you need.

A list of air cleaner manufacturers, type of filter, weight, and air flow speeds is shown on page 67. If you plan to use the air cleaner in a bedroom, a very slow speed is best for quiet operation. Use the noisier high speed to rapidly clean the air and then set it on a lower, speed for sleeping. Totally variable speeds are nice, but three speeds are adequate for the bedroom. In most other rooms, two-speeds are enough.

If there are older persons in your family, consider the weight of the air cleaner. You will often move it from room to room, from a kitchen to bedroom at night, for example. A light weight room air cleaner will be much easier to handle and to move around.

HEPA (high-efficiency particulate air) filters are the most effective, filtering out almost all particles down to .01 microns. For reference, the dot over the "i" is about 400 microns. Only a small percentage of smokes and dust are smaller than the filtration effectiveness of a HEPA filter.

Because of the high filter density of a HEPA, a more powerful blower is used. This uses a little more electricity and may be slightly noisier on the higher speeds. The filter element should last several years. Most will also have a carbon filter to remove some odors from the air. This is very helpful in a moist musty atmosphere.

Electronic room air cleaners are effective for removing small particles, like smoke and dust from the air. There are no filter elements to replace other than the charcoal element. Pull out the cleaning element and run it through a dishwasher cycle. These air cleaners can give off a little ozone. This results in a fresh scent inside your home; however, some individuals are hypersensitive to the ozone.

Self-charging electrostatic filters are the least effective for removing small particles like smoke. For larger particles like molds and pollen, they are effective. Mechanical filters are less effective for the smaller particles, but are less expensive than true HEPA filters.

Ozone models are used to purify the air by killing virus and bacteria, but they do not clean out fine particles. Electron generators are not rated by cfm of air flow. They just emit electrons to charge the dirt particles in the air. The small fan is just for mild circulation of the air.

The prices of room air cleaners varies substantially depending on different options. The prices range from less than $160.00 to more than $600.00 for these units.

Sizes of Air Contaminants - microns

Particulates	
Human Hair	100 - 20
Viruses	1 - .02
Bacteria	20 - .05
Skin Flakes	15 - .9
Pollen	100 - 5
Spores	100 - 9
Yeast Cells	20 - 2
Sneeze Droplets	100 - 15
Smoke	
Carbon Particles	1 - .005
Cooking/Grease	2 - .01
Tobacco Smoke	3 - .01
Wood Smoke	3 - .01
Dusts	
Household Dust	10 - .01
Insecticide Dust	20 - .01
Soil Dust	100 - 1
Coal Dust	100 - 1
Fly Ash	20 - 2
Animal Dander	10 - .2

figure #1

Manufacturers of High-Efficiency Room Air Cleaners

AIR QUALITY ENGINEERING, 3340 Winpark, Minneapolis, MN 55427 - (800) 328-0787 (612) 544-4426
model - "Smokemaster P600"   weight - 39.5 lbs   air flow rates/speeds - 235 to 420 cfm - three
filtration method - four-stage electronic — prefilter • ionizing section • oppositely charged plate • charcoal filter

AUSTIN AIR, 701 Seneca St., Buffalo, NY 14210 - (716) 856-3704
model - "Healthmate/Healthmate Plus"   weight - 45 lbs.   air flow rates/speeds - 75 to 400 cfm - three
filtration method - four stage HEPA — prefilter • 25 lbs. charcoal/ zeolite mixture • HEPA filter • mesh retaining filter

BIONAIRE CORP., 90 Boroline Rd., Allendale, NJ 07401 - (800) 253-2764 (201) 934-0755
model - "F70" • "F100" • "F150" • "F250"   weight - n/a   air flow rates/speeds - 100 to 250 cfm - three
filtration method - four-stage self-charge electrostatic — prefilter • electrostatic micro-filter • post-filter • charcoal filter
model - "SH1240" • "SH1860" • "CH3550"   weight - 11.6 • 14 • 39 lbs.   air flow rates/speeds - 60 to 350 cfm - three • four
filtration method - three-stage HEPA — prefilter for large particles • HEPA filter • charcoal filter

CLOUD 9, 777 Edgewood Ave., Wooddale, IL 60191 - (708) 595-5000
model - "Sterile-Aire 150 • 300"   weight - 22 • 39 lbs.   air flow rates/speeds - n/a cfm - two
filtration method - three-stage HEPA — prefilter for large particles • charcoal filter • HEPA filter

EMERSON ELECTRIC CO., 9797 Reavis Rd., St. Louis, MO 63123 - (314) 577-1300
model - "PWM" • "Console"   weight - 32 • 46 lbs.   air flow rates/speeds - 100 to 200 cfm - variable
filtration method - four-stage electronic — prefilter • charging section • collecting positive/negative plates • charcoal filter

ENVIRACAIRE CORP., 100 Jamison Ct., Hagerstown, MD 21740 (800) 332-1110
model - "10500" • "10520"   weight - 10 • 11.5 lbs.   air flow rates/speeds - 55 to 150 cfm - two
model - "12520" • "13520"   weight - 13.5 • 15.5 lbs.   air flow rates/speeds - 125 to 350 cfm - three
filtration method - two-stage HEPA — charcoal prefilter wrapper • HEPA filter

FRIEDRICH, PO Box 1540, San Antonio, TX 78295 - (210) 225-2000
model - "C-90"   weight - 28 lbs.   air flow rates/speeds - 230 to 390 cfm - three
filtration method - four-stage electronic — prefilter • charging section • oppositely charged plates section • charcoal filter

HEALTHWAY PRODUCTS CO., INC., PO Box 549, E. Syracuse, NY 13057 - (315) 463-0240
model - "HW130c"   weight - 7 lbs.   air flow rates/speeds - n/a cfm - two
filtration method - four-stage electronic — prefilter with charcoal • ionizing section • collection section • electron ionizer

HOLMES PRODUCTS CORP., 233 Fortune Blvd., Milford, MA 01757 - (508) 634-8050
model - "Climate Care"   weight - 6.12 lbs.   air flow rates/speeds - n/a cfm - single
filtration method - summer filter — HEPA filter • charcoal filter …winter filter — evaporating wicking filter • both filters operate
with an electrostatically charged electret filter with ionizer.
model - "HAP220" • "HAP240"   weight - 6.15 • 6.83 lbs.   air flow rates/speeds - 65 to 200 cfm - two • three
model - "HAP290" • "HAP300"   weight - 11.5 • 24.3 lbs.   air flow rates/speeds - 125 to 300 cfm - three
model - "HAP440" • "HAP475"   weight - 7.5 • 11.5 lbs.   air flow rates/speeds - n/a cfm - two
filtration method - HEPA + multistage — foam prefilter • HEPA filter • charcoal filter • electron ionizer

HONEYWELL, 1985 Douglas Dr. North, Golden Valley, MN 55422 - (800) 328-5111 • (612) 870-2682
model - "F29A1007"   weight - 15.5 lbs.   air flow rates/speeds - 125 to 300 cfm - three
filtration method - two-stage HEPA — charcoal prefilter wrapper • HEPA filter

KLEEN-RITE, 4444 Gustine, St. Louis, MO 63116 - (314) 353-1712
model - "Immacul-Aire"   weight - 30 lbs.   air flow rates/speeds - 180 & 435 cfm - two
filtration method - pleated media + charcoal — two layers, each has 27 square feet of surface

KRYSTIL KLEAR, Route 2, Box 300, Winamac, IN 46996 - (800) 869-0325 (219) 278-7865
model - "Klear Air 140"   weight - 15 lbs.   air flow rates/speeds - 140 cfm - two speeds
filtration method - four-stage HEPA — prefilter for large particles • charcoal filter • HEPA filter • safety net

LAKEAIR, PO Box 4150, Racine, WI 53404 - (800) 558-9436 (414) 632-1229
model - "LA250" • "LA500"   weight - 26 • 30lbs.   air flow rates/speeds - 70 & 275 cfm - two
filtration method - four-stage electronic — prefilter • ionizing section • oppositely charged plates section • charcoal filter

NEOLIFE, 3500 Gateway Blvd., Fremont, CA 94538 - (510) 651-0405
model - "Consolaire"   weight - 6 lbs.   air flow rates/speeds - 19 & 100 cfm - two
filtration method - three-stage self-charge electrostatic — charcoal • electrostatic collector grid • charcoal

NSA, 4260 E. Raines Rd., Memphis, TN 38118 - (901) 366-9288
model - "7100A" • "7100B"   weight - 32 lbs.   air flow rates/speeds - 89 & 120 cfm - two
filtration method - three-stage HEPA — prefilter for large particles • HEPA filter • Tri-media filter to remove gas and odor

OXYGEN TECH. CORP., 8229 Melrose, Lenexa, KS 66214 - (913) 894-2828
model - "FreshAire 500"   weight - 19 lbs.   air flow rates/speeds - 64 & 70 cfm - two
filtration method - ozone generator

QUANTUM ELECTRONICS, 110 Jefferson Blvd., Warwick, RI 02888 - (800) 966-5575 (401) 732-6770
model - "S200" • "S300" • "S400" • "S600"   weight - 7.5 lbs.   air flow rates/speeds - 15 to 105 cfm - variable
filtration method - ozone generator

RESEARCH PRODUCTS, PO Box 1467, Madison, WI 53701 - (800) 545-2219 (608) 257-8801
model - "Space-Gard 2275"   weight - 12 lbs.   air flow rates/speeds - 100 & 140 cfm - two
filtration method - pleated media — 21 pleats - 10.8 ft²

TELEDYNE-WATER PIK, 1730 E. Prospect Rd., Fort Collins, CO 80553 - (800) 525-2774 (303) 484-1352
model - "AFX10" • "AFX20"   weight - 6.6 • 8.10 lbs.   air flow rates/speeds - 60 to 135 cfm - two
filtration method - four-stage ionizer — prefilter • electrostatic filter • charcoal filter • ionizer brushes

TRION INC., PO Box 760, Sanford, NC 27331 - (919) 775-2201
model - "Super Clean II" • "Console 250"   weight - 9 • 38 lbs.   air flow rates/speeds - 55 to 250 cfm - three
filtration method - four-stage electronic — prefilter • ionizer • collector with aluminum plates • charcoal filter

UNITED AIR SPECIALISTS, 4440 Creek Rd., Cincinnati, OH 45242 - (513) 891-0400
model - "Crystal-Aire C10" • "C20"   weight - 27 • 39.5 lbs.   air flow rates/speeds - 90 to 340 cfm - variable
filtration method - four-stage electronic — prefilter • electrical charging section • collecting plates section • charcoal filter

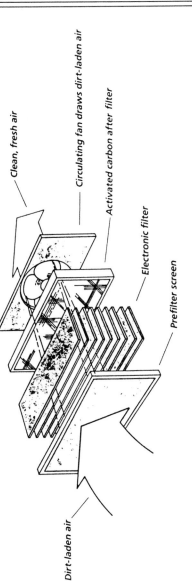

Clean, fresh air

Circulating fan draws dirt-laden air

Activated carbon after filter

Electronic filter

Prefilter screen

Dirt-laden air

The LA-500 complements any decor. The compact cabinet is constructed of metal and wood with a durable woodgrained or designer white vinyl covering. It's convenient tote handle allows for easy transport from room to room.

You're protected with LakeAir. We're so confident of our reliable performance that we offer you a five-year limited warranty on all units. You won't get this kind of protection with any other air cleaner available today.

Specifications

Capacity:	
low:	210 ft³/min. or 378 m³/hr.
high:	275 ft³/min. or 495 m³/hr.
Actual size:	17" x 13" x 15" or 42.5 cm x 32.5 cm x 37.5 cm
Shipping size:	18" x 15" x 15" or 47.5 cm x 37.5 cm x 37.5 cm
Shipping weight:	30 lbs. or 13.6 kg.
Power:	120 volts, AC/60 Hz 102 watts
Particle removal:	As small as .01 microns
Cabinet finish:	Wood-grained or designer white vinyl
Warranty:	Five-year limited

LakeAir - a complete line of air cleaners:

Portable Models	Residential Duct Mounted Models	Commercial/Industrial Self-contained Models
LA-250	LAD-1814	LA-1000
LA-500	LAD-2214	LA-1400
(ME-90)		LA-2000
LAFC		LAFC

LakeAir International, Inc. P.O. Box 4150
Racine On The Lake, WI 53404 414-632-1429

Five-year limited warranty

portable model
LA-500

UL LISTED

LakeAir Features and Benefits

LakeAir's triple action filtering system works like a pollution magnet—trapping 97% of all airborne particles (even those as small as one-millionth of an inch!) for a cleaner, healthier home or office. The prefilter screen removes lint, animal dander and dust particles. The electrostatic filter removes particles from the air as small as .01 microns (as in smoke) and the activated carbon after filter helps to eliminate even the most stubborn odors.

LakeAir units cost just pennies to run. The LA-500 requires less energy than a 125 watt bulb. And because the electrostatic filter is permanent, you'll save even more money because you never have to replace it. You may even be eligible for medical deductions on your income taxes if the air cleaner is prescribed by a physician to alleviate hay fever, asthma or other respiratory ailments. LakeAir also sharply reduces heating and air conditioning costs by eliminating the need to exhaust large quantities of contaminated air. Plus, when dust and grime are removed from the air, costly electronic and stereo equipment escape damage. You'll breathe easier with these savings.

LakeAir electronic air cleaners will save you time and money on cleaning. The super-efficient LA-500 is powerful enough to clean a 20'x20' area more than five times per hour. With less dirt in the air, you won't have to clean draperies, windows, carpets and furniture as often.

Two-speed controls adjust for the room size and the cleaning rate, giving you greater versatility.

The LA-500 is simple to operate, just a push of a button will bring you freshly scrubbed air.

Calculating the Number of Air Cleaners Needed:

Calculate the volume of the room or area in cubic feet.

Length X Width X Height of Area = Volume of Area

Multiply the volume of the area by the number of air changes desired in an hour to get the total volume of air to be cleaned in one hour.

Volume of Area X Number of Air Changes Required = Cubic Feet / Hour to be Cleaned

Divide the volume of air to be cleaned in one hour by sixty minutes to obtain the cubic feet per minute of air to be cleaned.

Cubic Feet/Hour ÷ 60 Minutes/Hour = Cubic Feet/Minute (CFM) to be Cleaned

Compare the Cubic Feet/Minute (CFM) to be cleaned with the LakeAir chart of electronic air cleaners and the CFM levels produced by each unit. By dividing the CFM of the proposed unit into the CFM required for the given area, you will obtain the number of units required to do the job effectively.

CFM of Area to be Cleaned ÷ CFM of Unit Desired = Number of Units

— or —

You may also calculate the number of air cleaners needed using international measurements (metric system).

Calculate the volume of the room or area in cubic meters.

Length X Width X Height of Area = Volume of Area

Multiply the volume of the area by the number of air changes desired in one hour to get the total volume to be cleaned in one hour.

Volume of Area X Number of Air Changes Required = Cubic Meters / Hour (CMH) to be Cleaned

Compare the Cubic Meters/Hour (CMH) to be cleaned with the LakeAir chart which gives the clean air delivery rate in CMH and CFM. You will then be able to determine the number of LakeAir units for your specific needs.

CMH of Area to be Cleaned ÷ CMH of Unit Desired = No. of Units

LakeAir MODELS AND CLEAN AIR DELIVERY RATES		
LA-250	Low 70 CFM (126 CMH)	High 100 CFM (198 CMH)
LA-500	Low 210 CFM (378 CMH)	High 275 CFM (495 CMH)
LAFC	Low 400 CFM (720 CMH)	High 1000 CFM (1800 CMH)
LA-1400	Low 800 CFM (1440 CMH)	High 1100 CFM (1980 CMH)
LA-2000	Low 1500 CFM (2700 CMH)	High 2100 CFM (3780 CMH)

Q: I want contemporary ceiling paddle fans for my living room and kitchen. They must be efficient and pay back the cost with utility bills savings. How can I tell which designs and features are best?

A: While all ceiling fans look basically alike, there are significant quality and structural differences among them. Definitely, do not shop for just the lowest priced one. Within a year, it will begin to hum and wobble.

Many new efficient contemporary designer fans have three to six blades. One five-blade model, called Petal, has wrap around, petal-shaped blades. Another high-output three-blade model has split hi-tech airfoil blades.

Key design features to look for are motor housing material, bearing type, motor size, blade pitch, range of speeds, automatic speed and lighting controls and sound/vibration isolating features.

Die cast or cast iron motor housings are best. These are made to close tolerances. This heavier metal, as compared to a thin steel stamping, dissipates heat better, is more durable and provides longer motor life.

A larger, more powerful motor also runs cooler and quieter. Double-shielded, permanently-lubricated bearings are most durable and quiet.

Look for sound and vibration reducing components between all metal parts.

A steeper pitch angle (twist) of the blades is better and moves more air at a lower speed. Most better-quality fans have a blade pitch of at least 14 degrees and even more on larger contemporary three-blade models.

Leave adequate ceiling clearance

Large, high output motor inside

Double-shielded bearings

Contemporary petal-shaped blades

Six-speed remote control

Three-speed reversible motor with pull chain

Sound-deadening blade hub

Balanced & matched blades

Balance (some blade sets are matched to within one gram of one another) and quality of the blade finish are more important than the blade material itself. Some of the best quality, most expensive fan blades are made of laminated or solid hardwoods, engineering plastics or fabric covered frames.

For the greatest convenience, select a fan with a hand-held remote speed and lighting control. These are often available only on the highest quality fans. Remote controls are ideal for bedrooms or when relaxing by the TV.

One hand-held remote, Air Design, provides six speeds and programmable preset speed/lighting combinations. A unique sleep setting gradually slows the fan speed as you sleep. The typical pull chain, three-speed settings on most fans are often not adequate for effective, quiet cooling.

Even an expensive fan can pay back its cost in utility bills savings. A properly-sized fan allows you to comfortably raise the thermostat setting five degrees. In winter, reverse the rotation and set the thermostat lower.

Q: I just had some firewood delivered which I plan to use next winter to heat my living room. How can I tell if it is seasoned wood? How small should I split the logs?

A: Look at the ends of the logs. If they are well seasoned, they should be checked and cracked. Knock two of the logs together. Seasoned wood makes a ringing sound, not a dull thud.

If they seem to be well seasoned and are small enough for you to knock together, you should not have to split them more. If the wood is still green, split it into smaller pieces so that it dries out by next winter.

Although most ceiling fans look similar at first glance, there are significant differences among them. Manufacturers of the highest quality ceiling fans are listed on the following pages along with information about their models. I have tried to describe some of the unique models each has available. Page 72 also shows illustrations of several of these styles and designs.

A good indication of fan quality is the pitch of the blades. A larger pitch moves more air and usually indicates a more powerful, heavy-duty motor (no hum). The pitch of blades is often indicated on the box or in the user manual. If not, use a protractor and measure the angle of the blade holders before buying. Less than 12° is considered shallow. 14° or steeper is common on many high quality fans.

There are many remote controls available with ceiling fans. A wall mounted, hard wired remote is least expensive. For the greatest convenience, purchase a multispeed hand-held remote. These allow you to program the speed, light intensity and timer. The most sophisticated remote, Air Design by Emerson, is shown below. These cannot be used on all Emerson models.

_ _ _ _ _ _ _ _ _ _ _ _ _ _ _ _ _ _ _ _

Manufacturers of Ceiling Fans

BEVERLY HILLS FAN CO., 6033 De Soto., Woodland Hills, CA 91367 - (800) 826-6192 (818) 992-3267

styles - 3, 4, 5 or 6 blades in traditional or contemporary styles — 6 multi-colored blades that are curved with a glass light globe with a sandblasted star design — 4 blades with an illuminated iridescent glass and a hummingbird design in the motor housing —clear acrylic housing and 4 blades with either a blue or pink neon light in the housing

blade size - 42", 44", 52", 60"   blade pitch - 12°, 14°, 20°   RPM range - 50 - 225
bearing type - sealed and permanently lubricated   motor housing - die cast
blade material - high-gloss wood, acrylic, aluminum
controls - wall mounted or hand-held soft touch computerized 3-way fan and light control switch

BROAN MFG. CO., 926 W. State St., Hartford, WI 53027 - (414) 673-4340

styles - 4 or 5 blades in traditional styles
blade size - 42", 52"   blade pitch - 12°   RPM range - 50 - 210
bearing type - sealed and permanently lubricated   motor housing - die cast   blade material - laminated hardwood
controls - wall-mounted control for 3 or 4 speeds and light on/off and dimming

CASABLANCA FAN CO., 450 Baldwin Park, City of Industry, CA 91746 - (800) 759-3267 (818) 369-6441

styles - 3, 4, 5 or 6 blades in traditional or contemporary styles — 3 blades with a unique bi-wing design and an integrated downlight — 3 split blades with an integrated downlight — 5 silk blades tensioned by fiberglass fishing rods and features a bicycle sprocket for the hub — 3 angular and vee-shaped blades with an extended point on the end of the blades
blade size - 29", 36", 38", 42", 44", 50", 52", 53", 54", 56", 58", 84"   blade pitch - 12°, 14°, 16°, 22°   RPM range - 20 - 270
bearing type - sealed and permanently lubricated   motor housing - die cast
blade material - 8-ply wood veneer, plastic, fabric
controls - wireless remote "Comfort-Touch" operates fan and light functions within a 50-foot radius, auto-program adjusts fan speed as the room temperature changes, even switching the fan off when no longer needed, "winter" program will reverse the fan, "security" automatically turns lights on and off in an irregular sequence

EMERSON ELECTRIC, 8400 Pershall Rd., Hazelwood, MO 63042 - (800) 325-1184 (314) 595-2500

models - 3, 4, 5 or 6 blades in traditional or contemporary styles — 5 blades uniquely shaped that wrap around and look like a flower petal — 3 angular shaped aluminum blades with a pyramid-shaped housing — 5 rectangular blades and flanges with a pentagonal housing
blade size - 42", 50", 52"   blade pitch - 14°   RPM range - 40 - 290
bearing type - sealed and permanently lubricated   motor housing - die cast
blade material - 8-ply hardwood veneer, plastic, fabric, aluminum
controls - hand-held "Air Design" remote with six fan speeds, forward and reverse, light dimmer with preset memory, independent dual light control, programs light at pre-set time with the security mode, "winter" mode forces hot air down, sleep setting automatically decreases the fan speed while you sleep

ENCON INDUSTRIES, 6901 Snowden Rd., Ft. Worth, TX 76140 - (800) 992-3267 (817) 293-7400

styles - 3, 4, 5 or 6 blades in traditional or contemporary styles — 4 chili pepper shaped blades with jalapeno green finish — 4 crayon shaped blades with multi-color finish — 5 multi-color finished blades with directional bullet lights

blade size - 30", 42", 48", 52", 56"	blade pitch - 12°	RPM range - 50 - 220
bearing type - sealed and permanently lubricated	motor housing - die cast	blade material - laminated hardwood

controls - hand-held remote provides five levels of light dimming, 3-speed fan control, operates up to a distance of 50 feet

FASCO, PO Box 150, Fayetteville, NC 28302 - (800) 334-4126 (910) 483-0421

styles - 4, 5 or 6 blades in traditional or contemporary styles — 5 blade contemporary angular style blade and oval-shaped housing with brushed chrome, gunmetal black or white finish with an integrated light kit

blade size - 30", 52", 56"	blade pitch - 14°	RPM range - 65 - 260
bearing type - sealed and permanently lubricated	motor housing - die cast	

blade material - laminated and solid hardwood, fabric, plastic

controls - hand-held remote to control the three speeds or the light

HUNTER FAN CO., 2500 Frisco Ave., Memphis, TN 38114 - (800) 971-3267 (901) 745-9222

styles - 3, 4 or 5 blades in traditional or contemporary styles — 4 blades with a sculptured floral design finished in burnished brass, glossy black or verde — 3 or 4 blades and the housing looks like an airplane propeller available with ceiling applique of "Snoopy"® or a replica of F4U Corsair — 4 blades shaped like baseball bats and the housing looks like a catchers mitt with an integrated 100 watt baseball style globe

blade size - 32", 42", 44", 48", 52"	blade pitch - 15°	RPM range - 45 - 330
bearing type - sealed and permanently lubricated, the "Original" is in an oil bath		
motor housing - cast iron	blade material - 6-ply hardwood veneer, fabric, aluminum	

controls - hand-held "Quiet Touch" remote with LCD display controls the fan speed, light intensity, and motor direction, features a reverse rotation after 4 hours for night time and an 8 hour automatic shut off, security delay light-off control

LITEX IND., 2002 Avenue R, Grand Prairie, TX 75053 - (800) 527-1292 (214) 641-3015

models - 3, 4 or 5 blades in traditional or contemporary styles — 5 pencil shaped blades with multi-color finish — 4 multi-color finished blades with directional bullet lights

blade size - 36", 42", 52", 56"	blade pitch - 13°, 14°	RPM range - 55 - 280
bearing type - sealed and permanently lubricated	motor housing - die cast	blade material - laminated hardwood

controls - wall-mounted control for 3 or 4 speeds, reversible air flow

NUTONE, Madison & Redbank Rds., Cincinnati, OH 45227 - (800) 543-8687 (513) 527-5100

models - 3, 4 or 5 blades in traditional or contemporary styles — 5 blades with raised floral motif in a weathered grey, sandstone or verdigris finish

blade size - 42", 48", 52", 56"	blade pitch - 14°	RPM range - 60 - 190
bearing type - sealed and permanently lubricated	motor housing - die cast	blade material - laminated hardwood

controls - remote control with wall-mounted holder, with 3 speeds, forward and reverse, light on/off and light dimmer

SEARS/KENMORE, 3333 Beverly Rd., Hoffman Estates, IL 60179 - (800) 359-2000 (708) 286-2500

models - 4, 5 or 6 blades in traditional or contemporary styles

blade size - 30", 42", 52"	blade pitch - 14°	RPM range - 65 - 240
bearing type - sealed and permanently lubricated	motor housing - die cast	blade material - laminated hardwood

controls - remote control with wall-mounted holder, with 3 speeds, forward and reverse, light on/off and light dimmer

SIERRA CEILING FANS, PO Box 3038, Amarillo, TX 79116 - (806) 358-1621

styles - 4, 5 or 6 blades in traditional or contemporary styles

blade size - 52"	blade pitch - 14°	RPM range - 80 - 205
bearing type - sealed and permanently lubricated	motor housing - die cast	blade material - laminated hardwood

controls - wall-mounted control for 3 or 4 speeds and light on/off and dimming

THOMAS IND., 4360 Brownsboro Rd., Ste. 300, Louisville, KY 40207 - (800) 365-4448 (502) 893-4600

styles - 5 blades in traditional styles

blade size - 42", 52"	blade pitch - 12°	RPM range - 80 - 210
bearing type - sealed and permanently lubricated	motor housing - die cast	blade material - hardwood veneer

controls - wall-mounted control for 3 or 4 speeds and light on/off and dimming

WIND CHASER PRODUCTS, 1842 Washington Way, Suit C, Venice, CA 90291 - (310) 827-8569

styles - 3, 4 or 5 blades in traditional or contemporary styles

blade size - 30", 36", 42", 52", 56"	blade pitch - 12°	RPM range - 50 - 200
bearing type - sealed and permanently lubricated	motor housing - die cast	blade material - hardwood veneer

controls - wall-mounted control for 3 or 4 speeds and light on/off and dimming

SONICA FAN INNOVATIONS, 13516 Imperial Highway, Santa Fe Springs, CA 90670 - (310) 926-2134

styles - 4 or 5 blades in traditional or contemporary styles — 4 blades that are contoured like airfoils/wings with an integrated light —5 blade contemporary angular style blade and oval-shaped housing with brushed chrome, brushed aluminum, white or verdi green finish with an integrated light kit

blade size - 42", 52", 72", 84"   blade pitch - 12°, 13°, 14° or 16° RPM range - 65 - 220
bearing type - sealed and permanently lubricated   motor housing - die cast
blade material - multiple layers of hardwood veneer, plastic
controls - hand-held operates up to 30 feet, three speed selection, memory functions include light dimmer or direction control

---

Broan - Collector Series

Hunter - Baseball Mitt   *Encon* - Chili Pepper

		Recommended Fan Size and Location			
Room	**Typical Activities**	**Recommended Location**	**Alternate Location**	**Minimum Fan Size**	**Ambient Air Temperature***
Bedroom	Sleeping	Over foot of bed	Off to either side of bed, but not directly over head of bed	36"—up to 150 sq. ft. 48"—up to 300 sq. ft. 52"—up to 600 sq. ft.	86°F
Living Family Dining	Sitting, walking, light housework	Center of room	In corner, minimum 24" blade tip clearance from wall	same as above	78°F
Kitchen	Cooking, washing dishes	Center of room	Away from stove	same as above	76°F
Garage Utility	Light work	Center of room	In corner, minimum 24" blade tip clearance from wall	same as above	74°F

*Maximum temperature at which occupants maintain "72°F comfort level" with fan in operation.

Standard Installation

Ceiling fans are easily adapted to standard, sloped and high ceilings for convenient installation in any room.

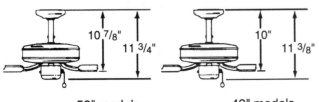

10 7/8"   11 3/4"   10"   11 3/8"

52" models   **42" models**

standard

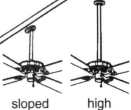

sloped   high

Q: My son has a whole-house fan and his home stays almost as comfortable as mine with air-conditioning. How much electricity does a whole-house fan save over air-conditioning and can I easily install one myself?

A: Using a whole-house fan, instead of air-conditioning continuously, can cut your electricity usage by 80%. I use one in my home on all but the hottest days. I prefer the breezy fresh air, even if it's a little warmer.

A whole-house fan, mounted in a hallway ceiling, keeps you comfortable in several ways. The gentle breeze throughout your home makes 80 degrees feel like 75 degrees. Just the quiet hum of a fan makes people feel cooler.

By drawing in the cooler air, the entire structure of your house, furniture, cabinets, etc. cool down over night. They absorb heat again in late morning and this delays and reduces the temperature rise indoors.

Since most whole-house fans are mounted so that they exhaust the air into the attic, the attic stays cooler too. This reduces the heat gain in your house, particularly in the early evening.

You have two basic whole-house fan designs to choose from - direct drive and belt drive. With direct drive (for small to medium-size houses), the fan blades are mounted directly under the motor and are attached to the motor shaft.

On a belt-drive fan design, the motor is offset to one of the corners of the fan housing. A belt connects a pulley on the motor to a pulley on the fan blades. Belt-drive fans have

Blades turn slowly for quiet operation

Powerful motor

Belt drive

Large pulley

Steeply-pitched blades for high air flow

Mount tight-sealing louver kit underneath

Designed to fit standard joist spacing

the highest air flows for larger houses.

These fans are also quieter than direct-drive fans. With different size pulleys on the motor and the fan blades, they can use steeply-pitched, slower-turning blades. This reduces noise. On either design, you can get a variety of speed controls including single, triple, and totally-variable.

Whole-house fans are easy to install yourself. Each fan manufac-turer has several sizes and models to choose from that fit typical attic joist spacing. You just saw a hole through the ceiling, reinforce the opening with 2x4's if necessary, and nail the fan in place. Install a louver kit under it.

One simple-to-install direct-drive fan is designed specifically for one-person installation. It has spring clips on the housing sides to hold it in place as you drive in the nails.

It is important to select the proper size fan (cubic feet per minute). A size estimate is to multiply the square footage of your house by three. The proper amount of attic exhaust vent area is equally important to minimize resistance.

Q: I am adding a large fireplace in my living room to help heat my house in the winter. I am having trouble getting a large chimney liner. How large a liner do I need and can I use two smaller ones side-by-side?

A: A rule of thumb is that the chimney flue area should be at least $1/10$ as large as the fireplace opening. It is acceptable to have two flue liners from one fireplace.

The flue liners should be separated from the chimney wall by a one half inch to one inch gap. This space allows for the large thermal expansion due to the heat of the fire.

Whole house ventilation fans not only cool your house, but they make you feel cooler because of the movement of air. If you air-condition, turn off your air conditioner on cool nights and run the fan. A typical whole-house fan uses less than 10% as much electricity as a central air conditioner. Another energy-saving advantage of a fan is that it forces cool air through your attic. This helps to keep it cool and reduces the heat transferred from your hot roof to the ceiling.

When you select a whole-house fan, choose one that is large enough for your house. The chart below shows the recommended air flow capacities of fans for various size houses. This chart is based on average ceiling heights. If your ceilings are unusually high, select a larger fan.

Whole-house fans are sized in cubic feet per minute (cfm) of air flow. This air flow rate assumes that there is adequate exhaust vent area in your attic. You can determine the amount of attic exhaust vent area, divide the fan cfm by 750. For example, a 6,000 cfm fan requires 8 sq.ft. of net free vent exhaust area. The free vent area is marked on most vent packaging.

You have two basic design choices - a direct-drive or belt-drive design. Direct drive is the simplest design and is adequate for small and medium size houses. The fan blade is attached directly to the motor so they both turn at the same speed. A belt-drive design positions the motor off to the side. This has several advantages. With a small pulley on the motor and large pulley on the fan, the fan turns much slower than the motor. This allows for a steeper pitch on the fan blades for more air flow. The highest capacity fans are belt driven. This design is also quieter because of the position of the motor and the slower speeds. The direct-drive model is designed for one person installation. There are spring clips on the sides of the fan housing. Once you saw the opening in your ceiling between the joists, you just push it up into the opening. The clips hold it in place while you secure it with screws or nails.

It is very important to install louvers under the whole-house fan. Each fan model has a set of louvers designed to fit flush in the ceiling below it. They open automatically from the air flow when the fan starts. When installing them, handle them with care so you don't deform any of the louvers. It is important that they seal well when the fan is not running. You can also buy insulated covers for the winter. They are made of rigid foam insulation and set over the entire top of the fan and the opening.

A variable-speed control is an advantage to fine-tune the speed, especially at night. The manufacturers list on page 75 lists the standard speed control for each model. Many have variable speeds standard and others have it as an option. A timer is also useful to switch it off after a predetermined length of time. If you do not centrally air-condition your home, a thermostatic control is a good option. An automatic high-temperature shut-off switch is a safety device. If, for some reason, the motor gets too hot, due to several possible problems, the motor will shut off.

Recommended Whole-House Fan Capacity		
House Size - ft^2	Air Flow - cfm	Free vent area - ft^2
1,000	3,000	4.0
1,200	3,600	4.8
1,400	4,200	5.6
1,600	4,800	6.4
1,800	5,400	7.2
2,000	6,000	8.0
2,200	6,600	8.8
2,400	7,200	9.6
2,600	7,800	10.4
2,800	8,400	11.2
3,000	9,000	12.0

Manufacturers of Whole-House Ventilation Fans

BROAN, PO Box 140, Hartford, WI 53027 - (800) 548-0790 (414) 673-4340

model - 2220 • 2224 • 2230   blade diameter - 20 inch • 24 inch • 30 inch   maximum air flow - 3300 • 3600 • 5100
rpm - 1060/650 • 825/525 • 700/400   drive type - direct-drive   motor - n/a
speed control - two-speed   amperage - 4.5 amps • 4.5 amps • 5.0 amps   wattage - 400 • 460 • 490
model - 2236   blade diameter - 36 inch   maximum air flow - 6850 cfm
rpm - 440   drive type - belt-drive   motor - n/a
speed control - single-speed   amperage - 5.5 amps   wattage - 500

features - A wall thermostat activates the fan when the house temperature rises above a preset comfort setting. A high temperature control shuts the fan off if there is a line overload. It has a manual on/off switch. An electronic variable speed control dial allows you to choose a selection of air speeds and/or sound levels. A 12-hour timer control allows the fan to operate continuously for any set period up to 12 hours. The shroud is made from Acoustek™ which is a sound absorbing material that is fire retardant and moisture resistant.

EMERSON ELECTRIC, 8400 Persall Rd., Hazelwood, MO 63042 - (800) 325-1184 (314) 595-2500

model - WH24FM • WH30FM   blade diameter - 24 inch • 30 inch   maximum air flow - 3600 cfm • 5100 cfm
rpm - 660 • 510   drive type - direct-drive   motor - 1/3 hp • 1/3 hp
speed control - variable-speed   amperage - 5.8 amps • 5.9 amps   wattage - 584 • 575
model - WH36FM   blade diameter - 36 inch   maximum air flow - 7200 cfm
rpm - 445   drive type - belt-drive   motor - 1/2 hp
speed control - variable-speed   amperage - 6.0 amps   wattage - 650

features - An automatic temperature control turns the fan off when the temperature drops to a pre-set level. It has a manual start. A 12-hour timer shuts the fan off at pre-selected times. The high temperature switch automatically turns the fan off at 204°F in case of a fire. It includes an on/off switch. A variable speed wall control lets you control the speed of the fan. The fans are equipped with rubber isolation mounting for quiet operation.

FASCO, PO Box 150, Fayetteville, NC 28302 - (800) 334-4126 (919) 483-0421

model - A20DD • A24DD • B30DD   blade diameter - 20 inch • 24 inch • 30 inch   maximum air flow - 3600 • 5500 • 6900
rpm - 1050 • 1065 • 625   drive type - direct-drive   motor - n/a
speed control - three-speed   amperage - 3.0 amps • 5.2 amps • 5.5 amps   wattage - 360 • 624 • 660
model - UF22 • UF30   blade diameter - 22 inch • 30 inch   maximum air flow - 3600 cfm • 6950 cfm
rpm - 1120/965 • 695/575   drive type - direct-drive   motor - 1/4 hp 1/3 hp
speed control - two-speed   amperage - 3.1 amps • 6.5 amps   wattage - 372 • 780
model - 2438 • 3038 • 3638   blade diameter - 24 inch • 30 inch • 36 inch   maximum air flow - 3900 • 5500 • 7100
rpm - 745 • 545 • 430   drive type - belt-drive   motor - n/a
speed control - three-speed   amperage - 5.7 amps • 5.5 amps • 7.2 amps   wattage - 684 • 660 • 864

features - Models "UF22" and "UF30" have self-contained shutters. They are easy to install in several minutes — nail brackets in place, snap into place and plug in the fan. Reversible models "3038R" and "3638R" are available for vertical or horizontal installation — you simply reverse the blades and leads.

KOOL-O-MATIC CORP., PO Box 310, Niles, MI 49120 - (616) 683-2600

model - 360 and 360T   blade diameter - 36 inch   maximum air flow - 7320/5400 cfm
rpm - 380/200   drive type - direct-drive   motor - 1/3 hp
speed control - variable-speed   amperage - 4.5/5.2 amps   wattage - 450/420

features - The speed control and timer can vary the fan speed to desired capacity for temperature conditions. The timer provides, hold, 0-12 hour automatic shut off. Models "240T" or "240TC" are for a single room with a 14" diameter blade, 1/4 hp motor and 1420 rpm.

LESLIE-LOCKE, 4501 Circle 75 Parkway, Atlanta, GA 30339 - (800) 755-9392 (404) 953-6366

model - Pace Setter   blade diameter - 30 inch • 36 inch   maximum air flow - 5800 cfm • 8800 cfm
rpm - 825/725 • 1725/1160   drive type - belt-drive   motor - 1/4 hp • 1/3 hp
speed control - two-speed   amperage - 6.8 amps • 6.8 amps   wattage - 500 • 500

features - A 12-hour timer control allows you to turn the fan on up to 12 hours before it will automatically shut off.

LOMANCO, PO Box 519, Jacksonville, AR 72076 - (800) 643-5596 (501) 982-6511

model - 2480 • 3082   blade diameter - 24 inch • 30 inch   maximum air flow - 3700 cfm • 5900 cfm
rpm - n/a   drive type - direct-drive   motor - 1/4 hp • 1/2 hp
speed control - variable-speed   amperage - 4.7 amps • 8.0 amps   wattage - 564 • 960

features - A variable-speed control is available that has a minimum speed setting adjustment. It is very easy and simple to install with just a two-wire hook-up.

NUTONE INC., Madison & Red Bank Rds., Cincinnati, OH 45227 - (800) 543-8687 (513) 527-5100

model - WHV20   blade diameter - 24 inch   maximum air flow - 3200 cfm
rpm - 1050 • 800   drive type - direct-drive   motor - 1/4 hp
speed control - single-speed   amperage - 8.0 amps   wattage - 550
model - WHV24DD • WHV30-02   blade diameter - 24 inch • 30 inch   maximum air flow - 2800 cfm • 4800 cfm
rpm - 800 • 850   drive type - direct-drive   motor - 1/5 hp • 1/4 hp
speed control - two-speed   amperage - 3.6 amps • 5.0 amps   wattage - 340 • 480
model - WHV30BD • WHV36BD   blade diameter - 30 inch • 36 inch   maximum air flow - 5600 cfm • 6800 cfm
rpm - 1725 • 1725   drive type - belt-drive   motor - 1/3 hp • 1/3 hp
speed control - two-speed   amperage - 6.5 amps • 6.5 amps   wattage - 545 • 615

features - A variable speed control switch gives you unlimited choices of the fan drive type speeds. A toggle/switch timer switches between high and low plus it has a 12-hour timer. Also available is a 12-hour timer control that turns the fan on for up to 12 hours before it will shut off automatically.

Emerson Whole House Attic Fans

high-efficiency Emerson Attic Fans

1 Unique quiet-design blade assembly.

2 Direct-drive ⅓ HP motors on 24″ and 30″ models. ½ HP motor on 36″ model. 5-year limited warranty on all motors.

3 Deep steel venturi funneling air through blades to produce maximum air flow efficiency.

4 Rigid, tight-fitting plenum sleeve liner and snap-in fasteners for quick assembly, which eliminate need for wood framing.

5 Rubber grommet isolates blade assembly from motor in direct-drive models

6 Rubber isolation mounting throughout assure smooth, quiet operation.

7 Fan isolated from ceiling structure.

8 Motor isolated from frame.

9 Quiet, flutter-free shutter automatically opens and closes with fan operation. Draft-free fit when not in operation.

Three sizes for virtually all home installations.
FAN SPECIFICATIONS

CATALOG NUMBER	BLADE SIZE	AIR FLOW* CFM WITH SHUTTER		FAN RPM*	AMPS*	WATTS*	REQUIRED ATTIC OPENING FOR PROPER EXHAUST	OPTIONAL VERTICAL SHUTTER FOR ADDITIONAL ATTIC EXHAUST
		AT 0.0″ S.P.	AT 0.1″ S.P.					
WH24FM	24″	4400	3600	660	5.8	584	7.1 SQ. FT.	WFS 24
WH30FM	30″	6300	5100	510	5.9	575	10.8 SQ. FT.	WFS 30
WH36WS	36″	8500	7200	445	6.0	650	15 SQ. FT.	WFS 36

*RATINGS AT HIGH SPEED AT 0.1″ S.P. WITH SHUTTER. SPECIFICATIONS SUBJECT TO CHANGE WITHOUT NOTICE.

DIMENSIONS

CATALOG NUMBER	FAN SIZE	FAN DIMENSIONS (inches) Length Width Height	CEILING SHUTTER OPENING (inches)	FAN WEIGHT
WH24FM	24″	29½″ x 29½″ x 12″	29½″ x 24⅛″	32 lbs.
WH30FM	30″	34½″ x 34½″ x 12″	34½″ x 30″	35 lbs.
WH36WS	36″	41″ x 41″ x 14″	33¾″ x 40½″	43 lbs.

FAN SELECTION GUIDE

FAN SIZE	NO. OF SPEEDS	TO MAKE ONE COMPLETE AIR CHANGE AT 0.1 INCH S.P.	
		EVERY 2 MINUTES RESIDENCE SIZE	EVERY 3 MINUTES RESIDENCE SIZE
24″	VARIABLE	1200 sq. feet	1800 sq. feet
30″	VARIABLE	1700 sq. feet	2550 sq. feet
36″	VARIABLE	2400 sq. feet	3600 sq. feet

NOTE: THE ABOVE RESIDENCE SIZE (SQUARE FEET) HELPS DETERMINE WHAT SIZE WHOLE HOUSE FAN IS REQUIRED TO MAKE A COMPLETE AIR EXCHANGE WITHIN THE OCCUPIED AREA EVERY TWO OR THREE MINUTES

Q: Our water tastes fine, but I worry that contaminants may harm my children's physical and mental health. Can I test the water myself? What types of water purifiers are there and do they cost much to operate?

A: There are many contaminants in water that can harm your entire family, especially children. Studies indicate that some heavy metals, such as lead, are linked to lower IQ's in children. Other organic compounds react with the chlorine in water to form cancer-causing trihalomethanes (THM).

Low concentrations of some chemicals, such as nitrates, which are harmless to adults, may be hazardous or fatal to infants.

Everybody should test their water, at least for lead concentrations, particularly with children in the home. Lead can get into the water from the city's water supply mains or from the plumbing inside your house.

Do-it-yourself tests cost from $17 to $40. Test kits contain two vials for samples to be sent to the laboratory for analysis. You take a "first draw" sample after the water has been undisturbed in your plumbing for hours.

A second "purged-line" sample is taken after the water has run for several minutes to clear out the pipes.

This helps to determine if the lead is coming from your plumbing or from the city's supply mains. The labs can also test for pesticides, herbicides, solvents, coliform bacteria, volatile organics, etc. These more comprehensive tests cost from $98 to $170.

The most common water purifiers/filters are activated carbon, dis-

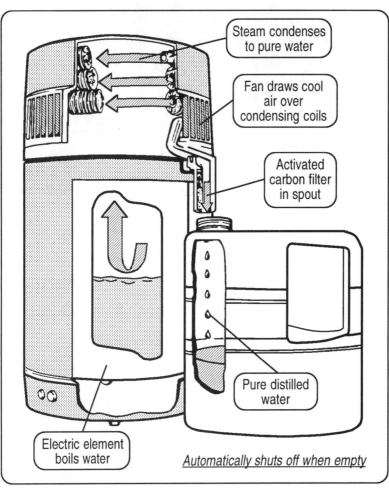

Steam condenses to pure water

Fan draws cool air over condensing coils

Activated carbon filter in spout

Pure distilled water

Electric element boils water

Automatically shuts off when empty

tillers, reverse osmosis (RO), ozone, and ultraviolet light. In my home, I use an activated carbon filter and a countertop distiller. It is important to select the proper purifier depending on the contaminants found in the test.

Activated carbon improves the water's taste and removes many chemicals and organics. Solid block carbon filter are more effective for

removing lead than granulated carbon. Some are treated with silver to stop bacteria growth in the filter. Operating costs (for replacement cartridges) range from $35 to $70 per 1,000 gallons.

A distiller produces very pure water and the boiling process kills bacteria and virus. A countertop model takes about seven hours to produce a gallon of pure water at a cost of about 25 cents of electricity (eight cents per kilowatt-hour). It has a small activated carbon filter in the outlet to freshen the taste.

RO systems (with built-in carbon filters) force water through a semi-permeable membrane to filter out contaminants. They use no electricity, but can waste three to five gallons of water for each gallon of purified water. Ultraviolet and ozone purifiers kill bacteria, but do not remove contaminants.

Q: I have a waterbed in my home. When I leave for the weekend, should I unplug it to save electricity? How much electricity does one use?

A: About one home in six has a waterbed with an electric heater. A typical queen-size bed can cost about $100 per year to keep warm. Turning it off saves, but it takes a long time to reheat when you return home. Instead, set the thermostat lower and cover the bed with two quilts when you leave.

The testing laboratories are listed on page 79. The labs send vials to you for the water samples. You mail the samples to them for testing. After your water is tested, the chart below will give you an idea of which common types of water purification methods will be effective for your water needs. The labs can also give you advice on the best method.

If you have a home with older plumbing, you should have a lead test done. This consists of two tests - one sample when you first turn on the faucet and one sample after the water has been running. When you contact the labs, they can advise you as to which tests are needed depending on your water source and region of the country. Most systems include some type of activated carbon filter.

Ozone gas and ultraviolet light are methods to sanitize the water. Both will kill bacteria and virus. Ozone also causes the contaminants to coagulate into larger particles so that your filter/purification system can remove them easier. Some of the carbon filters are treated with silver. The silver ions are harmless to you, but they kill bacteria that may live in the filter material.

The cost to operate each system varies. An activated carbon filter is usually the cheapest per gallon of water (only replacement cost of the filter). A reverse osmosis system wastes 3 to 5 gallons of water for each gallon of purified water you get. You can determine cost per gallon from your water rates. A distiller uses about 25 cents worth of electricity per gallon.

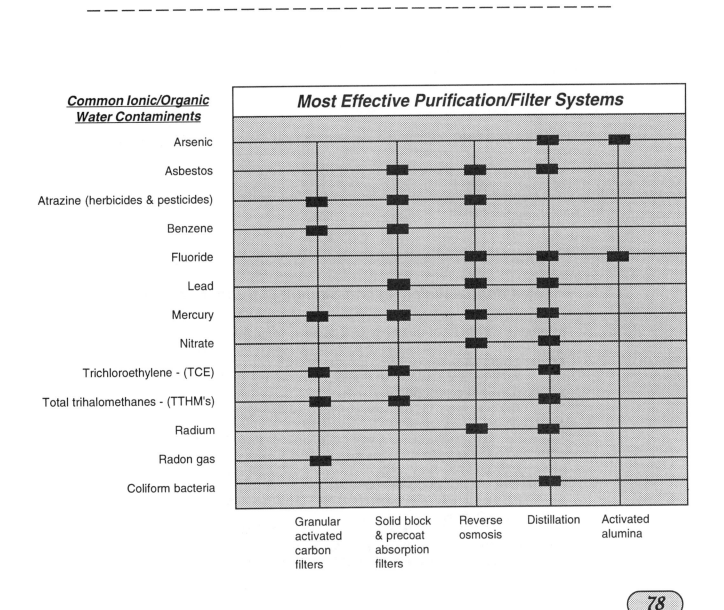

Residential Water Testing Laboratories

ANALYTICAL LAB & CONSULTING, 361 W. 5th Ave., Eugene, OR 97401 - (503) 485-8404

 Lead test

 TOD, arsenic, coliform, etc.

AQUA ASSOCIATES, P.O. Box 1251, Fairfield, NJ 07004 - (201) 227-0422

 Nine cancer-causing compounds

 General chemistry for wells

 Coliform bacteria

 Lead

 Radon gas

CLEAN WATER LEAD TESTING UNCA, 1 University High, Asheville, NC 28804 - (704) 251-6800

 Lead test for water

HYDRO-ANALYSIS, P. O. Box 242, 57 Noble St., Kutztown, PA 19530 - (610) 683-7474

 Heavy metal including lead

 FHA & coliform

 Coliform, nitrate, detergents, solvents, pesticide, lead

 Industrial solvents

NATIONAL TESTING LABS, 6555 Wilson Mills, Cleveland, OH 44143 - (800) 458-3330

 Lead test

 73 chemical test

 Above plus 20 pesticides

SPECTRUM LABS., 301 W. County Rd. E2, St. Paul, MN 55112 - (612) 633-0101

 Lead test

 Basic drinking water

 Basic drinking water + volatile organics (VOC)

 Basic + VOC + herbicides

SUBURBAN WATER TESTING, 4600 Kutztown Rd., Temple, PA 19560 - (800) 433-6595

 30 chemicals plus coliform bacteria

 Same as above less volatile chemicals

 Lead test

 Radon gas

 Trace metals (arsenic, barium, mercury, etc.)

 Pesticides and PCB scan

Residential Water Testing System Manufacturers

AMERICAN WATER PRODUCTS - Reverse Osmosis, Ultraviolet
 10885 Kalama River, Fountain Valley, CA 92708 - (714) 963-8490

AMWAY CORP. - Activated Carbon
 7575 E. Fulton Rd., Ada, MI 49355 - (800) 544-7167 (616) 676-6000

APLIED OZONE TECHNOLOGIES - Ozone
 7900B Fruitville Rd., Sarasota, FL 34240 - (813) 379-0000

AQUAFINE - Ultraviolet, Ozone
 25230 W. Avenue Stanford, Valencia, CA 91355 - (805) 257-4770

AQUA PRO OF TEXAS - Reverse Osmosis
 P. O. Box 8824, The Woodlands, TX 77387 - (713) 367-4312

ATLANTIC ULTRAVIOLET CORP. - Ultraviolet
 375 Marcus Blvd, Hauppage, NY 11788 - (516) 273-0500

B&R - Reverse Osmosis
 55 S. Country Club, Mesa, AZ 85210 - (602) 898-0008

BRUNER CORP. - Activated Carbon, Reverse Osmosis
 P.O. Box 7500, Milwaukee, WI 53207 - (414) 747-3700

CLEARBROOK - Activated Carbon with silver for bacteriostat
P.O. Box 100354, Birmingham, AL 35210 - (205) 956-2090

CULLIGAN - Activated Carbon, Reverse Osmosis
1 Culligan Pky., Northbrook, IL 60062 - (800) 285-5442 (708) 205-6000

CUNO INC. - Activated Carbon, Reverse Osmosis
400 Research Pky, Meriden, CT 06450 - (800) 733-1199 (201) 237-5541

DURASTILL INC. - Distiller
4200 NE Birmingham Rd., Kansas City, MO 64117 - (816) 454-5260

ECOWATER - Activated Carbon, Distiller
P.O. Box 64420, St. Paul, MN 55164 - (800) 869-2837

ELECTROLUX WATER SYSTEMS - Activated Carbon with Ultraviolet
2300 Windy Ridge Pky., Marietta, GA 30067 - (800) 243-9078

EVERPURE INC. - Activated Carbon, Reverse Osmosis
660 Blackhawk Dr., Westmont, IL 60559 - (800) 323-7873 (708) 654-4000

FILTERITE - Activated Carbon, Reverse Osmosis
2033 Greenspring Dr., Timonium, MD 21093 - (410) 252-0800

GREAT LAKES WATER SYSTEMS - Reverse Osmosis
P. O. Box 26, Alparaiso, IN 46384 - (219) 465-4043

HAGUE WATER QUALITY INTERNATIONAL - Distiller
4343 S. Hamilton Rd., Groveport, OH 43125 - (614) 836-2195

HAMMACHER SCHLEMMER - Distiller
147 E. 57th St., New York, NY 10022 - (212) 421-9000

HESS MACHINE - Ozone
1054 South State, Ephrata, PA 17522 - (717) 733-0005

HOME REVERSE OSMOSIS SYSTEMS - Reverse Osmosis
RR 1., Peru, IL 61354 - (815) 339-6300

HURLEY WATER SYSTEMS - Activated Carbon
12621 S. Laramie Ave., Alsip, IL 60658 - (708) 388-9222

IDEAL HORIZONS - Ultraviolet, Ozone
1 Ideal Way, Poultney, VT 05764 - (802) 287-4488

INNOVA PURE WATER - Activated Carbon - pour-through
5170 126th Ave. N., Clearwater, FL 34620 - (813) 572-1000

KINETICO INC. - Activated Carbon, Reverse Osmosis
9975 Kinsman Rd., Newberry, OH 44065 - (216) 564-9111

KISS INTERNATIONAL - Activated Carbon, Reverse Osmosis
965 Park Center Dr., Vista, CA 92083 - (619) 599-0200

LONGMARK OZONE INDUSTRIES - Ozone
P.O. Box 413, Yreka, CA 96097 - (916) 842-2788

MULTI-PURE CORP. - Activated Carbon
P. O. Box 4179., Chatsworth, CA 91313 - (800) 622-9206 (818) 341-7577

NERO SYSTEMS - Ultraviolet, Activated Carbon
1000 Valley Forge Circle St. 102A, King of Prussia, PA 19406 - (610) 783-5724

NSA - Activated Carbon with silver for bacteriostat
4260 E. Raines Rd., Memphis, TN 38118 - (901) 366-9288

OXYGEN TECHNOLOGIES - Ozone + ultraviolet + activated carbon in one unit
8229 Melrose, Lenexa, KS 66241 - (913) 894-2828

PLYMOUTH PRODUCTS - Activated Carbon, Reverse Osmosis
502 Indiana Ave., Sheboygan, WI 53081 - (800) 222-7558 (414) 457-9435

REGAL WARE - Activated Carbon, reverse Osmosis, Boiler/Carbon
P. O. Box 395, Kewaskum, WI 53040 - (414) 626-2121

SEARS - Activated Carbon, Reverse Osmosis, Distiller
Sears Tower, 233 S. Wacker Dr., Chicago, IL 60606 - (800) 366-3000 (312) 875-2500

SHAKLEE - Reverse Osmosis
444 Market St., San Francisco, CA 94111 - (415) 954-3000

TELEDYNE WATER PIK - Activated Carbon
1730 E. Prospect Rd., Ft. Collins, CO 80553 - (800) 525-2774 (303) 484-1352

WATERWISE INC. - Distiller
26200 U.S. Hwy. 27 South, Leesburg, FL 34748 - (904) 787-5008

Q: My clothes look dingy and wear out too fast, my skin feels dry, my bathtub and sink have deposits, etc. How can I tell if a water softener will help and will using one push up my water bills much?

A: More than 85% of the United States suffers from excessively hard water, so you most likely will benefit from installing a water softener. You can get a whole-house ion-exchange water softener or an inexpensive magnetic scale reducer just to protect your water heater and plumbing.

The benefits of soft water are many. Your clothes not only get cleaner, but they can last up to 35% longer. The calcium carbonate residue in clothes, due to hard water, cuts and grinds up the material fibers as you move. Your skin stays softer and your hair gets shinier without conditioners.

Some foods, especially fresh vegetables, cook and taste better when prepared with soft water. The calcium in hard water combines with a protein in the skins making them tough with a shriveled look.

Tests have shown that water heaters operate 22% to 30% more efficiently with soft water. This is due to the reduction of the heat blocking scale buildup on the heat exchanger and electric elements. This savings alone pays back more than the cost of the salt blocks.

You will also have a significant savings on your laundry and dishwashing costs. With soft water, you need less detergent, cooler wash water, and you can use a shorter wash cycle which saves electricity and water.

Most whole-house water softeners use an ion exchange process. Sodium ions replace calcium and

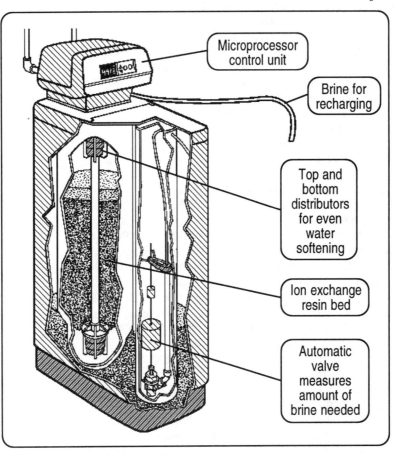

Microprocessor control unit

Brine for recharging

Top and bottom distributors for even water softening

Ion exchange resin bed

Automatic valve measures amount of brine needed

magnesium ions in the hard water. Salt, from the recharging brine, is completely rinsed out each regeneration cycle. The increased dietary intake of sodium ions from softened water is minimal.

The primary operating cost of an ion exchange softener is the salt (about $50/year) and the water used during the regeneration cycle. Some inefficient models consume up to 10,000 gal./year. They use a simple

timer that runs the cycle every night, whether it needs it or not.

Several newer water softeners use efficient electronics to control the frequency and duration of regeneration cycles. The microprocessor stores your water usage patterns in memory and reduces water consumption by 50%.

To just reduce the energy-robbing scale (calcium deposits) in your water heater and plumbing, an inexpensive magnetic scale reducer helps. A magnetic field is created around the incoming water line. This causes a change in the orientation of the ions so they do not stick to the pipes.

Q: Our builder neglected to put any sound insulation between the first and second floors of our home. Does this result in more heat loss upward into the attic and how can we soundproof it more?

A: For energy efficiency, insulation between floors is not generally used. If you keep several of the second-floor rooms unheated or air-conditioned, the temperature difference between floors may warrant some light insulation.

To improve the soundproofing, lift up the old carpeting and caulk any gaps around the baseboard to block the direct sound paths between the floors. Installing a new thick carpet pad helps a lot too.

The major water softener operating cost is the water for the regeneration cycle - see below. The regeneration cycle recharges the softening resin with sodium and flushes out the calcium. The salt cost is minimal ($5 for a 50 lbs. block). It uses about 4 to 5 lbs. of salt per cycle. Figure #1 shows a split resin and brine tank system.

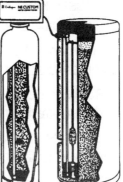

The least efficient and least expensive regeneration cycle control is an "*automatic timer*". It recharges based on time, not by how much water you consume, so both water and salt are wasted.

The best controls are "*demand*" types because they recharge the softener resin only when it is depleted of sodium. A computerized control or a mechanical flow meter measures the gallons of water used. Based on your water hardness, the softening resin must be recharged after a certain number of gallons of water softened (set by the installer). A demand hardness sensor measures the hardness of the softened water. If it is not adequately softened, it determines that it is time for the resin to be recharged. All of the above types of demand controls are effective.

figure #1 - 2-tank design

Magnetic scale reducers do not actually soften the water, so they will not help with cleaning, soft skin, etc. Their purpose is to magnetically effect the calcium ions so they do not stick to the inside of pipes or water heaters. These are either clamped around a water pipe or placed in-line. Page 84 shows an in-line design. These use either permanent or electromagnets. Permanent magnets are the simplest to install. The electromagnet models provide finer control of the magnetic field strength.

gallons per cycle	Combined water and sewage rate - $ per 100 cubic feet						
	1.00	2.00	3.00	4.00	5.00	6.00	7.00
One regeneration cycle every other day - 182 cycles per year							
40	9.76	19.52	29.28	39.04	48.80	59.56	68.32
50	12.20	24.40	36.60	48.80	61.00	73.20	85.40
60	14.64	29.28	43.92	58.56	73.20	87.84	102.48
70	17.08	34.16	51.24	68.32	85.40	102.48	119.56
80	19.52	39.04	58.56	78.08	97.60	117.12	138.74
90	21.69	43.38	65.07	86.76	108.45	130.14	151.83
One regeneration cyle every fourth day - 91 cycles per year							
40	4.88	9.97	14.64	19.52	24.40	29.28	39.16
50	6.10	12.20	18.30	24.40	30.50	36.60	42.70
60	7.32	14.64	21.96	29.28	36.60	43.92	51.24
70	8.54	17.08	25.62	34.16	42.70	51.24	59.78
80	9.76	19.52	29.28	39.04	48.80	58.56	69.37
90	10.85	21.69	32.54	43.38	54.24	65.07	75.92
One regeneration cycle every week - 52 cycles per year							
40	2.79	5.58	8.37	11.16	13.94	16.74	19.52
50	3.49	6.98	10.46	13.96	17.43	20.92	24.40
60	4.18	8.36	12.59	16.72	20.91	25.18	29.28
70	4.88	9.76	14.64	19.52	24.40	29.28	34.16
80	5.49	10.98	16.73	21.96	27.89	33.46	39.64
90	6.20	12.40	18.59	24.80	30.99	37.18	43.38

Annual Water Costs to Operate a Water Softener

Manufacturers of Effficient Water Softeners

AMERICAN WATER PROD., 10885 Kalama River, Fountain Valley, CA 92708 - (714) 963-8490
regeneration cycle control - automatic: timer; demand: computerized, flow meter, hardness sensor

AMETEK, PO Box 1047, Sheboygan, WI 53082 - (414) 457-9435
regeneration cycle control - automatic: timer; demand: flow meter

AQUA SYTEMS, 12505 W. Rockville Rd., Indianapolis, IN 46234 - (317) 272-3000
regeneration cycle control - automatic: timer; demand: computerized, flow meter, hardness sensor

ATLANTIC FILTER CORP., 3112 45th St., W. Palm Beach, FL 33407 - (407) 683-0101
regeneration cycle control - automatic: timer; demand: computerized, flow meter, hardness sensor

BRUNER CORP., PO Box 07500, Milwaukee, WI 53207 - (800) 288-1788 (414) 747-3700
regeneration cycle control - automatic: timer; demand: flow meter

CHARGER WATER TREATMENT, 8150 Lehigh Ave., Morton Grove, IL 60053 - (800) 642-4274
regeneration cycle control - automatic: timer; demand: computerized, flow meter, hardness sensor

CULLIGAN INTERNATIONAL, One Culligan Parkway, Northbrook, IL 60062 - (708) 205-6000
regeneration cycle control - automatic: timer; demand: computerized, flow meter, hardness sensor

CUNO INC., 400 Research Parkway, Meridan, CT 06450 - (800) 243-6894
regeneration cycle control - automatic: timer; demand: flow meter

ECOWATER SYSTEMS, INC., PO Box 64420, St. Paul, MN 55164 - (612) 739-5330
regeneration cycle control - automatic: timer; demand: computerized and flow meter

ENTING WATER CONDITIONING, INC., PO Box 546, Dayton, OH 45449 - (800) 735-5100
regeneration cycle control - automatic: timer; demand: computerized, flow meter, hardness sensor

HAGUE QUALITY WATER INTN'L, 4343 S. Hamilton Rd., Groveport, OH 43125 - (614) 836-2195
regeneration cycle control - automatic: timer; demand: computerized, flow meter, hardness sensor

HELLEBRAND WATER CONDITIONING, PO Box 187, Waunakee, WI 53597 - (608) 849-3050
regeneration cycle control - automatic: timer; demand: flow meter

INAQUA INTERNATIONAL, 6265 E. Sawgrass Rd., Sarasota, FL 34240 - (813) 377-1889
regeneration cycle control - automatic: timer; demand: flow meter

INTERMOUNTAIN SOFT WATER INC., 424 West 1200 North, Orem, UT 84057 - (801) 225-5233
regeneration cycle control - automatic: timer; demand: computerized, flow meter, hardness sensor

IONICS, INC., 3039 Washington Pike, PO Box 99, Bridgeville, PA 15017 - (412) 343-1040
regeneration cycle control - demand: flow meter

KINETICO INC., PO Box 193, Newbury, OH 44065 - (216) 564-9111
regeneration cycle control - demand: flow meter

LINK-O-MATIC MFG. CO., 600 N. 6th St., Richmond, IN 47374 - (800) 428-6928 (317) 962-1538
regeneration cycle control - automatic: timer

PURA-TECH, INTN'L, PO Box 298, Groveport, OH 43125 - (614) 836-2195
regeneration cycle control - demand: computerized and flow meter

QUANTUM/ALPINE WATER, 38th 900 West, Provo, UT 84604 - (801) 375-7555
regeneration cycle control - automatic: timer; demand: computerized and flow meter

QUANTUM MAGNETIC SYSTEMS, 8215 Crudele, Garfield Heights, OH 44125 - (216) 441-6873
magnetic scale reducer - permanent magnet, clamps around the pipe - no plumbing modifications

R & M MANUFACTURING, 146 South State St., Lindon, UT 84042 - (801) 785-5557
  regeneration cycle control - automatic: timer; demand: computerized and flow meter

RAINSOFT WATER COND. CO., 2080 Lunt Ave., Elk Grove Village, IL 60007 - (708) 437-9400
  regeneration cycle control - automatic: timer; demand: computerized and flow meter

SCALE WATCHER, 1150 Limestone Rd., Oxford, PA 19363 - (610) 932-6888
  magnetic scale reducer - electromagnet - insulated electric wire wraps around the pipe

SOFT WATER INC., PO Box 343, Waukesha, WI 53187 - (414) 547-3866
  regeneration cycle control - automatic: timer; demand: flow meter

SOPHTEC INTN'L, 930 West 16th, Costa Mesa, CA 92627 - (714) 548-7222
  magnetic scale reducer - permanent magnet which clamps around the pipe and in-line

SPRINGSOFT INTN'L, INC., 122 E. Lake St., Bloomingdale, IL 60108 - (708) 894-5000
  regeneration cycle control - automatic: timer; demand: flow meter

WATER FACTORY SYSTEMS, 68 Fairbanks, Irvine, CA 92718 - (800) 733-1199
  regeneration cycle control - automatic: timer; demand: flow meter

WATER SOFT INC., 220 Ohio St., Ashland, OH 44805 - (419) 289-0633
  regeneration cycle control - automatic: timer; demand: flow meter

WATERCARE CORP., PO Box 1717, Manitowoc, WI 54221 - (414) 682-6823
  regeneration cycle control - automatic: timer; demand: flow meter and hardness sensor

WSI INC., PO Box 100354, Birmingham, AL 35210 - (800) 343-1121 (205) 956-2090
  regeneration cycle control - automatic: timer; demand: flow meter

- -

Magnetic Scale Reducer with Permanent Magnet

The *SoPhTec* Model I-1020 is designed to properly condition water at flow rates between 0.5 gpm and 20 gpm. Higher flow rates may be attained by installing multiple units in parallel. When it is possible for the flow rate through the I-1020 to exceed 20 gpm, or when units are installed in parallel, the Model I-1020-FC (with integral flow control regulator) must be used.

The Model I-1020 has been permanently assembled and sealed. *Any attempt to disassemble the unit will void the warranty.* The only exception is the removal of the center core for servicing.

The I-1020 should be installed in the water line utilizing unions (attached to 1" Brass Nipples) for ease of installation and for ease of removal should this be required at any time. (See "Installation Diagram".) Direction of water flow through the I-1020 is not critical to unit's function. *Caution - make certain that there is a minimum of 16" clearance for removal of the center core.* (See "Installation Diagram".)

INSTALLATION DIAGRAM

To install fittings to the 1" pipe nipples on the I-1020 utilize the following procedure:
  1. Grip each brass end piece with a vice or wrench; *grip unit only by machined flats on end pieces;*
  2. Thread the male half of a PVC union to the nipple utilizing a paste type thread sealant on the nipple

SOPHTEC INT'L.

Q: I am concerned about the "sick house syndrome" in our energy efficient house. The air gets stale even with a furnace air cleaner. How can I bring in fresh air without driving up my utility bills?

A: In many airtight efficient homes, indoor air, both winter and summer, is more polluted with organic chemicals, molds, pesticides, carbon monoxide, etc. than outdoor air. These pollutants come from cleaners, paints, solvent, carpeting, even air fresheners, and get trapped indoors.

Heat recovery ventilators are the most effective and energy efficient method to bring in fresh air and exhaust stale air. They are available as small window units or larger whole-house models. Several states' building codes now require them in all new homes.

An efficient whole-house model can save up to 85% of the energy from the outgoing air. Some models also offer optional electrostatic air cleaners to pre-filter the incoming fresh air. Some whole-house models use only as much electricity as a 50-watt light bulb on the low quiet speed.

A heat recovery ventilator uses an efficient heat exchanger. In the winter, the stale indoor exhaust air transfers its heat to the incoming cold fresh air through the heat ex-

changer. The inlet and the outlet air streams are kept separate so no pollutants get back indoors.

In the summer, the cool outgoing stale air pre-cools the incoming fresh air. An enthalpy type of heat exchanger is often recommended in hot climates using more annual air-conditioning than heating. With this

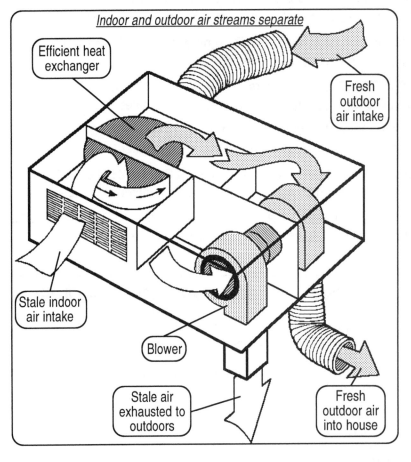

Indoor and outdoor air streams separate

Efficient heat exchanger

Fresh outdoor air intake

Stale indoor air intake

Blower

Stale air exhausted to outdoors

Fresh outdoor air into house

type, the outgoing stale air also helps to dehumidify the incoming fresh air.

Some whole-house models can be ducted into your existing duct system and others have their own duct system. You often locate the stale air intakes in a bathroom, kitchen, and hobby room. The fresh air outlets are located in a living room, family room, or dining room.

Heat recovery ventilators offer several types of controls - timed operation, variable-speed/cfm (cubic feet per minute of air flow), and humidity-level-controlled. The best model for your home depends on your climate, family size, and lifestyle. A minimum of two speeds is recommended.

Continuous low-speed operation is often used with an automatic speed-up when bathrooms are used, for example. You can also override the automatic controls when cooking or when entertaining a large group. A hand-held remote control is a convenient option for use from a bedroom at night.

Q: I am going to build a new home and I have heard about autoclaved cellular concrete. What is it and is it more efficient than regular concrete?

A: Autoclaved cellular concrete ACC has an insulating R-value of about R-1.25 per inch, about twice as high as regular concrete. It is about 25% lighter and costs about the same as regular concrete. It can be used for foundations instead of poured concrete.

It is made of cement, lime, aluminum powder, and fly ash from coal-fired utility plants. This mixture forms tiny insulating hydrogen bubbles. It is cut into flat pieces or blocks and cured in an autoclave.

With today's more energy efficient airtight homes, indoor air is often more polluted than outdoor air. A heat recovery ventilator brings in fresh outdoor air and recovers the heat (or "coolth") from the outgoing stale air. These ventilation systems save up to 90% (*"efficiency"*) of the energy as compared to opening a window. These ratings are listed with each manufacturer in the following table. I have listed the most efficient and high quality units.

The air flow capacity of heat recovery ventilators is rated in cubic feet per minute (cfm) of air *"flow rate"*. To select the proper capacity unit for your home use a general rule of thumb, from the Home Ventilating Institute, that you should have at least one air change in your house every two hours or .5 air changes per hour (ach). Multiply your total floor area by the ceiling height to get the total air volume. Divide this number by 120 to get the required cfm capacity. If you have specific moisture or other problems, you may need a higher capacity than .5 ach.

figure #1

If you plan to install a whole-house unit, have the contractor do an analysis of the number of inlets and outlets, and the capacity you need. It is usually not a do-it-yourself installation. Figure #1 shows a typical attic mounted layout.

The *"# of inlets and outlets"* shown in the manufacturers list is the recommended number, but your contractor may deviate from this number. The true *"power usage"* may be less than listed since the unit does not run continuously on high speed. It will vary depending on your specific home and needs.

The best *"heat exchanger type"* for your home depends on your climate. Cold climates require a unit with freeze protection. Warm climates often require one which also transfers moisture. Consult your local contractor.

- -

Manufacturers of Heat Recovery Ventilators

AIR X CHANGE, 401 VFW Dr., Rockland, MA 02370 - (617) 871-4816
    flow rate - 500 TO 2800 cfm   efficiency - 75% to 85%   heat exchanger type - rotary core
    # of inlets - six to eight   # of outlets -six to eight   power usage - 324 to 552 watt
    special features - self-cleaning energy transfer wheel, moisture stays in the vapor phase, no drains

AMERICAN ALDES, 4537 Northgate Ct., Sarasota, FL 34234 - (813) 351-3441
    flow rate - 90 to 180 cfm   efficiency - 70% to 90%   heat exchanger type - counterflow
    # of inlets - eight   # of outlets - four   power usage - 210 watts
    special features - eliminates the need of ventilating fans in the bathrooms

AMERIX CORP., 2796 5th Ave. S., Fargo, ND 58103 - (800) 232-4116 (701) 232-4116
    flow rate - 90 to 428 cfm   efficiency - 75% to 85%   heat exchanger type - crossflow
    # of inlets - four to six   # of outlets - four to six   power usage - 88 to 223 watts
    special features - auto defrost control

BOSSAIRE, 2901 S.E. 4th St., Minneapolis, MN 55414 - (612) 378-0049
    flow rate - 130 to 400 cfm   efficiency - 80%   heat exchanger type - crossflow
    # of inlets - six to eight   # of outlets - six to eight   power usage - 80 to 157 watts
    special features - external supply filter for allergy sufferers

BRYANT/CARRIER, PO Box 4808, Syracuse, NY 13221 - (800) 227-7437 (315) 432-6000

flow rate - 65 to 1270 cfm   efficiency - 75% to 84%   heat exchanger type - counterflow
# of inlets - two   # of outlets - two   power usage - 144 to 552 watts
special features - door swings open so no tools required to clean the filters and core

CONSERVATION ENERGY SYS, PO Box 582416, Minn'lis, MN 55458 - (800) 667-3717

flow rate - 75 to 700 cfm   efficiency - 80% to 93%   heat exchanger type - crossflow
# of inlets - six to eight   # of outlets - six to eight   power usage - 69 to 193 watts
special features - remote control with illuminated switches for one touch ventilation
*(through-the-wall unit)
flow rate - 50 to 113 cfm   efficiency - 78%   heat exchanger type - crossflow
# of inlets - n/a   # of outlets - n/a   power usage - 32 to 108 watts

DES CHAMPS LABORATORIES, 66 Okner Pky., Livingston, NJ 07039 - (201) 535-8300

flow rate - 110 to 415 cfm   efficiency - 70% to 85%   heat exchanger type - counterflow
# of inlets - six to eight   # of outlets - four to six   power usage - not available
special features - electrostatic air filter to pre-filter air before it enters your home

DURO DYNE, Rte. 110, Farmingdale, NY 11735 - (516) 249-900

flow rate - 50 to 200 cfm   efficiency - 70% to 80%   heat exchanger type - crossflow
# of inlets - two   # of outlets - two   power usage - not available
special features - contains a temperature sensor that protects against cell freeze-ups

ENVIRONMENT AIR LTD., PO Box 10, Cocagne, New Brunswick EOA 1KO Can. - (506) 576-6672

flow rate - 70 to 270 cfm   efficiency - 70% to 90%   heat exchanger type - heat pipe
# of inlets - four to eight   # of outlets - four to six   power usage - 192 watts
special features - automatic defrost and optional electronic wall mounted control unit

HONEYWELL, PO Box 524, Minneapolis, MN 55440 - (800) 328-5111 (612) 951-1000

flow rate - 70 to 250 cfm   efficiency - 70% to 90%   heat exchanger type - rotary core
# of inlets - four to eight   # of outlets - four to six   power usage - 156 to 1400 watts
special features - contains a dessicant-coated heat transfer disc

LAY INTERNATIONAL, 16247 Forest Meadows, St. Louis, MO 63005 - (314) 532-0517

flow rate - 50 and 80 cfm   efficiency - 75% and 80%   heat exchanger type - rotary core
* (through-the-window or wall unit)   power usage - 25 to 40 watts
special features - activated carbon filter available

NEWAIRE, 7009 Raywood Rd., Madison, WI 53713 - (800) 627-4499 (608) 221-4499

flow rate - 70 to 120 cfm   efficiency - 73% to 78%   heat exchanger type - crossflow
# of inlets - six to eight   # of outlets - four to six   power usage - 55 to 240 watts
special features - the core is treated with a resin for better moisture control

NUTECH ENERGY SYS, 511 McCormick Blvd., London, Ontario N5W 4C8 Can - (519) 457-1904

flow rate - 40 to 1200 cfm   efficiency - 70% to 90%   heat exchanger type - crossflow
# of inlets - two   # of outlets - two   power usage - 55 to 1300 watts
special features - lifetime warranty on the aluminum core

QDT CORP., 1000 Singleton Blvd., Dallas, TX 75212 - (214) 741-1993

flow rate - 150 cfm   efficiency - 70%   heat exchanger type - heat pipe
# of inlets - two   # of outlets - two   power usage - not available
special features - compact size less than four cubic feet

RAYDOT INC., PO Box 728, Cokato, MN 55321 - (800) 328-3813 (612) 286-2103

flow rate - 100 to 225 cfm   efficiency - 75% to 82%   heat exchanger type - counterflow
# of inlets - two   # of outlets - two   power usage - 80 to 100 watts
special features - HEPA filter and pre-sorber activated charcoal prefilter

RESEARCH PRODUCTS, PO Box 1467, Madison, WI 53701 - (608) 257-8801

flow rate - 120 to 150 cfm   efficiency - 77%   heat exchanger type - crossflow
# of inlets - six to eight   # of outlets - four to six   power usage - 168 watts
special features - front panel opens for easy access to filters

SNAPPY AIR DISTRIBUTION, PO Box 1168, Detroit Lakes, MN 56502 - (218) 847-9258

flow rate - 240 cfm   efficiency - 70% to 75%   heat exchanger type - crossflow
# of inlets - two   # of outlets - two   power usage - 100 watts
special features - removable core for easy cleaning

STIRLING TECHNOLOGY, PO Box 2633, Athens, OH 45701 - (800) 535-3488 (614) 594-2277

flow rate - 60 to 200 cfm   efficiency - 96%   heat exchanger type - rotary
# of inlets - six to eight   # of outlets - four to six   power usage - 256 watts
special features - corrosion resistant stainless steel heat exchanger

VENMAR VENTILATION, 1715 Haggerty, Drummondville, Quebec J2C 5P7 Can. - (819) 477-6226

flow rate - 65 to 265 cfm   efficiency - 76% to 95%   heat exchanger type - cross & counterflow
# of inlets - six to eight   # of outlets - four to six   power usage - 105 to 410 watts
special features - a variety of attractive wall-mounted countrols available

The new 1000 Thruwall™ brings to the unique 1000 design, simplified installation, with direct access for supply and exhaust air through a wall plenum. A white plastic, UV protected, intake/exhaust hood is supplied to make a clean and simple installation on the exterior of the building. The hood is designed to be installed before exterior siding or finish is applied and can be painted with an oil base paint. There are two exhaust ports to take air from the building. The decision on which port to use can be made by the installer, adding flexibility to the installation. Both ports are supplied closed and either the plastic top or side knockout is easily cut out by the installer at the job site.

The total depth 330mm (13") is the same as standard upper cabinets. The finish color is almond, to compliment cabinets and appliances.

The 1000 Thruwall™ is wall mounted using a convenient wall bracket and screws. The unit can be installed on a wall with a minimum stud spacing of 406mm (16") o/c. A 368mm x 280mm (14 1/2" x 11") hole is required to be cut in the wall between studs. An 203mm (8") long styrofoam plenum is supplied to be cut to the proper wall thickness and inserted into the wall opening. Additional plenums are available for applications which have walls more then 203mm (8") thick. On models with defrost, 152mm (6") of clearance must be allowed between the left side and adjacent cupboards and walls. A filler strip may be installed as long as either the top or bottom has been left open to allow air to enter the FrostBuster™ defrost system.

Through-the-wall design by <u>*Conservation Energy Systems*</u>

Q: Our bathroom vent fan sounds like the space shuttle Columbia at liftoff. What are the quietest and most efficient bathroom vent fans and how can I distinguish a good-quality fan from others?

A: Although most bathroom vent fans look identical on the outside, there are many design and quality differences inside. Compare the design features and sound level specifications. You can barely hear some of the new super-quiet fans running.

It is very important to adequately ventilate your bathroom when showering or bathing. Running a vent fan is much more energy efficient than just opening a window for ventilation. In a tightly sealed and energy efficient house, excessive moisture can quickly deteriorate your house and exacerbate mold growth and allergies.

The most quiet and powerful design is a small attic-mounted axial vent fan. One fan can vent all your bathrooms and utility room. Other super-quiet vent fans use a standard ceiling-mounting with specially-designed motors, sound and vibration isolation, and smooth contours for quiet air flow.

For the simplest installation, select one of the new ceiling-mounted models that is designed as a simple bolt-in replacement for your old noisy fan. You should very easily be able to install one yourself in half an hour.

It is also easy to install the axial vent fan in your attic. A six-inch diameter fan is most common. You attach it with its mounting bracket against a rafter or truss. Run six-inch diameter flexible duct down to the ceiling air inlet grill and another duct out the gable.

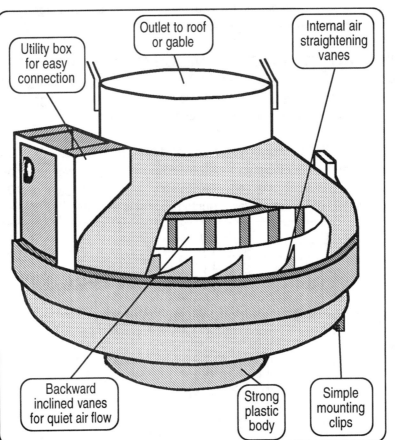

Utility box for easy connection

Outlet to roof or gable

Internal air straightening vanes

Backward inclined vanes for quiet air flow

Strong plastic body

Simple mounting clips

When comparing bathroom vent fans, the sound level is rated in units called "sones". One sone is about as loud as a new very-quiet refrigerator. A sound level rating of four sones is twice as loud as two sones.

Although an attic-mounted axial fan is rated at about 2.5 sones at the fan motor, the fan is located up in your attic. In your bathroom, you only hear the quiet sound of air move-

ment, not the motor. In a large bathroom, you can install two inlet grills in the ceiling, over the bathtub and the sink.

Some of the new super-quiet bolt-in replacement bathroom vent fans are rated at only 1.5 sones. These quiet fans often have slower, better-balanced motors. The motors are mounted in rubber bushings with bridge brackets to locate the motor out of the air stream and reduce turbulence.

It is important to select the proper size fan for your bathroom. Too small a fan will not be able to ventilate the bathroom quickly enough for highest efficiency. Too large a fan will be noisier than necessary.

Q: I have heard that putting crumpled newspapers in my freezer helps save electricity. Can newspapers really help?

A: You should try to keep your freezer reasonably full. This reduces the amount of cold air that rushes out each time you open the door. Packing it too full of foods, though, impedes necessary air circulation.

You can use frozen water-filled jugs or crumpled newspapers to fill a less-than-full freezer. Crumpled newspapers are most effective because if you take them out when you need space, you lose less energy than from ice.

By using your vent fan, you can reduce the moisture buildup and potential damage to the interior of your home. You should select the proper size vent fan for your bathroom. Too large a fan will be noisy and draw out excess air and too small a fan will not exhaust the moist air fast enough. See the chart below for the recommended sizes. Fan sizes are rated in cubic feet per minute (cfm) of air flow.

Axial attic-mounted vent fans are the quietest and most powerful fans. When you compare the sound levels rating on page 92, keep in mind that vent fans are rated at the fan itself.

Since the axial fan is mounted inside the attic, it is much quieter in your bathroom than the sound rating would indicate. Page 91 shows additional information and specifications on axiel vent fans.

An axial fan is easy to install in your attic with the mounting clips. Run flexible duct up to it from your bathroom. Figure #1 shows how you can install two ceiling intake grills to vent a large bathroom using only one axial fan in the attic.

BATH/SPA EXHAUST Powerful enough to exhaust 2 areas with just one fan. Eliminates moisture problems quickly and quietly.

figure #1

Bathroom vent fan noise levels are rated in sones of sound. One sone is about the noise level of a quiet running refrigerator. As the chart on page 92 shows, larger (higher air flow capacity - cfm) bathroom vent fans are generally noisier than small ones.

Recommended Bathroom Vent Fan Size	
Bathroom Size sq. ft.	Fan Capacity cfm
30	33
40	44
50	55
60	66
70	77
80	88
90	99
100	110
110	121
120	132

There are many internal design features which reduce the noise significantly and are not apparent on the outside. For the most effective operation, you should run your bathroom vent fan the entire time that you are showering or bathing. Several of new models have motion or humidity sensors to automatically start the fan when the bathroom is used.

For example, in the Broan line, **MS** in the model number refers to motion-sensing and **HS** to humidity-sensing. If your bathroom door is snug to the floor, saw a half inch off the bottom to allow air to get in when the fan is running.

Manufacturers of Bathroom Vent Fans

AUBREY MFG. CO., 6709 S. Main St., Union, IL 60180 - (800) 247-2273 (815) 923-2101

BOWERS MFG., 8685 Bowers Ave., South Gate, CA 90280 - (213) 566-2111

BROAN MFG. CO., PO Box 140, Hartford, WI 53027 - (414) 673-4340

* DEFLECTO CORP., PO Box 50057, Indianapolis, IN 46250 - (317) 849-9555

* FANTECH INC., 1712 Northgate Blvd., Sarasota, FL 34234 - (800) 747-1762 (813) 351-2947

FASCO CONSUMER PRODUCTS, PO Box 150, Fayetteville, NC 28302 - (910) 483-0421

FLORIDA POLYMERS, 1000 Sand Pond Rd., Lake Mary, FL 32746 - (407) 333-9225

NUTONE INC., Madison & Red Bank Rds., Cincinnati, OH 45227 - (513) 527-5100

PANASONIC, 1 Panasonic Way, Secaucus, NJ 07094 - (201) 392-6442

PENN VENTILATOR CO., 9995 Gantry Rd., Philadelphia, PA 19115 - (215) 464-8900

* ROSENBERG FANS, 2500 W. County Rd. B, St. Paul, MN 55113 - (612) 639 -0846

*   *Ceiling-mounted axial fan*

Motor

- totally enclosed
- class B insulation
- 115/1/60 supply
- permanently sealed ball bearings with special lubricant
- thermal overload protection with automatic reset
- fan blades attached to rotating motor
- 3 year warranty
- CSA and UL approved

- suitable for high moisture, dust and lint loading
- suitable for continuous operation in air streams up to 140º
- simple installation
- long and maintenance free operation over maximum load conditions
- electrical safety
- ensures long life

Corrosion Protection

- motor and blades dipped in waterproof lacque to resist corrosion
- fan housing molded of High

Impact GE plastic
- suitable for fume and moist atmospheres
- superior corrosion resistance

Fan Wheel

- backward inclined blades
- high air volumes
- quiet operation
- efficient performance

- high pressure
- non-overloading
- suitable for dust

Variable Speed

- 100% control of air flow

- set exact flow requirments
- energy saving
- quiet operation

Fan Housing

- aerodynamic shape
- internal air vanes
- molded from GE NORYL N190 plastic
- UL listed
- 1.75" lip collars
- external terminal box with prewired capacitor
- available in diameters 4, 6, 8, 10 & 12

- smooth airflow
- improved performance
- durable
- weather and corrosion resistant
- fire resistant
- easy installation
- easy access
- simple connection
- matches all standard duct sizes

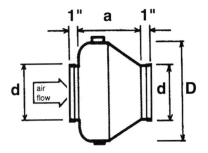

Performance Data for Fantech							
model	fan HP	Watts	RPMS	volt.	cfm 0"	duct dia.	sones
F-100	1/30	70	2500	115	160	4"	-
F-125	1/30	70	2500	115	205	5"	-
F-150	1/20	90	2500	115	270	6"	2.1
F-160	1/15	100	2150	115	360	6"	3.2
F-175	1/12	150	2700	115	415	6"	4.5
F-200	1/15	100	2150	115	410	8"	3.2
F-225	1/10	150	2700	115	520	8"	4.5
F-250	1/6	230	2400	115	700	10"	5.6
F-315	1/5	370	3100	115	900	12.5"	6.2

Fan Specifications for Fantech			
Dimensional Data			
Model	D	d	a
F-100	9 1/2	3 7/8	5 1/4
F-125	9 1/2	4 7/8	5 1/4
F-150	11 3/4	5 3/4	5 7/8
F-160	11 3/4	5 3/4	5 7/8
F-175	11 3/4	5 3/4	5 7/8
F-200	13 1/4	8	6 1/4
F-225	13 1/4	8	6 1/4
F-250	13 1/4	10	7
F-315	16	12 1/2	8 1/4

Bathroom Vent Fans

Manufacturer	Capacity	Sound	Manufacturer	Capacity	Sound
model #	cfm	sones	model #	cfm	sones
AUBREY MANUFACTURING			**FASCO CONSUMER PRODUCT**		
710	50	2.5	794	70	3.0
720	50	2.5	691W	70	3.0
7555	60	3.0	A692W	70	3.0
7564	80	3.0	7100	100	1.5
7610	110	3.0	7130	130	2.5
7650	50	3.0	7100L	100	1.5
			7150L	150	3.0
			1001	100	3.0
BOWERS/THERMADOR			1001F	100	3.0
VQT90M	90	2.1			
VQT200	225	2.7	**FLORIDA POLYMERS**		
			FP50	50	2.5
BROAN MANUFACTURING CO.			FP50L	50	2.5
S90	90	1.5			
HS90	90	1.5	**NUTONE INC.**		
MS90	90	1.5			
S120L	120	2.5	QT80	80	1.5
S120FL	120	2.5	QT90	90	1.5
HS120L	120	2.5	QT110	110	2.0
MS120L	120	2.5	QT130	130	1.0
MHS120L	120	2.5	QT140L	150	2.5
S130	130	2.5	QT150	160	2.5
HS130	130	2.5	QT200	200	2.0
MS130	130	2.5			
			PANASONIC		
DEFLECTO - Sound levels are at fan in attic					
			FV05VQ	50	0.5
TF4	160	2.4	FV08VQ	90	1.0
TF6	270	2.8	FV12VQ	110	1.0
TF8	410	3.2	FV08VQS	90	1.0
			FV12VQS	110	1.0
FANTECH - Sound levels are at fan in attic			FV08VQH	90	1.0
			FV12VQH	110	1.0
F/FR100	150	1.0	FV20VQ	190	1.5
F/FR125	205	1.0			
F/FR150	270	2.1			
F/FR160	360	3.2	**PENN VENTILATOR**		
F/FR175	415	4.5			
F/FR200	410	3.2	Z3	60	1.6
F/FR225	520	4.5	Z5	140	2.1
F/FR250	700	5.6	Z6	125	1.5

Q: I need a good humidifier because I have wintertime allergies and the static electricity could light the Astrodome. What type of whole-house console humidifier is most effective and cheapest to operate?

A: Maintaining the proper humidity level is important for comfort and allergy control. A whole-house console humidifier is often more effective than a furnace-mounted one. A console model can be set to run continuously on a low, quiet fan speed, not just when the furnace blower is on.

Generally, 40 to 60 percent relative humidity produces the best indoor air quality. Many bacteria and viruses thrive in both drier and more moist air. Dust mites and mold are worse at higher levels and ozone at lower levels. Your lungs will be happy, and your furniture will last longer.

Properly humidified air cuts your heating bills too. This allows you to set your furnace thermostat a couple of degrees lower and save energy without feeling chilly. The savings will pay back the $15 to $20 annual electricity cost to operate a humidifier many times over.

There are six basic types of humidifiers - evaporative (wicking), impeller, steam-mist, warm-mist, ultrasonic, and floor register covers.

Evaporative "wicking" designs are most often used for large whole-house console models. These use a special filter-type material which naturally draws up (wicks) water from a reservoir. A fan circulates room air through the damp filters to release moisture and clean the air.

In one model, Moist Air, the wicking filters rest on floats in the

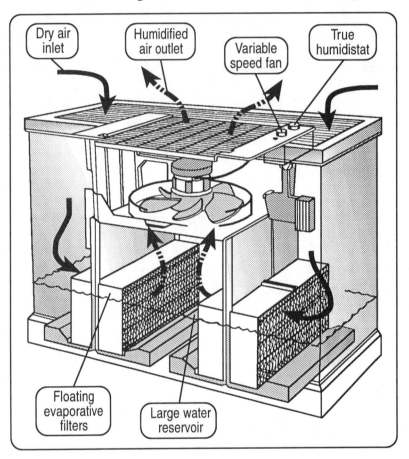

Dry air inlet

Humidified air outlet

Variable speed fan

True humidistat

Floating evaporative filters

Large water reservoir

water reservoir. As the water evaporates and its level drops, the filter stays in proper contact with it for the most effective humidification.

Some models use filters treated with an anti-bacterial material. Others use a built-in, replaceable high efficiency air filter with a secondary charcoal element to remove odors and carcinogenic volatile organic chemicals.

Be sure to select a model with a built-in "true" humidistat, not just a low/high switch. Without a true humidistat, the output does not respond to changing indoor conditions like cooking or a large group of guests.

A multi or variable-speed fan is best. Combined with a humidistat, this provides complete control over comfort. For nighttime use, select a whole-house model with a special quiet "sleep" setting. For extra bedroom humidity, small steam-mist and floor register designs are totally quiet.

Q: The pressure relief valve on my gas water heater leaks. I have replaced it, but it still leaks when the burner comes on. What can I do to make the relief valve stop leaking?

A: Chances are that the replacement valve is not faulty. Your tank may have sediment that is clogging the valve and making it leak. Open and close the lever several times.

If it still leaks, lightly tap the valve body, not the lever, with a plastic mallet. This often dislodges particles. In the future, drain a few gallons out of the lower tank valve several times a year to reduce sediment buildup. This also increases its life and maintains its efficiency.

Manufacturers of Humidifiers

BEMIS, PO Box 901, Sheboygan, WI 53085 - (800) 558-7651 (414) 467-4621

model - console 4973   type - evaporative   capacity - 5.5 gallons
coverage - 3,000 sq. ft.   output - 12.0 gal./day
special features - It has an automatic humidistat and a variable-speed fan. There is a replaceable two-stage filter with an activated charcoal trap that is located in the back of the unit to trap dust and pollen particles. It includes a refill hose.

model - tabletop 7376   type - evaporative   capacity - 1.7 gallons
coverage - 900 sq. ft.   output - 2.5 gal./day
special features - A removable water tank makes refilling easy. It has a three speed humidity control with a special quiet setting for nighttime use. There is a two-stage air cleaner and it comes with a replaceable filter. The grille on top is multi-directional.

BIONAIRE, 90 Boroline Rd., Allendale, NJ 07401 - (800) 253-2764

model - console W-9   type - evaporative   capacity - 9.0 gallons
coverage - 3,500 sq. ft.   output - 8.0 gal./day
special features - The unit has a power light to show it is running. It is equipped with an indicator to show when the filter needs to be cleaned and when the tank is empty. It has a three-speed control for ultra quiet nighttime operation and three easily removed tanks.

model - tabletop CM-3   type - warm mist   capacity - 3.0 gallons
coverage - 1,000 sq. ft.   output - 3.0 gal./day
special features - A power light shows when the unit is on and it shuts off when the water supply is low. There is an automatic humidistat.

DURACRAFT CORP., 355 Main St., Whitinsville, MA 01588 - (508) 234-4600

model - concole DH-8000-02   type - evaporative   capacity - 3.0 gallons
coverage - 4,100 sq. ft.   output - 3.1 gal./day
special features - It is available with an automatic and an adjustable humidistat. There is easy mobility with attached castors.

model - tabletop DH-836   type - evaporative   capacity - 3.0 gallons
coverage - 1000 sq. ft.   output - 3.1 gal./day
special features - A safety lock prevents the unit from running when the cover is off. A power light shows when the unit is on and it shuts off when the water supply is low. It has an ultra quiet two-speed fan for nighttime use.

model - table top DH-900's   type - warm mist   capacity - 2.4 gallons
coverage - 900 sq. ft.   output - 2.6 gal./day
special features - An indicator shows when the tank is empty and it shuts off when tank is empty, removed or tipped over.

EMERSON MOIST AIR, 8400 Pershall Rd., Hazelwood, MO 63042 - (800) 237-6511

model - console HD14W (Moist Air) type - evaporative   capacity - 12.0 gallons
coverage - 2,750 sq. ft.   output - 15.0 gal./day
special features - It is equipped with a 6-bladed fan with variable speeds. The TrapMax® Filter is a honeycomb that floats in the water reservoir and is treated with a special compound to retard bacterial growth.

model - table top 850   type - evaporative   capacity - 2.0 gallons
coverage - 750 sq. ft.   output - 2.2 gal./day
special features - Multi-directional air louvers put the air where you want it. It features a three-speed air flow control including a quiet night setting. It has an automatic humidistat. Three-speed fan includes a quiet nighttime setting. It has non-slip rubber feet.

model - floor heat register 500   type - evaporative   capacity - 2.0 gallons
coverage - 750 sq. ft.   output - n/a
special features - The furnace drives the air into the room. It is lightweight and, with no moving parts, it is ideal for a child's room.

HOLMES PRODUCTS CORP., 233 Fortune Blvd., Milford, MA 01757 - (508) 634-8050

model - table top HM2060   type - evaporative   capacity - 3.0 gallons
coverage - 1,200 sq. ft.   output - 4.0 gal./day
special features - It has an adjustable humidistat and 3 control speeds. A power light indicates when the unit is on.

model - table top HM460B   type - ultrasonic   capacity - 2.0 gallons
coverage - 850 sq. ft.   output - 2.3 gal./day
special features - It has a 2-speed fan for nighttime operation. The water purification system traps impurities to give a clean output.

model - table top HM5150   type - steam mist   capacity - 2.6 gallons
coverage - 900 sq. ft.   output - 2.5 gal./day

model - table top HMHV8005   type - impeller   capacity - 2.0 gallons
coverage - 650 sq. ft.   output - 1.2 gal./day

KAZ, INC., 41 Cross St., Hudson, NY 12534 - (518) 828-0450

model - tabletop 3300   type - evaporative   capacity - 1.2 gallons
coverage - 800 sq. ft.   output - 2.0 gal./day
special features - A water indicator tells you when to refill and how much water to add. There is a fill channel so you can fill without removing the cover. It is equipped with a whisper-quiet fan that won't disturb your sleep.

model - table top 2000   type - impeller   capacity - 2.5 gallons
coverage - 600 sq. ft.   output - 1.0 gal./day
special features - The container is translucent and unbreakable with a visible water supply.

SEARS (KENMORE), 3333 Beverly Rd., Hoffman Estates, IL 60179 - (800) 359-2000 (708) 286-2500

    model - console 14412   type - evaporative   capacity - 12.0 gallons

    coverage - 3,000 sq. ft.   output - 12.5 gal./day

    special features - It has a variable fan speed, an automatic humidistat and shuts off when the water supply is low.

    model - table top 14092   type - warm mist   capacity - 2.0 gallons

    coverage - 1,000 sq. ft.   output - 2.8 gal./day

    special features - Very quiet operation with the whisper quiet system - no fan or motor.

TOASTMASTER INC., 1801 N. Stadium Blvd., Columbia, MO 65202 - (314) 445-8666

    model - console 3445   type - evaporative   capacity - 12.0 gallons

    coverage - 2,750 sq. ft.   output - 8.7 gal./day

    special features - It has an infinite speed control with an automatic humidistat and automatic shutoff. An indicator light shows when the tank is empty. The control panel is concealed and located on the top of the unit. Moves easily on rollabout castors.

    model - tabletop 3412   type - evaporative   capacity - 2.0 gallons

    coverage - 1,250 sq. ft.   output - 4.0 gal./day

    special features - The louvers are directional and it has an automatic humidistat. It is equipped with a charcoal air cleaner.

Maximum Indoor Humidity Level to Avoid Window Condensation		
Outdoor Temperature	Maximum Indoor Humidity Level - Single Pane - %	Maximum Indoor Humidity Level - Double Pane - %
-30	3	27
-20	6	30
-10	8	35
0	13	40
10	20	46
20	26	52
30	32	59
40	44	68

The above chart is based on an indoor temperature of 70°F and a wind speed of 15 miles per hour. Use this only as a guideline. The actual humidity level where condensation forms depends on your specific window design, special coatings, thickness of air space, and type of gas in between glass panes. The frame may also begin to sweat before the glass itself.

Effect of Humidity on Health

Decrease in Bar Width Indicates Decrease in Effect

Optimum Zone

	Bacteria
	Viruses
	Fungi
	Mites
	Respiratory Infections
	Allergic Rhinitis and Asthma
	Chemical Interactions
	Ozone Production

% Relative Humidity	10	20	30	40	50	60	70	80	90

Selector Guide for Various Types of Humidifiers

Floor Heat Registers

How it works:

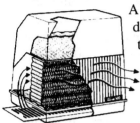

A filter element draws water from the reservoir on top of the unit. Warm air from the furnace blows through the filter and into the room.

Advantages:

• Low operating cost - the manufacturer recommends filters impregnated with bacteria killer. A package of two filters is $14.00 and this is the only future cost.
• No moving parts and it is very quiet.

Disadvantages:

• Variable output. Moisture output will drop if the airflow from the furnace is reduced or restricted.
• Humidification stops whenever the furnace turns off.
• No humidistat.
• Tank is difficult to fill and clean.
• The unit is easy to trip over.

Ultrasonic

How it works:

Water flows from a reservoir to a transducer and nebulizer (small electronic components). Nebulizer oscillates about 1.7 million times a second, churning the water into a cool mist.

Advantages:

• Uses little energy.
• Very few microorganisms are released into the air.
• Quiet.

Disadvantages:

• Emits annoying white dust if used with most tap water.
• May require soft or distilled water or a demineralization cartridge.
• Very hard water can leave hard to remove mineral deposits on nebulizer.
• Can emit bits of dead microorganisms causing allergic reactions.

Steam-Mist

How it works:

Water flows into a small heating chamber and it is kept at the boiling point. As the water boils, it releases moisture through a spout and into the air.

Advantages:

• Uses tap water.
• Needs no filters.
• No moving parts.
• Water vapor is sterile because the boiling water kills microorganisms.
• Emits little or no white dust.

Disadvantages:

• High energy consumption.
• Heating element may need extra cleaning to remove any buildup of hard water minerals.
• Mist and boiling water from tipped over tank can scald.
• Can emit bits of dead microorganisms causing allergic reactions.
• Noisy

Warm-Mist

How it works:

Basically the same as the steam-mist type described above. A fan in the spout mixes cool air with the steam which produces mist somewhat warmer than room air.

Advantages:

• Uses tap water.
• Needs no filters.
• Water vapor is sterile because the boiling water kills microorganisms.
• Emits little or no white dust.
• Slight risk of scalding from mist.

Disadvantages:

• High energy consumption.
• Heating element may need extra cleaning to remove any buildup of hard water minerals.
• Can emit bits of dead microorganisms causing allergic reactions.
• Noisy
• Boiling water from tipped over tank can scald.

Evaporative

How it works:

Water is drawn into a wick through capillary action. A fan pulls air through the filter, allowing the water to evaporate and sends it into the room.

Advantages:

• Uses little energy.
• Uses tap water.
• Easy to clean.
• No spray, not likely to spread bacteria and white dust.

Disadvantages:

• The fan and airflow can be noisy.
• Frequent filter replacement adds to operating cost. Filters often available only from manufacturer.
• Needs to be cleaned regularly to prevent growth of undesirable microorganisms
• Removes heat from the room.

Impeller

How it works:

The impeller and fan assembly dips into a water tank. When the cone spins, it pumps water upward. The fan blades throw water droplets out a nozzle and into the air.

Advantages:

• Uses little energy.
• Needs fewer refills than other types.
• Tank is very easy to clean.
• Very inexpensive to buy.

Disadvantages:

• Can spew microorganisms along with water.
• Can splatter water.
• Can emit white dust if used with hard tap water. It needs distilled or soft water or a demineralization cartridge. One year's running cost can be greater than purchase price.
• Sloshing noise from the fan and impeller can be distracting.

Q: I've heard that harmful formaldehyde gas levels are highest during the summer in efficient houses like mine. How can I determine if my house has a problem and how can I lower the gas level energy efficiently?

A: Formaldehyde gas is given off by many common materials and products in every home. Symptoms of high formaldehyde gas levels are often similar to colds and allergies - headaches, burning eyes, coughing, runny nose, etc. It is also a suspected carcinogen.

Indoor formaldehyde levels are generally highest in the summertime. Both heat and humidity increase the release of formaldehyde from furniture, carpeting, drapes, kitchen and bathroom cabinets, many adhesives, and many common household products.

If you have made energy improvements to your home, your central air conditioner may now be oversized for its cooling needs. The air conditioner runs less and does not dehumidify well, even though you may feel comfortable. This can increase the level of formaldehyde gas that gets trapped indoors. Typical central and room air cleaners do not effectively remove it.

Several laboratories offer inexpensive do-it-yourself home test kits (about $35 for three tests) to check the formaldehyde level inside your home. For one test, you just open a small bottle filled with a special water solution that absorbs formaldehyde gas.

After a day or two, you mix in a few drops of test liquid. The water solution changes color and you compare it to a color chart to determine the formaldehyde gas level.

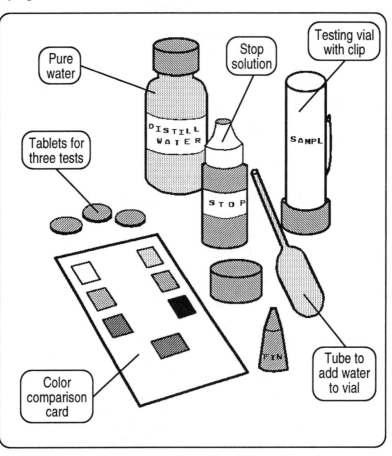

For $20 more, you can send the sample to the lab for more accurate analysis. If your do-it-yourself test shows a higher than acceptable level of gas, you should consider having the lab analyze the next sample. Other 7-day-average-level home tests require laboratory analysis.

Natural ventilation is the most energy-efficient method to lower the formaldehyde gas level inside your home. If you air-condition, open windows several minutes and several times per day on all but the hottest and humid days. The heat and moisture gain will not be great.

Installing a heat recovery whole-house fresh air ventilation system saves the energy from the stale air that it exhausts from your home. This is an effective option if you air-condition most of the time. This allows you to make your house even more airtight which also reduces air leakage through the walls, another possible source of formaldehyde gas.

Q: I want to add some more insulation to my walls and I can get a good buy on some one-inch rigid foam insulation. Can I just glue it over the old drywall and glue new drywall to it?

A: This method works, but you should use foil-faced (on both sides) rigid foam insulation board. The foil provides a good surface for the adhesive and it is a good vapor barrier to keep moisture out of the wall cavity.

Leave a narrow gap between the insulation boards. Fill that gap and the gaps around electrical conduit boxes with silicone caulk for an airtight wall. Silicone is effective because it adheres well, is elastic, and has a very long life.

According to the Department of Natural Resources at Ball State University, some of the symptoms of formaldehyde sensitivity may include - burning or sore eyes, sinus irritation, dry or sore throat, runny nose, coughing, difficulty in breathing, headaches, dizziness, nausea, chest or abdominal pains, diarrhea, and rashes.

This is a very long list of symptoms and there could be many other causes of them. If you have any of these symptoms, <u>contact your physician first</u>. Testing your home for formaldehyde would also be helpful so your physician has more information. Information on the home test kits is shown on page 99. A detailed formaldehyde background information booklet is supplied with the home test kits.

Individual sensitivity to formaldehyde varies significantly. According to National Indoor Environmental Institute, many people can detect the odor of formaldehyde gas at only 0.05 parts per million (ppm). At 0.5 ppm, most people perceive throat irritation. At .1 ppm, it is a strong irritant to most people.

Figure #1 lists several common sources of formaldehyde gas inside homes. Many of these products either use formaldehyde-based adhesives or are treated with formaldehyde in a finishing process. Particleboard is a major contributor. The release of formaldehyde gas decreases with time as a product ages. In many products and materials, it decreases about 50% per year. Therefore, after two years, it only gives off 25% as much as when it was brand new.

High heat and humidity increase the release of formaldehyde gas. This is why the concentrations of formaldehyde are usually highest in early afternoon in an inadequately air-conditioned home. Inadequate air-conditioning, due to an oversized unit or improper evaporator coil, can result in high indoor humidity levels with very little ventilation.

The shorter one- to two-day home test kit indicates the maximum level possible that the formaldehyde level can reach. You can close up your house, let it get a little warmer than usual, and do the laundry and shower to increase the humidity level.

If you test for one day under these conditions and no excess formaldehyde gas is detected, it is a good indication that your house does not have a problem. Sometimes, it may be the short-term peaks in the gas concentration that cause problems for you.

Page 100 lists steps to reduce formaldehyde gas inside your home if the tests show a high level. There are many types of heat recovery ventilators (formerly called air-to-air heat exchangers) available. Your heating and cooling contractors should be familiar with several brands they can recommend. They range from simple window units to complete whole-house ventilation systems.

The whole-house types of heat recovery ventilator use a separate duct system from your central heating and air-conditioning systems. Stale air is often drawn from kitchens or bathrooms and fresh air outlets are located in several other rooms throughout the house. The ventilator brings in fresh outdoor air.

A blower circulates the air through the system. In the heat exchanger, the two air streams transfer the heat between them. The system can be automatically controlled by a timer or by humidity levels inside the house. The amount of energy saved (cooled air in the summer and heated air in the winter) can range from 50% to 80% depending on the system.

Household Sources of Formaldehyde	
Adhesives	Lubricants
Carpeting	Paints
Clothing - perm. press	Paper products
Cosmetics	Particle board
Deodorants	in cabinets
Detergents	in walls
Draperies	in floors
Dyes	Plastics
Fertilizers	automobile
Foam insulation	appliances
Fungicides	sports equip.
Furniture	Plywood
Leathers & furs	Shampoo *figure #1*

Suppliers/Labs for Formaldehyde Test Kits for Homes

AIR TECHNOLOGY LABS, 6687 N. Blackstone Ave., Fresno, CA 93710
(800) 354-2702 (209) 435-3545

DIY* - $35.00 - 1 device and materials for three tests
kit contains materials to analyze test
LAB - $60.00 - 2 devices - lab results received in two weeks
test sampling period is ideally for 16 to 24 hours, but can be less
(*- DIY means do-it-yourself)

AIR QUALITY RESEARCH, 4310 Miami Blvd., Durham, NC 27703
(800) 242-7472 (919) 544-2987

LAB - $72.50 - 1 test with lab analysis
test sampling period is for 5 to 7 days

HOMECheck Formaldehyde Test Kit

ATL, Inc. Air Technology Labs — 6687 N. Blackstone Ave., Ste. 103, Fresno, CA 93710 • 209-435-3545 • FAX 435-8503 • 800-354-2702

Find out if *FORMALDEHYDE GAS* is causing *DISCOMFORT IN YOUR HOME*

FEATURES

☛ **Do-It-Yourself**
Easy to use, no special training required

☛ **Answers On-The-Spot**
Does not have to be returned to a laboratory.

☛ **Sensitive, Measures Low Levels**
As low as 0.1 ppm of formaldehyde in an afternoon, or 0.02 ppm with overnight sampling

☛ **Makes *Three* Tests**
Test different places in the home, or before & after reducing formaldehyde levels

☛ **Low Cost**
A fraction of alternative methods

☛ **Uses Sampler Found In ASTM Standard Method**
ASTM D5014-89 "Standard Test Method for Measurement of Formaldehyde in Indoor Air (Passive Sampler Methodology)"

☛ **Provides Practical Information**
Booklet explains about formaldehyde and gives practical advice on how to improve your indoor air quality.

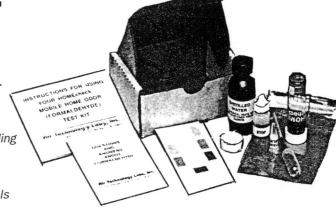

EACH HOMECheck TEST KIT PROVIDES

☛ **Complete Instructions**   ☛ **Simple Passive Bubbler™ sampler**

☛ **Supplies for three tests**   ☛ **Reference color comparison card**

☛ **Informational Booklet with practical advice on improving indoor air quality.**

Steps to Improve Indoor Air Quality and Lower Fomaldehyde Levels

A. Allow time

The source of formaldehyde vapors in new homes is often from particleboard products which use resins (glues) made from formaldehyde-containing products. The formaldehyde out-gasses in two forms. Free formaldehyde is formaldehyde that has not joined chemically with the product. Labile formaldehyde is formaldehyde that is only partially-combined with the product.

Over time, both sources of formaldehyde will decrease over time as it is slowly released by the product. The free formaldehyde will dissipate within weeks and its concentration will drop. Labile formaldehyde releases more slowly. On average, the total amount of formaldehyde given off by the product will decrease by about 50% per year. After two years, it will out-gas only 25% as much as it did initially.

B. Lower the humidity and temperature inside your home

Products containing formaldehyde resins out-gas more formaldehyde vapors as the temperature and humidity increase. In the winters, if the air in your house is dry and you keep your thermostat low, the level of formaldehyde will be low. The problem is often worst in the summer. Use your air conditioner because it both cools and dehumidifies. You can also just use a dehumidifier if your house stays cool enough in the summer.

C. Bring more fresh air into your home

Bringing more fresh air into your home, even if it is a little more humid, will dilute the formaldehyde vapors and therefore, lower the concentration. If you air-condition, you should only open the windows for a short period several times a day. This allows the air to change inside your home, but it does not allow time for the materials inside your home and the building materials themselves to absorb moisture from the humid summer air.

Using a heat recovery ventilator is the best method to bring in outdoor air efficiently. In the summer, the stale air exhausted outdoors, cools the incoming fresh air through a special heat exchanger. In the winter, it draws heat from the stale outgoing air and transfers it to the incoming air. These can save 50% or more of the energy that would otherwise be wasted. They are available through most ventilation contractors and some heat and cooling contractors.

If you do not air-condition in the summer, leave several windows open for cross-ventilation, not just one window. If you only open one window, depending on the direction of the breeze outdoors, it may create a slight negative pressure inside your home. This will draw air in through cracks and gaps in the walls and attic. Your walls and attic may have materials in them that contain an out-gas formaldehyde worsening the problem inside your home. This is particularly true during hot, humid summer weather.

D. Install the proper type of air cleaner

You must use a special air cleaner material (Purifil, permanganate, or alumina) to be effective for formaldehyde removal. Standard electronic or filter-type air cleaners will not remove it. Activated charcoal filters are not as effective as the materials listed above. Contact an air filtration specialist or contractor in your area.

E. Seal the formaldehyde-containing materials

Formaldehyde vapors may not only be coming out from products and materials you can see, but also from inside your walls. Carefully seal up all cracks and gaps (especially around sinks where plumbing penetrates the wall surface) with caulking or gaskets. Place inexpensive foam gaskets behind electrical wall outlet faceplates (switch off the circuit breakers before removing the faceplates.) Several effective finishes and coverings are two coats of polyurethane varnish, special low-perm vapor barrier paints, vinyl wallpaper and linoleum.

Q: My single pane windows are not in bad condition, but they waste a lot of energy and are hard to clean. How can I improve their efficiency without investing in entirely new thermal replacement windows?

A: There are several ways to improve the efficiency of your windows without a huge investment in all new replacement windows. These methods not only lower your heating and air-conditioning costs, but they reduce dust and outdoor noise inside your home and the fading of your furniture and curtains.

One excellent replacement window alternative is to install new do-it-yourself tilt-in replacement sash kits in your existing window frames. The tilt-in feature allows you to clean the windows from indoors. Installing these kits costs less than half as much as new replacement windows. You can install one yourself in less than an hour.

There are many glass options available, including super-efficient argon gas-filled low-e glass and tinted glass for hot climates. Filling the gap between the panes of glass with argon gas increases the efficiency and reduces outdoor noise. The sash frame is made of wood with options of aluminum-cladding.

If only the channels in your window frames are worn so that the sash is loose and leaky, you can buy inexpensive do-it-yourself replacement frame channels. One type of replacement channel is designed so you can easily remove the entire window sash from indoors for cleaning.

If your window sash won't stay open in the summer and keeps sliding down, you can install another design of airtight replacement channel. In addition to stopping air leaks, the channels create a snug spring-friction fit to allow your windows to slide up easily, yet stay open.

Applying new do-it-yourself insulating window film saves energy and greatly reduces the sun's fading rays on your furniture. This film has a special low-E coating on it, similar to the new super-high-efficiency window glass. Window film is very easy to install yourself.

There are several film options. You can install nearly-clear window film which you can't even tell is on your windows. This reduces heat loss in the winter and heat gain in the summer.

For greater heat reduction in the summer, you can apply a tinted low-e film. You may choose to use a clear film on east and north windows and a tinted film on south and west windows.

Q: I am concerned about global warming from using too much energy and inefficient products. About how much carbon dioxide (CO_2) gas is produced from various types of energy we use?

A: You will be surprised at how much CO_2 gas is produced. Each kilowatt-hour (KWH) of electricity you use produces from 2.14 to 2.37 pounds of CO_2 gas depending on whether oil or coal generation is used. One KWH is the amount of electricity used by one 100-watt light bulb in just 10 hours.

Based on the usable energy output, burning natural gas produces the least amount of CO_2 gas. For one million Btu's of energy, natural gas produces 118 pounds of CO_2 gas compared to 694 pounds from coal-generated electricity

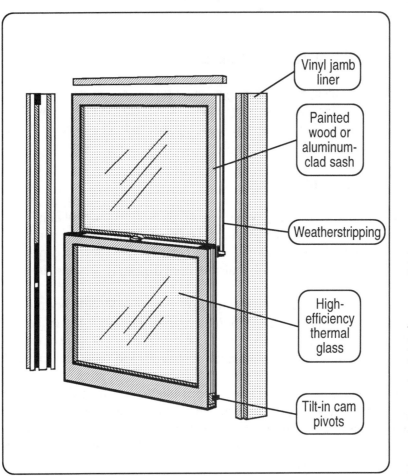

Vinyl jamb liner

Painted wood or aluminum-clad sash

Weatherstripping

High-efficiency thermal glass

Tilt-in cam pivots

Inefficient, leaky old windows not only waste energy, but they cause chilly drafts inside your home. There are several improvement options. Tilt-in replacement sashes cost less than complete replacement windows and you can save the labor cost by doing the installation yourself. The various glass and frame options are shown on the following pages. A less expensive option is installing new airtight frame channels in your existing double hung windows. One design allows you to remove the sash for cleaning. The other design has a spring-loaded center section for a tight fit. Product information is shown on the following pages.

Another option is applying low-e insulating window film to your windows. This keeps heat inside in the winter and blocks reflected heat from sidewalks and patios in the summer. The plastic film material itself blocks much of the sun's fading rays and the low-e coating blocks even more rays.

Manufacturers of Insulating Window Film

Product # - color	Solar heat reduction	Heat loss reduction	UV light reduction	Glare reduction
COURTAULDS PERFORMANCE FILMS, P. O. Box 5068, Martinsville, VA 24115				
"Vista" and "Llumar" brands - (800) 345-6088				
"Gila Sunshine" brand - (800) 528-4481				
"VISTA" brand - professionally installed only				
V30 - gray	59%	1%	99%	66%
V45 - gray	46%	1%	99%	48%
V58 - gray	35%	1%	99%	60%
"LLUMAR" brand - professionally installed only				
E-1220SR	79%	30%	99%	81%
DL15 - bronze	61%	8%	99%	84%
DL15G - gray	58%	10%	99%	83%
DL30GR - green	54%	4%	99%	66%
N-1020 - gray	63%	4%	99%	73%
N-1035 - gray	52%	4%	99%	60%
N-1050 - gray	44%	3%	99%	45%
N-1065 - gray	31%	1%	99%	28%
N-1020B - bronze	77%	14%	99%	77%
N-1035B - bronze	62%	11%	99%	58%
N-1050B - bronze	51%	8%	99%	57%
"GILA SUNSHINE" brand - do-it-yourself from retail outlets				
Low-e	55%	30%	99%	81%
3M ENERGY CONTROL PROD., 3M Center, St. Paul, MN 55144 - (800) 328-1684 ext. 228 (612) 736-2388				
Professionally installed only				
LE35AMARL - amber	70%	30%	99%	65%
LE20SIAR - silver	73%	23%	97%	81%
LE30CUARL - copper	64%	26%	98%	64%
LE50AMARL - amber	55%	29%	97%	44%
MADICO, 45 Industrial Pky., Woburn, MA 01888 - (800) 225-1926 (617) 935-7850				
Professionally installed only				
SB-340 - bronze	66%	17%	96%	65%
TSG-335 - gray	53%	12%	98%	55%
NG-50 - gray	51%	5%	96%	48%
NB-50 - bronze	51%	5%	96%	48%
NG-35 - gray	61%	10%	96%	59%
NB-35 - bronze	61%	10%	96%	59%
METALLIZED PRODUCTS, 2544 Terminal Dr. S., St. Petersburg, FL 33712 - (800) 777-1770 (813) 327-2544				
Professionally installed only				
SW150 SILVER 15	84%	29%	96%	84%
SW150 SILVER 30	65%	20%	96%	60%
Sold do-it-yourself or professionally installed				
SW150 GRAY 30	60%	15%	96%	58%
SW150 BRONZE 30	61%	15%	96%	57%

Manfacturers of Replacement Sashes and Channels

CRAFTLINE, 1125 Ford St., Maumee, OH 43537 - (800) 283-3311 (419) 893-3311
frame - ponderosa pine interior — wood or aluminum clad exterior   colors - white, bronze, gray, beige
glazing options - double insulated, low-e coatings, argon gas filled

CRESTLINE, PO Box 8007, Wausau, WI 54402 - (800) 552-4111 (715) 845-1161
frame - pine interior — aluminum exterior   colors - pewter-tone, white or almond — brown
glazing options - double insulated is standard, Smart R® is double insulated glass with low-e and argon gas filled airspaces

KOLBE & KOLBE, 1323 S. Eleventh Ave., Wausau, WI 54401 - (715) 842-5666
frame - pine interior — aluminum clad or K-Kron finish exterior   colors - rustic, white, beige, sand, green, custom
glazing options - low-e coating, argon gas filled, $^7/_8$" glazing is available

MARVIN WINDOWS, PO Box 100, Warroad, MN 56763 - (800) 346-5128 (800) 552-1167 in MN
frame - ponderosa pine interior — wood or aluminum clad exterior   colors - white, brown, gray, bronze or 50 optional
glazing options - double insulated, low-e coating, argon gas filled, solar gray or solar bronze glass, beveled, obscure glass

QUAKER CITY MANUFACTURING, 201 Elmwood Ave., Sharon Hill, PA 19079 - (215) 586-4770
type - "Window Fixer Replacement Channels" are spring-sealing replacement channels that are manufactured for 1$^3/_8$" thick double hung wood sash with ½" or $^3/_8$" parting bead. These channels will hold up to 20 pounds per sash; 20 for the upper and 20 for the lower.
type - "Takeout Channels" make windows removable for painting or cleaning. They must be used in conjunction with a set of "Window Fixer Replacement Channels".
type - "Power Lifters" are designed to balance and hold a window open. They replace worn-out or broken window balances.

SEMCO WINDOWS, PO Box 378, Merrill, WI 54452 - (800) 333-2206 (715) 536-9411
frame - southern pine interior — wood or aluminum clad exterior   colors - green, white, bronze, burgundy, taupe, brown
glazing options - double insulated, low-e coating, argon gas filled

VETTER, One Wausau Center, Wausau, WI 54402 - (800) 826-1707
frame - ponderosa pine interior — wood or aluminum clad exterior   colors - sandtone, white, shale or royal brown
glazing options - double insulated is standard, tempered, low-e coating, argon gas filled, bronze or gray tinted, quick frost — light film over the window or obscure so no one can see in

WEATHER SHIELD, PO Box 309, Medford, WI 54451 - (800) 477-6808 (715) 748-2100
frame - pine, maple, oak, cherry wood interior — natural primed, Poly I, Flexicolor™, Contempra aluminum exterior
colors - white, desert tan, adobe and Hartford green are standard colors — nine custom or an additional 120 "special-order"
glazing options - $^5/_8$" or $^7/_{16}$" Insul, low-e coating, argon gas

---

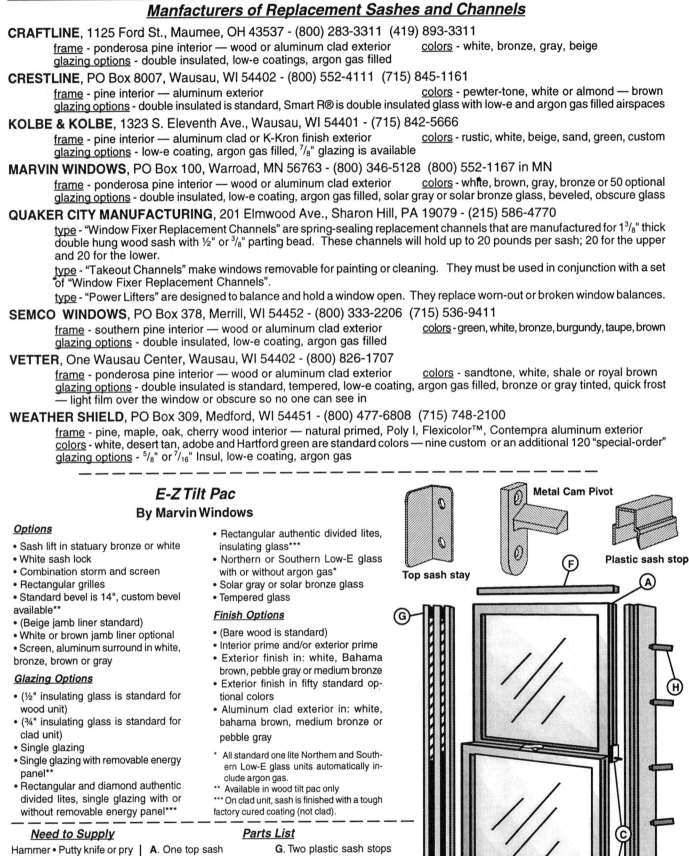

E-Z Tilt Pac
By Marvin Windows

Top sash stay   **Metal Cam Pivot**   **Plastic sash stop**

Options
- Sash lift in statuary bronze or white
- White sash lock
- Combination storm and screen
- Rectangular grilles
- Standard bevel is 14°, custom bevel available**
- (Beige jamb liner standard)
- White or brown jamb liner optional
- Screen, aluminum surround in white, bronze, brown or gray

Glazing Options
- (½" insulating glass is standard for wood unit)
- (¾" insulating glass is standard for clad unit)
- Single glazing
- Single glazing with removable energy panel**
- Rectangular and diamond authentic divided lites, single glazing with or without removable energy panel***

- Rectangular authentic divided lites, insulating glass***
- Northern or Southern Low-E glass with or without argon gas*
- Solar gray or solar bronze glass
- Tempered glass

Finish Options
- (Bare wood is standard)
- Interior prime and/or exterior prime
- Exterior finish in: white, Bahama brown, pebble gray or medium bronze
- Exterior finish in fifty standard optional colors
- Aluminum clad exterior in: white, bahama brown, medium bronze or pebble gray

* All standard one lite Northern and Southern Low-E glass units automatically include argon gas.
** Available in wood tilt pac only
*** On clad unit, sash is finished with a tough factory cured coating (not clad).

Need to Supply
Hammer • Putty knife or pry bar • Screwdrivers — standard and phillips • Finish nails • Common nails • Pliers • Inside casing • Fiberglass insulation • Shim stock • Nail set

Parts List
A. One top sash
B. One bottom sash
C. Four metal cam pivots, 2 left, 2 right with 8 screws
D. Left vinyl jamb liner
E. Right vinyl jamb liner
F. Inside header part stop

G. Two plastic sash stops
H. Metal jamb liner brackets (number will vary per unit size)
I. Two sash retainer clips (attached to bottom sash) with 6 screws, three per clip
J. Two exterior top sash stays

5. Modification of Sash

A. Before trimming left side of both sash to fit, measure between jambs, (Measurement A). Left side should be trimmed so the final width of sash is ¾" less than frame opening (Measurement A).

Example: If measurement A (distance between both jambs) is 32", sash should be cut to measure 31¼".

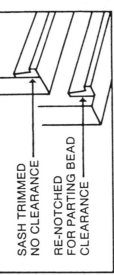

Sash preparation for Take-Out-Window Channels

STOP ANGLE
RIGHT JAMB
CHECK RAIL
SOFT SIDE
MEASUREMENT A
STANDARD BLIND STOPS BOTH SIDES
JAMBS WITH OR WITHOUT PLOW

Illustrations below show upper sash

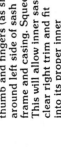

SASH TRIMMED NO CLEARANCE

RE-NOTCHED FOR PARTING BEAD CLEARANCE

B. After sash has been trimmed, you will note that check rail (section of meeting rail) clearance has been cut off on left sides of both sash.

These must be re-notched to establish a full ½" clearance so that they match notches on right sides of both sash.

C. Round off sharp corners, which may remain from trimming left side of sash, so windows will release easily.

D. Sash can now be inserted by pushing left side of outer sash against outer Take-Out Channel. This will allow right side of sash to clear right inside trim and parting bead, allowing sash to fit into its proper outer channel. Inner sash is easily installed by hooking thumb and fingers (as shown) around left side of sash frame and casing. Squeeze. This will allow inner sash to clear right trim and fit into its proper inner channel.

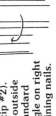

Window Fixer take-out channels

1. Temporarily remove inside stops (trim) at top and sides of window. Using a 2" wide putty knife and working from top to bottom, pry out only ⅛" before moving to the next nail, etc. Then working upwards pry out about ½" more at each nail; as you reach the top, the strip should lift out easily. Now remove the sash. Some older windows have wood side parting stops (beads), which must be removed and discarded. The top parting stop (bead) must be shortened to allow clearance of channels, (a full 1¼" on left side and a full ½" on right side). Reinstall the top parting stop (bead) after completing steps 2 & 3. Ropes or chains must be cut. Weights will then drop down within cover, remove pulleys. Also, metal-channels, (balances) in which the sash ride up and down, if used in your system, must be removed. To remove metal balances; if nailed, simply pry loose with putty knife, otherwise remove screws and lift out with the sash.

SHORTEN TOP PARTING BEAD
REMOVE SIDE PARTING BEAD

If there is any excess of lumpy paint along the edge of the sash, this should be scraped off and sanded so sash ride smoothly in the new channels.

2. Place Take-Out Channel in left side of window against outside stop.

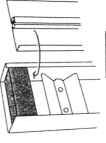

Attach with nails supplied. Snap left standard window channel into Take-Out channel (be sure it seats itself behind roll-over flanges). Left side of channel installation is now complete.

3. Install stop angle from Take-Out channel package (Note tip #2). Position it against right outside stop, now place right standard channel against stop angle on right jamb. Attach with remaining nails.

4. Re-install top parting stop (bead) and inside trim which was removed in Step 1.

Quaker City Mfg. Co.

How to install Window Fixer Replacement Channels

Take your time. Read the instructions carefully and follow them step by step. This is one job that usually goes rather easily.

1: Temporarily remove inside trim (stop) at top and side of the window. Using a 2" wide putty knife, work from the top of the trim down. Pry out trim about ⅛" at each nail. Then, working upwards, pry out about ½" more at each nail. When you reach the top, the trim should lift out easily.

2: Remove nails, screws or staples holding old metal channels. Pull sash and channels out of the window and place on a chair. Disconnect the old channels and discard. Scrape off any excess or lumpy paint along the edge of the sash and sand smooth.

If your windows have sash cord or chain, see "Special Instructions for Older Windows" below.

3: Before fitting sash in new channels, make sure that the new channels fit your window. Note that the angled end goes on the bottom and slants toward the outside. If the top parting bead interferes with channel fit at the top of the window, cut ½" off each end of the parting bead. If the channel must be trimmed, see "Cutting Instructions" below.

4: Fit the new channels on to each side of the sash. Make sure both sash are held securely by the channels.

5: Pick up both sash and channels together and place them into the window frame. Insert the bottom first. When the bottom butts against the outside stop, tilt the entire unit into the frame. Unit will now stand securely by itself.

6: Now test the channels. Move the sash up and down in the channels. If the sash are too tight, ease the flange of the channels away from the sash (picture A). If the sash are too loose, press flange towards the channels (picture B).

7: To leave sufficient space for future adjustment if required, use a putty knife as a spacer while nailing channels in place. Place putty knife blade between the channel and the outside stop at the top of the window. Now nail upper portion of each channel into place. Raise sash, again use putty knife to provide space at the bottom of the window between outside stop and channel. Now nail the bottom portion of the channel into place. Replace inside trim. Again, allow the thickness of the knife blade between the channel and the trim while nailing trim in place.

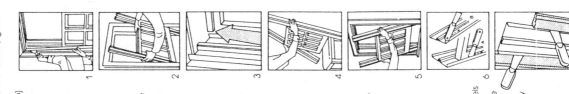

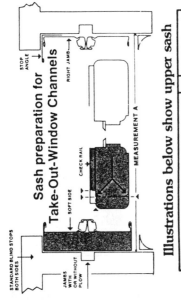

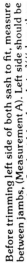

Q: I want to install new replacement windows to lower my utility bills and for the easy cleaning and neat appearance. Vinyl and fiberglass windows are maintenance-free, but are they efficient and durable?

A: High-quality vinyl or fiberglass frame replacement windows are very energy efficient. You can order some windows with super-efficient glass of R-8 insulation value. Installing these windows can cut the heat loss through your windows by up to 90%. Many designs tilt in for easy cleaning.

Fiberglass or vinyl frame and sash material offers many advantages. The material itself is a good insulator. Good-quality vinyl frames and sashes are made with many insulating air cavities inside the frames. This reduces heat loss and increases the strength and rigidity of the entire window.

Several replacement window manufacturers inject polyurethane foam inside of the frame and sash cavities. This further improves the insulation value. Since the frames are custom sized to your old window openings, the foam insulation can be injected as they are being assembled.

Vinyl and fiberglass windows are maintenance-free. Very little dirt sticks to these materials and they are easily hosed or wiped off. On vinyl windows, the color goes completely through the vinyl so small scratches are not apparent. Scratches on the fiberglass can easily be touched up.

Fiberglass, although more expensive than vinyl, is extremely durable and attractive. Since fiberglass expands and contracts with temperature changes much less than vinyl, it can be made to tighter toler-

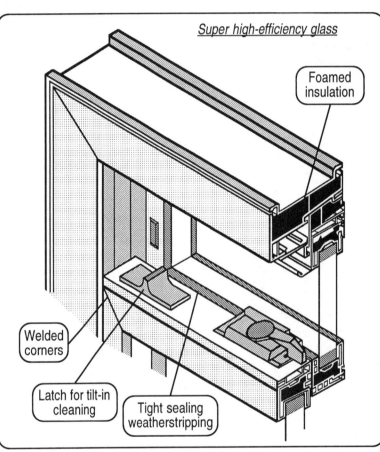

Super high-efficiency glass

Foamed insulation

Welded corners

Latch for tilt-in cleaning

Tight sealing weatherstripping

ances. This provides long-term air-tightness and smooth operation.

There are significant differences in the quality of various types of vinyl replacement windows. A poorly-constructed window often lacks adequate rigidity, especially in very hot weather. The internal frame supports and webbing, which you cannot see, affect both the rigidity and the insulation value of the window and sash frames.

The best types of vinyl windows use welded construction at the corners. This forms a much stronger unit than one assembled with screws. The expansion of the vinyl from temperature changes may cause the screws to loosen over time.

If you are going to the expense of having new replacement windows installed, you should select high-efficiency glass. Most replacement window manufacturers give you several glass options.

At the very least, insist on double pane, low-e, argon gas-filled windows for almost any climate. In addition to saving energy, the low-e coating blocks the fading rays and the argon gas cuts outdoor noise. You can also now get double pane glass with two low-e films stretched in between them. This forms three gaps filled with super-insulating krypton gas.

Q: Does it waste electricity to put hot food in the refrigerator right after we eat or should we wait until it cools down a little?

A: From an energy-efficiency standpoint, any hot food you put in your refrigerator forces the motor to run more. People often leave warm food out to cool too long and they run the risk of food poisoning. Check with your local health department for safe cooling time periods. If you do put hot food in your refrigerator, cover it with a tight-fitting lid.

In the information provided on each manufacturer's windows, all of the frames materials are vinyl unless noted as fiberglass. Unless indicated as *"foam filled"*, the frames are hollow. The available styles are listed (awning, double-hung, slider, etc.). The types of high efficiency glazing are also listed. Unless otherwise listed, all the manufacturers offer standard double pane glass. The high-efficiency glazing options are double pane low-e, with or without argon gas in the gap, triple pane (with or without low-e coatings or argon-gas), standard Heat Mirror, Heat Mirror Plus, and Heat Mirror Super Glass.

"Low-e" refers to a microscopically-thin layer of heat reflecting atoms on the surface of the glass. This is invisible to the eye, but it blocks heat loss in the winter and heat gain in the summer. It also blocks much of the sun's fading rays. The clear argon gas (instead of air) filling in between the panes of glass insulates better than air. It also deadens much of the sound transmission from outdoors. Argon is an inert gas so it is safe even if it leaks out of broken glass. Krypton (safe inert gas) is also sometimes used.

Heat Mirror is glass technology that suspends thin clear plastic films inside double pane windows. The low-e coating is applied to these pieces of film. Standard Heat Mirror uses one low-e coated film in between double pane glass. In Super Glass, there are two pieces of low-e film in between the two glass panes and the gaps are filled with krypton gas. This forms three insulating gaps overall. Heat Mirror Plus glass has one piece of low-e film and a low-e coating on the glass too. When selecting the type of glazing, compare the efficiency values for the entire window, not just the glass itself. The airtightness, insulation value of the frame, type of edge spacer between the panes are also very important. Just the R-value of the glass does not tell the entire story.

As a reference, single pane glass has an insulating R-value of R-0.8. Standard clear double pane glass is R-2. Double pane low-e coated glass is about R-2.9. Adding argon or krypton rasies it to about R-4. Standard heat mirror is about R-5. Heat Mirror Plus is about R-7. Heat Mirror Super Glass is about R-9. Triple pane with two low-e coatings and argon gas is about R-9.

Manufacturers of High-Efficiency Vinyl or Fiberglass Windows

ACORN BUILDING COMPONENTS, 12620 Westwood, Detroit, MI 48223 - (313) 272-5700
> styles - casement, double hung, slider
> type of glass - double pane low-e argon gas

ALENCO, P.O. Box 4466, Peachtree City, GA 30265 - (800) 476-8037
> styles - awning, casement, double hung, slider
> type of glass - double pane low-e argon gas

CERTAINTEED CORP., P.O. Box 860, Valley Forge, PA 19482 -(800) 274-8530 (215) 341-7000
> styles - awning, casement, double hung, slider
> type of glass - double pane low-e argon gas

CRESTLINE, P.O. Box 8007, Wausau, WI 54402 - (800) 552-4111
> styles - casement, double hung, slider
> type of glass - double pane low-e argon gas

FIBERLUX INC., 59 S. Terrace Ave., Mt. Vernon, NY 10461 - (800) 688-7711 (914) 664-7111
> styles - double hung, slider
> type of glass - double pane low-e argon gas

KAUFMAN WINDOW & DOOR, 13271 Mt. Elliott, Detroit, MI 48212 - (313) 893-9500
> styles - awning, casement, double hung, slider
> type of glass - double pane low-e argon gas

L. B. PLASTICS, INC., P.O. Box 907, Mooresville, NC 28115 - (800) 752-7739 (704) 663-1543
> styles - awning, casement, double hung, slider, tilt-turn
> type of glass - double pane low-e argon gas, Heat Mirror®

LOUISIANA-PACIFIC, 324 Wooster Rd. N., Barberton, OH 44203 - (800) 358-2954 (216) 745-1661
    <u>styles</u> - awning, casement, double hung, slider
    <u>type of glass</u> - double pane low-e argon, Heat Mirror Plus®

KENSINGTON MFG., P.O. Box 572, Leechburg, PA 15656 - (800) 444-4972 (412) 845-8133
    <u>styles</u> - awning, casement, double hung, slider   <u>frame</u> - foam insulation-filled
    <u>type of glass</u> - double pane low-e argon gas or krypton gas

PEERLESS PRODUCTS, P.O. Box 2469, Shawnee Mission, KS 66201 - (800) 279-9999 (913) 432-2232
    <u>styles</u> - awning, casement, double hung, slider
    <u>type of glass</u> - double pane low-e argon gas

PORTAL, INC., 10 Tracy Dr., Avon Industrial Park, Avon, MA 02322 - (800) 966-3030 (508) 588-3030
    <u>styles</u> - awning, casement, double hung, hopper, slider
    <u>type of glass</u> - double pane low-e

THERMAL INDUSTRIES, 301 Brushton Ave., Pittsburgh, PA 15221 - (412) 244-6400
    <u>styles</u> - awning, casement, double hung, slider   <u>frame</u> - foam insulation-filled
    <u>type of glass</u> - double low-e argon gas and triple pane

THERMETIC GLASS, INC., Rt. 1, Box 1A, Toluca, IL 61369 - (800) 747-4774 (815) 452-2371
    <u>styles</u> - awning, casement, double hung, slider
    <u>type of glass</u> - double pane low-e argon gas, also with two low-e coatings

TRACO, P.O. Box 805, Warrendale, PA 15095 - (800) 837-7002 (412) 776-7000
    <u>styles</u> - awning, casement, double hung, slider
    <u>type of glass</u> - double low-e argon gas, Heat Mirror®

ULTRA BUILDING SYSTEMS, 1000 Main Ave., Clifton, NJ 07011 - (800) 843-9353 (201) 777-1112
    <u>styles</u> - awning, casement, double hung, slider
    <u>type of glass</u> - double pane low-e argon gas, Heat Mirror®, Super Glass®

VINYL THERM, 321 W. 83rd St., Bloomington, MN 55420 - (800) 876-4884 (612) 884-4329
    <u>styles</u> - awning, casement, double hung, hopper, slider
    <u>type of glass</u> - double pane low-e, triple pane, also with argon gas

VINYLUME PRODUCTS, INC., 4021 Mahoning Ave., Youngstown, OH 44515 - (216) 799-2000
    <u>styles</u> - casement, double hung, slider
    <u>type of glass</u> - double pane low-e, also with argon gas

VINYLMAX CORP., 891 Redna Ter., Cincinnati, OH 45215 - (800) 837-9103 (513) 772-0364
    <u>styles</u> - double hung, slider   <u>frame</u> - foam insulation-filled
    <u>type of glass</u> - double pane low-e argon gas

VYNEX CORP., 135 40th St., Pittsburgh, PA 15201 - (800) 666-8969 (412) 681-3800
    <u>styles</u> - casement, double hung, slide
    <u>type of glass</u> - double pane low-e argon, Heat Mirror®

WEATHER SHIELD MFG., P.O. Box 309, Medford, WI 54451 - (800) 477-6808 (715) 748-2100
    <u>styles</u> - awning, casement, double hung, slider
    <u>type of glass</u> - double pane low-e argon gas, triple pane two low-e argon gas

WILMES WINDOW MFG. CO. INC., 234 W. 23rd St., Ferdinand, IN 47532 - (812) 367-1811
    <u>styles</u> - awning, casement, double hung, slider
    <u>type of glass</u> - double pane low-e, also with argon gas

WINSTROM MFG. CORP., P.O. Box 310, Park Forest, IL 60466 - (708) 748-8200
    <u>styles</u> - awning, casement, double hung, slider
    <u>type of glass</u> - double pane low-e argon gas

WINTER SEAL, 5500 Enterprise Blvd., Toledo, OH 43612 - (419) 729-8520
    <u>styles</u> - casement, double hung, slider   <u>frame</u> - fiberglass frame
    <u>type of glass</u> - double pane low-e argon gas

Builder's Quick Reference Guide

All vinyl construction
Virtually maintenance-free — never requires painting; thermal efficiency helps to lower fuel costs; moving parts glide easily on non-stick surface.

Welded frame construction
Helps eliminate racking and twisting during installation; increases energy efficiency.

Multi-chamber frame sections
Add structural strength; enhance the natural insulation properties of vinyl.

Perimeter center fin weatherstripping
Creates a tight seal against air and water infiltration and reduces sound transmission; exceeds industry standards.

Insulating glass
Provides energy efficiency; substantially reduces outside noises.

Removable operating sash
Provides a port for transporting building materials; removes from the inside for easy cleaning.

Telescoping sash construction
Increases rigidity and strength to help eliminate racking and twisting.

Interlocking meeting rail
Reduces air and water infiltration; resists lock tampering.

Pick-resistent meeting rail cam locks*
Provide added security; meet AAMA 1302.5 voluntary specifications for forced-entry-resistant prime windows.

Sill latches*
Lock automatically when ventilating sash is closed.

Channel glazing on operating sash
Reduces glass breakage; makes glass replacement easy.

Sloped step sill with drain slots
Drains rainwater to the outside; provides a tight seal to reduce air infiltration; protects weatherstripping from the elements.

Screens with fiberglass cloth
Fit into concealed channels to prevent accidental dislodgement; easily cleaned fiberglass will not rust, crease or corrode.

Heavy-duty brass rollers (on Horizontal Slider)
Provide strength and ensure smooth, quiet operation.

Full frame fins
Help reduce air and water leakage; fin holes speed installation.

Full-length sash handle
Easy to grasp; no screws to pull loose.

Snap-off fin
Convenient for multiple unit mulling and stacking.

Factory-adjusted sash balances
Operate smoothly; hold the sash in the proper open position.

Decorator shapes and colors
Provide design options for the most demanding home buyers.

*Either cam lock or sill latch is standard depending on model

Fusion welding at the corners of the master frame add strength and insure durability

All-vinyl construction protects against inclement weather while glazing channel protects glass

Operating sash can be removed from inside the building so cleaning is simple

Center fin pile weatherstripping increases energy efficiency by sealing out air and water

Meeting rail interlock design plus cam lock reduce air infiltration and provide security

Drainage slot in sill allows water to drain off quickly and easily

Corrosion-resistant rollers insure smooth, quiet operation every time (on slider model window)

Block-and-tackle balancing system provides steady, even sash operation (on single hung model window)

Lift handle designed as an integral part of the sash and latch engages automatically when window is closed

Q: I saw some very attractive inexpensive interior storm windows. My old windows are ugly and leaky, but I cannot afford replacement windows now. How efficient are storm windows and what type do you recommend?

A: The new designs and materials used for interior storm windows are very efficient, attractive, and durable. With the many frame colors and paintable magnetic strips, you often don't even notice the storm windows.

At a cost of about 25% as much as replacement windows, storm windows are an excellent do-it-yourself alternative. If you air-condition, leave them up all year. It only takes a few minutes to put them up or take them down.

In addition to saving energy year-round and improving your comfort, especially at night, interior storm windows block the sun's fading rays. I installed a magnetic acrylic storm window under my skylight to reduce fading.

Good-quality frames and attachment methods are important to realize the maximum savings on your utility bills. If you install the storm windows properly with an airtight seal, you'll notice how much more quiet it is. A rigid plastic (often vinyl) frame is usually used. The most common glazing materials are clear acrylic (Plexiglas) or polycarbonate plastic sheets. Acrylic remains crystal clear for years. Polycarbonate (bullet-proof glass) is more expensive, but virtually unbreakable.

The primary difference among the various storm windows is the method that the frame is attached and sealed to the wall or window frame. The most common methods are magnetic strips, hook-and-loop, and tape.

The magnetic attachment method is one of the easiest to install and best sealing. A thin magnetic strip is formed into the storm window frame. An adhesive-backed paintable steel strip is stuck to the window frame or wall. You just press the storm frame against the strip and it sticks and seals.

One unique design uses tiny flexible bellows (like a refrigerator door seal) between the storm window frame and the magnetic strip. This allows it to conform to uneven old window frames and handle temperature expansion.

One hook-and-loop (Velcro®) attachment method uses an extra inner gasket next to the hook-and-loop strips. This produces an airtight seal and is compliant with rough and warped window frames.

Super-efficient low-e glass has recently become available for storm windows. Although it is somewhat heavier and more expensive than the clear plastic glazings, low-e glass saves more energy and is durable.

Q: What is the cause of an ice dam on a roof? Is it a sign of good energy efficiency since the roof stays so cold?

A: An ice dam is a sign of energy inefficiency. It is formed when heat, escaping from the ceiling into the attic, causes snow to melt on the roof. At night, the water refreezes and forms the dam. This blocks the water flow down the roof and forces it up under the shingles causing leaks.

The best way to stop the formation of damaging ice dams is to improve the energy efficiency of your ceiling. Also, increase the attic ventilation to make sure the roof stays cold enough so the snow does not repeatedly melt.

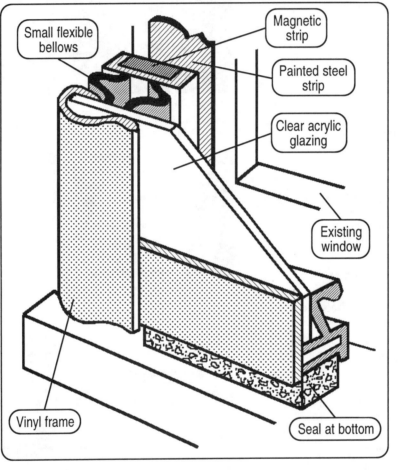

Small flexible bellows

Magnetic strip

Painted steel strip

Clear acrylic glazing

Existing window

Vinyl frame

Seal at bottom

Interior storm windows are effective and energy efficient both during heating and air-conditioning. They also block much of the sun's fading rays and the transmission of outdoor noise. On a cold winter night, you will feel more comfortably warm sitting near a window covered by an interior storm window. I have listed the highest-quality interior storm windows available.

These energy-efficient types of interior storm windows are easy to install yourself. Many of the manufacturers and retail dealers will sell you the materials (frame pieces, magnetic, steel, or Velcro strips, acrylic glazing, etc.) to install the storm windows yourself. It is much less expensive to install them yourself. Some manufacturers sell the assembled frame/window units and others sell the parts to join together. It is often easier and less expensive to buy the clear acrylic glazing at a local plastics outlet than to have it shipped from the storm window company.

When selecting the proper interior storm window for your house, consider the evenness of the surface where it will attach. If it is very uneven, a bellows design or Velcro attachment method is a good choice. You can also mount a narrow metal angle inside the window frame and attach any of these storms windows to it. If you plan to leave your storm windows up year-round, this is a good installation method. For very large windows, a heavy gauge frame will hold its shape and seal best.

Using low-e (low-emissivity) glass is the most efficient and scratch-resistant storm window material. It is called pyrolitic or hard coat low-e coating. It is invisible, but it blocks much of the heat flow through windows, both from going out in the winter and coming in in the summer. It is also very effective for blocking the sun's fading rays. Check your Yellow Pages under windows or storm windows. Ask local dealers if they will make these windows for you. They are almost always custom-made and are not for the do-it-yourselfer. Several of the major glass manufacturers that make pyrolitic low-e glass are LOF and Ford Glass.

— —

Manufacturers of Interior Storm Windows

ENERGY CONTROL PROD., 1214 Charles St., Huntington, IN 46750 - (800) 258-8468 (219) 356-6256
frame - vinyl (extra-rigid heavy duty) - nine colors   attachment - magnetic
glazing - acrylic (has a special gasket around the glazing inside the frame),

MAGNETITE, 8356 Tom Dr., Baton Rouge, LA 70815 - (800) 624-8483 (504) 927-8712
frame - vinyl   attachment - magnetic
glazing - acrylic

MODERN PLASTICS, 678 Howard Ave., Bridgeport, CT 06605 - (800) 243-9696 (203) 333-3128
frame - vinyl   attachment - magnetic or mechanical clips
glazing - acrylic or polycarbonate

PANELAIR, 203 Sparks St., Brockton, MA 02402 - (508) 588-8900
frame - vinyl   attachment - magnetic
glazing - acrylic or polycarbonate

PLASKOLITE, P.O. Box 1497, Columbus, OH 43216 - (800) 848-9124 (614) 294-3281
frame - vinyl   attachment - magnetic (uses flexible bellows design)
glazing - acrylic
note - only available through dealers - The dealers may sell the materials to you for do-it-yourself installation, but they are generally only sold installed.

SEAL MASTER, 10431 Lexington Dr., Knoxville, TN 37932 - (615) 966-3000
frame - vinyl   attachment - magnetic
glazing - acrylic
note - only sold installed through a dealer network - If you want to purchase a do-it-yourself kit, Panelair (listed above) will sell these windows in kit form.

THERMO-PRESS, 5406 Distributor Dr., Richmond, VA 23225 - (804) 231-2964
frame - vinyl   attachment - Velcro or mechanical clips
glazing - acrylic

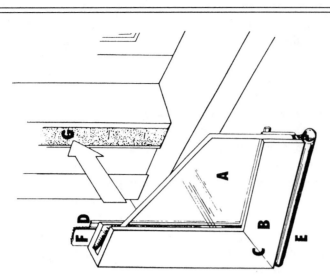

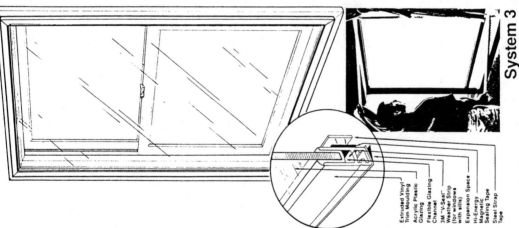

System 3

Extruded Vinyl
Trim Moulding
Acrylic Plastic
Glazing
Flexible Glazing
Channel
3M "V-Seal"
Weather Strip
(for windows
with sills)
Expansion Space
Hi-Energy
Magnetic
Sealing Tape
Steel Strap
Tape

ECP Brand Magnetic Rigid Insulating Window

How much of your home heat goes out the windows? Think about it a minute. If you have a dozen 4' x 4' windows in your home, that's almost 200 square feet of window area. If those windows aren't well insulated, it's a big hole in your insulation program.

The Energy Control People from ECPcan help plug that hole with an insulating system to fit your needs and budget. One of our answers is the Magnetic Rigid Insulating Window.

Inside installation
☐ Easy to put up and take down
☐ Reduces air infiltration more effectively than most exterior storm windows
☐ Installs on any wood, steel or aluminum window

Heavy-duty crystal-clear acrylic glazing
☐ Good visibility; non-yellowing
☐ High impact strength — many times greater than that of equivalent thickness of glass
☐ Minimal care and maintenance required

Strong extruded-vinyl trim moulding with flexible channel gasket
☐ Reduces conductive heat loss much more effectively than metal
☐ Flexible glazing channel is additional seal against air infiltration and noise; also helps prevent bowing of frame

Continuous hi-energy magnetic sealing tape
☐ Attracted to steel strap tape on window moulding
☐ Provides easy mounting and removal
☐ Seals tightly around entire frame like magnetic refrigerator door to reduce air and noise infiltration

Creates dead-air insulating space
☐ Reduces heat loss by 55% on a single-glazed window.
☐ Makes a single-glazed window a double-glazed window
☐ Makes a double-glazed window a triple-glazed window
☐ Reduces noise transmission significantly
☐ Added to present storm window systems, this system can provide the benefits of quadruple glazing

A **ACRYLIC.** .125 (1/8" thick). This material is known for its fine clarity, and its non-yellowing, distortion-free tendencies. In fact, our acrylic has shown itself to be as transparent as the finest optical glass, weighs half as much, and has 17 times the impact resistance! Thermo-Press Windows are available in clear as well as tinted and ultra-violet filtering acrylics.

B **PVC FRAME.** Our frames are multi-durometer Poly-Vinyl Chloride. This PVC extruded frame attaches permanently to the acrylic used. Thermo-Press frames are white, but can be painted or stained to match your existing window trim.

C **JOINTS.** All frames are constructed with mitred joints. Such precision of construction is not only functionally imperative, but certainly lends to the beauty that these windows convey.

D **INTER-GASKET.** Providing extra insulation and air-tight construction is a flexible vinyl gasket, much the same as you find on your refrigerator door. This gasket, on the inside of the PVC frame is the key to virtually eliminating air infiltration. To insure a proper working relationship between the PVC frame and our inter-gasket, they are extruded as one component.

E **BULB GASKET.** We have insured the gasket seal all around by having a separate vinyl "ubular gasket which is utilized to "snug up" the panel when it rests on a window sill.

F **LOOP VELCRO®.** A 1/2" loop velcro strip is chemically bonded to the PVC frame and attaches to a 1/2" hook velcro strip.

G **HOOK VELCRO®.** A continuous 1/2" hook velcro strip is mechanically stapled to the window trim or an added subframe to insure a secure and durable closure. The hook is available in colors to enhance the product's attractiveness.

H **QUALITY OF VELCRO®.** Velcro is a durable woven nylon hook and loop fastening tape with a minimum life of 10,000 openings and closings. Velcro tapes are manufactured by a weaving process considered to be one of the most precise and refined in the entire textile industry.

Thermo-press® Corporation

Energy Control Products

Our vinyl and acrylic windows help reduce condensation. First, because of a magnetic seal that's virtually airtight. Second, by installing over your existing window cavity, an insulating air space is created. This separates the warm inside air from cold prime window glass. And with our exclusive "Bellows" design (that expands or contracts as temperatures change), the seal is maintained and annoying drafts are eliminated.

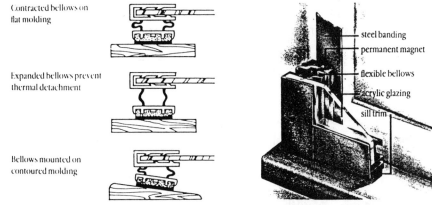

Contracted bellows on flat molding

Expanded bellows prevent thermal detachment

Bellows mounted on contoured molding

Still more reasons to have the Flex-Tite Winsulator installed:

■ Acrylic will not yellow, is lighter and 17 times more impact resistant than glass of an equal thickness.

■ Easy to store, maintain and clean

■ Invisible from outside

■ White, brown or tan trim blends with any decor

■ Custom-made to fit any size window

steel banding
permanent magnet
flexible bellows
acrylic glazing
sill trim

The Flex-Tite Winsulator window. At home in residential, commercial and industrial locations.

Winsulator windows are custom-made to go almost anywhere. So if those Three Little Pigs lived in a mobile home or a high-rise, they could still keep the wolf away from their door as well as their windows.

Our windows also install over basement, jalousie and crank-out casement windows. The Winsulator is even an ideal choice in commercial/industrial buildings where outside window installation is impractical and window replacement too expensive.

PLASKOLITE, INC.

P.O. Box 1497 ■ Columbus, Ohio 43216 ■ (614) 294-3281

Q: I need more security and it is drafty and noisy near my windows, but I cannot afford replacement windows. How can I make inexpensive and burglar resistant, yet attractive, reusable storm windows myself?

A: For about $20 and a little elbow grease, you should be able to build an efficient reusable storm window. By using clear, virtually unbreakable polycarbonate plastic (bullet-proof glass) sheets, it can deter a burglar.

Well-made storm windows will cut your heating and air-conditioning bills and greatly improve your comfort year-round. However, if you don't design and build them properly, you will just waste your time and money. You'll know how good a job you did by the reduction in outdoor noise transmission.

The air gap width between your primary and storm window affects the energy savings. Too narrow an air gap does not insulate well. Too wide an air gap allows energy-robbing air currents to form in between the windows.

Overall, the energy efficiency of outdoor storm windows is higher than indoor ones. Design them large enough to cover the entire window opening and to mount against the wall. This blocks most of the air leaks too. Outdoor storm windows protect your primary windows from the wrath of storms, baseballs, heads,

etc. Indoor ones needn't be built as rugged, but you should finish them more carefully for an attractive appearance.

A thin film indoor design is the simplest and least expensive storm window to make. Build the frame with 1x2 lumber. Size it slightly smaller than the window opening. This provides clearance for com-

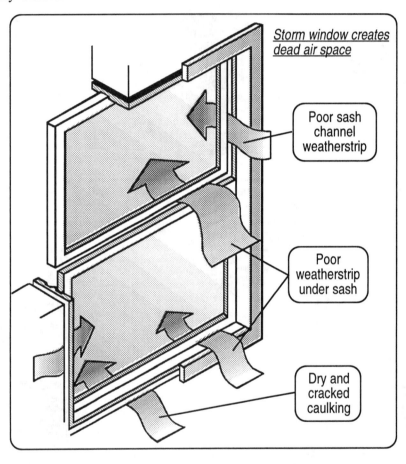

Storm window creates dead air space

Poor sash channel weatherstrip

Poor weatherstrip under sash

Dry and cracked caulking

pression weatherstripping around the frame. Staple clear thin plastic film to the back of the frame.

A more durable exterior storm uses a heavier wood frame and glass or rigid plastic sheeting. Seal the pane in the frame with caulk. Drill weep holes in the bottom of the frame to allow moisture to escape. Make it easily removable. Most codes require one emergency escape window in each room.

The most efficient and sound-proof exterior storm window uses double plastic or glass panes. Make the wood frame deep enough to allow for a one-inch air gap between the two storm panes. Use a wood or aluminum channel as a mullion to evenly space the panes apart.

Paint the frame and the mullion with two coats before assembly. This reduces moisture transmission and possible fogging. Also use a caulk with low moisture permeability. Don't forget to drill weep holes.

Q: We use our wood burning stove often in the winter. Can you tell me how to get stains off our light-colored roof?

A: It will be difficult to remove the dark stains from your roof. There is very fine carbon dust in smoke and it gets down into the pores of any material. This fine soot even has a greasy feel to it. Try scrubbing the roof with a strong detergent. Then use a matching roof paint on the stains.

Excessively sooty smoke indicates incomplete and inefficient combustion of the wood. You are either burning unseasoned damp wood or not providing adequate combustion air. Both of these problems can cause a creosote buildup inside your chimney and the possibility of a chimney fire. Have your chimney cleaned and your wood stove inspected.

Do-it-yourself storm windows are easy to make and can increase the overall energy efficiency of your home. Installing storm windows also reduces chilly drafts throughout your home. This allows you to set your thermostat lower and save more energy, yet still be comfortable.

Another advantage of storm windows is that they reduce window condensation during cold weather. Chart #1 shows how humid you can keep your home without causing window condensation. Since storm windows, especially exterior ones, keep your primary windows warmer, condensation is reduced. Keep in mind, as it gets colder outdoors, you must reduce the humidity level inside your home.

Before building and installing any storm windows, make sure your primary windows are properly caulked and weatherstripped. This not only blocks outdoor air leakage, but it also reduces condensation between the primary and storm windows.

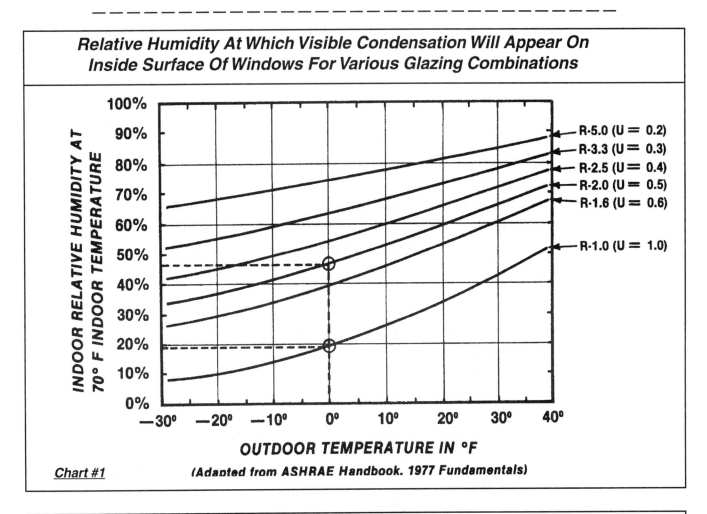

Relative Humidity At Which Visible Condensation Will Appear On Inside Surface Of Windows For Various Glazing Combinations

INDOOR RELATIVE HUMIDITY AT 70° F INDOOR TEMPERATURE

R-5.0 (U = 0.2)
R-3.3 (U = 0.3)
R-2.5 (U = 0.4)
R-2.0 (U = 0.5)
R-1.6 (U = 0.6)
R-1.0 (U = 1.0)

OUTDOOR TEMPERATURE IN °F

Chart #1   **(Adapted from ASHRAE Handbook. 1977 Fundamentals)**

Recommended Materials List

a) 1x2 pine lumber
b) 1-1/8x2-1/2 redwood lumber
c) 1/2x1 wood strips
d) 1/2x1/2 wood strips
e) 1/4x1/2 wood strips
f) 1/4x3/16 wood strips
g) acrylic or polycarbonate glazing
h) heat shrink film
i) double strength glass

j) silicone caulk
k) butyl rubber caulk
l) waterproof glue (epoxy or resorcinol)
m) nails, screws, hooks, hook & loop strips
n) good-quality exterior paint
o) open-cell foam weatherstripping
p) vinyl bulb weatherstripping
q) double-sided tape
r) anchors for screws

DESIGN #1 MATERIALS REQUIRED: a,b,e,f,i,j,k,l,m,n,o,p,r

Used as indoor or outdoor storm windows. The double pane storms are usually used outdoors. Has a high-quality wood frame and glass glazing. For outdoor use, redwood lumber is recommended.

1) Build a frame for the storm window using 1x2 lumber for single pane. For double pane, you will have to size redwood lumber to $1^1/8$x$2^1/2$. Use waterproof glue and nails or screws to make the corner lap joints. Size the outside frame dimensions to the window opening size plus 4 inches if you plan to cover the entire opening. Size it $1/2$-inch smaller than the window opening size if you want it to fit inside the window opening.

2) Attach one set of $1/4$x$1/2$ face strips - see diagram with nails and waterproof glue.

3) Have the panes of glass cut to a size $1/4$-inch smaller than the inside dimensions of the frame. This will leave $1/8$-inch clearance all around the edge of the glass.

4) For the double pane storms, lay one piece of glass flat on a table. Cut lengths of the $1/4$x$3/16$ spacer strips to fit around the edge of the glass pane. Place a thin bead of butyl caulk on the edge of the glass pane and lay the spacer strip on it. Then put another layer of caulk on the top of the spacer and lay the other glass pane over it to form the double pane assembly.

5) Lay the frame on the table and lay the panes/pane assembly on top of the face strip. Fill the gap between the edge of the glass and the frame with caulk. Use silicone caulk for the single pane storms and butyl caulk for the double pane storms. Make sure to completely fill the gap.

6) Set the other face strip on top of glass; make sure it seals into the caulk. Attach this to face strip.

7) Prime and paint the frame with good-quality exterior paint.

8) If you made it larger than the window opening, you can mount it to the wall surface with screws or hooks. For this mounting method, put the foam weatherstripping on the surface of the frame so it is compressed against the wall.

9) If you plan to mount it inside your window opening, put $3/8$-inch thick foam weatherstripping on the outside edge of the frame. Then carefully push it into the window opening so the foam is compressed against the sides of the opening. Since these are fairly heavy, you will have to fix it in place with screws or hooks.

DESIGN #2 MATERIALS REQUIRED: a,h,l,m,n,o,p

Used as indoor storm windows. Has wooden frame and thin film glazing. The thin film heat-shrink glazing is not durable enough to be used for an outdoor storm window.

1) Measure your indoor window opening on the wall. Let the frame lumber set indoors for several days to acquire the stable moisture content of your house.

2) Use the 1x2 lumber to make a rectangular frame. If you plan to cover the entire window opening, make the frame with outside dimensions 4 inches larger than the window opening. If you plan to have the storm window fit inside the window opening, make the frame with outside dimensions that are ½ inch smaller than the window opening. You won't need redwood lumber since it won't be exposed to the weather. Use a lap joint at the corners for a strong and attractive frame. Use waterproof glue at the corner joints and secure with nails or screws.

3) Paint the frame with good-quality exterior house paint. This will seal the wood and minimize size changes and warpage.

4) Using scissors, cut out a rectangular piece of the thin film that is slightly larger than the frame.

5) Lay it over the frame and staple it to the frame. Blow your hair dryer on the shrink film so it pulls taut. Then cut off the excess near the outer edge of the frame.

6) If you made it larger than the window opening, you can mount it to the wall surface with screws or hooks. For this mounting method, put the foam weatherstripping on the surface of the frame so it is compressed against the wall.

7) This is also a good application for the Velcro-type of hook and loop fasteners. If you use a continuous strip of the fastener on the wall and the frame, you won't need to use weatherstripping. The hook and loop fastener will provide a fairly airtight seal.

8) If you plan to mount it inside your window opening, put ³/₈-inch thick foam weatherstripping on the outside edge of the frame. Push it into the window opening so the foam is compressed against the sides of the opening. Since these are lightweight storms, the compression of the foam should hold them in place.

DESIGN #3 MATERIALS REQUIRED: c,g,m,n,o,p,q,r

Used as outdoor storm windows. Has no frame and uses wood strips to attach an acrylic or polycarbonate sheet directly over the window opening against the wall.

1) Measure your outdoor window opening on the wall. Cut the plastic glazing panel to a size 2 inches larger than the window opening.

2) Cut four support strips from ½x1 inch lumber to fit on the outside surface near the edge of the glazing. These will be approx. 2 inches shorter than the dimensions of the glazing panel.

3) Using some double sided tape, stick the wood support strips in position on the glazing.

4) Drill clearance holes through the wood and the plastic glazing at three locations on each strip.

5) Have a helper hold this assembly against the wall over window. Mark the hole locations on the wall. Drill holes through the siding into the sheathing beneath. For masonry houses, you will have to drill larger holes and install anchors for the mounting screws. Remove and paint the wood strips.

6) Attach foam weatherstripping to the plastic glazing, opposite the wood support strips and screw the storm window to the wall. This will compress the weatherstripping against the wall.

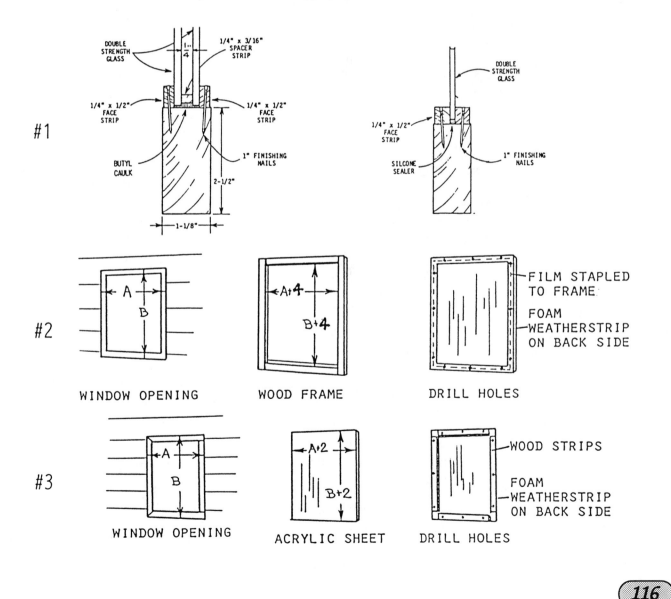

Q: I need to replace my old ugly, drafty windows, but each salesman says something different. What are the best wood replacement windows and can they really stop condensation and the fading of my curtains?

A: There have been recent efficient and convenience design improvements in wood window frame. Also, new types of high-efficiency glass not only stop 90% of energy loss and condensation, but some also block 99% of the sun's fading rays. Argon gas-filled windows stop most of the outdoor noise.

With new multistage painting processes and exterior vinyl or aluminum cladding, many new wood frame windows are almost maintenance-free. The indoor sash and frame surfaces are solid wood for a warm attractive look and feel. Wood, with its tiny air cells, is a natural insulator.

Most wood windows come with primed wood surfaces. Although more expensive, you can select unprimed specialty woods like cherry, oak, teak, and mahogany for an elegant natural wood look. The aluminum and vinyl cladding is usually available in white, gray, and earth-tones.

Tight-sealing tilt-turn wood windows, popular in Europe, swing in like casement or tilt in like tilt windows. This gives the option of opening it for maximum ventilation (casement) or just a little for security (tilt-in).

Most new double-hung replacement windows are designed so both sashes tilt-in for easy cleaning. In another easy-to-clean design, the entire sash pivots 180 degrees so you can clean both sides of the glass from indoors. New types of foam-filled and bulb weatherstripping make them more airtight.

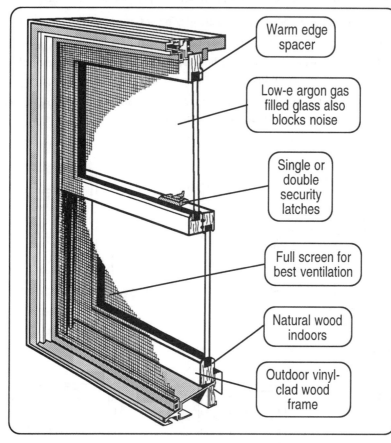

Warm edge spacer

Low-e argon gas filled glass also blocks noise

Single or double security latches

Full screen for best ventilation

Natural wood indoors

Outdoor vinyl-clad wood frame

To stop the fading of your curtains and furniture, select new windows with Heat Mirror XUV glass. This blocks the sun's fading rays like the best window films, but the window is totally clear like ordinary glass. Heat Mirror Insol-8 is eight times more efficient than your old window glass.

"Warm edge" spacers (between panes around perimeter) are another recent advancement in high-efficiency window glass. One design has a break in one side of the metal spacer to cut the heat transfer in half. This also looks better because you cannot see the metal spacer between the glass.

Another warm edge design uses a vinyl strip to thermally isolate the panes of glass. Still another design uses a thin S-shaped metal strip embedded in durable sealant to separate and seal the panes of glass.

Unique high-efficiency wood corner windows use a continuous piece of double pane glass that is bent at 90 degrees to form a corner. There is no break or support at the corner. It gives an attractive and open feel to a room.

Q: I have a battery operated calculator and a battery charger at home. When I am not actually using the calculator or charger, does the small AC wall plug adapter use any electricity and should I unplug it.

A: The small adapter that you plug into the wall is basically a small transformer. It converts the 110-volt AC house current to the correct DC voltage equivalent to batteries.

You should unplug them when you are not using the device. They continue to consume some electricity - just feel how warm they stay. Also, it is always much safer to unplug any electrical device when it's not in use.

High-efficiency wood replacement windows are some of the most efficient windows made because the wood itself is a natural insulator with millions of tiny air cells. I have listed the highest quality, most-efficient wood window manufacturers on the following pages along with information about their products.

The type of frame material has an impact on the amount of maintenance and the appearance of the window. Vinyl- and aluminum-clad wood windows require the least maintenance. They are clad only on the outdoor surfaces.

The indoor surfaces are usually just primed wood. This allows for more detailed contours and allows you to paint it any color you want. Many of the unclad wood windows come with special extra-durable paint on the outdoor surfaces or you can just specify primed wood.

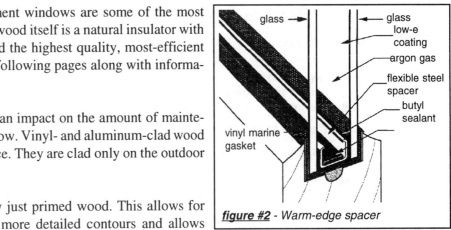
figure #2 - Warm-edge spacer

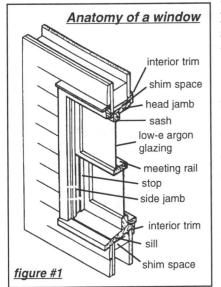
Anatomy of a window

interior trim
shim space
head jamb
sash
low-e argon glazing
meeting rail
stop
side jamb
interior trim
sill
shim space

figure #1

The type of glass has the greatest impact on the energy efficiency of replacement windows. The chart below shows the relative insulating values of several different glass options. On the following pages under *"type of glass"*, "double" refers to standard thermal pane glass. Low-e is a special clear glass coating that blocks heat transfer. Argon refers to argon gas in the gap between the glass panes.

Krypton gas is also sometimes used. Heat Mirror glass is even more efficient and expensive XUV glass is a special type of Heat Mirror glass design to also block nearly all of the sun's fading rays. Regular low-e and Heat Mirror glass block only some of the fading rays.

A unique style of window, common in Europe, is the tilt-turn window. It opens two different ways. You can tilt it in from the top or swing it in from the side depending on which handle you turn.

Don't confuse this type of window with windows called just "tilt". These are usually just double-hung windows that tilt in for easy cleaning. The rest of the window designs are self-explanatory listed on the following pages under *"styles"*.

Warm-edge technology (figure #2) is one of the newest advancements in windows. It provides insulation at the spacer area between the indoor and outdoor panes of glass. This is a typical area of heat loss and condensation in the winter. There are several effective design variations of warm-edge technology used to achieve the energy savings. The manufacturers that use warm-edge technology are indicated in *"special features"*.

Thermal Insulating Values for Glass Types*

	U-Value	R-Value
Wood Casement		
Double pane	0.432	2.31
Low-e	0.288	3.47
Low-e argon	0.236	4.24
Aluminum Clad Casement		
Double pane	0.436	2.29
Low-e	0.296	3.38
Low-e argon	0.243	4.12
Wood Slider		
Double pane	0.448	2.23
Low-e	0.323	3.09
Low-e argon	0.270	3.71
Wood Double-Hung		
Double pane	0.470	2.13
Low-e	0.362	2.76
Low-e argon	0.302	3.31
information from Clawson specs.		

Manufacturers of High-Efficiency Wood Windows

ANDERSEN CORP., 100 Fourth Ave., N., Bayport, MN 55003 - (612) 439-5150

styles - casement, geometric, bays, bows, awning, double-hung, slider
frame - pine, vinyl-clad wood   colors - white, brown, sand
type of glass - double, low-e, low-e argon   warranty - 20 years
special features - eighty-seven standard arch sizes available

ARCHITECTURAL COMPONENTS, 26 N. Leverett Rd., Montague, MA 01351 - (413) 367-9441

styles - casement, geometric, awning, double-hung, hopper   colors - n/a
frame - white pine, oak, cypress, cherry, mahogany   warranty - n/a
type of glass - double, low-e
special features - removable interior or exterior wood framed storm sashes, moulded sills and casings

BILT BEST, 175 Tenth St., Ste. Genevieve, MO 63670 - (314) 883-3571

styles - casement, geometric, awning, double-hung, slider   colors - white, bronze, sand, gray
frame - wood, aluminum-clad wood   warranty - 20 years
type of glass - double, low-e, low-e argon
special features - narrow slat venetian blinds between insulating glass, lexan corner key stabilizes the extruded aluminum frame; fourteen special colors in stock

CARADCO CORP., PO Box 920, Rantoul, IL 61866 - (217) 893-4444

styles - casement, french casement, geometric, bays, bows, awning, double-hung, slider
frame - western pine, aluminum-clad wood   colors - white, bronze, sand
type of glass - double, low-e, low-e argon   warranty - 10 years
special features - extruded aluminum brick mold is available for all-clad windows

CENTURY WINDOWS, 1301 Newark Rd., Mt. Vernon, OH - (614) 397-2131

styles - casement, geometric, bays, bows, awning, double-hung   colors - white, brown, beige
frame - pine, aluminum-clad wood   warranty - 25 years
type of glass - double, low-e, low-e argon
special features - warm edge technology

CLAWSON MANUFACTURING, Box 8891, Missoula, MT 59807 - (406) - 543-3161

styles - casement, geometric, bays, bows, awning, double-hung, slider   colors - white, bronze, sand
frame - pine, aluminum-clad wood, wood   warranty - 10 years
type of glass - double, low-e, low-e argon
special features - a special powder coating process to allow any colors to match your decor

CRAFTLINE, 1125 Ford St., Maumee, OH 43537 - (800) 283-3311 (419) 893-3311

styles - casement, geometric, bays, bows, awning, double-hung, slider   colors - white, bronze, beige, gray
frame - ponderosa pine, aluminum-clad wood   warranty - 20 years
type of glass - double, low-e, low-e argon
special features - blind system between the glass which is adjustable and operated by a corner knob

CRESTLINE, PO Box 8007, Wausau, WI 54402 (800) 444-1090 (715) 845-1161

styles - casement, geometric, bays, bows, awning, double-hung, slider
frame - western pine, aluminum-clad wood   colors - white, almond, pewter
type of glass - double, low-e argon   warranty - 20 years
special features - mini blinds available with a unique tilt-control knob for easy operation indoors

THE H WINDOW COMPANY, PO Box 206, Monticello, MN 55362 - (612) 295-5305

styles - geometric, bays, bows, awning, hopper   colors - white, brown, tan
frame - ponderosa pine, oak and other woods optional, aluminum/wood   warranty - 10 years
type of glass - double, triple, low-e, low-e argon, heat mirror
special features - rotates 180° for easy cleaning, with limited lifetime warranty on hinges

HURD MILLWORK, 575 S. Whelan Ave., Medford, WI 54451 - (715) 748-2011

styles - casement, geometric, bays, bows, awning, double-hung, slider   colors - white, bronze, sand
frame - ponderosa pine, aluminum-clad wood   warranty - 10 years
type of glass - double, triple, quad, low-e, low-e argon, heat mirror, heat mirror XUV, Insol - 8
special features - warm edge technology and hidden hinges available

KOLBE & KOLBE MILLWORK, 1323 S. Eleventh Ave., Wausau, WI 54401 - (715) 842-5666

styles - casement, french casement, geometric, bays, bows, awning, double-hung, slider
frame - pine, aluminum-clad wood
type of glass - double, low-e, low-e argon
colors - white,beige,sand,rustic
warranty - n/a
special features - removable grilles and true divided lites, 24 preapproved special colors available

LOUISIANA-PACIFIC, 324 Wooster N., Barberton, OH 44203 - (800) 358-2954 (216) 745-1661

styles - casement, geometric, bays, bows, awning, double-hung, slider
frame - pine, aluminum-clad wood, all wood
type of glass - double, triple, low-e, heat mirror, heat mirror XUV
colors - white, sand, brown
warranty - 20 years
special features - available with leaded, etched and beveled glass

MARVIN WINDOWS, PO Box 100, Warroad, MN 56763 - (800) 346-5128 (218) 386-1430

styles - casement, geometric, bays, bows, awning, double-triple-hung, slider, hopper, tilt-turn
frame - wood, aluminum-clad wood
type of glass - double, triple, low-e, low-e argon, low-e krypton
colors - white, bronze, brown, gray
warranty - 10 years
special features - warm edge technology also available is a unique corner or curved window; a flip handle is offered which features smooth styling for a contemporary look

MW MANUFACTURERS, PO Box 559, Rocky Mount, VA 24151 - (703) 483-0211

styles - casement, geometric, bays, bows, awning, double-hung
frame - wood, vinyl-clad wood
type of glass - double, low-e
colors - white, beige, brown
warranty - 10 years
special features - removable wood grilles for divided light appearance

OSLO AMERICA, 1060 Worcester Rd., Framingham, MA 01701 - (508) 875-5514

styles - casement, geometric, double-hung, tilt-turn
frame - mahogany, spruce, oak, teak, pine and other woods
type of glass - double, triple
colors - n/a
warranty - 10 years
special features - special tilt & swing (tilt-turn) options are available

PEACHTREE WINDOWS, PO Box 5700, Norcross, GA 30091 - (404) 497-2000

styles - casement, geometric, bays, bows, awning, double-hung
frame - wood, aluminum-clad wood
type of glass - double, low-e
colors - white, beige, brown
warranty - 10 years
special features - tilt-in window for cleaning using only two fingers

PELLA CORP., 102 Main St., Pella, IA 50219 - (515) 628-1000

styles - casement, geometric, bays, bows, awning, double-hung
frame - pine, aluminum-clad wood
type of glass - double, triple, low-e, low-e argon, heat mirror
colors - white, brown, tan
warranty - 10 years
special features - custom colors available, inside the pane mini blinds are operated by a corner knob

TISCHLER UND SOHN, 51 Weaver St., Greenwich, CT 06830 - (203) 622-8486

styles - casement, french casement, single-double-hung, geometric, bays, awning, tilt-turn
frame - mahogany, pine with flexicron paint
type of glass - double, low-e, heat mirror
colors - white, ivory, taupe, bronze
warranty - 2 years
special features - burglar resistant glazing and soundproofing is available

WEATHER SHIELD, PO Box 309, Medford, WI 54451 - (715) 748-2100

styles - casement, french casement, geometric, bays, bows, awning, double-hung, slider
frame - pine, oak, cherry, aluminum-clad wood
type of glass - double, triple, low-e, low-e argon, Supersmart® triple pane with 2 low-e and 2 argon
colors - white, adobe, tan
warranty - 20 years
special features - insulated true divided lite available

WENCO WINDOWS, 335 Commerce Dr., Mt. Vernon, OH 43050 - (614) 397-3403

styles - casement, geometric, bays, bows, awning, double-hung
frame - ponderosa pine, aluminum-clad wood
type of glass - double, low-e, low-e argon
colors - white, bronze, beige
warranty - 20 years
special features - warm edge technology, the sashes are screwed together for extra strength

J. ZELUCK, 5300 Kings Highway, Brooklyn, NY 11234 - (718) 251-8060

styles - casement, geometric, awning, double-hung, slider
frame - mahogany, teak, oak, cedar, walnut, cherry
type of glass - double, low-e, heat mirror
colors - n/a
warranty - 5 years
special features - twenty five different types of windows available

Q: I am building a new house and I want a natural wood front door, but I cannot afford one. How efficient and durable are the new stainable fiberglass doors that look and feel like real wood?

A: Inexpensive fiberglass front doors are an excellent alternative to real hard wood doors. Fiberglass doors are more durable than wood because fiberglass resists moisture, shrinking, warping, and scratching - common problems with real wood. With a built-in triple latch point deadbolt, they are very secure.

It is often difficult to distinguish a stained fiberglass door from a real wood door. Some fiberglass door manufacturers use pieces of real wood for the deep graining pattern to get the authentic look and feel of wood.

You can stain or paint a fiberglass door just like a wood door. Using oil-based stain is the easiest method to achieve a natural wood look. Although it requires more work, hand rubbing artist oil into the fiberglass door gives a more luxurious deep grained appearance.

Insulated fiberglass doors are significantly more energy efficient than wood doors. With rigid foam polystyrene insulation inside the fiberglass skins, the insulation value is four times greater than a solid wood door.

Using polyurethane foam offers even higher insulation than polystyrene foam. When this is injected inside the door cavity during assembly, all of the voids and gaps are completely filled with insulation.

Another efficiency advantage of fiberglass is that it expands and contracts very little with temperature and humidity changes. This

Stainable fiberglass

Double pane insulated glass

Pre-hung assembly

Magnetic weatherstripping

Filled with foam insulation

ensures a long-term airtight seal. Reinforcing wood pieces are used inside the perimeter of the door and at the lockset area for strength.

Fiberglass doors are usually sold as prehung assemblies, complete with the threshold. This makes installation easy. Select a model with jamb-jack adjusting screws. Using a special socket wrench, one person can easily fine tune the position door/frame inside the wall opening.

Most fiberglass doors use multi-finger (up to five) sweep weatherstripping under the door and compression weatherstripping around the door. You will immediately notice fewer drafts and less outdoor noise. This also reduces friction so the door closes easily with little wear.

The most airtight fiberglass doors use a refrigerator-type of magnetic seal in the door frame. A narrow decorative brass-plated steel strip is inset around the door perimeter. When you close the door, the seal sticks to the brass-plated strip. This seals well even if the door settles over time.

Q: Does it make sense to install rigid foam insulation directly under the roof? Do I need attic ventilation?

A: Generally, you should have adequate attic ventilation to remove moisture from the attic in the winter before it condenses. Even with a vapor barrier under the attic floor insulation, some indoor moisture still gets through.

Another option is to block off all the attic vents and install additional foam insulation under the roof itself. Tests in Sweden have shown that this results in a drier attic. You must have an airtight house to block most of the indoor air from reaching the attic. Open the vents again in the summer.

Do-It-Yourself "Jamb-Jack" Door Installation Method

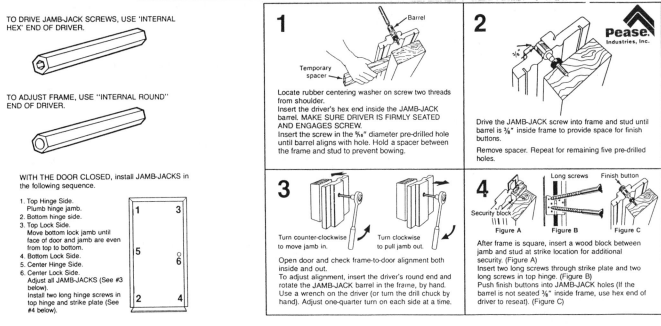

TO DRIVE JAMB-JACK SCREWS, USE 'INTERNAL HEX' END OF DRIVER.

TO ADJUST FRAME, USE "INTERNAL ROUND" END OF DRIVER.

WITH THE DOOR CLOSED, install JAMB-JACKS in the following sequence.

1. Top Hinge Side.
   Plumb hinge jamb.
2. Bottom hinge side.
3. Top Lock Side.
   Move bottom lock jamb until face of door and jamb are even from top to bottom.
4. Bottom Lock Side.
5. Center Hinge Side.
6. Center Lock Side.
   Adjust all JAMB-JACKS (See #3 below).
   Install two long hinge screws in top hinge and strike plate (See #4 below).

1 — Barrel. Temporary spacer.
Locate rubber centering washer on screw two threads from shoulder.
Insert the driver's hex end inside the JAMB-JACK barrel. MAKE SURE DRIVER IS FIRMLY SEATED AND ENGAGES SCREW.
Insert the screw in the ⁹⁄₁₆" diameter pre-drilled hole until barrel aligns with hole. Hold a spacer between the frame and stud to prevent bowing.

2 — Pease Industries, Inc.
Drive the JAMB-JACK screw into frame and stud until barrel is ³⁄₈" inside frame to provide space for finish buttons.
Remove spacer. Repeat for remaining five pre-drilled holes.

3 —
Turn counter-clockwise to move jamb in.
Turn clockwise to pull jamb out.
Open door and check frame-to-door alignment both inside and out.
To adjust alignment, insert the driver's round end and rotate the JAMB-JACK barrel in the frame, by hand. Use a wrench on the driver (or turn the drill chuck by hand). Adjust one-quarter turn on each side at a time.

4 — Long screws. Finish button. Security block. Figure A. Figure B. Figure C.
After frame is square, insert a wood block between jamb and stud at strike location for additional security. (Figure A)
Insert two long screws through strike plate and two long screws in top hinge. (Figure B)
Push finish buttons into JAMB-JACK holes (If the barrel is not seated ³⁄₈" inside frame, use hex end of driver to reseat). (Figure C)

Staining and Finishing Instructions for Fiberglass Door

For professional results, read all instructions before finishing your fiberglass door. Be sure to follow stain, paint, and topcoat manufacturer's instructions and warnings on product labels.

DO apply coatings in temperatures between 50ºF and 90ºF with humidity below 85%. The recommended stains and artist oils require oxygen to dry. High elevations slow drying time.

DO reapply the topcoat approximately every two years or when the gloss fades.

DO use high quality, exterior oil-based paint.

DO use high quality, 100% acrylic-latex exterior paint.

DO NOT use turpentine.

DO NOT apply coatings or topcoat in damp or cold weather.

DO NOT apply coatings in direct sunlight. This may affect application and performance of coatings.

DO NOT apply while dew is present or within one hour of dusk.

DO NOT use sandpaper on the door skins.

DO NOT use translucent, transparent or penetrating stain. They will not bring out the door's grain and color texture.

DO NOT apply pressure when cleaning lite frames. The primer could be removed.

DO NOT use lacquer thinner on specially labeled lite frames and decorative panels.

PREPARATION

What you will need:

Clean cloth rags or cheesecloth.
Mineral spirits or an all-purpose household cleaning solution such as Top Job, Pine Sol or Mr. Clean.

1. Using a clean, dry rag, wipe the entire surface with mineral spirits or the all-purpose cleaning solution prepared according to manufacturer's recommendations. (If cleaning many doors, change rags frequently.)

2. If using an all-purpose cleaner, *rinse thoroughly* and allow the surface to *dry completely* before applying stain.

3. Mask glass and remove or mask lock/handle-set hardware. Re-move weatherstripping from the jambs.

4. Stain or paint your fiberglass door immediately after cleaning to prevent dirt and other residue from settling on the clean surface.

STAIN COLOR TEST

It's best to stain a small area of your door to see if the result is what you want before proceeding too far. If you are not satisfied, remove and clean thoroughly with mineral spirits.

1. Practice stain application according to instructions. Color can be controlled by the amount of pressure used when brushing out the stain. For a darker look, let stain set several minutes, then brush lightly. For a lighter finish, brush immediately with a little more pressure.

STAINING

What you will need:

Artist oil application
Mineral spirits
2 tubes (37 ml.) artist oil
  A. Grumbacher
  B. Winsor & Newton

Stain application
Zar® Wood Stain (1pt.)

Clean cloth rags
3" Natural bristle brush

APPLICATION

1. A. Artist oil : Mix <u>one</u> 37 ml. tube of artist oil and 2 oz. of mineral spirits in a small clean container. *Mix thoroughly.*
   B. Zar® Wood Stain: Follow manufacturer's instructions.

2. Door Face - Using a clean rag, apply the stain in a circular motion.
   A. Apply stain to embossed panels first.
   B. Next, stain the flat horizontal sections.
   C. The vertical sections should be stained last.

3. Using a clean, dry 3" natural bristle brush, "feather" the stain in the direction of the grain. Wipe excess stain from brush onto rag. Feather the entire door, brushing each section separately and always with the grain.

4. Door Edges - Apply per component instructions below.

COMPONENTS

Doorlite frames and jambs can be stained to match your fiberglass door using the same materials as for the door. Apply *lightly* with a stain-saturated rag for greater control in matching the door color.

TOPCOATING

What you will need:

One quart of exterior-grade clear topcoat. **NOTE:** Must have ultraviolet (UV) stabilizers printed on the label. (For best results, use the following brand name topcoat - Zar® Exterior Polyurethane.)

NOTE: Reapply the topcoat every two years or when the gloss fades. Fading varies depending on exposure to the sun.

APPLICATION

1. Stain must be **completely dry** before you can topcoat the door. Allow stain to cure and dry for at least 24-48 hours.

2. Mask off the glass and hardware, and remove weatherstripping from the jambs before topcoating.

3. Apply topcoat following manufacturer's directions.

4. Topcoat all surfaces including wood edges.

NOTE: Because of weather conditions, drying times can vary. If the door skin is not totally dry, the topcoat may blister. Also, brush-on topcoat may move the stain if it is not completely dry.

PAINTING

What you will need:

Clean cloth rags or cheesecloth
Clean, dry 4" soft paint brush
Oil-base applications:
A. One quart of high quality, solvent of alkyd-based primer
B. One quart of high quality, oil-based exterior-grade house paint
Latex applications:
A. One quart of high quality, alkyd-based primer

B. One quart of high quality, 100% acrylic-latex, exterior house paint.
NOTE: It is recommended to prime your fiberglass door. Primer and topcoat should be the same brand and made to work together.

PRIMING & PAINTING

1. Apply primer with a brush in the direction of the grain.
   A. Use solvent or alkyd-based primer for oil-based applications.
   B. Use an alkyd-based primer for latex applications.
   C. Follow manufacturer's directions for drying time before reapplying.

2. Primer must be completely dry before applying overcoat.

3. Apply paint with a brush in the direction of the grain.

4. Allow to dry overnight when applying a second coat.

5. **All exposed surfaces** (except weatherstrip) **must be painted**.

No clear topcoat is necessary when painting your fiberglass door.

REPAIRS

1. Scratches
   A. Wipe the entire surface with mineral spirits or all purpose cleaner, such as Top Job or Mr. Clean, prepared according to manufacturer's recommendations. If using an all-purpose cleaner, **rinse thoroughly**.

NOTE: At this time, fine white scratches may disappear.

2. Light scratches or scuff
   A. Lightly mist the scratched area with primer.
3. Deep scratches
   A. Fill with crayon or patch pencil.
   B. Wipe off excess with rag dampened with mineral spirits or with an all purpose cleaning solution.
   C. Lightly apply primer.
4. Allow area to **dry thoroughly** before finishing.

- -

Manufacturers of Fiberglass Entry Doors

CASTLEGATE, 911 E. Jefferson, Pittsburgh, KS 66762 - (800) 835-0364
> type of insulation - foamed-in-place polyurethane core
> weatherstripping - compression with triple contact and drip fin on bottom sweep with adjustable aluminum or oak threshold

CECO ENTRY SYSTEMS, One Tower Lane, Oakbrook Terrace, IL 60181 - (312) 242-2000
> type of insulation - foamed-in-place polyurethane core
> weatherstripping - compression with a combination bottom consisting of double blade and bulb type sweep

EAGLE WINDOW AND DOOR, PO Box 1072, Dubuque, IA 52004 - (800) 453-3633 (319) 556-2270
> type of insulation - foamed-in-place polyurethane core
> weatherstripping - compression with adjustable threshold combined with bulb-shaped vinyl bottom

KAYLIEN INC., PO Box 711599-1599, Santee, CA 92072 - (800) 748-5627 (619) 448-0544
> type of insulation - solid particle board core or cellular honeycomb core - wood and paper
> weatherstripping - compression with adjustable threshold

LOEWEN WINDOWS, 1397 Barclay, Buffalo Grove, IL 60089 - (800) 245-2295 (708) 215-8200
> type of insulation - solid urethane foam core
> weatherstripping - compression with adjustable bottom sweep on metal sill that separates outside/inside metal with a wide thermal break

PEACHTREE DOORS, 4350 Peachtree Ind., Norcross, GA 30071 - (800) 477-6544 (404) 497-2000
> type of insulation - polyurethane foamed panels
> weatherstripping - compression with a rubber bottom sweep and an adjustable oak threshold

PEASE IND., PO Box 14-8001, Fairfield, OH 45014 - (800) 883-6677 (513) 870-3600
> type of insulation - polystyrene foam core
> weatherstripping - hinge weatherstrip is compression, lock and head weatherstrip is magnetic creating a "refrigerator-tight" seal to the brass/steel edge strip with a flexible five finger bottom cap on an adjustable sill

PERMA DOOR, 9017 Blue Ash Rd., Cincinnati, OH 45242 - (800) 543-4456 (513) 870-3600
> type of insulation - injected solid urethane foam core
> weatherstripping - compression with five fin sweep, an integrated drip cap, wool pile in the corner and an adjustable thermal break threshold

STANLEY DOOR SYSTEMS, 12 E. Maple Rd., Troy, MI 48084 - (313) 528-1400
> type of insulation - foamed-in-place polyurethane core
> weatherstripping - compression with a triple seal bottom sweep with an aluminum thermal break, also latch and hinge jamb corner seals

THERMA TRU, 1684 Woodlands Ste. 150, Maumee, OH 43537 - (800) 537-8827 (419) 891-7400
> type of insulation - foamed-in-place polyurethane foam core
> weatherstripping - compression with self adjusting and self sealing sill and door bottom system

Manufacturers of High-Quality Wood Entry Doors

ARCTIC SUPPLY, INC., I-94 at Co. Rd. T, Hammond, WI 54015 - (800) 428-9276   (715) 796-2292
    type of construction - solid oak, pine or fir
    type of weatherstripping - compression bulb, adjustable threshold meets door sweep

ATRIUM DOOR & WINDOW, 9001 Ambassador Row, Dallas, TX 75247 - (800) 935-2000   (214) 634-9663
    type of construction - solid pine
    type of weatherstripping - combination compression bulb and leaf (single sheet seals two surfaces) perimeter/no additional weatherstripping

BEND DOOR COMPANY, P.O. Box 5249, Bend, OR 97708 - (800) 346-5252   (503) 382-4411
    type of construction - solid fir
    type of weatherstripping - compression bulb (not pre-fixed)

BUFFELEN WOODWORKING, 1901 Taylor Way, Tacoma, WA 98421 - (800) 423-8810   (206) 627-1191
    type of construction - solid fir
    type of weatherstripping - compression bulb (not pre-fixed)

CONCEPT DOOR COMPANY, 110 W. Borderland Rd., El Paso, TX 79932 - (915) 585-1187
    type of construction - butcher-block laminated core, oak or mahogany veneer
    type of weatherstripping - compression bulb

CONNOISSEUR DOORS, INC., P.O. Box 29947, San Antonio, TX 78229 - (800) 336-6763   (512) 698-3280
    type of construction - solid oak (or other hardwood)
    type of weatherstripping - Q-lon, door threshold has sweep weatherstripping

CUMBERLAND WOODCRAFT, P.O. Drawer 609, Carlisle, PA 17013 - (800) 367-1884   (717) 243-0063
    type of construction - solid hardwood
    type of weatherstripping - customer specifications on weatherstripping (not pre-fixed)

DEINES CUSTOM DOORS, 325 Cherry St., Ft. Collins, CO 80521 - (303) 482-4806
    type of construction - solid hardwood
    type of weatherstripping - Q-lon, aluminum and oak,adjustable door sweep

DOOR SYSTEMS, INC., English Creek Ave., McKee City, NJ 08232 - (800) 257-8641   (609) 484-1600
    type of construction - laminated particle core, oak veneer
    type of weatherstripping - compression bulb (not pre-fixed)

ELEGANT ENTRIES, 240 Washington St., Auburn, MA 01501 - (800) 343-3432   (508) 832-9898
    type of construction - solid hardwood
    type of weatherstripping - Q-lon

INDUSTRIAL MILLWORK, W. Hwy. 36, Seneca, KS 66538 - (800) 462-3667   (913) 336-6001
    type of construction - solid hardwood
    type of weatherstripping - compression bulb (not pre-fixed)

INTN'L WOOD PROD., 10883 Thornmint Rd., San Diego, CA 92127 - (800) 468-3667   (619) 565-1122
    type of construction - solid hardwood
    type of weatherstripping - Q-lon

JESSUP DOOR CO., P.O. Box 240, Dowagiac, MI 49047 - (800) 826-2367   616) 782-2183
    type of construction - laminated wood core, oak veneer
    type of weatherstripping - compression bulb (not pre-fixed)

MAYWOOD, INC., P.O. Box 30550, Amarillo, TX 79101 - (800) 879-6299   (806) 374-2835
    type of construction - solid pine or oak
    type of weatherstripping - compression bulb

NANA WINDOWS & DOORS, 707 Redwood Hwy., Mill Valley, CA 94941 - (800) 873-5673   (415) 383-3148
    type of construction - solid fir
    type of weatherstripping - Q-lon (not pre-fixed)

ODL INC., 215 E. Roosevelt Ave., Zeeland, MI 49464 - (800) 288-1800   (616) 772-9111
    type of construction - butcher-block laminated wood core, oak and mahogany veneer
    type of weatherstripping - compression bulb (not pre-fixed)

PEASE INDUSTRIES, INC., P.O. Box 14-8001, Fairfied, OH 45014 - (800) 875-3691   (513) 870-3600
    type of construction - butcher-block laminated, oak, teak, or mahogany veneers
    type of weatherstripping - magnetic and polished brass-plated edge insert

PINECREST, 2118 Blaisdell Ave., Minneapolis, MN 55404 - (800) 443-5357   612) 871-7071
    type of construction - solid hardwood construction
    type of weatherstripping - compression bulb

VIKING INDUSTRIES INC., 18600 N.E. Wilkes Rd., Portland, OR 97220 - (503) 667-6030
    type of construction - solid pine construction
    type of weatherstripping - compression bulb (not pre-fixed)

WEATHER SHIELD MFG., INC., P.O. Box 309, Medford, WI 54451 - (800) 477-6808   (715) 748-2100
    type of construction - steel/cross-banded wood construction, oak veneer - Note - this type of construction is actually a narrow insulated steel door covered with a thick high-quality wood veneer
    type of weatherstripping - compression bulb

Q: I want to replace several windows with ones that are more efficient and burglar-proof. Are clear glass block windows very efficient? Can I do the installation job myself and how can I get ventilation?

A: For security, privacy, and energy efficiency, new designs of glass block windows are an excellent choice. There are simple do-it-yourself installation kits and custom-made preassembled glass block panels. Once installed, glass block windows are virtually maintenance-free.

Although not burglar-proof, glass block windows are much more difficult to break through than any ordinary single or double pane glass window.

A burglar first has to break many blocks and then has to deal with the mortar joints between them. For basements or other high-risk windows, you can install extra thick or even solid glass blocks for greater security.

Depending on the degree of privacy you desire, you can choose from clear undistorted-view blocks to one of many privacy patterns. Reflective (from outdoors) glass blocks reduce the summer sun's heat and add more privacy. Gold-tone or bronze-tinted blocks also provide a more contemporary look.

Even with a heavy privacy pattern, 90% of the outdoor light still

comes through the glass blocks for natural lighting. This is more efficient and attractive than having to draw curtains or lower blinds and turn on lamps.

Glass block windows are efficient for several reasons. Each glass block is not solid glass. It is made of two hollow halves fused together under high temperature. As they

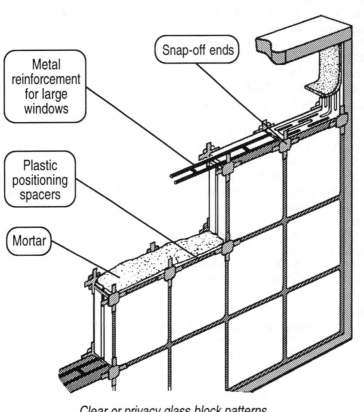

Clear or privacy glass block patterns

cool, an insulating vacuum forms inside them.

Since they are often set in mortar, glass block windows are airtight. This reduces drafts, dirt, and outdoor noise. The many horizontal mortar joints between the blocks act as louvers to block the direct summer sun's heat.

For natural ventilation, you can install screened vent panels that

crank out casement-style. The vent panel can be made of double pane glass, or for ultimate security, unbreakable clear double-pane bulletproof plastic.

For the do-it-yourselfer on a tight budget, one simple installation method uses clear plastic spacers and clear silicone caulking. This is easy to install and provides a totally clear view with nearly invisible joints.

If you prefer the standard mortar joints, you can use special plastic corner spacers to accurately position the glass blocks in the mortar. After the mortar is set, you twist off the exposed spacer ends and repoint those spots. The spacers strips are totally hidden inside the mortar.

Q: We have a crawl space with a dirt floor. I was told to cover the dirt with plastic and insulation. Is this the correct procedure?

A: You should put plastic film over the dirt to block moisture, but do not cover it with insulation. If your crawl space is unvented, hang insulation down the crawl space walls. Run it out several feet onto the floor. Since the earth stays warm, there is no need to cover the entire floor.

For a vented crawl space, insulate the floor above the crawl space, not the walls. Staple wire mesh under the floor to hold the batt insulation above it.

Glass block windows provide security against break-ins, privacy, and they are more energy efficient than ordinary single pane windows. There are several unique privacy glass patterns. You can find samples of the unique and common patterns at most glass block retailers and installers.

If you want ventilation in the summer, yet still have security, you can install a durable ventilation window panel (see page 128). These panels use clear double-pane bulletproof lexan plastic. You can also order them with insulation.

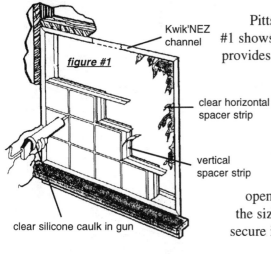

Kwik'NEZ channel

figure #1

clear horizontal spacer strip

vertical spacer strip

clear silicone caulk in gun

Pittsburgh Corning offers several do-it-yourself installation methods. Figure #1 shows the simplest method using silicone caulk and clear spacer strips. This provides a clear opening with the joints barely perceptible.

Another simple method is detailed below and on page 127. This method creates a true professional mortar joint look and the best security. The mortar joints also act as louvers in the summer to block the direct summer sun.

The third method is to order a pre-made glass block panel to fit your opening. Since the glass blocks are a fixed size, you will have to shim or adjust the size of the wall opening slightly. You simply slip the panel into place and secure it in the opening.

Do-it-yourself installation - "Mortar with Veritru® spacers" by Pittsburgh Corning

PREPARATION

1. Determine the opening size (Drawing A) into which your glass block panel will be built as follows:
When using:

8" Block: (No. Block x 8) + 1/2" = rough opening
6" Block: (No. Block x 6) + 1/2" = rough opening
4" Block: (No. Block x 4) + 1/2" = rough opening
12" Block: (No. Block x 12) + 1/2" = rough opening
NOTE: Above based on 1/4" mortar joints.

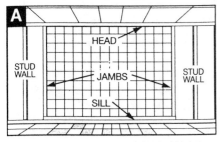

A

HEAD

STUD WALL   STUD WALL

JAMBS

SILL

2. Your panel should be built on a secure surface. A built-up sill is suggested to protect the bottom row of glass block from damage (Drawing B).

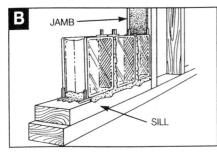

B

JAMB

SILL

3. Panel anchors must now be installed along the jambs and head in order to tie the panel into the frame (anchors will be embedded into the mortar joint). Do not install anchors on the sill. Anchors are supplied in 24" lengths and can be cut into two anchors, 12" long. They should be

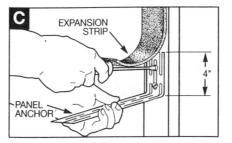

C

EXPANSION STRIP

4"

PANEL ANCHOR

bent to produce both a short and a long arm (Drawing C). Screw the short arms of the anchors to the jambs and head (Drawing C) after every **third 6" block** (anchors 18" apart) and after every **second 8" or 12" block** (anchors 16" and 24" apart, respectively). Use two screws per

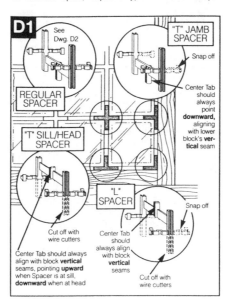

D1

See Dwg. D2

"T" JAMB SPACER

Snap off

REGULAR SPACER

Center Tab should always point **downward,** aligning with lower block's **vertical** seam

"T" SILL/HEAD SPACER

"L" SPACER

Snap off

Cut off with wire cutters

Center Tab should always align with block **vertical** seams, pointing **upward** when Spacer is at sill, **downward** when at head

Center Tab should always align with block **vertical** seams

Cut off with wire cutters

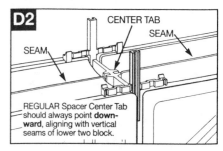

D2

CENTER TAB

SEAM

SEAM

REGULAR Spacer Center Tab should always point **downward**, aligning with vertical seams of lower two block.

anchor. If you are attaching to tile or masonry, screw plugs should be used.

4. Trim expansion strip as follows: The width should be 2 1/4" for THINLINE SERIES block and 2 3/4" for REGULAR SERIES block. The length should also cover the anchor short arm. Strips are installed between the anchors for full lengths of jamb and head (Drawing C) by stapling, nailing or gluing.

5. Spacers to be installed where four block come together (REGULAR Spacers) are used as supplied (Drawings D1 and D2); others ("T" and "L" Spacers) should be modified now for use at head, sill and jambs (Drawing D1).

Mortar Preparation
WHITE PREMIXED GLASS BLOCK MORTAR

The following gives an idea of the quantity of premixed mortar needed:

25-lb. Bag		50-lb. Bag	
Block Size	No. You Can Install	Block Size	No. You Can Install
12"	9 Blocks	12"	18 Blocks
8"	16 Blocks	8"	32 Blocks
6"	18 Blocks	6"	36 Blocks

Follow instructions on premixed mortar bag. Freshly mixed mortar may cause skin irritation. Avoid direct contact where possible and wash exposed skin areas promptly with water. If any gets into eyes, rinse immediately with water and seek prompt medical attention. Mixed mortar should be of a consistency that will allow it to stick to the edge of the glass block when the block is turned 90°. It's best to test the mortar on the block (Drawing E), and add water or mortar to the mix as needed.

Preparing mortar is an important step. If you have ever laid

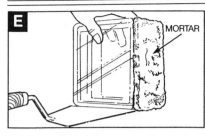

brick or concrete block, be aware that **glass block are nonabsorbent** and, accordingly, the mortar must be much less moist. The consistency should be spreadable, but not dry to the point of separating or crumbling.

Mix what you think you'll use in about an hour.

MIX-IT-YOURSELF MORTAR

The recommended proportions are:
  1 Part White Portland Cement
  1/2 Part Lime
  4 Parts White Sand

INSTALLATION

NOTE: No mortar is to be placed where expansion strips are used (jambs and head). For panels over 25 ft², you will have to install panel reinforcing.

Laying The First Course

1. Using the trowel, apply a full mortar bed to the sill. Sufficient mortar should be used so that a 1/4" joint will remain when the block are in place (Drawing F).

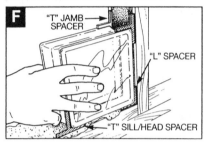

SERIES block.) Overlap reinforcing 6" where more than one is used (Drawing I).

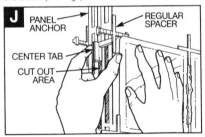

6. As the panel nears the head, the block will meet with the vertical, downward arms of the head panel anchors (top two courses for 6" and 8" block; top course for 12" block). These anchors should be positioned with the anchor between the spacer and the block. Make sure the center spacer tab fits in the cut out area of the panel anchor (Drawing J).

7. Because the top course meets the expansion strip of the head, no mortar is placed at the top edge of these block. Block and spacers for this final course are installed per Drawings K, L & M.

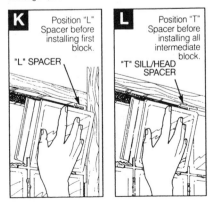

2. Install first block against expansion strip at the jamb location with modified spacers in place (Drawings D1, F). Note that **no mortar** is applied to this block.

3. After the block is positioned on the mortared sill, make certain that it is seated tightly against the spacers by pushing the block snugly into place. This seating check should be done for all the block you place.

4. Take the next glass block and apply approximately 3/8-1/2" of mortar to the vertical edge that will be contacting the preceding block.

5. Lay this block in place on the sill with appropriate spacers (Drawing G).

6. Continue the first course by repeating steps 3, 4 & 5 for each block.

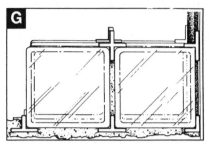

7. Periodically for this course and all others, use the small and large levels to check that all block are being placed level and plumb. If they are not, adjust accordingly before proceeding to the next course.

8. Using a damp sponge or polyfoam brush, press back into the joints any mortar that may have been forced out—no voids should remain in the joints. This replacing of squeezed out mortar should be done as required, and becomes increasingly important as you proceed.

Laying the Remaining Courses

1. Apply mortar to the top edge of the course of block just laid. Again, sufficient mortar should be used so that a 1/4" joint will remain when the next course is in place. Spread and smooth the mortar, but take care to keep the cross legs of the spacers as free of mortar as possible. This will ensure that the following course of block sits flat on the spacers.

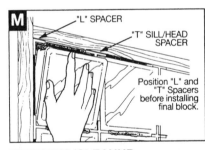

FINISHING/CLEANUP

1. Remove excess mortar from block faces using damp sponge or cloth—**rinse frequently**; do not use abrasive products for this cleanup. Be careful not to let any mortar on the faces totally dry before attempting to remove. At this point the block will still have a dry film over them which will be cleaned off later.

2. After the joint mortar has set up for approximately one hour, smooth all joints using a striking tool to remove excess mortar and produce a clean, professional-looking job (Drawing N). This smoothing procedure also compacts the mortar to create a moisture-proof seal. Striking should leave all joints completely filled with mortar.

NOTE: For shower wall panels you may want to rake out joints approximately 1/4" deep. After a 24-hour cure, fill the joints with a tub-and-tile grout.

2. Install second and remaining courses, except for the top, as was done for the first. Now, however, only REGULAR Spacers are needed on those block between the first and last of each course.

3. At the top of the second or third course (depending on block size being used) you will encounter the first jamb panel anchors. The top edge of the block **with spacer** should fit just **under** this anchor (Drawing H).

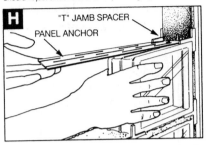

When mortar is applied to the top of this course, the anchors will be embedded in the between-joint course. For panels over 25 ft², you will have to install panel reinforcing after every third horizontal course for 6" block; after every other course for 8" and 12" block.

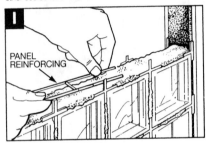

4. Apply a bed of mortar to the top edge of the already-installed block in that course.

5. Lightly press panel reinforcing into mortar bed. (2" wide for REGULAR SERIES block, 1 5/8" wide for THINLINE

3. One or two hours after striking, wipe the block faces with a soft, clean cloth to remove any remaining film.

4. At jambs and head, use caulk to seal the panel; trim molding may also be applied at these areas, if desired (Drawing O). Where a wooden curb has been used, cover it with trim molding.

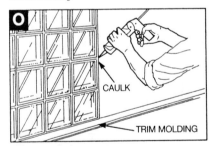

MAINTENANCE

An important part of the functional beauty of PC GlassBlock® products is that they are virtually maintenance-free! There is nothing to rot, rust, peel or paint.

All that is needed is an occasional wiping with a damp, soft cloth on interior panels...and a hosing on exterior panels. With this minimal attention, your PC GlassBlock® panel will remain sparkling and beautiful for years!

IF YOU NEED ASSISTANCE

We hope these instructions are clear and answer your questions about the installation of basic, straight panels of PC GlassBlock® products. A "How-To Install" video is available at your PC GlassBlock Distributor or local home center. If, however, you have questions, we are standing by to assist you at 412-327-6100, Monday through Friday, 8:00 a.m. to 5:00 p.m. Eastern Time. We'll be happy to help you in any way we can.

Manufacturers/Suppliers of Glass Blocks and Block Panels

ACRYMET INDUSTRIES, 42-05 10th St, Long Island, NY 11101 - (718) 786-7654
(manufacturers of do-it-yourself acrylic strip spacer system)

CIRCLE REDMONT, 2760 Business Center, Melbourne, FL 32940 - (800) 358-3888 (407) 259-7374

EUROGLASS CORP., 123 Main St., White Plains, NY 10601 - (914) 683-1390

GLASHAUS, INC., 415 W. Golf Rd., Ste. 13, Arlington Heights, IL 60005 - (708) 640-6910

GLASS BLOCK DESIGNS, 381 11th St., San Francisco, CA 94103 - (415) 626-5770

INTERNATIONAL GLASS BLOCK, 1316 E. Slauson, Los Angeles, CA 90011 - (213) 585-6368

PITTSBURGH CORNING, 800 Presque Isle, Pittsburgh, PA 15239 - (800) 992-5769 (412) 741-5082
(manufacturers of glass blocks, do-it-yourself installation kits and ventilation panels)

SHELTON GLASS BLOCK SYSTEMS, 6915 SW 57th Ave., Coral Gables, FL 33142 - (305) 667-4471
(manufacturers of framed glass block windows in glass block walls)

TAFCO CORP., 5024 N. Rose St., Schiller Park, IL 60176 - (708) 678-8425
(manufacturers of ventilation panels)

UNITED PANEL SYSTEMS, INC., 38 Kinkel St., Westbury, NY 11590 - (516) 997-2507

WATKINS CONCRETE BLOCK CO., 14306 Giles Rd., Omaha, NE 68138 - (402) 896-0900

WECK GLASS BLOCK, 415 W. Golf #13, Arlington Heights, IL 60005 - (708) 640-6910

- -

Tafco Vinyl Security Window

Features

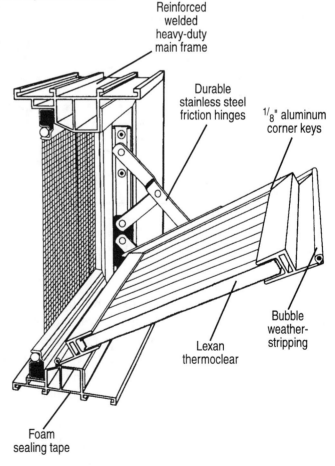

Reinforced welded heavy-duty main frame

Durable stainless steel friction hinges

$^1/_8$" aluminum corner keys

Lexan thermoclear

Bubble weather-stripping

Foam sealing tape

- Glazed with ribbed GE Lexan Thermoclear for impact strength **250 times** greater than glass. It can withstand repeated sledge hammer blows without breaking or cracking, and is listed as a Burglary-Resistant Glazing by Underwriters Laboratories. May also be glazed with $^5/_8$" insulated glass.

- Our security window insulates better than glass block.

- Our double sealing system, a bubble gasket on the door along with a foam seal on the main frame, insures a weather-tight seal.

- Welded main frame measures 3-$^1/_8$" deep for easy installation in a frame (buck), masonry, or glass block opening.

- Stainless steel friction hinges allow you to position door at any angle to control air flow.

- Window can be hinged to open up, down, to the right or to the left—making it truly multi-purpose.

- Available in all sizes.

- Cast zinc sash locks.

Q: The summer sun bakes me through my windows and skylight and fades my furniture. How can I inexpensively block the sun's direct heat, yet see clearly outdoors and still get free solar heat in the winter?

A: Blocking the sun's intensity through your windows can lower your air-conditioning costs significantly. In addition to blocking heat and glare, you must block the sun's invisible fading rays. These ultraviolet (UV) fading rays also slowly break down the fabrics and cause premature wear.

There are several inexpensive do-it-yourself summer-only methods to reduce the intensity of the sun through your windows without obstructing the view. These sun control methods are designed to be easily removed each winter to let free solar heat in through your windows.

I use a reusable summer-only self-cling film on several of my own south- and west-facing windows. It is available in lightly tinted gray or bronze and you can reapply it year after year. It is available in rolls or in do-it-yourself kits that include the film, knife, and squeegee for installing it.

This window film is made of self-cling vinyl. The vinyl creates a natural static charge that makes it adhere tightly to your window glass. There is no permanent adhesive. It blocks 55% of the sun's heat and most of the fading rays, yet still provides an undistorted view outdoors.

To install it, spray the window with water so the film slides easily. Lay the film against the window, cut it to size, and squeegee away the excess water. In the winter, you just pull one corner loose and peel it off.

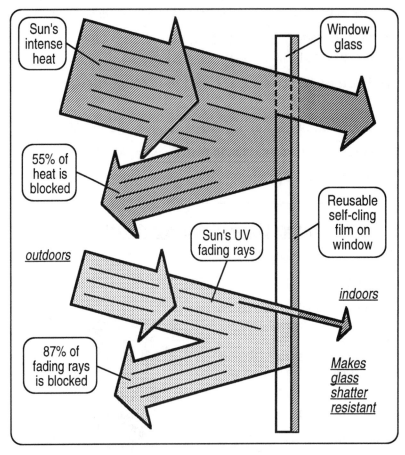

Roll it onto a paper tube or fold it up until next summer.

Another option is see-through roll-up interior shades that block heat and stop fading. One type uses a durable tinted mylar film that blocks 96% of the UV fading rays. It is mounted on a spring- or pull-chain roller.

Sun-control fiberglass screening can also be used for the roll-up shade. It blocks 50% to 70% of the sun's heat depending on the weave and color. The most effective new shade is aluminum foil embedded in tough fabric. It blocks all the fading rays and much heat, but you cannot see through it.

For a skylight, you can install a removable interior fiberglass screen shade. You attach narrow channels on either end of your skylight. You then wrap the screen ends around the rods to the desired length and tightness and snap them into the channels. There are also exterior skylight screen covers that attach with elastic bungie cords.

Q: My bathroom faucet drips and I wondered if the water saved by fixing it is worth the expense of calling the plumber. About how much water does a dripping faucet waste?

A: I opened a bathroom faucet a little in my own home to measure the amount of water wasted. The faucet dripped eight times per minute. Over six hours, it dripped a pint of water. This is equivalent to 182 gallons per year.

You should have the drip fixed. Although the amount of water wasted from your one faucet is not great, the total water wasted from many homes across the country is significant. Also it may be hot water which wastes energy too. A slow hot water drip feels cold by the time it gets to the faucet.

Do-it-Yourself Instructions for Installing an Interior Skylight Shade

Tools Required for Installation: screw driver, hack saw, mallet, tape measure, scissors

1) Measure width and length of skylight opening. Cut vinyl strip clips and sun screen retainer strips the width of skylight opening with a hacksaw.

2) Cut sun screen with scissors the width of the skylight opening. Sun screen width should be equal to vinyl clip strips and screen retainer strips.

3) With mallet or hammer, carefully line up and snap sun screen male and female retainer strips onto one end of sun screen. Roll screen out onto a flat surface and measure length of skylight opening and add four inches. Place second pair of retainer strips on this mark. Cut excess screen.

4) Attach vinyl clips to top and bottom widths of skylight opening with enclosed screws. Be sure to attach screws close to the edge of vinyl clip for added strength.

5) Roll screen at least two turns around screen retainer strips to get desired length and tightness.

6) Snap sun screen retainer strip with screen attached into top and bottom clip.

SCREEN TIGHT

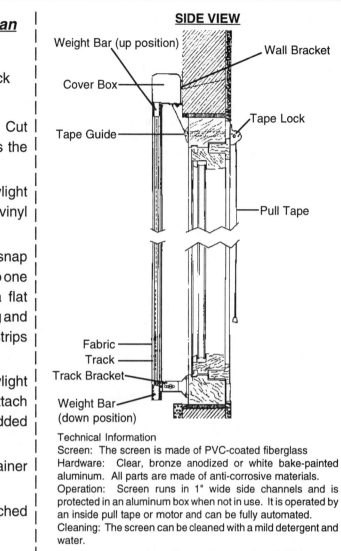

SIDE VIEW

Weight Bar (up position)
Wall Bracket
Cover Box
Tape Guide
Tape Lock
Pull Tape
Fabric
Track
Track Bracket
Weight Bar (down position)

Technical Information
Screen: The screen is made of PVC-coated fiberglass
Hardware: Clear, bronze anodized or white bake-painted aluminum. All parts are made of anti-corrosive materials.
Operation: Screen runs in 1" wide side channels and is protected in an aluminum box when not in use. It is operated by an inside pull tape or motor and can be fully automated.
Cleaning: The screen can be cleaned with a mild detergent and water.

EGE SYSTEMS SUN CONTROL

Do-it-Yourself Instructions for Installing an Exterior Skylight Shade

NO TOOLS REQUIRED

1) Gently wipe the skylight clean with a clean, damp cloth to remove dust and residue. Remove excess moisture by drying the glass thoroughly. Be careful not to scratch the skylight glass.

2) Unroll the sunshade carefully and position it over the skylight glass with the bungee strap knots face down.

3) Attach the sunbungee straps shade to the skylight by stretching and pulling the the lip on the sky around each corner. Pull the bungee straps under of the bungee light curb. It may be necessary to adjust the length sunshade firmly in place. straps to obtain an acceptable fit. Be sure to hold the

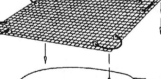
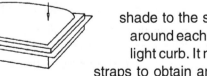

4) To achieve a snug fit and uniform appearance, reposition, and rewrap each corner of the sunshade individually.

SHADECRAFTERS

Manufacturers of Removable/Operable Sun-Control Products for Windows/Skylights

CLEAR-VIEW SHADE CO., 6124 N. Broadway, Chicago, IL 60660 - (312) 262-2360

description - These are interior roll-up shades using either a reflective or non-reflective sun control tinted film. It uses a chain-operated or spring roller shade. The shade material is available in a 4-mil thick reflective and a 3-mil thick non-reflective tinted film. It blocks up to 99% of the sun's fading rays and 95% of the sun's glare. The view through the tinted shade is <u>not</u> distorted.

* price - *film:* $44 spring roller for 3 ft. by 4 ft. tinted mylar shade - $10 additional charge for chain operation
sizes available - can go up to 12 ft. wide for single roller, but recommend 8 ft. to 9 ft. max. for shipping

EGE SYSTEMS SUN CONTROL, 15203 N.E. 95th St., Redmond, WA 98052 - (206) 746-7006

description - The operable exterior screens are made of PVC-coated fiberglass and block 80% to 90% of the sun's heat. You raise and lower the screen with an indoor pull tape. The screen slides up and down in 1" wide exterior side channels. When raised, it is stored in a small box above the window. Side channels and hardware are available in clear, tan or white coated aluminum. Motorized and automatic sun and wind controls are available.

price - *screen:* $333 for a 3.5 ft. x 5 ft. shade (to fit a 3 ft. x 4 ft. window)
sizes available - up to 10 ft. x 10 ft. shade with pull tape, larger for multiple shades and motors

MIDWEST MARKETING, 2000 E. War Memorial, Peoria, IL 61614 - (800) 638-4332 (309) 688-8858

description - These are interior roll-up shades using either sun control tinted mylar films or fiberglass shade material. The 4-mil thick 3-ply mylar shade material blocks from 51% to 72% of the sun's heat, depending on the color of the tinting (gray or bronze). It blocks 96% of the sun's fading rays and 90% of the sun's glare. The view through the mylar shade is <u>not</u> distorted. The fiberglass screening blocks up to 70% of the sun's heat. Spring rollers are often used on the shades with mylar film. Chain-operated shade rollers are often used on shade with fiberglass screening and very large windows.

price - *film:* $42 chain-operated or spring roller for 3 ft. by 4 ft. tinted mylar shade
sizes available - 146 in. max. width for mylar shade, 84 in. max. width for fiberglass screen shade

MOORE INDUS. COATINGS, P.O. Box 832, Boring, OR 97009 - (800) 448-6697 (309) 688-8858

description - The "Fabrifoil 7018" material is a foil-fabric hybrid. The aluminum foil is embedded deeply into the fabric and is virtually wrapped around each yarn. This combines the energy saving properties of aluminum foil with the durability of high quality fabrics. Blocks 85% of heat and all the fading rays.

price - *reflective fabric:* $42 for 21 ft. long x 54 in. wide roll - you buy the material and have it installed on a shade locally.
sizes available - 54 in. wide x any length in 21-ft. increments

SCREEN TIGHT, 221 N. Fraser, Georgetown, SC 29440 - (800) 768-7325 (803) 527-7658

description - This removable interior skylight shade uses sun control fiberglass screening. Mounting channels permanently mount on opposite ends of a skylight opening. You wrap the ends of the screening around plastic tubes and these tubes snap into the channels. It is very easy to remove in the winter for full light and sun's heat. When installed under the skylight, the screening blocks 70% of the sun's heat, glare, and fading rays.

price - *screen:* $30 for a 2 ft. x 4 ft. skylight
sizes available - 2, 3, or 4 ft. wide x any length to 4 ft.

SHADECRAFTERS, 1500 Beville Rd., #606-283, Daytona Beach, FL 32114 - (904) 788-4019

description - This is an exterior removable shade for any skylight with a raised curb. It uses fiberglass screening as the shading material. An elastic "bungee" cord is fed through brass grommets at each corner. To install it, you just stretch the bungee cords under the lip on the skylight curb. It is very easy to install and remove. It blocks 70% of the sun's heat.

price - *screen:* $25 for shade for a 2 ft. x 4 ft. skylight
sizes available - kits for 2 ft. x 2 ft., 2 ft. x 4 ft., and 4 ft. x 4 ft. skylights

SOLAR STAT, 511 N.E. 190th St., Miami, FL 33179 - (800) 783-0454 (305) 652-0454

description - This is an easily removable 4-mil thick tinted vinyl window film (does not obstruct or partially block the view like screening does). It uses the natural static charge of the vinyl to stick to the window. This is the same "peel-off" label material used on new TV picture tubes, for example. You can roll it on the window in the summer remove it in the winter and reinstall it next summer. With proper care, it should last for many years. It blocks 55% of the sun's heat, 88% of the sun's fading rays, and 62% of the glare. It can be applied to plastic or glass windows.

price - *film:* approx. $1 per sq. ft.

sizes available - 2, 3, 4, 5 ft. wide x 6.5, 15, 50 ft. long rolls; complete do-it-yourself kits, with film, knife, and squeegee, are available at retail outlet.

VIMCO, 9301 Old Staples Mill Rd., Richmond, VA 23228 - (800) 446-1503 (804) 266-9638

description - This removable interior skylight shade uses sun control fiberglass screening. It is a simple spring-loaded attachment which requires no holes, brackets or tools. You measure the opening and trim your fabric to fit the opening width. Adjust lock screws on compression rods and place the rods into the pockets in the screen. Attach three clips on each rod and position rods in the skylight opening. The skylight shade blocks 70% of the sun's heat, glare, and fading rays.

price - *screen:* $30 for 2 ft. wide and $60 for 4 ft. wide

sizes available - 2, 3, or 4 ft. wide x any length up to 5 ft.

description - This is an interior movable or fixed window shade that gives 100% complete blackout where total darkness is required. Operation can be by hand strap, pole crank, or electric motor with a wide selection of electronic controls. It features a fully enclosed head box and side channel allowing the shades to disappear into the pocket,

price - *screen:* $96 for a 3 ft. x 4 ft. clutch operated, $669 for a 12 ft. x 8 ft. motorized

sizes available - all are custom made

--- --- --- --- --- --- --- --- --- --- --- --- --- --- --- ---

Do-it-Yourself Instructions for Installing Self-Clinging Vinyl Window Film

Tools Required for Installation: Squeegee, Tape Measure, Straight Edge Ruler, Sharp Razor Blades, Exacto Knife, Glass Cleaner, Lint Free Cloth

Sun-Blocking Specifications for Solar Stat		
Color	Gray	Bronze
Total Solar Energy Rejection	55.2%	55.3%
Total Solar Energy Transmission	44.8%	44.6%
Total U.V. Rejection	82.3%	87.5%
Total U.V. Transmission	17.7%	12.4%
Visible Light Transmittance	37.2%	38.0%
Shading Coefficient	0.58	0.58
R - Factor	1.75	1.75
U - Factor	0.57	0.57

1) Avoid working in direct sunlight or wind. For best results apply when the temperature is between 45 and 90 degrees. Clean window thoroughly with a glass cleaner. Use a single edge razor blade to scrape excess build up. Make sure all corners and edges are as clean as possible. Wipe window dry with a lint free cloth.

2) Measure window. Unroll *Solar Stat* on a flat surface and cut one inch larger on each side to insure proper sizing.

3) Spray the window thoroughly with a glass cleaner before applying *Solar Stat*. **Wet generously.** Never install on a dry surface. For easier handling, spray the surface of *Solar Stat* before applying. This will prevent the film from clinging. Starting at the top, apply *Solar Stat* to the inside window. There is no front or back so either side may be applied. Position *Solar Stat* by using your hands to work out wrinkles until it overlaps the frame on all sides. On larger windows and doors some assistance will be helpful. The superior quality and durability of *Solar Stat* allows trouble free installation concerning wrinkles, creases, or if it should self cling.

4) Spray the surface of *Solar Stat*. **Wet generously.** Beginning at the center of the window firmly squeegee out bubbles and water towards the sides, working in a side to side, up and down direction.

5) After you have squeegeed out excess water and bubble, use a straight edge ruler to press *Solar Stat* to the inside edge of the window frame and trim excess with a sharp razor blade or exacto knife.

6) After trimming excess around entire window, firmly squeegee the edges towards the frame. At this point you may wish to repeat step #4. Any remaining small bubbles or excess water should evaporate in a few days. During the first 10 hours after installation Solar Stat should not be disturbed. On vehicles, do not roll windows up or down for the same time period.

Q: It is chilly near our windows and I want to try to make some inexpensive insulating shades myself. Can you tell me how to design and make them for high efficiency, yet have an attractive appearance?

A: Attractive energy-efficient window shades are easy to make yourself and can cut the heat loss (and sun's fading rays in the summer) through your windows by up to 75%. Another do-it-yourself option is a storm window kit. The rigid plastic storm window attaches and seals with magnetic strips.

Three key elements in designing and sewing an insulating shade are - 1) high insulation value, 2) airtightness, and 3) ease of operation. If the shades are difficult to open and close, you'll just end up leaving them open.

Making multi-layer shades provides the highest insulation level (R-value). Many thin layers are more effective than just one thick one. The small air gaps created with multiple layers blocks heat flow. Multiple layers also allow the shade to roll or fold up easier and flatter.

You can increase the efficiency of the shade by sewing a reflective layer in the center of the shade layers. This layer, either reflective mylar or foil (the type used in attics) helps to block radiant heat transfer year-round, especially in the summer.

It also minimizes the wasteful flow of indoor air, through the shade material itself, to the cold window glass. In cold climates, this reduces window condensation during severe weather. The reflective layer makes the shade hang flatter, so it looks better when it is closed.

To be most efficient, a shade should be as airtight as possible.

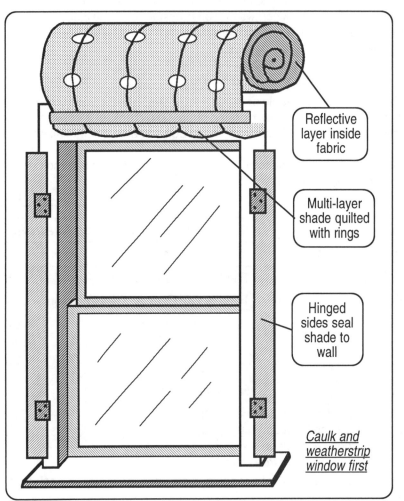

Reflective layer inside fabric

Multi-layer shade quilted with rings

Hinged sides seal shade to wall

Caulk and weatherstrip window first

Sticking adhesive-backed Velcro strips on the wall and the back of the shade forms an airtight seal. Decorative vertical wood strips, hinged to the wall or window frame, hold the shade tightly against the wall when it is closed.

A roll-up or pull-up (accordion-style) shade is easy to open and close. You can attach multiple pull strings, fed through an eyelet on the window frame, to raise and lower the shade various amounts.

Interior rigid (often one-eighth-inch clear acrylic) storm window kits can double the efficiency of your windows. The kits include all the materials. Various designs are attached by magnetic seals, Velcro, or clips.

One magnetic seal design uses a flexible magnetic seal like a refrigerator door. It seals well against an uneven wall or window frame and absorbs impacts from children. With proper care, these inexpensive storm windows last for many years.

Q: I am installing one of the new efficient temperature-controlling water faucets in my bathtub. Can you tell the proper ways to replace the ceramic tile that I accidentally cracked?

A: First clean out the grout around the tile. Using a chisel and a hammer, gently crack the tile in an X-pattern from corner to corner. Then slowly chip it away with the chisel working from the center to the edges.

Apply any standard waterproof tile adhesive to the back of the tile and press it in place. Wear rubber gloves and grout the joint, smoothing with your finger.

Instructions for making an insulating window shade yourself are listed on the following pages. To be most effective, the shade should have four major components - two layers of fiberfill, a layer of reflective film material, a layer of heavy inner-facing, and an envelope of fabric.

The reflective film layer is optional. The shade is still an effective insulator without it, but you will not feel as warm when sitting close to it. The reflective film is also effective in the summer to block heat from coming in through your windows. The air leakage through the shade itself is also reduced by the layer of plastic film inside.

You can also purchase insulating shades and kits for your windows. Window shade companies and some sewing supply outlets have kits available. One of the most energy efficient is "Window Quilt" brand. It is made by Appropriate Technology, P.O. Box 975, Brattleboro, VT 05302 - (800) 257-4501 (802) 257-4501.

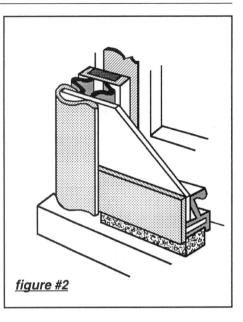
figure #2

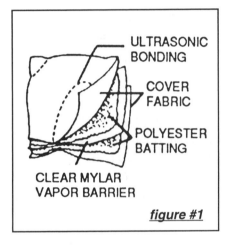

ULTRASONIC BONDING

COVER FABRIC

POLYESTER BATTING

CLEAR MYLAR VAPOR BARRIER

figure #1

They make two designs of shades - one attaches to a spring roller mounted above the window. The other design attaches around its perimeter with Velcro® to a mating strip on the wall around the window. Figure #1 shows the insulating multi-layers.

Installing interior insulating storm windows is another option. There are several effective attachment methods - magnetic, Velcro®, spring-loaded, and mechanical clips. Figure #2 shows a flexible bellows magnetic attachment. This conforms to irregularities on the window frame and absorbs impacts from children or objects.

Before you consider insulating window shades or interior storm windows, make sure your present windows are airtight. Caulk the non-moving joints and weatherstrip the moving joints. You can test the airtightness of your windows by holding a stick of lighted incense near them on a windy day. Move the incense around all the cracks and gaps that are weatherstripped and caulked. The trail of smoke from the incense will quickly indicate the leaky areas.

One of the most durable types of caulking is silicone. If you want it to match your wall exactly, make sure to buy a paintable silicone caulking. Most silicone is not paintable unless it is specifically marked as paintable. For double hung windows, a vinyl-bulb or other type of compressible weatherstripping is best. If you heat and air-condition year-round and never open windows, use a rope caulk to seal the sliding joints too.

Required Materials for Insulating Shade

muslin, duck, kettlecloth
½"-thick polyester or acrylic fiberfill
heavy inner-facing
reflective mylar film or standard window film
½" diameter plastic rings
crochet thread and nylon cord
¼" & ½" screw eyes
1-½" size spring hinges
1 x 2 and ½ x ¾ lumber
flat head wood screws
staple gun
2" size cleat
caulking and weatherstripping materials
general sewing supplies

figure #3

Do-it-Yourself Instructions for Making Insulating Shade

1) Measure the height of the window from the tip edges of window sill to the inner edge of upper casing. Measure the width of the window sill between the inner edges of the window casing.

2) Layout fabric and cut two rectangles whose dimensions are:

> 5 - ½" wider than the width measurement
> 3 - ½" longer than the height measurement.

3) Pin the fabric pieces together so that right sides face in. Leaving the top open, sew one side and bottom. On the other side, leave a 1-¼" opening near the bottom edge for the weight stick. Turn the shade right side out and press.

See Diagram #1

4) Sew a seam 1-¼" above bottom edge of shade. Cut the weight stick to 2" less than width of shade so the weight stick does not rub against the window casing. Insert the weight stick and sew the seam closed by hand.

See Diagram #2

5) Place the heavy inner-facing and fiberfill on top of it. Fold these layers in half lengthwise. You can also wrap this first with optional thin shiny mylar plastic film or reflective window film to help reflect the radiant heat or just lay on a sheet of film before you fold the layers over. You can buy the window film at most home center stores and the mylar film at many wallpaper stores. Then stuff the materials into the shade. The inner layers must fit tightly against the side and bottom seams.

6) Sew a ½" seam across the top edge of the shade cover and trim away the excess fiberfill. Leave at least ¼" of material above seam to allow room to attach the shade to the mounting strip.

See Diagram #3

7) Make marks on the back side of the shade for quilting. The first row of vertical stitches should be 2" in from the bottom edge. Allow 8" between stitches in vertical rows. The next rows of vertical stitches should be 2" in from the left side. Mark as many rows as fit, allowing 6" to 8" between rows.

8) With the front side of the shade facing you, staple the top to the mounting strip. Insert the screw eyes onto the top edge of the strip. The screw eyes should line up with the vertical rows of marks. Insert one ¼" screw eye per vertical row through the fabric into the bottom weight stick.

9) Thread two strands of crochet thread through a needle. Quilt where you marked the shade by pushing the needle from the back of the shade. Leave a 2" tail of thread on back. Push the needle back through and slip a plastic ring over needle. Secure it by tying threads around the ring.

See Diagram #4

10) Cut the nylon cords measuring twice the length plus the width of the shade. Cut as many cords as there are vertical rows. Tie each cord to the screw eye in the weight stick and thread the cords up through the plastic rings. Each cord is threaded through the screw eye at the top of the vertical row and through all the screw eyes to the left.

See Diagram #5

11) Cut two 1 x 2's each 4" shorter than the shade. Attach two hinges to each side clamp - 3 to each if the side clamp is longer than 60". Mount the side clamps to the window casing with screws, so it covers at least 1" of the shade when closed. Attach one additional screw eye to the outside of the opened left side clamp and thread all the cords through it. Attach the cleat under the sill, and tie the cords to it when the shade is open.

12) With the back side of the shade facing you, turn the shade upside down - mounting strip toward the floor and weight stick up. Place the raw stapled edge of the shade to the window casing and attach with screws. Adjust the shade so the edges are placed evenly over the side window casing and so the bottom edge of the shade extends 1" below top edge of sill.

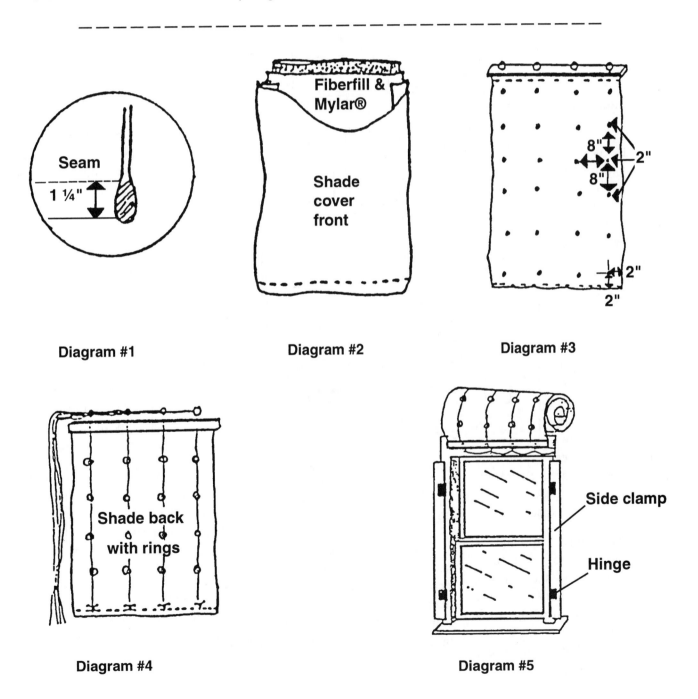

Diagram #1

Diagram #2

Diagram #3

Diagram #4

Diagram #5

Q: It gets chilly in our living room near the windows in the evening. Are there many types of simple inexpensive and attractive indoor shutters that we can build ourselves to block the cold?

A: Building inexpensive, yet attractive, insulating window shutters is a simple do-it-yourself weekend job. These shutters not only save energy year-round, but they also provide privacy and increased security. You will be amazed at how much warmer you will feel sitting near them.

For the best appearance with the most effective use of wall space, build a combination bookcase/window shutter. You can use inexpensive purchased or homemade shutters and build a bookcase around them.

When you open the shutters, they are hidden against the side walls of the bookcase around the window. Extending the lower portion of the bookcase further from the wall gives you a wider window sill and more storage space.

For maximum comfort and efficiency, make sure to weatherstrip the gaps around the shutters and between the hinged shutter sections. Vinyl bulb weatherstripping is effective and easily installed. It compresses when the shutters are closed, keeping out the cold air.

Solid shutter panels are the easiest to use. Much of the energy savings is gained just by blocking room air circulation against the cold window. Insulated shutters are somewhat more efficient, but they are thicker.

Mount the shutters close to the window. A narrower gap between the shutters and the window glass is

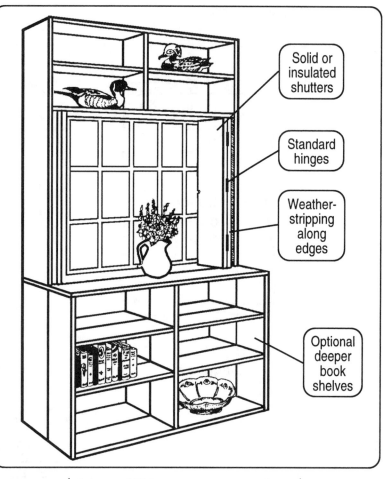

Solid or insulated shutters

Standard hinges

Weather-stripping along edges

Optional deeper book shelves

better. With a narrower gap, less energy-wasting air currents circulate between the shutter and the cold glass surface.

Louvered shutters are particularly attractive, but you will sacrifice some efficiency. If you install them, position the slats so, from top to bottom, they slant from indoors to outdoors. This helps keep the colder air near the window from flowing out into your room.

If you make your own shutters, without the bookcase, an accordion-style bi-fold design is easiest to make. When they are opened and folded flat against your wall, they extend out from your wall only double the width of the shutter material. You can also make insulated shutters by gluing thin rigid foam insulation between two thin wood veneers.

If you use many narrow sections (instead of a bi-fold), the shutters are thicker when opened, but don't extend out as far along the wall. While these shutters look nice, they aren't as energy efficient since there are more gaps between the additional sections allowing more air leakage through the gaps.

Q: I had a new central air conditioner installed last summer. My neighbor told me to cover it with a vinyl cover in the winter. Does it need to be covered and what type of cover should I get for my unit?

A: There is really no reason to cover the outdoor central air conditioner unit in the winter. It is designed to withstand the weather. In fact, most corrosion occurs in the summer when it is warmer.

Your neighbor probably confused central air conditioner with window units. It is a good idea to cover a window unit because cold may leak indoors through it during cold windy weather.

...fficiency double- and triple-
...more energy than even a
...ddition to losing energy,
...ld, you feel chilly sitting
...esults from radiant heat
...lf, especially at night.
...her, needlessly wast-
ing...

prove... ...other energy im-
caulki... ...e condition of the
candle... ...indy day, hold a
...ar the window.
(TAKE... ...Move the incense around all the window joints and where the window frame
meets the... ...u see leaky spots repair them. Putting up shutters over a leaky window will
waste both...

Install... ...e way to save energy and feel more comfortable. Shutters are more
effective than... ...lation value of the shutters reduces the conductive heat loss. They also
effectively blo... ...ainst the cold window glass. Shutters also save energy in the summer
by blocking the... ...rough your windows. They also block the direct sun in the summer,
especially on th...

To be most e... ...ints in the shutters. This reduces the air leakage past them. During
very cold weather,... ...or even ice on your windows when the shutters are closed. This
is because the glass... ...d, yet water vapor in the air still permeates through to the glass.
Therefore, it condens... ...a sign that your shutters are reducing the heat loss.

One attractive tec... ...build a bookcase around the window and shutters. When the
shutters are opened, they... ...kcase and are hidden. The bookcase also provides additional
storage and a larger wi... ...cks. Do-it-yourself plans and illustrations for making a
combination bookcase/sh... ...ages.

...kcase/Shutter

1) Plan the design of the bookca... ...e. Unless your window is extremely wide, plan on using bi-
   fold shutters (4 panels - 2 on ea... ...y wide, the depth of the bookcase would have to be too great
   to hide the shutters when they... ...e panel) shutters for wide windows.

2) You can make the shutters from... ...ood grade of plywood is an excellent choice. You can add rigid
   foam insulation to increase the i... ...minimize the weight. When the shutters are closed, all of the weight is
   supported by the side hinges.

3) Once you have determined the thickness of the shutters that you plan to use, quadruple that amount to calculate the opened
   thickness of both shutters. Add this number to the width of the window to determine the inside dimension of the vertical shutter
   side panel supports. Therefore, when the shutters are folded open, they will not block any of the window glass or be seen from
   outdoors.

4) Make your shutters halves (for bi-fold ones) using the plywood. Use standard hinges to attach the shutter halves (**A**) and (**B**)
   together. Drill the holes for hinges (**C**) so there is about a $1/_8$-inch gap between the shutters half edges when they are in the closed
   position. You will need this gap for space to attach the weatherstripping between them. Make the shutters the height of the window
   frame or slightly larger.

5) Lay the two shutter hinged assemblies flat on the floor with the center edges touching. Measure the total width of both shutters
   and add $1/_2$ inch to that dimension. This will allow for $1/_4$-inch clearance in the center and $1/_8$-inch clearance on each end for
   weatherstripping (**D**). You need more clearance in the center because the wood will grow and shrink with changes in humidity
   and temperature throughout the year. Soft compression-type weatherstripping will handle the changes in size.

Materials List for Bookcase/Shutter

good grade of plywood, hardwood or particle board
foam insulation board (1/2-inch thick)
thin wood or plastic veneer wood cover
hinges
foam or compression-bulb weatherstripping
wood glue
polystyrene foam glue
nails
screws
paint (exterior grade for insulated shutters)

6) Make side panels supports (**E**) for the bookcase using $1/2$-plywood or any other type of hardwood or particleboard. The length of the side panel supports will depend on the number of upper bookcase shelves you desire. The diagram shows two upper shelves. Since plywood is usually sold in 8-foot long sheets, you may want to run the bookcase from the floor to ceiling to simplify the construction. The depth of the side panel supports should be about 1 inch greater than the width of each panel (**A, B**). Therefore, the edges of the shutters and weatherstripping will not extend out past the edge of the side panels supports when they are opened.

7) Make the top and upper intermediate horizontal members (**F, G**) sized to fit in between the side panel supports. Make the center vertical support (**H**).

8) If you plan to make removable bookcase shelves (**I**), rout a slot in the side panels supports and the center vertical support to hold the shelves. Use 1-inch thick lumber for the center support if you rout slots, because there will be a slot routed in each side of it. You can also use plastic shelf support pins in drilled holes, but this does not look as finished.

9) Make the lower intermediate (**J**) and bottom horizontal pieces (**K**) the same size as the upper two. Make two vertical (**P**) supports and one center (**O**) support. Rout or use plastic shelf supports as above. The diagram shows an optional extended deeper lower shelves. It is best to make this as a completely add-on unit so that it can be removed without removing the entire unit from the wall and window.

10) Using screws and wood glue, assemble all of the members in a horizontal position on the floor, if the overall height is less than from floor to ceiling, usually 8 feet. If you are making it from floor-to-ceiling height, you will not have clearance to stand it up once it is completed, so assemble it vertically.

11) Cut the shelves to size and slip them into the routed slots. Attach the assembled shutter/bookcase to the wall using angle brackets on the inside surface of the side support panels (**E**).

12) It is best to wait to attach the shutters themselves until after the unit is attached to the wall. You may have to make some minor final adjustments on the shutters. Mount the hinges (**L**) for the shutters against the side support panels as close to the window as possible. The smaller the air gap thickness between the windows and the shutters, the better. This minimizes convection air currents.

13) Install $1/8$ to $1/4$-inch adhesive-backed foam weatherstripping between all of the vertical joints in the shutters themselves. Use vinyl bulb weatherstripping (**M**) on the edge of one of the shutters where they meet when they are closed. This is durable and compliant to changes in the gap size due to changes in weather conditions and temperatures.

14) Attach a knob and hook (**N**) to hold the shutters in the closed position. For the greatest efficiency, close them as soon as it gets dark enough outdoors that you are not getting usable light through the window. Also, if you are not using a room, close the shutters. On extremely cold and windy days, by closing the shutters you may save more energy in reduced heat loss than you spend for electricity to switch on a light in the room.

- -

Do-it-Yourself Insulated Shutters

1) Make the insulated shutters using $1/2$-inch thick rigid foam insulation board. You should be able to find this type of polystyrene foam board at most home centers or building supply outlets.

2) Measure the window to determine how big to make the shutters. It is most efficient to have the shutters recessed inside the window wall opening. This reduces the air gap between the shutters and the window and the air current between them. If you recess the shutters in the wall opening, they will extend out perpendicular from the wall when they are open.

3) If you want the shutters to lay flat against the wall when they are opened, you will have to make them larger than the opening and mount them on the wall.

4) Cut the foam insulation (**A**) 1 inch smaller than the final size of the shutter panels you want. Accordion double panel shutters are thicker than single panel ones when they are opened, but they don't extend out as far along the wall. If you make double panels, size the insulation piece 1 inch smaller for each panel.

5) Cut the outside wood veneer panels (**B**) from $1/16$ or $1/8$ sheets. These should be cut to the exact size of the panels that you want. Glue the foam pieces to one side of the wood panels using special adhesive for foam insulation. Some adhesives will dissolve the insulation, so be sure to use the proper type of glue. Center the insulation pieces on the wood panels. This will leave a $1/2$-inch gap around the perimeter.

6) Glue pieces of $^1/_2$x$^1/_2$ inch wood (**C**) against the insulation around the perimeter of the panel. Use the special glue for the foam insulation where the $^1/_2$-inch wood strips contact the insulation. Use standard wood glue on the surface that lays against the wood veneer. These wood strips serve several purposes - to finish the edge, add rigidity to the shutter panel, and provide a base for attaching hinges. Glue the remaining wood panels to the insulation and wood edge strip in the same manner. This produces the finished shutter panels.

7) Attach hinges (**D**) to the edges to connect the panels together and to the wall or window opening. Although it is not necessary, it is best to select hinges that leave a small gap between the panels. This provides room for narrow foam or compression bulb weatherstripping on the edge. When the panels are closed, the weatherstripping seals between the panel edges.

8) Paint the shutters with exterior-grade wall paint because it is durable. There may be some condensation on the outside surface (closest to the window) of the shutters when they are closed, particularly at night. If you want the natural look of the wood, apply a durable clear urethane finish.

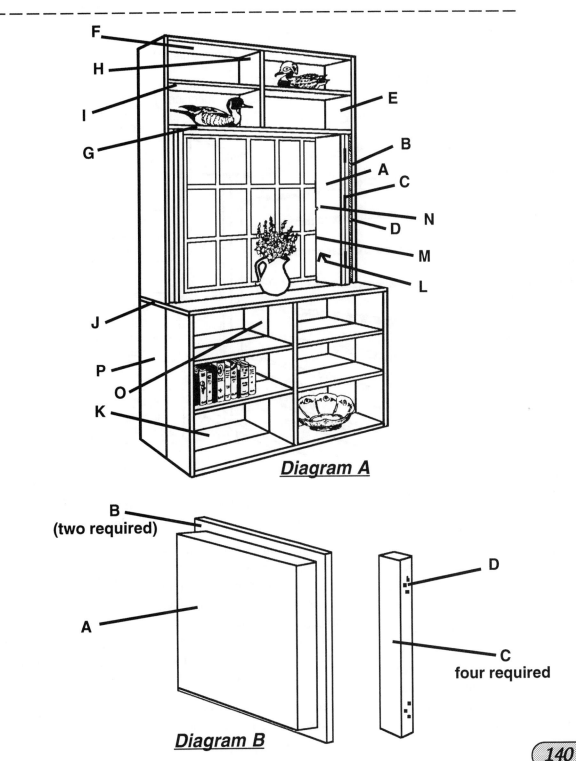

Diagram A

B
(two required)

A

D

C
four required

Diagram B

Q: I want to add some type of energy-efficient window covering for privacy and security against break-ins, but still allows for an unobstructed view when I open it. What do you recommend?

A: Exterior insulating rolling shutters are your best choice to provide the features you mention - energy savings, security, privacy, and a clear view. They are attractive on your home (available in 10 colors) and they have been popular on homes in Europe for many years.

Exterior rolling shutters also provide protection from hurricane or tornado force winds, over 100 mph for a standard shutter. You can get double and triple-strength models to withstand even higher winds and flying objects. Also, it would take a burglar a long while to break through one.

Insulating rolling shutters reduce the heat loss or heat gain through windows by about 50%. This results from the insulation of the shutter, the dead air space, and the reduced air leakage around your window. In the summer, it blocks the sun's heat and UV fading rays, but still lets in light.

Exterior rolling shutters are made of interlocking horizontal vinyl or foam insulated aluminum slats. These slide in aluminum channels on each side of the window and roll up into a small housing. This housing is located above the window, often under the roof soffit, so it is out of sight.

You can adjust the rolling shutter in several positions depending on your individual needs. For the maximum protection, efficiency, light and sound control, you completely lower and close the shutter. It can block 100% of the light for

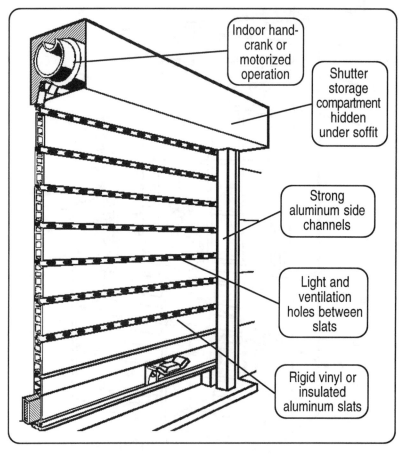

Indoor hand-crank or motorized operation

Shutter storage compartment hidden under soffit

Strong aluminum side channels

Light and ventilation holes between slats

Rigid vinyl or insulated aluminum slats

people who need total darkness to rest or sleep.

If you want some light and ventilation, roll up the shutter slightly to expose the interlocking flanges. There are small holes in the flanges. In this slightly-raised position, the holes are exposed. There are enough holes to allow you to visually distinguish forms outside the window.

For more light and ventilation or when seeking passive solar heat-ing in the winter, roll up the shutter to any position. When it is completely rolled up, it is totally out of sight from indoors.

You operate an exterior rolling shutter from indoors. The simplest method is a hand crank or counterbalanced strap. The most convenient method is an electric motor that you control with a wall switch or a hand-held remote.

For maximum protection from burglars and the weather, the shutter can be automatically closed by wind, sun, rain, or heat sensors or timers. When you leave your home, your house will be automatically protected.

Q: I have a wood-burning fireplace with large glass doors and a built-in blower. Should I be concerned that the glass may break when I am away from home?

A: Never leave home with a raging fire in your fireplace. Even if the glass appears to be free of flaws, it can shatter and blow sparks out into your room. I know because the glass in my fireplace door shattered for no apparent reason. Luckily, I was home at the time.

Do not build too hot a fire. The intense heat can cause the glass to lose its temper and develop fine stress cracks. Try to avoid hot flash fires from adding too much crumpled newspapers at one time.

Exterior rolling shutters have been popular in Europe for many years because they provide energy savings, privacy, and security. The energy savings come from the insulation value of the shutter slats and the dead air space created between the shutter and the window.

A unique feature of all exterior rolling shutters is the small slots or holes in the horizontal flanges between the slats (figure #2). These slots allow for ventilation and light without actually raising the shade. You just start to raise the shutter until the slats begin to separate and the slots are exposed. In the fully lowered position, with the slots covered, these shutters virtually block all the light.

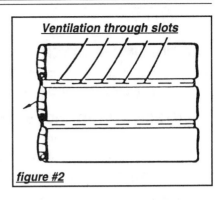

Ventilation through slots

figure #2

Although these rolling shutters are most often used on vertical windows, they also are ideal for mounting under a skylight. Figure #1 shows how one can be mounted. The one shown is made by Pioneer Roll Shutter Co. This particular model can be operated with a crank, 12-volt motor, or 120-volt motor. A 12-volt motor makes it easier to run an electric wire to the motor.

Page 143 lists information about the various manufacturers' shutters. The foam-filled aluminum slats are flatter, so they roll up tighter into a smaller storage box above your window. The PVC slats are strong and come in various cross-sections.

For large windows, a heavy cross-section slat design is needed. This also requires a larger storage box. The manufacturers or local dealers can recommend the best slat design for your specific home and weather conditions - tornadoes, hurricanes, extreme temperatures, sun exposure, etc.

Page 144 shows detailed information about exterior rolling shutters. Foam insulation filled aluminum and hollow (air-filled) are the most common slat materials. Several manufacturers also offer Lexan. This is a very tough plastic (used as bulletproof glass) and it is often lightly tinted in shutters. It is more often used for commercial installations.

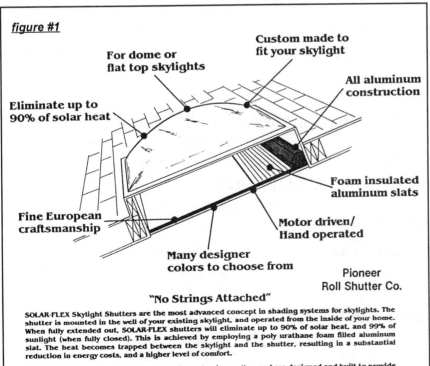

figure #1

Custom made to fit your skylight

For dome or flat top skylights

All aluminum construction

Eliminate up to 90% of solar heat

Fine European craftsmanship

Foam insulated aluminum slats

Motor driven/ Hand operated

Many designer colors to choose from

Pioneer Roll Shutter Co.

"No Strings Attached"

SOLAR-FLEX Skylight Shutters are the most advanced concept in shading systems for skylights. The shutter is mounted in the well of your existing skylight, and operated from the inside of your home. When fully extended out, SOLAR-FLEX shutters will eliminate up to 90% of solar heat, and 99% of sunlight (when fully closed). This is achieved by employing a poly urathane foam filled aluminum slat. The heat becomes trapped between the skylight and the shutter, resulting in a substantial reduction in energy costs, and a higher level of comfort.

All SOLAR-FLEX shutters are constructed from aluminum alloy, and are designed and built to provide years of lasting service. SOLAR-FLEX shutters come in a wide variety of colors to choose from, to accent any home decor.

Most rolling shutters work in a similar fashion. The unique special features of some are the types of automatic controls. In areas where there are sudden storms, automatic wind sensors can close the shutters before the storm strikes.

In hot climates, sun sensors are useful. A hand-held remote, like a TV control, is also a convenience. Seven-day programmable timers allow for a different schedule each day.

A typical installed cost for a 3.5 ft. wide by 5 ft. high PVC shutter with a hand crank is $650 and an aluminum shutter is $715. Motorized controls and special wind and sun sensors can cost an additional $300 depending on your specific home. For large shutters, generally over 6 feet wide, a motorized control is recommended.

Manufacturers of Rolling Shutters

AC ROLLING SHUTTER, 2310 Superior Ave., Cleveland, OH 44114 - (216) 621-4577
material - aluminum or PVC   insulation - air
operation - manual crank or electric motor   colors - aluminum - 5, PVC - 3

ALUTECH UNITED, INC., 512 N. Crain Highway, Glen Burnie, MD 21061 - (410) 768-7742
material - aluminum   insulation - foam
operation - manual crank/strap or electric motor   colors - unlimited
unique features - remote control, timers, temperature and wind sensors

AMERICAN ROLL SHUTTER, 31843 W. 8 Mile, Livonia, MI 48152 - (800) 331-1205 (313) 478-9311
material - aluminum, extruded aluminum or PVC   insulation - foam for Al, air for PVC
operation - manual crank or electric motor   colors - aluminum - 12, PVC - 4

PIONEER ROLL SHUTTER CO., PO Box 21240, Reno, NV 89515 - (702) 355-8686
material - aluminum   insulation - foam
operation - manual crank or electric motor   colors - 7 standard
unique features - remote, wireless, sun and wind control, light sensor, temperature advance

ROLLAC SHUTTER OF TEXAS, INC., 10800 Blackhawk, Houston, TX 77089 - (713) 485-1911
material - aluminum, extruded aluminum, PVC or Lexan   insulation - foam for Al, air for PVC
operation - manual crank/strap or electric motor   colors - aluminum - 10, PVC - 5
unique features - seven day programmable digital timer

ROLL-A-SHIELD, 3964 N. Oracle Rd., Tucson, AZ 85705 - (800) 457-8723 (602) 293-0666
material - aluminum with a baked enamel finish   insulation - foam
operation - manual crank/pull strap or electric motor   colors - 5 standard, 10 special order
unique features - remote control, wind and sun sensor, quick release system and a manual override

ROLL-A-WAY, 10597 Oak St. NE, St. Petersburg, FL 33716 - (800) 683-9505 (813) 576-1143
material - aluminum, PVC, or Lexan   insulation - foam for Al, air for PVC
operation - manual crank/pull strap or electric motor   colors - aluminum - 3, PVC - 4

SHUTTERHAUS-NUSASH, 2501 N. Anvil St., St. Petersburg, FL 33710 - (800) 330-7210 (381) 6522
material - PVC   insulation - air
operation - manual crank or electric motor   colors - 7 standard

SOLAROLL SHADE & SHUTTER, 915 S. Dixie Hwy E., Pompano Bch., FL 33060 - (305) 782-7211
material - aluminum or PVC   insulation - foam for Al, air for PVC
operation - manual crank or electric motor   colors - 6 standard

THERMO ROLLING SHUTTER, 5100 Jackson Rd., Ann Arbor, MI 48103 - (313) 995-0577
material - PVC   insulation - air
operation - manual crank/pull strap or electric motor   colors - 3 standard

TOP ROLL SHUTTERS, PO Box 2585, Salmon Arm British Columbia, VIE 4R5 - (800) 665-5550
material - aluminum or PVC   insulation - foam for Al, air for PVC
operation - manual crank/pull strap or electric motor   colors - 8 standard

WHEATBELT INC., PO Box 201, Hillsboro, KS 67063 - (800) 264-5171 (316) 947-2323
material - aluminum   insulation - air
operation - manual crank/strap or electric motor   colors - 3 standard
unique features - remote radio control, seven day programmable timer

Mini/Standard J
PVC Slat/RAW 30

Mini/Reverse J
PVC/SLAT/RAW 35

Mini/Curved
PVC/SLAT P20

1.25"   1.25"   1.25"

CP / COMPONENT PARTS

Slat Configurations:

Roll-A-Way Insulating Security Shutters are available in a variety of slat configurations to meet the most rigid shutter applications. There is a choice of six (6) PVC, two (2) aluminum foam filled, one (1) extruded double wall aluminum and one (1) Lexan® slat. This selection offers a number of advantages in residential and commercial applications where space and security is critical.

PVC slats are constructed of either white, ivory, beige or gray extruded BF Goodrich GEON® polyvinyl chloride #85887 which is UV stabilized. After years of field testing in Arizona, Ohio and Florida against hot, cold, humid and dry climates and conditions, this outdoor, weatherable PVC was chosen over imported PVC extrusions because of its excellent performance in strength and color retention.

The standard J and reverse J slats are superior to curved slats due to the following: The wall thickness of the J hook provides superior strength and support; the flat side creates better seating between slats; the step-down side provides additional wall strength and disruption of wind velocity; internal webbs provide additional strength; a wider hollow cavity provides added insulation; larger vent holes provide additional light and ventilation, creating excellent mood-lighting and visibility to the outside.

The foam filled slats are made from 3005H26 alloy, double wall cavity profile with a polyurethane insulating core available in standard colors of white, ivory and bronze.

The extruded double wall slat is made from 6063-T5 aluminum with a nominal wall thickness of 0.045" available in a white or bronze ESP paint or a clear anodized finish.

The Lexan® slats are made from Lexan® 153 polycarbonate resin which is UV stabilized, available in bronze tint. Slat L200 can be incorporated with RAW 60/65 slat to form a "window" within the shutter.

Slat Reinforcement:
6005-T5 alloy extruded aluminum.

Bottom Slat:
6063-T5 alloy extruded aluminum, typical wall 0.062".

Stormbar or Purlin:
6005 or 6105-T5 alloy extruded aluminum for fixed and removable application as requested.

Deluxe/Standard J
PVC SLAT/RAW 60

Deluxe/Reverse J
PVC SLAT/RAW 65

Large Curved 3-Rib
PVC SLAT P 55

Large
LEXAN® L200

2"   2"   2.16"   1.94"

Large aluminum
FOAM-FILLED SLAT
AF200

Mini aluminum
FOAM-FILLED SLAT
AF-150

Large extruded
ALUMINUM SLAT
US60

2.16"   1.57"   2.16"

Mini 6, 7, 8 & 10
4-SIDED

STANDARD
5-SIDED 10 & 12

STANDARD
6-SIDED 10 & 12

STORMBAR
(PURLIN)

TRACK HEIGHT
OPENING HEIGHT

Box:
ESP finished aluminum 3105-H14 with wall thickness of 0.032" is used for all configurations.

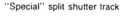

Typical Multi-Span Configuration
Multiple systems are connected to span virtually any width.

A   B

Y

Single track

"Special" split shutter track

TRACKS:

TYPE	A	B	Y
Mini	2⅛	3⅛	1³⁄₁₆
Std.	3	4.5	1.0

Roll-A-Way insulating security shutters offer a choice of two single and two split tracks to meet the most demanding configuration. The single tracks can be installed either jamb mounted or surface mounted as shown.

Track

JAMB MOUNT

SURFACE MOUNT

ROLL-A-WAY

Q: I would like some type of awning over my deck and large sliding glass door for blocking the sun's heat and rain. How durable and effective are the automatic retractable awnings that need no supports?

A: Retractable awnings are an excellent choice for decks and patios. They can be as wide as 40 feet and extend out from the house wall up to 12 feet or just as far as you need it. They need no supports that can get in your way.

Not only do they shield your deck and party guests from unexpected summer showers, but they block the sun's heat and fading rays. Extending the awning out over a large glass patio door can lower the indoor room temperature by eight degrees and protect your furniture from fading.

When you crank the retractable awning open, an elbow joint in each of two lateral support arms straightens. This extends the awning out over your deck. The arms are spring-loaded to keep the awning fabric stretched tight.

When the awning is retracted, the fabric rolls up and is stored in a small square box high on the house wall. With special covers, it is barely perceptible. The arms are fully collapsed at the elbows, they lay flush against the wall and are hidden too.

The least expensive awnings use a hand crank mechanism to open and close them. For easier operation, you can get an electric motor drive with a hand-held remote control, like a TV remote.

Special sun and wind sensors and 24-hour timer controls are also available. These automatically extend or retract the awning depend-

Adjust awning angle with screwdriver

- Stores in box when retracted
- Durable, waterproof multi-color fabric
- Control
- Folding lateral arms
- Extends 12 feet without supports

ing on weather conditions. For example, you can preset it to close the awning at a particular wind speed to protect the awning.

Most designs are supported by a single torsion rod that is attached to the wall. This makes installation simple. By just turning a few screws, you can adjust the angle of the aw-

ning to give the desired head clearance and shading. The lateral arms are usually made of special light-weight, high-strength aluminum alloys. With an anodized or baked-on finish, they are completely maintenance-free.

There are many choices of fabrics for retractable awnings depending on your specific needs. The most common fabric for residential use is solution-dyed acrylic. Laminated polyester materials are more waterproof for hard rains, but they are heavier and require a larger storage box.

Q: I have read where air leaks along the sill plate in a house are the greatest air leakage source. Where is the sill plate and how can I seal the leaks?

A: Many tests have indicated that the sill plate is the area of greatest air leakage. The sill plate is the piece of lumber that lays on top of the foundation. The walls attach to the sill plate. The top of the foundation, especially a poured foundation, is sometimes uneven and creates gaps.

I sealed the sill plate area in my home from the indoors using expanding foam caulk from a can. If you do not have access to it from indoors and must caulk from outdoors, make sure to paint it or the sun will degrade it.

All of the manufacturers of retractable awnings listed on page 147 use a similar design. A typical design is shown on the bottom of page 147 and typical installation instructions are shown on pages 148. This gives an idea of how they work. Basically, the two folding support arms are spring-loaded to pull the awning material taut. You can open only as far as you want.

I installed a 10 ft. x 12 ft. awning at my own home. It operates very easily with a simple hand crank. The hand crank method is least expensive. It takes about 30 seconds to open or close my awning. You can also get a motorized roller for easier and quicker operation. In areas where there are many storms and high winds, you can install a wind sensor to close it automatically in high winds. Sun sensors are also available to open or close the awning.

Solution-dyed acrylic is the most common residential fabric. It is durable and rolls up into the smallest storage box. Other fabrics are available (see selector guide below).

Awning Fabric Selector Guide

Generic Classification	Painted Army Duck	Vinyl Coated Cotton	Vinyl Laminated Polyester	Solution Dyed Acrylic	Acrylic Coated Polyester	Vinyl Coated Poly Cotton Blend	Solution Dyed Modacrylic
DESCRIPTION AND TYPICAL WEIGHT	Acrylic-painted cotton duck fabric. Typical weight is 11 oz. per square yard. Resistant to ultraviolet light, mildew and water.	Vinyl coated on cotton duck fabric. Typical weight is 15 oz. per square yard, resistant to ultraviolet light, mildew and water.	Tri-layer fabric, top and bottom layers are vinyl, middle layer is a polyester scrim. Typical weight range is 15 oz. per square yard, resistant to ultraviolet light, mildew and water.	Woven fabric, made of 100% acrylic solution dyed fibers with a fluorocarbon finish. Typical weight is 9.25 oz. per sq. yd. Resistant to ultraviolet and color degradation, also water and mildew.	Acrylic coated on each side of a polyester base fabric. Weights range from 9.5 oz. to 12.5 oz. per square yard. Resistant to ultraviolet light and mildew. Water repellent.	Vinyl coated on each side of a 50% polyester. Weight is 13 oz. per square yard. Resistant to ultraviolet light and mildew. Water repellent.	Woven fabric made of 100% modacrylic solution-dyed fibers with flourocarbon finish. Typical weight is 9.25 oz. per sq. yd. Resistant to ultraviolet and color degradation. Water repellent.
COLORS	Stripes or solids, primary colors, pastels, some earth tones	Solids or stripes - all colors are available.	Stripes, solids, primaries and pastels.	Wide variety - primaries and earth tones, solids and stripes.	Predominantly solids with some stripes. Same color, both sides.	Solid colors; same color both sides.	Solid colors and tweeds. Same color, both sides.
UNDERSIDE	Pearl gray, green or pearl gray with floral print.	Solid pearl gray.	Linen-like pattern, solid coordinating color to match top-side or same color as top.	Same as top surface.	Same as top surface.	Same as top surface.	Same as top surface.
SURFACE	Matte finish, with linen-like visible texture.	Smooth, non-glare surface with little or no texture.	Smooth or matte, with slight woven or linen-like texture.	Woven texture.	Surface is textured, with cloth appearance.	Surface is textured.	Woven texture surface.
TRANSPARENCY LEVEL	Opaque.	Opaque.	Translucent, depending on color.	Translucent, depending on color.	Translucent, depending on color.	Opaque.	Translucent, depending on color.
ABRASION RESISTANCE	Very good.	Very good.	Good. Base fabric is very strong.	Good.	Very good.	Very good.	Good.
DIMENSIONAL STABILTY (Stretch)	Very good.	Very good.	Very good.	Good. Some shrinkage in cold weather, some stretch in hot weather.	Very good.	Very good.	Good.
MILDEW RESISTANCE	Good. Not recommended for areas of constant high humidity.	Good. Not recommended for areas of constant high humidity.	Very good. Recommended for sustained high humidity.	Very good.	Very good.	Very good.	Very good.
DURABILITY/ AVERAGE LIFE SPAN	5-8 years (depends on climate and proper care of fabric)	5-8 years (depends on climate and proper care of fabric)	5-8 years (depends on climate and proper care of fabric)	5-10 years (depends on climate and proper care of fabric)	5-8 years (depends on climate and proper care of fabric)	5-8 years (depends on climate and proper care of fabric)	5-10 years (depends on climate and proper care of fabric)
FLAME RESISTANCE	Some colors are available with flame retardant treatment.	Some colors are available with flame retardant treatment.	All colors are flame resistant.	Non-flame resistant.	All colors are flame resistant.	All colors are flame resistant.	All colors are flame resistant.

Manufacturers of Retractable Awnings

ALCAN BLDG. PRODUCTS, 227 Town East Blvd., Mesquite, TX 75149 - (214) 285-8811

ARBOR AWNINGS, 5100 Jackson Rd., Ann Arbor, MI 48103 - (313) 995-0577

ARISTOCRAT FABRIC AWNINGS, 2901 N 18th, Philadelphia, PA 19132 - (800) 422-8577 (215) 228-6700

ASTRUP, 2937 W 25th St., Cleveland, OH 44113 - (800) 786-7616 (216) 696-2800

CANVAS PRODUCTS OF JACKSONVILLE, PO Box 57249, Jacksonville, FL 32241 - (904) 268-8000

CAPITAL CITY AWNING, 577 N Fourth Street, Columbus, OH 43215 - (614) 221-5404

DURASOL SYSTEMS, 197 Stone Castle Rd., Rock Tavern, NY 12575 - (914) 778-2686

EGE SYSTEM SUN CONTROL, 15203 NE 95th St., Redmond, WA 98052 - (206) 869-6575

STANDARD AWNINGS, 7 Conover Pl., Little Silver, NJ 07739 - (908) 741-0696

UNITEX, 5175 Commerce Dr., Baldwin Park, CA 91706 - (818) 962 - 6282

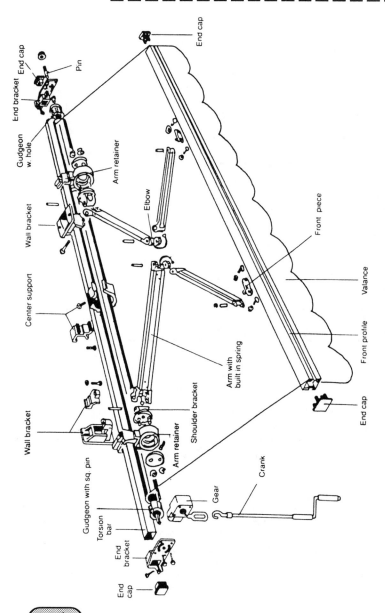

EGE *Elegant*

is a unique retractable and self-storing window awning that will add value to your house and improve your lifestyle. The tough, spring-loaded, folding arms extend generously without any need for cumbersome supporting posts. You can set the pitch or angle infinitely. Custom made to your specifications in any width with electric or manual operation.

- Add elegance to residential and commercial buildings
- Built-in heavy duty springs assure proper fabric tension
- Choose from over 60 fabric colors and patterns
- Mildew-resistant EGE 100% acrylic awnings can be rolled up wet
- Maintenance-free anodized aluminum
- 5 Year EGE warranty on hardware

TECHNICAL INFORMATION:

Width:	6'-40'; multiple units to any width
Height of unit:	9"-11", depending on installation
Projection:	Six projections available: 4'1", 5'9", 6'10", 8'6", 10'2", 12'0"
Pitch:	0-45 degrees
Arms:	Retractable with built-in heavy duty springs
Operation:	Manual gear/ hand-crank or electric tubular motor
Hardware:	100% maintenance-free, anodized, white, clear or bronze-finished aluminum; torsion bar made of galvanized steel or aluminium
Optional:	Aluminum hood. Fully automatic with sun and wind control

NOTE: Do not remove Red Plastic Protector from Arm Shoulder until awning is installed and ready to open. Use caution when removing Red Plastic Protectors. Arms are under tension.

IMPORTANT : If optional protective hood cover is used, it is **important** to refer to the enclosed hood cover instructions **first** — before continuing with installation.

Mounting

- Decide where awning is to be located.
- Mark center line.
- If door swings out, bottom of bracket must be at least 9" above top of door (Fig. 3).
- Top of bracket must be at least 2" below any overhang for proper clearance on electric units, or 1" below any overhang for manual units (Fig. 3).

UNITS WITH ODD NUMBER OF BRACKETS
- Measure 5' to each side of center line.
- End brackets must attach to Torque Bar no more than 12" on inside of Arm Shoulder. Locate on nearest stud or vertical mortar joint (Fig. 1).

UNIT WITH EVEN NUMBER OF BRACKETS
- Measure 7' to each side of center line.
- End brackets must attach to Torque Bar within Arm Shoulder and end of Torque Bar (Fig. 2). This allows approximately 12" to locate a stud or vertical mortar joint.
- Evenly space middle brackets to closest stud or vertical mortar joint (Fig. 2).

Wood-Mounting Installations — All brackets must mount to studs.
- Mount end brackets by drilling ¼" holes and mount using 5/16" dia. lagbolts and washers (Fig. 4).
- Using a chalk line, snap a line from opposite end brackets. Using chalk line as a guide, mount remaining brackets.

Mortar-Mounted Installations — All bottom bracket holes must line within a horizontal mortar line and top holes within a vertical mortar line.
- Mount brackets by drilling ½" holes and mount using stud bolt, washers and sleeve anchors (Fig. 5). Align sleeves so they expand against the brick instead of in the mortar line.

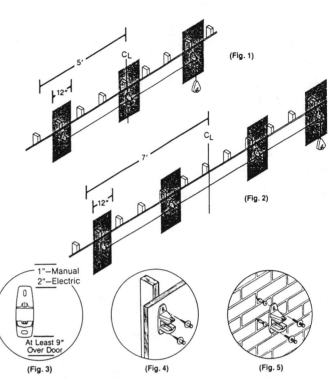

(Fig. 1)

(Fig. 2)

1"—Manual
2"—Electric

At Least 9"
Over Door

(Fig. 3)   (Fig. 4)   (Fig. 5)

Optional Installations — In cases where the awning is being installed on an irregular surface such as aluminum siding, it may be necessary to install a 2"x8"x10'/14' weatherized header to provide a solid support.

Mounting Unit To Brackets

Insert ¼" rod or something similar (not supplied) into Mounting Bracket as shown. This is an optional step to ease sliding of bar into "U" of bracket. This is not a mandatory step (Fig. 10).

Lift awning and hardware assembly onto rods and slide Torque Bar into "U" of the Mounting Brackets. (Remove ¼" rod if used.) Secure Torque Bar with supplied round head bolts and hex nuts. Insert bolts from the bottom. The nuts will lock in top of brackets (Fig. 11.)

At this time tighten all Mounting Bracket lagbolts securely. Press Plastic Cover over bolt.

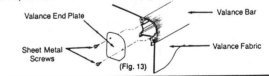

Hex Nut

Torque Bar

Plastic Cover

(Fig. 11)

¼" Rod

Round Head Bolts

(Fig. 10)

Remove Red Plastic Protectors from Arms.
(CAUTION: *Arms are under tension.*)

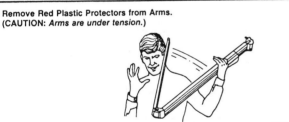

Valance Fabric

Insert Aluminum Rod into Valance fabric loop. (Rod is packed inside of the Valance Bar.) Slide fabric with rod into the bottom opening of the Valance Bar. Replace end cover on Valance Bar (Fig. 13).

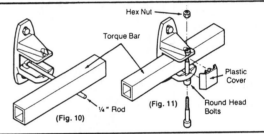

Valance End Plate

Valance Bar

Sheet Metal Screws

Valance Fabric

(Fig. 13)

Adjustments

Awning is extended to its maximum open position when the arms are almost straight and the awning fabric is still taut. There should be 1-2 turns of fabric remaining on the awning roll.

If the unit is slightly out of parallel as shown in Figure 14, or if the fabric rolls to one side during operation, the fabric has not been located properly on the awning roll. Extend the awning to the maximum open position, continue cranking until the starter strip is visible. Realign fabric on the starter strip.

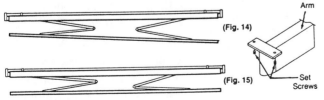

(Fig. 14)

(Fig. 15)

Arm

Set Screws

If the valance bar is parallel with the awning roll but the arms at different angles as shown in Figure 15, loosen set screws on retainer pins that hold the arms to the valance bar and reposition so that the arms are centered with each other. This adjustment should be done when the awning is in the retracted position.

Awning can be adjusted to vary the pitch of the awning for different valance heights. Extend the awning to full open position.

Have one person hold the valance bar at mid-point (Fig. 17). Loosen both Shoulder Bolts (Fig. 16). A tap on the bolt will loosen the joint so the arms will lower or raise to desired height. Raise the Valance Bar 12-18" higher than the final desired height during adjustment (Fig. 17). Generally, the Valance Bar will sag slightly after tightening the Shoulder Bolts.

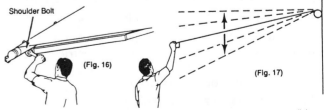

Shoulder Bolt

(Fig. 16)   (Fig. 17)

Align the Awning Roll with the Valance Bar by sight to assure they are parallel.

NOTE: Shoulder may not release even though shoulder bolt has been loosened. This is due to the friction lock of the shoulder. If this happens, loosen bolts and grasp the arm near the shoulder. Exert an up and down motion on the arm, which will release the friction lock.

Q: I like a hot shower in the morning, but we run out of hot water after the kids' showers. Keeping the water heater temperature set high wastes energy. Will a new instantaneous tankless water heater help?

A: An instantaneous water heater is the most energy efficient option available. It can supply enough steamy water for ten consecutive showers in the morning, yet use much less energy than your current water heater. A standard tank-type electric water heater easily can account for $200 to $300 of your annual utility bills.

With an instantaneous water heater, you can immediately run your dishwasher or clothes washer after showering without having to wait for the water in the tank to heat again. Standard water heaters, especially electric, have slow heat recovery rates.

To supply enough hot water for many showers with a typical water heater, you either must set the water temperature higher or have a very large tank. The tank walls continually lose about 15% of the heat. This increases your utility bills year-round and the air conditioner load in the summer.

An instantaneous (also called tankless) water heater has no inefficient tank of hot water. It heats the water only when you need it. When you turn on a hot water faucet, the heater senses the water pressure difference and immediately switches on the high-intensity heater.

High output gas burners or electric heater elements are used. As the cold water passes through the water heater, it is heated instantly. The gas units have the greatest hot water heating capacity.

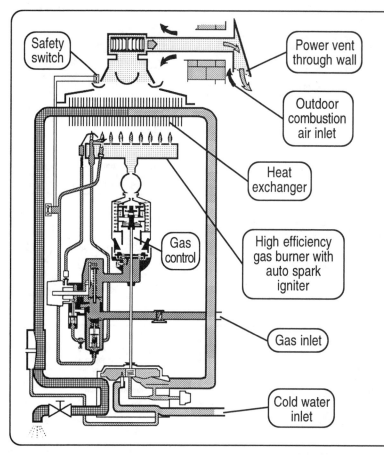

Safety switch

Power vent through wall

Outdoor combustion air inlet

Heat exchanger

Gas control

High efficiency gas burner with auto spark igniter

Gas inlet

Cold water inlet

These heaters are small and can be mounted on a wall in your utility room or basement. Some gas models have power vents to exhaust the flue gases outdoors through a small horizontal pipe. This is ideal if you want to convert from a costly electric water heater to a gas or propane instantaneous model. You will not have to build a chimney.

Although the initial cost of an instantaneous water heater is slightly higher than a conventional high-efficiency tank-type water heater model, one should last a long time. They are designed with replaceable parts, so they can be repaired if needed. There is no tank to get rusty and leaky.

A lower cost option is to install a tiny instantaneous electric water heater under the sink just to serve that bathroom. If your bathroom is like mine, it takes over a minute to get hot water after you turn on the faucet. The tiny instantaneous unit will provide hot water in seconds.

Q: I save styrofoam egg cartons, fast food hamburger containers, etc. because they are not biodegradable. Will these be effective insulation to put behind the paneling in my study which I'm remodeling?

A: Polystyrene foam material is good insulation, but I would not recommend it for that application. Polystyrene foam will burn and building fire codes usually require it to be covered with drywall.

If you want to find a good use for the waste foam containers, contact recyclers in your area. They can direct it for use in many types of products. For example, one new type of house construction method uses a cement/recycled polystyrene foam mixture for energy efficient wall blocks.

Instantaneous tankless water heaters, available in natural gas, bottled gas, or electricity, have no large tank of hot water. Instead, they have high-intensity gas burners or electric elements to heat the water on demand. This saves energy and can provide a continuous flow of hot water. A typical water heater loses up to 15% of its heat to the room air surrounding it. The loss is compounded in the summer. Your air conditioner must run longer to remove this waste heat from your house.

Your standard water heater relies on the reservoir of hot water in the tank, so it doesn't need as fast a heat recovery rate. This is fine until you try to take several consecutive showers or run your clothes washer right after showering. Then you run out of hot water. Since the tankless water heaters have such high-intensity heaters inside, you could take 100 consecutive showers and still have plenty of hot water. There is a pressure sensor in the water heater that senses when you open a hot water faucet. This starts the heater immediately.

Although you can take unlimited numbers of consecutive showers, you cannot do several hot water-using tasks at one time. The total output of hot water (in gallons per minute - gpm) is limited to the maximum output of the tankless water heater. As is shown on page 151, different models have different hot water output capacities. For example, a small gas unit at 2 gpm would be adequate for a simultaneous shower and perhaps handwashing the dishes. If you have two family members taking showers at the same time, you should select a larger capacity model. The chart below shows estimates of water usage for several household tasks.

Before you buy a tankless water heater, consider your water usage patterns. Make a list of any simultaneous hot water-consuming task that your family usually does. Estimate the amount of hot water in gpm that each task uses and add them together. This will indicate the maximum capacity of the tankless water heater you will need. By varying your water usage patterns a little, you may be able to get by with a smaller capacity unit at a lower cost.

If you contact the manufacturers listed on page 151 or their dealers, they should be able to advise you about the hot water consumption of various tasks. A sample list is shown below. Keep in mind that these are only estimates and the actual mount used varies by your specific habits.

Some models have automatic two-stage or variable-stage outputs to match the heat output to the amount of hot water that you need for a specific task. This gives more even water temperatures. For example, taking a shower with a low-flow shower head needs less hot water than filling your clothes washer. Other models have a manual dial that you can adjust. Where the manufacturers offer automatic two- and variable-stage outputs or manual adjustments, it is indicated on page 151 in the specifications.

The output specifications are shown in hot water flow in gpm for a **certain temperature rise** of the water. This means that if the incoming cold water is at 55 degrees, a 60-degree temperature rise would heat it to 115 degrees and supply a 3.5 gpm flow rate, for example.

If you plan to install a whole-house electric tankless water heater in place of your tank-type water heater, you will have to run a heavier electric line to it. This is needed because of the high-intensity element. The natural and bottled gas water heaters have the greatest output. Some of them have power vents so you do not need a chimney. These units have a blower that forces the exhaust fumes out through a horizontal pipe in the wall. This is ideal if you have an electric water heater now and you want to convert the heater to gas.

Another excellent use of a small (**point of use**) electric tankless water heater is in a bathroom. Typically, it takes a long while to get hot water to the faucet in the morning. This wastes energy and it wastes water down the drain. Installing a small tankless water heater under the sink can supply hot water in seconds.

Hot Water Usage for Several Tasks - in gpm	
*Showering - low-flow shower head	1.5
*Bathing	2
*Kitchen faucet	1
*Bathroom faucet	1
Dishwasher	3
Clothes washer - hot setting	3
* total water flow is greater than hot water flow because you are generally mixing in some cold water too.	

Manufacturers of Instantaneous Water Heaters

ADVANCED TECH IND., 7441 NW 8th St., Suite J, Miami, FL 33126 - (305) 265-7751

CHRONOMITE LABS, 21011 S. Figueroa St., Carson, CA 90745 - (800) 447-4962 (213) 320-9452

CONTROLLED ENERGY CORP., Fiddler's Green, Waitsfield, VT 05673 - (800) 642-3199 (802) 496-4436

EEMAX INC., 472 Pepper St., Monroe, CT 06468 - (800) 543-6163 (203) 261-0684

HOT AQUA INDUSTRIES, INC., 5916 Smiley Dr., Culver City, CA 90232 - (800) 441-0011 (310) 202-0111

KELTECH INC., PO Box 405, Richland, MI 49083 - (800) 999-4320 (616) 629-4814

KILO ALPHA CO., PO Box 768, Chatham, MA 02633 - (508) 945-4747

    model - "Original Pipe Water Heater"   type - electric   voltage - 120 volts

    features - This is not a tankless water heater but is attached to copper pipes only to heat the water.

PALOMA INDUSTRIES, 1440 Howard St., Elk Grove Village, IL 60007 - (708) 806-1010

VAILLANT CORP., 2607 River Rd., Cinnaminson, NJ 08077 - (609) 786-2000

WOLTER SYSTEMS, 1100 Harrison Ave., Cincinnati, OH 45214 - (513) 651-2666

Hot Water Output Capacities							
Company	**Model and Type**	**Voltage**	**Gallons per Minute (GPM) at**				
			50°	**60°**	**70°**	**80°**	**90°**
Advanced Tech Ind.	Supreme	I220	240	2.20	1.83	1.57	1.38	1.22
		S220	240	2.60	2.17	1.86	1.63	1.44
Chronomite Labs	Instant Flow	S-30L	120/240	0.41	0.34	0.29	0.26	0.23
		S-461	240	0.63	0.53	0.45	0.39	0.35
		S60C	240	0.82	0.68	0.59	0.51	0.46
		S70C	240	0.96	0.80	0.69	0.60	0.53
		S901	240	1.24	1.03	0.88	0.77	0.69
	Instant Temp	E-30	120/240	0.40	0.33	0.28	0.25	0.22
		E-46	240	0.62	0.52	0.44	0.39	0.34
		E-60	240	0.82	0.68	0.59	0.51	0.46
		E-70	240	0.96	0.80	0.69	0.60	0.53
		E-80	240	1.08	0.90	0.77	0.68	0.60
		E-90	240	1.22	1.02	0.87	0.76	0.68
Controlled Energy	Aquastar	80	gas	2.30	1.80	1.67	1.44	1.30
		125	gas	3.80	3.25	2.85	2.37	2.11
		170	gas	5.30	4.41	3.77	3.31	2.95
	Ariston	P10S	120	0.23	0.20	0.17	0.15	0.13
		P15S	120	0.31	0.26	0.22	0.19	0.17
	Powerstream	RP1-4	240	1.28	1.07	0.91	0.80	0.71
		RP1-2	240	0.64	0.53	0.46	0.40	0.36
		RP3	120	0.40	0.33	0.29	0.25	0.22
EEMax Inc.	Series-Two	EX144	240	1.95	1.63	1.39	1.22	1.08
		EX190	240	2.61	2.18	1.86	1.63	1.45
Hot Aqua Ind.	Hot Aqua	32	120	0.44	0.37	0.31	0.27	0.24
		59	240	0.80	0.67	0.57	0.50	0.45
Keltech Inc.	Acutemp	100	240	1.36	1.13	0.97	0.85	0.75
		120	240	1.64	1.37	1.17	1.03	0.91
		150/15	240	2.04	1.70	1.46	1.28	1.13
		180/18	240/480	2.44	2.03	1.74	1.53	1.36
Paloma Industries	Constant Flo	PH-6	gas	1.40	1.17	1.00	0.88	0.78
		PH-12	gas	2.86	2.39	2.04	1.79	1.59
		PH-24	gas	5.71	4.76	4.08	3.57	3.17
Vaillant Corp.	Valliant Mag	325	gas	2.03	1.69	1.45	1.27	1.13
Wolter Systems	Wolter	300	gas	1.20	1.00	0.86	0.75	0.67

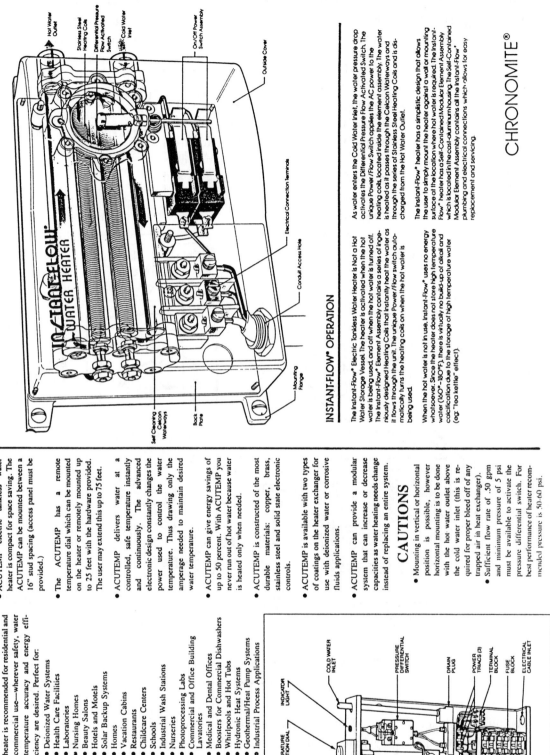

![Acutemp logo] ETL

KELTECH INC.

TANKLESS ELECTRIC WATER HEATERS

[PP] Product Presentation

The ACUTEMP tankless water heater is a modulating heater that incorporates a control system to allow the user to select the desired output temperature from 40° to 160° F within the limits of the flow chart. A thermostatic dial, graduated in degrees Fahrenheit, can be remotely mounted from the heater itself. The advanced electronic design constantly changes the power used to control the water temperature. A temperature sensor in the outlet side of the heat exchanger signals to the control system to regulate the temperature of the outlet water flow.

[UA] Uses, Applications

The ACUTEMP instant tankless water heater is recommended for residential and commercial use—wherever safety, water temperature accuracy and energy efficiency are desired. Perfect for:

- Deionized Water Systems
- Health Care Facilities
- Laboratories
- Nursing Homes
- Beauty Salons
- Hotels and Motels
- Solar Backup Systems
- Homes
- Vacation Cabins
- Restaurants
- Childcare Centers
- Schools
- Industrial Wash Stations
- Nurseries
- Photoprocessing Labs
- Commercial and Office Building Lavatories
- Medical and Dental Offices
- Boosters for Commercial Dishwashers
- Whirlpools and Hot Tubs
- Hydronic Heat Systems
- Geothermal/Heat Pump Systems
- Industrial Process Applications

ADVANTAGES

- ACUTEMP electric tankless water heater is compact for space saving. The ACUTEMP can be mounted between a 16" stud spacing (access panel must be provided.)
- The ACUTEMP has a remote temperature dial which can be mounted on the heater or remotely mounted up to 25 feet with the hardware provided. The user may extend this up to 75 feet.
- ACUTEMP delivers water at a controlled, safe temperature instantly and continuously. The advanced electronic design constantly changes the power used to control the water temperature. Thus drawing only the amperage needed to maintain desired water temperature.
- ACUTEMP can give energy savings of up to 50 percent. With ACUTEMP you never run out of hot water because water is heated only when needed.
- ACUTEMP is constructed of the most durable materials: copper, brass, stainless steel and solid state electronic controls.
- ACUTEMP is available with two types of coatings on the heat exchanger for use with deionized water or corrosive fluids applications.
- ACUTEMP can provide a modular system that can increase or decrease capacities as water heating needs change instead of replacing an entire system.

CAUTIONS

- Mounting in vertical or horizontal position is possible, however horizontal mounting is to be done with the hot water outlet above the cold water inlet (this is required for proper bleed off of any trapped air in heat exchanger).
- Sufficient flow rate of .50 gpm and minimum pressure of 5 psi must be available to activate the pressure differential switch. For best performance of heater recommended pressure is 50-60 psi.

INSTANT-FLOW® OPERATION

The Instant-Flow® Electric Tankless Water Heater is Not a Hot Water Storage Vessel. The heater is activated when the hot water is being used, and off when the hot water is turned off. The Instant-Flow® Element Assembly contains a series of ingeniously designed Heating Coils that instantly heat the water as it flows through the unit. The unique Power/Flow switch automatically turns the heating coils on when the hot water is being used.

When the hot water is not in use, Instant-Flow® uses no energy whatsoever. Since the heater does not store high temperature water (160°-180°F), there is virtually no build-up of alkali and calcification due to the storage of high temperature water (eg: "tea kettle" effect).

As water enters the Cold Water inlet, the water pressure drop activates the Differential Pressure Flow Activated Switch. The unique Power/Flow Switch applies the AC power to the heating coils, located inside the element assembly. The water is heated as it passes through the Celcon Waterways and through the series of Stainless Steel Heating Coils and is discharged from the Hot Water Outlet.

The Instant-Flow® heater has a simplistic design that allows the user to simply mount the heater against a wall or mounting surface at the location where hot water is required. The Instant-Flow® heater has a Self-Contained Modular Element Assembly which is located in the cast-aluminum housing. The Self-Contained Modular Element Assembly contains all the Instant-Flow® plumbing and electrical connections which allows for easy replacement and servicing.

CHRONOMITE®

Q: I have heard about a new super-efficient water heater accessory that can cool and dehumidify my house for free. How do these work and can I attach one to my existing water heater?

A: You are referring to a small add-on heat pump water heater (HPWH). The super-efficient ones can cut water heating costs by 60% and save more than $200 per year. As they heat the water, they produce up to 7,000 Btu/hr of free cooling. Other models cool and dehumidify fresh outdoor air.

An add-on HPWH operates similarly to a small window air conditioner. You can locate it near your existing water heater or in another room. Some models mount directly on top of the water heater to save floor space.

A HPWH draws heat from the surrounding air. Instead of exhausting this heat outdoors and wasting it as an air conditioner does, it is used to heat water in your existing water heater. The electric heating element or gas burners in your water heater seldom have to come on.

A small add-on HPWH (1.5 ft. wide) can be located anywhere in your home and plumbed to the water heater. Locate it in a room that you want to cool and dehumidify - a kitchen or musty basement, for example. Some models allow you to

duct the cool dry air to another room or to your central A/C ducts.

It is easy to install an add-on HPWH. Some do-it-yourself installation kits include a special coaxial water fitting that replaces the tank drain valve. This carries cold incoming water to the HPWH and hot water from it naturally follows back into the tank through the same fitting with no pumps.

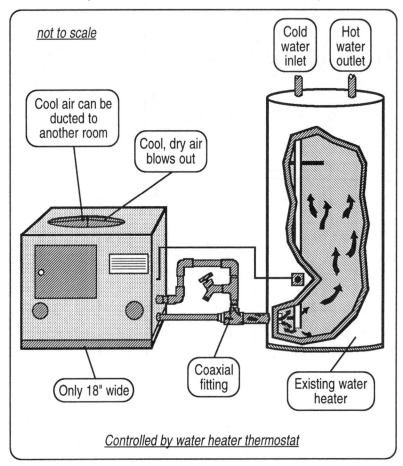

not to scale

Cool air can be ducted to another room

Cool, dry air blows out

Cold water inlet

Hot water outlet

Only 18" wide

Coaxial fitting

Existing water heater

Controlled by water heater thermostat

Complete integral HPWH/tank systems are also available. Venting models draw heat and humidity from incoming fresh outdoor air. This produces positive fresh and cool ventilation while heating your water for free.

For people with allergies or indoor pollutant sensitivity, it is a cost-effective and efficient method to improve indoor air quality.

If you have central air, a hot plate heat exchanger is effective for free hot water. The refrigerant lines from the air conditioner unit run through a heat exchanger plate under your existing water heater. Using no pumps or electricity, it transfers heat to the water heater for free hot water.

For an inefficient old central air conditioner, installing a dehumidifying heat pipe can reduce the muggy feeling inside your home without using more electricity. This pre-cools the air over the coils so more moisture is condensed out. It is a simple add-on device with no wiring or motors.

Q: I have an old self-defrost freezer that I keep in the utility room. The self-defrost feature in my freezer no longer works. Does this make it more inefficient and waste electricity?

A: It probably uses less electricity now than when it was new. The self-defrost feature on refrigerators and freezers uses a lot of extra electricity. They self defrost by briefly switching on heaters inside the compartment to melt the frost several times a day.

If yours is not working, it is not using the heater electricity. To maintain its efficiency, you should manually defrost it whenever the frost reaches .25 inches thick. If it gets thicker, it slows heat transfer.

A heat pump water heater (HPWH) produces hot water while cooling and dehumidifying your home. These units draw heat from the air inside your home and transfer this heat to your water heater tank. They operate similar to a window air conditioner, except that the heat is not exhausted outdoors.

These units operate very efficiently, providing up to $2.50 worth of heat for each $1.00 on your monthly electric bill (an *"energy factor"* of 2.5). The chart below compares the cost of heating water with a HPWH to using a standard electric water heater. Page 155 lists the manufacturers of HPWH's and detailed information. The *"recovery rate"* indicates how fast the HPWH produces hot water.

You must determine your home's specific needs to decide which model of HPWH is best for you. If you want to air-condition the room where your water heater is located, the HPWH model that mounts on top of your existing water heater is ideal (Crispaire #R106K2). It saves floor space and minimizes plumbing modifications.

For cooling other areas of your home, away from the water heater room, you can choose a remote add-on HPWH (Crispaire's #WH-6 or #B108K2). Model B108K2 can be located away from the water heater. The model WH-6 can be located near the water heater, but the cool air can be ducted to another room or into your central duct system. This keeps the noise level lower in other rooms. Therma-Stor model HP-80 is an integral unit with the tank. This is ideal for new construction where you have to install a new water heater anyway.

If you want to get fresh air into your home most efficiently year-round , the Therma-Stor VHP-80 HPWH draws heat from the incoming warm air in the summer. In the winter, it saves the heat from the warm outgoing stale air.

If you have a central air conditioner and do not need additional cooling from a HPWH, you can install a "Hot Plate". This transfers the waste heat from your central air conditioner into your water heater tank. Your air conditioner contractor will have to extend the refrigerant lines to the base of the water heater.

Just lowering the humidity level inside your home can make you more comfortable at a higher, more-efficient temperature. A dehumidifying heat pipe (either add-on or complete coil assembly by Heat Pipe Technology) can increase the dehumidification. This is ideal for older, oversized central air conditioners. Installing a new super-efficient whole-house dehumidifier can also increase comfort.

Cost to Use Standard Electric Water Heater versus Heat Pump		
Electric Rate	Electric	Heat Pump
$ per kwh	$ per 80 gallon	$ per 80 gallon
0.06	0.82	0.31
0.07	0.96	0.37
0.08	1.09	0.42
0.09	1.23	0.47
0.10	1.37	0.52
0.11	1.50	0.57
0.12	1.64	0.63
0.13	1.77	0.68
0.14	1.91	0.73

Manufacturers of Heat Pump Water Heaters

CRISPAIRE CORP., 3570 America Dr., Atlanta, GA 30341 - (404) 458-6643

general description - This is a very-high-efficiency add-on HPWH. It has an axial fan so that the cooled and dried air can be ducted to another room or into your central duct system.

model no. - WH-6	energy factor - 2.5	wattage - 500 watts
heating capacity - 6,000 Btuh	cooling output - 4,000 Btuh	dehumidification - 1 pint/hr.
recovery rate - 10 gal./hr. @135°	dimensions - 12 w x 10 d x 15 h in.	

special features - Can operate down to 35° before automatically switching over to water heater's resistance element, fast recovery option to provide quick hot water for high volume usage periods

general description - This is an add-on HPWH that mounts on top of an existing water heater. Since it mounts on top of the tank, no additional external plumbing is needed for most existing water heaters.

model no. - R106K2	energy factor - 2.1	wattage - 1,200 watts
heating capacity - 12,000 Btuh	cooling output - 7,100 Btuh	dehumidification - 1.2 pints/hr.
recovery rate - 17 gal/hr @135°	dimensions - 22 dia. x 20 h in.	

special features - Switch to set to heat pump, resistance elements in tank, or no heating. If room temperature drops below 50°, the HPWH shuts off automatically and water heater resistance elements come on.

general description - This is a remote add-on HPWH. It can be located in room away from the water heater to cool that room. This is an advantage if the water heater is located in a basement or garage that you do not want to cool.

model no. - B108K2	energy factor - 1.8	wattage - 1,200 watts
heating capacity - 12,000 Btuh	cooling output - 7,100 Btuh	dehumidification - 1.2 pints/hr.
recovery rate - 17 gal/hr @135°	dimensions - 18.2 w x 10.4 d x 25.1 h in.	

special features - It installs with a special coaxial valve for simple plumbing. Switch can be set to heat pump, resistance elements in tank, or no heating. If room temperature drops below 50°, the HPWH shuts off automatically and water heater resistance elements come on.

THERMA-STOR PRODUCTS, P.O. Box 8050, Madison, WI 53708 - (800) 533-7533

general description - This is an integral HPWH with the compressor mounted on top of the 80 gal. hot water heater tank. There is electric resistance backup heat.

model no. - HP-80	energy factor - 2.5	wattage - 600 watts
heating capacity - 10,100 Btuh	cooling output - 8,000 Btuh	dehumidification - 5 pints/hr.
recovery rate - 13 gal./hr. @ 80°	dimensions - 24 dia. x 72 h in.	tank size - 80 gal.

special features - double anode rods to reduce corrosion, built-in heat traps, R-15 foam tank insulation

general description - This is a whole-house fresh air ventilation system with an 80 gal. hot water heater tank and backup electric resistance heat. In the summer, the incoming fresh outdoor air is cooled and dehumidified by the HPWH. This heat is transferred to the 80 gal tank. In the winter, heat from the outgoing stale warm indoor air is used by the HPWH and is transferred to the water heater for hot water.

model no. - VHP - 80	energy factor - 2.5	wattage - 600 watts
heating capacity - 10,100 Btuh	cooling output - 8,000 Btuh	dehumidification - 5 pints/hr.
recovery rate - 16 gal./hr. @ 80°	dimensions - 24 dia. x 76 h in.	tank size - 80 gal.

special features - ventilation rate is adjustable from 80 to 200 cfm, controlled by a 24-hour timer or dehumidistat, built-in high-efficiency air filter (HEPA), can use it as an air conditioner even if you need no additional hot water

general description - This is a very-high-efficiency whole-house dehumidifier which uses a special heat exchanger coil to pre-cool the air for more dehumidifcation. This coil increases the efficiency to 6.5 lbs. of water vapor removed per kwh of electricity used from only 2 lbs. per kwh for a typical dehumidifier.

model no. - "Sahara"	dehumidification - 5 pints/hr.	efficiency - 6.8 pints/kwh
dimensions - 30 w x 17 d x 36 h in.	wattage - 780 watts	air flow - 245 cfm

special features - six-foot drain hose, continuous blower operation switch, can be attached to your central air conditioner duct system

Dehumidifying Heat Pipes Coils and Add-On Units

HEAT PIPE TECHNOLOGY, P.O. Box 999, Alachua, FL 32615 - (800) 393-3464 (904) 462-3464

general description - This is a flat (only 2.5-in. high) heat exchanger that you set your existing water heater on top of. The hot refrigerant from your central air conditioner transfers its heat to the water inside the water heater. No electricity or pumps are needed (see product details below).

model no. - "Hot Plate"

water heating output - n/a - enough hot water for family of four

sizes - 22.5 octagon x 2.5 h in.

output water temperature - 140° to 160°

general description - This is a evaporator coil assembly to replace the existing coil in your air handler (furnace/air conditioner blower). The dehumidifying heat pipe is built into the new coil assembly.

model no. - "Z-coil series"

cooling/heating output - 36,000; 48,000; and 60,000 Btuh

sizes - 21 w x 22 to 32 d x 25 h in.

nominal air flow - 1,200; 1,600; and 2,000 cfm blower

general description - This is an add-on dehumidifying heat pipe that is used with your present air handler evaporator coil. (Note the height dimension is only 3.5 in.)

model no. - "DHP series"

use with - 24,000 through 60,000 Btuh air conditioners

sizes - 43 w x 17 to 33 d x 3.5 h in.

nominal air flow - 1,200; 1,600; and 2,000 cfm blower

Free Hot Water from Waste Heat

The "Hot Plate" Heat Recovery Unit from Heat Pipe Technology is a revolutionary, trouble-free method of preheating water by capturing waste heat from air conditioners. Under normal conditions, heating hot water for domestic use can account for up to 30 percent of the electric costs to the average family. In the summer, a heat recovery unit can provide all the hot water needed by a family of four from the waste heat recovered from an air conditioner, or the excess heat from a heat pump.

How they work

Air conditioning systems by design collect heat from the conditioned space and waste it to the atmosphere. The hot plate captures the waste heat and uses it to heat water to 120° to 140°F for domestic use. The process of taking this heat from the A/C lowers operating pressures and condensing temperatures, thus lowering the operating costs of the air conditioning unit.

It is a proven way to cut electricity or gas use, based on solid engineering principles.

Trouble-free

Through thermosyphoning, the Hot Plate requires no electrical wiring and no water pumps that use energy or create maintenance problems. Because the Hot Plate is placed under the water heater inside the conditioned space, it needs no freeze protection or additional controls. No moving parts or extra energy are used.

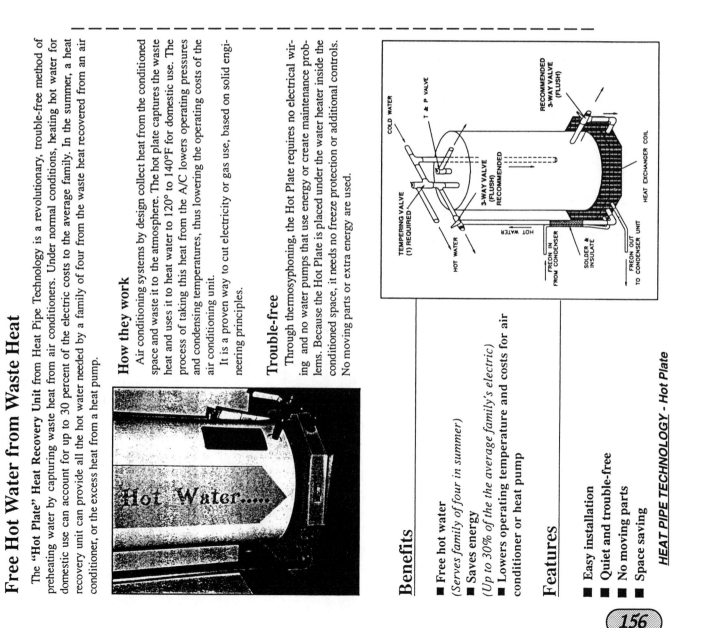

Benefits

- Free hot water
  (Serves family of four in summer)
- Saves energy
  (Up to 30% of the the average family's electric)
- Lowers operating temperature and costs for air conditioner or heat pump

Features

- Easy installation
- Quiet and trouble-free
- No moving parts
- Space saving

HEAT PIPE TECHNOLOGY - Hot Plate

Q: My old gas water heater doesn't supply enough hot water. Will installing one of the new designs with a lifetime no-leak warranty also cut my utility bills? How can I compare the many high efficiency models?

A: The new gas water heaters with a lifetime no-leak warranty are also the most energy efficient models. These also have no-rust stainless steel burners. Most water heaters have only a five or ten year no-leak warranty.

For a typical family of four, installing one of these super efficient models can lower your annual utility bills by more than $100. This can easily pay back its higher initial cost many times over its life.

Inside a no-leak water heater, the inner tank is made of durable non-toxic polybutylene plastic. The outer tank is made of durable polyethylene. Most other water heaters use glass-lined steel tanks which eventually leak.

A small super efficient stainless steel burner and heat exchanger system is located on the side of the plastic tank. A small pump circulates the water through the heat exchanger to the tank. An intermittent igniter eliminates the cost of burning a pilot light continuously.

Another efficient design, called Nautilus, uses a submerged burner design. The sealed burner is completely surrounded by water. This design transfers more of the heat to the water and less is lost up the flue.

Dip tube design, which brings in the cold inlet water to the burner heat exchanger, affects efficiency and tank life. One design creates a turbo action over the burner. Another design uses numerous small jet openings for more turbulence. Baffles in the exhaust flue also improve efficiency.

You can compare efficiencies and operating costs by the energy factors (EF). The EF for various models can range from a low of about 0.52 to a high of 0.70 for the super efficient no-leak plastic models. A water heater with an EF above 0.60 is considered very efficient. The level and type of tank wall insulation is also a good indication of the efficiency and overall quality of a water heater. The best ones use 2-inch thick rigid foam insulation for an insulating value of about R-16. Foam insulation also provides more support than fiberglass and resists denting.

If you are very concerned about getting enough hot water for morning showers, the "first hour rating" (FHR) in gallons is more important than just the size of the tank. A smaller, more efficient tank, with a high output burner, can provide more hot water than some models with larger tanks.

Q: My house has settled some over the years and there is a fairly wide and deep crack around one door frame. When I seal it, how far down in the gap should I push the foam backer rod?

A: You are correct in using a foam backer rod for a deep wide crack. You should not attempt to fill the entire crack with caulk. Push the backer rod in to a depth (measure where the edge of the rod touches the sides of the crack) equal to the width of the crack.

Use a silicone or polyurethane caulk. Polyurethane takes longer than silicone to cure, but it can be painted. Polyurethane also sticks to about anything.

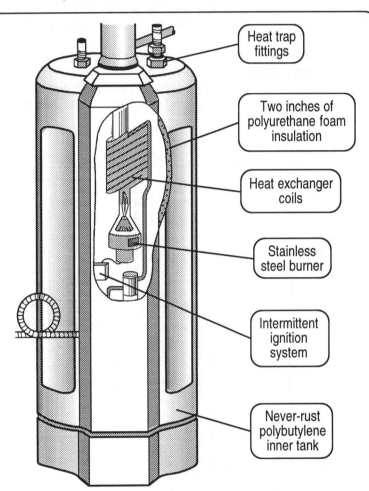

Heat trap fittings

Two inches of polyurethane foam insulation

Heat exchanger coils

Stainless steel burner

Intermittent ignition system

Never-rust polybutylene inner tank

The Energy Factor takes all factors into account - the combustion and heat transfer efficiency and the heat losses from the water tank. Your old water heater may have an EF as low as .40. You can use the charts on page 160 to determine the payback from installing a new water heater or to compare the paybacks from installing various super efficient models.

The highest efficiency water heater (made by Rheem) uses plastic construction. This eliminates corrosion and the possibility of leaks. Although it is very expensive initially, it usually provides a good lifetime payback because it lasts much longer than other water heaters. Sears & Roebuck also sells this same plastic water heater under its own label.

Heat traps are small one-way check valves installed in the water pipes at the top of the water heater. These block the natural energy-robbing circulation of water in these pipes. They can be easily installed in any new or old water heater.

Two-inch thick foam tank insulation is best. If you do not select one of the super efficient models listed on page 159, check the insulation specifications on the models you are considering.

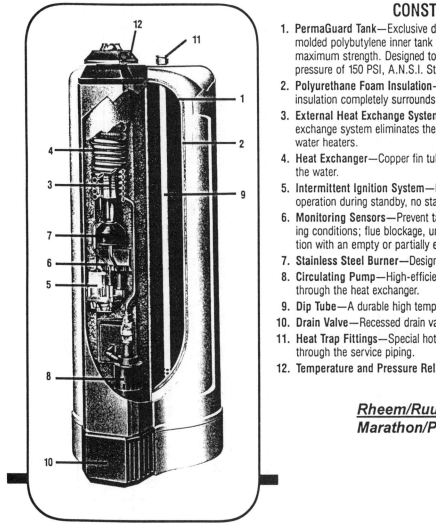

CONSTRUCTION FEATURES

1. **PermaGuard Tank**—Exclusive design, non-metallic construction...A seamless blow molded polybutylene inner tank reinforced with a filament wound fiberglass outer tank for maximum strength. Designed to withstand 300 PSI hydrostatic test pressure for working pressure of 150 PSI, A.N.S.I. Standard.
2. **Polyurethane Foam Insulation**—2 full inches (R16-7) of pre-formed polyurethane foam insulation completely surrounds the tank—sides, top and bottom!
3. **External Heat Exchange System**—No central flue pipe! Innovative external heat exchange system eliminates the major sources of heat loss found in conventional gas water heaters.
4. **Heat Exchanger**—Copper fin tube heat exchanger gives high efficiency heat transfer to the water.
5. **Intermittent Ignition System**—Energy efficient time proven design eliminates pilot operation during standby, no standing pilot!
6. **Monitoring Sensors**—Prevent tank damage by shutting down operation under the following conditions; flue blockage, unusual down drafts; thermostat malfunction and operation with an empty or partially empty tank (dry fired).
7. **Stainless Steel Burner**—Designed for efficient quiet operation and efficient heat transfer.
8. **Circulating Pump**—High-efficiency low volume pump circulates water from the tank through the heat exchanger.
9. **Dip Tube**—A durable high temperature plastic formula.
10. **Drain Valve**—Recessed drain valve protects against accidental damage.
11. **Heat Trap Fittings**—Special hot outlet and cold inlet fittings reduce convective heat loss through the service piping.
12. **Temperature and Pressure Relief Valve**—Factory installed.

Rheem/Ruud
Marathon/Performer

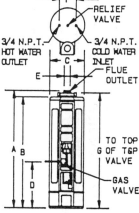

Model No.	Tank Cap Gal.	Nat. Gas Input BTU/Hr.	Recovery G.P.H. 90° Rise	First Hour Delivery Rating G.P.H.	Energy Factor	Appx. Shpg. Wght/Lbs.	Roughing In Dimensions (Shown in Inches)						
							A	B	C*	D	E	F	G
MG40345	40	34500	38	77.3	.70	152	66³/₈	61⁷/₈	21¹/₄	24¹/₂	3	8	65⁷/₈
MG50345	50	34500	38	84.6	.68	164	67¹/₄	62³/₄	23¹/₈	24¹/₂	3	8	66³/₄

*Front to back dimension: Add 7³/₈" on 40 Gal. and 7¹/₄" on 50 Gal.
NOTE: These units comply with SCAQMD Rule 1121 (California)

WATER CONNECTIONS ALL 3/4" N.P.T.

High Efficiency Gas Water Heaters

Water-heater Manufacturers	American Water Heater Group	A. O. Smith	Bradford White	Rheem/Ruud	State
Address	500 Princeton Rd. Johnson City, TN 37601 (615) 283-8000	5605 N. MacArthur Blvd. Irving, TX 75038 (214) 518-1990	323 Norristown Rd. Ambler, PA 19002 (800) 523-2931	P. O. Box 244040 Montgomery, AL 36124 (205) 260-1500	500 By Pass Rd. Ashland City, TN 37015 (800) 365-0024
Model	Nautilus	Conservationist Gold	Deluxe M-II	Marathon/Performer	Turbo Super Saver 85+
First Hour Rating	72 and 81	72 and 80	67 and 80	77 and 84	73 and 80
EF rating*	.60/.59	.65/.62	.62/.60	.74/.71	.64/.63
R-value	8.30	16.00	16.00	16.70	8.30
Insulation	1 in. of foam	1 15/16 in. of foam	2 in. of foam	2 in. of foam	1 in. of foam
Gallon capacity	40 and 50	40 and 50	40 and 50	40 and 50	40 and 50
Btu	38,000/40,000	40,000	40,000	34,500	40,000
Heat traps	No	Yes	Yes	Yes	Yes
Burner type	No burner	Cast iron	Cast iron	Stainless steel	Aluminized steel
Miscellaneous	Direct flame into submerged chamber, brass drain valve, energy-saving pilot, built in delimer, comes with T & P relief valve mounted on side of tank	Brass drain valve, push-button electric ignition, comes with relief valve, T & P relief valve mounted on side of tank	Brass drain valve, energy-saving pilot, condensation elimination system, no T & P relief valve, relief-valve opening is on top of tank	No central flue, has heat-exchange system, intermittent ignition system, comes with T & P relief valve mounted on top of tank, comes in natural gas only	Brass drain valve, energy-saving pilot comes with T & P relief valve mounted on side of tank
Limited warranty	10 year	10 year	10 year	Lifetime	10 year
List price**	$350	$450	$250	$900	$425

* The EF (energy factor) rating takes all losses (standby, heat transfer, etc.) into consideration for the efficiency rating. The higher, the better.

** Manufacturers won't give out list prices for their water heaters, referring customers instead to local distributors. These are ballpark prices listed for comparison. Actual prices will vary with geographical region, professional discounts and special-order shipping charges. Propane models typically cost another 10%.

Estimated Annual Operating Costs (in $) for Gas Water Heaters Using Natural Gas

Energy Factor

Fuel Cost (¢ per Therm)	0.44	0.46	0.48	0.50	0.52	0.54	0.56	0.58	0.60	0.62	0.64	0.66	0.68	0.70	0.72	0.74	0.76	0.78
42	143	137	131	126	121	117	112	108	105	101	98	95	93	90	87	85	83	81
46	157	150	144	138	133	128	123	119	115	111	108	105	102	99	96	93	91	88
50	170	163	156	150	144	139	134	129	125	121	117	114	111	107	104	101	99	97
54	184	176	169	162	156	150	144	139	135	130	126	123	119	116	113	109	107	104
58	197	189	181	174	167	161	155	150	145	140	136	132	128	124	121	118	114	112
62	211	202	194	186	179	172	166	160	155	150	145	140	136	132	129	125	122	119
66	225	215	206	198	190	183	177	170	165	159	154	149	145	141	137	133	130	126
70	238	228	218	210	202	194	187	181	175	169	164	159	154	150	145	141	138	134
74	252	241	231	222	213	205	198	191	185	179	173	168	163	158	154	150	146	142
78	266	254	243	234	225	216	209	201	195	188	183	176	172	167	162	158	153	150
82	279	267	256	246	236	227	219	212	205	198	192	185	180	175	170	166	161	157
86	293	280	268	258	248	239	230	222	215	208	201	195	189	184	179	174	169	165

How to Determine the Payback Period

Determining the payback period will help you decide what model water heater is most economical for you. The table above illustrates that the higher the EF, the lower the annual operating cost. However, a more efficient water heater generally has a higher purchase price. Therefore, there is a period of time before the savings in the lower operating cost of a more efficient water heater make up for the increased price of that water heater as compared to a less efficient water heater; this is the payback period. It is only after the payback period that you obtain a net savings with the more efficient water heater.

Accordingly, the shorter the payback period, the better.

EXAMPLE: Assume you are intending to buy a gas water heater and your local gas cost is $0.62 per therm. You are comparing two water heaters, Model A and Model B, which both have the same first hour rating.

	Price of Water Heater	EF	Estimated Annual Cost of Operation
Model A	$300	0.60	$155
Model B	$400	0.70	$132
Additional Cost of More Efficient Model (Model B)	$400 - $300 = $100		
Estimated Annual Savings in Operating Cost for Model B	$155 - $132 = $23		
Payback Period	$100/$23 per year = 4.3 year		
NOTE: As fuel prices increase, the greater the savings obtained from a more efficient water heater and the shorter the payback period becomes			

Q: My old electric water heater is getting leaky and it doesn't supply enough hot water for morning showers. What are the most efficient and durable electric water heaters made and what size should I get?

A: The cost of hot water for a family of four using an electric water heater can be as much as $400 per year. Even a small increase in overall efficiency (called "Energy Factor") can result in a substantial savings on your utility bills.

The Energy Factor (EF) can range from about .80 to .96. For example, with an electric rate of 8.5 cents per kilowatt-hour, the savings from upgrading from an EF of .80 to an EF of .96 can be about $80 per year. Water heaters with heavy foam tank wall insulation provides the highest EF.

One of the most durable and energy efficient new electric water heater designs uses a heavily-insulated all plastic tank. Since plastic won't rust, the water heater tank carries a lifetime no-leakage guarantee.

A durable plastic tank offers several other advantages. The internal shape of the tank can be designed to provide for optimum water circulation. It allows for more foam insulation at the tank top where the water is hottest. A smooth con-cave bottom allows the sediment to settle and flow out when you open the tank clean-out drain.

Also, an anode rod (used to reduce corrosion in a standard glass-lined steel tank) is not needed. With certain types of water, an anode rod can cause the hot water to have a peculiar odor.

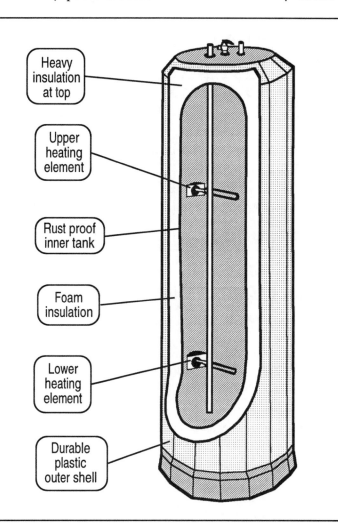

Heavy insulation at top

Upper heating element

Rust proof inner tank

Foam insulation

Lower heating element

Durable plastic outer shell

When determining the size of the water heater you will need to know the "First Hour Rating" (FHR) which indicates how much hot water it can provide. This includes the volume of the hot water heater tank plus the amount of incoming cold water it heats in one hour. A high-efficiency 52-gallon electric water heater can provide about 59 gallons

of hot water for the first hour in the morning.

If you don't have enough hot water in the morning, you can install a small point-of-use electric instantaneous tankless water heater in your bathroom. This heats the water as it is needed at the shower. Since it doesn't have to keep a large tank of water hot, it is very efficient.

By installing a small instantaneous water heater, you may be able to lower the water temperature in your regular water heater. This further reduces the heat loss from your water heater tank.

Q: I had new replacement windows installed two months ago. I was told by the installer (and paid extra) that these had low-emissivity (low-e) glass. How can I tell if they really are low-e glass?

A: The newer energy-efficient low-e window glass is difficult to detect with the eye. They almost look totally clear without the slight bluish tint of the older type of low-e glass.

There are special detectors available that can sense the low-e coating. Some window contractor have them. Your utility company may also have them to test installations before giving conservation rebates or credits.

Before buying a water heater, you should determine the peak (maximum) one-hour water usage your family needs. You can use the worksheet below to determine your hot water needs. Select a water heater that has a "first hour rating" equal to or exceeding your peak demand. The first hour rating includes the hot water volume of the tank plus the recovery rate - how much water the burner can heat in one hour.

The manufacturers list on page163 shows specifications for high-efficiency electric water heaters. Capacity, first hour rating (amount of hot water available in one hour) and the energy factor are listed with each manufacturer's name. These are the specifications for the highest efficiency models.

If you install a new electric water heater, make sure that it has heat trap fittings built in the nipples or your plumber installs them. Most water heater manufacturers sell them. A heat trap fitting is basically a one-way check valve that stops the natural upward flow of hot water into the pipes immediately above the water heater. Hot water slowly flows up, cools off and becomes more dense, then flows back down into the tank. This can waste a lot of heat over time.

Even if you install a new, well-insulated water heater, adding an insulation jacket on it helps some. The savings may not justify the expense of an insulation jacket kit, but if you have some old fiberglass insulation around the house, wrap a layer over it. This will save some energy. Also, by requiring the elements to come on less often, there is less scale build up in hard water areas. Reducing scale buildup prolongs the life of the heating elements.

Worksheet to Estimate Peak Hour Demand			
Use	Average Gallons of Hot Water per Usage	Times Used During One Hour	Gallons Used in One Hour
Shower	20	x _____	= _____
Bath	20	x _____	= _____
Shaving	2	x _____	= _____
Hands & Face Washing	4	x _____	= _____
Hair Shampoo	4	x _____	= _____
Hand Dishwashing	4	x _____	= _____
Automatic Dishwasher	14	x _____	= _____
Food Preparation	5	x _____	= _____
Clothes Washer	32	x _____	= _____
TOTAL		Peak Hour Demand	_____

To use this chart: Determine during what general time of day (morning, noon, evening) there is usually the most use of hot water in your home, keeping in mind the number of people in your home. Using the table, determine what your maximum usage of hot water in one hour could be; this is your peak hour demand. The right size water heater for your needs will be within one to two gallons of your peak hour demand.

NOTE: This table does not estimate total daily hot water usage. As an example, an average of 4 gallons of hot water is used each time dishes are washed by hand but dishes washed by hand are usually done 3 times a day. The average daily hot water usage for hand dishwashing, 12 gallons, is about the same as the average hot water usage for an automatic dishwasher, used once a day.

Example: Your household uses the most hot water in the morning. In the busiest one hour period of the morning, the uses are: 3 showers/20x3=60, 1 shave/2x1=2, 1 shampoo/4x1=4, handwashing of dishes/4x1=4, Total Peak Hour Demand = 70 gallons.

Chart courtesy of GAMA

Manufacturers of High-Efficiency Electric Water Heaters

AMERICAN WATER HEATER GROUP, 500 Princeton Rd., Johnson City, TN 37601 - (615) 283-8000

tank size - 30 gallons	first hour rating - 43 gallons	energy factor - .93
38 gallons	45 gallons	.91
40 gallons	50 gallons	.95
45 gallons	52 gallons	.89
50 gallons	58 gallons	.93
65 gallons	73 gallons	.92
80 gallons	89 gallons	.91

BRADFORD WHITE, 323 Norristown Rd., Ambler, PA 19002 - (800) 523-2931

tank size - 30 gallons	first hour rating - 44 gallons	energy factor - .93
38 gallons	45 gallons	.88
40 gallons	54 gallons	.92
47 gallons	53 gallons	.92
50 gallons	64 gallons	.93
65 gallons	73 gallons	.91
80 gallons	88 gallons	.91

NORDYNE, 1801 Park 270 Dr., St. Louis, 63146 - (314) 878-6200

tank size - 20 gallons	first hour rating - 29 gallons	energy factor - .90
30 gallons	40 gallons	.92
40 gallons	49 gallons	.90
47 gallons	48 gallons	.87
50 gallons	57 gallons	.86
65 gallons	68 gallons	.84
80 gallons	80 gallons	.82

RHEEM/RUUD, PO Box244040, Montgomery, AL 36124 - (205) 260-1500

tank size - 30 gallons	first hour rating - 38 gallons	energy factor - .95
40 gallons	48 gallons	.94
47 gallons	48 gallons	.87
50 gallons	54 gallons	.94
60 gallons	66 gallons	.93
65 gallons	67 gallons	.91
80 gallons	80 gallons	.87
85 gallons	90 gallons	.92

SEARS/KENMORE, Sears Tower, BSC 12-34, Chicago, Il 60684 - (800) 359-2000 (708) 286-2500

tank size - 20 gallons	first hour rating - 29 gallons	energy factor - .90
27 gallons	38 gallons	.89
30 gallons	41 gallons	.90
40 gallons	49 gallons	.93
52 gallons	56 gallons	.93
66 gallons	64 gallons	.91
82 gallons	76 gallons	.91

A. O. SMITH, 5605 N. MacArthur Blvd., Johnson City, TN 37601 - (615) 283-8000

tank size - 30 gallons	first hour rating - 42 gallons	energy factor - .93
40 gallons	50 gallons	.93
50 gallons	58 gallons	.95
66 gallons	70 gallons	.91
80 gallons	79 gallons	.91

STATE, 500 By Pass Rd., Ashland, TN 37015 - (800) 365-0024

tank size - 30 gallons	first hour rating - 42 gallons	energy factor - .90
40 gallons	49 gallons	.93
47 gallons	50 gallons	.90
50 gallons	56 gallons	.86
52 gallons	60 gallons	.93
66 gallons	71 gallons	.91
82 gallons	81 gallons	.91

Helpful Hints Checklist

If your water heater fails to work right, make the following easy checks. Often, you will find what's wrong yourself and you won't have to call and wait for service and hot water. If you do not find what's wrong when making the checks, then call for service.

A. NOT ENOUGH OR NO HOT WATER

1. Used more hot water than the water heater holds, or faster than the water heater can heat the water.
2. Hot water wasted through leaking or partially open faucet.
3. If the water heater is newly installed, check the installation steps to be sure it's installed correctly.
4. Make sure the electrical supply is turned on and that the cold water supply valve is fully open.
5. Check for a blown fuse or popped circuit breaker (circuit breakers weaken with age and may not handle the rated load).
6. During winter months, the colder supply water takes longer to heat.
7. The temperature limit switch may have opened the circuit if water temperature reached the maximum limit.
8. Temperature controls for the heating elements set too low.
9. Possible burned out element(s).

B. WATER TOO HOT

1. Temperature controls for the heating elements set too high.
2. Temperature control thermostat not working.

C. WATER LEAKS

NOTE: Always check for condensation first as the source of the "leak". Wipe all wet surfaces dry and check again. Also, the temperature and pressure relief valve may have opened to vent high pressure or temperature. Points to check on the water heater for possible leaks are as follows.

CAUTION: TURN OFF ELECTRICAL POWER IF YOU WILL REMOVE THE ACCESS PANELS. Before repairing a leak, turn off the water supply and drain the tank.

1. Inlet and outlet fittings.
2. Temperature and pressure relief valve connection, or the valve itself.
3. Drain valve, or drain valve threads to tank.
4. Gaskets around heating element(s).

NOTE: Improperly installed heat traps could cause reduced or restricted water flow.

Key No.	Description of Part
1	Seal ring (3 req.)
2	Drain valve
3	Heating element
4	Screw
5	Protector (lower)
6	Temperature control thermostat (lower)
7	Retaining spring
8	Gasket
9	Front panel
10	Control box cover (upper)
11	Control box cover (lower)
12	Protector (upper)
13	Temperature and control thermostat
14	Junction box cover
15	Seal ring
16	Reducer bushing
17	Dip tube
18	Temperature and pressure relief valve
19	Hot and cold heat traps
*	Owners manual
*	Element wrench

Repair Parts List

REPAIR PARTS

KENMORE SURVIVOR ELECTRIC WATER HEATERS

SINGLE ELEMENT
MODEL NUMBER
449.314410

DUAL ELEMENT
MODEL NUMBERS
449.310310 449.320310
449.310410 449.320410
449.310510 449.320510
449.310530

NOTE: The above listed Kenmore Survivor water heaters are shipped with a factory installed Temperature and Pressure Relief Valve. Key No 18

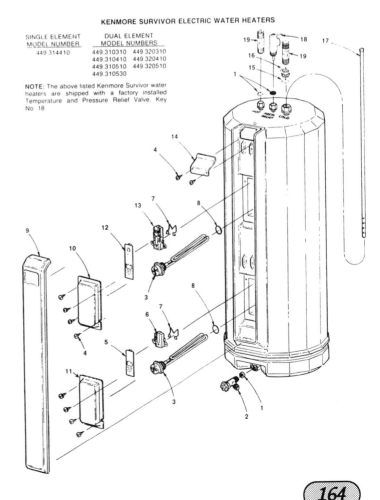

Q: I'm tired of my old shower and I want to install one of the new solid-state, four-head shower/body spray massage kits. Are these easy to install and are there any other new low-cost bathroom water savers?

A: Bathrooms (flushing toilets and showering) are the major water consumer in most homes. There are many new low-cost, do-it-yourself bathroom water-saver products that quickly pay back their cost and improve convenience.

The solid-state, multi-head shower/massage kit is a tall thin unit that mounts against the shower wall. All of the plumbing and controls are self-contained for simple installation. A ten push-button control panel is built in.

The shower/massage kit includes one overhead waterfall, two (high and low) oscillating and pulsating body spray nozzles and one three-way adjustable pulsating hydro-massage showerhead. Push buttons instantly switch among the heads and nozzles. The buttons provide all combinations of the spray heads.

There are many new low-flow standard and pulsating showerheads available. The price of some good quality metal ones is less than $10. These high-tech designs create turbulence and air mixing for a forceful shower. Some have nine different spray patterns and adjustments for low water pressure areas.

One new device, an auto faucet control, screws on and replaces the aerator on a bathroom faucet. A short rod hangs down to start and stop the water. Leave the hot and cold (temperature adjusted) handles turned on. Nudge the rod with your hand or cup for a trickle. For full flow, push the rod further.

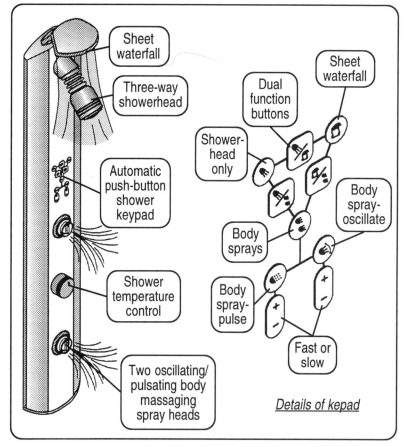

Sheet waterfall

Three-way showerhead

Automatic push-button shower keypad

Shower temperature control

Two oscillating/ pulsating body massaging spray heads

Dual function buttons

Sheet waterfall

Shower-head only

Body spray-oscillate

Body sprays

Body spray-pulse

Fast or slow

Details of kepad

A similar convenient faucet water saver, Flip Aerator, allows you to adjust the water from a trickle to full flow with a short flip lever. Adjusting the flow does not effect the hot/cold mix (water temperature).

These devices save water and time when shaving or washing. Adjust the water temperature once and it stays constant. These are ideal for people with arthritis who have prob-

lems turning handles. These protect against children walking away with the faucet on and also stop drips from leaky faucets.

A Zippy Rinse kit is a decorative hand-washing basin and water spout that sets on the toilet tank lid. Another model includes a complete replacement lid with a built-in water spout. When the toilet is flushed, the incoming fresh water first flows out the high spout into the basin for hand washing.

From the basin, it drains back into the toilet tank as always. This is ideal for children who don't often take the time to wash their hands or for incapacitated or arthritic people.

Q: I have a high-efficiency electronic air cleaner in my central air conditioner. What is the proper method to clean the filters?

A: An electronic air cleaner is very effective and does not impede air flow through your ducts as some other air filters can. When the filters (called cells or elements) collect dirt as they clean the air, they gradually loose their cleaning effectiveness.

Read the manufacturer's instructions first. One cleaning method is to place the cells in an automatic dishwasher on the bottom rack with the arrows upward. Also, hand cleaning them in a strong, hot detergent solution works.

Manufacturers of Low-Flow Shower Heads

ALSONS CORP., PO Box 282, Hillsdale, MI 49242 - (800) 421-0001 (517) 439-1411

model - "Lady Alsons 610 BX"	type - wall mount	flow - 2.7 gpm
number spray patterns - continuous	material - metal	
features - good range of swivel movement		
model - "665C"	type - wall mount - massage	flow - 2.3 gpm
number spray patterns - 2	material - plastic*	
features - easy to adjust		

AMERICAN STANDARD, PO Box 6820, Piscataway, NJ 08855 - (800) 524-9797 (908) 980-3000

model - "Sport"	type - wall mount	flow - 2.5 gpm
number spray patterns - 8	material - plastic*	
features - optional adjustable body/side spray, face spray adjusts up to 40° in any direction		

CHATHAM BRASS CO., 5 Olsen Ave., Edison, NJ 08820 - (800) 526-7553

model - "202"	type - wall mount	flow - 2.7 gpm
number spray patterns - continuous	material - metal	
features - spray control on side		
model - "44-3S"	type - wall mount	flow - 2.75 gpm
number spray patterns - continuous	material - metal	
features - spray control on side, self cleaning		

INTERBATH, 665 N. Baldwin Park Blvd., City of Industry, CA 91746 - (800) 800-2132 (818) 369-1841

model - "Intouch II Massage"	type - wall mount - massage	flow - 2.1 gpm
number spray patterns - 8	material - plastic	
features - shut-off setting, larger than most, 5-year warranty		
model - "Classic II Massage"	type - wall mount - massage	flow - 2.3 gpm
number spray patterns - 5	material - plastic	
features - shut-off setting, 5-year warranty		
model - "Intouch II Massage"	type - hand-held - massage	flow - 2.4 gpm
number spray patterns - 8	material - plastic	
features - shut-off setting, larger than most, bracket holds head 8 inches higher than shower pipes		

KOHLER CO., Kohler, WI 53044 - (414) 457-4441

model - "Mastershower Tower - electronic"	flow - variable depends on heads (functions) you select
number spray patterns - variable	material - plastic*
features - electronic control panel selects water action and speed - showerhead, sheet waterfall, two bodysprays	

model - "Mastershower Ultra Low Flow"	type - wall mount	flow - 1.9 gpm
number spray patterns - continuous	material - metal	
features - needle-sharp stream, spray control in center		
model - "Trend K-11741"	type - wall mount	flow - 1.8 gpm
number spray patterns - continuous	material - plastic*	
features - spray control in center		
model - "Mastershower 3-Way"	type - hand-held - massage	flow - 2.6 gpm
number spray patterns - 3	material - plastic*	
features - needle-sharp stream, spray control in center		

MELARD, 153 Linden St., Passaic, NJ 07055 - (800) 635-2731

model - "361"	type - wall mount - massage	flow - 2.5 gpm
number spray patterns - continuous	material - plastic*	
features - spray control on side		
model - "373"	type - wall mount - massage	flow - 2.5 gpm
number spray patterns - 2	material - plastic*	
features -spray control on side		

* Metal connector

Manufacturers of Low-Flow Shower Heads

MOEN INC., 25300 Al Moen Dr., N. Olmsted, OH 44070 - (800) 553-6636

model - "Pulsation 3934"
number spray patterns - 2
features - spray control on side

type - wall mount - massage
material - metal

flow - 2.3 gpm

model - "Moenflo 3905"
number spray patterns - continuous
features - spray control on side

type - wall mount
material - metal

flow - 2.2 gpm

POLLENEX, 217 E. 16th St., Sedalia, MO 65301 - (800) 767-6020

model - "Power Shower"
number spray patterns - 9
features - rotating spray head, larger than most

type - wall mount - massage
material - plastic*

flow - 2.5 gpm

model - "Ultra Dial Massage"
number spray patterns - 4
features - larger than most

type - wall mount - massage
material - plastic

flow - 2.7 gpm

model - "Power Shower"
number spray patterns - 9
features - rotating spray head, larger than most

type - hand-held - massage
material - plastic*

flow - 2.4 gpm

model - "Shower Miser"
number spray patterns -2
features - very concentrated massage stream

type - hand-held - massage
material - plastic

flow - 2.2 gpm

RESOURCES CONSERVATION, PO Box 71, Greenwich, CT 06836 - (800) 243-2862 (203) 964-0600

model - "Incredible Head"
number spray patterns - 1
features - aerated mist, shut-off setting

type - wall mount
material - metal

flow - 2.1 gpm

SPEAKMAN, PO Box 191, Wilmington, DE 19899 - (302) 764-9100

model - "S-2292-AF"
number spray patterns - continuous
features - spray control on side

type - wall mount
material - metal

flow - 1.8 gpm

TELEDYNE WATER PIK, 1730 E. Prospect Rd., Fort Collins, CO 80553 - (800) 525-2774

model - "SM80" series
number spray patterns - 8
features - wide massage pattern, reduced-flow setting, removable spray rings for easy cleaning

type - wall mount - massage
material - plastic*

flow - 2.5 gpm

model - "SM60" series
number spray patterns - 5
features - strong, wide massage pattern, reduced-flow setting

type - wall mount - massage
material - plastic*

flow - 2.5 gpm

model - "SM80" series
number spray patterns - 8
features - strong, wide massage pattern, reduced-flow setting, extra long six-foot hose

type - hand-held - massage
material - plastic*

flow - 2.5 gpm

model - "Super Saver"
number spray patterns - 8
features - aerated mist, five-foot hose

type - hand-held
material - plastic

flow - 2.5 gpm

WHEDON PRODUCTS, 21A Andover Dr., W. Hartford, CT 06110 - (800) 541-2184 (203) 953-7606

model - "Saver Shower"
number spray patterns - 1
features - aerated mist, 5-year warranty

type - wall mount
material - metal

flow - 2.6 gpm

model - "Pulsator Plus"
number spray patterns - 2
features - easy turn faceplate, 3-year warranty

type - wall mount - massage
material - plastic*

flow - 2.6 gpm

* _Metal connector_

Manufacturers of Water-Saving Devices

CONSEPT SALES, 1418 Ponderosa, Fullerton, CA 92635 - (714) 255-0481

> _type_ - water saving tank lid
> _size_ - model 100 — 15" - 18", model 200 — 18" - 2½", model 300 — 20½" - 22"
> _description_ - "The Lid" supplies a continuous flow of clean water that is activated by the flush mechanism that automatically shuts off. It provides easier access for persons with arthritis and it encourages small children to wash hands with germ-free cleaning. There are no moving parts. Remove tank lid and old inlet hose. Attach spout, new inlet hose to fresh water supply and drain hose and center and place "The Lid."

ENERGY TECHNOLOGY LABS, 2351 Tenaya Dr., Modesto, CA 95354 - (800) 344-3242 (209) 529-3546

> _type_ - control faucet aerator
> _description_ - Simply replace your old faucet. A simple touch of the flip-touch-control lever shuts off the flow of water. Flip the control level up for a full flow or down for a trickle. There is no need to adjust the hot and cold knobs.

ENVIRONMENTAL DESIGNWORKS, PO Box 26A88, Los Angeles, CA 90026 - (213) 386-5812

> _type_ - water saving fingerinse fountain
> _description_ - A ceramic basin sits atop the toilet tank lid. When the toilet is flushed, the system redirects fresh water to the wash basin, making it easy to wash your hands. After washing, the water drains into the toilet for the next flush. (See installation instructions below.)

INTERNATIONAL ENVIRONMENTAL SOLUTIONS, PO Box 8111, Clearwater, FL 34618 - (813) 367-4660

> _type_ - automatic faucet control
> _description_ - Unscrew end of faucet and remove all washers. Screw-in the automatic faucet control which has a plastic rod hanging down. Simply press the rod for water. When the pressure is released the water stops. For continuous water push rod gently upwards with your fingertip at the end of the rod, twist ¼ turn. To stop water, twist rod in circular direction.

NIAGARA CONSERVATION, 230 Route 206, Flanders, NJ 07836 - (800) 831-8383 (201) 927-4545

> _type_ - control faucet aerator
> _description_ - Simply replace your old faucet. Just flip the lever for full flow or a trickle. The trickle allows the user to save water while maintaining water temperature.

RESOURCES CONSERVATION, PO Box 71, Greenwich, CT 06836 - (800) 243-2862 (203) 964-0600

> _type_ - control faucet aerator
> _description_ - Simply replace your old faucet. The low flow faucet aerator has an on/off control. Flip the lever up for a trickle and down for a full flow.

Installation Instructions for "Zippy Fingerinse" System

1. Lift the top off the tank and look at the tank's back wall. There needs to be a passage way for the supply and drain tubes between the tank and its top. If your toilet already has "notches" in the tank's back wall that will adequately allow the tubes to pass through unobstructed, go to step 3. If your toilet's tank does not have notches, or even if it does have notches, but cannot use them due to an adjacent wall or other reason, you will need the Zippy Lifter. See step 2.

2. Slide the Zippy Lifter over the edge of the tank with the "IN" arrow pointing towards the inside of the tank. Firmly press down on the lifter for a secure fit. Position one lifter near each corner of the tank. Gently replace the tank's top and check it for stability. Most tank tops are not flat and you may need to adjust the Zippy Lifters' placement to achieve the optimum fit.

3. While connecting the fountain have a second person help hold the tank top as it may become awkward depending upon the available space.

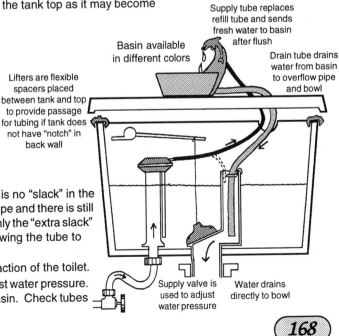

Supply tube replaces refill tube and sends fresh water to basin after flush

Basin available in different colors

Drain tube drains water from basin to overflow pipe and bowl

Lifters are flexible spacers placed between tank and top to provide passage for tubing if tank does not have "notch" in back wall

Supply valve is used to adjust water pressure

Water drains directly to bowl

   a. First, turn the water supply valve off.
   b. Carefully remove the existing refill tube from the ballcock nipple and from the overflow pipe. Remove overflow pipe cap if necessary.
   c. Position the fountain on the tank top using Q-hold. Form 4 equal size balls from the Q-hold strip, place one on each mark on the bottom of the fountain. Clean and dry the tank top. Press the fountain down onto the tank top with a slight twisting motion.
   d. Connect Zippy's ¼" supply tube to the ballcock nipple.
   e. Slide the ½" drain tube into the overflow pipe so that the tube clip attaches to the overflow pipe. Slide it until there is no "slack" in the tube. If the drain tube reaches the bottom of the overflow pipe and there is still "extra slack", cut the drain tube as necessary to eliminate only the "extra slack" (this helps drainage, water wants to go downhill), still allowing the tube to reach the bottom of the overflow pipe.

4. Be careful not to allow the tubes to interfere with the flushing action of the toilet.

5. Flush the toilet and slowly turn on the water supply valve to adjust water pressure. Set pressure to where there is no water splashing out of the basin. Check tubes to insure they are open and water flows unobstructed.

Q: I don't want to replace my old water heater yet, but I would like to cut my water heating costs. What can I do to make my old water heater more efficient without spending a lot of money on it?

A: Making low-cost improvements to your gas or electric water heater is well worth the expense. A water heater is typically responsible for about 20% of your monthly utility bill. For example, a family of four can spend in excess of $200 each year to operate an electric water heater.

Although you may not realize it, your old water heater wastes 10% to 15% of the heat through standby losses. This is heat lost through the tank walls and pipes into the surrounding air of your utility room or basement.

There are several simple ways to reduce stand-by losses. You can install inexpensive pipe nipple fittings, known as heat traps, in the water heater inlet and outlet pipes. These stop wasteful circulation of hot water right above your water heater. Touch these water pipes and feel how much warmer they are than the other water pipes.

Because hot water is less dense than cold water, it tends to rise in the inlet and outlet pipes at the top of the tank. As a result, a continuous (and wasteful) circulation takes place. The hot water slowly rises into the

copper pipes, cools off, and sinks back into the tank.

A glass ball in the hot water outlet heat trap fitting is just slightly heavier than water. When you are not using hot water, the ball gently sinks against a seat in the heat trap fitting and forms a tight seal. This blocks the water circulation. When you turn on a hot water faucet, the

Hot water outlet pipe

Cold water inlet pipe

Thermo-plastic ball is slightly lighter than water

Water flow

Special glass ball is slightly heavier than water

Hot　　Cold
Water heater

water pressure lifts the ball off its seat and the hot water flows freely through.

The inlet cold water heat trap has a small plastic ball which is slightly lighter than water. It floats up against a seat to block circulation. The ball is moved by water pressure when you turn on the cold water faucet. A plastic collar in the heat trap reduces corrosion of the pipes and tank.

Most older water heaters, and some new ones, lack adequate tank insulation. Adding a tank insulation jacket can really help. There is a new insulation jacket available that uses thin radiant reflective foil bubble insulation. Standard fiberglass batt tank jackets are more bulky, but very effective.

For zero cost, you can make your own insulation jacket from extra wall batt insulation. There is a simple bent-coat-hanger method to make support hooks to hold the insulation in place. This is very important, especially with a gas water heater, because you must not block the air inlet.

Finally, use the drain outlet near the bottom of the tank to drain a few gallons from the bottom of the tank once a month. This removes sediment.

Q: The back of our house is built into a small grade. Several of the windows are in window wells and they don't let in much light. What can we do so we don't have to turn on as many lamps?

A: One method that works well is to paint the inside of the window well with white enamel paint. Cover the bottom of the window well with crushed white rock. This reflects much more of the natural light into your windows. Cover the window well with an inexpensive domed clear plastic cover.

Manufacturers of several efficiency-improving products are listed below. Instructions for making your own water heater jacket using leftover wall batt insulation are shown on Page 171. Page 172 also includes a list of energy-saving tips for hot water usage.

Stand-by heat losses (10% to 15% of your total costs), from the water heater tank walls and pipes immediately above it to the surrounding air, offer the greatest potential for energy savings. With an old gas water heater, there isn't much you can do to increase the combustion efficiency. They generally don't burn the gas completely and the design of the heat exchanger, which transfers the heat to the water, is not the best.

The only way to increase the combustion and heat transfer efficiency is to purchase a new high-efficiency gas water heater. An electric water heating element is almost 100% efficient since there are no hot exhaust gases that lose heat up a flue.

There are two ways to reduce the stand-by heat losses - install a tank insulation jacket and install heat trap pipe fittings in the top of the water heater. Both products are described on the following pages.

A water heater insulation jacket is very effective since most older water heaters have inadequate tank insulation. It is important to purchase one that is big enough to completely cover the tank and top. With a gas water heater, **MAKE SURE TO LEAVE CLEARANCE AROUND THE FLUE VENT DAMPER AT THE TOP AND THE COMBUSTION AIR INLET AT THE BOTTOM.** You can completely cover an electric water heater. If the insulation is too short, make sure the upper end is covered because the water is hotter at the top. You can find conventional fiberglass jackets at most home center or plumbing stores. If you cannot find one, I have included a list of manufacturers to contact for names of local dealers.

There is a new type of insulation jacket made of aluminum foil covered bubble insulation. This insulation is less than ½ inch thick. It is ideal for water heaters that are located very close to a wall. Although the insulation value of the bubble material is not as high as a thicker conventional fiberglass jacket, the reflective nature of the foil itself cuts down on radiant heat loss from the hot tank.

Heat trap tank fittings keep the hot water from circulating up into the pipes above the tank when no hot water is being used. Since hot water is less dense, it naturally rises in the pipes. There it loses its heat, sinks back into the tank, and is replaced by more hot water. Over time, this continuous process cools off the water inside your water heater. Heat trap fittings block this wasteful circulation of the hot water. When you turn on a hot water faucet, the balls move and allow the water to pass unimpeded through the pipes.

Manufacturers of Tank Insulation Jackets and Heat Trap Fittings

INNOVATIVE INSULATION, 2710 S.E. Loop 820, Ft. Worth, TX 76140 - (800) 825-0123
    type - foil-bubble insulation jacket

OWENS-CORNING, Fiberglas Tower, Toledo, OH 43659 - (800) 438-7465
    type - fiberglass insulation jacket

PERFECTION CORP., 222 Lake St., Madison, OH 44057 - (800) 544-6344 (216) 428-1171
    type - heat trap fitting
    sold in most hardware and plumbing supply outlets under various names

RELIANCE, 500 Bypass Rd., Ashland City, TN 37015 - (800) 365-7782
    type - fiberglass insulation jacket

THERMWELL PRODUCTS, 150 E. 7 th St., Patterson, NJ 07524 - (201) 684-5000
    type - fiberglass insulation jacket

Instructions for Making a Water Tank Jacket

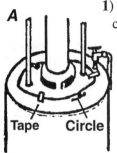

A — Tape, Circle

1) For a standard-sized water heater, untwist about 12 metal coat hangers. Using the pliers, straighten them as much as possible. You will use these to form the hooks that support the insulation around the tank.

2) Measure the diameter of the top of the water heater tank. Using the coat hangers, form a circle, three inches smaller in diameter, around the flue on top of the tank. This will be used to support the coat hanger hooks below.

3) Once the circle is formed, use the duct tape to secure it to the top of the tank. (See diagram A.) Clean the dust off the top of the tank first, or the tape will not stick well enough.

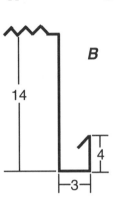

B — 14, 4, 3

4) Bend four coat hangers into the hook shape shown in diagram B. The 3-inch dimension is used for standard 3 ½ wall insulation. If you are using thicker insulation, increase that dimension accordingly.

5) Bend the straight end of the coat hanger hooks around the wire support circle on top of the tank. Just a single-bend loop is adequate. Tape the hooks to the side of the tank. (See diagram C.)

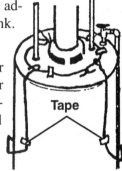

C — Tape

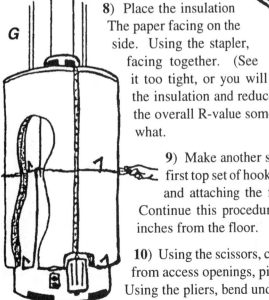

D

6) Measure the circumference of the water heater tank. Cut a length of insulation to that length plus four inches. One easy method to cut fiberglass batts insulation is to lay it on a cutting board and lay another board across it. (See diagram D.) Wear a mask to avoid breathing the fiberglass dust.

7) Using a scissors, cut the insulation back 2 inches on each end of the length of insulation, leaving the paper backing intact. (See diagram E.) You will use this 2-inch flap to staple the ends together.

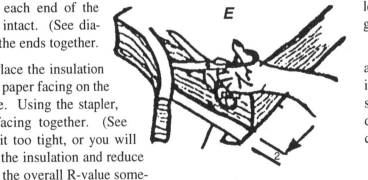

E — 2

8) Place the insulation around the tank in the hooks. The paper facing on the insulation should be to the outside. Using the stapler, staple the ends of the paper facing together. (See diagram F.) Don't try to pull it too tight, or you will compress the insulation and reduce the overall R-value somewhat.

F

9) Make another set of four hooks and hang them from the first top set of hooks. Follow the same procedure for making and attaching the fiberglass insulation. (See diagram G.) Continue this procedure until the tank is covered to about six inches from the floor.

10) Using the scissors, cut back the insulation at least three inches from access openings, pipes, combustion air inlet, and thermostat. Using the pliers, bend under the exposed ends of the wire hooks.

G — 1

Tips for Using Your Water Heater More Efficiently

1) Set the water heater thermostat as low as possible to satisfy your needs. 120 degrees is generally considered the recommended minimum temperature. With a lower hot water temperature, less heat is lost from the water heater tank. Also, less energy is lost from your hot pipes after you turn off the hot water at the faucet.

2) If you have a dishwasher without a water preheater, you should keep the hot water temperature at 140 degrees. Temperatures lower than this may not adequately clean your dishes. If you plan to buy a new dishwasher, select one with a water preheater.

3) Drain several gallons of water once a month from the drain valve in the bottom of your water heater. This will remove any sediment that collects there over time. The build-up of sediment can insulate the hot surfaces from the water, so the heating efficiency is reduced.

4) Unless you have a very new high-efficiency water heater, you probably should add insulation to the tank. You can test it by feeling the temperature of the water heater tank. If it feels warm, then it is losing heat and you should add an insulation jacket.

5) If someone is home during the daytime and uses hot water throughout the day, you should add insulation to your hot water pipes. The heat from a lot of hot water is lost from the pipes each time your turn off the hot water at the faucets.

6) If you have a gas water heater, check the color of the burner flames and the flow of air into the draft diverter at the flue. The flame should be a steady blue color. If it is yellow and seems to jump around, you should have it checked.

7) Install low-flow shower heads or flow restrictors. These will reduce the hot water usage by 50 percent. Showers generally use less hot water than a bath. When you purchase a low-flow shower head, select one with a shutoff valve. This allows you to turn off the water temporarily while you are lathering.

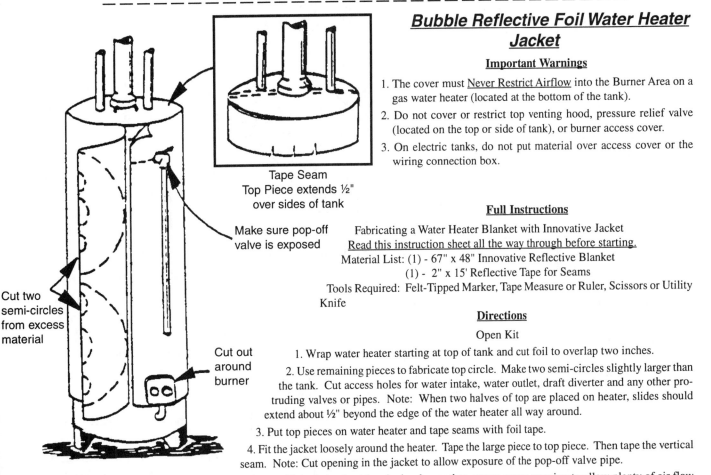

Tape Seam
Top Piece extends ½"
over sides of tank

Make sure pop-off
valve is exposed

Cut two
semi-circles
from excess
material

Cut out
around
burner

Bubble Reflective Foil Water Heater Jacket

Important Warnings

1. The cover must <u>Never Restrict Airflow</u> into the Burner Area on a gas water heater (located at the bottom of the tank).

2. Do not cover or restrict top venting hood, pressure relief valve (located on the top or side of tank), or burner access cover.

3. On electric tanks, do not put material over access cover or the wiring connection box.

Full Instructions

Fabricating a Water Heater Blanket with Innovative Jacket
<u>Read this instruction sheet all the way through before starting.</u>
Material List: (1) - 67" x 48" Innovative Reflective Blanket
(1) - 2" x 15' Reflective Tape for Seams
Tools Required: Felt-Tipped Marker, Tape Measure or Ruler, Scissors or Utility Knife

Directions

Open Kit

1. Wrap water heater starting at top of tank and cut foil to overlap two inches.

2. Use remaining pieces to fabricate top circle. Make two semi-circles slightly larger than the tank. Cut access holes for water intake, water outlet, draft diverter and any other protruding valves or pipes. Note: When two halves of top are placed on heater, slides should extend about ½" beyond the edge of the water heater all way around.

3. Put top pieces on water heater and tape seams with foil tape.

4. Fit the jacket loosely around the heater. Tape the large piece to top piece. Then tape the vertical seam. Note: Cut opening in the jacket to allow exposure of the pop-off valve pipe.

5. Cut out holes for burner cover, controls, drain, etc. Make hole about two inches larger than access cover opening to allow plenty of air flow around burner area.

Note: When installed properly, the jacket should hang loosely, and slightly extended away from the sides of the water heater.

Optional: You may want to tape jacket to tank around access hole. This will keep edges secure.

Q: My gas water heater is 15 years old and it does not seem to heat water as fast as it used to. Can I tune it up myself and what might cause the reduced hot water volume?

A: Heating water accounts for about 20 percent of the typical family's utility bills. A simple tune-up will not only lower your utility bills, but it will increase the hot water volume for morning showers.

Every month or two, drain several gallons of water from the valve at the bottom of the water heater. This removes some of the sediment that settles to the bottom of the tank.

A thick layer of sediment can insulate the hot burner heat exchanger from the water. This results in less hot water output and a slower recovery rate (time required to heat the incoming cold water).

For more effective cleaning, close the cold water inlet valve. Open the hot water faucet in the nearest bathroom. With an electric water heater, turn the electricity off first so the top element does not overheat and burn out.

Quickly open and close the cold water inlet valve several times. This stirs up the sediment in the bottom of the tank. Drain out a few more gallons. Close the tank drain and

open the water inlet valve. When all the air is forced out of the bathroom faucet, close it too.

Feel the top portion of the water heater tank. If it feels warm, add an insulation jacket. Make sure to allow for clearance around the draft hood at the top and the combustion air inlet near the bottom.

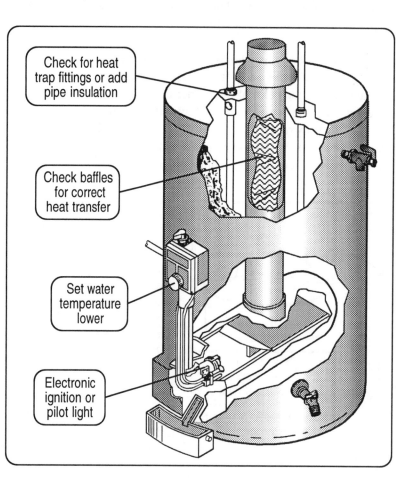

Check for heat trap fittings or add pipe insulation

Check baffles for correct heat transfer

Set water temperature lower

Electronic ignition or pilot light

If your water heater does not have heat trap pipe fittings (one-way valves), either install them or insulate the water pipes above the water heater. Insulating a three foot length is usually adequate.

There are several possible causes for reduced hot water supply. You can troubleshoot some of these causes yourself. The thermostat may

have accidentally been set lower. Check the hot water temperature at the nearest faucet. It should be 120 degrees.

The burner orifice may be dirty. Check it by looking at the flame. It should be steady and blue, not yellow. Cleaning requires a service call.

Setting the thermostat above 120 degrees will increase the hot water volume, but it wastes energy. If everything checks out okay, but there's not enough hot water, consider a new super efficient water heater. Some have lifetime no-rust warranties and can cut your water heating costs by $100 per year.

Q: We are building a sunspace and we want to install a heat circulating fireplace. We want the chimney to obstruct as little of the view as possible. How can we build one?

A: If you have a source of inexpensive firewood, a heat circulating fireplace can provide economical heat. A prebuilt zero clearance model is probably your best choice and easiest to install yourself.

Use an approved (flow manufacturer's recommendations) double wall flue pipe. Instead of covering it with wood or brick, slip large green vinyl piping (for storm drains) over it. This will block less of the view.

Troubleshooting Guide for Gas Water Heater

It is important that *ALL* causes of a condition be checked - even after you have found the one that is giving trouble. Here is why. Suppose the problem is that the burner will not ignite and you find dirt in the main burner orifice. There are 15 other causes for the same condition! Some may be just developing and some may develop after you fixed the original condition.

Causes indicated with (X) should be given immediate attention.

Possible Cause and Solution

#	Possible Cause	Solution
1	Excess primary air	Adjust air shutter to reduce air
2	Insufficient primary air	Adjust air shutter to increase air supply
3	Insufficient secondary air	Provide ventilation to heater
4	Low gas pressure	Check with utility - change orifice for available pressure
5	High gas pressure	Check with utility - check orifice for correct pressure
6	No gas	Check with utility
7	Wrong regulator pressure	Adjust regulator to 3 1/2" W.C. Pressure
8	Dirt in main burner orifice	Clean orifice - check for source of dirt and eliminate
9	Dirt in pilot burner orifice	Clean orifice - check for source of dirt and eliminate
10	Dirt in gas lines	Notify utility - if necessary install dirt trap in gas line
11	Dirt under thermostat valve seat	Clean carefully - check for source of dirt and eliminate
12	Orifice too large	Replace with correct orifice
13	Orifice too small	Replace with correct orifice
14	Venturi clogged	Clean - check for source of trouble and correct
15	Flue clogged	Clean - check for source of trouble and correct
16	Pilot line clogged	Clean - check for source of trouble and correct
17	Main burner line clogged	Clean - check for source of trouble and correct
18	Wrong pilot burner	Replace with correct pilot burner

Water Heater Problem Matrix

(Cause numbers correspond to the table above; ✓ = possible cause, X = give immediate attention)

Water Heater Problem	1	2	3	4	5	6	7	8	9	10	11	12	13	14	15	16	17	18
GAS ODOR AND/OR TASTE IN WATER																		
SOOTING OR SMOKING BURNER																		
BURNER BURNS IN VENTURI																		
BURNER IS NOISY																		
FLAMES FLOAT OFF BURNER																		
BURNER BURNS YELLOW																		
BURNER WILL NOT IGNITE																		
PILOT LIGHTS GO OUT WHEN BUTTON RELEASED																		
TANK BULGED - REVERSED HEADS											X							
PILOT FLAME TOO LARGE					X		✓											✓
PILOT FLAME TOO SMALL				✓			✓		✓	✓						✓		✓
SMOKING AND CARBON FORMATION		✓	✓		X		✓	✓			X	✓		✓			X	
COMBUSTION ODORS	✓	✓	✓		X		✓	✓				✓		✓			X	
CONDENSATION	✓						✓				X	✓					X	
THERMOSTAT FAILS TO CLOSE											X		✓					
EXCESSIVE RELIEF VALVE OPERATION																		
DRIP FROM RELIEF VALVE																		
OVERHEATED WATER - STEAMING					X		✓				X							
SLOW HOT WATER RECOVERY	✓	✓	✓	✓			✓					✓	✓	✓	X			
INSUFFICIENT HOT WATER				✓			✓	✓				✓	✓					
HIGH OPERATING COST					X		✓	✓			X	✓	✓	✓	X			
PILOT WILL NOT REMAIN LIT	✓			✓	X	✓	✓			✓	✓					X		✓
BURNER POPS WHEN TURNED ON OR OFF	✓			✓			✓	✓						✓				
BURNER FLAME TOO HIGH		✓	✓		X		✓									✓		
BURNER FLAME NOISY	✓				X		✓							✓				
BURNER FLAME YELLOW - LAZY		✓	✓	✓			✓	✓						✓	X		✓	
BURNER FLAME FLOATS LIFTS OFF PORTS	✓				X		✓					✓			X		✓	
BURNER WILL NOT IGNITE	✓					✓	✓	✓		✓		✓		✓		✓		✓

Troubleshooting Guide for Gas Water Heater

It is important that *ALL* causes of a condition be checked - even after you have found the one that is giving trouble. Here is why. Suppose the problem is that the burner will not ignite and you find dirt in the main burner orifice. There are 15 other causes for the same condition! Some may be just developing and some may develop after you fixed the original condition.

Causes indicated with (X) should be given immediate attention.

Possible Cause / Solution

#	Possible Cause	Solution
C1	Wrong pilot adjustment	Adjust pilot screw in thermostat
C2	Pilot flame does not engulf thermocouple	Adjust pilot screw in thermostat
C3	Thermocouple lead connection loose	Tighten snug with fingers, then take 1/4" turn with wrench
C4	Defective thermocouple lead	Replace with new thermocouple lead
C5	Defective thermostat	Replace or repair in accordance with mfg's. instructions
C6	Defective magnetic valve	Replace in accordance with mfg's. instructions.
C7	Improper calibration	Recalibrate in accordance with mfg's. instructions
C8	Pilot filter clogged	Replace with new filter
C9	Thermostat set too high	Turn temperature knob to desired temperature
C10	Thermostat set too low	Turn tempurature knob to desired temperature
C11	Heater installed in confined space	Provide ventilation by use of louvers in wall or door
C12	Overbaffled	Replace with correct baffle
C13	Heater not connected to flue	Provide and connect to proper flue
C14	Wrong burner ports	Replace with correct burner head
C15	Sediment or lime in tank	Drain - check to see if water treatment is necessary
C16	Heater too small for job	Install adequate heater
C17	Wrong piping connections	Correct piping - dip tube in cold inlet
C18	Leaking faucets	Repair faucets

Water Heater Problem (cause codes C1–C18 per table above; ✓ = check, X = give immediate attention)

Water Heater Problem	Marked Causes
GAS ODOR AND/OR TASTE IN WATER	
SOOTING OR SMOKING BURNER	
BURNER BURNS IN VENTURI	
BURNER IS NOISY	
FLAMES FLOAT OFF BURNER	
BURNER BURNS YELLOW	
BURNER WILL NOT IGNITE	
PILOT LIGHTS GO OUT WHEN BUTTON RELEASED	
TANK BULGED - REVERSED HEADS	C6 ✓
PILOT FLAME TOO LARGE	C1 ✓
PILOT FLAME TOO SMALL	C1 ✓; C7 ✓
SMOKING AND CARBON FORMATION	C5 ✓; C6 ✓; C12 X; C13 ✓; C14 ✓
COMBUSTION ODORS	C11 X; C13 ✓; C14 ✓
CONDENSATION	C11 X; C13 ✓; C14 ✓
THERMOSTAT FAILS TO CLOSE	C5 ✓; C6 ✓; C7 ✓
EXCESSIVE RELIEF VALVE OPERATION	C5 ✓; C9 X
DRIP FROM RELIEF VALVE	C5 ✓; C9 X; C15 ✓
OVERHEATED WATER - STEAMING	C1 ✓; C5 ✓; C7 ✓; C9 X
SLOW HOT WATER RECOVERY	C5 ✓; C10 ✓; C12 ✓; C15 ✓; C16 ✓; C17 ✓
INSUFFICIENT HOT WATER	C5 ✓; C10 ✓; C12 ✓; C15 ✓; C16 ✓; C17 ✓
HIGH OPERATING COST	C5 ✓; C9 X; C12 ✓; C15 ✓; C16 ✓; C17 ✓; C18 ✓
PILOT WILL NOT REMAIN LIT	C1 ✓; C2 ✓; C3 ✓; C4 ✓; C6 ✓; C7 ✓; C11 ✓
BURNER POPS WHEN TURNED ON OR OFF	C12 ✓; C14 ✓
BURNER FLAME TOO HIGH	C14 ✓
BURNER FLAME NOISY	C14 ✓
BURNER FLAME YELLOW - LAZY	C11 X; C12 ✓; C13 ✓; C14 ✓
BURNER FLAME FLOATS LIFTS OFF PORTS	C11 X; C12 ✓; C13 ✓; C14 ✓
BURNER WILL NOT IGNITE	C3 ✓; C4 ✓; C5 ✓; C6 ✓; C8 ✓; C10 ✓; C11 X

Troubleshooting Guide for Gas Water Heater

It is important that *ALL* causes of a condition be checked - even after you have found the one that is giving trouble. Here is why. Suppose the problem is that the burner will not ignite and you find dirt in the main burner orifice. There are 15 other causes for the same condition! Some may be just developing and some may develop after you fixed the original condition.

Causes indicated with (X) should be given immediate attention.

Possible Cause / Solution

Possible Cause	Solution
Gas leaks	Check with utility - repair at once
Excess draft	Check source and correct
Cold drafts	Check source and correct
Return circulating lines	Recommend change to one pipe system
Furnace coil hooked direct	Disconnect coil
Long runs of exposed piping	Insulate
Hot water piping in outside walls	Insulate
Excessive water pressure	Use pressure reducing valve and pressure relief valve
Surge from auto washer solenoid valve	Install blind pipe air cushion
Check valve in water line	Use pressure relief valve
Heater stacking	Install adequate heater and relief valve
No relief valve	Install relief valve
Pressure reducing valve in water line	Install relief valve
Dip tube in hot water outlet	Remove and replace in cold water inlet
Thermocouple loose at thermostat	Replace thermocouple
Thermocouple not in pilot flame	Replace thermocouple
Pilot is lit	Replace thermostat
Control set to "ON"	Replace thermostat
Thermostat set to "HIGH"	Replace thermostat
Proper gas pressure to thermostat	Replace burner
Adjust air shutter	Replace burner
Condition of anode	Replace anode rod

Water Heater Problem (matrix of causes, X = immediate attention)

GAS ODOR AND/OR TASTE IN WATER	Condition of anode (√)
SOOTING OR SMOKING BURNER	Adjust air shutter (√)
BURNER BURNS IN VENTURI	Proper gas pressure to thermostat (√)
BURNER IS NOISY	Proper gas pressure to thermostat (√)
FLAMES FLOAT OFF BURNER	Proper gas pressure to thermostat (√)
BURNER BURNS YELLOW	Proper gas pressure to thermostat (√); Adjust air shutter (√)
BURNER WILL NOT IGNITE	Pilot is lit (√); Control set to "ON" (√); Thermostat set to "HIGH" (√)
PILOT LIGHTS GO OUT WHEN BUTTON RELEASED	Thermocouple loose at thermostat (√); Thermocouple not in pilot flame (√)
TANK BULGED - REVERSED HEADS	Excessive water pressure (X); Surge from auto washer solenoid valve (√); Check valve in water line (X); Heater stacking (√); No relief valve (X); Pressure reducing valve in water line (X)
PILOT FLAME TOO LARGE	
PILOT FLAME TOO SMALL	
SMOKING AND CARBON FORMATION	
COMBUSTION ODORS	
CONDENSATION	
THERMOSTAT FAILS TO CLOSE	Return circulating lines (√)
EXCESSIVE RELIEF VALVE OPERATION	Excessive water pressure (X); Surge from auto washer solenoid valve (√); Heater stacking (√)
DRIP FROM RELIEF VALVE	Excessive water pressure (X); Surge from auto washer solenoid valve (√); Check valve in water line (√); Heater stacking (√)
OVERHEATED WATER - STEAMING	Furnace coil hooked direct (√); Heater stacking (√)
SLOW HOT WATER RECOVERY	Excess draft (√); Cold drafts (√); Furnace coil hooked direct (√); Heater stacking (√)
INSUFFICIENT HOT WATER	Cold drafts (√); Return circulating lines (√); Long runs of exposed piping (√); Hot water piping in outside walls (√); Heater stacking (√)
HIGH OPERATING COST	Gas leaks (X); Excess draft (√); Cold drafts (√); Return circulating lines (√); Furnace coil hooked direct (√); Long runs of exposed piping (√); Hot water piping in outside walls (√); Heater stacking (√); Dip tube in hot water outlet (√)
PILOT WILL NOT REMAIN LIT	Cold drafts (√)
BURNER POPS WHEN TURNED ON OR OFF	
BURNER FLAME TOO HIGH	
BURNER FLAME NOISY	Gas leaks (√)
BURNER FLAME YELLOW - LAZY	
BURNER FLAME FLOATS LIFTS OFF PORTS	Gas leaks (√); Excess draft (√)
BURNER WILL NOT IGNITE	

176

Q: I don't have allergies, but I want a super-high-filtration "allergy-safe" vacuum cleaner to cut down on dust. How are they different and do the filters require a more powerful, electricity-guzzling motor?

A: True "allergy-safe" vacuum cleaners have more than just a better bag. The best ones have multiple high-efficiency filters and seals to eliminate leaks of allergens (allergy-causing dust) back into your room. Even if you don't have allergies, these vacuum cleaners are worthwhile.

The first time you use one of these vacuum cleaners, you will be amazed by the lack of that "just vacuumed" smell. The room actually smells fresher than before you vacuumed. With a HEPA and a charcoal filter, the air coming out of the vacuum cleaner is more pure than the air going in.

I have allergies and use an allergy-safe vacuum cleaner. In addition to stopping sneezing and eliminating itchy, watery eyes, the first bag was full after two weeks. It picked up more dirt in two weeks than my other one did in two months.

There are two keys to allergy-safe vacuuming. First, the vacuum cleaner must be very powerful to deep clean and pick up the dirt,

dander, mold, pollen, dust mites, etc. It must also highly filter the return air so the allergens don't blow out again into your room.

The cleaning power of a vacuum cleaner is measured by the suction (inches of water lift) and the volume of air flow (cubic feet per minute - cfm). The most powerful allergy vacuums have a suction

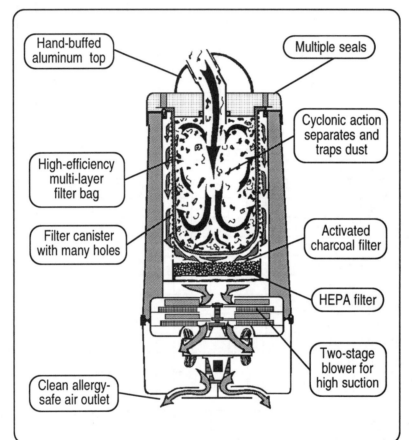

Hand-buffed aluminum top

Multiple seals

Cyclonic action separates and traps dust

High-efficiency multi-layer filter bag

Filter canister with many holes

Activated charcoal filter

HEPA filter

Two-stage blower for high suction

Clean allergy-safe air outlet

of 85 inches and an air flow of 100 cfm. Most allergy-safe vacuum cleaners use a canister design with a power nozzle (beater bar and brush) for carpeting.

There are several designs for keeping the dirt and allergens inside the vacuum cleaner. One design uses a double wall, 28-layer cellulose filter bag, a charcoal filter, and a final fiberglass or HEPA filter. A thin metal or reinforced plastic housing stays rigid for a long-term seal.

A rapidly spinning (cyclonic) flow of dirty air inside the filter bag helps to separate the dirt particles. They also hit the filter bag pores at an angle. This makes it more effective at trapping them inside. One design has 3,500 very tiny air holes in the metal canister for the filter bag. This makes more effective use of the entire filtering surface of the bag.

The motors in allergy-safe vacuum cleaners are more powerful, up to 9 amps, than a standard model. (Don't be fooled by the marketing hype of 3 or 4 "peak" horsepower motors.) Considering the few hours that a vacuum cleaner is used, the extra electricity used by an allergy-safe model is insignificant.

Q: I leave a door to an uncooled room open a little for my dog and cat to get to their food, water and litter box. The door gradually swings open all the way and wastes energy. I can feel a cool draft from the opened door. What can I do to keep it in position so that energy is not wasted?

A: Since you have to go in and out of the room often, you still want the door to operate smoothly. One simple no-cost trick I have used is to remove the bottom hinge pin.

Hit it with a big hammer to bow it slightly. Grease it and drive it back into the hinge. This provides just enough drag to keep the door from swinging open by itself, yet you will still be able to open it very easily.

Allergy-safe vacuum cleaners are good for allergy sufferers. Even if you do not have allergies, these specially-designed vacuum cleaners reduce the level of dust inside your home.

I have allergies and I started using one of these vacuum cleaners in my own home. It not only eliminated the dust and my sneezing, but it cleaned much better. After the first two weeks of using the new vacuum cleaner, it deep cleaned so well, that the bag was full. It picked up the dirt that my regular vacuum cleaner had missed. After that, I changed the bag on a normal schedule.

The chart below shows the sizes of various allergens (allergy-causing particles). The vacuum cleaner filter system (bags and other filters) must be effective at filtering out particles at least that small. Cigarette and other smoke are some of the smallest particles and you will need a HEPA filter to effectively remove them.

The chart on page 179 lists the manufacturers of special allergy-safe vacuum cleaners, along with other detailed information on them. Page 180 shows where common allergens are trapped in a typical home and the best methods to vacuum to remove them.

When you vacuum to eliminate allergens, it is important to 1) deep clean to remove them, and 2) to keep them inside the vacuum cleaner. The cleaning power of vacuum cleaner is basically determined by the air flow rated in cfm (cubic feet per minute). A higher suction force (measured in inches of water lift) usually creates greater air flow. It is the air flow that draws up the dirt, not the suction.

Don't just judge the most powerful vacuum cleaner by the advertised "peak horsepower". It is marketing hype. Some vacuum cleaners are rated a 4 peak horsepower, but they never attain that level when they operate. They would blow a fuse in your house if they did. You should always compare cfm of air flow and suction in inches of water lift to get a true comparison.

In addition to having high-efficiency filters and bags, these allergy-safe vacuum cleaners are designed to be very airtight with many seals. This keeps the dust inside the vacuum cleaner. You can buy high-efficiency filter bags for ordinary vacuum cleaners, but some of the smaller allergen particles will still leak out around the bag and the cover.

A HEPA filter is the most efficient for home use. There are more effective filters, ULPA, but they are expensive and are usually only used in special rooms, like computer manufacturing. A charcoal filter is effective because it also removes odors and unhealthy organic chemicals from the air. The charcoal filter should be replaced several times a year.

The Vita-Vac and the Air-Way models are very similar. The Vita-Vac basically replaces Air-Way's fiberglass filter with a HEPA filter and uses a different replaceable bag. Several of the models use a cyclonic (spinning) action of the air. This spinning of the air separates the dirt particles and makes a filter bag more effective.

Sizes of Typical Allergens - microns	
Particulates	
Human Hair	100 - 20
Viruses	1 - .005
Bacteria	20 - .05
Skin Flakes	15 - .9
Pollen	100 - 5
Spores	100 - 9
Sneeze Droplets	100 - 15
Smoke	
Carbon Particles	1 - .005
Cooking/Grease	2 - .01
Tobacco Smoke	3 - .007
Wood Smoke	3 - .001
Dusts	
Household Dust	10 - .001
Insecticide Dust	20 - .001
Soil Dust	100 - 1
Coal Dust	100 - 1
Animal Dander	10 - .2

Manufacturers of Allergy-Safe Vaccum Cleaners

AIR-WAY SANITIZOR, P.O. Box 701, Talladega, AL 35160 - (800) 537-1073 (205) 362-2299
model - "Sani-Clean"   style - canister   water lift - 96.4"   air flow -109 cfm
filtering system - 4 stages — 1) + 2) double wall 28-layer cellulose bag • 3) charcoal filter • 4) fiberglass filter

EUREKA CO., 1201 E. Bell St., Bloomington, IL 61701 - (800) 688-4583 (309) 828-5616
model - "Excalibur 6404"   style - upright   water lift - 32.2"   air flow - n/a
filtering system - 2 stages — 1) paper bag • 2) 6-layer filter system — the final layer is electrostatically charged
features - 25 foot power cord, on-board attachments with built-in hose

FANTOM TECHNOLOGIES, 1979 E. Everleigh Cir., Sandy, UT 84093 - (800) 668-9600 (801) 255-9685
model - "Fantom - F11051"   style - upright   water lift - 50.0"   air flow - 38 cfm
filtering system - 2 stages — 1) dual cyclonic action - no bag • 2) HEPA filter after motor
features - 30 foot cord, 3 on-board attachments, 7 foot hose extension available creating a 17 foot cleaning reach

HEALTH-MORE INC., 3500 Payne Ave., Cleveland, OH 44114 - (800) 344-1840 (216) 432-1990
model - "Filter Queen Majestic"   style - canister   water lift - 85.0"   air flow - 68 cfm
filtering system - 4 stages — 1) cyclonic action - no bag • 2) cellulose filter cone • 3) charcoal filter • 4) secondary filter

MIELE APPLIANCES, 22D Worlds Fair Dr., Somerset, NJ 08873 - (800) 843-7231 (908) 560-0899
model - "White Pearl - S434i"   style - canister   water lift - 94.5"   air flow -125 cfm
model - "S401i"   style - canister   water lift - 94.5"   air flow -125 cfm
filtering system - 5 stages — 1) double layer bag • 2) electrostatic nylon filter before motor • 3) charcoal filter before motor
• 4) electrostatic nylon filter after motor • 5) HEPA filter
model - "S174i"   style - upright   water lift - 55.2"   air flow - 65 cfm
model - "S170i"   style - upright   water lift - 47.8"   air flow - 60 cfm
filtering system - 5 stages — 1) two-ply layer bag • 2) filter before motor • 3) flows through motor exhaust filter • 4) + 5)
two-stage exhaust filter - the first one is electrostatically charged
features - built-in tools

NILFISK, 300 Technology Dr., Malvern, PA 19355 - (800) 645-3475 (610) 647-6420
model - "GS90"   style - canister   water lift - 75.0"   air flow - 87cfm
filtering system - 4 stages — 1) two-ply primary cellulose bag • 2) cotton main filter • 3) micro filter around motor • 4) HEPA
filter or optional ULPA filter

SHARP ELECTRONICS CORP., Sharp Plaza, Mahwah, NJ 07430 - (800) 237-4277
model - "EC-12TWT7" — "EC-12TWT9" — "EC-14TWT7" — "EC-14TWT9"
          style - upright   water lift - 80.0"   air flow - n/a
filtering system - 4 stages — 1) 2-ply filter bag • 2) + 3) + 4) 3-filter system
features - 35 foot power cord, on-board tools, 9 foot cleaning reach

SILVER KING INTN'L, 3009 W. Colorado Ave., Colorado Springs, CO 80904 - (800) 864-1658 (719) 578-5260
model - "73-B-2"   style - canister   water lift - 72.0"   air flow - 97cfm
filtering system - 2 stages — 1) cyclonic action - no bag • 2) 24-layer cellulose filter after motor
features - wet and dry vacuum, plastic pillow bag to clean your pillows

VITA-MIX CORP., 8615 Usher Rd., Cleveland, OH 44138 - (800) 848-2649 (216) 235-4840
model - "Vita-Vac"   style - canister   water lift - 88.0"   air flow - 91cfm
filtering system - 4 stages — 1) + 2) double wall 14-layer filter cellulose bag • 3) charcoal filter • 4) HEPA filter

Sani-Clean by Air-Way Sanitizor

GS90 by Nilfisk

Various attachments

GUIDELINES FOR CLEANING WITH THE VITA-VAC:

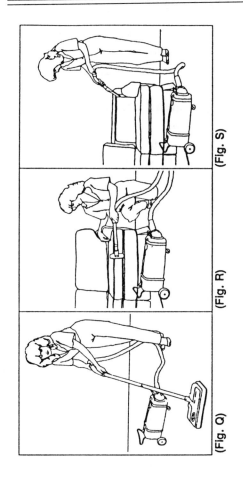

(Fig. Q) (Fig. R) (Fig. S)

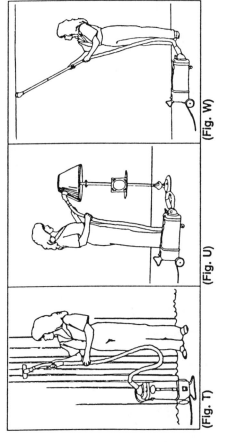

(Fig. T) (Fig. U) (Fig. W)

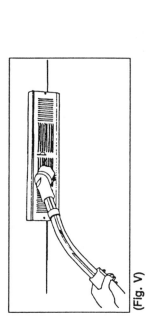

(Fig. V)

Item to be cleaned	What can be found*	Vita-Vac tool**	Comments
Rugs and carpets	1, 2, 3, 4 5, 6, 7, 11	A, D	Contaminants hide deep in the carpet, and are hard to get out. Power (water lift) and airflow (cfm) are both very important in getting rugs and carpets clean. (Fig. Q)
Upholstered furniture	1, 2, 3, 4 5, 6, 7, 11	C, D	Upholstered furniture is considered to be the worst place for dust mites. The Vita-Vac's superior cleaning system even captures their "feces." (Fig. R) and (Fig. S)
Hardwood, ceramic, linoleum and tile floors	1, 2, 4, 5 6, 7, 11	B, D E	Wet-mopping does not get rid of all the dust, dirt, etc; when the water dries the remaining dust is still a problem. The Vita-Vac's special filters eliminate dust. **It can also be a great electric broom.**
Curtains	2, 4, 6, 7, 11	C, E	Curtains must be vacuumed often to be kept clean. (Fig. T)
Fans, lamps, tables, TV, books, etc.	2, 11	E	The discharge from most vacuums makes you re-dust each time you vacuum. Vita-Vac does not let any dust out, so you only need to dust occasionally. Use the Vita-Vac to do the dusting to make sure you actually eliminate it from your home. (Fig. U)
Air returns and registers	1, 2, 3, 4, 6, 7, 8, 9 10, 11	D, E	Need to be cleaned often to prevent dust, dust mite feces, pollens, and mold spores, etc. from being circulated throughout the home. (Fig. V)
Ceilings and walls	1, 2, 11	B, C, D	Eliminates dust, dirt, smoke, and cobwebs, etc. rather than just spreading them around with a dust cloth. (Fig. W)

*1-dirt, 2-dust, 3-dust mites, 4-lint, 5-food, 6-pollens, 7-ragweed, 8-mold 9-mildew, 10-fungi, 11-smoke

**A-Power Head, B-Floor Brush, C-Upholstery Tool, D-Crevice Tool, E-Dust Brush

Q: I plan to install a home-size central vacuum cleaner myself. I have allergies, so I need clean, dust-free air. Since these central units are powerful, do they use a lot of electricity and are they efficient?

A: A central vacuum system does have a larger, more powerful motor than a standard portable vacuum cleaner. It can still be plugged into a standard electric outlet. Considering the length of time that you run a vacuum cleaner each month, the electricity usage difference is not significant.

Central vacuum cleaners are easy to install yourself, even in a two-story home. They offer many advantages over standard portable vacuum cleaners. They are much more powerful for deep cleaning of furniture and carpets. This deep cleaning can extend the life of your carpeting.

Since the central unit is located in a utility room, basement, or garage, there is little noise when you are vacuuming. You just hear the sound of the air flowing into the hose and attachment. A telephone ring or a baby crying can easily be heard.

The combination of the deep thorough cleaning and the fact that the dust and dirt are collected in the central unit, should reduce allergens inside your home. The exhaust air is often vented outdoors. Even with the best filter bag, a standard por-

table vacuum cleaner allows fine dust to pass through the bag and get back into your room.

To install a central vacuum cleaning system, mount the central unit on a wall near a standard electric outlet and plug it in. Run a small plastic pipe from the central unit with branches off to wall outlets. With a lightweight 30-foot hose,

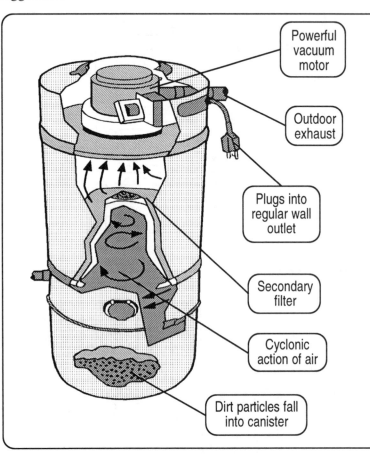

Powerful vacuum motor

Outdoor exhaust

Plugs into regular wall outlet

Secondary filter

Cyclonic action of air

Dirt particles fall into canister

you often need only three outlets on each floor.

To get to a second story, you can run the plastic pipe up through a first-floor closet. A low-voltage wire is run along with the pipe. When you flip up the outlet cover and insert the hose, it automatically switches on the central vacuum motor.

There are several types of central vacuum system designs. One

type uses a large disposable filter bag. Since it is big, it generally needs to be replaced only once or twice a year. Another type uses cyclonic action. The incoming dirty air spins around very fast inside the central unit and the dust and dirt drop into a canister. You empty it twice a year.

The cleaning power of central vacuum systems is rated in air power watts. This power rating is based on the amount of suction force and the amount of air flow. A higher air power means more overall cleaning power.

Q: I have a furnace hot air outlet register in my garage. I only open the register the few times that I work in the garage, but it doesn't seal well when it is closed. How can I block the heated air leaks?

A: Most hot air registers don't seal well when they are closed. Go to your hardware store and check out some new ones. Hopefully you can find one that seals better than your old one.

In my garage, I made a mini magnetic acrylic interior storm window to cover the register. Put the steel strip on the wall around the register. When you don't need heat, close the register and stick the mini storm window over it. Some storm window companies will sell you the small amount of materials that you will need.

The major advantages of central systems are deep-cleaning power, no exhaust dust and dirt in air, low noise, an easy-to-handle lightweight hose, and easy maintenance.

You should mount the central vacuum unit in your basement, utility room, or garage. Most of the residential-size models plug into a regular 110-volt electrical outlet. The vacuum piping is often standard two-inch-diameter PVC plastic water pipe. This is very easy to work with and glues together at the joints. Try to keep the pipes as straight as possible with few elbows for the greatest vacuuming power.

Most central vacuum cleaner manufacturers rate their cleaning power in calculated maximum "air power watts". This takes into account the suction pressure, the air flow volume, and the size of the pipe and hose. Several manufacturers just publish the suction pressure, maximum air flow, and electric current draw (amps). Generally, higher air power watts or higher amps indicates more powerful vacuum motors.

There are several designs of central vacuum cleaning systems - disposable bags or filters, cyclonic (rapidly spinning air), a combination of cyclonic and filters, and an inverted permanent filter bag. It is best to vent them all outdoors to minimize residual dust in the indoor air. Several of the disposable bag models may be vented indoors.

When selecting a specific design type, make a decision as to whether you would rather buy replacement disposal filters or take time to clean a reusable washable filter. The disposable bags should have to be replaced only once or twice a year. The air passing through the vacuum motor is cleaner in the disposable bag and filter types. The true cyclonic type just needs to be emptied twice a year. The combination cyclonic and filter units are either a small inexpensive disposable filter or a cloth or washable foam filter. All of these central vacuum cleaner designs should clean very effectively with proper maintenance.

- -

Correct Vacuuming Extends Life and Beauty of Carpeting

Carpet nap does what it is trained to do. It is designed to spring up and down as we walk on it. However, if our vacuum does not brush the carpet, and train it to stand up,

When carpet is matted the carpet nap needs to be returned to the upright postion to release trapped dirt.

more than we walk on it and train it to lay down, the carpet will mat and pack in the traffic trails. There are two problems with packed or matted carpet. First, it is unsightly and secondly with the nap laying down flat, you can't pull the dirt through the sides of the carpet yarn. The heavy dirt, like sand and grit stays in the carpet and acts like little knives, the sharp edges on the sand cut the fiber every time you walk across the nap.

To properly vacuum your carpet, you must determine which way the nap is laying. You can determine this by taking the edge of your shoe and pulling it across the surface of the carpet all four ways until you

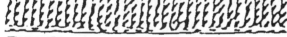

determine which direction pulls the nap up. Your brush roll on your vacuum turns towards the front of the machine and then back, so push your vacuum forward the same direction the nap is laying. In so doing, the for-

Dirt is easily removed in carpet that is not matted.

ward turning brush will pull the nap up brushing it hundreds of times, training it to stand up, restoring the beauty to your carpet, and deep cleaning it at the same time.

Proper vacuuming, the proper vacuum cleaner, and eliminating packed or matted carpet are all important. Packed or matted carpet cannot be cleaned. Every time you walk across packed or matted carpet, you kick up a small cloud of dust that affects respiratory problems, allergies, sinus problems and asthma. Packed or matted carpeting quickly becomes dirt laden, and a breeding ground for carpet mites, germs and many other microscopic creatures, all of which affects the health of your family. Proper vacuuming eliminates all of these problems, giving you a healthier and cleaner home.

By pushing the vacuum forward in the same direction the nap is laying it lets the brushroll pull the nap up. By pushing the vacuum in the other direction it causes a matting condition.

182

Model Numbers, Design, and Specifications on Each

BEAM INDUSTRIES, PO Box 788, Webster City, IA 50595 - (800) 369-2326 (515) 832-4620

model	type	air watts	power
model - 167S	type - filtered cyclonic	air watts - 404	power - 11.7 amps
model - 189S	type - filtered cyclonic	air watts - 404	power - 11.7 amps
model - 197S	type - filtered cyclonic	air watts - 368	power - 11 amps
model - 287S	type - filtered cyclonic	air watts - 455	power - 12 amps
model - 297S	type - filtered cyclonic	air watts - 406	power - 12 amps
model - 677S	type - filtered cyclonic	air watts - 778	power - 12 amps

BROAN MFG., PO Box 140, Hartford, WI 53027 - (800) 548-0790 (414) 673-4340

model	type	air watts	power
model - CV40	type - cyclonic	air watts - NA *	power - 13.5 amps
model - CV30	type - cyclonic	air watts - NA	power - 11 amps
model - CV20	type - cyclonic	air watts - NA	power - 10 amps
model - CV10	type - cyclonic	air watts - NA	power - 8 amps

* NA = Calculations not available

CENTRAL VAC INT'L, 3133 E. 12th St., Los Angeles, CA 90023 - (800) 666-3133 (213) 268-1135

model	type	air watts	power
model - CV-7	type - disposable bag	air watts - 274	power - 8.0 amps
model - CV-7DPS	type - disposable bag	air watts - 490	power - 16.0 amps
model - CV-11	type - disposable bag	air watts - 407	power - 12.8 amps
model - CV-16	type - disposable bag	air watts - 423	power - 12.6 amps

ELECTROLUX, 2300 Windy Ridge Pky., Marietta, GA 30067 - (800) 892-5678 (404) 933-1000

model	type	air watts	power
model - 1590	type - cyclonic/filter	air watts -481	power - 13.0 amps

FASCO INDUSTRIES, PO Box 150, Fayetteville, NC 28302 - (800) 334-4126 (910) 483-0421

model	type	air watts	power
model - 852SVDM	type - permanent filter **	air watts - 449	power - 13.3 amps
model - 851DM	type - permanent filter	air watts - 424	power - 11.6 amps
model - A853	type - permanent filter	air watts - 310	power - 8.7 amps
model - 858	type - cyclonic	air watts - 404	power - 12 amps

** Cloth filter bag has a weight on it. When the vacuum starts the bag is sucked upward as the air is drawn through it. When it shuts off the weight pulls the bag down and the dirt automatically falls off into the removeable canister at the bottom.

HOOVER CO., 101 E. Maple, North Canton, OH 44720 - (216) 499-9200

model	type	air watts	power
model - S5567-011	type - cyclonic/wash filter	air watts - NA	power - 12 amps
model - S5569-011	type - cyclonic/wash filter	air watts - NA	power - 12 amps
model - S5567-011	type - cyclonic/wash filter	air watts - NA	power - 10.5 amps

HP PRODUCTS, 512 W. Gorgas, Louisville, OH 44641 - (800) 822-8356 (216) 875-5556

model	type	air watts	power
model - 260	type - cyclonic	air watts - 371	power - 12.6 amps
model - 360	type - cyclonic	air watts - 279	power - 12.7 amps
model - 99	type - cyclonic	air watts - 734	power - 13.5 amps
model - 200	type - disposable bag	air watts - 389	power - 11.6 amps

LINDSAY MANUFACTURING, PO Box 1708, Ponca City, OK 74602 - (405) 762-2457

model	type	air watts	power
model - P125	type - cyclonic	air watts - 390	power - 11.5 amps
model - P110	type - cyclonic	air watts - 380	power - 11 amps
model - P100	type - washable foam filter	air watts - 490	power - 11 amps
model - P70	type - disposable bag	air watts - 370	power - 8.4 amps

M&S SYSTEMS, 2861 Congressman Ln., Dallas, TX 75220 - (800) 877-6631 (214) 358-3196

model	type	air watts	power
model - AV425	type - cyclonic	air watts - 410	power - 11 amps
model - AV525	type - cyclonic	air watts - 500	power - 13 amps
model - FX500A	type - disposable bag	air watts - 490	power - 13 amps
model - FX675A	type - disposable bag	air watts - 500	power - 13 amps

NUTONE, Madison & Red Bank Rds., Cincinnati, OH 45227 - (800) 543-8687 (513) 527-5100

model	type	air watts	power
model - CV450	type - disposable bag	air watts - 584	power - 12.6 amps
model - CV353	type - disposable bag	air watts - 406	power - 12 amps
model - CV350	type - disposable bag	air watts - 396	power - 11 amps
model - CV553	type - cyclonic	air watts - 378	power - 12 amps

Cyclonic Vacuum System

Fasco's newly designed Cyclonic Vacuum System with the Turbo Tornado design uses centrifugal separation for a filter-free design.

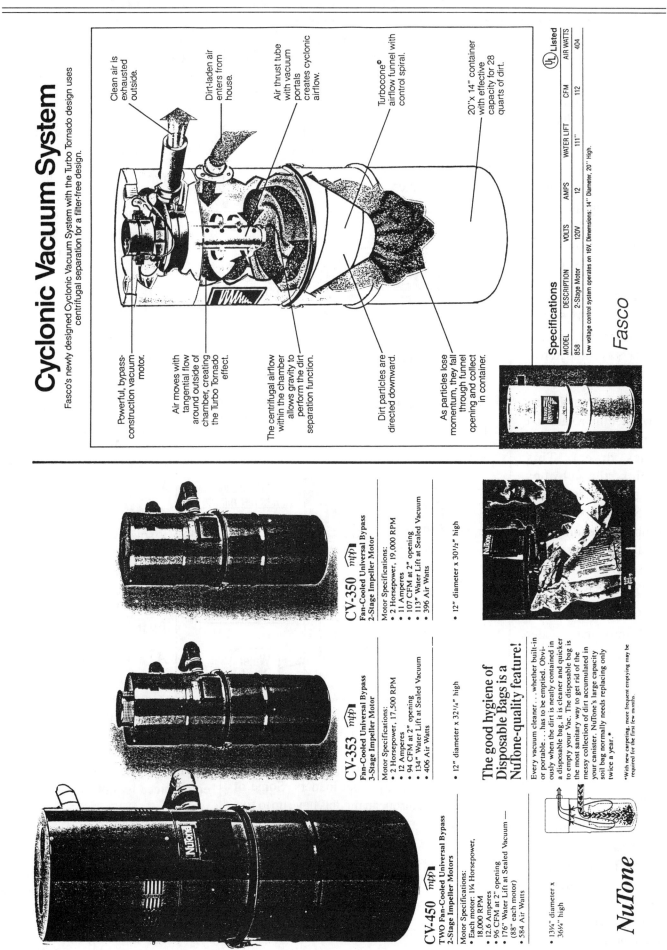

Clean air is exhausted outside.

Dirt-laden air enters from house.

Air thrust tube with vacuum portals creates cyclonic airflow.

Turbocone® airflow funnel with control spiral.

20" x 14" container with effective capacity for 28 quarts of dirt.

Powerful, bypass-construction vacuum motor.

Air moves with tangential flow around outside of chamber, creating the Turbo Tornado effect.

The centrifugal airflow within the chamber allows gravity to perform the dirt separation function.

Dirt particles are directed downward.

As particles lose momentum, they fall through funnel opening and collect in container.

Specifications

MODEL	DESCRIPTION	VOLTS	AMPS	WATER LIFT	CFM	AIR WATTS
858	2-Stage Motor	120V	12	111"	112	404

Low voltage control system operates on 16V. Dimensions: 14" Diameter, 20" High.

®L Listed

Fasco

CV-350
Fan-Cooled Universal Bypass 2-Stage Impeller Motor

Motor Specifications:
- 2 Horsepower, 19,000 RPM
- 11 Amperes
- 107 CFM at 2" opening
- 113" Water Lift at Sealed Vacuum
- 396 Air Watts

- 12" diameter x 30½" high

CV-353
Fan-Cooled Universal Bypass 3-Stage Impeller Motor

Motor Specifications:
- 2 Horsepower, 17,500 RPM
- 12 Amperes
- 94 CFM at 2" opening
- 134" Water Lift at Sealed Vacuum
- 406 Air Watts

- 12" diameter x 32¼" high

CV-450
TWO Fan-Cooled Universal Bypass 2-Stage Impeller Motors

Motor Specifications:
- Each motor: 1¼ Horsepower, 18,000 RPM
- 12.6 Amperes
- 96 CFM at 2" opening
- 176" Water Lift at Sealed Vacuum — (88" each motor)
- 584 Air Watts

- 13¾" diameter x 36¾" high

The good hygiene of Disposable Bags is a NuTone-quality feature!

Every vacuum cleaner...whether built-in or portable...has to be emptied. Obviously when the dirt is neatly contained in a disposable bag, it is cleaner and quicker to empty your Vac. The disposable bag is the most sanitary way to get rid of the messy collection of dirt accumulated in your canister. NuTone's large capacity soil bag normally needs replacing only twice a year.*

*With new carpeting, more frequent emptying may be required for the first few months.

NuTone

184

Q: My skin is sensitive to detergent residues in clothes and I need to buy a new clothes washer. What clothes washer design is the most efficient and provides the best cleaning and rinsing?

A: Front-loading clothes washers provide the most thorough cleaning and rinsing. Some models even have allergy rinse cycles for people sensitive to detergents. Over its lifetime, a new front-loader can save over $1,500 in water, detergent, and energy costs as compared to a standard top-loader.

With a front-loader, the washer tub rotates on a horizontal axis (like a clothes dryer). This tumbles the clothes through the sudsy water up to 50 times per minute for superior cleaning. The typical top-loader model just swirls the clothes slowly through the water

Since the clothes tumble through the water in a front-loader, the tub has to be only partially filled for effective cleaning. These designs use 30% to 50% less water and 60% less detergent than a top-loader. This saves water and energy and reduces pollution in our rivers.

One front-loader uses a unique "hydromatic" cleaning process. The agitator fins in the tub are designed like ladles too. First, the tub rotates slowly for 5 seconds as the fins lift the sudsy water and it then falls onto the clothes.

For the next four seconds, it stops and lets the clothes soak. Then it spins faster for 5 seconds to agitate the clothes through the water. This cycle repeats every 17 seconds. Another model reverses the tub rotation every 13 seconds. This improves cleaning and reduces tangles and wrinkles.

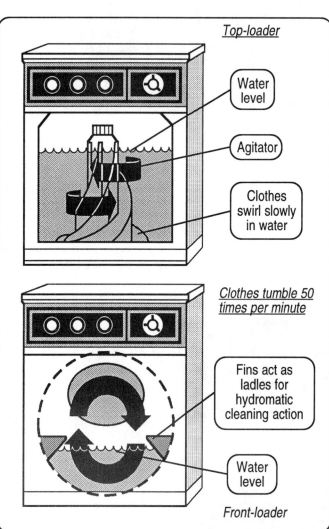

Top-loader

Water level

Agitator

Clothes swirl slowly in water

Clothes tumble 50 times per minute

Fins act as ladles for hydromatic cleaning action

Water level

Front-loader

Very thorough rinsing is a plus with many front-loaders. Some of the European models have up to five separate rinses per cycle. This virtually eliminates all the detergent residue and the dinginess from your clothes.

With the horizontal axis tub, front loaders can spin as fast as 1,500

rpm (revolutions per minute). This extracts more water and detergent residue. A typical top-loader spins at about 700 rpm. High-speed spinning also reduces the required time in your dryer, another significant energy savings.

Front-loaders are smaller (only about 27 inches wide) than top-loaders because the large agitator is not needed. Since the door is in the front of the washer, you can stack the dryer on top of the washer to save floor space.

Some models have built-in water heating elements so you only need to run a cold water line to it. The top quality European front-loaders have built-in shock absorbers for vibration-free spinning and are very quiet.

Q: Several years ago, I built a solar window heater that you recommended. It works great, but the clear acrylic plastic cover is starting to crack. What should I do to fix it?

A: You will have to replace the clear acrylic plastic cover. You apparently installed the acrylic cover too tightly or did not allow for clearance holes. Once the tiny cracks start in acrylic, they tend to grow until the entire piece is shot.

Acrylic, like most plastics, expands and contracts a lot with temperature changes. You should use some type of compliant weatherstripping below it and make large clearance holes at the screws to allow for expansion.

The typical family does eight loads of laundry per week using over 10,000 gallons of water per year. Front-loading washing machines are the most efficient design of washer. These use one third less water than a top-loading washing machine and two-thirds less detergent. A front-loader uses less water. This is better for both the environment and your savings account. The annual savings for the typical family can be as high as $150. This can pay back the cost of the washing machine several times over its life.

Top-loaders are more popular in Europe where energy and space are at a premium. Information on the manufacturers (some are imported from Europe) of front-loaders are shown on page 186 and 187.

Front-loaders also wash and rinse much more thoroughly than top loaders. The tumbling action of the clothes through the water provides better cleaning. With the horizontal rotation of the washer tub in a front-loader, the tub can spin faster for more thorough rinsing. Whereas a typical top-loader spins at 700 rpm, a front-loader can spin as faster as 1,600 rpm. This extracts more suds and water and speeds drying too.

If you have little floor space, you can mount the dryer on top of a front-loading washer. This is common in Europe. For Asko on page 187, there are two depth dimensions listed. The first is with the door closed and the second depth dimensions is with the door opened.

Since they are often located in kitchens in Europe, the European washers are designed to be extremely quiet. The Asko washer is mounted on heavy shock absorbers to deaden sound and stop vibration of the washer cabinet.

The Miehle washer uses a special "hydromatic" cleaning process. The agitator rotates slowly for 5 seconds, as the fins lift up and dump sudsy water over the clothes. For the next 4 seconds, it stops and soaks the clothes. Then it agitates fast for 5 more seconds.

"Pre-programmed cycles" lists only the most common preset cycles. The European models allow you to adjust the time of each portion of the cleaning cycle. This gives you an infinite number of possible cleaning cycles. You can also adjust the water level and the thoroughness of the rinsing. This is important if you are sensitive to detergent residues.

If you do prefer a top-loader because of its larger load capacity, the most efficient ones are listed on page 188. The chart on this page shows the typical cost to do a load of wash with a gas or an electric water heater at different water temperatures and wash/rinse settings.

Manufacturer of a Combination Washer/Dryer

MALBER USA INC. (manufactured in Europe)

model - Malber WD800

dimensions - 33 $\frac{1}{2}$" h x 23 $\frac{1}{2}$" w x 20 $\frac{7}{8}$" d

water consumption - 11.5 to 23 gallons

hook up - cold or hot

load capacity - 13 pounds

spin speed - 700 to 850 RPM

drum material - stainless steel

pre-programmed cycles - nine individual wash and rinse programs - pre-soak, super wash, normal wash, permanent press, hi-speed spin, delicates, knits, rinse and spin, gentle spin – two 120 minute drying programs - one for normal fabrics with 1300W heating element and one for delicate with 1000W

features - A fully automatic combination of a washing machine and a condensing tumble dryer that does not require a vent. It has four speeds - 56 rpm for the wash, 100 rpm pre-spin tumbling, 500 rpm gentle for delicates, and 800 rpm silent hi-speed spin for regular wash. Optional casters are available if you would like to move the machine.

Specifications of Front-Loading Clothes Washers

A. E. G. (manufactured in Europe)

model - lavamat 508, lavamat 850

dimensions - 33 $^1/_2$" h x 23 $^5/_8$" w x 23 $^5/_8$" d

water consumption - 11.5 to 23 gallons

load capacity - 13 pounds

spin speed - 700 to 850 RPM

drum material - stainless steel

hook up - cold or hot and cold water with an internal water heater to 203ºF

pre-programmed cycles - cotton, permanent press, extra gentle/delicates, short wash, pre-wash, energy saving program*, and half load

features - It contains an automatic detergent and fabric softener dispenser in the control panel which handles both powder and liquid. Other options include special spin programs with gentle start and short spins for delicate items. The machine automatically adjusts the water intake according to the amount and the weight of the laundry.

ASKO (manufactured in Europe)

model - Premier, Superior, Excellence

dimensions - 32 $^1/_4$" - 33 $^1/_2$" h x 23 $^1/_2$" w x 34 $^3/_8$" - 41 $^3/_8$" d (open)

water consumption - 11 to 17 gallons

load capacity - 14 to 16 pounds

spin speed - 600 to 1500 RPM

drum material - stainless steel

hook up - cold water with an internal water heater to 194ºF

pre-programmed cycles - main wash, extra gentle/delicates, short wash, pre-wash, energy saving program, short spin, delay spin and super rinse which is ideal for someone with skin sensitivity to detergents

features - The controls are easy to reach in the front and are also child proof. Up to 22 cycles are available depending on the various options that are chosen, including five rinses which will remove virtually all of the detergent. A fabric softener and liquid detergent dispenser are also available. The Excellence model has touch controls and digital displays.

MIEHLE (manufactured in Europe)

model - W1918A, W1930

dimensions - 33 $^1/_2$" h x 22 $^7/_{16}$" w x 23 $^5/_8$" d

water consumption - 17 to 30.9 gallons

load capacity - 15 pounds

spin speed - 400 to 1600 RPM

drum material - stainless steel

hook up - cold and hot water with an internal water heater to 203ºF

pre-programmed cycles - cottons, permanent press, extra gentle/delicates, woolens, short wash, pre-wash, depending upon the cycle chosen 3 to 4 rinses will take place

features - A water plus option is available that increases the water level and provides an extra rinse which is ideal for soft water or allergies to detergent. Other options include hydromatic cleaning process, gentle action and a delayed start. The control panel is electronic with single dial program and temperature setting with sequence lights.

WHITE WESTINGHOUSE

model - LT350R

dimensions - 34 $^5/_8$" h x 26 $^7/_8$" w x 27" d

water consumption - 14.5 to 28 gallons

load capacity - not available

spin speed - 585 RPM

drum material - porcelain

hook up - hot and cold water required

pre-programmed cycles - regular wash, permanent press, extra gentle/delicates, pre-wash

features - A buzzer sounds after each wash cycle and a fabric softener signal is also available. It has a unique, electronically controlled, two-way drive system which monitors the washer's speed and direction automatically. This reverses the tub rotation every 13 seconds. It contains a bleach diluting container and a self cleaning lint filter vane.

* saves electricity by using a lower water temperature and longer wash cycle

Manufacturers of Efficient Clothes Washers

A.E.G., 65 Campus Plaza, Edison, NJ 08837 - (800) 344-0043 (908) 225-8837

AMANA REFRIGERATION INC., Amana, IA 52204 - (800) 843-0304 (319) 622-5511

ASKO, INC., 903 N. Bowser, Ste. 200, Richardson, TX 75081 - (214) 644-8595

FRIGIDAIRE CO., 6000 Perimeter Dr., Dublin, OH 43017 - (800) 685-6005 (614) 792-4100

GE APPLIANCES, Appliance Park, Louisville, KY 40225 - (800) 626-2000 (502) 452-4311

GIBSON, 6000 Perimeter Dr., Dublin, OH 43017 - (800) 685-6005 (614) 792-4211

KELVINATOR, 6000 Perimeter Dr., Dublin, OH 43017 - (800) 685-6005 (614) 792-4211

KENMORE/SEARS, 3333 Beverly Rd., Hoffman Estates, IL 60179 - (800) 359-2000 (708) 286-2500

MALBER USA INC., 90 Arrandale Rd., Rockville Centre, NY 11570 - (516) 678-8300

MAYTAG CO., 1 Dependability Sq., Newton, IA 50208 - (515) 792-7000

MIELE APPL., 22 D Worlds Fair Dr., Somerset, NJ 08873 - (800) 843-7231 (908) 560-0899

MONTGOMERY WARD, Montgomery Ward, Chicago, IL 60671 - (800) 323-1965 (312) 467-2000

PHILCO INTERNATIONAL, 10 Parkway Center, Pittsburgh, PA 15220 - (800) 537-5530

SPEED QUEEN, PO Box 990, Ripon, WI 54971 - (800) 843-0304 (414) 748-3121

WHITE WESTINGHOUSE, 6000 Perimeter, Dublin, OH 43017 - (800) 245-0600 (614) 792-4100

Most Efficient Top-Loading Clothes Washers							
Brand	Model #	Electric Use (kWh)	Energy Cost ($)	Brand	Model #	Electric Use (kWh)	Energy Cost ($)
Standard size machines (over 16 gallon capacity)							
Frigidaire	WA	562	46	Maytag	LAT5004	840	69
Montgomery Ward	LAT4914	562	46	Maytag	LAW9304	840	69
White Westinghouse	LA271	562	46	Maytag	LS*7804	840	69
Montgomery Ward	LAT5914	794	66	Gibson	27F2	844	70
Kelvinator	AW700	823	68	Frigidaire	LCE752*	849	70
Kelvinator	AW701	823	68	General Electric	WSM2700R	849	70
Gibson	27M6	823	68	Kenmore/Sears	93701	849	70
Philco	S6B2	823	68	White Westinghouse	L*400M	852	70
General Electric	WWA5600S	836	69	Frigidaire	WADL	856	70
General Electric	WWA7600S	836	69	White Westinghouse	LA450	856	71
Maytag	LAT2914	840	69	Amana	LWD553	857	71
Maytag	LAT8204	840	69	Speed Queen	AWM5*1	857	71
Maytag	LAT8214	840	69	Frigidaire	LCE772	859	71
Maytag	LAT8234	840	69	Frigidaire	WA**L	863	71

Q: I am considering buying a new no-vent electric condensing clothes dryer so it does not have to be on an outside wall. Are condensing dryers efficient and which new dryer features are best?

A: No-vent condensing clothes dryers have been popular in Europe for many years. By not having to vent it outdoors, you can locate the dryer in any convenient closet, bedroom, utility room, etc.

Condensing dryers use a tiny blower to circulate room air across a heat exchanger inside the dryer. As the room air draws heat from the hot damp dryer air, moisture condenses out and drips into a removable container.

The dry air then circulates across the heating element and through the clothes drawing out more moisture. This process continues until the clothes are dry. Condensing dryers are the same size and look like an ordinary dryer.

Although the small extra motors in a condensing dryer use slightly more electricity than in a vented dryer, no heated or cooled indoor air is exhausted outdoors. This can cut your electric bills and eliminate chilly drafts.

The drying chamber is sealed so no moisture escapes into your home. This is better than just pulling the duct loose and venting your ex-isting dryer indoors. Excessive humidity can exacerbate allergies and window sweating.

Condensing dryers, because they are often located in a living area, are designed to be extremely quiet. This requires very high quality motors, bearings, vibration isolation materials and balanced construction.

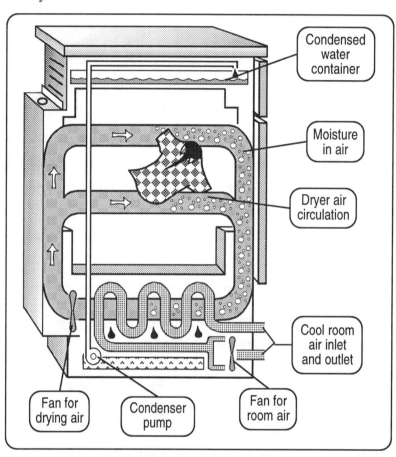

Condensed water container

Moisture in air

Dryer air circulation

Cool room air inlet and outlet

Fan for drying air

Condenser pump

Fan for room air

Reversing, two-direction drum rotation is used on several condensing and vented models. This fluffs your clothes, reduces wrinkling, and reduces drying times by 35 percent. By keeping the clothes fluffed and open, different weight materials can be effectively dried together in one load.

The clothes first spin in the forward direction for four minutes with a high air flow rate. The drum reverses for 25 seconds with a lower air flow rate. This allows the dryer air to draw more moisture out of the clothes.

A true electronic moisture sensor saves energy and reduces shrinkage and ironing time. By touching and "feeling" the dampness of the clothes, the sensor turns the dryer off at the precise time. This is more effective than "automatic sensors" that just measure the air temperature to estimate dryness.

A "no-wrinkle" feature keeps the dryer slowly spinning, without heat, for up to one hour after the clothes are dry. It beeps every five minutes to alert you. A stainless steel drum is more durable than porcelain over steel.

Q: I have siding on the top half of my house and stucco over concrete blocks on the first-floor walls. The stucco is deteriorated. Does it make sense to cover the stucco with siding too?

A: If you like the appearance of stucco on the lower half of your house, do not cover it with siding. There are durable plastic based stucco look-a-like coatings that you can apply yourself.

Stucco is an energy efficient wall finish. It seals all the tiny cracks and gaps where air, dust, and noise can enter your home. If you want additional wall insulation, attach rigid foam insulation boards to the wall first.

The most important considerations when buying a dryer are the design (condensing or vented), type of moisture sensor, and drum rotation directions.

No-vent condensing dryers are manufactured by European companies and are imported into the United States. These are the "Cadillacs" of dryers and are priced as such. They also make regular vented models.

Electronic "true" moisture sensors provide the most precise drying control. A sensor in the drum actually touches the clothes as they tumble against it. The other type of automatic sensor just measures the dryer exhaust air temperature to estimate the dryness of the clothes.

Reversing tumbling action is a new and effective drying feature. The drum switches between primary and reversing rotation during the drying cycle. This provides quicker and more even drying with less wrinkles. You can also dry loads with fabrics of mixed weights better. Frigidaire is the only U.S. manufacturer with a reversing drum.

A reversing drum also shortens drying time, so it saves electricity. In the winter, a condensing model can save energy overall because heated air from your house is not blown outdoors and lost.

— —

Manufacturers of Efficient Clothes Dryers

ADMIRAL, 1 Dependability Sq., Newton, IA 50208 - (515) 792-7000

model - 20/20 Line
dimensions - 44" h x 27" w x 27" d
moisture sensor type - automatic air temperature sensor
drum rotation direction - one-way
drum material - steel with polyester powder coat
pre-programmed cycles - permanent press, cotton/linen, fluff, delicate, wrinkle out
features - This is a heavy duty dryer with a 7.0 cubic foot drum that is capable of holding 20 pounds of clothing. It has an end-of-cycle signal and a large side swinging door which opens 180 degrees.

A.E.G., 65 Campus Plaza, Edison, NJ 08837 - (800) 344-0043 (908) 225-8837

model - Lavatherm 520
dimensions - 33 $\frac{1}{2}$" h x 23 $\frac{5}{8}$" w x 23 $\frac{5}{8}$" d
drum rotation direction - reversing
drum material - stainless steel
pre-programmed cycles - auto/time regular, permanent press, special care for heat sensitive fabrics, cool air anti-crease cycle
moisture sensor type - electronic true moisture sensor
features - This is a condenser dryer that requires "no venting". It is equipped with an illuminated light to show when the condenser drawer is full. It has a cooling down phase with "no-wrinkle" cycle, if the clothes are not removed the dryer will reverse tumble for 30 minutes.

AMANA REFRIGERATION INC., Amana, IA 52204 - (800) 843-0304 (319) 622-5511

model - LE9207/LG9209
dimensions - 43" h x 26 $\frac{7}{8}$" w x 28" d
drum rotation direction - one-way
drum material - stainless steel
pre-programmed cycles - auto/time regular, auto/time delicate, auto/time permanent press, auto/time knits, auto permanent press/knit, time no heat, preferred*, favorite*
moisture sensor type - electronic true moisture sensor
features - A reversible door can be converted in minutes to open from right to left. The interior light comes on every time the door is opened.

ASKO, INC., 903 N. Bowser, Ste. 200, Richardson, TX 75081 - (214) 644-8595

model - Excellence
dimensions - 42 $\frac{1}{4}$" - 33 $\frac{1}{2}$" h x 23 $\frac{1}{2}$" w x 46 $\frac{1}{2}$" d (open)
drum rotation direction - one-way
drum material - stainless steel
pre-programmed cycles - sensor controlled extra dry, normal dry, damp dry, iron dry, anti-crease, low temperature, fluff/no heat
moisture sensor type - electronic true moisture sensor
features - "No vent required" with this condensing dryer with an internal trap for easy drainage and removal.

FRIGIDAIRE CO., 6000 Perimeter Dr., Dublin, OH 43017 - (800) 685-6005 (614) 792-4100

    model - DE/DG9000AWW   drum rotation direction - reversing

    dimensions - 43 $5/_8$" h x 26 $7/_8$" w x 27" d   drum material - steel with polyester powder coat

    pre-programmed cycles - regular, permanent press, delicate, heavy/dense, knits, ultra delicate, air fluff, press saver, refresher, gentle heat, favorite*

    moisture sensor type - automatic air temperature sensor

    features - A "no-wrinkle" cycle senses when the clothes are dry, turns off, then gently tumbles your clothes with fresh air and signals every 10 minutes.

GE APPLIANCES, Appliance Park, Louisville, KY 40225 - (800) 626-2000 (502) 452-4311

    model - DDE9605S/DDG9685S   drum rotation direction - one-way

    dimensions - 43" h x 25" w x 27 " d   drum material - steel with polyester powder coat

    pre-programmed cycles - automatic regular, automatic permanent press, automatic knits, automatic cottons, delicates, extra care, fluff/no heat

    moisture sensor type - electronic true moisture sensor

    features - The door can reverse from right-hand to left-hand swing. A red indicator light on the panel shows which cycle or option is being used. * *favorite and preferred cycles are cycles that you program for your preferences*

HOTPOINT, Appliance Park, Louisville, KY 40225 - (800) 626-2000 (502) 452-4311

    model - DLB/DLL2650R   drum rotation direction - one-way

    dimensions - 43" h x 25" w x 27" d   drum material - porcelain-enamel

    pre-programmed cycles - automatic permanent press, automatic knits, automatic normal, automatic heavy, press guard, timed normal

    moisture sensor type - electronic true moisture sensor

    features - The dryer continues with no heat tumbling for 60 minutes and beeps every 5 minutes to alert you.

KENMORE/SEARS, 3333 Beverly Rd., Hoffman Estates, IL 60179 - (800) 359-2000 (708) 286-2500

    model - 26-65952/26-75952   drum rotation direction - one-way

    dimensions - 43" h x 27" w x 28 $3/_8$" d   drum material - porcelain-enamel

    pre-programmed cycles - cotton/sturdy, cotton, normal, permanent press, knit/delicates, knits, delicates/low and ex-low, touch up, air-dry, soft heat, auto dry, wrinkle guard

    moisture sensor type - electronic true moisture sensor

    features - The dryer is available with a dryer rack and the interior drum light comes on when the door is opened.

KITCHENAID, St. Joseph, MI 49085 - (800) 422-1230

    model - Superba Selectra KEYE/KGYE960W   drum rotation direction - one-way

    dimensions - 42" h x 29" d x 27 $3/_4$" w   drum material - steel with polyester powder coat

    pre-programmed cycles - automatic regular/heavy, automatic permanent press, regular/heavy, permanent press, air tumble, quick press

    moisture sensor type - electronic true moisture sensor

    features - The electronic custom dry control automatically dries to the degree of dryness you select.

MALBER USA INC., 90 Arrandale Rd., Rockville Centre, NY 11570 - (516) 678-8300

    model - Malber WD800   drum rotation direction - reversing

    dimensions - 33 $1/_2$" h x 23 $1/_2$" w x 20 $7/_8$" d   drum material - stainless steel

    pre-programmed cycles - nine individual wash and rinse programs - pre-soak, super wash, normal wash, permanent press, hi-speed spin, delicates, knits, rinse and spin, gentle spin – two 120 minute drying programs - one for normal fabrics with 1300W heating element and one for delicate with 1000W

    moisture sensor type - electronic true moisture sensor

    features - A fully automatic combination of a washing machine and a condensing tumble dryer that does not require a vent. It has four speeds - 56 rpm for the wash, 100 rpm pre-spin tumbling, 500 rpm gentle for delicates, and 800 rpm silent hi-speed spin for regular wash. Optional casters are available if you would like to move the machine.

MAYTAG CO., 1 Dependability Sq., Newton, IA 50208 - (515) 792-7000

model - Dependable Care Plus LDE9904

dimensions - 43 $5/_8$" h x 28 $1/_2$" w x 26 $3/_4$" d

pre-programmed cycles - regular fabric, permanent press, knits/delicates, wrinkle release, air fluff, custom

moisture sensor type - electronic true moisture sensor

drum rotation direction - one-way

drum material - steel with polyester powder coat

features - A dryness monitor lets you know what stage of dryness your load is in at all times.

MIELE APPL., 22 D Worlds Fair Dr., Somerset, NJ 08873 - (800) 843-7231 (908) 560-0899

model - Novotronic

dimensions - 33 $1/_2$" h x 23 $7/_{16}$" w x 23 $5/_8$" d

pre-programmed cycles - auto cottons, cottons, permanent press, anti-crease, delicates, air-dry

moisture sensor type - electronic true moisture sensor

drum rotation direction - reversing

drum material - stainless steel

features - This is a "no vent" condenser dryer with an air cooling system. There is an indicator light for the condenser drawer when it needs to be emptied.

WHIRLPOOL CORP., Benton Harbor, MI 49022 - (800) 253-1301

model - Clean Touch

dimensions - 42 $3/_8$" h x 29" w x 27 $13/_{16}$" d

pre-programmed cycles - permanent press, air-dry/fluff, delicates, heavy, damp dry, tumble press

moisture sensor type - electronic true moisture sensor

drum rotation direction - one-way

drum material - stainless steel - enamel

features - The Tumble Press® cycle is for previously cleaned items that need a quick press, or for clothes that have been packed in a suitcase.

WHITE WESTINGHOUSE, 6000 Perimeter, Dublin, OH 43017 - (800) 245-0600 (614) 792-4100

model - WDE/WDG846RB

dimensions - 34 $5/_8$" h x 27" w x 25 $1/_2$" d

pre-programmed cycles - Regular, permanent press, knits/delicate, time/auto dry, air fluff, wrinkle rid,refresher

moisture sensor type - automatic air temperature sensor

drum rotation direction - one-way

drum material - steel with polyester powder coat

features - A quick and easy clean lint filter is located in the front for easy cleaning.

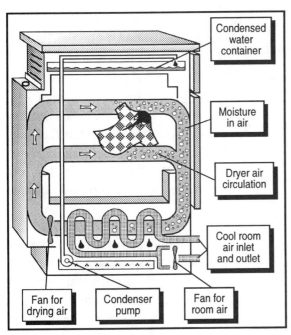

Condensed water container

Moisture in air

Dryer air circulation

Cool room air inlet and outlet

Fan for drying air

Condenser pump

Fan for room air

How a No-Vent Condensing Clothes Dryer Works

With a condensing dryer, all that is required is a 220-volt receptacle for the electric plug. The condensing dryer operates with a closed air circuit, i.e., the clothes drying air is cooled so that the moisture condenses inside the machine. Indoor room air is used to cool the clothes drying air.

The condensed water is then collected and pumped to the condensate drawer within the control panel. Once the drawer is full of water, the drying cycle stops and an electronic indicator on the control panel is illuminated. The drawer is easily removed for emptying. As soon as this is done and the empty drawer is reinserted, the drying cycle will restart.

Using an optional water drawer elimination kit, the condensed water can be pumped off directly into a drain. This saves having to remove and empty the container every time the dryer is used. this is useful if the clothes dryer is located near a drain or a sink.

Q: The clothes dryer outdoor vent flapper sticks open sometimes. It gets chilly near the dryer and in the summer, mosquitoes get indoors through it. What is the best sealing, most efficient vent cover?

A: Many homes have similar problems, but the homeowners never realize that the source of drafts, bugs, molds, etc. is from a leaky dryer vent. In my own home, a mouse crawled indoors through a leaky flapper.

A leaky dryer vent cover wastes energy dollars year-round. In the winter, a chilly draft often forces you to set your furnace thermostat a little higher for comfort. This produces a double energy loss. In the summer, you may not feel the draft, but humidity leaks in and reduces comfort.

It is sometimes difficult to determine if your vent flapper is always closing properly. When it is warm immediately after the dryer stops, it may get stuck open until it cools off and the materials contract.

Just a fine layer of lint near the hinge area can keep it from closing properly. In the winter, this lint absorbs moisture. When the dryer shuts off, the damp lint can freeze solid and hold it open. After each use, go outdoors and wipe off any lint.

I installed a slightly more expensive vent cover design (available at hardware stores that uses a "floating cap" seal. A round cap, inside the vent, slides up and opens when the dryer is on and blows against it.

When the dryer shuts off, the cap slides back down and seals tightly over the end of the vent outlet. It is made of smooth plastic to eliminate lint buildup and the exte-

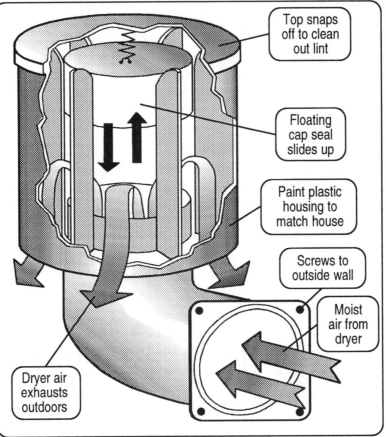

Top snaps off to clean out lint

Floating cap seal slides up

Paint plastic housing to match house

Screws to outside wall

Moist air from dryer

Dryer air exhausts outdoors

rior shell is paintable to match your house.

Another simple option is to install an indoor draft blocker. It mounts in the duct between the dryer and the wall. It has built-in one-way only louvers.

If you ever need to run a humidifier in your home, try venting your electric dryer indoors occasionally. This really cuts your utility bills.

One do-it-yourself indoor vent kit ducts the dryer air into a small water reservoir and through a filter to remove the lint. Another design is indoor and outdoor switchable. By moving a lever, the warm moist dryer air can be directed indoors through a replaceable filter during cool weather or outdoors.

If you need a new clothes dryer, you might consider one of the European no-vent condensing dryers. These are expensive units, but they are very quiet and last a lifetime. Installing a combination condensing washer/dryer (both in one standard size cabinet) saves space and requires no venting.

Q: I plan to install a new high-efficiency gas furnace in my utility room. The furnace installer insists that it needs fresh outdoor air piped in for combustion. Is he correct?

A: He is right. He is installing a high efficiency condensing furnace. These furnaces attain their high efficiency by condensing the moisture in the flue gases. In your old furnace, the moisture did not condense.

Indoor air from a laundry room contains traces of bleach, detergent, etc. When these chemicals mix with the hot condensed water inside the new furnace, the condensate becomes acidic and corrodes the heat exchanger.

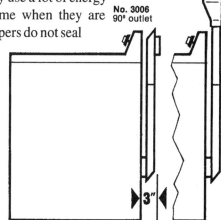

Transition Fitting
No. 3006
90° outlet

3"

Clothes dryers are one of the greatest energy wasters in most homes. They use a lot of energy and draw a lot of heated or cooled air out of your home when they are running. When they are not running, most vent flappers do not seal well and more conditioned indoor air is lost. A leaky vent can also let dust, allergens and insects get indoors.

The best-sealing dryer vent cover is the "floating cap" design shown on page 195. These are available at many home center and discount retail outlets. If you cannot find one in your area, the manufacturer, Heartland Products, will sell one to you directly. The price is generally lower if you buy it at a retail outlet. Simple installation instructions are also shown on page 195.

If your outdoor vent cover seems to be sealing well, but you still feel air leaking in, you can install an indoor in-line draft blocker. It is a one-way valve which only lets air flow out.

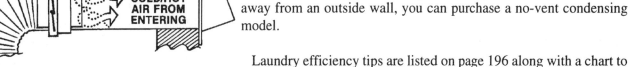

If you use an electric clothes dryer and do not have a humidity problem in your home in the winter, you can vent the dryer indoors with a heat recovery kit. The top kit shown traps lint in a water bath and a filter. The bottom kit has a lever so you can easily vent it indoors through a lint filter or outdoors. If space is tight, there are new telescoping ducts that allow you to locate the dryer within 3" of the wall. See above.

PREVENTS COLD/HOT AIR FROM ENTERING

If your dryer needs to be replaced, and you would like to move it away from an outside wall, you can purchase a no-vent condensing model.

Laundry efficiency tips are listed on page 196 along with a chart to estimate the cost of using your clothes washer at various temperature settings.

- -

Manufacturers of Tight-Sealing Dryer Vents

DEFLECTO CORP., PO Box 50057, Indianapolis, IN 46250 - (800) 428-4328 (317) 849-9555
<u>type</u> - standard outdoor vents, heat recovery - water lint trap & indoor/outdoor vent lever

DUNDAS JAFINE INDUSTRIES, 11099 Broadway, Alden, NY 14004 - (800) 387-2578 (716) 681-9690
<u>type</u> - standard outdoor vents, heat recovery - water lint trap & switchable indoor/outdoor vent lever, tight space adjustable telescoping duct

HEARTLAND PRODUCTS, PO Box 777, Valley City, ND 58072 - (800) 437-4780 (701) 845-1590
<u>type</u> - floating outdoor cap vent cover

LAMBRO INDUSTRIES, PO Box 367, Amityville, NY 11701 - (516) 842-8088
<u>type</u> - standard outdoor vents, indoor in-line draft blocker, heat recovery - dry lint trap & switchable indoor/outdoor vent lever, tight-space adjustable telescoping duct

NEMCO, 14260 - 172nd Ave., Grand Haven, MI 49417 - (616) 842-9511
<u>type</u> - standard outdoor vents

OATEY, 470 W. 160th, Cleveland, OH 44135 - (800) 321-9532 (216) 267-7100
<u>type</u> - standard outdoor vents, heat recovery - water lint trap & indoor/outdoor vent lever

Installation Instructions for "Sliding Cap" Dryer Vent

1) Assemble:

Insert the smooth edge of the plastic elbow into the bottom of the plastic vent body.

2) Prepare Dryer Vent Opening:

Remove the old hood and flipper of the existing dryer vent by removing screws or cutting with hacksaw blade. Clean lint accumulated in tube through wall.

3) Install:

Place the flat portion of the elbow on the wall, lining up holes in wall and elbow. Mount the vent in a vertical position as shown. Secure the 6 screws provided through the top bracket of vent and flat portion of elbow.

4) Paint:

HeartlandProducts

Paint with water base paint.

5) Maintenance:

Remove the vent lid periodically and clean out any lint build-up which may restrict free movement on the floating member.

Dimensions: 6$\frac{1}{2}$" w x 7" d x 13"h

Special Installation Instructions

Window Well Installation: For the dryer vent to function properly, it must be installed in a vertical position. Remove the window pane and replace with exterior grade plywood. Cut a 4" hole in the plywood. A surface area of 14" in ht. is required to mount the dryer vent flush with the window. Mount the dryer vent in a vertical position over the existing hole. If there is not a 14" space, mount the top of the canister to the siding of the house above the window, lining up the elbow and the sq. flange (the flat portion of the elbow) with the existing hole. Use exterior, high density styrofoam 6½" by 6½" pieces) to fill the space between the sq. flange and the window plywood. The number of pieces of syrofoam needed will vary with the distance between the flange and window. Be sure there are no gaps between the flange and window. If multiple pieces of styrofoam are used secure the pieces to the sq. flange and window. If multiple pieces of styrofoam are used, secure the pieces to the sq. flange with rubber bands. The rubber bands can be cut and removed after the vent is installed. Before inserting the styrofoam, be sure and cut a 4" vent hole in all pieces. To secure the bottom flange to the window plywood, insert wood screws through the flange and styrofoam into the window plywood. The screw length needed is determined by the distance between the sq. flange and plywood window.

Siding Installation: The vent can be adapted to many different types of siding. For the vent to function properly, it must be installed in a vertical position. In most instances, the vent will fit flush to the outside wall. Simply remove the existing vent and cut the existing vent pipe flush with the outside wall. The existing vent pipe must not protrude into the vent. **NOTE:** The positive closing dryer vent does not include vent pipe ducting. The 6 ½" sq. flange on the vent mounts over the top of the existing hole, allowing the air to flow from the existing duct through the 4" elbow and out the bottom of the vent canister.

Aluminum Siding: For the vent to function properly, it must be installed in a vertical position. Install according to "General Directions", except use 1 ½" wood screws. If it doesn't appear to be airtight, you may have to caulk around the sq. flanges.

Lap Siding: For the vent to function properly, it must be installed in a vertical position. Do not assemble the vent before mounting. Mount the sq. flange on the elbow to the existing vent hole. Place the canister in position on top of the elbow. With pen or chalk, outline the rectangular canister flange on the siding at the appropriate mounting placement. Cut out this portion of the siding. This enables the vent to be mounted in a true vertical position. Caulk with silicon around the canister flange to seal out moisture.

Brick, Block or Concrete: For the vent for function properly, it must be installed in a vertical position. Mount with masonry screw anchors. Secure the vent with appropriate screws. Silicon the edge of the sq. flange to prevent leakage.

Clothes Washing and Drying Efficiency Tips

• Use lower temperature settings. Use warm or cold water for the wash cycle instead of hot and only use cold for rinses. Experiment with different laundry detergents to find one that works well with cooler water. By presoaking heavily soiled clothes, a cooler wash temperature may be fine. The temperature of the rinse water does not affect cleaning, so always use the cold water rinse setting.

• Turn down the water heater thermostat. 120°F is adequate for most home needs, with the possible exception of dishwashing. By reducing your hot water temperature, you will save energy with either hot or warm wash cycles.

• Load the washing machine to capacity when possible. Most people tend to underload rather than overload their washers. Check your machine's load capacity in pounds, then weigh out a few loads of laundry to get a sense of how much laundry 10 or 20 pounds represents. Then use your eye to judge the volume of clothes for a load.

• Washing one large load will take less energy than washing two loads on a low or medium setting. Don't go to the other extreme and overload your machine, though. The clothes won't get as clean and you may end up having to wash them again. When you don't have a full load, match the water level to the size of the load. Most washing machines, even older ones, offer several different settings. Note: Permanent press fabrics should be washed on a "permanent press cycle" to minimize wrinkling.

• If washing lightly-soiled clothes, use the suds-saving feature if available on your washing machine. This saves the wash water to be reused on the next load. Only use this feature if the second load is to be washed right away.

• When drying, separate your clothes and dry similar types of clothes together. Lightweight synthetics dry more quickly than bath towels and natural fabrics.

• Don't overdry clothes. Take clothes out while they are still slightly damp to reduce the need for ironing - another big energy user. Overdrying also causes shrinkage, generates static electricity, and shortens the fabric life of your clothing. If your dryer has a setting for auto-dry, be sure to use it instead of the timer to avoid wasting energy.

• Don't add wet items to a partially-dried load.

• Dry items in consecutive loads when possible to take advantage of the residual heat from the previous load. When used in this manner, less energy is required initially to heat the dryer.

• If your dryer is located in an unheated space, consider moving it to a heated space to improve its efficiency.

• Clean the dryer filter after each use or as necessary. A clogged filter will restrict air flow and reduce dryer performance.

• Dry full loads when possible, but be careful not to overfill the dryer. Drying small loads wastes energy. Overloading causes wrinkling and uneven drying. Air should be able to circulate freely around the drying clothes. If your washer and dryer are properly-matched, a full washer load will be about the right size for the dryer.

• Check the outside dryer exhaust vent cover. Make sure it is clean and that the flapper on the outside hood opens and closes freely. If the flapper stays open, cold air will blow into your house through the dryer and increase heating costs. Replace the outside dryer vent hood with one that seals well.

• In good weather, consider hanging clothes outside and using totally-free solar energy to do the drying. Your clothes will also smell fresh.

Cost of a Load of Laundry					
Electric Water Heater [1]			Gas Water Heater [2]		
Wash/Rinse Settings	kWh used	Avg. Cost per Load (cents)	Wash/Rinse Settings	Therms Used	Avg. Cost per Load (cents)
Water Heater Thermostat Set at 140 F					
Hot/Hot	8.3	66	Hot/Hot	.329	20
Hot/Warm	6.3	50	Hot/Warm	.247	15
Hot/Cold	4.3	34	Hot/Cold	.164	10
Warm/Warm	4.3	34	Warm/Warm	.164	10
Warm/Cold	2.3	18	Warm/Cold	.082	5
Cold/Cold	0.4	3	Cold/Cold	-	3
Water Heater Thermostat Set at 120 F					
Hot/Hot	6.5	52	Hot/Hot	.248	15
Hot/Warm	4.9	39	Hot/Warm	.186	10
Hot/Cold	4.3	27	Hot/Cold	.124	7
Warm/Warm	3.4	27	Warm/Warm	.124	7
Warm/Cold	1.9	15	Warm/Cold	.062	4
Cold/Cold	0.4	3	Cold/Cold	-	3
1. Assumes 8 cents per kWh. 2. Assumes 60 cents per therm.					

Q: My TV repairman said that common high-voltage surges in my electric lines caused my VCR and microwave oven to break. Will installing a whole-house surge suppressor protect them and does one waste electricity?

A: The electronic circuitry in today's appliances has become very sensitive to common high-voltage surges in your electric lines. Even clothes dryers and furnaces now have electronic microprocessors.

Everyday, there are hundreds of high-voltage surges (up to 6,000 volts) in your home. These surges can be caused by external sources such as motors switching on and off in a nearby home or business, lightning, car accidents involving an electric pole, etc. Even running your own vacuum cleaner, furnace blower, or refrigerator, any appliance with a motor, causes surges.

These numerous surges, only a fraction of a second in duration, can slowly degrade the insulation and solid state components in your electronic appliances. Then one day, for no apparent reason, they just stop working properly. Surges also make light bulbs burn out more often.

A whole-house surge suppressor can protect all the circuits in your home from high-voltage surges. You can mount one on the circuit breaker panel with only three or four wires. Another design, offering more heavy-duty protection, is installed as a mounting adapter behind your electric meter.

The newest, least expensive, and easiest to install whole-house surge suppressor is built into a standard double circuit breaker. Mount it into your breaker panel like any other circuit breaker and attach a single wire to ground. These use virtually no electricity to work.

When you select a whole-house surge suppressor, compare the performance specifications. The level of protection varies among similar-looking surge suppressors. The best models react to block high-voltage surges within one nanosecond (one billionth of a second).

The key specifications are the clamping voltage (when the suppressor begins to block the surge) and the total energy it can dissipate without burning out. A lower clamping voltage and a higher total energy dissipation are better. For sensitive equipment like computers and VCR's, a combination of a whole-house and plug-in point-of-use suppressors is effective.

Compare the warranties. Several manufacturers will replace any damaged electronic appliances up to $5,000 caused by surges. One manufacturer sells an inexpensive surge suppressor for laptop computers with a full two-year computer replacement warranty, even if the computer is damaged by dropping it.

Q: I plan to reshingle my roof. Should I select light- or dark-colored shingles? I have heard that light ones reflect summer heat, but lose heat in the winter.

A: Light-colored shingles are the best choice for almost any climate. In the summer, your roof stays cooler with light-colored shingles. This saves energy and reduces the deterioration of the roofing materials.

In the winter, light-colored shingles do not lose more. With dark shingles, the roof does get slightly warmer in the winter. With proper attic ventilation and insulation, this warmer air is exhausted out the roof vents and adds very little heat to your home.

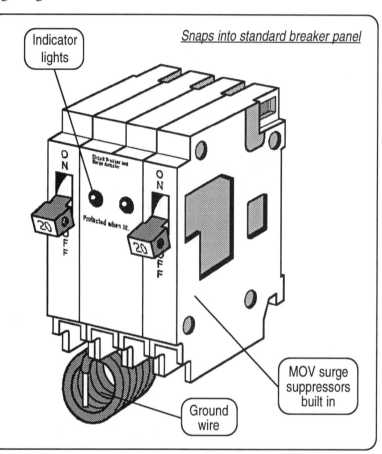

Indicator lights

Snaps into standard breaker panel

ON
20
OFF

Circuit Breaker and Surge Arrester

Protected when lit.

ON
20
OFF

MOV surge suppressors built in

Ground wire

Using surge suppressors can protect the electronic equipment in your home. You may not realize how many of your appliances have sophisticated electronics which may be damaged by a surge - coffee makers, clothes washers and dryers, refrigerator/freezers, clocks, CD players, VCR, etc.

Each several thousand-volt surge is of such short duration, that you seldom notice them in the operation of your appliances until they seem to break for no apparent reason. These voltage spikes slowly breakdown the insulation and the solid state components.

It is best to use a combination of a whole-house surge suppressor and point of use suppressors (at the electric plug) for your expensive appliances and electronic equipment. Several types of point-of-use surge suppressors are shown in figure #1. This group of products is made by Intermatic.

If you have a computer modem or answering machine, don't forget to use a surge suppressor for telephone lines too. A lightning strike near a telephone pole can easily destroy a modem. I lost a $200 modem that way several years ago.

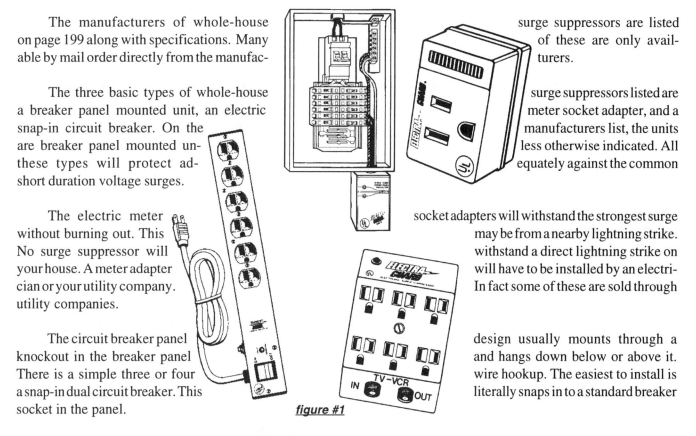

The manufacturers of whole-house surge suppressors are listed on page 199 along with specifications. Many of these are only available by mail order directly from the manufacturers.

The three basic types of whole-house surge suppressors listed are a breaker panel mounted unit, an electric meter socket adapter, and a snap-in circuit breaker. On the manufacturers list, the units are breaker panel mounted unless otherwise indicated. All these types will protect adequately against the common short duration voltage surges.

The electric meter socket adapters will withstand the strongest surge without burning out. This may be from a nearby lightning strike. No surge suppressor will withstand a direct lightning strike on your house. A meter adapter will have to be installed by an electrician or your utility company. In fact some of these are sold through utility companies.

The circuit breaker panel design usually mounts through a knockout in the breaker panel and hangs down below or above it. There is a simple three or four wire hookup. The easiest to install is a snap-in dual circuit breaker. This literally snaps in to a standard breaker socket in the panel.

figure #1

Both of these later types have indicator lights to let you know they are working. If you notice the indicator light is ever out, it means that a very large voltage surge (often from lightning) has hit your house and burned out the MOV's in the suppressor. It probably protected all your appliances though. It must be replaced.

The key specifications to consider when selecting a whole-house surge suppressor are the clamping voltage and total energy dissipation. A higher total energy dissipation indicates that it can withstand a higher surge. A faster reaction time also offers more protection. All of the units listed on page 199 have acceptable performance specifications for home use.

The warranty varies a lot for the various models. Several of the manufacturers have warranties that cover electrical equipment damaged by a surge. EFI offers a unique warranty for laptop computers. If you buy a surge suppressor, the laptop is insured for any type of damage, not just a surge.

Manufacturers of Whole-House Surge Suppressors

ACI, P.O. Box 306, Walnut Ridge, AR 72476 - (800) 541-5590 - (501) 886-6625
  reaction time - less than 1 nanosecond   clamping voltage - 340 volts
  total energy dissipation - 320 joules for SK and 160 joules for 2ND
  warranty - 5 years

ACT COMMUNICATIONS, P.O. Box 375, Ector, TX 75439 - (903) 961-2300
  reaction time - less than 1 nanosecond   clamping voltage - 390 volts
  total energy dissipation - 300 joules   warranty - 5 years

ADVANCED RESEARCH, P.O. Box 3131, Billings, MT 59103 - (800) 333-7254 (406) 259-7254
  reaction time - less than 1 nanosecond   clamping voltage - 130 volts
  total energy dissipation - 600 joules   warranty - 15 years

CONTROL CONCEPTS, P.O. Box 1380, Binghamton, NY 13902 - (800) 288-6169 (607) 724-2484
  reaction time - less than 1 nanosecond
  clamping voltage -uses a special capacitive circuit - no rated voltage
  total energy dissipation - 480 joules   warranty - 10 years

EFI ELECTRONICS, 2415 South 2300 West, Salt Lake City, UT 84119 - (801) 977-9009
  reaction time - less than 1 nanosecond   clamping voltage- 240 volts
  total energy dissipation - 425 joules   warranty - 5 years-up to $2,500 for damaged equip.

ELECTRICAL SYSTEMS MFG., P.O. Box 265, Swansea, SC 29160 - (803) 568-4141
  reaction time - less than 5 nanosecond   clamping voltage - 180 volts
  total energy dissipation - 180 joules   warranty - 5 years

INNOVATIVE TECHNOLOGY, 15470 Flight Path Dr., Brooksville, FL 34609 - (904) 799-0713
  reaction time - less than 1 nanosecond   clamping voltage - 130 volts
  total energy dissipation - 400 joules   warranty - 10 years

INTERMATIC, Intermatic Plaza, Spring Grove, IL 60081 - (815) 675-2321
  reaction time - less than 1 nanosecond   clamping voltage - 325 volts
  total energy dissipation - 400 joules   warranty- 3 years

LEA DYNATECH, 6520 Harney Rd., Tampa, FL 33610 - (800) 654-8087 (813) 621-1324
  reaction time - less than 1 nanosecond   clamping voltage - 420 volts
  total energy dissipation - 405 joules   warranty - lifetime & up to $5,000 for any equipment damaged

METER-TREATER, 5700 Columbia Circle, West Palm Beach, FL 33407 - (800) 638-3788
  reaction time - less than 1 nanosecond   clamping voltage - 240 volts
  total energy dissipation - 2,000 joules   warranty - 5 years

MVC, P.O. Box 8171, Amarillo, TX 79109 - (806) 358-4024
  reaction time - less than 1 nanosecond   clamping voltage - 190 volts
  total energy dissipation - 160 joules   warranty - 5 years

SIEMENS CORP., P.O. Box 89000, Atlanta, GA 30356 - (800) 678-9888 (404) 751-2000
  reaction time - less than 1 nanosecond   clamping voltage - 600 volts
  total energy dissipation - 460 joules   warranty - 1 year

TRANS-ORBER CORP., 1812 Hillcrest, Ft. Worth, TX 76107 - (817) 735-9128
  reaction time - less than 1 nanosecond   clamping voltage - 184 volts
  total energy dissipation - 208 joules   warranty - 5 years

TYTEWADD POWER FILTERS, 704 W. Battlefield Rd., Springfield, MO 65807 - (417) 887-3770
  reaction time -1.5 nanoseconds   clamping voltage - 150 volts
  total energy dissipation - 200 joules   warranty - 1 year

Technical Specifications for EFI Electronics Corp.

General Data	120/240 Single-Phase 120/208/Three-Phase
Nominal Line Voltage	120 Volt
Maximum Continuous Line Voltage	150 VRMS
TVSS Circuit Type	Semi-conductor/Solid state
Fusing	Independent per phase
EMI/RFI Noise Rejection (10Hz - 50 MHz)	-20 dB
Frequency	50, 60, 400 Hz
Operating Temperature	-10 to 60 degrees Centigrade
Dimensions: Housing alone/With face plate	6" x 6" x4" / 7" 7" x 4.06"
Weight	4 lbs.

TVSS Performance Specifications	
Nominal Clamp Level (V Peak @ 1 mA)	240 V
Clamp Level @ 300 A (V Peak 8 x 20 us)	330 V
Capacitance Per Phase	6,000 pF
Peak Transient Current	50,000 Amps

	ANSI/IEEE C62.41-1980 Dynamic Clamping Voltage L-N
Category A# Ringwave (6kV, 200A, 100kHz)	440 V
Category B3 Ringwave (6kV, 500A, 100kHz)	455 V
Category C1 Impulse (6kV 1.2 x 50 us, 3kA 8 x 20 us)	500 V
Category C3 Impulse (20kV, 10kA)	650 V

Circuit Breaker/Surge Arrester

Features:

- Compact design incorporating (2) 15A or 20A
  1-pole circuit breakers in series with surge
  arrester module.
- Plug-in load center mounting is easy to install.
- One device will protect the entire residence.
- Can withstand high impulse currents
  (40,000A per phase).
- Illuminated LED's indicate surge protection
  functioning.
- Perfect for retrofit - replaces (2) 1" breakers
  without losing any circuits.
- UL listed - meets UL 1449 and
  ANSI C62.11-1987 requirements.

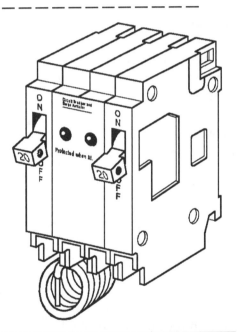

SIEMENS

Catalog Number	Circuit Breaker Ampere Rating[1]	Number of 1-Pole Breakers	Carton Quantity/ Master Quantity	Weight (lbs. each)
QSA1515	15	2	1/28	0.5
QSA2020	20	2	1/28	0.5

1 All terminals are UL Listed for 60/75° C cu/Al conductors. Wire range is #10 - 14 AWG.

Specifications	
Secondary Surge Arrester Voltage Rating - 175V AC maximum, phase to neutral.	Discharge Current Withstand Rating - 10,000 amps, phase to neutral.
Transient Energy Rating - 460 joules per phase.	
Peak Current Rating - 40,000 amps per phase.	Circuit Breaker Interrupting Rating - Maximum RMS Symmetrical, 10,000 amps, 120/240V AC. (not for use on 240 volt systems)
Discharge Voltage/Current Characteristic Rating - at 1500 amps, 600 volts, phase to neutral at 5000 amps, 800 volts, phase to neutral.	

Q: I am considering replacing my old gas range with a fast-heat electric induction cooktop. Easy clean-up and my children's safety are concerns. How efficient are induction elements and do they cook as well as gas?

A: Easy-to-clean electric induction cooktops (and ranges) are just one of many recent improvements in electric cooking. They offer instantaneous response and precise control over cooking heat just like a gas burner does.

Induction elements work by creating magnetic friction (instant heat) in the pot or pan without heating the smooth ceramic glass cooktop. The glass cooktop stays relatively cool so spills do not cook on and wipe clean with a damp cloth. This also makes it safe around children.

Induction elements can provide intense initial heat. They can bring a quart of water to a boil in four and one half minutes, yet provide precise low level heat for simmering a sauce or melting chocolate without a double boiler.

When a pot is removed from an induction element, the current automatically stops. If you remove the pot just briefly to stir or add some water and return it quickly, the heat automatically comes back on to the same level.

This makes it impossible to forget and accidentally leave the

heat on, possibly starting a fire. Even if a child can manage to turn it on (built-in child-safe locks), and climbs onto the cooktop, it will not heat.

Induction is the most energy efficient method to cook. All of the heat goes into the pot and food, not

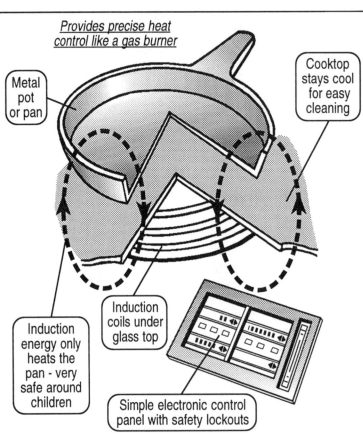

Provides precise heat control like a gas burner

Metal pot or pan

Cooktop stays cool for easy cleaning

Induction energy only heats the pan - very safe around children

Induction coils under glass top

Simple electronic control panel with safety lockouts

the stove top or surrounding air. This is a real benefit in the summer because it keeps your kitchen cooler and reduces the load on your air conditioner.

Metal cooking utensils (iron, steel, stainless) must be used on an induction element. A favorite old pot with a warped bottom, that won't heat well on other electric elements, works great on induction elements.

Electric quartz halogen elements also provide quick heat initially. These elements use light

energy to transfer heat to the pot. There is usually a radiant coil in the center of the halogen ring for even heating. Halogen does not provide as instantaneous a heat response as induction does.

Smooth top radiant glass cooktops clean easily. Any flat bottom pot can be used, but radiant elements heat slower than halogen. Dual units combine a six and eight-inch coil in a single element for various size pots.

Some manufacturers offer modular cooktops so you can mix and match various types of cooking elements, grills, woks, etc. for your needs.

Q: We use our central air conditioner the majority of the summer. I would like to find a simple method to seal off my fireplace opening in the summer. Is much cool air lost and how can I seal it?

A: Even though cool air is dense and tends to sink, it can be drawn up a chimney in the summer. As the sun shines on a brick chimney, it gets warm. This heats the air inside and creates a strong upward draft.

Cut a clear acrylic cover, similar to an interior storm window, several inches larger than the fireplace glass door opening. Use adhesive-back magnetic tape on the acrylic to hold and seal it against the door frame.

Although electricity is a more expensive source of energy than gas in most areas of the country, an electric cooktop, especially induction elements, is more energy efficient inside your home. This is because most of the heat generated goes into cooking the food and less is lost to the surrounding room air

An induction cooktop heats by passing a magnetic field through a metal cooking utensil. This heats the metal utensil and thus cooks the food. Most of the halogen light cooktops also have a resistance coil inside of the halogen light. The halogen light gives quick heating and precise control and the electric resistance coil provides even heating across the cooking surface. Most halogen cooktops have two halogen elements and two standard resistance elements. This is to reduce the cost since you don't need the quick heating feature of a halogen element for all your cooking needs.

— —

Manufacturers of Induction, Halogen and Radiant Cooktops

ADMIRAL HOME APPLIANCES, 740 King Edwards Ave., Cleveland, TN 37320 - (615) 472-3371

| <u>type</u> - radiant | <u># of elements</u> - 4 | <u>heating output ranges</u> - 1,200 to 2,000 |

<u>features</u> - It has a hot surface indicator light and the control knobs are removable.

AEG/ANDI-CO. APPLIANCES, 65 Campus Plaza, Edison, NJ 08837 - (800) 344-0043 (908) 225-8837

<u>type</u> - halogen/radiant	<u># of elements</u> - 2 halogen — 2 radiant	<u>heating output ranges</u> - 1,200 to 2,400
<u>type</u> - radiant	<u># of elements</u> - 4	<u>heating output ranges</u> - 1,200 to 2,400
<u>type</u> - solid disk	<u># of elements</u> - 4	<u>heating output ranges</u> - 1,500 to 2,000

<u>features</u> - One unit has touch control for the selection of the dual zones. There are residual heat indicators for all cooking areas.

AMANA REFRIGERATION, INC., Amana, IA 52204 - (800) 344-0043 (319) 622-5511

| <u>type</u> - halogen/radiant | <u># of elements</u> - 2 halogen — 2 radiant | <u>heating output ranges</u> - 1,200 to 2,400 |
| <u>type</u> - radiant | <u># of elements</u> - 4 | <u>heating output ranges</u> - 1,200 to 2,400 |

<u>features</u> - The units can be installed two different ways - counter-flush or on-counter. There are five optional interchangeable cartridges available for right or left side for some models — smoke control grill, griddle, two coil element, two solid disk element, or halogen/radiant element.

CREDA INC., 5700 W. Touhy, Chicago, IL 60648 - (708) 647-8024

| <u>type</u> - halogen/radiant | <u># of elements</u> - 2 halogen — 2 radiant | <u>heating output ranges</u> - 1,200 to 2,200 |
| <u>type</u> - radiant | <u># of elements</u> - 4 | <u>heating output ranges</u> - 1,200 to 2,000 |

<u>features</u> - A range of modular, design-integrated cooktops are available styles are a barbecue grill, a two solid disk element unit, a deep fryer, a two halogen/radiant element unit and a downdraft module. One model is available with a telescopic downdraft.

FRIGIDAIRE CO., 6000 Perimeter Dr., Dublin, OH 43017 - (800) 451-7007 (614) 792-4100

<u>type</u> - halogen/radiant	<u># of elements</u> - 2 halogen — 2 radiant	<u>heating output ranges</u> - 1,200 to 2,200
<u>type</u> - radiant	<u># of elements</u> - 4 or 5	<u>heating output ranges</u> - 1,200 to 2,100
<u>type</u> - solid disk	<u># of elements</u> - 4	<u>heating output ranges</u> - 1,500 to 2,600

<u>features</u> - The glass top comes with marble styling in almond, white or black. It is available in 30" and 36" models.

GAGGENAU USA CORP., 425 University Ave., Norwood, MA 02062 - (617) 255-1766

| <u>type</u> - halogen/radiant | <u># of elements</u> - 1, 2, 3 or 4 halogen/radiant | <u>heating output ranges</u> - 1,000 to 4,400 |

<u>features</u> - One model is uniquely designed with a six-sided shape. With the sensor buttons you lightly touch them for precise heat settings — 1 to 9. There are several different modules that are available for your own unique design or cooking preferences — two halogen elements, two or three solid disk elements, deep fryer, barbecue grill, griddle plate and a downdraft ventilator.

GE APPLIANCES, Appliance Park, Louisville, KY 40225 - (800) 626-2000 (502) 452-4311

<u>type</u> - induction	<u># of elements</u> - 4	<u>heating output ranges</u> - 1,300 to 2,200
<u>type</u> - halogen/radiant	<u># of elements</u> - 1 halogen — 3 or 4 radiant	<u>heating output ranges</u> - 1,000 to 2,500
<u>type</u> - radiant	<u># of elements</u> - 4	<u>heating output ranges</u> - 1,200 to 1,900

<u>features</u> - Individual modular units are available to design your own unit — two coil elements, two cast iron solid disk elements, two radiant elements, grill module or a griddle. The induction cooktop has electronic controls that offer ten power settings for each of the four heating elements. The unit has a control lockout feature that prevents unwanted operation.

JENN-AIR, 3035 Shadeland, Indianapolis, IN 46226 - (317) 545-2271

type - induction/radiant   # of elements -2 induction — 2 radiant   heating output ranges - 1,200 to 2,100
type - halogen/radiant   # of elements - 1 halogen — 2 or 3 radiant   heating output ranges - 1,200 to 2,200
type - radiant   # of elements -4 or 5   heating output ranges - 1,000 to 2,400

features - You can customize your cooktop with the modular cartridges available — two solid disk elements, two halogen elements, two coil elements, two halogen/radiant elements, a griddle, a grill, and a cooker/steamer. Also available are additional grill grates, a kebab rotisserie, a wok, and a grill cover.

KING REFRIGERATOR CORP., 76-02 Woodhaven Blvd., Glendale, NY 11385 - (718) 897-2200

type - solid disk   # of elements - 2 to 4   heating output ranges - 1,250

features - The cooktops are made of stainless steel.

KITCHENAID, 701 Main St., St. Joseph, MI 49085 - (800) 253-3977 (616) 982-4500

type - halogen/radiant   # of elements - 2 halogen — 2 or 3 radiant   heating output ranges - 1,200 to 2,400
type - radiant   # of elements - 4   heating output ranges - 1,200 to 2,400

features - Separate components are available for a custom design — side-mount downdraft ventilation system, grill, plug-in griddle, two cast-iron elements or two halogen/radiant elements.

MAYTAG CO., 1 Dependability Sq., Newton, IA 50208 - (515) 792-7000

type - radiant   # of elements -4   heating output ranges - 1,200 to 2,100
type - solid disk   # of elements - 4   heating output ranges - 1,500 to 2,000

features - The cooktops have drip-retaining edges to contain spills and boil-overs. The control knobs are removable for easy cleaning.

MIELE APPLIANCES, INC., 22 D Worlds Fair Dr., Somerset, NJ 08873 - (800) 843-7231 (818) 765-9870

type - radiant   # of elements -4 or 5   heating output ranges - 1,400 to 2,000

features - Individual component pieces are available to design your own unit — two cast iron solid disk elements, two radiant elements, electric barbecue, steamer/boiler/fryer, a downdraft ventilator or a griddle.

MODERN MAID, Amana, IA 52204 - (800) 843-0304

type - halogen/radiant   # of elements - 2 halogen — 2 radiant   heating output ranges - 1,400 to 1,900
type - radiant   # of elements -2 to 4   heating output ranges - 1,400 to 1,800

features - Some of the units are offered with a choice of six interchangeable cartridges — two solid disk element, two coil element unit, two radiant element, a halogen/radiant unit, a griddle or a smoke control grill.

REGENCY VSA APPLIANCES LTD., 1442 Irvine Blvd., Tustin, CA 92680 - (714) 544-3530

type - halogen/radiant   # of elements - 1 halogen — 3 radiant   heating output ranges - 1,200 to 2,000
type - radiant   # of elements -4   heating output ranges - 1,200 to 2,000

features - The cooktop is available with smooth touch pads. There is an LED indicator which gives precise readout of heat levels to each element.

SEARS, 3333 Beverly Rd., Hoffman Estates, IL 60179 - (708) 286-2500

type - induction/radiant   # of elements -2 induction — 2 radiant   heating output ranges - 1,200 to 2,200
type - halogen/radiant   # of elements - 1 halogen — 3 radiant   heating output ranges - 1,200 to 2,200
type - radiant   # of elements -4 or 5   heating output ranges - 1,000 to 2,400

features - Some models are available as a flush to counter design. They include hot surface and a unit "on" indicator lights.

TAPPAN, 6000 Perimeter Dr., Dublin, OH 43017 - (800) 685-6005 (818) 765-9870

type - radiant   # of elements -4   heating output ranges - 1,200 to 2,100
type - solid disk   # of elements - 4   heating output ranges - 1,200 to 2,600

features - On the radiant unit a red indicator light stays lit until the surface is safe to touch. A heat sensor element automatically adjusts the heat to maintain the set cooking time on some of the solid disk models.

THERMADOR, 5119 District Blvd., Los Angeles, CA 90040 - (213) 562-1133

type - halogen/radiant   # of elements - 1 halogen — 3 radiant   heating output ranges - 1,000 to 2,000
type - radiant   # of elements -4   heating output ranges - 1,000 to 2,000

features - The cooktop has an extra low setting — the full-size burner head and on/off cycling process evenly distributes heat so you can cook temperature-sensitive foods. The halogen model is available in either updraft or downdraft for use with the Cook'n'Vent hoodless downdraft ventilation system.

WHIRLPOOL CORP., 2000 M-63, Benton Harbor, MI 49022 - (800) 253-1301 (616) 926-5000

type - radiant   # of elements -4   heating output ranges - 1,400 to 2,400

features - The unit has individual hot surface element indicators. It comes with a textured pattern to help hide finger prints.

Solid-Element
Electric Cooktop

Cast-iron cooking units (called hobs in Europe) contain electric resistance wires embedded in ceramic insulation. When turned on, heat spreads evenly throughout element and is conducted to pot or pan placed on element.

Types of solid elements:

1. Thermostatically-controlled, incorporates metal-sensing device to monitor and regulate temperature of pan it contacts. Begins heating at full wattage, reduces power when it reaches selected setting, then maintains steady temperature by cycling on and off.

2. Thermal limiters, identified by red dot in element center, use heat sensors to lower heat automatically if pan boils dry or its bottom is too warped to make contact with element.

3. Low-wattage solid elements use reduced wattage to protect against overheating.

Design/Features

Cooktop surface surrounding slightly raised solid elements; porcelain enamel, brushed metal, or tempered black or white glass.

Solid elements sealed into cooktop surface.

Infinite heat settings, from high to low.

Sleek, contemporary appearance.

Use/Care/Cleaning

Use characteristics similar to electric coil units, with more even heat distribution and longer heating and cooling times.

No drip pans. Raised elements allow spills to flow away from hot unit for easier cleaning.

Can develop rust spots. Elements require periodic "seasoning" with oil and type of care required for cast-iron cookware.

Use only flat-bottomed pans.

Not suitable for canners, woks or specialty cookware.

Sooth-Glass Cooktop
High-Speed Radiant Elements

Ceramic surface is a durable, translucent material which efficiently conducts heat from high-speed radiant elements positioned beneath it. Heat transfers to cookware by conduction and radiation. Cooking areas have permanent designs which glow red when unit is turned on and as it cycles on and off to maintain heat setting. Most heating elements include a temperature sensor or thermal limiter (similar to those on solid-elements) to protect glass from overheating.

Design/Features

Smooth, flat ceramic cooking surface installs flush with countertop. Heating elements installed beneath glass have no drip pans/rings to remove and clean. Four heating surfaces in various arrangements: two small and two large units, or two small, one large and one dual (small or large) element.

Withstands high temperatures, extreme changes in temperature, impact from heavy utensils, and is stain resistant.

Infinite heat settings, from high to low.

Indicator lights glow when surface unit is on, stay on as long as sensor indicates unit is off but too warm to touch.

Sleek, contemporary appearance.

Versatile black ceramic-glass panels offer pattern and color decorating options. Light colored surfaces (such as white or almond) are permanently integrated into the black glass, allowing color coordination of cooktop with other kitchen appliances.

Use/Care/Cleaning

Easy-clean smooth glass surface, with most spatters/spills on cooler cooktop surfaces rather than heating areas.

Use flat-bottomed metal cookware for best results. Glass and ceramic cookware take longer to heat, are less efficient than metal utensils, but can be used.

Smooth-Glass Cooktop
Halogen Elements

Beneath the ceramic-glass cooktop, heat transfers to cooking areas from quartz halogen lamp tubes which encircled electric resistance coils. Both heat sources are positioned in ceramic fiber insulation in a cup underneath glass. This combination provides quick even heat.

Some cooktops combine quartz halogen elements with high-speed radiant units, offering two sources for cooking.

Halogen lamps glow instantly, with heat transfer to glass surface and utensil on it by both conduction and radiation.

Design/Features

Smooth, flat ceramic cooking surface installs flush with countertop. Heating elements are installed beneath glass, have no drip pans/rings to remove and clean. Four heating surfaces in various arrangements: two small and two large units, or two small, one large and one dual (small or large) element.

Withstands high temperatures, extreme changes in temperature, impact from heavy utensils.

Infinite heat settings, from high to low.

Halogen elements provide immediate visible glow which increases in intensity as temperature rises. More rapid response to control settings than electric resistance heating systems.

Indicator lights glow when surface unit is on, stay on as sensor indicates unit is off but too warm to touch.

Sleek contemporary appearance.

Use/Care/Cleaning

Easy-clean smooth glass surface with most spatters/spills on cooler cooktop surfaces rather than heating areas.

Use flat-bottomed metal cookware for best results. Glass and ceramic cookware take longer to heat, are less efficient than metal utensils, but can be used.

Smooth-Glass Cooktop
Induction Elements

Positioned under a ceramic cooking surface are induction wire coils connected to solid-state controls. When controls are turned on, electric current to coils is converted into high-frequency alternating current. As current flows through coils, it creates a magnetic field that generates heat in cookware made of magnetic materials (iron, steel, nickel or various magnetic alloys). Hot utensil cooks food while cooktop surface remains relatively cool.

Magnetic induction cooking is similar to gas cooking: instant on and off; infinite temperature range with immediate response to controls to raise or lower cooking speed. It provides very quick initial heat.

Design/Features

Fastest heating, cooling and response to control changes of electric cooktop systems.

Turns off if no utensil is on unit or if cookware is nonmagnetic.

Uses only amount of energy needed to heat size of utensil.

Sleek, contemporary appearance with various patterns and color surface options available.

Use/Care/Cleaning

Requires changes in cooking practices: magnetic utensil must be centered on cooking area and must be larger than 4 inch diameter; start foods at lowest heat setting recommended to avoid scorching/burning.

Requires use of magnetic cookware - cast iron, steel, and some stainless steels. Test by seeing if a magnet sticks to it. Aluminum, copper, glass and other nonmagnetic materials will not work.

Warped pans may cause uneven cooking; thin-gauge pans may result in scorching/burning.

Q: My friend has a new gourmet "professional-type" gas range with six special burners and boiler, grill, griddle, warming tray ... Do these use more gas and heat up a kitchen more than an ordinary gas range?

A: Even though these special professional gas ranges have many features and super-high-output burners, they actually can consume less energy overall than an ordinary gas range. With one of these ranges anyone can become a gourmet cook. They are commercial-quality and should last a lifetime.

Professional home-use "restaurant" ranges have burners with heat outputs as high as 15,000 Btuh. The largest burners on ordinary ranges are only 9,000 Btuh. When boiling water or cooking, the pot heats up faster with the higher-output burners.

This reduces the overall cooking time and the total amount of heat that is wasted and lost into your kitchen. When cooking or entertaining, your kitchen will stay more comfortable, especially in the summer.

Professional ranges also have special burner designs and controls to provide more precise; and therefore, more efficient cooking. One model has a multi-stage burner that varies the heat output from 14,000 Btuh down to only 400 Btuh. This is ideal for extremely delicate simmering or sauteing.

Other professional ranges use special star burners. Instead of a round burner flame on an ordinary burner, a star burner has eight fingers projecting from the center. There are many holes in the top of each finger, so the flame is in contact with the entire bottom of the pot for even cooking with no burning.

Many professional ranges have six burners, built-in grills with lava rocks, and griddles. The ovens are very large capacity, big enough to handle a commercial bun tray. Some models have the option of gas or electric ovens, or one of each. If you do prefer an electric oven, you can get an optional convection oven which allows you to switch the fan on or off.

Special infrared broilers produce evenly-cooked, juicy meats and seafood. Instead of just an open flame above the meat or seafood, the gas flows out into a large rectangular honeycomb box. As the gas burns in the hundreds of tiny holes, the entire honeycomb piece glows red and sears the meat perfectly. You can also get a super-hot 30,000 Btuh accessory burner just for oriental wok cooking.

Don't just go out and buy a commercial-grade restaurant range. They are not certified by the AGA for home use. Certified professional "home-use" ranges have child-proof knobs, cool air-wash oven doors, electronic ignition, and insulated/multi-wall construction for zero-clearance against cabinets.

Q: I hear that the furnace or air-conditioner filter should be changed often. How often is often and how can I tell when it is dirty?

A: It is important to have a free flow of air through the blower filter for maximum efficiency, especially when air-conditioning. Hold the filter up to the light to see if it is badly clogged with dust, pet hair, etc.

Standard furnace filter elements cost only a couple of dollars at most. To be safe, just schedule a change every two months, whether or not it looks dirty.

Six star burners

Warming shelf

Griddle

Cool air-wash oven doors

Waste-level broiler

Commercial-size ovens

Painted or brushed stainless steel construction

With proper care, professional restaurant gas ranges can last a lifetime. A list of the major manufacturers and some detailed information on each is presented on pages 207 and 208.

These gas ranges look just like true commercial-grade restaurant ranges (and many are converted from them), but they have been modified for residential safety. Although the commercial models are slightly less expensive because they do not have these safety features, do not install one in your home.

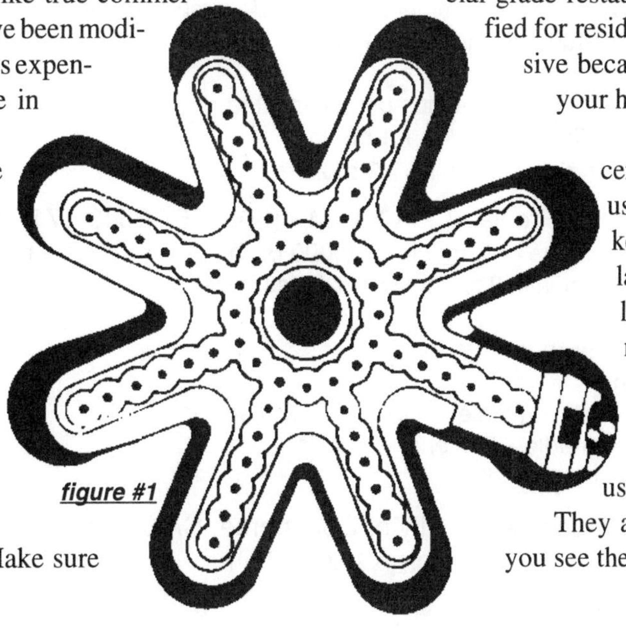

The residential models are certified by the American Gas Association (AGA) for residential use. They have safety modifications such as air wash oven doors, keeping the outside surface cool to eliminate burns, particularly around children. The sides and back are either insulated or have several layers so they can be placed against cabinets and not be a fire hazard (zero-clearance).

Residential certified models have electronic ignition instead of a standing pilot light used on true commercial models. This is safer and saves gas. They also have childproof knobs that snap into the off position. Make sure you see the AGA residential certification.

figure #1

Detailed product information is shown on pages 207 and 208. There are many options available such as griddles, grills, woks and even the number of burners can be variable.Under the features listed, *"B"* stands for cooktop burners. *"6B"* means 6 burners. As you can see, you can mix and match many of the options to get the specific configuration that you want. Most 48" and 60" models have two ovens.

The heat outputs are measured in Btu per hour (Btuh). The following pages list the *maximum* heat outputs for the cooktop burners, griddles, grills, ovens, etc. The maximum outputs range from 14,000 to 15,000 Btuh.

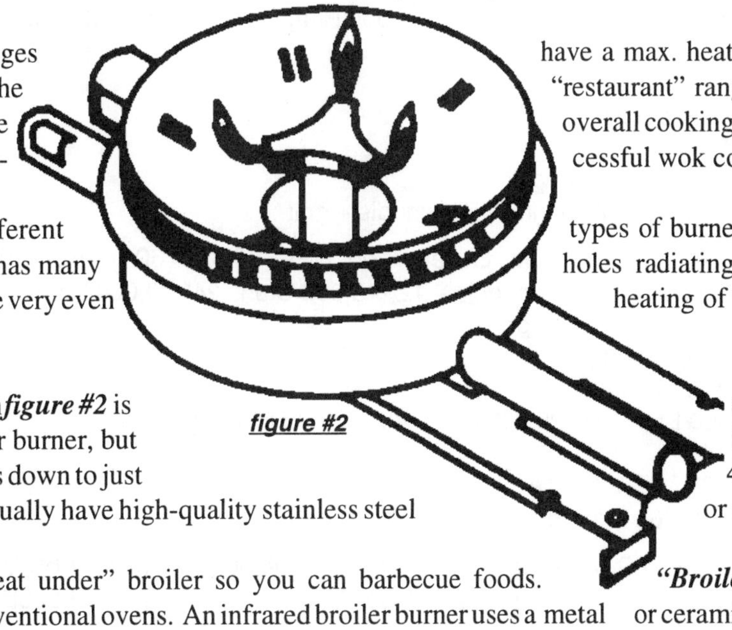

Most standard home ranges have a max. heat output of about 9,000 Btuh. The higher output of the "restaurant" range allows you to bring water to boil faster and reduce overall cooking time. A very-high heat output is also essential for successful wok cooking.

figure #2

There are several different types of burners (see figure1 and 2). The star burner in *figure #1* has many holes radiating out from the center. These are supposed to provide very even heating of the bottom of any size pan on the burners.

The other type shown in *figure #2* is a vari-flame design. It uses a fairly standard circular burner, but it also has a tiny burner inside for simmering. It drops down to just 400 Btuh, which is extremely low. These ranges usually have high-quality stainless steel or cast iron burners.

"Grill" refers to a "heat under" broiler so you can barbecue foods. *"Broiler"* is a regular "heat over" broiler like in most conventional ovens. An infrared broiler burner uses a metal or ceramic honeycomb box with many tiny holes in it. The gas burns in these holes and the entire box glows red. This does an excellent broiling job and cooks the meat evenly.

Several of the range ovens have an optional convection fan. This circulates the heated air throughout the oven for faster and more-even cooking and baking. You can also choose an electric element in one of the ovens from some manufacturers or combinations of the above.

Manufacturers of Home-Use Professional Gas Ranges

BROWN STOVE WORKS, P.O. Box 2490, Cleveland, TN 37320 - (800) 251-7485 (615) 476-6544
    model - "Five Star"   griddle - 10,500 Btuh   grill - no
    burner type - Vari-flame - Small simmer burner inside circular burner
    burner type - 14,000 Btuh down to only 400 Btuh
    broiler type - open flame
    oven - 18,000 Btuh, electric convection oven available
    features - 36" - 4B + griddle + 1 oven + 1 broiler,
              48" - 6B + griddle + 2 ovens + 2 broilers

GARLAND, 185 E. South St., Freeland, PA 18224 - (800) 257-2643 (717) 636-1000
    model - "Restaurant Range"   griddle - 18,000 Btuh   grill - no
    burner type - star burner with 8 fingers with 7 holes in each
    burner type - 14,000 Btuh
    broiler type - infrared burner
    oven - 35,000 Btuh
    features - 36" - 6B or 4B + griddle + 1 oven + 1 broiler
              60" - 6B + griddle + 2 ovens + 2 broilers
              and 1 waist-high broiler

JADE RANGE, 7335 E. Slausen Ave., City of Commerce, CA 90040 - (213) 728-5700
    model - "Dynasty"   griddle - 16,000 Btuh   grill - 24,000 Btuh
    burner type - circular burner
    burner type - 15,000 Btuh
    broiler type - infrared burner
    oven - 30,000 Btuh - (convection fan optional)
    features - 30" - 4B + 1 oven
              36" - 6B or 4B + griddle or 4B + wok
              48" - 8B or 6B + wok or griddle or grill, or 4B + both
              60" - 8B or 6B + two of griddle, grill, or wok, or 4B + all options

THERMADOR, 5119 District Blvd., Los Angeles, CA 90040 - (800) 735-4328
    model - "Prorange"   griddle - 30,000 Btuh   grill - 30,000 Btuh with lava rock
    burner type - circular
    burner output - 15,000 Btuh
    broiler type - infrared burner
    oven - 30,000 Btuh
    features - 36" - 4B + griddle or grill
              48" - 6B + griddle or grill, 4B + griddle + grill

VIKING RANGE CORP., 111 Front St., Greenwood, MS 38930 - (601) 455-1200
    model - "Professional"   griddle - 12"-15,000 Btuh, 24"-30,000 Btuh
    burner type - circular   grill - no
    burner output - 15,000 Btuh
    broiler type - infrared burner
    oven - 30"-24,000 Btuh, 36"-28,000 Btuh, 48"-20,000 Btuh (2 ovens)
    features - 30" - 4B
              36" - 6B, 4B + griddle
              48" - 8B, 6B + 12" griddle, 4B + 24" griddle

WOLF RANGE CO., 19600 S. Alameda St., Compton, CA 90221 - (800) 866-9653 (310) 637-3737
    model - "The Gourmet Series"   griddle - 18,000 Btuh   grill - 18,000Btuh - infrared burner
    burner type - circular
    burner output - 15,000 Btuh
    broiler type - electric in left oven
    oven - 24,500 Btuh - (convection fan optional)
    features - 36" cooktops available only, not 36" full range
              48" - 8B, 6B + griddle or grill, 4B + griddle + grill
              60" - 6B + griddle + grill

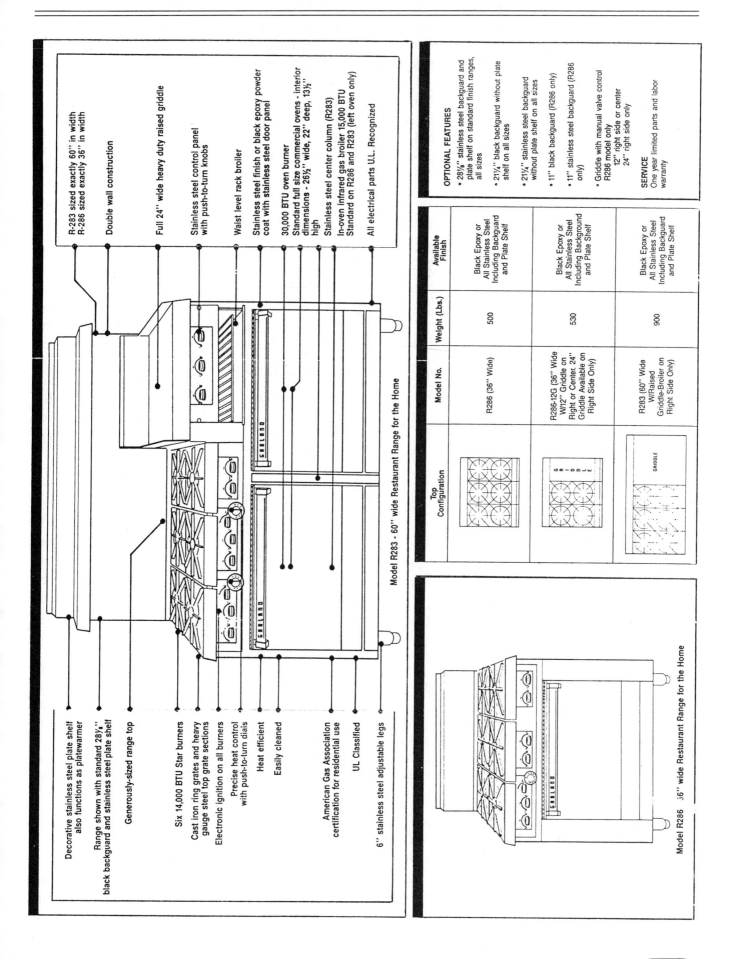

Left callouts (Model R283):

- Decorative stainless steel plate shelf also functions as platewarmer
- Range shown with standard 28⅛" black backguard and stainless steel plate shelf
- Generously-sized range top
- Six 14,000 BTU Star burners
- Cast iron ring grates and heavy gauge steel top grate sections
- Electronic ignition on all burners
- Precise heat control with push-to-turn dials
- Heat efficient
- Easily cleaned
- American Gas Association certification for residential use
- UL Classified
- 6" stainless steel adjustable legs

Top/right callouts:

- R-283 sized exactly 60'' in width
- R-286 sized exactly 36'' in width
- Double wall construction
- Full 24'' wide heavy duty raised griddle
- Stainless steel control panel with push-to-turn knobs
- Waist level rack broiler
- Stainless steel finish or black epoxy powder coat with stainless steel door panel
- 30,000 BTU oven burner
- Standard full size commercial ovens - interior dimensions - 26½'' wide, 22'' deep, 13½'' high
- Stainless steel center column (R283)
- In-oven infrared gas broiler 15,000 BTU Standard on R286 and R283 (left oven only)
- All electrical parts U.L. Recognized

Model R283 - 60'' wide Restaurant Range for the Home

Model R286 36'' wide Restaurant Range for the Home

OPTIONAL FEATURES

- 28⅛" stainless steel backguard and plate shelf on standard finish ranges, all sizes
- 21¼'' black backguard without plate shelf on all sizes
- 21¼'' stainless steel backguard without plate shelf on all sizes
- 11'' black backguard (R286 only)
- 11'' stainless steel backguard (R286 only)
- Griddle with manual valve control R286 model only
  12'' right side or center
  24'' right side only

SERVICE

One year limited parts and labor warranty

Top Configuration	Model No.	Weight (Lbs.)	Available Finish
	R286 (36" Wide)	500	Black Epoxy or All Stainless Steel Including Backguard and Plate Shelf
	R286-12G (36" Wide W/12" Griddle on Right or Center. 24" Griddle Available on Right Side Only)	530	Black Epoxy or All Stainless Steel Including Background and Plate Shelf
	R283 (60" Wide W/Raised Griddle-Broiler on Right Side Only)	900	Black Epoxy or All Stainless Steel Including Background and Plate Shelf

Q: I want to buy a new microwave oven both for the convenience and to lower my electric bills. What are the newest designs of microwave ovens available and what features should I look for?

A: If you have an older microwave oven, you'll be amazed at the new convenience features available and how fast some of the new models cook. Combination microwave/convection ovens are available. Use these as a microwave for fast cooking, a convection oven for fast efficient baking, or a combination of both for speed and browning.

Some of the newest microwave ovens have super-fast-cooking power as high as 1,000 watts. These increase cooking speeds by 25% over the standard high-output models. This reduces overheating of your kitchen and overworking of your air conditioner in the summer.

When selecting a new microwave oven, choose one with as many of the new convenience features as your budget will allow. These features include automatic moisture-sensing reheat/cooking, multi-stage programming, specific foods cooking memory, super-high-output cooking power, automatic defrost by weight, etc.

Using a microwave oven requires much less electricity than using your conventional range or oven.

With more convenience features, you will tend to use it more often instead of your rangetop or large oven. Whereas an oven may use 3,400 watts (or an equivalent for gas) for an hour, the most powerful microwave oven uses only 1,400 watts for a fraction as long.

An automatic moisture-sensing feature makes cooking most food

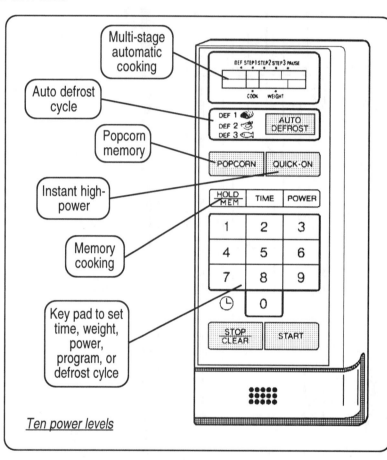

Ten power levels

simple. A sensor inside the microwave oven detects the presence of steam. This tells the microwave oven's "brain" how the cooking or reheating is progressing.

For example, when cooking frozen vegetables, it will start on the high cooking power level. When steam is sensed, indicating that the vegetables are at the proper cooking temperature, it automatically switches to a lower cooking power

level for the proper length of time. Make sure you are getting a "true" moisture-sensing feature, not just a sound alike name.

Multi-stage programming allows you to automatically defrost, then cook at two different time and power settings, and then incorporate a standby warming. Put in the food and walk away until it is done.

Memory cooking allows you to preprogram the cooking times for several often made microwave foods like potatoes, pizza slices, cups of coffee, etc. You just touch the "potato" button and the oven automatically cooks it properly.

Q: I have a heat pump. My house always seems to stay warm, but when I put my hand by the warm air register, the air feels chilly. How can it keep my house warm?

A: The heated air output from your heat pump is cooler than that from an electric, gas, or oil furnace. Its temperature, as it reaches your hand, is lower than your body temperature. The cooler air feels even colder because of the wind chill effect.

Since you keep your house in the 68 to 70 degree range, the air output is hot enough to keep it warm. Heat pumps tend to run longer and move more air than gas or oil furnaces because the air coming out isn't as hot.

Increased power and a variety of convenience features distinguish today's microwave ovens from those made several years ago. You can buy a combination microwave/convection oven for the speed and efficiency of a microwave with the browning and baking abilities of a regular oven. I have listed several of the best models on the page 211. A sample keypad is shown on page 212.

A convection oven uses a fan to constantly recirculate heated air over the food. You can set an oven temperature like a conventional oven, but the need for preheating is mostly erased. The heat circulation browns food nicely and seals in moisture. Since the heat is fan forced rather than radiant like a conventional oven, food cooks in about $1/_3$ the time.

A combination microwave/convection oven can be used as a microwave for fast heating, a convection oven for baking, or a combination of the two for full meal preparation. Oven capacity ranges from .3 cubic feet in subcompacts to 1.5 cubic feet in full-size ovens. See the chart on page 211 for a comparison of features on mid-size (approximately 1 cubic foot) ovens.

Generally you should buy the largest size your space and budget allow. Always check the inside, usable space in relation to the outside dimensions. You may be able to get the space you want inside in an oven with smaller outside dimensions.

Most ovens offer one-button convenience for popcorn, but some also have beverage and pizza pre-sets. You simply press the button and enter the number of cups of coffee or slices of bread you are heating. The oven does the rest. Many ovens offer pre-set codes for a wide variety of commonly-made items. Usually these codes are listed on the keypad but some ovens list the codes inside the door. Look for an oven that will let you re-program the pre-sets to your particular tastes.

Most mid- to large-size microwave ovens today have an automatic defrost feature. Some ovens accomplish this by alternating between full power and no power (standing time). Others are able to run at reduced power levels. On some ovens you program the weight of food being defrosted, on others you program the type of food. Many require you to turn the food at intervals indicated by "beeping." Defrosting is one of the most popular features, so look for one that best meets your needs.

The auto cook and moisture sensor feature controls the cooking cycle by measuring steam as it escapes from the heated food. In auto cook mode, you program information about the type and amount of food you are cooking, and the oven does the rest by measuring how long it takes to detect steam, then calculating the full cooking time.

The moisture sensor takes the guesswork out of reheating food by setting the cooking time based on the amount of escaping steam, and turning itself off when a certain level has been reached. This eliminates the need for you to turn or stir the food.

The most important thing to remember when using auto cook or moisture sensor is that food must be properly covered or the sensor will be activated prematurely, resulting in undercooked food.

Similarly, a probe inserted in casseroles and roasts measures the internal temperature of food. You plug the cord extending from the probe into a receptacle in your oven, then program the temperature you want the food to reach. Once the temperature is reached, the probe will either signal the oven to turn off or to maintain a lower "holding" temperature.

Multi-stage programming allows you to do several tasks automatically. Most ovens feature four-stage programming. This means if your recipe calls for cooking at two different power levels, you set the oven to defrost the dish, then cook at high power, switch to low power, and then stand for the specified length of time. Once you tell the oven what to do, you walk away until it is time to eat.

None of these convenience features will help if the keypad or instructions are hard to read or understand. Look for a keypad that logically leads you through the necessary steps, is easily receptive to your touch and that emits a distinctive sound to let you know your commands are being received.

Manufacturers of Microwave and Combination Convection/Microwave Ovens

Manufacturer	Model #	Oven Size	Output Wattage	Cooking Stages*	Temp. Probe	Auto Cook	Convection/ Microwave?
AMANA REFRIGERATION, INC. Amana, IA 52204 (800) 843-0304 (319) 622-2142	M85T	.8	700	4	No	No	RMC720A
	Convection oven is 1.1 cu. ft. and 750 watts with temperature settings from 200°-450°						
FRIGIDAIRE COMPANY 6000 Perimeter Drive, Dublin, OH 43017 (800) 685-6005 (614) 792-4911	MCT1080A	1.0	1000	4	No	Yes	No
GE APPLIANCES Appliance Park Building 6, Room 106 Louisville, KY 40225 (800) 626-2000	JVM150J	1.0	750	5	Yes	Yes	JET342H
	Convection oven is 1.4 cu. ft and 800 watts with temperature settings from 200°-475°						
KITCHENAID (Division of Whirlpool) 701 Main St., St. Joseph, MI 49085 (800) 422-1230	KCMS125Y	1.2	800	2	No	Yes	KHMC107Y
	Convection oven is .9 cu. ft. and 800 watts with temperature settings from 200°-450°						
MCD 2510 Electronics Drive, Anniston, AL 36201 (205) 831-5790	M125/6 M46-14T	1.2 cu.ft.	800	3	No	Yes	No
PANASONIC CO. One Panasonic Way, Secaucus, NJ 07094 (201) 348-7000	NN2408	1.0	700	3	No	No	NN-2959
	Convection oven is 1.0 cu. ft. and 700 watts with temperature settings from 200°-450°						
SEARS ROEBUCK & CO. 3333 Beverly Rd., Hoffman Estates, IL 60179 (800) 359-2000 (708) 286-2500	Kenmore	1.2	800	4	No	No	89969
	Convection oven is 1.3 cu. ft. and 700 watts with temperature settings from 200°-450°						
SHARP ELECTRONICS Sharp Plaza, Mahwah, NJ 07430 (201) 529-8703	R-4A84	1.2	900	No	No	Yes	R9H83
	Convection oven is 1.5 cu. ft. and 900 watts with temperature settings from 200°-450°						
TAPPAN 6000 Perimeter Drive, Dublin, OH 43017 (800) 685-6005 (614) 792-4911	56-3872	1.0	1000	4	No	Yes	No
WHIRLPOOL CORP. 2000 M-63, Benton Harbor, MI 49022 (800) 253-1301	MT2100XYR	1.0	800	NA	No	Yes	MC8990XT
	Convection oven is 1.3 cu. ft and 700 watts with temperature settings from 200°-450°						

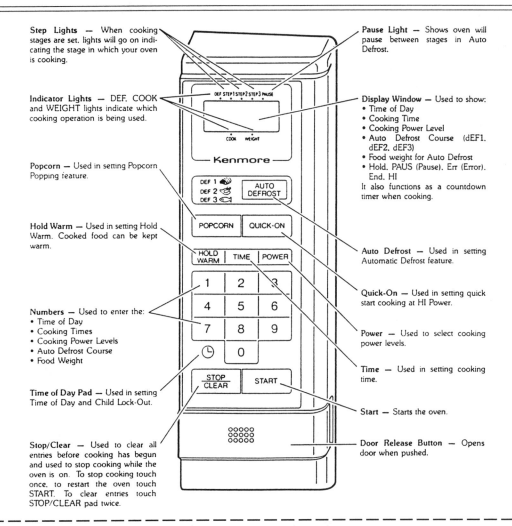

Step Lights — When cooking stages are set, lights will go on indicating the stage in which your oven is cooking.

Pause Light — Shows oven will pause between stages in Auto Defrost.

Indicator Lights — DEF. COOK and WEIGHT lights indicate which cooking operation is being used.

Display Window — Used to show:
• Time of Day
• Cooking Time
• Cooking Power Level
• Auto Defrost Course (dEF1. dEF2. dEF3)
• Food weight for Auto Defrost
• Hold. PAUS (Pause). Err (Error). End. HI
It also functions as a countdown timer when cooking.

Popcorn — Used in setting Popcorn Popping feature.

Hold Warm — Used in setting Hold Warm. Cooked food can be kept warm.

Auto Defrost — Used in setting Automatic Defrost feature.

Quick-On — Used in setting quick start cooking at HI Power.

Numbers — Used to enter the:
• Time of Day
• Cooking Times
• Cooking Power Levels
• Auto Defrost Course
• Food Weight

Power — Used to select cooking power levels.

Time — Used in setting cooking time.

Time of Day Pad — Used in setting Time of Day and Child Lock-Out.

Start — Starts the oven.

Stop/Clear — Used to clear all entries before cooking has begun and used to stop cooking while the oven is on. To stop cooking touch once. to restart the oven touch START. To clear entries touch STOP/CLEAR pad twice.

Door Release Button — Opens door when pushed.

Microwave Cooking Tips

Arrange food carefully. Place thickest areas toward outside of dish. Rotate or stir during cooking to help distribute heat evenly.

Turn over dense pieces of food such as meat and whole baked potatoes.

Watch cooking time. Cook for the shortest amount of time indicated and add more as needed. Food severely overcooked can smoke or ignite.

Add standing time. Stir food after cooking, if possible, and leave it rest awhile so the heat distributes evenly. Carry-over heat actually continues the cooking and raises internal temperature by several degrees.

Cover-up: Glass covers, plates, saucers, plastic wrap and wax paper hold in heat and speed cooking, defrosting and heating. Place a wax paper tent on roast poultry or meat to help retain heat and prevent spattering.

Baked goods with fillings. Cut filled pastry, cake or doughnuts open after heating to release the steam; let stand awhile before eating. Baked goods that feel warm to the touch may contain fillings hot enough to burn the mouth.

Food with skins. Pierce unpeeled potatoes, squash, apples, tomatoes and sausage in casing to prevent a build-up of steam that may cause the food to splatter.

Liquids. Briskly stir liquids before heating and reheating to incorporate air. This prevents abrupt boilovers that sometimes occur after air-depleted liquids are heated (especially in tall, narrow containers).

Check for "doneness". Look for signs indicating that cooking temperatures have been reached. Some common signs are:
• Food steams throughout, not just around edges
• Center bottom of dish is very hot to the touch
• Poultry thigh joints move easily
• Meat and poultry show no signs of pinkness and meat juices run clear when meat is cut close to the bone.
• Fish is opaque and flakes easily with a fork.

Don't overload the oven. Three groups of 2 items generally heat more evenly than 6 at once.

Avoid steam burns by directing steam away from the face and hands. Slowly lift the farthest edge of a dish's covering; carefully open popcorn and oven cooking bags away from the face.

Always use potholders to prevent burns when handling containers and utensils that are in contact with hot food. Enough heat from the food can transfer through utensils to cause skin burns.

Packaging from microwavable foods. Never reuse packaging, trays or containers provided with microwavable foods unless the label clearly states that they are designed for reuse.

Q: I need to replace my old refrigerator/freezer with a new high-efficiency model with more convenience features. What features should I look for when selecting a new one and how much electricity will I save?

A: An old refrigerator/freezer is one of the most electricity guzzling appliances in your home. New high-efficiency refrigerator/freezers operate for less than $50 per year, a 50% savings over old ones. They also maintain more constant temperature and humidity levels and have many features.

New convenience features allow you to store and find foods faster, so the door is not opened for as long. Some energy efficient models have a small door within the large refrigerator door. You put frequently-used items there so you won't have to open the large door as often. An exterior ice and water dispenser may also save energy.

New high efficiency wall and door insulation systems require smaller motors and compressors. This contributes to quiet operation. One efficient model has two totally separate refrigerator and freezer compressor units. This provides precise control over the refrigerator and freezer temperatures.

During a power outage, the extra insulation keeps food frozen

and fresh for a longer time. There should also be less sweating around the door gasket area in the summer, even with the energy saver/door heaters switched off.

The most efficient design has the freezer on the top. The cooling coils are in the freezer section and some of this cold air is circulated down with a fan to cool the refrig-

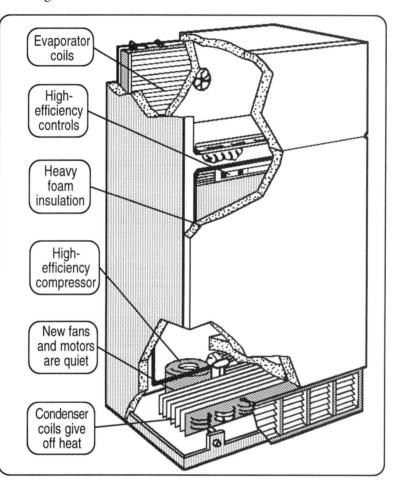

- Evaporator coils
- High-efficiency controls
- Heavy foam insulation
- High-efficiency compressor
- New fans and motors are quiet
- Condenser coils give off heat

erator section. With the freezer above, the colder, more dense air naturally falls into the refrigerator.

A typical side-by-side refrigerator/freezer uses about 25% more electricity than a comparable freezer-on-top model. It is less efficient because it is more difficult to keep a tall vertical freezer cold enough. There is more uninsulated door gasket area with a side-by-side model.

Select the smallest refrigerator/freezer that is an adequate size for your needs. A larger one loses more energy through its greater wall surface area. Also, a reasonably-full refrigerator uses less electricity than a more-empty one, especially if it is opened often.

Although a manual-defrost model is most energy-efficient, you must periodically defrost it. If you don't and the frost builds up, it rapidly loses efficiency. Unless you have time to defrost it, select an automatic defrost model and you'll save electricity overall. I use a freezer-on-top automatic defrost model in my own kitchen.

Q: I went up into my attic and the blown-in insulation was high in some spots and low in others. Is it worthwhile to take a rake and level it better?

A: It would probably be a good idea to go up and inspect the insulation closer. Leveling it reduces the over all energy loss through your attic floor. Just a small inadequately insulated area can have a significant effect on your utility bills.

Wear a breathing mask and goggles when handling the insulation. Also, check to make sure that the insulation did not settle over the soffit vents and block them. This can cause energy loss both summer and winter.

Tips for Using Your Refrigerator/Freezer Efficiently

1) Clean condenser coils on back or underneath the refrigerator every three months.

2) Set the refrigerator temperature at 38 to 40 degrees.

3) If you have a separate freezer control, set the freezer temperature at 0 to 5 degrees.

4) Level the refrigerator so the door closes reasonably quick. Don't tilt it back too much or the door will slam and jar the refrigerator.

5) If you have a manual defrost model, defrost the freezer when the frost reaches 1/4-inch thickness.

6) Locate the refrigerator away from the stove or direct sun.

7) Store frequently-used items in a specific location near the front of the refrigerator.

8) Use a very low-wattage light bulb in the refrigerator.

9) Periodically clean off door gasket and metal surface. It will seal better and reduce mildew.

10) Clearly label packages in the freezer for quick identification.

11) Keep refrigerator and freezer full. Keep milk cartons full of water in it when not full of foods.

12) Cover any containers filled with liquids. This reduces moisture and frost buildup.

13) Turn off door "anti-sweat" heaters - (energy-saver switch).

14) Check the magnetic door gasket seal. It should hold a dollar bill in place when it's closed.

15) Install clear vinyl door curtain.

16) Put warm foods in shallow containers for quicker cooling.

17) A refrigerator needs ventilation. Near a window is good. Don't tuck it next to cabinets in a corner.

18) Decide what you want before opening the door. Use glass containers so you can quickly identify foods in the refrigerator.

19) Add only 2-3 lb. of fresh food for each 1 cu. ft. of freezer capacity. This allows the food to freeze quick enough without warming the freezer compartment.

Most Energy-Efficient Refrigerator/Freezers				
Brand	Model	Size (cu. ft.)	Energy Use(kwh/yr.)	Electric Cost ($/yr.)
Side-by-side - 19.5 - 22.4 cubic feet - with through the door ice				
Sub-Zero	561	21.4	755	62
Kenmore	5226	21.7	759	63
General Electric	TFH22*RS	21.7	759	63
Montgomery Ward	62273	21.7	759	63
Kitchen Aid	KSR*22QA**0	21.6	761	63
Whirlpool	ED22DQ*A*0*	21.6	761	63
Gibson	MRS22WH***	22.1	774	64
Westinghouse	MRS22WH***	22.1	774	64
Tappan	MRS22WH***	22.1	774	64
Frigidaire	*RS22WH***	22.1	774	64
Side-by-side - 22.5 to 24.4 cubic feet - with through-the-door ice				
General Electric	TFH24*RS	23.6	799	66
Montgomery Ward	64273	23.6	799	66
Frigidaire	*RS24WH***	24.1	807	67
Gibson	MRS24WH***	24.1	807	67
Kelvinator	MRS24WH***	24.1	807	67
Tappan	MRS24WH***	24.1	807	67
Westinghouse	MRS24WH***	24.1	807	67
Side-by-side - 24.5 - 27 cubic feet - with through-the-door-ice				
Kenmore	5357	25.2	828	68
Whirlpool	ED25DQ*A*0*	25.2	828	68
Kitchen Aid	KSR*25QA**0*	25.1	851	68
Kenmore	5376	26.6	851	70

The electric costs are based on a rate of $.0825 per kilowatt hour, each (*) in the model number indicates there is a number or letter that changes based on color, style, etc.

Most Energy-Efficient Refrigerator/Freezers				
Brand	Model	Size (cu. ft.)	Energy Use (kwh/yr)	Electric Cost ($/yr.)
Top freezer - 14.4 - 16.4 cubic feet				
Kenmore	6742	14.4	496	41
Hotpoint	CTH14CYS	14.4	496	41
General Electric	TBH14*AS	14.4	496	41
RCA	MTH14CYS	14.4	496	41
Whirlpool	ET14UK*A*0	14.4	498	41
Roper	RT14HK*A*0	14.4	498	41
RCA	MTH16CYS	15.6	515	42
Hotpoint	CTH16*YS	15.6	515	42
Kenmore	334*	14.4	526	43
Whirlpool	ET14J**A*0*	14.4	526	43
Roper	RT14D**A*0	14.4	526	43
Estate	TT14*K*A*0	14.4	526	43
Top freezer - 16.5 - 18.4 cubic feet				
Gibson	*RT17DHA**	16.8	561	46
Frigidaire	FRT17*HA**	16.8	561	46
Westinhouse	*RT17*HA**	16.8	561	46
Tappan	MRT17DHA**	16.8	561	46
Kelvinator	MRT17DHA**	16.8	561	46
Maytag	RT*17EOCA*	16.6	566	47
Admiral	AT17EM6*	16.5	566	47
Norge	RBE170P*	16.5	566	47
Jenn-Air	JRTE175	16.5	566	47
Montgomery Ward	HMG77133*	16.5	566	47
Crosley	RBE170P*	16.5	566	47
Magic Chef	RBE170P*	16.5	566	47
Amana	T*18*3	17.8	582	48
Estate	TT18HK*A*0*	18.1	589	49
Roper	RT18HK*A*O*	18.1	589	49
KitchenAid	KTR*18KA**1*	18.1	589	49
Whirlpool	ET18*K*A*1*	18.1	589	49
RCA	MTH18EAS	18.2	591	49
General Electric	TBH18*AS	18.2	591	49
Hotpoint	CTH18EAS	18.2	591	49
Kenmore	*787	18.2	591	49

Most Energy-Efficient Refrigerator/Freezers				
Brand	**Model**	**Size (cu. Ft.)**	**Energy Use (kwh/yr.)**	**Electric Cost ($/yr.)**
Top freezer - 18.5 - 20.4 cubic feet				
Amana	T*19R3	18.6	595	49
Maytag	RT*19E0CA*	18.7	599	49
Admiral	AT19EM6*	18.6	599	49
Norge	RBE193P*	18.6	599	49
Montgomery Ward	HMG791*3*	18.6	599	49
Crosley	RBE193P*	18.6	599	49
Magic Chef	RBE193P*	18.6	599	49
Jenn-Air	JRTE197*	18.6	599	49
Top freezer - 20.5 - 22.4 cubic feet				
Amana	T*21*3	20.7	626	52
General Electric	TBH21*AS	20.6	631	52
Kenmore	*717	20.6	631	52
Hotpoint	XRH21GAS	20.6	631	52
RCA	MTH21GAS	20.6	631	52
Amana	T*22R3	21.6	640	53
Magic Chef	RBE214R*	21.1	642	53
Maytag	RT*21E0CA*	21.1	642	53
Norge	RBE214P*	21.1	642	53
Admiral	AT21EM9*	21.1	642	53
Crosley	RBE214P*	21.1	642	53
Jenn-Air	JRTE217*	21.1	642	53
Montgomery Ward	HMG711*3*	21.1	642	53
Westinghouse	*RT22NHA**	21.6	645	53
General Electric	TBH22PAS	21.6	650	54
Top freezer - 20.5 - 22.4 cubic feet - with through-the-door ice				
Crosley	GT22X8D*	22.3	726	60
Magic Chef	RB234RD*	22.3	726	60
Admiral	AT22XLD*	22.3	726	60
Norge	*T22XLD*	22.3	726	60
Jenn-Air	JRTD227**	22.3	726	60
Montgomery Ward	HMG321*3*	22.3	726	60
Maytag	RTW22E*CA*	22.1	726	60
Refrigerator with bottom freezers				
Amana	B*22A2	21.7	592	49
Montgomery Ward	72373	21.7	634	52
General Electric	TCX22ZA	21.7	634	52
Kenmore	8628	21.7	634	52

216

Q: My old dishwasher is noisy and doesn't always clean completely. How well do the new efficient, super-quiet models clean? What are some of the new convenience and efficiency features to consider?

A: There are many new super-quiet dishwashers that provide very effective cleaning. Some models cost less than $40 per year to operate using an electric water heater and even less with a gas water heater.

The newest and most efficient features are electronic "brains" to select and fine tune the cycles automatically, super hot sanitizing cycles and high quality internal filters for better cleaning with less hot water.

The most energy efficient and quiet dishwashers use a two-pump system. By using two single-direction pumps instead of one large reversing pump, the water reservoir can be smaller. This cuts hot water usage by 40 percent to only 5.3 gallons on the normal cycle.

Two-pump systems are inherently quieter. One single-direction pump, with a quiet quick-start feature, is used for the high pressure washing spray. Another small quiet pump is used to drain the water after each cycle. Two-pump systems do not require the extra valving of a single reversing pump.

Insulation level is important for efficiency and noise reduction. Several of the well insulated single-pump models are quiet too. Multiple layers of asphalt/felt/foil insulation or fiberglass batt wraps are effective. Motors and pumps mounted to the base pan instead of the tank also reduce noise.

One new efficient model uses sensors and a computer brain (Intellisense) to automatically mea-

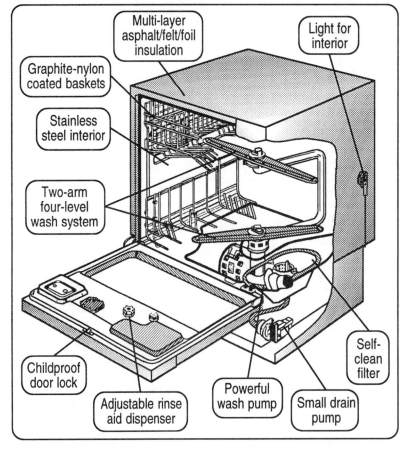

Multi-layer asphalt/felt/foil insulation

Light for interior

Graphite-nylon coated baskets

Stainless steel interior

Two-arm four-level wash system

Childproof door lock

Adjustable rinse aid dispenser

Powerful wash pump

Small drain pump

Self-clean filter

sure how dirty the dishes are. The electrical conductivity of the water, its cloudiness, its temperature and the spray arm rotation speed are continually measured by the brain.

The brain determines the minimum cycle time for cleaning and drying. It even remembers the last time you washed. If it has been more than a day, the brain assumes the food is dried on and uses a slightly

longer cycle. The cycle can also be manually selected, like light/china, for example.

Many of the super-efficient European designs offer a super hot sanitizing cycle. The water is heated by an internal heater to 165 degrees for a minimum wash cycle of 24 minutes. A final 7-minute rinse is also super-hot.

High quality filters, some self-cleaning, and built-in waste grinders improve cleaning. Multi-level spray wash systems, up to four levels from two rotating arms, require shorter wash cycles. One model uses two rotating mini arms on the ends of the regular arm to insure every dish gets sprayed.

Q: I have a gas furnace with a manual wall thermostat. I set the temperature 10 degrees lower at night. When I set it up in the morning, should I increase it in steps over an hour or all at once.

A: With a gas or oil furnace, it doesn't make much difference in energy usage if you set it back up in several, two-steps or all at once. It is more convenient to set it up the full ten degrees initially. Consider purchasing an automatic clock setback thermostat for less than $50.

If you have a heat pump with backup electric heat, set it higher in several-degree steps. This keeps the backup heaters from coming on.

Manufacturers of Quiet and Efficient Dishwashers

A.E.G., 65 Campus Plaza, Edison, NJ 08837 - (800) 344-0043 (908) 225-8837

number of pumps/gal - two/5.3 gal
racks - nylon coated
internal water heater/temp. - yes/162°
internal food disposer - no

cycles/options - pots & pans, normal, light, heavy, china/crystal, 2 quick washes, 2 economy washes, rinse & hold, start delay, heated dry on/off

wash spray system - three-level - the spray system alternates spray arms in short cycles, the lower level sprays water up, the water is controlled by a valve and then sprays up from the top arm and to the sides from the tower

features - The interior of the dishwasher is stainless steel. It is equipped with an internal water softener. There is a safety valve that senses a change in the water pressure and cuts off the water supply at the faucet in case of flooding. It also sounds an alarm to warn you if the protection system has been activated.

AMANA, Amana, IA 52204 - (800) 843-0304

number of pumps/gal - one/7.7 gal
racks - nylon coated
internal water heater/temp. - yes/140°
internal food disposer - no

cycles/options - pots & pans, normal, light, heavy, china/crystal, short, rinse & hold, start delay, heated dry on/off

wash spray system - three-level - lower level is a wash arm that rotates in a starlike pattern with five nozzles spraying upward, next level is a telescoping tower which sprays from the center, top level is an arm that sprays water down

features - Spring loaded clamps hold down lightweight plastic cups and Tupperware® containers preventing them from flipping over. An adjustable rack on the upper level allows you to double-stack cups. A self-cleaning filter removes food waste early in the wash cycle and keeps it from redepositing the food in later cycles.

ASKO, INC., 903 N. Bowser, Richardson, TX 75081 - (800) 367-2444 (214) 644-8595

number of pumps/gal - two/5.3 gal
racks - graphite nylon coated
internal water heater/temp. - yes/165°
internal food disposer - no

cycles/options - pots & pans, normal, delicate/light china, rinse & hold, heated dry on/off

wash spray system - four-level - an upper spray arm and a counter-rotating lower spray arm, both spray up and down simultaneously with constant pressure

features - The interior tub and spray arms are stainless steel. A compact dishwasher is available which measures only 19½"h x 21⅞"w x 22⁷/₁₆"d that can sit on a countertop or can be built-in and it can handle six full place settings and an additional eight cups or glasses. It is equipped with two glide-out baskets. This is ideal for a one or two-person household. The insulating materials are asphalt/felt/ foil. The pumps and motors are mounted on a steel base pan away from the tank so the dishwasher is very quiet.

BOSCH CORP., 2800 S. 25th Ave., Broadview, IL 60153 - (800) 866 -2022 (708) 865-5585

number of pumps/gal - two/5.4 gal
racks - nylon coated
internal water heater/temp. - yes/161°
internal food disposer - no

cycles/options - pots & pans, normal, delicate/light china, quick, economy, rinse & hold, heated dry on/off

wash spray system - four-level - lower level sprays water up as the arms rotates, the upper arm rotates and sprays water both up and down, and a small nozzle on the top sprays water down

features - The tub, inner door and spray arms are stainless steel. An optional stainless steel control panel and door front are available. An integrated series is available that allows the control panel to be adjusted to match a drawer height of up to 6", a cabinet door mounting that can be used with almost any kitchen cabinet, and a dishwasher door that is recessed to accept a ¾" thick door panel to provide a flush look.   An optional extra long stemware caddy which can accomodate glasses of up to 12 inches is available.

CALORIC, Amana, IA 52204 - (800) 843-0304

number of pumps/gal - one/7.7 gal
racks - nylon coated
internal water heater/temp. - yes/140°
internal food disposer - no

cycles/options - pots & pans, normal, light, short, plate warmer, rinse & hold, start delay, heated dry on/off

wash spray system - three-level - lower level is a spray arm with six nozzles that rotate, the tower sprays water in the middle and the top sprays down from two sides

features - The upper rack has two cup shelves which fold down to allow for a second layer of cups. The silverware basket has a center compartment that closes for keeping small items from floating away.

CREDA INC., 5700 W. Touhy Ave., Niles, IL 60714 - (800) 992-7332 (708) 647- 8024

number of pumps/gal - one/7.3 gal
racks - nylon coated
internal water heater/temp. - yes/150°
internal food disposer - no

cycles/options - pre-rinse, pots & pans, normal, light, economy wash, china/crystal, short, plate warm, rinse & hold, start delay, heated dry on/off

wash spray system - three-level - powerful top, middle, and bottom spray action

features - The interior of the tub and door are manufactured of stainless steel. It is available as an integrated unit that allows your cabinet door to be attached to the front of the dishwasher.

FRIGIDAIRE, 6000 Perimeter Dr., Dublin, OH 43017 - (800) 451-7007

number of pumps/gal - one/7.7 gal
racks - nylon coated
internal water heater/temp. - yes/140°
internal food disposer - yes
cycles/options - pots & pans, heavy, normal, water saver, rinse & hold, custom, delay start, heated dry on/off
wash spray system - three-level - lower level is a wash arm that rotates with nine nozzles spraying upward, the tower has three nozzles that spray out and up, the upper level sprays water down
features - A rinse aid dispenser has a clear cap indicator to show when to refill it. A space saving cup shelf folds down to create extra room for another row of cups or small dishes.

GAGGENAU, 425 University Ave., Norwood, MA 02062 - (617) 255-1766

number of pumps/gal - two/7.5 gal
racks - nylon coated
internal water heater/temp. - yes/175°
internal food disposer - no
cycles/options - pots & pans, heavy, normal, water saver, rinse & hold, delicate/china, delay start, heated dry on/off
wash spray system - three-level - top spray nozzle and lower and middle stainless steel wash arms
features - The interior is stainless steel and it is equipped with an automatic built-in water softening system. The dishwasher fits perfectly into the bottom row of cupboards, the controls are located along the top edge of the door.

GENERAL ELECTRIC, Appliance Park, Louisville, KY 40225 - (800) 626-2000

number of pumps/gal - one/7.6 gal
racks - nylon coated
internal water heater/temp. - yes/140°
internal food disposer - yes
cycles/options - pots & pans, normal, light, china/crystal, rinse & hold, delay start, heated dry on/off
wash spray system - three-level - two small arms rotate on the ends of a large wash arm creating a random pattern of water jets. A tower sprays a 25º V shaped pattern from top, middle, and bottom
features - An adjustable utility shelf allows you to double stack cups, to secure light items or to use for large knives and utensils. A special jet in the bottom of the wash arm automatically keeps the filter clean.

GIBSON, 6000 Perimeter Dr., Dublin, OH 43017 - (800) 458-1445

number of pumps/gal - one/7.6 gal
racks - nylon coated
internal water heater/temp. - yes/140°
internal food disposer - yes
cycles/options - pots & pans, heavy, normal, light, rinse & hold, delay start, heated dry on/off
wash spray system - three-level - wash arm spins and sprays water from nine nozzles, the tower sprays water up and to the sides from three nozzles, the top sprays from two nozzles to the side and down
features - A fold down divider in the upper rack allows it to hold larger items such as bowls or pots.

JENN-AIR, 3035 N. Shadeland, Indianapolis, IN 46226 - (800) 536-6247

number of pumps/gal - one/7.6 gal
racks - nylon coated
internal water heater/temp. - yes/140°
internal food disposer - yes
cycles/options - heavy, normal, light, quick, rinse & hold, delay start, heated dry on/off
wash spray system - three-level - full size upper arm forces water down from the top, the tower rises and sprays water out from the center, full size lower spray arm forces water up from the bottom
features - The rack insert is designed to pop out to accommodate oversized items.

KELVINATOR, 6000 Perimeter Dr., Dublin, OH 43017 - (800) 323-7773

number of pumps/gal - one/7.6 gal
racks - nylon coated
internal water heater/temp. - yes/140°
internal food disposer - yes
cycles/options - pots & pans, heavy, normal, light, rinse & hold, delay start, heated dry on/off
wash spray system - three-level - wash arm spins and sprays water from nine nozzles, the tower spray water up and to the sides from three nozzles, the top sprays from two nozzles to the side and down
features - A self cleaning filter quickly removes leftover food and insures a clean wash and rinse.

KENMORE/SEARS, 3333 Beverly Rd., Hoffman Estates, IL 60179 - (800) 359-2000 (708) 286-2500

number of pumps/gal - one/7.6 gal
racks - nylon coated
internal water heater/temp. - yes/140°
internal food disposer - yes
cycles/options - pots & pans, normal, water saver, light, china/light, rinse & hold, quick rinse, custom, delay start, heated dry on/off
wash spray system - three-level - lower level is a wash arm that rotates spraying upward, the upper lever is a spray arm that sprays water, the tower sprays water up and out
features - It is equipped with a small items basket and a fold down fence rack.

KITCHEN AID, 2303 Pipestone Rd, Benton Harbor, MI 49022 - (800) 422-1230

number of pumps/gal - one/7.6 gal
racks - nylon coated
internal water heater/temp. - yes/160°
internal food disposer - yes
cycles/options - pots & pans, normal, light/china, sani rinse, rinse & hold, start delay, heated dry on/off
wash spray system - four-level sweep wash arm system - lower level arms rotate and sprays water up, upper spray arms rotates and sprays water up and down - a wash impeller forces 40 gallons of water per minute through the wash arm
features - The upper rack is adjustable to 16 positions. Simply raise, lower or tilt to accommodate your individual load.

MAYTAG, One Dependability Square, Newton, IA 50208 - (515) 792-7000

number of pumps/gal - one/6.5 gal

internal water heater/temp. - yes/140°

racks - nylon coated

internal food disposer - yes

cycles/options - pots & pans, heavy, normal, light, rinse hold, delay start, heated dry on/off

wash spray system - three-level with small spray holes - full size upper arm forces water down from the top, the tower rises and sprays water out from the center, full size lower spray arm forces water up from the bottom

features - This dishwasher senses (Intellisense® system) the amount of food, the presence of detergent, rinse aid, the wash arm rotation and the water temperature. It tracks the amount of time elapsed between loads so it can adjust for dried-on food particles, and it even remembers the number of times the door was opened. It chooses the right cycle to clean your dishes. The dishwasher bases its cycle on your habits.

MIELE, 22D Worlds Fair Dr., Somerset, NJ 08873 - (800) 843-7231 (908) 560-0899

number of pumps/gal - two/6.2 gal

internal water heater/temp. - yes/150°

racks - nylon coated

internal food disposer - no

cycles/options - pots & pans, heavy, normal, light, rinse hold, delay start, heated dry on/off

wash spray system - three-level - three spray arms, the top and bottom rotate in one direction and the one in the center rotates in the opposite direction

features - There is an adjustable top basket with a double cup layer and special inserts are available for plates and stemware. It also has a built-in water softener. The interior tub and door is stainless steel. It is available as an integrated unit you simply install in your own custom front panel.

REGENCY VSA APPLIANCES, PO Box 3341, Tustin, CA 92681 - (714) 544-3530

number of pumps/gal - two/5.9 gal

internal water heater/temp. - yes/165°

racks - nylon coated

internal food disposer - yes

cycles/options - pots & pans, heavy, normal, fast, rinse & hold, delay start, heated dry on/off

wash spray system - four-level - dual spray arms, the bottom rotates and sprays water up, the top rotates and sprays water up and down, on the top the water is sprayed down and to the sides

features - The interior tub and door liner are constructed of stainless steel. The door latch is easy to release and is combined with a built-in child safety lock.

TAPPAN, 6000 Perimeter Dr., Dublin, OH 43017 - (800) 537-5530

number of pumps/gal - one/7.6 gal

internal water heater/temp. - yes/140°

racks - nylon coated

internal food disposer - yes

cycles/options - pots & pans, heavy, normal, light, rinse & hold, delay start, heated dry on/off

wash spray system - three-level - lower level is a wash arm that rotates with nine nozzles spraying upward, the tower has three nozzles that spray out and up, the upper level sprays water down

features - The lower rack has a fold down rack to hold big items and the upper rack has a cup shelf.

VIKING RANGE CORP., PO Drawer 956, 111 Front St., Greenwood, MS 38930 - (601) 455-1200

number of pumps/gal - two/5.3 gal

internal water heater/temp. - yes/165°

racks - graphite nylon coated

internal food disposer - no

cycles/options - pots & pans, normal, light/china, rinse & hold, plate warm, delay start, heated dry on/off

wash spray system - four-level - lower level is a wash arm that rotates and sprays up, the upper level turns in the opposite direction and sprays water up and down

features -The tank and inner door are made of stainless steel. The upper rack has two dual-level cup racks and the left side holds stemware to prevent movement during washing. There is triple-layer insulation of asphalt/felt/foil on the top, back and both sides of the tank.

WHIRLPOOL CORP., 2303 Pipestone Rd., Benton Harbor, MI 49022 - (800) 253-1301

number of pumps/gal - one/7.6 gal

internal water heater/temp. - yes/140°

racks - nylon coated

internal food disposer - yes

cycles/options - pots & pans, heavy, normal, hi temp, light, china, rinse & hold, delay start, heated dry on/off

wash spray system - three-level - two full-size spray arms reach every part of the inside and in the door silverware basket, an upper rack tower and a special deflector on the top creates a showering action

features - The racks on the top are adjustable. Adjust them upward for larger platters or pizza pans on the bottom or lower them to hold long-stemmed or larger glasses in the top.

WHITE WESTINGHOUSE, 6000 Perimeter Dr., Dublin, OH 43017 - (800) 245-0600

number of pumps/gal - one/7.6 gal

internal water heater/temp. - yes/140°

racks - nylon coated

internal food disposer - yes

cycles/options - pots & pans, heavy, normal, light, rinse & hold, delay start, heated dry on/off

wash spray system - three-level - lower level is a wash arm that rotates with nine nozzles spraying upward, the tower has three nozzles that spray out and up, the upper level sprays water down

features - The utensil basket has compartments with snap down lids to hold small items so they stay in place in the washer. The upper rack comes with utensil basket, fold down cup shelf and divider.

Q: For Christmas, I want to get my mother some new cooking gadget, like an automatic complete breakfast maker or bread maker. Do these cooking appliances use much more energy than using the range or ovens?

A: Most countertop cooking appliances use much less energy than your range and large oven. A typical oven uses more than 3,000 watts, compared to about 1,300 watts for a small countertop roaster/cooker. Rangetop elements vary from about 1,250 watts to 2,250 watts.

One of the newest cooking gadgets is an automatic "breakfast express" machine that makes a complete breakfast. You put in two eggs (still in their shells), two pieces of bread, and enough coffee and water for one to four cups.

Set its alarm timer to wake you and turn on the unit. It automatically opens the shells and fries the eggs, toasts the bread (light to dark settings), and brews the coffee, all in ten minutes. The electric usage is about 1,500 watts, much less than using the range, toaster, and coffee maker.

Automatic bread makers are also energy and time savers. You put all the ingredients for making a loaf of bread into the bread maker. In about 2.5 to 4.0 hours, depending on the loaf size and type of bread,

you have a fully baked loaf of homemade bread.

You can select the darkness of the crust from light to dark. There are preprogrammed automatic bake settings for different types of breads and recipes. Some bread makers have up to eight settings for basic white, quick baking, raisin, french, dough only, cake, jam, and homemade.

Makes square or round loaf of bread

Viewing window

Kneading hook inside

Automatic controls and timer

Heavily insulated walls for efficient baking

Mixes, kneads, rises, and bakes automatically

These bread makers use from about 400 to 800 watts during the baking cycle and very little electricity for the kneading and rising cycles. With no preheating, as required with a standard oven, the energy cost is about only 10 cents per loaf, depending on the type of bread.

Many other countertop appliances, particularly automatic potato bakers, are efficient. An automatic

potato baker bakes one or two potatoes in less than 30 minutes at only 900 watts, less wattage and time than your oven. They taste like real baked potatoes, not like ones "nuked" in a microwave.

A "cookie factory" is another convenient and efficient alternative to oven baking. Special non-stick pans with patterns recessed in them make shaped cookies without rolling and cutting. It uses 850 watts and makes nine gingerbread men cookies in eight minutes.

Q: I plan to install a sunroom (greenhouse) kit on the south side of my house. How do I determine how many roof vents to order?

A: Unfortunately, there is no simple rule of thumb to help you. A sunroom can easily overheat in the summer sun, especially on the south side. The heat gain depends on many variables specific to your individual house. Even on mild winter days, a sunroom can get uncomfortably warm.

You should consult the sunroom kit manufacturers for their recommendations. If the roof vents seal well when they are closed, it will not hurt to install more than you think that you will need. It will cost a little more initially, but it is cheaper to install them now than later if it overheats.

There are many efficient convenience appliances now available. The types of products that each manufacturer offers, the electricity usage, and the cost per use of each is listed on pages 223 and 224. Keep in mind that many of these countertop appliances have on-off thermostats built into them. Since the heating elements are off much of the time, they actually use less electricity than the listed wattages would indicate. A toaster oven or roaster set on a lower temperature uses less electricity than on a higher temperature. The slow cooker made by Presto has a very high wattage rating (also used as a deep fryer). Its high output heating elements are just off for longer periods of time.

You can easily calculate how much it costs to operate any electric appliance. You just multiply the rated wattage (usually on the name plate or label) by the number of hours you use it. Multiply that answer by the electric rate ($/kilowatt-hour) in your area and divide it by 1,000 to get the cost in dollars. As an example, a slow cooker that uses an average of 250 watts of electricity, costs 16 cents for an eight-hour cooking cycle. The calculation is as follows - 250 watts x 8 hours x $.08 per kilowatt-hour ÷ 1,000.

On pages 222 and 223, I have replaced the *"cost per use"* figures for the bread makers with their suggested retail price. Since the baking cycle length varies by more than an hour, depending on the type of bread you are making, an estimate would not be appropriate. These are suggested retail prices and you will generally find them less expensive at most retail outlets.

— —

Manufacturers of Efficient Countertop Cooking Appliances

appliance type	wattage	minutes per use	cost per use
BLACK & DECKER, 6 Armstrong Rd., Shelton, CT 06484 - (800) 231-9786 (203) 926-3000			
Electric tea kettle	1500 watts	5 min.	$ 0.01 / use
Steamer/cooker	650 watts	40 min.	$ 0.03 / use
Waffle Baker	550-900 watts	3 min.	$ 0.01 / use
CUISINART, 150 Milford Rd., E. Windsor, NJ 08520 - (800) 726-0190			
Electric tea kettle	1500 watts	5 min.	$ 0.01 / use
DAZEY, One Dazey Circle, Industrial Airport, KS 66031 - (800) 255-6120 (913) 782-7500			
Griddle	1500 watts	10 min.	$ 0.02 / use
Indoor grill	1500 watts	15 min.	$ 0.03 / use
Pick-A-Pocket	1000 watts	10 min.	$ 0.01 / use
Skillet	1200 watts	30 min.	$ 0.05 / use
Slow cooker/fryer	1400 watts	8 hours	$ 0.19 / use
Steamer/cooker	1400 watts	40 min.	$ 0.07 / use
Waffle baker	1000 watts	3 min.	$ 0.01 / use
DELONGHI, 625 Washington Ave., Cartlstadt, NJ 07072 - (800) 322-3848 (201) 507-1110			
Indoor grill	1500 watts	15 min.	$ 0.03 / use
FABERWARE, INC., 1500 Bassett Ave., Bronx, NY 10461 - (718) 863-8000			
Electric tea kettle	1500 watts	5 min.	$ 0.01 / use
Griddle	1440 watts	10 min.	$ 0.02 / use
Indoor grill	1175 watts	15 min.	$ 0.02 / use
Skillet	1250-1500 watts	30 min.	$ 0.05-0.06 / use - 3 models
Steamer/cooker 1	500 watts	40 min.	$ 0.08 / use
Wok	1200 watts	10 min.	$ 0.02 / use
HITACHI, 3890 Steve Reynolds Blvd., Norcross, GA 30093 - (800) 448-2244			
Bread maker	810 watts	2 hours and 50 min.	*$349.99
MAVERICK INDUSTRIES, 265 Rariton Center Parkway, Edison, NJ 08837 - (908) 417-9666			
Indoor grill	750-1200 watts	15 min.	$ 0.01-0.02 / use - 6 models
Steamer/cooker	700 watts	40 min.	$ 0.04 / use
MR. COFFEE, 24700 Miles Rd., Bedford Heights, OH 44146 - (800) 321-0370 (216) 464-4000			
Iced tea pot	700 watts	10 min.	$ 0.01 / use
Potato baker	900 watts	30 min.	$ 0.04 / use

* Suggested retail price. See above for discussion of costs to operate bread maker.

Manufacturers of Efficient Countertop Cooking Appliances

appliance type	wattage	minutes per use	cost per use

NESCO, THE METAL WARE CORP., PO Box 237, Two Rivers, WI 54241 - (414) 793-1368

Steamer/cooker	600 watts	40 min.	$ 0.03 / use

PANASONIC, One Panasonic Way, Secaucus, NY 07094 - (201) 348-7000

Bread maker	410-630 watts	4 hours	*$279 to $400
Steamer/cooker	450-630 watts	40 min.	$ 0.03 / use

PRESTO, 3925 N. Hastings Way, Eau Claire, WI 54703 - (715) 839-2121

Electric tea kettle	750 watts	5 min.	$ 0.01 / use
Griddle	1000-1500 watts	10 min.	$ 0.01-0.02 / use - 3 models
Skillet	1000-1300 watts	30 min.	$ 0.04-0.05 / use - 3 models
Slow cooker/fryer	1300 watts	8 hours	$ 0.19 / use

REGAL WARE, 1675 Reigle Dr., Kewaskum, WI 53040 - (414) 626-2121

Breadmaker	430 watts	2 hours & 20 min.	*$349.95
Indoor grill	1175 watts	15 min.	$ 0.02 / use
Hot pot	500 watts	5 min.	$ 0.01 / use

RIVAL, 800 E. 109 Terrace, Kansas City, MO 64129 - (816) 943-4100

Cookie Factory	850 watts	8 min.	$ 0.01 / use
Hot pot	750 watts	5 min	$ 0.01 / use
Indoor grill	830 watts	15 min.	$ 0.02 / use
Skillet	1000-1250 watts	30 min.	$ 0.04-0.05 / use - 2 models
Slow cooker	250 watts	8 hours	$ 0.16 / use
Steamer/cooker	600 watts	40 min.	$ 0.03 / use

SALTON, 550 Business Center Dr., Mt. Prospect, IL 60056 - (800) 233-9054 (708) 803-4600

Breadmaker	550 watts	2 hrs & 20 min.	*$150.00 to $200.00
Sandwich maker	600 watts	10 min.	$ 0.01 / use
Skillet	1200 watts	30 min.	$ 0.05 / use
Steamer/cooker	800 watts	40 min.	$ 0.04 / use
Waffle baker	760 watts	3 min.	$ 0.01 / use
Wok	1600 watts	10 min.	$ 0.02 / use

SUNBEAM-OSTER, PO Box 247, Laurel, MS 39441 - (800) 597-5978 (601) 425-7800

Indoor grill	800-1000 watts	15 min.	$ 0.02 / use - 5 models
Steamer/cooker	800 watts	40 min.	$ 0.04 / use
Waffle baker	625 watts	3 min.	$ 0.01 / use

TOASTMASTER, 1801 N. Stadium Blvd., Columbia, MO 65202 - (800) 947-3744 (314) 445-8666

Bread maker	550 watts	3 hours and 40 min.	*$200.00 to $250.00
Griddle	1400 watts	10 min.	$ 0.02 / use
Indoor grill	1200 watts	15 min.	$ 0.02 / use
Snackster	850-900 watts	10 min.	$ 0.01 / use - 2 models
Waffle baker	650-1400 watts	3 min.	$ 0.01 / use - 9 models

WEST BEND, 400 Washington Street, West Bend, WI 53095 - (414) 334-2311

Bread maker	575 watts	3 hours and 40 min.	*$179.95
Egg cooker	600 watts	5 min.	$ 0.01 / use
Electric tea kettle	1000 -1500 watts	5 min.	$ 0.01 / use - 2 models
Fondue pot	600 watts	10 min.	$ 0.01 / use
Griddle	1300-1470 watts	10 min.	$ 0.02 / use - 2 models
Hot pot	600 watts	5 min.	$ 0.01 / use
Skillet	1200-1300 watts	30 min.	$ 0.05 / use - 9 models
Slow cooker	200-300 watts	8 hours.	$ 0.13-0.19 / use - 9 models
Steamer/cooker	600 watts	40 min.	$ 0.03 / use
Wok	1000-1500 watts	10 min.	$ 0.01-0.02 / use - 4 models

WELBILT APPLIANCE, PO Box 3618, New Hyde Park, NY 11042 - (516) 365-5040

Bread maker	650-750 watts	4 hours	*$99.99 to $289.99
Breakfast express	280-1,540 watts	10 min.	*$469.99

ZOJIRUSHI, 5628 Bandini Blvd., Bell, CA 90210 - (800) 733-6270 (213) 264 6270

Bread maker	500 watts	3 hours and 50 min.	*$249.95 to $349.95
Steamer/cooker	600-930 watts	40 min.	$ 0.03-0.05 / use - 6 models

Features of Automatic Bread & Dough Makers

Manufacturer	West Bend	Panasonic		Hitachi	
Model #	41040	SD-BT55P	SD-BT10P	HB-B101	HB-B201
Loaf Size	1 & 1.5-lb.	1-lb.	1-lb.	.5, 1, 1.5-lb.	.5, 1, 1.5-lb.
Loaf Shape	Tall Square	Rectangular	Rectangular	Tall Square	Tall Square
Bread Pan Capacity	93-oz.	65-oz.	65-oz.	100-oz.	100-oz.
Machine Dimensions	13-in. high / 13-in. wide / 9.5-in. deep	13-in. High / 14-in. Wide / 9.5-in. Deep	12-in. High / 9-in. Wide / 11-in. Deep	13.6-in. High / 10-in. Wide / 14.4-in. Deep	13.6-in. High / 10-in. Wide / 14.4-in. Deep
#Bake Settings/ Description	Six/ Basic, Basic Rapid, Whole Wheat, Whole Wheat Rapid, French, Sweet	Four/ Basic Bake, Basic Rapid, Whole Wheat, Whole Wheat Rapid	Four/ Basic Bake, Basic Rapid, Whole Wheat, Whole Wheat Rapid	Four/ Bread, Bread Rapid, Mix Bread, Dough	Five/ Bread, Bread Rapid, Mix Bread, Rice, Jam
Shortest Loaf Time	3-Hrs.	3-Hrs.	3-Hrs.	2-Hrs. 50-Min.	2-Hrs. 50 Min.
Longest Loaf Time	4-Hrs. 20-Min.	5-Hrs.	5-Hrs.	4-Hrs. 20 Min.	4-Hrs. 20-Min.
Delay Start/Max Time	Yes/13 Hrs.	Yes/13 Hrs.	Yes/13 Hrs.	Yes/13 Hrs.	Yes/13 Hrs.
Dough Cycle	Yes	Yes	Yes	Yes	Yes
Keep-Warm Cycle	Yes, 3-Hrs.	Yes, 1 Hr.	Yes, 1 Hr.	Yes, 30-Min.	Yes, 30-Min.
Crust Color Control	3 Settings for Light,Med,Dark	1 Setting for Basic Light Only	1 Setting for Basic Light Only	2 Settings for Light, Dark	3 Settings for Light,Med,Dark

Manufacturer	Regal		Zojirushi		Welbilt	
Model #	K-6773	K-6774	BBCC-S15	BBCC-N15	ABM-100	ABM-300
Loaf Size	1 & 1.5-lb.	1-lb.	.5, 1.0, 1.5-lb.	.5, 1.0, 1.5-lb.	1.5-lb.	1.0-lb.
Loaf Shape	Tall Square	Tall Square	Tall Square	Tall Square	Round	Round
Bread Pan Capacity	78-oz.	70-oz.	94-oz.	94-oz.	92-oz.	92-oz.
Machine Dimensions	13-in. High / 13-in. Wide / 9-in. Deep	13-in. High / 13-in. Wide / 9-in. Deep	14-in. High / 8.5-in. Wide / 14.5-in. Deep	14-in. High / 8.5-in. Wide / 14.5 in. Deep	14.5-in. High / 11.5-in. Wide / 12-in. Deep	14.5-in. High / 11.5-in. Wide / 12-in. Deep
#Bake Settings/ Description	Three/ French, Dough, Sweet	One/ Baking	Eight/ Basic White, Quick Baking, Raisin,French, Dough, Cake,Jam, Homemade	Six/ Dough, White Bread (Dry Milk), White Bread (Fresh Milk), Raisin Bread (Dry Milk), Raisin Bread (Fresh Milk), Sweet Bread/Cake	Three/ White Bread, French Bread, Sweet Bread	Three/ White Bread, French Bread, Sweet Bread
Shortest Loaf Time	2-Hrs. 20-Min.	2-Hrs. 20-Min.	2-Hrs. 50 Min.	2-Hrs. 50 Min.	4-Hrs.	2-Hrs. 15-Min.
Longest Loaf Time	3-Hrs. 40-Min.	2-Hrs. 20-Min.	4-Hrs. 30 Min.	4-Hrs. 30 Min.	4-Hrs. 40-Min.	4-Hrs. 40-Min.
Delay Start/Max Time	Yes/13 Hrs.	No	Yes/13 Hrs.	Yes/13 Hrs.	Yes/12 Hrs.	Yes/12 Hrs.
Dough Cycle	Yes	No	Yes	Yes	Yes	Yes
Keep-Warm Cycle	Yes, 1 Hr.	Yes, 1-Hr.	No	No	Yes, 30-Min.	No
Crust Color Control	2 Settings for Light & Dark	No	3 Settings for Light,Med,Dark	3 Settings for Light,Med,Dark	2 Settings for Light & Dark	3 Settings for Light,Med,Dark

Q: I am considering painting my house with the same type of insulating paint used on the space shuttle. Can this type of paint really lower my utility bills? Can I roll it on like ordinary paint?

A: You are referring to "ceramic-filled" paint and it is ideal for use on houses. It is available in many grades of exterior, interior wall, and roof paints that can lower your heating and cooling costs.

This paint is not actually used on space shuttles, but it contains the same type of insulating ceramic particles in the shuttles' heat shield tiles. On your house exterior or interior walls, it looks just like ordinary paint.

Ceramic-filled paints use durable water-based acrylic paint with fine ceramic particles (often borosilicate) mixed in it. These are tiny hollow ceramic spheres, several times smaller in diameter than a human hair.

Ceramic materials possess unique heat-resistant and insulation properties. They block heat radiation (loss or gain) and they dissipate heat rapidly. You can hold a cigarette lighter under a metal strip coated with ceramic-filled paint and touch the top of the metal strip without getting burned.

With ceramic paint on your indoor walls, heat that is normally lost through the wall is reflected back indoors. This not only reduces your heating bills, but it makes you feel warmer in the winter and cooler in the summer. This also allows you to set your thermostat back and save more energy.

In the summer, you get the greatest reduction in air-conditioning costs and improvement in comfort by painting the exterior of your house with ceramic-filled paint. Painting your existing roof with a light color is effective for lowering cooling costs and it can increase the life of your shingles.

You can roll, brush, or spray on ceramic-filled paint. You apply it several times thicker (10-dry mils) than ordinary wall paint. The thicker layer helps seal tiny cracks to block outdoor and indoor noise transmission. The ceramic paint particles themselves are a very good sound insulator.

There are several new types of non-ceramic "easily cleanable" flat wall paints available. These can save energy because the walls remain bright for years. A clean bright wall reflects more light, so you need fewer lamps turned on.

One type of easy to clean paint, called Ever-clean, has a unique non-porous surface, although it looks like ordinary wall paint. Typical stains, like crayons, coffee, grease, etc., wipe right off. Another paint, called Silken Touch, has fine teflon particles in it to reject dirt and stains.

Q: I replaced my incandescent bulbs in my garage/work area to reduce my electric bills. Sometimes, late at night, they tend to flicker. Why?

A: Your fluorescent lights probably are flickering because it is colder at night than during the day, and they do not operate well at colder temperatures. The problem will probably disappear in the summer.

Fluorescent lights are much more efficient than your old lights. Because they are more efficient, they give off less heat into the room. This is a real advantage in a small garage in the summer. Installing several two-tube fixtures is best with pull chain switches. This allows you to turn on only as many as you need.

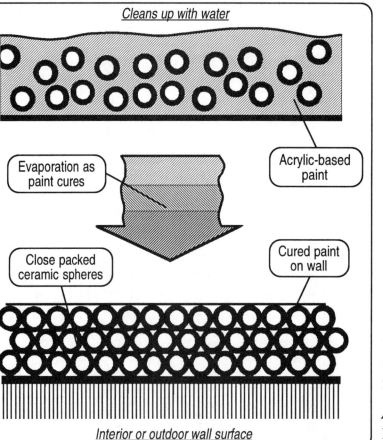

Cleans up with water
Evaporation as paint cures
Acrylic-based paint
Close packed ceramic spheres
Cured paint on wall
Interior or outdoor wall surface

New types of paints can help make your house more energy efficient. Ceramic-filled paints actually increase the effective insulation value of your house (interior and exterior). The new wall paints stay clean. A clean wall absorbs less light than a dirty wall, so you will need fewer lights turned on with this paint.

The manufacturers of ceramic-filled paint are listed below along with the thickness of the cured paint. Thickness is measured in mils (one mil is equal to 1/100 of an inch.)

Most of these paints use hollow borosilicate ceramic spheres. This is the same material used on the space shuttle heat tiles (see illustration). Super Therm by Moore, uses several different types of flat ceramic particles for higher efficiency. This requires less paint thickness. This gives you more wall coverage per gallon. With a typical interior wall coating of 8 dry mils, you can expect a coverage of about 125 sq. ft. per gallon. Heavier coverage is often used on the exterior, especially on rough masonry, which yields 75 to 125 sq. ft. per gallon.

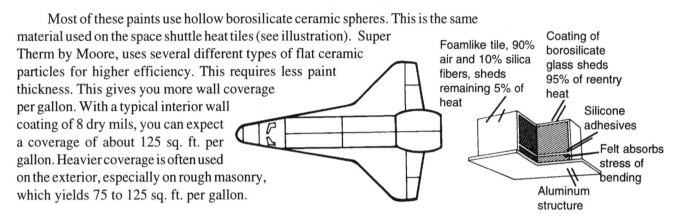

The thickness listed below gives you some idea of the relative coverage of the various manufacturers' paints. Also a thicker coating tends to fill small cracks and may block noise better. The bottom of page 227 shows typical application instructions and page 228 shows background information on the benefits of indoor and outdoor use of ceramic-filled paint.

Several manufacturers of paints that clean easily are shown on page 227. The Ever-Clean paint by Sherwin Williams has a non-porous surface to eliminate stains and dirt. It is available in flat or satin wall paint. It looks like ordinary paint on your walls. The teflon-filled paint by Porter also resists dirt. The Benjamin-Moore paint allows you to paint over a dirty old glossy surface.

Manufacturers of Ceramic-Filled Paints

CERAMA-TECH INTNL., 1646 Via del Mesonero, San Diego, CA 92173 - (619) 690-0773
name - "Cerama-Tech" thickness - 8 dry mils

E.E.R. INTERNATIONAL, 3000 N.E. 30th Pl. #411, Ft. Lauderdale, FL 33309 - (305) 561-4244
name - "Ceramicoat" thickness - 10 dry mils

HYDRO-THERM, 3701 Rio Grande, Amarillo, TX 79104 - (800) 766-2066 (806) 372-1255
name - "Hydro-Therm" thickness - 10 dry mils

INSULATED COATINGS CORP., 956 S. Hwy. 41, Inverness, FL 32650 - (800) 345-5306
name - "Astec" thickness - 8 dry mils

KEY SOLUTIONS, P.O. Box 5090, Scottsdale, AZ 85261 - (800) 776-9765
name - "Therm-O-Flex" thickness - 9 dry mils

MOORE INDUST. COATINGS, P.O. Box 832, Boring, OR 97009 - (800) 448-6697 (503) 665-8344
name - "Super Therm" thickness - 7 dry mils

SPM THERMO-SHIELD, Rt. 2 - Box 208A, Custer, SD 57730 - (605) 673-3201
name - "Thermo-Shield" thickness - 5 dry mils

SUPERIOR PRODUCTS INTNL., 6459 Universal Ave., Kansas City, MO 64120 - (816) 241-1976
name - "Super Therm" thickness - 7 dry mils

* Manufacturers of Easily Cleanable Wall Paints and Other New Paints

BENJAMIN MOORE, 4400 E. 71st St., Cleveland, OH 44105 - (216) 341-1611
"Regal Aquagrip" - primer allows you to put latex directly over glossy surface

PORTER PAINTS, 400 S. 13th St., Louisville, KY 40203 - (502) 588-9200
"Silken Touch" - paint has fine teflon particles in it to reject dirt

SHERWIN-WILLIAMS CO., 101 Prospect Ave., Cleveland, OH 44115 - (216) 566-2000
"EverClean" - non-porous surface resists stains and dirt

* Contact retail outlets of these paint manufacturers for local prices

---

Typical Ceramic-Filled Paint Application Instructions

Primers:

No primer is usually required.   Follow instructions for proper application and film buildup.

Surface Preparation:

All surfaces must be clean and free from dust, dirt, oil, and grease. Minimally, all house exterior surfaces should be cleaned with a power washer prior to coating.

Color:

Tinting many be achieved with Thermo-Shield wall coating by the addition of universal colorants. Darker colors reduce the reflectivity and emissivity of the surface.

Theoretical Coverage:

132 square feet per gallon at 5 mils dry film thickness and no loss

Drying Time:

To set - 20 minutes
To recoat - 4 hours
Complete - 12 hours (at 75° F and 50% relative humidity)

Thinning:

None required. Clean water in small amounts (up to one pint per gallon) may be added to replace evaporation losses or to adjust for spray equipment.

Equipment:

Roll or airless spray applications is recommended. Small areas may be brushed. When Thermo-Shield wall coating is applied by brushing, two coats are required applying both coats in the same direction.

Airless Spray:

Tip orifice - .031 inches
Atomizing pressure - 2200-2500 psi
Fan spread - 60 degrees

Cleanup:

Clean tools and equipment with warm soapy water. Rinse with clean water.

EverClean™
Interior Latex Flat Wall Paint
A96 Series

SURFACE PREPARATION

STEEL
RUST AND MILL SCALE MUST BE REMOVED USING SANDPAPER, STEEL WOOL, OR OTHER ABRADING METHOD. BARE STEEL MUST BE PRIMED THE SAME DAY AS CLEANED.

WOOD
SAND ANY EXPOSED WOOD TO A FRESH SURFACE. PATCH ALL NAIL HOLES AND IMPERFECTIONS WITH A WOOD FILLER OR PUTTY AND SAND SMOOTH.

MILDEW
MILDEW MUST BE REMOVED BEFORE PAINTING BY WASHING WITH A SOLUTION OF 1 QT. HOUSEHOLD BLEACH AND 3 QTS. OF WARM WATER. APPLY THE SOLUTION AND SCRUB THE MILDEWED AREA. ALLOW THE SOLUTION TO REMAIN ON THE SURFACE FOR 10 MINUTES. RINSE THOROUGHLY WITH CLEAN WATER AND ALLOW THE SURFACE TO DRY 48 HOURS BEFORE PAINTING. WEAR RUBBER GLOVES AND PROTECTIVE CLOTHING. **DO NOT ADD DETERGENTS OR AMMONIA TO THE BLEACH SOLUTION.**

CARE AND WASHING INSTRUCTIONS

TO ASSURE MAXIMUM WASHABILITY AND DURABILITY WAIT AT LEAST TWO WEEKS BEFORE WASHING THE DRY PAINT FILM. WHEN REMOVING STAINS, DIRT AND MARKS, USE A SOFT CLOTH OR SPONGE WITH WATER OR A GENERAL PURPOSE HOUSEHOLD CLEANER. STUBBORN STAINS MAY REQUIRE THE USE OF AN AMMONIATED HOUSEHOLD CLEANER FOR TOTAL REMOVAL. DO NOT USE AN ABRASIVE CLEANER OR SCRUB BRUSH TO REMOVE STAINS.

APPLICATION

BRUSH
NO REDUCTION NECESSARY. USE A NYLON BRUSH.

ROLLER
NO REDUCTION NECESSARY. USE A 3/8" NAP SYNTHETIC ROLLER COVER ONLY.

PAD
NO REDUCTION NECESSARY.

SPRAY - AIRLESS
PRESSURE .... 2000 PSI
TIP .... .017-.021"
REDUCTION .... NONE

SPRAY - CONVENTIONAL
NOT RECOMMENDED

CLEANUP INFORMATION

CLEAN SPILLS AND SPATTERS IMMEDIATELY WITH SOAP AND WARM WATER. CLEAN HANDS AND TOOLS IMMEDIATELY AFTER USE WITH SOAP AND WARM WATER. FLUSH SPRAY EQUIPMENT AFTER CLEANING WITH MINERAL SPIRITS TO PREVENT RUSTING OF THE EQUIPMENT. FOLLOW MANUFACTURER'S SAFETY RECOMMENDATIONS WHEN USING MINERAL SPIRITS.

LABEL ANALYSIS
A96W24

PIGMENT BY WEIGHT	46.1%
TITANIUM DIOXIDE	21.2%
SILICA/SILICATES	24.9%
VEHICLE BY WEIGHT	53.9%
ACRYLIC RESIN	12.1%
WATER	35.5%
ADDITIVES	6.3%
TOTAL	100%

CAUTIONS

DO NOT APPLY BELOW 50° F.

NON-PHOTOCHEMICALLY REACTIVE.

PROTECT FROM FREEZING.

SEE LABEL FOR ADDITIONAL CAUTIONS.

CAUTIONS
CONTAINS CRYSTALLINE SILICA
Use only with adequate ventilation. To avoid overexposure, open windows and doors or use other means to ensure fresh air entry during application and drying. If you experience eye watering, headaches, or dizziness, increase fresh air, or wear respiratory protection (NIOSH/MSHA TC23C or equivalent) or leave the area.
Adequate ventilation required when sanding or abrading the dried film. If adequate ventilation cannot be provided wear an approved particulate respirator (NIOSH/MSHA TC21C or equivalent). Follow respirator manufacturer's directions for respirator use.
Avoid contact with eyes and skin. Wash hands after using. Keep container closed when not in use. Do not transfer contents to other containers for storage.
FIRST AID: In case of eye contact, flush thoroughly with large amounts of water. Get medical attention if irritation persists. If swallowed, get medical attention immediately.
DELAYED EFFECTS FROM LONG TERM OVEREXPOSURE: Abrading or sanding of the dry film may release crystalline silica which has been shown to cause lung damage and cancer under long term exposure.
DO NOT TAKE INTERNALLY. KEEP OUT OF THE REACH OF CHILDREN.

GB48 (11/93)

Q: Even with our air conditioner running, the sun still bakes us, especially in second-story rooms. Are there any methods to use the sun's intense heat to help cool our house in the summer?

A: The same intense heat from the sun that bakes you can be used to cool your house for free. Solar power is an ideal fit with cooling because the greatest amount of solar energy is available during the hottest times.

There are new solar-powered devices that use the sun's heat to cool and dehumidify your house. These bring in fresh dehumidified outdoor air. In the winter, the solar heat also can be used to heat your home for free.

Since the incoming fresh air is not humid, your air conditioner needs to run less. The drier air also allows you to set your thermostat a little higher and still be comfortable. This saves even more electricity.

One new system, made by New Thermal Technologies, uses free heat from solar collectors to dry out (recharge) a slowly rotating desiccant wheel. A desiccant is a material which readily absorbs moisture. The only cost to run this unit is the electricity for a small motor and blowers.

As humid fresh outdoor air is drawn across the solar recharged desiccant, it is dehumidified before it enters your home. In some climates, a small amount of moisture is reintroduced into the air stream for evaporative cooling.

Stapling reinforced reflective foil under your roof rafters provides double solar cooling. First, foil blocks heat transfer from the hot roof to the ceiling below. In my own

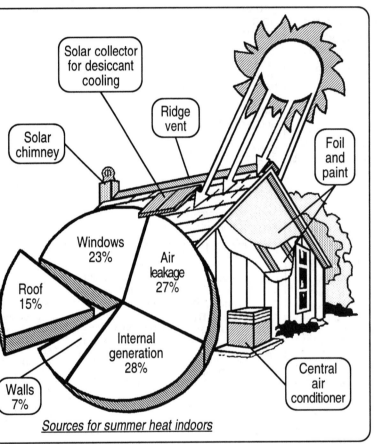

Solar collector for desiccant cooling

Ridge vent

Solar chimney

Foil and paint

Windows 23%

Air leakage 27%

Roof 15%

Internal generation 28%

Walls 7%

Central air conditioner

Sources for summer heat indoors

home, it lowered my bedroom temperature by 10 degrees.

Second, the solar heated air, between the roof and foil, naturally flows up and out roof vents. This draws cool air in the lower soffit overhang vents to cool the roof. It is important to install the roof vents near the peak. A continuous ridge vent is best.

If you use the least expensive single-sided foil (about $.09 per sq.

ft. with a kraft paper backing), face the shiny side down. It will not be dulled by dust buildup over time. Applying special heat reflective attic paint on the underside of the roof reduces heat transfer downward. Just apply it from inside the attic to the sheathing.

The sun shining on a simple do-it-yourself wooden solar chimney creates a natural upward draft. Extend the chimney from above the roof down to a room ceiling. Adding a clear window and insulation increases the draft.

Q: I have older double-hung windows in my house with counterbalance weights inside the frame. How can I insulate this cavity in the frame without interfering with the movement of the weights?

A: One effective method is to install 1-½ inch plastic pipe for the weights to slide in. Pull the trim loose from the frame to get access to the cavity. Cut the appropriate lengths of pipe. Drop the weights, with the ropes attached, into the pipes. Pack insulation around the pipes.

Another option is to remove the weights and pack the entire frame cavity with insulation. Install spring-type sash guides that will hold the window in any open position. Sash guide kits are available at many hardware stores.

Several natural methods to help cool your house are reflective attic foil, lo-emissivity attic paint, attic ventilation, a solar chimney, and a solar-powered dehumidifier/cooler.

Manufacturers and prices of reflective attic foil and vents are shown on page 231. Figure #2 on this page shows how foil is stapled under the roof rafters. Instead of foil, you can spray low-emissivity silver paint on the underside of the roof sheathing. This paint, Lo/Mit-1, is made by Solar Energy Corporation (SOLEC), Box 3065, Princeton, NJ 08543 - (609) 883-7700.

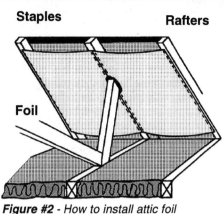

Staples   **Rafters**

Foil

Figure #2 - How to install attic foil

Adequate roof ventilation, especially if you install foil or paint, is very important. The chart below shows the recommended amount of roof vent area. A list of roof ridge vent manufacturers are shown on page 231. A solar chimney (page 232) naturally draws hot air out of your house and creates a breeze.

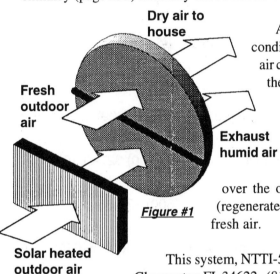

Dry air to house

Fresh outdoor air

Exhaust humid air

Figure #1

Solar heated outdoor air

A solar-powered desiccant system can reduce the load on your air conditioner. It provides fresh dehumidified outdoor air into your home. Your air conditioner has to run less because it does not have to dehumidify also. All the electricity used goes to cooling.

Figure #1 shows how a desiccant works. A desiccant is a material that naturally attracts moisture. As fresh outdoor air is drawn across one half of the desiccant wheel, the moisture is sucked out of it. This dehumidified air flows into your house. Dry solar-heated air is blown over the other moisture-laden half of the desiccant wheel and this dries it out (regenerates it). This wheel slowly rotates to continually dehumidify more incoming fresh air.

This system, NTTI-500S, is made by New Thermal Technologies, 12900 Automobile Blvd., Clearwater, FL 34622 - (813) 571-1888. The company can help you to determine the payback period from the electricity savings. If you are installing a totally new central air conditioning system, you can install a smaller A/C unit if you also install a NTTI solar unit. The total installed combination system cost will be about the same as just installing a larger central A/C unit.

Recommended Net Free Vent Area for Attics - (sq. in.)

	Attic Width in feet										
		20	**22**	**24**	**26**	**28**	**30**	**32**	**34**	**36**	**38**	**40**
Attic Length in feet	**20**	192	211	230	269	288	307	326	348	365	384	403
	24	230	253	276	300	323	346	369	392	415	438	481
	28	269	296	323	349	376	403	430	484	511	538	564
	32	307	338	369	399	430	461	492	522	553	584	614
	36	346	380	415	449	484	518	553	588	622	657	691
	40	384	422	461	499	538	576	614	653	691	730	768
	44	422	465	507	549	591	634	676	718	760	803	845
	48	461	507	553	599	645	691	737	783	829	876	922
	52	499	549	599	649	699	749	799	848	898	948	998
	56	538	591	645	699	753	807	860	914	967	1021	1075
	60	576	634	691	749	807	864	922	979	1037	1094	1152

Manufacturers of Continuous Ridge or Soffit Vents

AIR VENT INC., 4801 N. Prospect Rd., Peoria Hts., IL 61614 - (800) 247-8368 (309) 688-5020
"Filter Vent" - $20 for 10 ft. section

BENJAMIN OBDYKE, J. Fitch Indust. Park, Warminster, PA 18974 - (800) 458-2309
"Roll Vent" - $49.95 for 20 ft. roll

COBRA VENTILATION CO., 1361 Alps Rd., Wayne, NJ 07470 - (800) 688-6654
"Cobra Ridge Vent" - $45 for 20 ft. roll

COR-A-VENT INC., P.O. Box 428, Mishawaka, IN 46546 - (800) 837-8368 (219) 255-1910
"Cor-A-Vent" - $12 for 4 ft. section

LOMANCO, P.O. Box 519, Jacksonville, AR 72078 - (800) 643-5596 (501) 982-6511
"SOV-4" - 17.89 for 4 ft. section

Manufacturers of Do-it-Yourself Reflective Attic Foils

AAE SYSTEMS INC., 780 Camino de la Reina #149, San Diego, CA 92108 - (619) 296-0970
price - n/a

ADVANCED FOIL SYSTEMS, 4471 E. Santa Ana St. #F, Ontario, CA 91761 - (909) 390-5125
price - $.15/sq. ft.

DENNY SALES CORP., 3500 Gateway Dr., Pompano Beach, FL 33069 - (800) 327-6616
price - $.12/sq. ft.

INNOVATIVE ENERGY, 1119 W. 145th Ave., Crown Point, IN 46307 - (800) 776-3645
price - n/a

INNOVATIVE INSULATION, 6200 W. Pioneer Pkwy., Arlington, TX 76013 - (800) 825-0123
price - $.15 - .25/sq. ft.

KEY SOLUTIONS, 7529 E. Woodshire Cove, Scottsdale, AZ 85258 - (800) 776-9765
price - n/a

LAMOTITE, 2909 E. 79th St., Cleveland, OH 44104 - (800) 841-1234
price - $.15/sq. ft.

RABAR PRODUCTS INC., 3243 Blair St., Cocoa, FL 32926 - (407) 636-4104
price - $.12/sq. ft.

RICH'S ENTERPRISES, 2734 El Dorado Pl., Snellville, GA 30278 - (404) 979-9671
price - $.15 - .25/sq. ft.

RISI, P.O. Box 2846, Wichita, KS 67201 - (800) 798-3645 (316) 265-6712
price - $.15 - .25/sq. ft.

SIMPLEX PRODUCTS DIV., P.O. Box 10, Adrian, MI 49221 - (517) 263-8881
price - n/a

SOLAR SHIELD, 1054 Branch Dr., Alpharetta, GA 30201 - (800) 654-3645 (404) 343-8091
price - $.13 - .14/sq. ft.

THERMONICS INTERNATIONAL, 776C Lakeside Dr., Mobile, AL 36693 - (334) 666-2343
price - $.15 - .20/sq. ft.

*VAN LEER, 9505 Bamboo Rd., Houston, TX 77041 - (800) 825-3766 (713) 462-6111
price - $.20/sq. ft.

Cross-laminated high density polyethylene film

Instructions For Making A Solar Chimney

A) To keep the costs down and simplify the availability of the materials, build the solar chimney with standard size building materials. Make it a size that divides evenly into 4 x 8 sheets (both glazing and plywood) to minimize waste.

B) Go up into your attic and find the exact location where you plan to cut through the ceiling. Cut the 2-foot square hole in the ceiling. Frame the hole with double 2 x 4's. Make sure to keep the blocking plumb because you will cover it with plywood to connect the hole in the ceiling to the hole in the roof. This will create the lightwell channel for the breeze and provide natural lighting to your room or hall.

C) Using a plumb line, find the locations for the four corners of the hole in the roof directly above the hole in the ceiling. Drill small holes through these four spots in the roof. These will mark the desired location of the opening in the roof.

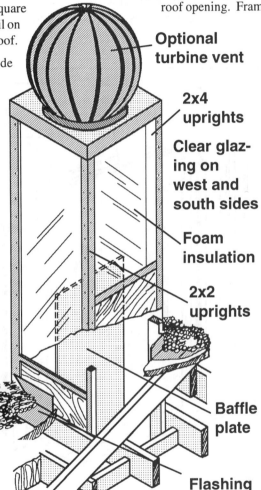

D) Go up on your roof and carefully remove the shingles surrounding the four locator holes. Saw through the roof sheathing at the holes to make the square roof opening. Frame the opening with 2x4's making sure to keep them plumb for when you nail on the vertical 2x4's to form the lightwell channel between the ceiling and the roof.

E) Cut and nail vertical 2x4's to the inside of the openings to form the lightwell channel from the roof to the ceiling. These should then be recessed so the inside surface is flush with the very edge of the hole in the ceiling. You will nail the uprights for the chimney portion to these 2x4's in the lightwell. You will then later cover the inside of these 2x4's with plywood so they will enclose and finish the lightwell.

F) For three of the corners, between east and south, east and north, and north and west, you will nail other vertical chimney 2x4 uprights to the ones below. Attach these in a suitable manner for adequate support. These 2x4's will form the corners of the solar chimney above the roof. Use a 2x2 on the south and west corner so that less of the glazed area is blocked. Nail horizontal 2x4's between the surface for the top cover and turbine uprights and provide a mounting vent.

G) If you have a very short lightwell, the sun at high noon may shine down into your room through the lightwell. If you find that this happens in your area, secure a horizontal 2x4 across the east to west side at the top of the lightwell. Cut and nail a plywood baffle to the 2x4 and to the plywood on the sides. This baffle will block any sun from shining directly down into your room below.

H) Cut foil-faced rigid foam insulation board to cover all the inside unglazed surfaces in the chimney. Paint the foil surface flat black and glue and nail it to the plywood surfaces with the black foil facing inward. This black surface becomes the solar absorber to capture the sun's heat.

I) Use some type of clear plastic sheets for the south and west sides. The various types of materials are listed in the materials list. Glaze the entire west side and only the upper half of the south side to avoid direct sunlight from shining in your room around noontime.

J) Lay a bead of silicon caulking on the 2x4 and 2x2 uprights and place the sheets against the uprights. Cut four lengths of the aluminum angle trim and drill holes in it every one foot. Place a bead of caulking under each leg and screw these in place through the glazing sheets along the exterior corners to finish them.

K) You can either have a 2-foot square sheet metal top made to cover the chimney and mount the turbine vent or you can make a plywood top. If you make a plywood top, use the aluminum angle to finish the edges. Use silicon caulking under the top.

L) Paint all the unglazed exterior surfaces with house paint to match your house or roof. Attach flashing around the chimney and replace the shingles. Finish the inside of the lightwell with plywood or drywall.

M) Make a plywood door to fit the opening in your ceiling. Attach a ½x½ strip around the inside of the opening about ¾ of an inch above the opening. Stick adhesive-backed foam weatherstripping against the strip. Attach the door with hinges and attach a latch to hold it closed when you are air-conditioning or in the winter. Glue several inches of foam insulation board on top of it to block heat flow when it's closed.

Q: I want to build a conventional-looking 2,500 sq. ft. super-efficient house. My sons and I want to do some of the work ourselves. What construction method do you recommend?

A: Your question is timely because I plan to build a similar house. I would recommend stress-skin panel construction. These houses are well insulated (up to R-40 walls) and airtight. Your heating and cooling bills should be at least 50% less than a standard 2x4 studded wall house.

The term "stress-skin" panel refers to the fact that the wall and roof panels carry all the load themselves. They do not need any framing or other supporting structure. Once the panels are delivered to your site, you can usually have the house closed in just a couple of days.

This makes them ideal for the do-it-yourself builder. You send your floor plan to the stress-skin panel manufacturers. Their computers design all the panels and components. The panels, numbered per the assembly plan, are delivered to your building site with window and door openings already cut.

Each panel (up to 24 feet long and 8 feet wide) consists of thick rigid foam insulation with structural plywood or waferboard bonded to each side. They may be ordered with paneling or drywall already attached. You may also purchase uncut panels and install windows and doors yourself.

The panels are manufactured in a "house factory" with rigid quality control. Since they are not exposed to the outdoor weather for weeks or months like conventional building materials, the fit and finish is excellent. This speeds up construction at your site.

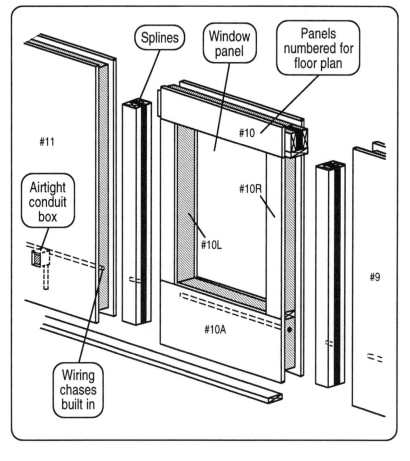

Wiring chases are routed into the insulation before the stress skins are attached. This makes for simple electrical wiring and very airtight construction. These houses are quiet and dust-free. In most construction, there is much air leakage around poorly sealed conduit boxes.

With most manufacturers' panels, the insulation in the bottom of the panel is routed out to accept a lumber sill plate on top of a standard foundation. Each panel is joined vertically and sealed along the joints with standard lumber or insulated splines.

You work your way around the foundation until all of the wall panels are up and properly positioned. The corners are nailed together through studs that are in the routed-out ends of the corner panels. This forms an extremely strong and rigid house.

Q: When I hold my hand over the end of my vacuum cleaner hose, the motor races faster. Does the same thing happen to my furnace blower when I close registers to unused rooms and does this waste electricity?

A: It is a common misconception that a blower motor uses more electricity when the air flow is restricted. Your vacuum cleaner motor speeds up when you block the hose because it is doing no work when no air is moving. In this unloaded "clogged" state, it is actually using less electricity.

This is similar to your furnace blower. As you close off registers to unused rooms, the resistance in your duct system increases. This reduces the load on your furnace blower. If you close too many registers, however, the air flow is overly restricted and the heat exchanger becomes inefficient.

Stress-skin panel house construction is one of the most energy-efficient methods to build a house. This is due to the high insulation value and air-tightness. Stress-skin panels are also called structural foam building panels. By structural, it is meant that they are self-supporting and do not need additional framing or other supporting structures. The term "foam panels or curtainwall panels" are similar, but they are not as strong as stress-skin panels. These panels require a post and beam or timber framed structure for support.

Stress-skin panels usually are produced by permanently bonding particleboard or plywood on both sides of rigid foam insulation. The insulation can be any thickness (often available in increments of one-inch) depending on the insulation level you desire. Insulation levels as high as R-40 are available. These panels or special vented designs are used for the roof too.

The two most common types of foam insulation used are expanded polystyrene (EPS) or polyisocyanurate of which urethane foam is the most common. Polyisocyanurates are made with CFC's or HCFC's which give them a higher insulation value per inch thickness than EPS.

The drawback to this foam insulation is that it slowly releases these chemicals into the air and this degrades the earth's ozone layer. Information and specifications on a typical stress-skin panel are shown on page 236.

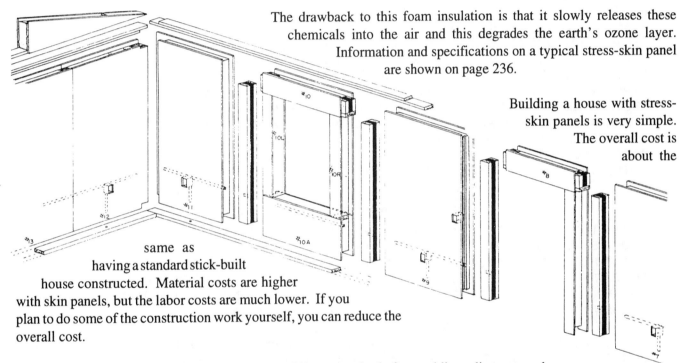

Building a house with stress-skin panels is very simple. The overall cost is about the same as having a standard stick-built house constructed. Material costs are higher with skin panels, but the labor costs are much lower. If you plan to do some of the construction work yourself, you can reduce the overall cost.

Each stress-skin panel manufacturer has a different method of assembling adjacent panels. The illustration above shows a method that uses a separate insulated spline to join the panels. Caulk and sealer is used between adjacent panels for an airtight fit. I have listed the manufacturers of highest-quality stress-skin panels on page 235.

On other panels, vertical slots are routed in the insulation at each end. You slide two 1x4 wood splines in the slots on each side (4 total) and nail them to the stress skin particleboard. Still others use a tongue and groove method. They are all very effective. The particular joining method should not be of critical concern to you when selecting a manufacturer or design.

You can buy complete stress-skin panel house kits. The illustration on this page shows a typical kit. The panels are numbered, so you know exactly where each goes. You can also provide the panel manufacturers with your own architectural drawings, and they will design, build, and number all pieces for your house.

Since these houses are very airtight, you should install a whole-house heat recovery ventilation system. This provides continuous fresh air into your house without wasting much energy. There is a heat exchanger that saves the energy from the stale exhaust air and transfers it to the incoming fresh air.

Manufacturers of Stress-Skin Panels

AFM CORP., P.O. Box 246, Excelsior, MN 55331 - (612) 474-0809
ALLIED FOAM PRODUCTS, P.O. Box 2861, Gainesville, GA 30503 - (404) 536-7900
ATLAS INDUSTRIES, 6 Willow Rd., Ayer, MA 01432 - (508) 772-0000
BRANCH RIVER FOAM PLASTICS, 15 Thurber Blvd., Smithfield, RI 02917 - (401) 232-0270
CORNELL CORP., P.O. Box 338, Cornell, WI 54732 - (715) 239-6411
ENERCEPT INC., 3100 9th Ave. S.E., Watertown, SD 57201 - (605) 882-2222
ENGINEERED PANEL TECH., P.O. Box 120427, Nashville, TN 37212 - (615) 254-1381
FIBERGLASS TECHNOLOGY IND., N. 3808 Sullivan #31, Spokane, WA 99216 - (509) 928-8880
FISCHER CORP., 1843 Northwestern Pky., Louisville, KY 40203 - (502) 778-5577
FOAM PRODUCTS CORP., P.O. Box 2217, Maryland Hts., MO 63043 - (800) 824-2211
FUTUREBILT INTERN'L., A104 Plaza del Sol, Wimberly, TX 78676 - (512) 847-5721
GREAT LAKES INSULSPAN, 9012 E. U.S. 223, Blissfield, MI 49228 - (517) 486-4844
J-DECK BULDING SYS., 2587 Harrison Rd., Columbus, OH 43204 - (614) 274-7755
KORWALL INDUSTRIES, 326 N. Bowen Rd., Arlington, TX 76012 - (817) 277-6741
MARNE INDUSTRIES, P.O. Box 465, Grand Rapids, MI 49588 - (616) 698-2001
MURUS CO., P.O. Box 220, Mansfield, PA 16933 - (717) 549-2100
PANEL BUILDING SYS., 431 Second St., Greenville, PA 16125 - (412) 694-8082
PERMA-R-PRODUCTS, P.O. Box 5235 EKS, Johnson City, TN 37603 - (615) 929-8007
RADVA CORP., P.O. Box 2900, FSS, Radford, VA 24143 - (703) 639-2458
SCHMUCKER MFG. CO., 417 E. Fourth St., Derry, PA 15627 - (412) 694-8082
STRUCTURAL PANELS, 350 Burbank Rd., Oldsmar, FL 34677 - (813) 855-2627
TECTUM INC., P.O. Box 920, Newark, OH 43055 - (614) 345-9691
VERMONT STRESSSKIN PANEL, RR1, Box 2794, CAmbridge, VT 05444 - (802) 644-8885
W.H. PORTER, 4240 136th Ave., Holland, MI 49424 - (616) 399-1963
WING MANUFACTURING, 1638 Clearview Dr., Latrobe, PA 15650 - (412) 537-7755
WINTER PANEL CORP., R.R. 5, Box 168B, Brattleboro, VT 05301 - (802) 254-3435

- -

Manufacturers of Panelized Houses

ALH BUILDING SYSTEMS, P.O. Box 288, Markle, IN 46770 - (219) 758-2141
ACORN STRUCTURES, P.O. Box 1445, Concord, MA 01742 - (508) 369-4111
ACTIVE HOMES CORP., 7938 S. Van Dyke, Marlette, MI 48453 - (517) 635-3532
ARMSTRONG LUMBER CO., 2709 Auburn Way N., Auburn, WA 98002 - (206) 852-5555
AUTOMATED BUILDING SYS., 309 Lafe Cox Dr., Johnson City, TN 37601 - (615) 926-2158
BARDEN & ROBESON, P.O. Box 210, Homer, NY 13077 - (607) 749-2641
BRISTYE INC., Box 818, Mexico, MO 65265 - (314) 581-6663
CAROLINA BUILDERS CORP., P.O. Box 58515, Raleigh, NC 27658 - (919) 850-8270
CEDAR FOREST PRODUCTS, 107 W. Colden St., Polo, IL 61064 - (815) 946-3994
COASTAL STRUCTURES INC., P.O. Box 631, Gorham, ME 04038 - (800) 341-0300 (207) 854-3500
CRESTMANOR HOMES, P.O. Box 884, Martinsburg, WV 25401 - (304) 267-4444
EMDURE-A-LIFETIME, 7500 N.W. 72 nd Ave., Miami, FL 33166 - (305) 885-9901
FOREST HOME SYSTEMS, RD #1, Box 131K, Selinsgrove, PA 17870 - (800) 872-1492 (717) 374-0131
HARVEST HOMES, 1 Cole Rd., Delanson, NY 12053 - (518) 895-2341
K-K HOME MART, 420 Curran Hwy., North Adams, MA 01247 - (413) 663-3765
MIRON BUILDING SYS., Center St., Box 1538, Green Island, NY 12183 - (518) 273-5473
NEW ENGLAND HOMES, 270 Ocean Rd., Greenland, NH 03840 - (603) 436-8830
NORTHERN COUNTIES HOMES, P.O. Box 97, Upperville, VA 22176 - (703) 592-3232
NORTHERN HOMES, 51 Glenwood Ave., Queensbury, NY 12804 - (800) 933-3931 (518) 798-6007
REGIONAL BUILDING SYS., 5560 Sterrett Pl, Columbia, MD 21044 - (800) 367-7512 (410) 997-7200
RYLAND GROUP, 1100 Broken Land Pky., Columbia, MD 21044 - (410) 715-7000
U.S. HOUSING COMPONENTS, 5890 Sawmill Rd., Dublin, OH 43017 - (614) 766-5501
UNIFIED CORP., 4844 Shannon Hill Rd., Columbia, VA 23038 - (804) 457-3622
UNIHOME CORP., Iron Horse Park, N. Billerica, MA 01862 - (508) 663-6511
WAUSAU HOMES, P.O. Box 8005, Wausau, WI 54402 - (715) 359-7272
WOODLAND HOMES, P.O. Box 202, Lee, MA 02138 - (413) 623-5739
YANKEE BARN HOMES, HCR 63, Box 2, Grantham, NH 03753 - (800) 258-9786 (603) 863-4545

General Description

Woodclad™, manufactured by Winter Panel Corporation, is a structural-grade stresskin panel with an interior wood facing of pine, cedar, oak or cherry. Panels provide a complete roof or wall system, including both exterior and interior structural sheathings, high R-value insulation and a finished interior wall surface. The laminated construction affords tremendous strength and rigidity.

Only the highest quality wood facings are used in Woodclad™ panels, providing an extremely attractive, yet economical paneled wood surface. Facings include tongue-and-groove pine, tongue-and-groove cedar, and either oak or cherry veneer-wrapped tongue-and-groove waferboard.

The pine and cedar facings are kiln-dried to 7% moisture content — well below conventional standards for lumber — then milled to 6-27/32" width with tongue-and-groove routing. Any change in moisture content will tend to swell rather than shrink the boards, tightening joints between them.

The hardwood facings are produced from high-quality veneers wrapped around 3-7/16"-wide strips of 3/8" tongue-and-groove OSB waferboard. Bonding the hardwood veneers to narrow tongue-and-groove OSB virtually eliminates any possibility of veneer delamination. The panels have the look and feel of solid hardwood paneling, yet they are both more affordable and more stable under changing moisture conditions.

All the wood facings are permanently bonded to the stresskin panels using high-quality, durable adhesives. Groove edges of the facing boards are flush with the panel edge; tongues extend out past the edge for connection to adjoining panels.

The Woodclad™ panel system offers excellent insulation performance. High-density isocyanurate foam insulation (an advanced formulation of urethane) provides more insulation than 9" of fiberglass or 6" of 1-lb density expanded polystyrene (EPS).

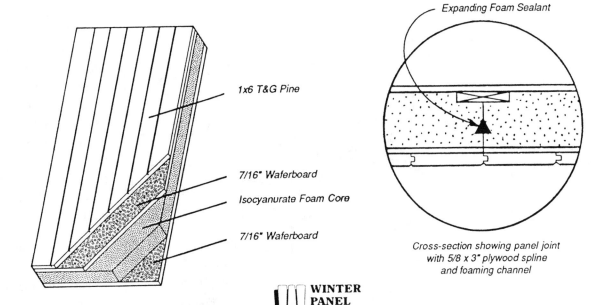

1x6 T&G Pine

7/16" Waferboard

Isocyanurate Foam Core

7/16" Waferboard

Expanding Foam Sealant

Cross-section showing panel joint with 5/8 x 3" plywood spline and foaming channel

WINTER PANEL CORP.

Applications

Woodclad™ panels provide an all-in-one roof or wall system with a finished interior paneled wood surface. The most popular Woodclad™ application is roof systems for houses with cathedral ceilings and exposed timber or log rafters. Panels can be installed very quickly, with an entire roof often being closed in during a single day. No interior finish work is required after panels are installed.

At joints of the 48"-wide panels, extending tongues on the wood facings fit into grooves on the adjoining panels, totally concealing the panel joint. For roof applications, WoodClad™ panels are generally installed horizontally, perpendicular to the rafters, with 4' panel end joints on rafter centers. This both conceals and strengthens panel end joints. Panels are secured into rafters using nails or screws from the exterior. Single 5/8 x 3" plywood splines, installed into routed grooves along the panel

exterior, are used to reinforce panel joints. As panels are installed, a bead of foam sealant is applied in the pre-routed triangular grooves in adjoining panels, assuring a tight seal.

Woodclad™ can also be used as wall panels in timber frame and post-and-beam houses. For wall applications, all panels should be nailed or screwed into horizontal wood framing members (girts/plates and sills) along the top and bottom edges and into every vertical post along the wall (posts do not need to align with panel joints).

The tongue-and-groove configuration of facings on Woodclad™ panels allows panel waste to be kept to a bare minimum. By ripping panels at a T&G joint and carefully separating the facing boards so as to leave the tongue intact (tongue-and-groove joints are not glued), panel remnants can be fully utilized.

DIMENSIONS AND WEIGHT:

Overall Thickness	5-5/16" (pine and cedar)
	4-15/16" (oak and cherry)
Thickness Tolerance	+/- 1/8"
Width	48" (with tongue extending 3/8" further)
Width Tolerance	+0" -1/8"
Standard Lengths (ft)	8, 9, 10, 12, 14, 16
Length Tolerance	+0" -1/4"
Weight	5.4 lb/ft² (pine and cedar)
	4.8 lb/ft² (oak and cherry)

THERMAL PERFORMANCE:

Conductivity of Foam (k value) (aged 6 months)	.13 -.15 [Btu-in/ft²hr°F]
Minimum R-Value of Panel (aged 6 months)	26 [Ft²hr°F/Btu]
WATER VAPOR PERMEABILITY:	less than 1 perm
WATER ABSORPTION:	2.4%

Q: I am considering building a 3,000 sq. ft. "snap together" insulating foam block house. It must be economically priced and super-strong to resist tornadoes. Is this construction method efficient?

A: There are several new construction methods, including the snap together blocks, that use a combination of rigid foam insulation and concrete. All of these methods produce a super efficient house with utility bills 50 percent less than most similar sized houses.

All are also extremely strong. Some even survived a direct hit by Hurricane Andrew in otherwise destroyed neighborhoods. From indoors and outdoors, they look identical to any conventionally-built house.

The simplicity of building with snap together foam blocks is ideal for the do-it-yourself builder/helper. Interlocking hollow rigid foam blocks are designed to literally snap together like a huge Lego house. The insulation value of foam blocks is as high as R-32.

The hollow foam insulation blocks snap together to form the foundation and walls. Openings for windows and doors are easily cut into the foam. The entire assembly is then reinforced with steel rods in the hollow cavities. Using a pump

truck, concrete is poured into the cavities at the top of the walls. The concrete flows throughout all the cavities and forms a solid strong monolithic insulated concrete wall. With the foam on the interior and exterior surfaces, the walls can be finished by any common method.

Each foam block (often made of expanded polystyrene) is roughly

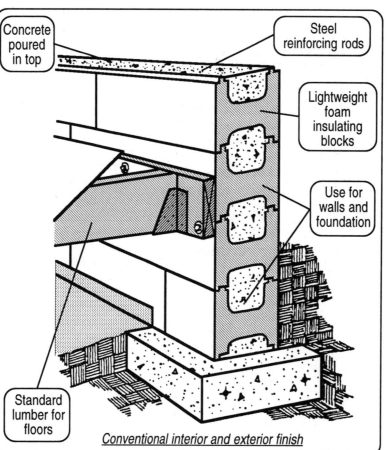

one foot square by 40 inches long and costs from $4 to $5 per block. A block weighs less than four pounds and the blocks for the construction for an entire house weigh only several hundred pounds.

In addition to low-energy usage, strength, and termite resistance, these houses are quiet. The combination of the heavy concrete mass in the center, foam on both sides, and

no air leakage, stops most outdoor noise.

A similar type of construction uses larger hollow foam panels that are made of a mixture of 14% concrete and 86% foam beads. This concrete/foam mixture is still lightweight, about 180 pounds per 10-foot wall section.

Another method uses sheathing backed foam wall panels. Concrete is poured onto the foam panels at your building site. When cured, the complete panels are tilted up on the foundation. Still another method uses steel mesh on the outside of foam panels. Concrete is blown on the panels at your site.

Q: I need to buy a new electric range and I was considering a self-cleaning oven. Does it use much electricity during the self-cleaning cycle?

A: A self-cleaning cycle can use a substantial amount of electricity. This is used to reach and maintain the high oven temperature to break down spills and spots that have accumulated in the oven over time.

Overall, a self-cleaning oven can be more efficient than a standard one. These ovens have thicker wall insulation to maintain a safe exterior temperature during the hot self-clean cycle. If you bake often, this heavier insulation saves more electricity than is used when self cleaning.

Image labels (figure):
- Concrete poured in top
- Steel reinforcing rods
- Lightweight foam insulating blocks
- Use for walls and foundation
- Standard lumber for floors

Conventional interior and exterior finish

Insulating concrete-filled foam blocks and other similar building methods form a very strong super energy efficient house.

The manufacturers and detailed information on their products are shown on pages 238 and 239. All of these manufacturers use the stack-together insulating foam blocks, unless otherwise indicated in "*description*".

With the foam block method, hollow blocks are first stacked together. Concrete is poured in the top and it flows throughout the cavities inside all the foam blocks. Figure #4 shows how a window opening is formed.

Figure #1 shows the Rastra system. The larger rigid concrete/foam mixture (fire resistant) panels are tilted up on end. The concrete is then poured in as with the blocks.

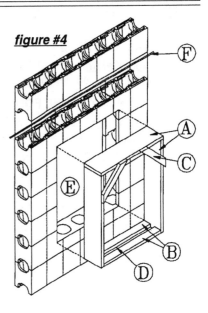

figure #4

(A) 2x10's framed as the Rough Opening

(B) 2-2x4's used for sill

(C) Bracing made of scrap wood to hold frame square

(D) Slot in sill used to fill below opening

(E) Opening fashioned around the installed frame

(F) Rebar, must be 4 feet longer than width of opening, placed in the center depression of the rebar chairs

- - - - - - - - - -

Liteform uses nylon snap ties to form walls from 4" to 24" thick. Re-usable corner clamps & retainer plates make assembly go faster. For traditional concrete walls, forms are stripped. How-

Figure #2 shows the Liteform system. This uses insulating foam sheets that are held together with plastic ties. These create the forms for the concrete to be poured into. The cost depends on your local costs for rigid foam insulation sheets.

Figure #3 is another foam/concrete panel method. This method is the Corotherm system. These insualted and structural panels are cast on site and then tilted up into position.

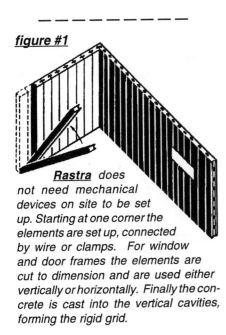

figure #2

snap ties

rebar

foam insulation sheets

ever, one or both sides of the form can be left in place to insulate your project.

- - - - - - - - - -

figure #1

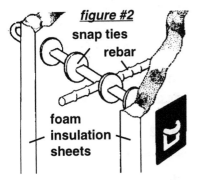

Rastra does not need mechanical devices on site to be set up. Starting at one corner the elements are set up, connected by wire or clamps. For window and door frames the elements are cut to dimension and are used either vertically or horizontally. Finally the concrete is cast into the vertical cavities, forming the rigid grid.

- - - - - - - - - - - - - - - - -

Corotherm insulated panels are structural, site-cast, tilt-up concrete panels. They have a concrete exterior and concrete ribs on 2' centers verters horizonmost panels additional ments or may dicis eascon

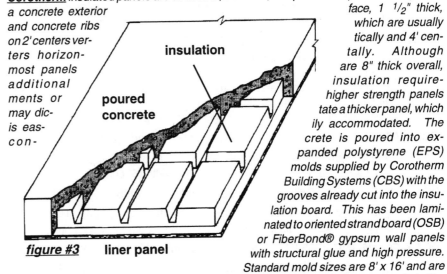

insulation

poured concrete

figure #3   **liner panel**

face, 1 $1/2$" thick, which are usually tically and 4' centally. Although are 8" thick overall, insulation requirehigher strength panels tate a thicker panel, which ily accommodated. The crete is poured into expanded polystyrene (EPS) molds supplied by Corotherm Building Systems (CBS) with the grooves already cut into the insulation board. This has been laminated to oriented strand board (OSB) or FiberBond® gypsum wall panels with structural glue and high pressure. Standard mold sizes are 8' x 16' and are combined for larger walls as needed. The liner becomes the interior face of the panel. The mold is laid face down on the slab with the EPS board up. Rebar is placed in the grooves of the insulation along with weld plates and lifting inserts. Regular weight concrete, 5000 psi, is poured into the molds and allowed to cure for 60 hours before erecting.

Manufacturers of Foam/Concrete House Blocks and Panels

3.10 INSULATED FORMS, PO Box 46790, Omaha, NE 68128 - (402) 592-7077

    <u>type of foam</u> - expanded polystyrene   <u>finished R value</u> - R22+   <u>weight of block</u> - 5 pounds
    <u>block size</u> - 48" length x 16" height x 9 $^1/_4$" or 11" width (6" or 8" core)

AMERICAN POLY STEEL FORM, 106 Horton Rd., Newfield, NY 14867 - (607) 564-7332

    <u>type of foam</u> - expanded polystyrene   <u>finished R value</u> - R22+   <u>weight of block</u> - 5 pounds
    <u>block size</u> - 48" length x 16" height x 9 $^1/_4$" or 11" width (6" or 8" core)

CONFORM INC.,1820 S. Santa Fe St., Santa Ana, CA 92705 - (800) 266-3676 (714) 662-1100

    <u>type of foam</u> - expanded polystyrene   <u>finished R value</u> - R22 to R24   <u>weight of block</u> - 2 pounds
    <u>block size</u> - 40" length x 16" height x 10" width (6.5" core)
                40" length x 12" height x 8", 10" or 12" width (4", 6" or 8" core)

COROTHERM BUILDING SYS., 12824 Highway 431 S., Guntersville, AL 35976 - (205) 582-0808

    <u>type of foam</u> - expanded polystyrene   <u>finished R value</u> - R16+   <u>weight of panel</u> - 40 to 44 lbs sq. yd.
    <u>panel size</u> - site-cast to your specifications
    <u>description</u> - These are large insulated molds made with chipboard sheathing and formed polystyrene insulation. Steel reinforcing is installed and the molds are sprayed with concrete to create the structure and exterior surface. The forms are stood in place on the foundation or concrete slab.

ENER G CORP., 4205 W. Adam, Phoenix, AZ 85009 - (602) 470-0223

    <u>type of foam</u> - expanded polystyrene   <u>finished R value</u> - variable   <u>weight of panel</u> - not available
    <u>panel size</u> - 2' length x 8' height
    <u>description</u> - This is a poured in place forming system for post and beam concrete construction. The OSB furring strips are secured into concrete posts for finishing the exterior and interior with nails or screws. The electrical and plumbing chases are built-in. The panels can be customized upon request to suit specific applications.

GREENBLOCK, PO Box 749, Woodland Park, CO 80866 - (719) 687-0645

    <u>type of foam</u> - expanded polystyrene   <u>finished R value</u> - R22 to R30+   <u>weight of block</u> - 3 pounds
    <u>block size</u> - 39" length x 9 $^3/_4$" height x 8 $^1/_2$" width (5 $^3/_4$" core)

I.C.E. BLOCK, 570 S. Dayton-Lakeview, New Carlisle, OH 45344 - (800) 423-2557 (513) 845-8347

    <u>type of foam</u> - expanded polystyrene   <u>finished R value</u> - R28 to R32   <u>weight of block</u> - 5 pounds
    <u>block size</u> - 48" length x 16" height x 10" or 11" width (6.5" or 8" core)

INSTEEL, 2610 Sidney Lanier Dr., Brunswick, GA 31525 - (800) 545-3181 (912) 264-3772

    <u>type of foam</u> - expanded polystyrene   <u>finished R value</u> - R22 to R24   <u>weight of panel</u> - 38 pounds
    <u>panel size</u> - 4' wide x any length from 6' to 24' long
    <u>description</u> - The components of the 3-D System consists of the core of 2 $^1/_2$" of expanded polystyrene, flanked by 11 gauge 2" x 2" wire mesh on each side and connected with 9 gauge galvanized truss wires, and field-coated with concrete. The wire used in the panels is manufactured from recycled steel.

LITEFORM INC., PO Box 774, Sioux City, IA 51102 - (712) 252-3704

    <u>type of foam</u> - extruded polystyrene   <u>finished R value</u> - R20+   <u>weight of block</u> - 2 pounds
    <u>sheet size</u> - 4' x 8' sheets of 2" rigid insulation cut into 8" planks
    <u>description</u> - Vertical sheets of rigid foam insulation are used as concrete forms. The inner and outer sheets are held together with easy-to-assemble plastic forming ties. Once the rigid foam insulation wall forms are tied together and rebar is slipped inside, concrete is poured in the top. Available in a re-usable form.

OUTWATER PLASTICS INDUS., 4 Passaic St., Wood-Ridge, NJ 07075 - (201) 340-1040

    <u>type of foam</u> - expanded polystyrene   <u>finished R value</u> - R22   <u>weight of block</u> - 3 pounds
    <u>block size</u> - 48" length x 12" height x 9 $^1/_2$" width (6" core)

PDQ BUILDING BLOCKS, PO Box 395, Pablo, MT 59855 - (406) 675-2525

    <u>type of foam</u> - expanded polystyrene   <u>finished R value</u> - R22   <u>weight of block</u> - 3 pounds
    <u>block size</u> - 48" length x 16" height x 9" or 11" width (6" or 8" core)

POLY-FORM, INC., 722 W. Euless Blvd., Euless, TX 76040 - (817) 283-8916

    <u>type of foam</u> - expanded polystyrene   <u>finished R value</u> - R20+   <u>weight of block</u> - 1 $^3/_4$ pounds
    <u>block size</u> - 40" length x 10" height x 8", 10" or 12" width (4", 6", or 8" core)

PRECISION FOAM MOLDERS, INC., 101 S. 30th St., Phoenix, AZ 85034 - (602) 275-5524

    <u>type of foam</u> - molded polystyrene   <u>finished R value</u> - R20+   <u>weight of block</u> - 3 pounds
    <u>block size</u> - 48" length x 16" height x 9" or 11" width (6" or 8" core)

RACINE FORM WORKS, INC. (IGLOO), 905 Prospect St., Racine, WI 53404 - (414) 632-6898

    type of foam - expanded polystyrene   finished R value - R17+   weight of block - 2 pounds
    block size - 40" length x 10" height x 10" width

RASTRA INC., 501 E. Plaza Circle, Litchfield Park, AZ 85340 - (602) 935-3545

    type of foam - polystyrene & concrete   finished R value - R24   weight of panel - 180 pounds
    panel size - 10' length x 10" height x 15" width
    description - This is a 90% recycled lightweight, honeycomb-like mixture of small polystyrene beads completely covered with a cement skin. The mixture is molded into blocks which contain interior horizontal and vertical cavities. Reinforcement bars are inserted and concrete is poured into the wall giving it rigid stability. The material is fire resistant.

REDDI-FORM INC., 1415 Orchard Dr., Chambersburg, PA 17201 - (800) 334-4303

    type of foam - expanded polystyrene   finished R value - R22   weight of block - 3 pounds
    block size - 48" length x 12" height x 9 1/2" width

SOUTHWEST ICE BLOCK, INC., PO Box 208, Litchfield Park, AZ 85340 - (602) 935-5428

    type of foam - expanded polystyrene   finished R value - R30   weight of block - 5 pounds
    block size - 48" length x 16" height x 9 1/4" width or 11" width (6" or 8" core)

THERMALOCK PRODUCTS, INC., 162 Sweeney St., N. Tonawanda, NY 14120 - (716) 695-6000

    type of foam - expanded polystyrene   finished R value - R15 to R24   weight of block - 35 to 42 pounds
    block size - 16" length x 8" height x 8", 10" or 12" width
    description - This block is made of various concrete aggregates with the center containing 15% to 30% recyled expanded polystyrene insert. The block can be made using a large variety of aggregates, added color, and added waterproofing.

IGLOO™ Concrete Forms

Sample Cost Comparison-Crawl Space Igloo Forms Versus Concrete Block

This analysis assumes material and labor costs as shown. Rates for Igloo forms are based on erecting, bracing and pouring 30ft2 of wall area per labor hour for a wall up to 5 courses high. Other costs and rates may be substituted in the calculations.

Diagram: Crawl Space 30' x 40'; Garage 24' x 24'

IGLOO FORM FOUNDATION

Crawl space wall: 5 courses (50 2/3')		
Garage wall: 4 courses (40 2/3')		
Footings	same as for block	
Igloo forms		
290 @ $5.25/ea		$1,523
30 ends @ .80/ea		24
Steel		
#4 rebar, 500' @ .25/ft		125
Ties and adhesive		30
Concrete 13.5 yards @ $50/yd		675
Labor 28 hours @ $15/hr		420
Dampproofing	same as for block	
Total		$2,797

CONCRETE BLOCK FOUNDATION

Crawl space wall: 6 courses (48")		
Garage wall: 6 courses (48")		
Footings	same	
Concrete block (10")		
950 @ $2.55/ea		$2,423
Extruded foam board to insulate crawl space only (2" board)		
18 sheets @ $16/ea		288
Labor to insulate		
2 hours @ $15/hr		30
Dampproofing	same	
Total		$2,741

Advantages of Igloo forms:
  Control scheduling
  Control quality
  Save time
  Allow design flexibility
  Provide a super-insulated foundation

Q: I have heard of conventional-looking 2,500 sq. ft. houses that can be heated and air-conditioned for less than $200 per year. How are these houses constructed and are they expensive to build?

A: You are referring to extremely energy efficient construction called superinsulation. There are many construction techniques for superinsulated houses and they needn't be a lot more expensive to build than any other house. While they look like any typical house, superinsulated houses cost only a fraction as much to heat and cool.

Both conventional and some new construction methods can be used to build a superinsulated house. Thick conventional studded walls are filled with new high-density insulation. The exterior, which can later be finished with brick, stucco, or siding, is covered with thick rigid foam insulation. This blocks energy-wasting thermal bridges through the wall studs.

In addition to being high-insulated, superinsulated houses are also very airtight. This not only saves energy, but it reduces noise, dirt, and allergens inside the home.

A continuous air/vapor barrier plastic film is attached and sealed under the drywall. Another method seals all the drywall joints and corners to block air leakage. Heat re-covery fresh air ventilation systems are sometimes used. Since you can control the fresh air, the air quality inside these homes is typically better than an average house.

Do-it-yourselfers have several new low-cost superinsulation construction options - concrete-filled insulating hollow foam blocks, self-supporting foam core wall panels,

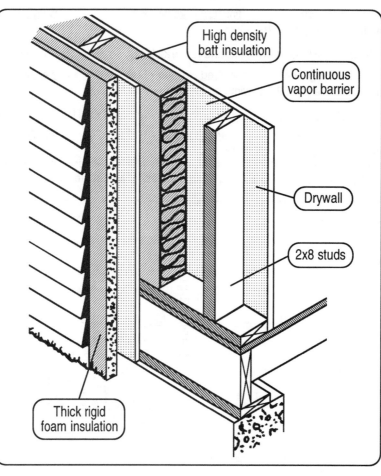

High density batt insulation

Continuous vapor barrier

Drywall

2x8 studs

Thick rigid foam insulation

low-density insulating concrete blocks, etc. Doing some of the construction work yourself can really lower the overall costs.

To use the hollow foam blocks, you stack them together like a giant Lego set to build the wall. Once the wall is built, concrete is pumped into the top of the wall. The concrete fills the interlocking cavities in the foam blocks forming a very strong superinsulated, airtight, and sound-proof wall. Finish the interior and exterior surface any way you like.

Self-supporting superinsulated foam core wall panels are very effective. These lightweight 8-foot high panels consist of up to eight inches of rigid foam insulation bonded between plywood panels on each surface. You simply saw holes in the panels to install framing for doors and windows.

The finished panels are so strong that they can be attached directly to the foundation and to each other without any other supporting framework. This makes construction quick and simple. With the high insulation value and few joints and gaps, these houses are extremely airtight and efficient.

Q: I am in the process of installing a new medium-efficiency gas furnace in my home. I am replacing a 20-year-old furnace. My furnace contractor says I need a brand new flue liner. Is he correct?

A: He probably is right. Sometimes when you install a new furnace, especially one in the 80% efficiency range, you must install a new flue liner. Since the new furnace is more efficient and captures more heat for your home, the exhaust flue gases are much cooler. With a large older flue, the water vapor in the gases may condense and cause corrosion problems.

Superinsulation houses can be heated and cooled for less than $200 per year, even in severe climates. In addition to saving much on your utility bills, superinsulated houses are also very quiet, clean, and airtight.

Superinsulation refers to more than just conventional construction with extra heavy insulation in the walls and ceiling. These houses are very airtight, many with less than one-quarter air change per hour. The combination of high insulation, high-quality windows and doors, and airtightness are all needed to produce such low heating and cooling needs.

There are several methods for building a superinsulated house using more conventional building methods. Three wall diagrams are shown on page 244. You have two options for making the house airtight. The first, and most common, is to staple a 4-mil thick polyethylene plastic film on the indoor surface of the wall studs and under the ceiling joists.

It is important to seal all the seams in the film with tape and caulk. Don't forget to seal around the electrical outlets in outside walls. You can get special electrical conduit boxes with flanges to attach and seal the plastic film. Your contractor must be careful when installing the interior drywall. Any small tears in the film can result in substantial energy losses. Discuss your contractor's or builder's experience with these construction techniques.

Another sealing method is to use the drywall itself as the air/vapor barrier - page 243. This is called the Airtight Drywall Approach (ADA). With this method, you do not need the plastic film. All the joints in the drywall, corners, windows, doors, etc., are sealed with gaskets, not caulked. These gaskets provide a long-term airtight seal. The gaskets are often round or square closed-cell backing rods, or vinyl or neoprene glazing tape commonly used in commercial construction. You will definitely need a builder who has prior experience with this technique.

There are several do-it-yourself superinsulation construction methods that can significantly reduce the overall building costs. These methods produce very conventional-looking houses. One method is the large hollow insulating foam blocks and other similar building methods, see pages 237 through 240. Another simple do-it-youself superinsulation building method uses stress skin foam core wall panels. These panels come in two types - self supporting and non self supporting. Please see pages 233 through 236 for more information.

The chart below shows how to determine savings by adding wall insulation. Look up the amount of heat (therms) needed for your current wall. Adding insulation requires fewer therms. Multiply the therms saved by your local utility rates to determine the dollar savings.

Wall Insulation

therms of natural gas burned per season to replace heat lost through 1,000 sq. ft. of wall

Wall stud size	R-value of insulation in stud space	Degree-day zone								
		2,000	3,000	4,000	5,000	6,000	7,000	8,000	9,000	10,000
2 x 4	none	144	223	306	389	474	555	637	723	807
	R-6	58	89	122	156	189	222	255	289	323
	R-11	37	59	82	105	128	151	175	198	222
	R-13	33	52	72	92	112	133	153	174	195
2 x 6	R-19	21	35	49	63	78	92	107	122	137
double stud 8 1/2" space	R-30	11	19	28	37	46	56	65	74	84
double stud 10 1/2" space	R-38	9	16	23	30	38	45	52	60	68

Manufacturers of Special Building Products

Air/Vapor & Air Barriers:

STO CORP., 6175 Riverside Dr. S. W., Atlanta, GA 30331 - (404) 346-3666
RAVEN INDUSTRIES, Box 1007, Sioux Falls, SD 57117 - (605) 336-2750
DUPONT - FIBERS DEPT., Centre Rd., Wilmington, DE 19898 - (302) 774-1000

Sealants and Tapes for Air/Vapor Barriers:

TREMCO, 3735 Green Rd., Beechwood, OH 44122 - (216) 292-5000
PARSEC INC., P.O. Box 38534, Dallas, TX 75238 - (214) 341-6700

Insulation Ventilation Baffles:

POLY FOAM INC., 116 S. Pine St., Lester Prairie, MN 55435 - (612) 445-4089

Foundation Coatings:

THORO SYSTEMS, 7800 NW 38th St., Miami, FL 33166 - (800) 322-7825
DRYVIT SYSTEMS, 1 Energy Way, West Warwick, RI 02893 - (800) 556-7752

ADA-Airtight Drywall Approach

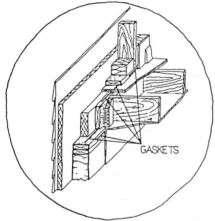

BAND JOIST

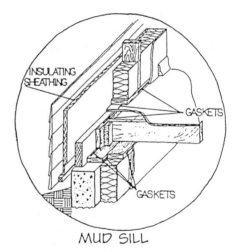

MUD SILL

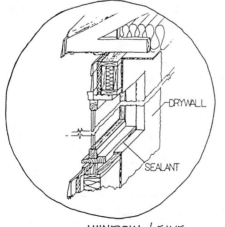

WINDOW & EAVE

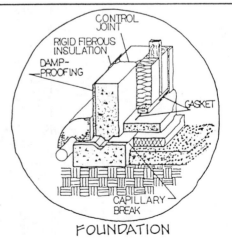

FOUNDATION

Superinsulated Walls

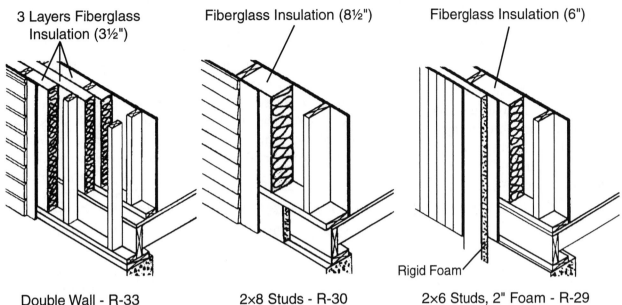

3 Layers Fiberglass Insulation (3½")

Fiberglass Insulation (8½")

Fiberglass Insulation (6")

Rigid Foam

Double Wall - R-33

2×8 Studs - R-30

2×6 Studs, 2" Foam - R-29

Superinsulated Attic

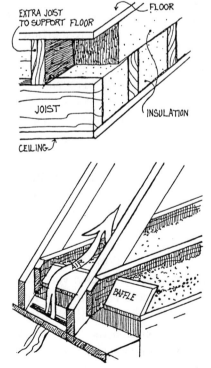

EXTRA JOIST TO SUPPORT FLOOR

FLOOR

JOIST

INSULATION

CEILING

AIR

BAFFLE

If insulation in an attic floor is the poured kind, wood baffles should be permanently installed to keep the insulation out of the overhang, whether or not it is ventilated.

If there is a need for a floor in the attic, extra joists are set at right angles to the original joists and extra insulation is put between them.

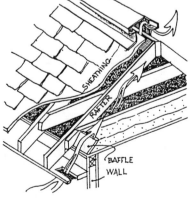

SHEATHING

RAFTER

BAFFLE WALL

Insulation must not go into the overhang of the roof. Baffles hold it back; soffit vent and ridge vent allow good ventilation.

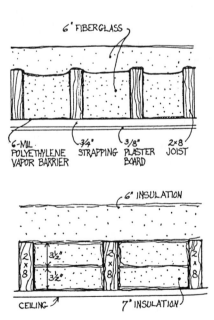

6" FIBERGLASS

6-MIL POLYETHYLENE VAPOR BARRIER

¾" STRAPPING

⅜" PLASTER BOARD

2×8 JOIST

6" INSULATION

CEILING

7" INSULATION

To avoid gaps in insulation, adjust the thicknesses of insulation so that the first layer or two comes to the top of the joists; then lay the next layer at right angles to the joists. This covers all gaps as well as the joists themselves.

244

Q: I want to replace my roof with one that is efficient, attractive, and long-lasting like slate, tile, or heavy shakes. With a limited budget, what are the best types of roofing to consider?

A: The type of roofing materials you select impacts not only upon the appearance of your house, but upon your utility bills. Many have warranties up to 50 years and can make your house more fire safe and valuable at resale.

Installing contoured shingles, shakes, tiles, or slate forms small air gaps above the roof sheathing. In the summer, this produces a natural air flow under the roofing to reduce the roof temperature in the hot sun. This increases your comfort and cuts your air-conditioning costs.

Some new roof materials simulate the look of expensive heavy slate, tiles, and shakes at a fraction of the cost and weight. For example, new lightweight fiber-cement roofs (now use cellulose fibers instead of asbestos) are difficult to distinguish from real clay or slate.

Fiber-cement tiles have a high insulation value of R-2.4, much higher than solid cement. Since they are relatively lightweight, your roof should be able to support them. Real slate weighs more than 1,000 pounds

per square (100 sq. ft.) and the slate may require extra-strong roofing construction.

Another option to simulate the expensive look of slate or clay tile is polymer roofing. It is made of the same high-strength plastics used in cars and aircraft. It costs only about one-third as much as real clay tiles and weighs only one-tenth as much. They are guaranteed for 50 years.

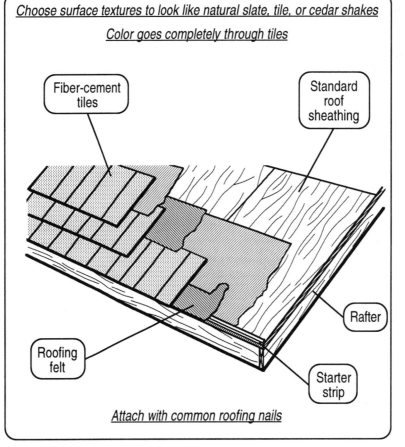

Choose surface textures to look like natural slate, tile, or cedar shakes
Color goes completely through tiles

Fiber-cement tiles

Standard roof sheathing

Rafter

Roofing felt

Starter strip

Attach with common roofing nails

Cedar shakes or shingles are also very attractive. Many are now treated with chemicals for fire and mold resistance. Cedar is lightweight enough to be used on any roof. They weather to a beautiful silvery color. Good-quality, heavy shakes should last for 40 to 50 years.

A less expensive alternative (about half the price of cedar) is treated pine shakes. These use yel-

low pine grown in the Southeast. As the old growth Western cedar forest gradually disappear, treated fast-growing pine is an environmentally preferable roofing material.

Another attractive option to cedar is wood fiber. This is made by pressure bonding wood fibers into shake and shingle shapes. Each piece is 25% larger than standard roofing, so they are much quicker to install. They have a temporary "walkable coating" for safer do-it-yourself installation. Extra-heavy architectural fiberglass shingles also are made to look like real slate or wood.

Q: I am planning to get replacement windows for my home. How can I compare the energy ratings of various windows? Each window manufacturer seems to use different efficiency tests.

A: Until recently, each manufacturer used its own performance tests for insulation value and airtightness. This makes it difficult, if not impossible, to use the figures for any meaningful comparison.

Some windows now come with an "energy-use" sticker very similar to appliances. The National Fenestration Rating Council (NFRC) sets the test standards. The window manufacturers who want to be rated must have their window tested by a private testing lab for impartial results. Ask for a NFRC rated window.

Some of the roofing materials are warranted for up to 50 years. They often actually last a lifetime. The chart below shows some of the important selection characteristics and specifications for many roofing materials.

The most durable roofing materials, clay and concrete tiles, slate, etc., are also the heaviest. They are not suitable for the typical reroofing job because the roof structure is not strong enough to handle the weight. In addition to the high cost of the roofing materials, you would have the additional cost of strengthening the roofing structure.

If you are building a new house, installing one of these heavy durable roofs makes long-term economic sense. During construction, the cost of the additional lumber in the roof is not great. These roofs require little maintenance and can improve the resale value of your house.

For reroofing an existing house, some of the newer alternative roofing materials are an excellent choice. Many of these materials are designed to look like real shakes, tiles, or slate, at a fraction of the cost and weight. In the chart below, the price is shown in dollars per 100 square feet of roofing area (called a "square" in the trade).

You should also consider the minimum slope allowable for the type of roofing you select. In most northern climates, the roofs have a steep enough slope for any type of roofing material.

In warmer climates, the slope of the roof may not be adequate for all types of roofing materials. The slope of a roof is measured by the vertical rise of the roof over the horizontal run. If your roof does not have an adequate slope, there is a greater chance of leaks from rain and snow, especially during storms.

Pages 247 and 248 list the manufacturers of roofing materials and the types of materials they offer. Contact them for specifications and names of local contractors.

Types of Roofing					
Type	Price $/sq.	Fire Rating	Life Years	Min. Slope	Weight lbs./sq.
Asphalt Shingles	50-200	C to A	15-25	2-in-12	235-390
Asphalt Roll	55-75	C to A	10-15	1-in-12	45-150
Bent Cedar Shingles	500-600	B to A	50+	4-in-12	250-500
Cedar Shingles/Shakes	300-400	C	15-50	4-in-12	160-300
Clay Tiles	180-850	A	50+	3-in-12	595-1500
Concrete Tiles	45-400	A	50+	4-in-12	750-1200
Fiber Cement Tiles	250-575	B to A	50	3-in-12	200-250
Fiberglass Shingles	50-200	A	20-50	2-in-12	200-400
Polymer Tiles	200-250	A	50	4-in-12	100-150
Slate Shingles	160-700	A	50+	4-in-12	500-3200
Transparent Glass Tiles	1500	A	50+	8-in-12	1000
Treated Pine Shakes	150-200	n/a	50	4-in-12	375-400
Wood Fiber Shingles	75-125	n/a	15+	4-in-12	225-250

Manufacturers of Roofing Materials

ASPHALT ROOFING MANUFACTURERS, 6000 Executive Blvd, Rockville, MD 20852 - (301) 231-9050
(Association of manufacturers - contact for local suppliers)

ATLAS ROOFING CORP., Box 5777 Valley Rd., Meridian, MS 39302 - (800) 933-2721
<u>type</u> - asphalt and fiberglass shingles and asphalt roll - Special granule surface with several colors available.

BENDER ROOF TILE IND., INC., PO Box 190, Belleview, FL 34421 - (800) 888-7074 (904) 245-7074
<u>type</u> - concrete tiles - Available in "S" shape or a flat tile which can be smooth or ribbed.

BIRD ROOFING CO., 1077 Pleasant St., Norwood, MA 02062 - (800) 247-3462 (617) 551-0656
<u>type</u> - asphalt, fiberglass and organic shingles, roll roofing - A unique construction of embedding oversized opaque ceramic granules.

BUCKINGHAM-VIRGINIA SLATE, PO Box 8, Arvonia, VA - (804) 581-1131
<u>type</u> - roofing slates - The color is blue-black and unfading which can be matched at any future time.

CAL-SHAKE INC., PO Box 2265, Irwindale, CA 91706 - (800) 736-7663 (818) 969-3451
<u>type</u> - fiber cement tiles - Available styles are shake, clay and slate in natural colors.

CEDAR SHAKE & SHINGLE BUREAU, 515 116TH Ave., NE, Belluvue, WA 98004 - (206) 453-1323
(Association of manufacturers - contact for local suppliers)

CELOTEX CORP., PO Box 31602, Tampa, FL 33631 - (800) 235-6839 (813) 873-1700
<u>type</u> - asphalt and fiberglass shingles, asphalt roll - The Presidential Shingle has a curved edge design which gives the appearance of a fine wood shake.

CERTAIN TEED CORP. ROOFING, PO Box 860, Valley Forge, PA 19482 - (215) 341-6801
<u>type</u> - asphalt, fiberglass and organic shingles - Available with a wood-grain finish or a slate appearance.

C&H ROOFING INC., PO Box 2105, Lake City, FL 32056 - (800) 327-8115 (904) 755-1102
<u>type</u> - bent cedar shingles - Resembles an English cottage thatch roof with gently flowing contours.

ELK CORP., 14643 Dallas Pkwy., Dallas, TX 75240 - (214) 851-0400
<u>type</u> - asphalt and fiberglass shingles - Has the natural appearance of wood shingles, tile and slate.

ETERNIT INC., Box 679, Blandon, PA 19510 - (800) 233-3155 (215) 926-0100
<u>type</u> - fiber cement tiles - Slates are available in two sizes and five colors which are predrilled.

EVEREST ROOFING PROD., 2500 Workman Mill Rd, Whittier, CA 90601 - (800) 767-0267 (714) 594-7647
<u>type</u> - lightweight polymer tiles - Molded tiles to simulate natural slate and split cedar shakes.

EVERGREEN SLATE CO. INC., PO Box 248, Granville, NY 12832 - (518) 642-2530
<u>type</u> - roofing slates - Available in ten colors, either unfading or semi-weathering.

FIBRECEM CORP., PO Box 411368, Charlotte, NC 28241 - (800) 346-6147 (704) 527-2727
<u>type</u> - fiber cement tiles - An authentic slate appearance and design available in four colors and three styles.

GAF BUILDING MATERIALS, 1361 Alps Rd., Wayne, NJ 07470 - (201) 628-3000
<u>type</u> - fiberglass shingles, asphalt roll - Available in 7 styles and colors with a slate or wood shake appearance.

Manufacturers of Roofing Materials

GEORGIA PACIFIC, PO Box 105605, Atlanta, GA 30303 - (800) 447-2882 (404) 652-4000
   type - asphalt, fiberglass and organic shingles, roll roofing - Three styles are available.

GS ROOFING CO., 5525 Macarthur Blvd., Irving, TX 75038 - (800) 666-7005 (214) 580-5600
   type - asphalt and fiberglass shingles - Featuring the style and appearance of natural wood shakes.

IMPRESSION, 22599 Western Ave., Torrance, CA 90501 - (310) 618-1299
   type - clay tile and transparent glass - Seven styles are available with a custom or standard glaze.

JAMES HARDIE BUILDING, 10901 Elm Ave., Fontanta, CA 92335 - (800) 426-4051 (714) 355-6500
   type - fiber cement tiles - Manufactured with a natural wood look and texture in six colors.

LIFEPINE ROOFING PRODUCTS, PO Box 1386, Savannah, GA 31402 - (800) 735-7663 (912) 232-0786
   type - pressure treated pine shakes - Easy to install due to the square sides and ends.

LUDOWICI-CELADON, INC., PO Box 69, New Lexington, OH 43764 (800) 945-8453 (614) 342-1995
   type - clay tiles - Ten different styles are available in twenty-two standard colors that do not fade.

MANVILLE/SCHULLER, PO Box 5108, Denver, CO 80217 - (800) 654-3103
   type - fiberglass shingles, roll roofing - Designed to create a three dimensional appearance with shadow lines.

MARLEY ROOF TILES, 1990 E. Riverview, San Bernardino, CA 92408 - (800) 344-2875 (714) 796-8324
   type - concrete tiles - The color is all the way through and never needs painting.

MASONITE, 1 S. Wacker Dr., Chicago, IL 60606 - (312) 750-0900
   type - compressed wood fiber shingle - Deep shadow lines and a rugged texture give the look of cedar shakes.

MAXITILE, 17141 S. Kingsview Ave., Carson, CA 90746 - (800) 338-8453 (310) 217-0316
   type - fiber cement tiles and shakes - Color through out so it is resistant to chipping and peeling.

MONIER ROOF TILE, PO Box 5567, Orange, CA 92613 - (800) 432-2715 (714) 750-5366
   type - concrete tiles and fiber cement tiles - Available in terra cotta clay, shake, split shake and slate styles.

OWENS CORNING FIBERGLASS, Fiberglass Tower, Toledo, OH 43659 - (800) 527-7718 (419) 248-8000
   type - fiberglass shingles - A unique staggered-edge shingle system with a blend of color and pattern.

REDLAND CLAY TILE, 443 B. Tecate Rd. #386, Tecate, CA 91980 - (800) 354-5983 (619) 744-3717
   type - clay tiles - Available in the "Two Piece Mission" or"S" shape style in ten standard color combinations.

SUPRADUR MFG. CORP., PO Box 908, Rye, NY 10580 - (800) 223-1948 (914) 967-8230
   type - clay tiles and fiber cement tiles - Available in slate, wood-grain shake and traditional styles.

TAMKO ASPHALT PRODUCTS, 220 W. 4th St., Joplin, MO 64801 - (800) 641-4691 (417) 624-6644
   type - asphalt and fiberglass shingles - Available in a variety of designs and styles.

VANDE HEY-RALEIGH MFG., 1665 Bohm Dr., Little Chute, WI 54140 - (800) 236-8453 (414) 766-1181
   type - concrete tiles - Twenty standard colors, all styles and colors are available with custom weathering.

VINTAGE WOOD WORKS, Hwy 34 S. PO Drawer R 2521, Quinlan, TX 75474 - (903) 356-2158
   type - cedar shingles - Fancy cut shingles.

Q: I want new siding on my house and to add some insulation under it. What new types of very low-maintenance siding are available? Is there a way to simulate real brick, stone, or stucco with siding?

A: There are unique new siding materials with profiles that can provide any look you want, from cedar shakes to brick to stucco. Some of these "no-maintenance" materials have 25-year to lifetime warranties. You can order efficient siding with the insulation already attached to the back surface.

To add heavy insulation and change to a brick appearance, you can use special insulation panels. The panels have horizontal tracks spaced the width of standard bricks. You attach the panels with a screw/washer assembly.

Simply glue the lightweight ½-inch thick bricks into the horizontal tracks (weighs only 6 lbs./sq. ft. installed.) Formed corner sections make finishing easy. Gun mortar in between the bricks and brush off the excess.

Installing lightweight polypropylene siding panels (lifetime warranty) also simulates true brick or wood shingles and adds some insulation value. The panels interlock on all four sides, so little alignment is required. Only 20 panels are required per 100 sq. ft. making installation easy.

These siding panels are also made to simulate stone for your entire house or just as accents. For the most natural stone look at half its cost and weight, use new imitation stones set in mortar. These fake stones (hundreds of shapes) are made from cement, lightweight aggregate, and natural color.

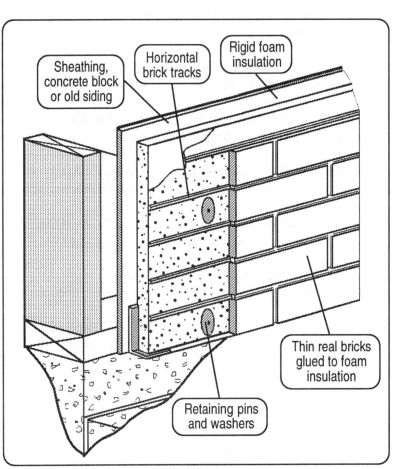

Sheathing, concrete block or old siding

Horizontal brick tracks

Rigid foam insulation

Thin real bricks glued to foam insulation

Retaining pins and washers

Inexpensive hardboard panel siding can give the authentic look of stucco, lap, or panel siding. Wood particles and tough resins are formed under extreme pressure and temperature. The deep stucco or wood texture is formed into the surface. When painted, you cannot tell it from the real thing.

Oriented strand board (OSB) siding is similar to hardboard except several layers of wood fibers are directionally-oriented for higher strength. With no knots or imperfections, it provides an attractive appearance at low cost.

In wet climates, composite concrete siding, 50-year warranty, looks like wood lap or panel siding when painted. It is a lightweight mixture of cement, paper fibers, and fillers. You'll need a special saw to cut it.

New types of vinyl siding have natural, no-shine, wood surface textures. Some are formed in real cedar molds for authentic graining. Others use a seven-layer painting process to attain deep natural graining.

Q: Does cold water in the toilet tank draw much heat from a house? In the summer, the cold water in it sweats and drips on the floor.

A: In cold areas of the country, a toilet can indirectly use up to 1,400 kilowatt-hours of energy each year. Each time the tank fills with cold water, the water slowly warms. This draws heat from your house. In warm climates, a sweating tank in the summer can be an annoying problem.

Solve the energy loss problem by installing water saving devices. There will be less water each flush to heat up. Since the incoming cold water mixes with unused warm water still in the tank, the combined water temperature is warm enough to minimize sweating.

Residing materials for your house increase the insulation level of your walls. You can install rigid foam wall insulation under the new siding. Depending on the type of siding you select and the condition of your old siding, you can often install it directly over the old siding.

There are several new types of siding materials that are excellent choices for an existing house or a new house. Many of them are designed to look like real wood siding, cedar shakes, brick, etc. The table to the right compares the approximate costs.

"Profiles" refers to the shape of the siding. For example, "double 4" refers to one piece of 8" lap siding that looks like two 4" laps. It is much quicker to install one 8" lap than two separate 4" laps. *"Surface textures"* refers to what the installed siding looks like.

Siding Material	Cost per sq. ft.
aluminum/steel	$0.75 - $1.25
brick panels	$1.75 - $3.85
cedar shingle panels	$1.50 - $1.75
cement and aggregates	$3.50 - $4.15
crushed stone	$2.15 - $2.25
fiber cement	$4.80 - $5.10
hardboard	$0.40 - $0.90
oriented strand board	$0.75 - $1.10
plywood	$0.90 - $2.70
polypropylene	$1.40 - $1.75
tongue and groove	$0.75 - $3.40
vinyl	$0.50 - $1.75

Fiber cement is a lightweight, yet strong, combination of cement and natural fibers. It can be formed into many shapes and surface textures. U.S. Brick comes complete with the rigid insulation for simple installation. Cedar shingle panels have many shingles already attached together. It gives a real individual shingle or shake look with easy and quicker installation.

Oriented strand board is like hardboard (Masonite), but the fibers are oriented for strength. This allows the use of thinner, lighter, and less expensive material. Polypropylene is a very durable plastic material. It is often used as hinge that can handle repeated flexing.

Manufacturers of Exterior Siding

ABTCO, INC., PO Box 98, Roaring River, NC 28669 - (919) 696-2751
material - hardboard   profiles - triple 4, double 6, single 8, laps
surface textures - cedar lap, textured & smooth beaded lap, shakes, cedar panel, stucco, smooth
special features - a multi-lap hardboard with the look of authentic beveled narrow lap siding
warranty - 5 to 25 years depending on siding

ALCAN BLDG PROD., 11 Cragwood, Woodbridge, NJ 07095 - (800) 729-2522 (908) 381-0900
material - aluminum/steel, and vinyl   profiles - triple 3, double 4 & 5, single 8, vertical 8 & 12
surface textures - random woodgrain with a natural low gloss finish or a soft brushed pattern
special features - a complimentary line of soffit, fascia and trim to help you get a distinctive design
warranty - limited lifetime

ALCOA, PO Box 716, Sidney, OH 45365 - (800) 962-6973
material - aluminum/steel, and vinyl   profiles - triple 3 & 4, double 4 & 5, vert 6 & 12, single 8
surface textures - rich stained cedar woodgrain or woodgrain with a subtle brushed finish
special features - a unique accent panel in fishscale style with a smooth brush stroke finish
warranty - limited lifetime - vinyl, 50 years - aluminum

ALSCO BUILDING PROD., 3101 Poplarwood Court, Raleigh, NC 27604 - (800) 521-2930 (919) 599-2151
material - vinyl   profiles - triple 3, double 4 & 5, single 8
surface textures - natural woodgrain finish
special features - the panel has a depth of $5/8$" which allows for greater strength and rigidity
warranty - limited lifetime

ALSIDE, PO Box 2010, Akron, OH 44309 - (216) 929-1811
material - vinyl   profiles - triple 4, double 4 & 6, single 8
surface textures - deep woodgrain with a multi-colored shading pattern and a smooth matte finish
special features - shock resistant panels and breather holes to allow built-up moisture to evaporate
warranty - limited lifetime

ALUMINUM INDUSTRIES, PO Box 31489, St. Louis, MO 63131 - (800) 228-1840 (314) 821-7200
material - vinyl bonded aluminum   profiles - double 4 & 5, single 8
surface textures - woodgrain finish
special features - fire resistant, lightweight, yet super strong
warranty - 40 years

BIRD INC., PO Box 329, Bardstown, KY 40004 - (800) 626-1524 (502) 348-9231
    material - vinyl   profiles - triple 3, double 4 & 5, single 8
    surface textures - rich woodgrain look with a low-gloss satin finish
    special features - softly curved for a natural profile with uniform color throughout
    warranty - limited lifetime

CEDAR VALLEY SHINGLE SYSTEMS, 943 San Felipe Rd., Hollister, CA 95023 - (800) 521-9523
    material - cedar shingle panels   profiles - 8 foot panels in 2, 3, 4 & 5 course
    surface textures - mixed grain cedar which is rough or vertical grain which is knot-free
    special features - Requires only 14 nails per panel with interlocking end joints
    warranty - n/a

CERTAINTEED CORP., PO Box 860, Valley Forge, PA 19482 - (800) 233-8990
    material - vinyl and polypropylene   profiles - triple 2, 3 & 4, double 4 & 5, single 4, 6.5 & 8
    surface textures - low gloss, rough-cedar-like or smooth-brushed finish, cedar shingle
    special features - full 3/4" clapboard base provides distinctive shadow lines.
    warranty - limited lifetime

CLADWOOD, 427 Main St., Oregon City, OR 97045 - (800) 547-6633 (503) 650-4274
    material - plywood   profiles - single 8 & 9
    surface textures - geniune cedar, roughcast stucco, hand-split shakes, rough-sawn finish
    special features - bonded with exterior resins, lightweight and easy to handle
    warranty - 20 years

GEORGIA PACIFIC CORP., PO Box 105605, Atlanta, GA 30348 - (404) 521-4000
    material - vinyl   profiles - triple 3, double 4 & 5, single 8
    surface textures - subtle woodgrain embossed finish
    special features - available in decorator colors with a full line of matching accessories and trims
    warranty - limited lifetime

HEARTLAND, PO Box 880, Boonesville, MS 38829 - (800) 432-7801 (601) 728-6261
    material - vinyl   profiles - triple 3, double 4 & 5, single 8
    surface textures - low gloss, freshly painted wood finish
    special features - aerated and non-aerated soffit panels to help make your insulation more effective
    warranty - limited lifetime

JAMES HARDIE BUILDING PROD., 10901 Elm Ave., Fontana, CA 92337 - (800) 426-4051 (909) 356-6300
    material - fiber cement   profiles - single 7.5 & 9.5 laps in 12-ft lengths, panels
    surface textures - smooth and rough sawn wood appearance, stucco finish
    special features - resists water damage, mildew, salt spray, termites and it is non-combustible
    warranty - 50 years

L - B STONE, PO Box 276, Apple Creek, OH 44606 - (216) 698-3931
    material - cement   profiles - single pieces
    surface textures - smooth and natural stone appearance
    special features - since it is lightweight it can be used where stone is not structurally feasible
    warranty - 20 years

LOUISIANA PACIFIC, 111 SW Fifth Ave., Portland, OR 97204 - (503) 221-0800
    material - oriented strand board   profiles - single 6, 8, 9.5 & 12 laps - 8, 9 & 10 panels
    surface textures - smooth and cedar finish
    special features - exterior trim and fascia available with a smooth exterior grade resin
    warranty - 25 years

MASONITE, 1 South Wacker Dr., Chicago, IL 60606 - (312) 750-0900
    material - hardboard and oriented strand board   profiles - triple 3, double 4 & 5 & 6, single 8 laps
    surface textures - rough sawn cedar, stucco, smooth, textured & smooth beaded lap
    special features - grainless and uniformly thick, free of wood's imperfections
    warranty - 5 to 25 years depending on siding

MASTER SHIELD, 1202 N. Bowie Dr., Weatherford, TX 76086 - (800) 433-5524
    material - vinyl   profiles - triple 3, double 4 & 5, single 8
    surface textures - millwood grain finish provides a natural wood look
    special features - deep panel ridges form a wide shadow line
    warranty - limited lifetime

NAILITE, 1251 Northwest 165th St., Miami, FL 33169 - (800) 328-9018 (305) 620-6200
    material - polypropylene   profiles - 4 foot panels
    surface texture - shake and shingle pattern, stone and brick finishes
    special features - a patented 4-sided interlock with expansion features allows the walls to breathe
    warranty - limited lifetime

NORANDEX, PO Box 8000, Macedonia, OH 44056 - (216) 468-2200
    material - vinyl   profiles - triple 3 & 4, double 4 & 5, single 8
    surface textures - soft rich matte finish that looks like painted wood
    special features - a unique locking system that locks siding panels
    warranty - limited lifetime

OREGON STRAND BOARD, 34363 Lake Creek , Brownsville, OR 97327 - (800) 533-3374 (503) 466-5177
    material - plywood - tongue and groove   profiles - single 6 & 8 & 10 laps
    surface texture - wood beauty in natural clear, or rustic knotty finish
    special features - the strength of the siding can reduce your exterior stud requirements
    warranty - 20 years

PANEL BRICK MFG, INC., PO Box 907, Owensboro, KY 42301 - (502) 684-7268
    material - brick cement board   profiles - 4 foot panels
    surface texture - 12 color blends with sand and smooth faces
    special features - the brickettes are $1/2$" thick bonded to high density fiberboard
    warranty - 20 years

REAL BRICK, PO Box 907, Owosso, MI 48867 - (517) 625-6000
    material - brick   profiles - 4 foot panels
    surface texture - the finish can run from rough to smooth depending on style
    special features - the brick is $1/2$" fitted snugly into an insulated and gooved panel which is screwed on
    warranty - 100 years

ROLLEX CORP., 2001 Lunt Ave., Elk Grove Village, IL 60007 - (800) 251-3300 (708) 437-3000
    material - vinyl   profiles - triple 3, double 4 & 5
    surface textures - natural woodgrain with low gloss finish
    special features - color coordinated soffits complement your exterior siding in vented or solid panels
    warranty - limited lifetime

ROXITE, PO Box 830, Rock Falls, IL 61071 - (815) 625-8112
    material - 60% crushed stone with fiberglass   profiles - 4 foot panels
    surface textures - cedar shakes, natural brick and stone finishes
    special features - lightweight, weighing less than 1-$1/2$ pounds per square foot
    warranty - limited lifetime

ROYAL PRODUCTS, 30A Vinyl Ct., Woodrige, Ontario, L4L 4A3 - (800) 387-2789
    material - polypropylene   profiles - 4 foot panels
    surface textures - cedar shakes, red or buff brick finish, stone
    special features - zero clearance, flame retardant, very easy to clean with no maintenance
    warranty - lifetime pro-rated

SHAKERTOWN, 1200 Kerron St., Winlock, WA 98596 - (800) 426-8970 (206) 785-3501
    material - cedar shingle panels   profiles - 8 foot panels in single or double courses
    surface textures - vertical grain for modern look or mixed grain for rustic look
    special features - self-aligning with concealed nailing system hiding nails and prevents rust stains
    warranty - 10 year limited

SIMPSON TIMBER PRODUCTS, Third & Franklin, Shelton, WA 98584 - (800) 445-2442 (206) 427-9624
    material - overlaid fir plywood   profiles - plain panel, pattern 4 or 8, inverted batten
    surface textures - rough sawn wood grain finish without knots
    special features - light and easy to handle, paint or stain goes on with less absorbtion for more uniform results
    warranty - 25 years

SKOOKUM LUMBER CO., PO Box 7309, Olympia, WA 98507 - (206) 352-7633
    material - tongue and groove, beveled   profiles - lap
    surface textures - western red cedar in smooth or rough finish
    special features - natural wood siding gives a warm and earthy appearance
    warranty - n/a

STONE PRODUCTS CORP., PO Box 270 , Napa, CA 94559 - (800) 255-1727
    material - cement and aggregates   profiles - 3 foot brick & wire panel, single pieces
    surface textures - cultured stone, cultured brick
    special features - because it is lightweight it can be applied to any structurally sound exterior wall
    warranty - 20 year limited

WOLVERINE TECH., 17199 Laurel Park Dr. N., Livonia, MI 48152 - (800) 521-9020 (313) 953-1100
    material - vinyl   profiles - triple 3 & 4, double 4, 4.5 & 5, single 6 & 8
    surface textures - smooth, satin or woodgrain surface
    special features - offers an Exterior Design System to replicate historical details
    warranty - limited lifetime

Q: I am planning an efficient room addition - a living room and a bedroom. Will insulation (for energy savings) in the walls also block noise? Can you give me some tips for blocking noise between other rooms?

A: The thermal insulation in outside walls will block much of the outdoor noise, but it won't quiet the noise transmission between rooms. Energy-efficient and airtight windows also help block outdoor noise.

The sound transmission class (STC) index is used to compare quietness of various wall construction methods. It rates how well each wall blocks noise between rooms. A higher STC rating is better. An STC of 58 is recommended for a family room-to-bedroom wall and 55 for a bedroom-to-bedroom wall.

As a reference, you can easily hear normal speech through a wall with an STC rating of 25. At an STC of 42, loud speech is audible as a murmur. At an STC of 50, loud speech is not audible. A typical 2x4 studded interior wall with one layer of drywall on each side has a STC of 34.

The simplest soundproofing wall construction method is to attach ½-inch soundboard under the drywall on each side of the studs. This increases the STC to 45. Several companies manufacture special soundproofing underlayment panels, often made from recycled products such as newsprint, tires, seagrass, etc.

Instead of using the soundboard, you can mount resilient metal channels between the drywall and the studs in one room and add fiberglass insulation inside the wall for a STC of 50. This method can also reduce energy loss if you

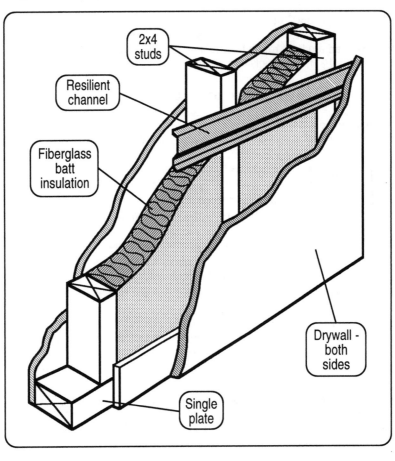

2x4 studs

Resilient channel

Fiberglass batt insulation

Single plate

Drywall - both sides

shut off the furnace or air conditioner registers to an unused room.

To further reduce noise, run separate heating ducts to each room. This blocks a direct path for noise between rooms and can also cut your utility bills. You have better control over the amount of heat going to each room so you can often set your thermostat lower and still be comfortable. Stagger electric outlets in common walls so they are not di-

rectly opposite one another. This eliminates another direct noise path.

The quietest wall design uses staggered studs, separate base plates, and batt insulation. The insulation is woven through the staggered studs. This completely isolates one side of the wall from the other side for a STC of 60.

For existing rooms, you can add a resilient channel to one wall and cover that with another layer of drywall. Another option is adding a layer of ½-inch soundboard covered with drywall.

Q: I have noticed carpet discoloration along the baseboards of my home. Someone told me that my furnace and air-conditioning ducts can cause this. Will you explain?

A: Leaky or poorly-designed ducts may cause the discoloration problem that you describe. It also is an indication of an energy inefficient heating system. This is particularly true if you close off unused rooms.

When your central blower comes on, it can create a slight positive pressure in some rooms and a slight negative pressure in others. In rooms with a negative pressure, dirty air from inside the wall cavity is sucked in by the baseboard and the carpet filters out the dirt. Have your duct system checked for leaks and duct dampers adjusted for even flow.

Soundproof qualities of walls and floors are rated by the sound transmission class (STC). A higher STC is more soundproof. Figure #1 shows both the minimum and optimum recommended STC ratings for walls between various rooms. They are related to bedrooms because quiet is usually most desirable there.

To reduce noise coming in from outdoors, tight-fitting windows and doors are particularly helpful. Replacement windows will make the most noticeable difference. Low-e double-pane windows, with the air gap filled with argon gas, are most effective. The inert argon gas is very dense and it naturally blocks sound transmission through the glass.

Recommended STC Wall Ratings Between Rooms		
figure #1	Minimum	Optimum
Living room/Bedroom	50	57
Bedroom/Bedroom	48	55
Kitchen/Bedroom	52	58
Dining room/Bedroom	52	58
Bathroom/Bedroom	52	59
Family room/Bedroom	52	58

Tips to Reduce Sound Transmission Through an Existing Wall

A) Since interior walls between two rooms don't have windows, it is fairly easy to add another layer of drywall. This will yield an STC of roughly 43.

B) Add a layer of soundboard and then another layer of drywall. You need the second layer of drywall for a smooth finished surface.

C) You can add resilient channels on one wall and another layer of drywall over the channels. This helps block both normal noise and impact noise from something bumping the walls.

D) Put small foam "draft sealers" behind all electrical outlet and switch covers on the common wall in both rooms. This blocks a direct route between rooms for airborne noise.

E) If you have a common heating duct running between the two adjacent rooms, you have several options. If possible, run a separate heating duct to one of the rooms and close off the old duct in that room. Remove the duct stub running to that wall register and drywall over the opening.

F) If you can't run a separate duct, place a dresser or chest in front of the register. This blocks and absorbs some of the sounds from the other room. DO NOT PLACE THE DRESSER TOO CLOSE TO THE WALL SO THE AIR FLOW IS IMPEDED. You can buy inexpensive plastic draft diverters to place over the register to redirect the air flow.

G) Make sure that your furniture, dressers and chests are not actually touching the wall. They can help transmit the sound through the wall. They can also vibrate a little from the sound vibration and cause an impact type of noise transmission through the wall.

H) Hang a tapestry or other cloth-type decoration on the wall. These damp out some of the sound vibrations before they contact the wall.

I) Run a small bead of caulk between the floor and the bottom edge of the wall. There often are small gaps that can allow sound to pass through into the wall. If you have wall-to-wall carpeting, pull one side loose and caulk. Be sure to stretch the carpet again when reattaching it to the tack strip.

Manufacturers of Soundproofing and Recycled Products

AKZO INDUSTRIAL SYSTEMS, PO Box 7249, Asheville, NC 28802 - (704) 665-5050
Sound control under-carpet matting.

ARMSTRONG WORLD IND., PO Box 3001, Lancaster, PA 17604 - (717) 397-0611
Acoustical wall systems, wall and floor coverings.

CARLISLE TIRE & RUBBER CO., PO Box 99, Carlisle, PA 17013 - (717) 249-1000
Softpave resilient tiles produced from recycled tires and a rubber binder.

DODGE-REGUPOL, INC., PO Box 989, Lancaster, PA 17603 - (800) 322-1932 (717) 295-3400
Natural cork flooring and recycled rubber flooring.

DURABLE MAT CORP., PO Box 290, Norwalk, OH 44857 - (800) 537-1603 (419) 668-8138
A variety of floor tiles and mats made from recycled rubber.

HENDRICKSEN FLOORING, 8031 Mill Station Rd, Sebastopol, CA 95472 - (707) 829-3959
Natural linoleum and carpet made from sisal, seagrass, and wool.

HOMASOTE CO., PO Box 7240, W. Trenton, NJ 08628 - (800) 257-9491 (609) 883-3300
Structural fiberboard made from 100% recycled newsprint.

LATICRETE INTERNATIONAL, 1 Laticrete Park N., Bethany, CT 06524 - (800) 243-4788 (203) 393-0010
Sound control mortar system and underlayment.

TRUS JOINT CORP., PO Box 60, Boise, ID 83707 - (208) 375-4450
Wooden floor joist I-beams.

Partition System	Absorptive Materials	STC	Fire Rating	Weight p.s.f.
Single Stud Walls Basic construction is 2" x 4" studs 16" o.c. with double top plate and single or double bottom plate. Faces are $5/8$" thick fire resistive type gypsum board applied, taped and finished in accordance with manufacturer's recommendations. Resilient channels are applied to studs 24" o.c. as shown with a $1/2$" x 3" gypsum nailing strip at the bottom. Absorptive material is paper-backed glass fiber or mineral wool batts stapled in the stud space as illustrated. Sound deadening board is sound-rated organic fiber board with a 15-18 pcf density.	None	34	1 Hr	$6 1/2$
	None	45	1 Hr	8
	$1 1/2$" glass fiber	50	1 Hr	$6 1/2$
	$1 1/2$" glass fiber	52	1 Hr	7
	3" glass fiber	53	1 Hr	7
	2" mineral wool	59	2 Hr	12
Double Stud Walls With a Common Plate Basic construction is a double row of 2" x 3" or 2" x 4" studs, each row 16" o.c. and each row aligned with an opposite edge of the 2" x 6" top and bottom plates. The rows of studs are offset 2" to 8" to prevent any chance contact. Other details and materials are as described for single stud walls.	2" mineral wool	49	1 Hr	7
	None	49	1 Hr	10
	$1 1/2$" glass fiber	50	1 Hr	8
	$1 1/2$" glass fiber	53	1 Hr	8
	$1 1/2$" glass fiber	56	1 Hr	10
Double Stud Walls on Seperate Plates Basic construction is a double wall of 2" x 3" studs on separate plates about 1" apart. Studs of each frame are 16" o.c. with the studs in one frame offset 2" to 8" from those of the other. Other details and materials are as described for single stud walls.	2" mineral wool	51	1 Hr	$7 1/2$
	None	53	1 Hr	9
	3" mineral wool	60	1 Hr	9
	3" mineral wool	58	1 Hr	8
	None	51	2 Hr	$12 1/2$
	3" mineral wool	59	2 Hr	$12 1/2$
	3" mineral wool	57	1 Hr	10

Wall Face	
Single gypsum board each side, applied with screws; no resilient channels.	
Single gypsum board laminated and nailed over sound board on each side; no channels.	
Single gypsum board applied with screws 1 side; opposite side on resilient channels.	
Single gypsum board laminated and nailed over sound board, opposite side on resilient channels.	
Single gypsum board on resilient channels each side.	
Double $1/_2$" gypsum board, base sheet vertical; face sheet horizontal; applied on resilient channels one side.	
Single gypsum board each side, applied with screws (2x3 studs - 16" o.c.); no resilient channels.	
Single gypsum board laminated and nailed over sound deadening board each side (2x4 studs - 16" o.c.); no resilient channels.	
Single gypsum board nailed one side. Single gypsum on resilient channels opposite.	
Single gypsum board laminated and nailed over sound deadening board 1 side. Single gypsum board on resilient channels opposite (2x3 studs - 16" o.c.).	
Double gypsum board ($1/_2$" over $5/_8$") nailed one side; single gypsum board on resilient channels opposite (2x4 studs - 24" o.c.).	
Single gypsum board each side applied with screws.	
Single gypsum board laminated and nailed over sound board each side.	
Single gypsum board laminated and nailed over sound board each side.	
Single gypsum board laminated and nailed over sound board 1 side; single gypsum board on resilient channels opposite.	
Double gypsum board; nailed each side.	
Double gypsum board each side; outer layer laminated and nailed; base layer nailed.	
Double gypsum board laminated and nailed one side. Single gypsum board on resilient channels opposite.	

Q: We are adding a room to our house with 2x4 studded walls. What type of insulation should we use in the walls? We are also considering increasing the insulation in our existing house.

A: There are several new types of insulation available that are very effective and reasonably-priced. Installing the proper type and amount of insulation can lower your utility bills significantly. Check your local building codes for minimum insulation requirements.

One very effective type of insulation mixes a special latex adhesive binder with blown-in insulation to provide rigidity. After the insulation is blown into the wall cavity, it becomes stiff enough to resist settling. Even a small insulation void area at the top of a wall cavity, due to settling with standard insulation, can result in a great energy loss.

For the existing uninsulated walls of your house, this non-settling insulation is blown in small installation holes from outdoors. With siding, one strip is removed and small holes are drilled. With brick veneer, bricks are carefully removed and replaced after blowing in the insulation. This is not foam insulation that can give off formaldehyde.

For your room addition, fine nylon netting is stapled over the indoor edge of the studs. Then the non-settling insulation is blown-in behind the netting where it becomes stiff. This eliminates any energy-wasting voids and gaps and provides an insulation value of R-4.3 per inch with fiberglass. Also, your house is more soundproof with fewer voids.

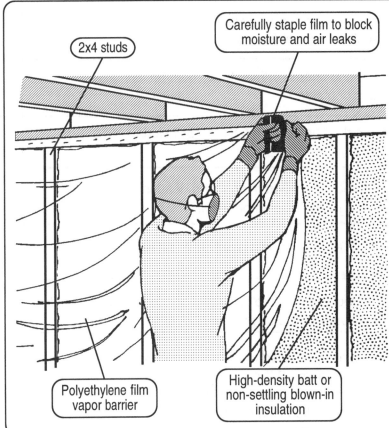

2x4 studs

Carefully staple film to block moisture and air leaks

Polyethylene film vapor barrier

High-density batt or non-settling blown-in insulation

With the 2x4 studded walls in your addition, you have about a 3½-inch width inside the walls for insulation. Some of the new high-density fiberglass batts (insulation value of R-13 or R-15) may be cost effective alternatives to standard R-11 batts.

For example, if your state codes require a R-16 wall insulation level, you can install high-density R-15 fiberglass batts and very inexpensive sheathing. Overall, this is less expensive than installing the cheaper standard R-11 batts with expensive rigid foam insulation sheathing. For R-19 walls, you can use high-density batts and thinner foam sheathing.

Always have your builder do an insulation level payback analysis for you. Often, while you are already building a new addition or retrofitting an existing house, adding extra insulation barely increases labor costs. Your building code minimums don't always offer the optimum payback.

Q: I burn my open fireplace often, both for the heat and the aesthetics. I use newspapers to get the fire started. Can I use old rolled up newspapers exclusively in my fireplace?

A: Old newspapers burn fairly well, but you should not use them exclusively. A mix of half wooden logs and half newspaper logs provides a more complete burn.

Be careful when burning newspapers in your fireplace. If you have glass doors on your fireplace, the newspaper can flare up and cause flash fires. Over time, these flash fires can reduce the temper of the glass and it can fracture. Hot ashes can then be blown out into your room. Also, be careful storing old newspapers since they can become a fire hazard.

Listed below are the new types of insulation and manufacturers of exterior insulation systems. The manufacturers of high-density fiberglass batts are shown below. The manufacturer (Ark-seal) of the equipment used to install the non-settling "Blown-in Batt" insulation is shown below. You can contact this company to find which insulation contractors uses its process in your area.

Charts to determine the payback from adding insulation are shown on the following pages. These are based on the annual number of heating degree days of your climate. The more heating degree days, the colder the climate is. Find the major city closest to your location and use its number of heating degree days. Round it up or down to the nearest 1,000 heating degree days.

These payback charts show the savings in therms of natural gas. Based on your local utility rates, you can determine the amount of dollars saved. To convert these figures to oil multiply the savings in therms by .7 to get the savings in gallons of oil per year. For LP gas, multiply the savings in therms by 1.08 to get the savings in gallons. For electric resistance heating, multiply the savings in therms by 21 to get the savings in kilowatt-hours. For a heat pump, multiply the savings in therms by the following factors depending on your climate to get the savings in kilowatt-hours -

2,000 - 3,000 heating degree days - multiplier of 12
4,000 - 5,000 heating degree days - multiplier of 15
6,000 - 7,000 heating degree days - multiplier of 17
8,000 - 9,000 heating degree days - multiplier of 18

The reason for the variable factors listed above for heat pumps is that heat pumps become less efficient in cold temperatures. Therefore, in colder climates with greater heating degree days, the utility bills are higher and the savings are greater.

Manufacturers of High-Efficiency Insulation

ARK-SEAL, 2190 S. Kalamath, Denver, CO 80223 - (800) 525-8992
 <u>type</u> - non-settling blown-in
CELOTEX CORP., 4010 Boy Scout Blvd., Tampa, FL 33607 - (813) 873-4000
 <u>type</u> - slag wool ceiling tiles
CERTAINTEED, P.O. Box 860, Valley Forge, PA 19482 - (800) 441-9850 (215) 341-7000
 <u>type</u> - high-density batts, fiber glass building insulation, pipe and board, duct and metal building insulations
EVANITE FIBER CORP., PO Box E, Corvallis, OR 97339 - (503) 753-1211
 <u>type</u> - fiber glass aerospace and cryogenic insulations
ISOLATEK INTERNATIONAL, 41 Furnace St., Stanhope, NJ 07874 - (201) 347-1200
 <u>type</u> - slag wool insulations (bulk), fire protection (sprayed), building insulation (sprayed)
KNAUF FIBER GLASS, 240 Elizabeth St., Shelbyville, IN 46176 - (800) 825-4434
 <u>type</u> - high-density batts, fiber glass building insulation, pipe and board, duct and metal building insulations
OWENS-CORNING, Fiberglas Tower, Toledo, OH 43659 - (800) 438-7465 (419) 248-8000
 <u>type</u> - high-density batts, fiber glass building insulation, pipe and board, duct and metal building insulations
PARTEK INSULATIONS, INC., 401 Westpark Ct., Peachtree City, GA 30269 - (404) 631-1200
 <u>type</u> - rock wool pipe, board and blanket insulations, rock wool roof insulations
ROCK WOOL MFG. CO., 203 N. 7th St., Leeds, AL 35094 - (205) 699-6121
 <u>type</u> - slag wool building, pipe and board and commercial insulations
ROXUL INC., 55 Harrop Dr., Milton, Ontario L9T 3H3 - (416) 878-8474
 <u>type</u> - rock and slag wool building, board, duct, metal building and roof insulations
SCHULLER INTERNATIONAL, P.O. Box 5108, Denver, CO 80217 - (800) 654-3103
 <u>type</u> - high-density batts, fiber glass building insulation, pipe and board, duct, metal building and aerospace insulations
SLOSS INDUSTRIES, 3500 35th Ave., N., Birmingham, AL 35207 - (205) 254-7802
 <u>type</u> - slag wool insulations (bulk)
USG INTERIORS, INC., 125 S. Franklin St., Chicago, IL 60606 - (312) 606-4000
 <u>type</u> - slag wool board and blanket insulations and ceiling tiles
WESTERN FIBERGLASS, INC., 4340 West 850 South, Salt Lake City, UT 84104 - (801) 972-1223
 <u>type</u> - fiber glass building and metal building insulations

Ceiling Insulation

therms of natural gas burned per season to replace heat lost through 1,000 sq. ft. of ceiling

R-value of insulation in ceiling	Degree-day zone								
	2,000	3,000	4,000	5,000	6,000	7,000	8,000	9,000	10,000
0	192	297	408	519	631	740	850	964	1076
1	144	223	306	389	474	555	637	723	807
3	96	148	204	260	316	370	425	482	538
5	72	111	153	195	237	278	319	362	404
7	52	83	115	147	179	212	245	278	311
9	43	69	96	123	149	177	204	231	260
11	37	59	82	105	128	151	175	198	222
13	33	52	72	92	112	133	153	174	195
15	29	46	64	82	100	118	136	154	173
17	23	38	54	69	85	102	118	134	151
19	21	35	49	63	78	92	107	122	137
21	19	32	45	58	71	85	98	111	126
24	17	28	40	51	63	75	87	99	112
30	14	23	33	42	52	62	71	81	91
38	9	16	23	30	38	45	52	60	68
44	8	14	20	26	33	39	45	52	59
50	7	12	18	23	29	35	40	46	52
56	6	11	16	21	26	31	36	42	47

Ceiling Insulation

The R-value for commercially available ceiling insulation materials may vary widely, from about 2.0 to 4.0 per inch depending upon the material, the density, the temperature, and the quality of installation. Settling or shrinking may, in time, reduce the effectiveness of the insulation.

The pre-calculated values for therms per season in the above table include an allowance for the R-value of the ceiling construction.

• If there is insulation in your attic now, you may use the following figures to approximate the R-value of the existing insulation: vermiculite - R-2 per inch of thickness; mineral wool, glass fiber, cellulose - R-3 per inch of thickness. By interpolation, use the R-value in the table.

• Ask your insulation supplier for the R-value of the insulation material to be used.

Example: A single-story house in the 4,000 degree-day zone has an attic floor area of 30 ft. by 50 ft. The 1,500 sq. ft. of ceiling area is not now insulated. The supplier offers insulation with an R-19 rating.

Fuel Requirement before and after changes.

1. Before: The values in the first line (R-0) are for ceiling-attic construction with no insulation. For each 1,000 sq. ft. the therms required are 408.

2. After: The values in the line for R-19 show 49 therms for each 1,000 sq. ft. of ceiling area.

3. Therm Savings: For each 1,000 sq. ft., the savings will be 408 - 49 = 359 therms per season.

4. Adjustment for Area: 359 x 1.5 = 538 therms for 1,500 sq. ft.

Annual Heating Degree Days for Various Cities

City	Days	City	Days	City	Days
ALABAMA		LOUISIANA		NORTH DAKOTA	
Birmingham	2,551	Baton Rouge	1,560	Bismarck	8,851
Huntsville	3,070	New Orleans	1,385	Fargo	9,226
Mobile	1,560	Shreveport	2,184	OHIO	
ALASKA		MAINE		Cincinnati	4,806
Anchorage	10,864	Caribou	9,767	Columbus	5,281
Barrow	20,174	Portland	7,511	Cleveland	6,351
Fairbanks	14,279	MARYLAND		OKLAHOMA	
ARIZONA		Baltimore	4,654	Oklahoma City	3,725
Flagstaff	7,152	Frederick	5,087	Tulsa	3,860
Phoenix	1,442	MASSACHUSETTS		OREGON	
Tucson	1,800	Boston	5,634	Medford	5,008
ARKANSAS		Nantucket	5,891	Portland	4,635
Fort Smith	3,292	Worcester	6,950	PENNSYLVANIA	
Little Rock	3,219	MICHIGAN		Erie	6,451
CALIFORNIA		Detroit	6,232	Philadelphia	5,101
Fresno	2,492	Grand Rapids	6,894	Pittsburgh	5,278
Los Angeles	1,204	Marquette	8,393	Scranton	6,254
San Diego	1,439	MINNESOTA		RHODE ISLAND	
Sacramento	2,843	Duluth	10,000	Providence	5,954
San Francisco	3,015	Minneapolis	8,382	SOUTH CAROLINA	
COLORADO		Rochester	8,295	Charleston	2,003
Alamosa	8,529	MISSISSIPPI		Spartanburg	3,074
Denver	6,283	Jackson	2,239	SOUTH DAKOTA	
Pueblo	5,462	Vicksburg	2,041	Huron	8,223
CONNECTICUT		MISSOURI		Rapid City	7,345
Bridgeport	5,617	Kansas City	4,711	TENNESSEE	
Hartford	6,172	St. Joseph	5,484	Chattanooga	3,254
New Haven	5,897	Springfield	4,561	Memphis	3,207
DELAWARE		St. Louis	4,980	Nashville	3,756
Wilmington	4,930	MONTANA		TEXAS	
FLORIDA		Great Falls	7,750	Amarillo	3,985
Jacksonville	1,239	Billings	7,212	Austin	1,711
Miami	199	Missoula	8,125	Dallas	2,405
Orlando	656	NEBRASKA		El Paso	645
Tampa	683	Lincoln	5,864	Houston	1,396
GEORGIA		Omaha	6,612	UTAH	
Atlanta	2,983	NEVADA		Salt Lake City	5,802
Augusta	2,568	Ely	7,733	Milford	6,497
Columbus	2,383	Las Vegas	2,709	VERMONT	
Savannah	1,819	Reno	6,332	Burlington	8,269
IDAHO		NEW HAMPSHIRE		VIRGINIA	
Boise	5,809	Concord	7,383	Lynchburg	4,166
Idaho FAlls	8,475	NEW JERSEY		Norfolk	3,421
ILLINOIS		Atlantic City	4,812	Richmond	3,960
Cairo	3,821	Newark	4,972	Roanoke	4,315
Chicago	6,155	Trenton	4,980	WASHINGTON	
Springfield	5,429	NEW MEXICO		Seattle	4,424
INDIANA		Albuquerque	4,348	Spokane	6,655
Evansville	4,435	Silver City	3,705	WASHINGTON DC	4,122
Indianapolis	5,699	NEW YORK		WEST VIRGINIA	
South Bend	6,439	Albany	6,875	Charleston	4,476
IOWA		Buffalo	7,062	Huntington	4,676
Des Moines	6,808	New York City	4,871	Parkersburg	4,754
Dubuque	7,376	NORTH CAROLINA		WISCONSIN	
KANSAS		Charlotte	3,342	Green Bay	8,029
Dodge City	4,986	Raleigh	3,393	La Crosse	7,589
Topeka	5,319			Madison	7,863
Wichita	4,787			Milwaukee	7,635
KENTUCKY				WYOMING	
Lexington	4,814			Lander	7,870
Louisville	4,660			Sheridan	7,683

Foundation Insulation									
therms of natural gas burned per season to replace heat lost through 10 ft. of foundation									
foundation type	Degree-day zone								
	2,000	3,000	4,000	5,000	6,000	7,000	8,000	9,000	10,000
basement									
not insulated	9	13	18	23	28	33	38	43	48
insulated	3	5	7	9	11	13	16	18	20
crawl space									
not insulated	4	6	8	10	12	14	16	18	20
insulated	2	2	3	4	5	6	7	8	9

Wall Insulation									
therms of natural gas burned per season to replace heat lost through 1,000 sq. ft. of wall									
Wall stud size	R-value of insulation in crawl space	Degree-day zone							
		2,000	3,000	4,000	5,000	6,000	7,000	8,000	9,000	10,000
2x4	none	144	223	306	389	474	555	637	723	807
	R-6	58	89	122	156	189	222	255	289	323
	R-11	37	59	82	105	128	151	175	198	222
	R-13	33	52	72	92	112	133	153	174	195
2x6	R-19	21	35	49	63	78	92	107	122	137
double stud 8½" space	R-30	11	19	28	37	46	56	65	74	84
double stud 10½" space	R-38	9	16	23	30	38	45	52	60	68

Foundations

(Diagram labels: R-19, R-11, vapor barrier — basement no insulation — basement insulated; R-19, R-7, vapor barrier — crawl space no insulation — crawl space insulated)

Basements

Many heating contractors overlook heat losses from basements, and assume that the basement will be kept warm by heat lost from the furnace or boiler casing plus heat from ducts and pipes which pass through the basement. The heat lost from the basement is as costly as heat lost from the living room. Any reduction in basement heat loss will result in a warmer basement and warmer floors for the rooms above.

Complete insulation in this case consist of: storm sash over basement windows, caulking between sill plate and foundation, insulation of the space next to the band joist, and insulation of the basement wall. The calculations in Table 3 are based upon insulating the basement walls with R-4 foam plastic board covered with ½-inch gypsum drywall, the band joist with R-19 batts, and double glazing on basement windows.

Crawl Spaces

All crawl spaces should be dry and well above the water table for the sire. The ground surface should be covered with a layer of polyethylene plastic to prevent the evaporation of water vapor from the ground into the crawl space and eventually into the house above.

One alternative that is frequently recommended in the case of houses with electrical resistance heating is to place insulating batts between the floor joists (as much as R-19) to prevent heat loss from the heated space to the crawl space. Any water pipes in the crawl space (both hot and cold) should be located above the insulation. Insulating the floor over a crawl space may increase cooling costs, since it prevents the radiation of summer heat to the cooler ground surface.

The second alternative, which is preferred in houses with heating ducts or heating pipes in the crawl space, is to insulate the crawl space walls and to close the foundation vents. In this case, the crawl space will be partially heated by the heat radiating from ducts and pipes. Complete insulation of the crawl space consists of: closing of all vent openings in the foundation walls, covering of the vent openings with insulating inserts, caulking between the sill plate and the top of the foundation, insulation of the band joist (R-19), and insulation of the crawl space walls (R-10).

Wall Insulation

The net wall area is obtained by subtracting total window and exposed doors from the gross wall area. Consider only the net wall areas that are to be improved by insulation. Since the R-values of insulation materials vary widely, a range of R-values from about 3.2 per inch to 3.7 per inch is shown.

• Obtain the R-value of the insulation material to be installed from the supplier.
• Find the value in the second column that most nearly corresponds to the insulation R-value. (Note that the R-value for the wall construction has been included in the pre-calculated table.) Interpolate when necessary.
• The 8½-inch and 10½-inch stud spaces are for double-wall construction.

Example: A single-story house in a locality with about 5,200 degree-days per season is 30' by 50' with walls 8' high. The frame walls (2x4 studs) are currently empty. The walls are to be filled with insulation. The supplier gives an R-13 value for the product.

Fuel Requirement before and after change.

1. **Before:** The values in the first line (R-0) are for 2x4 stud walls with no insulation. The gross wall area is (30 + 50 + 30 + 50) x 8 = 1,280 sq. ft. The door and window areas total 210 sq. ft. Therefore, the net wall area is 1280 - 210 = 1,070 sq. ft. Use the value under the 5,000 degree-day column without interpolation; 389 therms for 1,000 sq. ft.
2. **After:** From the table, the value in the line for R-13 insulation shows 92 therms for each 1,000 square feet of net wall area.
3. **Therm Savings:** For each 1,000 square feet, the savings would be 389 - 92 = 297 therms per season.
4. **Adjustment for Area:** 297 x 1.07 = 318 therms per season.

Basis for Calculations

The following assumptions were made in the calculation procedure used in this circular: A degree-day base of 65°F; an indoor-air temperature of 70°F; R-values and U-values for materials as published in ASHRAE tables; for natural gas, furnace and boiler efficiency of 70%; for fuel oil, calorific value of 140,000 Btu per gallon and efficiency of 70%; for electrical resistance heating, thermal value of 3412 Btu per kWh and efficiency of 100%; for electrical heat pump heating, performance as indicated; infiltration, based on crackage method, is included in the heat loss for doors and windows; R-value for ceiling-roof combination is based on an R of 3 (R-value of ceiling alone) and temperature difference taken from indoor to outdoor air.

Q: I have weatherstripped my front and side doors, but there's a draft coming in underneath them. How can I seal out the drafts under the doors without having the seal rub on my carpet when opening the door?

A: The threshold seal under a door is often neglected when weatherstripping. It receives the most abuse from opening and closing the door and from feet and objects being dragged over it. Just a small leak there can cause cold feet in the winter and can push up your utility bills year-round.

There are literally hundreds of different design, shapes, and materials of door threshold seals. Some use new resilient plastic materials that wear extremely well and retain their shape for a durable long-lasting seal.

Your problem with the door threshold seal rubbing and wearing your carpet is a common one. The best type of door threshold seal to protect your carpet is an automatic-lifting seal. There are several designs available.

The easiest design to install screws on to the surface of the door at the bottom. It is only about one to two inches high and barely noticeable. This is good for both wood and insulated steel doors. For solid wood doors, you can mount it the same way or rout out the door bottom to recess the seal. This is more work, but the seal is totally hidden under the door.

When you close the door, a tiny rod pushes against the door jamb on the hinge side. This forces the flexible seal down so it seals tightly against the floor or threshold. Although an automatic seal is more

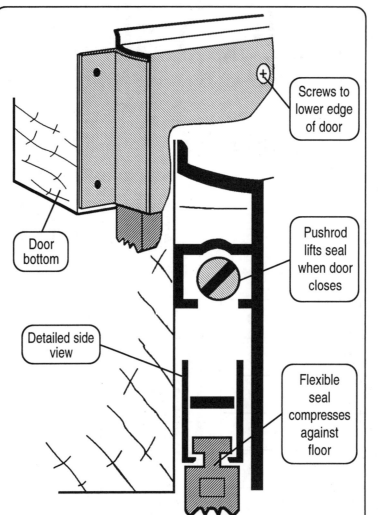

Door bottom

Screws to lower edge of door

Detailed side view

Pushrod lifts seal when door closes

Flexible seal compresses against floor

expensive than a standard one, it should last a long time since it doesn't rub.

Another option is to install an aluminum or wood threshold, with a built-in vinyl bulb seal, underneath the door. You will have to cut a small amount off the bottom of your door for clearance. This works well if the floor under your door is worn down.

Its only drawback is that the vinyl bulb can get damaged over time by the pitter patter of your children's feet and the friction of the door bottom. Replacement vinyl bulb seals are inexpensive and slip easily in place.

You can add an attractive wood threshold on the floor beneath your door and use a door sweep seal. Some new sweeps, made of silicon, are more durable than the common vinyl sweeps you usually find. They wear well and remain flexible at cold temperatures. You can get special multiple-sweep seals and door shoes to deflect rain too.

Q: I have a crawl space underneath my house. The floor above it is insulated. There are outdoor vents in the crawl space, but there is still mold on the underside of the floor lumber. Why?

A: Venting your crawl space was a good idea, but only a partial solution. You also should lay 6-mil thick plastic vapor barrier over the ground and up the crawl space walls to the top. This blocks the moisture.

To kill the mold on the joists, mix one-half to three-quarters cup of bleach to a gallon of water. Spray it on the joists. Be sure to wear safety goggles.

With all but the automatic types of door threshold seals, you should plan to install a replacement flexible seal strip every several years. These only cost a couple of dollars and take only a few minutes to replace. Automatic threshold seals, ones that lift up as soon as the door begins to open, are protected and do not drag across the floor or carpet. The actual flexible seal is only compressed when the door closes, so it lasts longer. When you select a door threshold seal of any type, make sure that you can purchase replacement seal elements.

The chart below shows the advantages and disadvantages of the most common types of seals. Page 263 shows general do-it-yourself installation instructions to help you determine which type to select. The packaging on most door threshold seals shows detailed installation instructions for that specific design. To attain a good airtight seal, the quality of the installation job is as important as the quality of the materials used.

To determine if your door needs a new threshold seal, hold a stick of lighted incense near the door bottom on a windy day. By watching the trail of the smoke, you can quickly determine the airtightness of the seal. While you are testing your door bottom with the incense smoke, check the rest of the door weatherstripping for leaks. One of the most durable and inexpensive types of weatherstripping is a spring metal strip. It is also easy to install, even for the inexperienced do-it-yourselfer. You will probably have to use several short pieces of adhesive-backed foam strip weatherstripping around the dead bolt latch area

The type of door that you have is also a factor in determining which type of threshold seal to select. Since solid wood doors expand and contract throughout the year, if you have one, you should select a taller type of flexible seal material. This is because it will have to seal over a wide range of gap widths from summer to winter. This is also an excellent application for an automatic seal.

- -

Advantages and Disadvantages of Common Types of Door Threshold Seals

STANDARD SWEEP
Advantages: Easy to install, low cost, easily replaced, moderate durability, no need to trim door bottom.

Disadvantages: May drag on carpet, door must be even, moderate sealing quality, visible on bottom of door.

AUTOMATIC SWEEP
Advantages: Very durable, will not wear carpet, very airtight seal, adjustable if floor settles

Disadvantages: Visible on bottom of indoor edge of door, more difficult to install, more expensive

DOOR SHOE
Advantages: Low cost, very durable, very airtight seal, not visible on door, rain drip cap available.

Disadvantages: Must remove and trim door to install, floor or threshold must be even.

VINYL BULB & THRESHOLD
Advantages: Useful where no present threshold or floor is worn, vinyl seal is easily replaced, attractive appearance.

Disadvantages: Exposed vinyl bulb is susceptible to wear, must remove and bevel bottom of door, higher cost.

INTERLOCKING
Advantages: Excellent seal, very durable, attractive, rain drip cap available.

Disadvantages: Must remove door to install, must be properly aligned, higher cost.

Do-it-Yourself Door Threshold Installation Instructions

SWEEP THRESHOLD

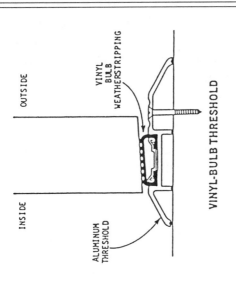

1) Make sure that the floor or threshold is even so the sweep seals against it.

2) Measure the width of your door and saw the sweep to a length about one-eighth inch shorter.

3) Center the sweep on the bottom of your door so it just touches the floor or threshold.

4) Mark the location of the slotted holes on your door.

5) Remove the sweep and drill holes in the marked spots.

6) Screw the sweep into place, leaving the screws loose.

7) Slide the sweep down so it rest firmly against the floor or threshold. Tighten the screws.

VINYL-BULB THRESHOLD

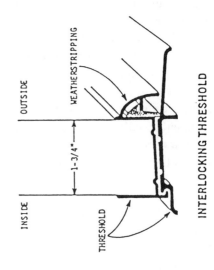

1) Saw the threshold to fit in the door opening on the floor.

2) Slip the vinyl bulb into the threshold and measure its height above the floor.

3) Mark the height of the uncompressed threshold on the bottom edge of the door.

4) Remove the door from the hinges.

5) Saw the bottom of the door on an angle so that it will slightly compress the vinyl bulb when the door closes.

6) Mark and drill mounting holes in the floor. Screw the threshold in place.

7) Snap the vinyl bulb in the slot in the threshold.

8) Replace the door on the hinges.

VINYL-BULB DOOR OVER THRESHOLD

1) Make sure that the floor or threshold is even so the shoe seals against it.

2) Measure up from the floor or threshold and mark a line about 1/2" high on the door.

3) Remove the door and saw along the marked line.

4) Center the door shoe over the bottom of the door with the rain drip cap to the outside.

5) Mark the mounting holes on the bottom of the door.

6) Remove the door shoe and drill the holes.

7) Screw the door shoe into place and replace the door.

INTERLOCKING THRESHOLD

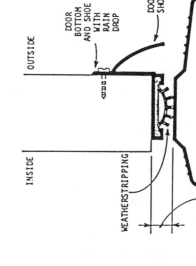

1) Saw the floor section of the threshold to fit the door opening.

2) Saw the door section to a length about 1/16" narrower than the width of the door.

3) Open the door and position the floor section on the floor.

4) Position the door section in its interlocking position and measure the height for the floor.

5) Mark that height on the bottom of the door.

6) Remove the door and saw the bottom off that exact height.

7) Drill holes and screw the door section to the door bottom.

8) Replace the door on the hinges and make sure the two pieces interlock properly.

9) If not, remove door and shim the door section until it fits.

263

Home Office & Plant
4226 Transport St.
Ventura, CA 93003
(805) 642-2600

Branch Office Plant
5535 Distribution Dr., Memphis, TN 38118 • (901) 365-2160

INSTRUCTIONS FOR INSTALLING
PEMKO AUTOMATIC DOOR BOTTOMS
#411 AR, 412CR, 4131 CR, 430CR, 434AR For wood or metal doors
U.S. Patent No. 3,703,788

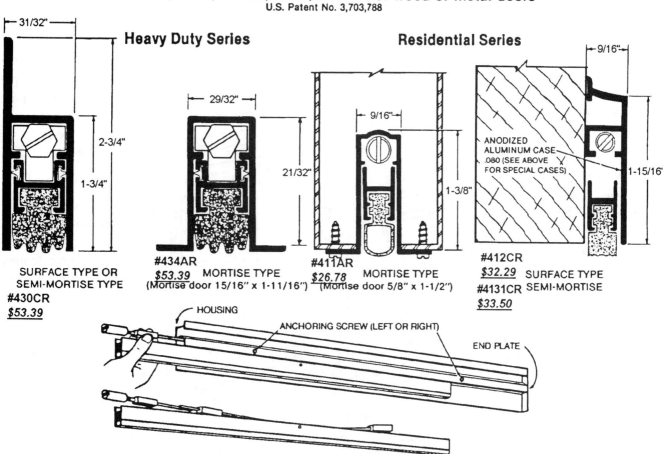

Heavy Duty Series

31/32"

2-3/4"

1-3/4"

SURFACE TYPE OR
SEMI-MORTISE TYPE
#430CR
$53.39

29/32"

21/32"

#434AR
$53.39 MORTISE TYPE
(Mortise door 15/16" x 1-11/16")

Residential Series

9/16"

1-3/8"

#411AR
$26.78 MORTISE TYPE
(Mortise door 5/8" x 1-1/2")

9/16"

ANODIZED
ALUMINUM CASE
.080 (SEE ABOVE
FOR SPECIAL CASES)

1-15/16"

#412CR
$32.29 SURFACE TYPE
#4131CR SEMI-MORTISE
$33.50

HOUSING

ANCHORING SCREW (LEFT OR RIGHT)

END PLATE

DROP BAR AND PUSH ROD ASSEMBLY

The SURFACE and SEMI-MORTISE models may be reversed for left or right hand installations. It is not necessary to reverse the full mortise model. All models may be trimmed down 3". However, it is necessary to determine the hand and reverse the mechanism, if required, prior to cutting down the unit to fit the door.

To reverse (see illustration) remove the small anchoring screw on back of the unit, and slide out drop bar push rod assemblies together. Replace these assemblies in the opposite end, line up the hole in the end anchor with the pre-drilled hole in the case, and replace the retaining screw.

After hand is determined and unit is cut to size (cut end opposite plunger), fasten to properly prepared door with screws for nails. (Nails furnished in addition to screws on #411 model.) Attach end plate to end opposite plunger and attach striker plate or screw to jamb.* Notice that some end plates are made with break-off sections to compensate for left or right hand installations.

The automatic may be set to seal up to 7/8" gap under the door by turning the adjusting screw on plunger counter clockwise until neoprene or felt just touches the floor surface when door is closed. It is not necessary to squash the neoprene or felt against the floor for a good seal.

Note that where the floor surface is not even and no saddle or threshold is being used for the automatic to seal against, it may be necessary to remove the drop bar and to contour it to fit the floor. The aluminum drop bar section may be curved slightly by bending carefully so that the center is approximately 1/32" off the floor with the ends touching. Avoid bending the aluminum bar sideways as this may cause the unit to jamb in the case.

* For wood jambs, a striker plate is mounted on jamb opposite plunger for Heavy Duty Series. With Residential Series, a flat head screw is provided to mount opposite plunger on wood doors.

A vestibule can reduce chilly drafts

Q: My children seem to run in and out the back door 100 times a day. This creates a chilly draft each time and much dust. Does it make sense to build a vestibule around the door and how can I build one myself?

A: Building a simple do-it-yourself exterior vestibule around your back door can help cut your utility bills, both winter and summer. If you are handy with tools, you should be able to build a very attractive and inexpensive vestibule over a weekend.

A vestibule saves even when the back door is not being opened. The dead air space provides additional insulation value to the back door and frame area. Also, most well-used exterior back doors no longer have a good airtight seal. A vestibule reduces the air leakage past your back door weatherstripping.

By reducing the drafts inside your house, you may be able to set your thermostat a degree or two lower and still be comfortable. Depending on your climate, you will save from 1% to 3% on your utility bills for each degree you lower your thermostat setting.

In addition to saving energy, a vestibule offers extra storage area for coats, wet boots, etc. and keeps muddy little feet out of your house. If you have allergies, the "air lock" it creates helps block the free flow of pollen and mold spores into your house each time the door is opened.

The simplest do-it-yourself exterior vestibule utilizes basic 2x4 wall framing and a simple built-up roof. You should install a large pre-hung door. Since the vestibule is not heated, an inexpensive non-insulated door should be adequate. Good weatherstripping, though, is an energy plus.

Install a window for natural lighting. An inexpensive single-pane window is adequate but a double or triple pane will be more energy efficient. If the window faces south, you should install a large window. The vestibule can then also function as a passive solar collector to further reduce heat loss from your house. You should still wire a single overhead light for nighttime use.

Although wall insulation is not required, you may want to use insulating foam sheathing instead of plywood. This is especially true if the window does face south for some solar heating. You can cover the walls with aluminum or vinyl siding for low maintenance.

Q: I am told that I should tighten up my home to save energy. Can you tell me how much heat is contained in that air that leaks out?

A: Each cubic foot of air holds very little heat, only .018 Btu per degree temperature. This means it takes .018 Btu of heat to raise one cubic foot of air one degree higher in temperature.

With an older house, it is not uncommon to have two complete air changes per hour. A 1,500 square foot home with 8 foot ceilings has a volume of 12,000 cubic feet. It can lose 24,000 cubic feet of air each hour.

If it's 40 degrees outdoors and 70 degrees indoors, your furnace must heat that incoming cold air 30 degrees. By multiplying 24,000 cubic feet of air times 30 degrees and then that number by the .018 factor, you get the total amount of heat lost to air leaks. For the example above, it would average about 13,000 Btu per hour.

Large window

Built-up roof

Pre-hung door

Siding

Insulating sheathing

By building an exterior vestibule around your back door the key energy-saving feature of a vestibule is the air lock it creates when the door is opened and the overall reduction in air leakage through your existing back door.

In cold climates, if your back door is on the south side of your house, the vestibule can also be used as a passive solar heater. In this case, you should install a fairly-large window on the south side of it and insulate it so it stays warm.

In warm climates, you should install an awning over the window to minimize heat buildup in the summer. Installing insulating clear low-e window film can help both summer and winter.

Do-it-Yourself Instructions for Building a Vestibule

1) Before beginning to build this vestibule, plan your project. You can make the unit to fit any size door. Try to size it to be consistent with the rest of your house.

2) Make all your measurements carefully and stake out the corners of the foundation of your vestibule. Dig the trench for your foundation footings to be at least one foot below the frost line.

3) Pour the concrete in the trench for the footings and allow enough time for it to set up. Build the foundation with concrete blocks. Make it high enough so that there is at least one course of blocks above the ground level. Pour concrete in the cavities in the blocks and set foundation bolts in the concrete.

Required Materials for Vestibule
lumber - 2x4, 2x6, 2x8
pre-hung door
window
plywood sheathing
foam insulation board sheathing
silicone caulk
metal flashing
paint
floor covering
concrete blocks
concrete
nails
sill seal

4) Lay sill seal on top of the concrete blocks. Then attach 2x6 sill plates (A) to the foundation. Bolt the sill plates to the foundation bolts. Set 2x8's (C,D) on top of the sill plates as shown.

5) Nail 2x8 joists (E) to the sill plates and to the skirt. Nail down the plywood decking (F).

6) Construct sidewall for the vestibule separately. It is easiest to build them on the ground first. Use double studs at the corners and around the openings for windows and doors. Raise the sidewalls one by one in to position on the plywood decking and nail them to both the 2x8 skirt and to each other at the corners. Also attach the walls together by lapping a second top plate.

7) Build the roof on the ground. First build a frame of 2x6's (G,H). The outer edges of the frame should be flush with the finished siding. Then nail 2x6 rafters (I) in between them. Sheathe the roof with exterior-grade plywood (J).

8) Nail metal flashing around the perimeter of the roof. Fashion a built-up roof with layers of building paper and tar. Then set the roof on the wall framing and nail it to the wall top plates. Make sure the roof slopes away from the house wall.

9) Run electrical wiring for the light between the framing members.

10) Bolt 2x4 bench supports (K) to the sidewall studs and to the roof rafters.

11) Nail plywood sheathing to the outside surface of the walls. If it does face south and you are in a cold climate, you may want to use foam insulation board sheathing instead of plain plywood.

12) Install the window and door in the openings and caulk them with silicone caulk.

13) Nail aluminum or vinyl siding to the outside of the wall sheathing.

14) Finish the inside wall surface if you want a more finished appearance from the inside.

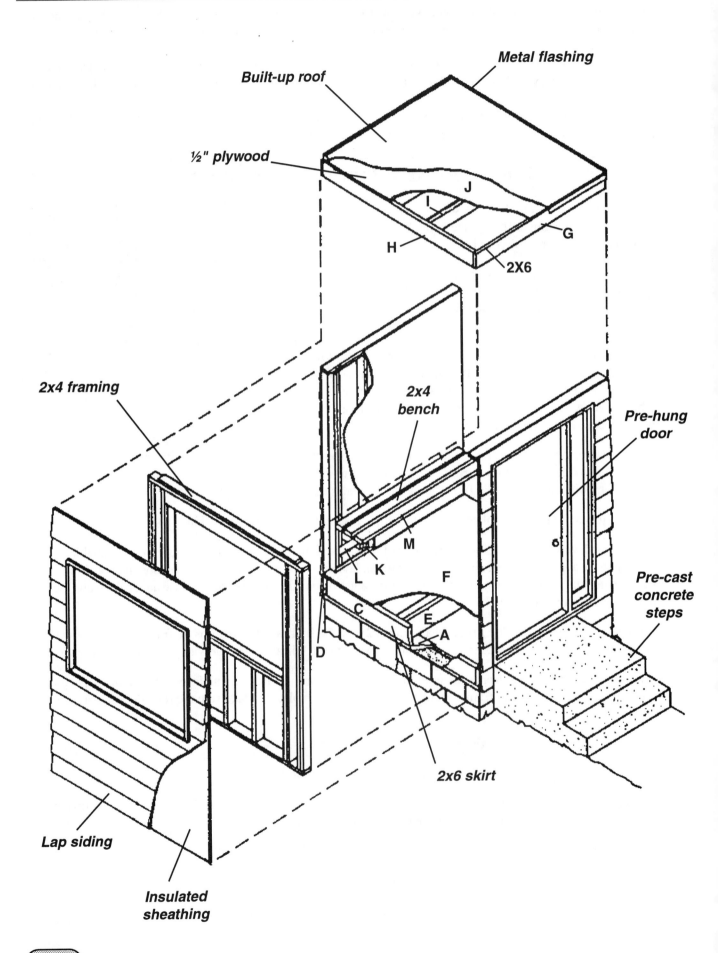

Metal flashing

Built-up roof

½" plywood

J

I

H

G

2X6

2x4 framing

2x4 bench

Pre-hung door

M

K

L

F

D

C

E

A

Pre-cast concrete steps

2x6 skirt

Lap siding

Insulated sheathing

Do-it-Yourself Instructions for Building an Indoor Bookcase/Vestibule

1) First, check which way your ceiling joists run because you will want to nail the top plates of the vestibule to the joists. Nail the three top plates (A, B, C,) to the joists.

2) Cut and pull back the carpeting and the carpet pad where the vestibule will be built. Mark the location of the soleplates (D, E, F) on the floor directly under the top plates on the ceiling. Nail the soleplates to the floor.

3) Following the diagram, nail the studs (G) between the top and soleplates.

4) Attach the door header pieces (H) in between the studs (G) as shown. Also nail the header for the bookcase (I, J) in place. Brace these headers with studs (K). Nail pieces (L,M) into place for added support.

5) Next make the bookshelf divider using 2x4's (N,O). Center the divider in the bookshelf opening and nail it to the frame and floor. Attach the halves with angle brackets.

6) Cut away the section of the   soleplate under the door opening to make room for the pre-hung   door. Nail the pre-hung door into place.

7) Finish the walls with drywall may also finish the and nicer look.

Required Materials for Indoor Bookcase/Vestibule

lumber - 2x4's
lumber - ½" plywood
drywall
drywall tape
pre-hung door
door threshold
wood trim molding
bookshelf supports
bookshelf clips
angle brackets
latex caulk
weatherstripping
interior paint
nails
screws

and tape all the joints. You inside too for a more finished

8) Attach the adjustable shelf supports to the sides of the shelf opening and to each side of the divider.

Pre-hung door

9) Cut the shelves from the ½" plywood and finish them. Attach the clips for the shelf supports and slide in the shelves.

Shelf supports

10) Cut the door trim to size and nail it around the door.

11) Install a door threshold under the door. You will probably have to cut off the bottom of the door for clearance. A vinyl bulb type of threshold would be a good choice.

12) Caulk all the joints and weatherstrip the door. Then paint the vestibule with interior wall paint.

13) Lay the carpeting back against the vestibule and cut and fit it for a snug fit. Finish it off with a molding around the bottom of vestibule.

Windbreak shields patio door; saves energy

Q: I have a large glass patio door. It always seems hot near it in the summer and drafty and cold in the winter. What can I do inexpensively to block the sun and cold and reduce the drafts?

A: A large glass patio door is one of the greatest energy guzzlers year-round. This is due to the large amount of mating edges that must be sealed and the huge glass surface area.

In the summer, the majority of the heat is from the direct sun and from heat reflected off of the patio. Even if the door itself is shaded, direct sun on the patio radiates upward. Air leakage is not as significant a problem in the summer as in the winter.

In the winter, some of the chilly drafts are not caused by air leaks at all. Warm room air near glass gets cold, even with thermal glass. This cold air is heavier than the rest of the heated room air, so it sinks to the floor and causes an apparent chilly draft from outdoors.

It is important to caulk and weatherstrip the rest of your windows and doors. Air that leaks in through your patio door must push air out from your house somewhere else. If it didn't leak out, your house

would explode. Tightening up the rest of your house also reduces your utility bills and dust in your house.

Blocking the direct force of the wind against your door reduces leaks. The amount of cold outdoor air leaking in through a small unsealed spot increases several times when a stiff wind blows against it.

Pitched shingled roof

Make larger roof overhang if facing west

Window or shutter toward summer breezes

Make deep enough to block afternoon sun

Building an attractive covered wind/sun shield around your patio door helps year-round. A simple framed plywood wall on each side of your door is adequate. Cover it with a pitched shingled roof.

This provides an ideal location to hang plants under the roof. If you rely on natural ventilation or fans for cooling, build a hinged shutter or operable window in the side that faces the prevailing summer breezes.

If you have swinging hinged patio doors instead of a sliding door, install a new door threshold seal. There are many types available - automatic, sweep, vinyl bulb, door shoe, etc. and each has its advantages.

With carpeting on the floor, install an automatic lifting threshold seal. As the door starts to open, a cam mechanism raises the seal so it does not drag on the carpeting.

Q: Is it always best to remove the old shingles before installing new shingles on my roof? Does this affect the amount of the sun's heat that is transferred down through the hot roof?

A: Removing the old shingles first is definitely the preferred method, especially if they are badly cupped and curled. Reroofing over them may look very good at first. After the sun heats the new shingles through the summer, irregularities from the old shingles underneath may appear.

From an energy efficiency standpoint, the extra layer of shingles will not have a great effect. Shingle color and material are most important. Light colored shingles reflect more of the sun's heat than dark ones. Metal roofs, especially aluminum, also reflect heat.

Instructions for making a sun/wind shelter for your patio door to block the force and pressure of the wind are on the following pages. The further north you live, the deeper the shelter must be. This is because the sun is lower in the sky in the northern latitudes than it is in the south. The deeper shelter blocks the lower sun better. It is also effective for growing hanging plants and for shelter from the rain and sun for your pet.

It is also important to seal the mating edge between the sliding and the fixed doors. If you cannot find the proper-sized replacement seal, a vinyl-bulb or a brush-type of seal is effective. Mount it on the sliding door so it just touches the fixed door edge as it closes.

If you have a swinging/hinged door, you should weatherstrip the door bottom with a threshold seal. The chart on page 262 lists advantages and disadvantages of several methods for sealing the threshold. If your patio door swings in over a thick carpet, you should consider an automatic lifting threshold seal. The surface mount types are the easiest to install. These and the other threshold seals are available at most hardware and home center stores.

- -

Do-It-Yourself Instructions for Flowerbox Window Sun Shield

1) Make the window unit a little taller than the window you're shielding and wide enough to clear the trim and sill.

2) You should use redwood, cedar or pressure-treated lumber to build the unit. If you use any other wood, you need to finish it with a good exterior paint or applying a penetrating stain and sealer.

3) Assemble the flower box from ¾-inch exterior plywood. Butt the sides (1,2) together, and attach the bottom (3) using screws and glue. Drill ½-inch holes in the bottom to facilitate drainage, and treat the inside of the box with a wood preservative to keep it from rotting. Set aside for at least two days to dry.

4) Frame window top and sides with 1x2 strips (4, 5) screwed directly into the wall studs. After the flower box dries, attach it with screws to the wall studs just below the sill.

5) Cut six lengths of 1x6 boards (6) to fit, trimming the tops at a 30° angle. Butt the boards together (or leave spaces between each, if desired) and screw them to the flower box. Brace the siding at the top with 1x2 ledgers (7), cut to fit and attach flush with the top inside edge of the siding boards.

6) Have a piece of ⅛-inch translucent acrylic plastic of the appropriate dimensions formed to match the shape shown in the diagram. Drill holes through the plastic sheet and screw it into the top of the 1x6 boards (6), then caulk wherever necessary for a weathertight seal.

Note: Before drilling holes in acrylic, secure the material so it won't move around. Also, back the plastic with a wood scrap to prevent it from chipping when the drill penetrates the plastics's backside.

Required Materials for Flowerbox Window Sun Shield

lumber - 1x2, 1x6 pressure treated
scrap lumber
exterior plywood
screws
wood glue
optional exterior paint
optional stain and sealer
optional wood preservative
reinforcing rods
acrylic plastic

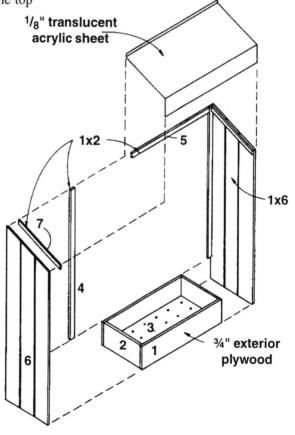

⅛" translucent acrylic sheet

1x2

5

1x6

7

4

3

2 1

6

¾" exterior plywood

Instructions for Making a Patio Door Shelter

1) Before starting to build this shelter, plan the size and slope of roof that you want. It will depend on the size and style of your house. Also consider the orientation to the sun. A door facing toward the east or west will require a deeper shelter to block the sun. (The sun is lower in the sky in the morning and afternoon.) Determine the type of plywood siding that will look best. It may be desirable to use pressure treated plywood (CCA) except the additional cost must be considered. When handling or sawing pressure treated lumber, follow recommended safety procedures. Cedar siding is also an option.

2) You should determine if you want a window or shutter in one of the sides of the shelter. Depending on your house orientation, it may allow for more natural ventilation in the summer.

Required Materials for Patio Door Shelter

lumber - 2"x4"x8' - 10 pieces pressure treated for framing
lumber - 1"x6"x8' - 3 pieces cedar or redwood for trim
plywood - $3/_8$"x4"x8' - 2 sheets exterior grade
plywood siding - $5/_8$"x4"x8' - 1 sheet
galvanized metal flashing - 2"x3"x16' (45° angle type)
narrow metal strip
caulking sealant cartridge type - 1 or 2 cartridges
building paper (dimensions same as size of roof sheathing)
#8 penny nails - 1 pound cement coated or galvanized
#16 penny nails - 1 pound cement coated or galvanized
$3/_4$" length galvanized roofing nails - 1 pound
roof shingles
galvanized lag bolts required only if attachment is needed at masonry or cement surfaces
exterior grade latex paint for prime and finish coats
optional - exterior grade stain, varnish or polyurethane

Note: Material list based on door shelter of 2' maximum depth and overall length of not more than 8'. Material list adjustment required for deeper or longer shelter.

3) First assemble the frames for the side walls of the shelter. It is usually easiest to assemble these flat on the ground. Make sure the frame is square. Cut the vertical pieces (1) from the 2x4 lumber (pressure treated lumber is recommended) to a length to give adequate headroom under the shelter. Cut the horizontal pieces (2,3) to provide the depth of shelter you want.

4) Nail the horizontal pieces together to walls. Use #16 long) either cement galvanized type. If window or shutter, header supports in it.

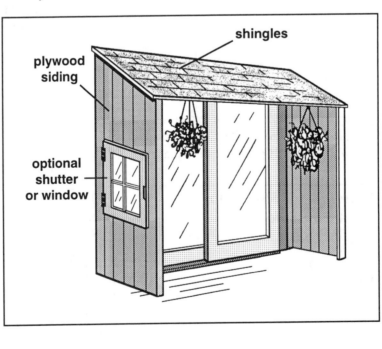

and vertical form two side penny nails (3 ½" coated or you plan to add a cut and nail the the side wall for

5) Cut vertical door and the cross piece lumber. Nail these to the sliding glass door will be used to attach house.

opening pieces (4) (5) from the 2x4 the house around opening. These the shelter to the

6) Nail the side wall opening pieces (4,5). diagonal wood scrap wood) may be

frames to the door Temporary bracing (light used to ensure the

unit is true square, plumb, level and perpendicular. Remove bracing as permanent outer siding is installed.

7) Cut a piece of 2x4 lumber for the front roof support (6) and nail it to the top of the side wall frames. This will tie the ends together. Add two cross supports (7) from the top piece (6) to piece (5).

8) After you have determined the pitch of the roof that you want, cut and nail the horizontal roof support (8) to the house. Locate the wall studs before you drive in the nails.

9) Cut the roof rafters (9) and nail them securely to the roof support (8) and to the front support (6). You may want to bevel the ends of the rafters to the angle of the roof.

10) Cut the $^5/_8$" siding to make the covers for the side walls. Nail these covers to the side wall frames.

11) Cut the $^3/_8$" plywood for the inside surface of the side walls and underneath the roof. Nail these pieces into place.

12) Cut trim pieces (10,11) from the 1x6 lumber and nail them to the front of the shelter.

13) Cut a piece of the $^3/_8$" plywood (14) to use for the roof sheathing. Nail it in place over the roof frame. #8 galvanized nails will resist the dampness the best. Cover the roof sheathing with building paper. Nail a metal drip strip (12) to the lower end of the roof.

14) Cover the roof with shingles using $^3/_4$" length galvanized roofing nails. Lighter-colored shingles will not get as hot in the summer. Nail metal flashing (13) against the house. Seal it with a good quality caulking sealant.

15) You should paint the completed unit both inside and out with several coats of good quality exterior paint or stain and apply exterior grade varnish or polyurethane.

NOTE: Optional storage compartment may also be incorporated into a longer door shelter as conditions allow or personal preference.

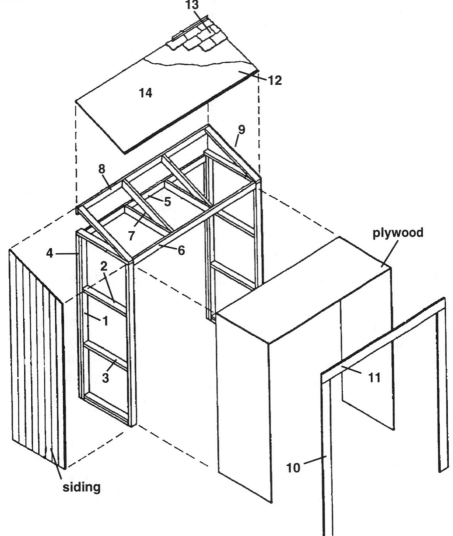

Q: My electric bills are outrageous and my children never turn off lights. I heard that I will save $50 for each bulb that I replace with a compact fluorescent bulb. How is the light quality from the compacts?

A: New compact fluorescent light bulbs are now designed to fit nearly every size and style of lamp or fixture. If you tried one several years ago, you'll be surprised at the excellent light quality of some of the new ones. Although all brands look similar, there are major differences among them.

In general, an 18-watt compact fluorescent bulb produces as much light as a standard 75-watt bulb. Over its 10,000-hour life, each one saves up to $50 in electricity as compared to a standard bulb. Multiply this by the number of lamps and fixtures in your house and the total savings is tremendous.

These bulbs are also environmentally friendly. Using electricity produced from a coal-fired power plant, each 18-watt compact fluorescent bulb saves 500 pounds of coal, produces 1,300 pounds less carbon dioxide (global warming gas) and 20 pounds less sulfur dioxide (acid rain) over its life.

Although compact fluorescent bulbs cost more to buy initially than standard incandescent bulbs, they last 13 times longer. If you use a lamp for four hours every night, a compact fluorescent bulb lasts six years. This is ideal for hard to reach fixtures, like above stairs.

Not all compact fluorescent bulbs produce the same quality of light. How true colors look under a light is referred to as color rendition index (CRI). Some bulbs have CRI's as low as 60. Most are in the 82 range and some are above 85. A CRI of 100 is perfect color rendition.

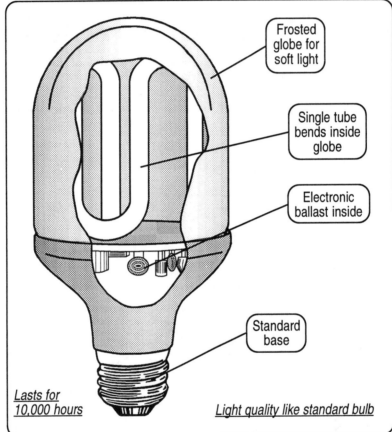

Frosted globe for soft light

Single tube bends inside globe

Electronic ballast inside

Standard base

Lasts for 10,000 hours

Light quality like standard bulb

Compact fluorescent bulbs are available in two designs. Integral units include the ballast, base and bulb in one piece. Modular units have replaceable bulbs. Since ballasts last 50,000 hours (20 years of typical use), only having to replace the light element saves another five to ten dollars.

When buying a bulb, consider the type of ballast used. The new ones with electronic ballasts start instantly with no buzz. Less expensive ones with magnetic ballasts take longer to reach full brightness and flicker initially.

There are many shapes and styles of compact fluorescents - globe, twin, triple, and quad tubes, indoor and outdoor floods, and reflector bulbs for recessed lighting. Some are tinted various colors for contemporary lighting.

For small table and floor lamps, use a three-piece adapter kit. A small ballast plugs into the wall and the lamp cord plugs into the ballast. The very small fluorescent bulb screws into the standard lamp socket.

Q: We have a small enclosed barn that we plan to use occasionally as a workshop. Our house has natural gas, but not the barn. What type of small space heater is best?

A: The best type of heater depends on how often you will use the workshop and your activities in it. If you most often work in just one area of the workshop, install electric radiant heat panels. These provide quick effective spot heating without having to heat the entire barn.

If you work there for extended lengths of time and throughout the entire area, a small direct vent gas heater is best. Even though there will be an expense to pipe the gas to it, it will be less expensive in the long term.

The chart below shows the annual cost comparison of compact fluorescent bulbs versus standard bulbs for various lengths of time each night. Even though the compact fluorescent bulbs costs 30 times as much to buy, it will save from $30 to $40 over its life. If you are going to replace existing bulbs, use the following guide for sizing the new bulb - (incandescent/equivalent compact fluorescent) 25 watts/9 watts, 40 watts/11 watts, 60 watts/17 watts, 75 watts/20 watts, 90 watts/23 watts.

Compact fluorescent bulbs are available in many shapes and sizes to fit almost any lamp or fixture. These are listed under *"styles/shapes"* on pages 275 and 276. Sketches of the various shapes are shown below. The chart on page 276 shows the suggested types of compact fluorescent bulbs for various applications in your house. For a recessed cannister fixture, use a reflector light whenever possible.

Annual Cost Comparison - 75 Watt Incandescent vs. 18 Watt Compact Fluorescent								
	75 Watt Incandescent				18 Watt Compact Fluorescent			
Hours on per Day	Bulb Life Years	Bulb Replacement Cost [1]	Electric Operating Cost	Total Cost	Bulb Life Years	Bulb Replacement Cost	Electric Operating Cost [2]	Total Cost
2	1.03	0.48	4.38	4.86	13.70	1.09	1.05	2.14
4	0.51	0.97	8.76	9.73	6.85	2.19	2.10	4.29
6	0.34	1.46	13.14	16.06	4.57	3.28	3.15	6.43
8	0.26	1.95	17.52	19.47	3.42	4.39	4.20	8.59
10	0.21	2.43	21.90	24.38	2.74	5.47	5.26	10.73
12	0.17	2.92	26.28	29.20	2.28	6.58	6.31	12.89

Notes - [1] *$0.50 per bulb*   [2] *$15.00 per bulb*

Compact Fluorescent Shapes and Styles

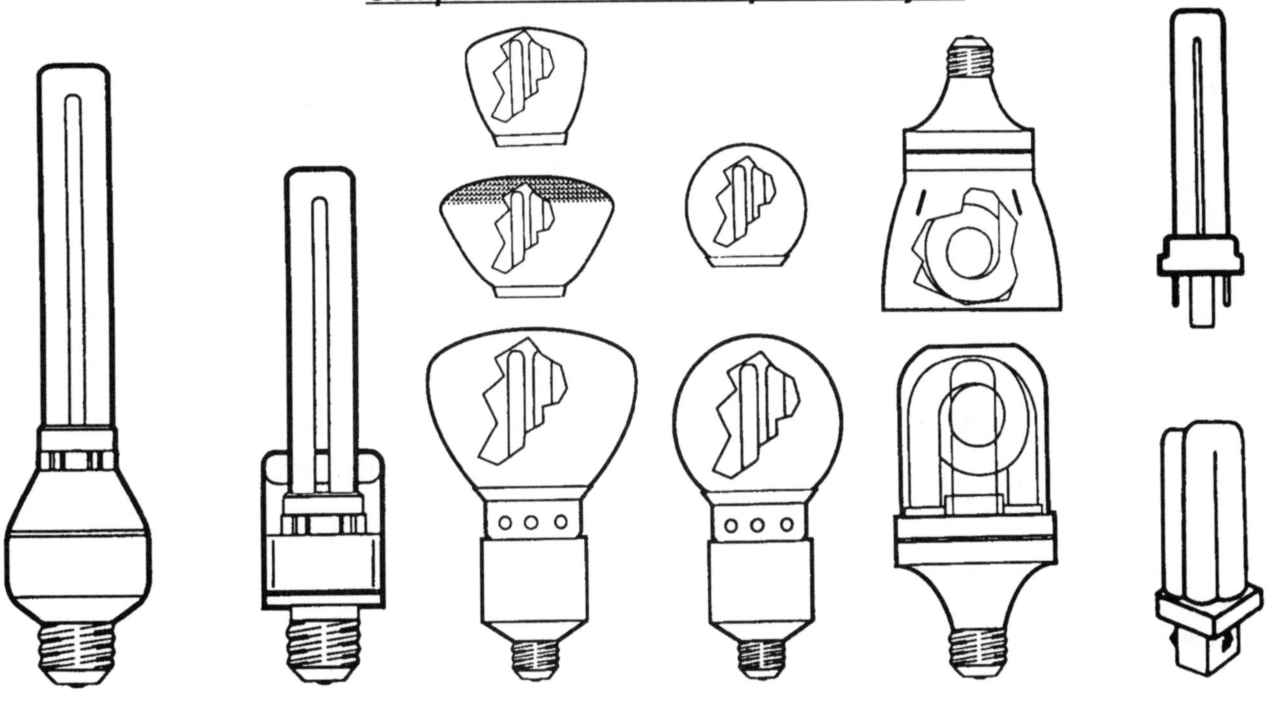

Manufactuers of Compact Fluorescent Bulbs and Kits

AERO-TECH LIGHT BULB CO., 534 Pratt Ave., N., Schaumburg, IL 60193 - (708) 351-4900

type - modular unit
ballast type - magnetic
wattages - 9, 13

style - double tube, floodlight
light quality CRI - 82 and 85

FEIT ELECTRIC CO., 2042 E. Vernon Ave., Los Angeles, CA 90058 - (800) 543-3348

type - integral unit

styles/shapes - single tube, double tube, quad tube, circular, spiral, floodlight, globe, reflector

ballast type - magnetic
wattages - 5, 7, 9, 13, 18, 22, 27, 28

light quality CRI - 82

GENERAL ELECTRIC CO., 1975 Noble Rd., Nela Park, Cleveland, OH 44112 - (800) 626-2000

type - integral unit
ballast type - electronic
wattages - 15, 20, 23, 25, 26, 28

styles/shapes - double tube, triple tube, quad tube, reflector
light quality CRI - 82

type - modular unit

styles/shapes - single tube, double tube, triple tube, circular, downlight, u-shape

ballast type - electronic and magnetic
ballast type - magnetic (circular)
wattages - 9, 11, 15, 16, 20, 22, 24, 39

light quality CRI - 82
light quality CRI - 52 (circular)

LIGHTS OF AMERICA, 611 Reyes Dr., Walnut, CA 91789 - (909) 594-7883

type - modular unit

styles/shapes - double tube, triple tube, quad tube, reflector, globe, tubular, circular, u-shape

ballast type - electronic
ballast type - magnetic (circular)
wattages - 5, 7, 13, 18, 20, 21, 22, 26, 27, 30, 38, 55

light quality CRI - 84
light quality CRI - 52 (circular)

OSRAM SYLVANIA, 100 Endicott St., Danvers, MA 01923 - (508) 777-1900

type - integral unit
ballast type - electronic
wattages - 7, 9, 11, 15, 20, 23,

styles/shapes - double tube, triple tube, reflector, globe
light quality CRI - 82

type - modular unit
ballast type - magnetic
wattages - 9, 13

styles/shapes - double tube
light quality CRI - 82

PANASONIC LIGHTING CO., One Panasonic Way, Secaucus, NJ 07094 - (800) 553-0384

type - integral unit
ballast type - electronic
wattages - 15, 16, 20, 25

styles/shapes - double tube, globe, tubular
light quality CRI - 84 and 88

PHILIPS LIGHTING CO., PO Box 6800, Somerset, NJ 08875 - (908) 563-3000

type - integral unit
ballast type -electronic
wattages - 9, 11, 15, 17, 18, 20, 23

styles/shapes - double tube, triple tube, reflector, tubular
light quality CRI - 82

SK AMERICA, INC., 460 Bergen Blvd., Pallisades Park, NJ 07650 - (800) 793-1212 (201) 585-1177

type - integral unit
ballast type - electronic

styles/shapes - reflector, globe, tubular, circular
light quality CRI - 82

type - modular unit
ballast type - electronic
ballast type - magnetic for 22 and 30 watt circular
wattages - 15, 17, 18, 20, 23, 30
features - available in red, green, and blue colored bulbs

styles/shapes - reflector, globe, tubular, circular
light quality CRI - 82

SUPREME LIGHTING CO., 1605 John St., Fort Lee, NJ 07024 - (800) 221-1573

type - integral unit
ballast type - magnetic
wattages - 9, 13, 16

styles/shapes - double tube, floodlight
light quality CRI - 82 and 85

type - lamp conversion kit with wall outlet and bulb socket adapter
ballast type - magnetic
wattages - 7, 9, 13

styles/shapes - double tube

light quality CRI - 82

US-PAR ENTERPRISES, 13404 S. Monte Vista Ave., Chino, CA 91710 - (909) 591-7506

type - integral unit
ballast type - magnetic
ballast type - magnetic (circular and u)
wattages - 5, 7, 9, 12, 13, 15, 22, 30

styles/shapes - double tube, floodlight, circle, globe, u-shape
light quality CRI - 82
light quality CRI - 60 (circular and u-shape)

Application Selector Guide									
	Shaded Lamp[1]	Enclosed Indoor	Open Indoor	Bare Bulb	Track	Recessed Can	Enclosed Outdoor	Energy $ Saved[2]	vs. Replaces Incand.[3]
Double Tube									
15w	X	X	X	X	X	X	X	$36.00	60w
15w HPF	X	X	X	X	X	X	X	$36.00	60w
20w	X	X	X	X	X	X	X	$44.00	75w
26w	X		X	X	X		X	$51.20	90w
Triple Tube									
15w	X	X	X	X	X	X	X	$36.00	60w
15w HPF	X	X	X	X	X	X	X	$36.00	60w
20w	X	X	X	X	X	X	X	$44.00	75w
20w HPF	X	X	X	X	X	X	X	$44.00	75w
23w	X		X	X			X	$52.80	90w
25w HPF	X		X	X			X	$52.00	90w
Quad Tube									
28w	X		X	X			X	$57.50	100w
Fluorescent Reflectors									
15w			X	X	X	X	X	$48.00	75w R40
20w HPF			X	X	X	X	X	$44.00	75w R40
Floodlight									
16w							X	$36.00	75w
Globe									
16w			X	X				$36.00	60w
Tubular									
16w	X	X	X	X	X	X	X	$36.00	60w

1 One piece lamp systems do not work with clip-on shades
2 Energy dollars saved vs. incandescent lamps formula: energy rate used national average, $.08 per KWH . This does not include replacement bulb costs.

HPF means High Power Factor

(A)		(B)		(C)		(D)
Watts Saved	x	Energy Rate	x	Rated Life Hours	=	Energy Dollars Saved
		1,000				

3 Comparison is to standard incandescent bulbs, except 90w is Watt-Miser® bulb

Q: There were several break-ins in my neighborhood. I want to install outdoor security lights, but they are so expensive to operate. Are there any bright lights that don't use a lot of electricity?

A: Lighting the exterior of your house, especially the backyard, is one of the best methods to deter a thief. There are new bright super-efficient outdoor lights (high intensity discharge - HID) that you can install yourself. They use only a couple of cents worth of electricity per night.

High-pressure sodium lights are the most efficient HID light commonly used for homes. One small 35-watt high-pressure sodium floodlight is brighter than five standard 40-watt bulbs combined.

Although these fixtures and bulbs are more expensive initially, they quickly pay back their higher cost in lower electric bills. The bulbs last 20,000 hours as compared to less than a 1,000 hours for standard floodlights, so there is savings in bulb replacement costs too.

There are many new HID light styles designed for home use. These fixtures are now smaller and more attractive. You can buy antique-designer light posts, contemporary bollard lights for use near a deck or pool, wall floodlights, in-ground lights, etc., many with high-pressure sodium bulbs.

If you plan to illuminate a large area and are not concerned about the light's color rendition quality, low-pressure sodium bulbs use even less electricity. You will only find these low pressure sodium bulbs at commercial electrical outlets.

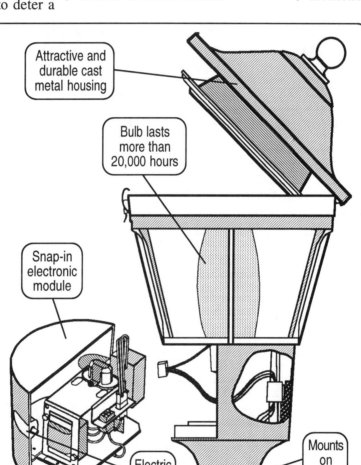

Attractive and durable cast metal housing

Bulb lasts more than 20,000 hours

Snap-in electronic module

Electric eye

Mounts on post

The most common HID floodlights sold at home centers are mercury vapor. These are twice as efficient as standard floodlights, but still much less efficient than high-pressure sodium lights. The color rendition quality from mercury vapor lights is good, but they tend to kill the reds.

Motion-sensing lights are one of the best crime deterrents and use the least amount of electricity. They can sense motion as far away as 60 feet and you can adjust the on-time from one minute to 30 minutes.

A floodlight's switching on usually scares a thief away. Some models have an interior module into which you can plug lamps. When the motion-sensing floodlight comes on, it switches on the interior lamps. When you are away at night, it appears that someone switched on the lights.

In my own home, I use solar-powered motion-sensing floodlights. These need no wiring, so they are ideal for backyard or storage shed locations. With powerful internal batteries, they will switch on 120 times on just one day's charge from the sun.

Q: I want to add insulation to my attic. Fiberglass is easy to use, but it irritates my skin. What other insulation options are there?

A: Fiberglass insulation batts can be itchy if you do not dress properly. Wear heavy coveralls and gloves. Put rubber bands around the wrist area of the coveralls over the gloves to seal the arms. Wear a breathing face mask.

Blown-in rock wool or cellulose is another effective insulation option. If you can wait several months, a Canadian company is developing a "non-itchy" fiberglass-like batt insulation made from recycled plastic bottles.

Many people do not realize how much it costs to keep common incandescent floodlights on all night long. The chart below shows these electric costs. Also, standard floodlight bulbs must be replaced twenty times more often than the more efficient bulbs.

For home use, high-pressure sodium (HPS) lights are becoming much more popular. A 35-watt HPS produces almost as much light as a 150-watt standard incandescent floodlight. These HPS bulbs also last more than 20,000 hours, several years of every-night operation.

Style of Lights

1. bollard
2. flood
3. inground
4. path
5. post
6. wall

figure #1

Colors will look slightly different (color rendition index) under HPS than under standard floodlights, but it is still very acceptable. Don't confuse HPS with low pressure sodium (LPS) lights used in many supermarket parking lots. LPS, although more efficient than HPS, gives off a monochromatic yellowish light. This make most colors look gray and would be objectionable in areas, like   a deck or pool, where you entertain.

Page 279 and 280 lists
ciency residential outdoor se-
type of design and shape of the
eral styles and the illustrations
each style of light.

the manufacturers of the highest effi-
curity lights. *"Styles"* indicates the
light fixture. Figure #1 lists the gen-
below show a descriptive picture of

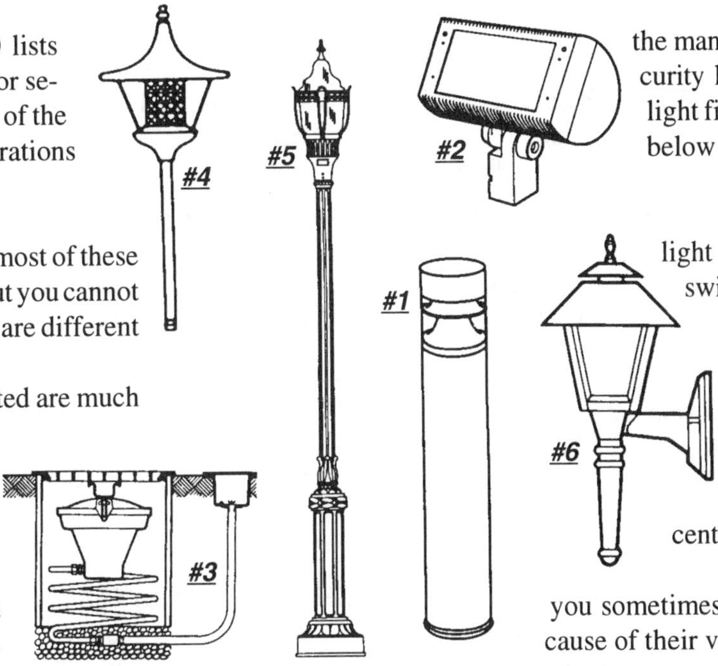

You can purchase most of these
type of bulb than HPS, but you cannot
one fixture. The ballasts are different

light fixtures for use of another
switch various types of bulbs in
for each type of bulb.

All of the bulbs listed are much
descent floodlights.
bulb types are as fol-
sodium, *LPS* - low
halide, *FL* - fluores-

more efficient than incan-
The abbreviations for the
lows: *HPS* - high pressure
pressure sodium, *MH* - metal
cent, and *MV* - mercury vapor.

For areas where
MV or *MH* bulbs be-

you sometimes entertain, you may consider
cause of their very white light.

#4   #5   #2   #1   #6   #3

Annual Lighting Cost Comparison																
Watts	**Your Electric Rate (cents per Kilowatt-hour)**															
	5.5	**6**	**6.5**	**7**	**7.5**	**8**	**8.5**	**9**	**9.5**	**10**	**10.5**	**11**	**11.5**	**12**	**12.5**	**13**
35	8.41	9.17	9.94	10.70	11.47	12.23	12.99	13.76	14.52	15.29	16.04	16.82	17.57	18.34	19.10	19.10
40	9.61	10.48	11.36	12.23	13.10	13.98	14.85	15.72	16.60	17.47	18.35	19.22	20.10	20.96	21.85	22.72
60	14.41	15.72	17.04	18.35	19.66	20.97	22.28	23.59	24.90	26.21	27.51	28.82	30.13	31.44	32.75	34.08
75	18.02	19.66	21.29	22.93	24.57	26.21	27.85	29.48	31.12	32.76	34.40	36.04	37.67	39.32	40.95	42.58
80	19.22	20.97	22.71	24.46	26.22	27.96	29.70	31.45	33.20	34.94	36.69	38.44	40.18	41.94	43.68	45.42
90	21.62	23.59	25.55	27.52	29.48	31.45	33.42	35.38	37.35	39.31	41.29	43.24	45.22	47.18	49.15	51.10
100	24.02	26.21	28.39	30.58	32.76	34.94	37.13	39.31	41.50	43.68	45.86	48.04	50.23	52.42	54.60	58.78
105	25.23	27.52	29.81	32.10	34.40	36.69	38.98	41.28	43.57	45.86	48.15	50.46	52.74	55.04	57.33	59.62
135	32.43	35.38	38.33	41.28	44.23	47.17	50.12	53.07	56.02	58.97	61.91	64.86	67.80	70.76	73.70	76.66
150	36.04	39.31	42.59	45.86	49.14	52.42	55.69	58.97	62.24	65.52	68.79	72.08	75.35	78.62	81.90	85.15

To use this chart: *Find the column corresponding to your utility rate. Use the figure in that column with the wattage of the bulb. It is a dollar figure for 12 hours of use, seven days a week for a year.*

Manufacturers of High-Efficiency Outdoor Security Lights

ADJUSTAPOST MFG., PO Box 71, Norton, OH 44203 - (216) 745-1692

style	*bulb*	*style*	*bulb*
bollard	MV, HPS	flood	FL, HPS, MH, MV
path	FL	post	FL, HPS, MV
wall	FL, HPS, MV		

COOPER LIGHTING, PO Box 824, Vicksburg, MS 39180 - (601) 638-1522

style	*bulb*	*style*	*bulb*
bollard	FL, HPS, MH, MV	flood	HPS, MH, MV
post	HPS, MH	wall	HPS, MH, MV

GE LIGHTING, Nela Park #4162, Cleveland, OH 44112 - (800) 626-2000

style	*bulb*	*style*	*bulb*
flood	HPS, MH, MV	post	HPS, MH
wall	HPS, MH		

HOLAPHANE CO., 250 E. Broad St. Suite 1400, Columbus, OH 43215 - (614) 345-9631

style	*bulb*	*style*	*bulb*
bollard	HPS, MH, MV	post	HPS, MH, MV

HUBBELL LIGHTING, 2000 Electric Way, Christiansburg, VA 24073 - (703) 382-6111

style	*bulb*	*style*	*bulb*
bollard	HPS, MH, MV	flood	HPS, MH, MV
inground	HPS, MH, MV	path	FL, MV
post	FL, HPS		

KIM LIGHTING, PO Box 1275, Industry, CA 91749 - (818) 968-5666

style	*bulb*	*style*	*bulb*
bollard	HPS, MH, MV	flood	HPS, MH, MV
inground	HPS, MH, MV	path	FL
post	FL, HPS, MH, MV	wall	FL, HPS

LITEFORM DESIGNS, PO Box 3316, Portland, OR 97208 - (800) 458-2505

style	*bulb*	*style*	*bulb*
bollard	FL, HPS	path	FL, HPS
post	FL, HPS	wall	FL, HPS

LITHONIA, Box A, Crawfordsville, IN 47933 - (800) 428-0960

style	*bulb*	*style*	*bulb*
bollard	HPS, MH, MV	flood	HPS, MH, MV

PRESCOLITE, 1251 Doolittle Dr., San Leandro, CA 94577 - (510) 562-3500

style	*bulb*	*style*	*bulb*
bollard	FL, HPS, MV	flood	HPS, MV
inground	HPS, MH, MV	path	MV
post	HPS, MV		

RAB ELECTRIC CO., 170 Ludlow Ave., Northvale, NJ 07647 - (201) 784-8600

style	*bulb*	*style*	*bulb*
path	FL	post	HPS, MH, MV

WF HARRIS LIGHTING, PO Box 5023, Monroe, NC 28111 - (704) 283-7477

style	*bulb*	*style*	*bulb*
path	FL	post	HPS, MH, MV
wall	FL, HPS, LPS, MH, MV		

Manufacturers of Solar and 110-Volt Motion Sensing Lights

BRINKMAN CORP., 4215 McEwen Rd., Dallas, TX 75244 - (214) 387-4939
    power source - solar   model - "Home Guard"

BRK ELECTRONICS, 780 McClure Rd., Aurora, IL 60504 - (708) 851-7330
    power source - 110 volt   model - "PIR835"

HEATH ZENITH, PO Box 1288, Benton Harbor, MI 49023 - (616) 925-6000
    power source - solar   model - "SL-7001"

HUBBELL LIGHTING, 2000 Electric Way, Christiansburg, VA 24073 - (703) 382-6111
    power source - 110 volt   model - "Presence Sense"

INTERMATIC, Intermatic Plaza, Spring Grove, IL 60081 - (815) 675-2321
    power source - solar   model - "Solar Tech"

RAB ELECTRIC CO., 170 Ludlow Ave., Northvale, NJ 07647 - (201) 784-8600
    power source - 110 volt   model - "Light Alert"

SIEMENS SOLAR, PO Box 6032, Camarillo, CA 93011 - (800) 325-9325 (805) 482-6800
    power source - solar   model - "Sensor Light"

Siemens Solar
SENSOR LIGHT™

Built-in motion detector automatically turns on light when triggered. Automatically shuts off when you leave. Bright energy-efficient DULUX® fluorescent bulb lasts over 5 years. Unit mounts easily to wall, fascia, soffit or roof eave. No wiring or electrician required.

Solar powered convenience/security light with built-in motion sensor.

- Safety and security where you need it with no wiring.

- Up to 2 weeks of operation with no sun.

- Activated automatically by heat and motion (no timers or switches to set); welcomes you home and alerts you for safety.

- Bright energy efficient DULUX® bulb. Illuminates large areas evenly. Equivalent to a 75-watt flood light. 5-year bulb life.

- Installs in minutes with our universal mounting bracket. Hardware and bulbs included.

- SENSOR LIGHT™ mounts on eaves, soffits, walls, even posts. Place anywhere on or around your home or yard. For additional flexibility, solar module can be detached from unit. 14-foot cord included.

- Adjustable sensitivity control reduces 'false "triggers."

- No utility bills. Saves you money. Works even when the power is off.

- Full 2-year warranty.

MODEL 17935

NO SUN? NO PROBLEM. Thanks to our high efficiency solar cell and storage batteries, you'll get peak performance out of your Siemens Solar SENSOR LIGHT™ even up to two weeks with no sun.

Technical Information

Solar Panel Cell Type/Protection:	Single crystalline; laminated EVA - Tedlar®
Solar Panel Output:	2.75 watts (± 5%)
Battery:	Sealed lead acid; 6.5 Amp-hr., up to 24-month shelf life; up to 5-year red LED light to tell when battery is low
Hours to Fully Charge:	12 hours
PIR:	Pulse count technology, eliminating false triggers; 40' range @ 110° view angle; full sensitivity and light level adjustments
Functions:	Dual operating switch modes; 3-position main operating switch: Auto -- Off -- Charge; 3-position run-time switch: Test -- 30 sec. -- 60 sec.
Run Time:	Maximum capacity = 130 60-second trips; up to 2 weeks without sun
Bulb:	9-watt DULUX® fluorescent SE; light output equivalent to 75-watt incandescent; quick start; replaceable; 5-year life

111-700030-01 REV. D

Q: I want to install outdoor lighting for security and landscaping myself because I cannot afford an electrician. What is new this year in efficient do-it-yourself low-voltage lighting?

A: There have been many improvements to do-it-yourself outdoor low-voltage (12-volt) lighting over the past several years. There are new designs which are easier to install with brighter lights, automatic controls and more styles available (tier, brick, flood, globe, well, spot, deck, bollard and spread).

Low-voltage lights are energy efficient. A do-it-yourself kit with six low-voltage lights uses less electricity than one standard 75-watt bulb. Since they operate on only 12 volts, low-voltage light kits are simple and safe to install. Just lay the wiring in the grass or on top of the ground.

There are two basic categories of low-voltage lights. Many inexpensive plastic kits are available at your local hardware stores. More expensive decorator die cast metal, solid brass and redwood kits are available through lighting outlets. Even though kits may look similar, there are major differences in features and light output.

Simulated brick paving or edging low-voltage lights are one of the newest innovations. High-strength (can support a car) plastic paving lights are the exact size of a brick. The outside housing looks just like a real brick.

Place these in a patio, driveway or walkway to light the path or accent landscaping. Another design uses snap-together bricks to form edging along a walk or garden. Wiring is built into these bricks for simple installation.

Reflective dome inside

Interchangeable top section

High efficiency light bulb

Light focused in different directions

Simple two-clip wire connectors

Several manufacturers offer adjustable low-voltage spot/floodlights. By turning a knob on the back or rotating the lens, the light beam ranges from a wide flood to a tight spot. You only need one light for two purposes.

For additional versatility, select a new convertible design. Interchangeable prismatic lens (multi-angle lens distributes light evenly) tier or floodlight tops snap onto the same base.

Since only the top light section needs to be changed, the entire fixture does not have to be removed and rewired. Santas, jack-o-lanterns and snowmen tops can be snapped on during the holidays.

Several kits have new wire connection methods for easier installation. One method uses two small clips that snap together over the wire. Another method uses a cam lever action. Both hit the conductor on the first try.

Some new decorator die cast post lights have ivy leaves or cattails cast into them. With a natural variegated green color, they blend into the garden. Contemporary redwood and perforated spherical lights are attractive.

Q: My toilet always seems to be hissing and gurgling. I am sure that it is wasting a lot of water. How can I fix it myself?

A: A leaky toilet increases your water bills because it runs continuously. The noise is often caused by water leaking past a deteriorated stopper bulb in the tank. A bad float bulb or shut-off valve which lets the water level rise too high may be the culprit.

Replacement parts cost only about $10 to fix either problem. Simple installation instructions are shown on the packaging or check your library for "fix it" books. They all cover simple toilet repair.

If you have ever tried to install low-voltage lighting in the past, you know how hard it was to get the prongs on the light to hit the wire inside the main cable. Two new simple to use, "hit-on-the-first-try" connection methods are shown below. Another connector design by Brinkmann, which uses a lever action, is simple to use.

The chart below shows the proper sizing of transformer, wire gauge, and length of wire. As you expand your system, it is important to use the proper gauge wire for maximum lighting output.

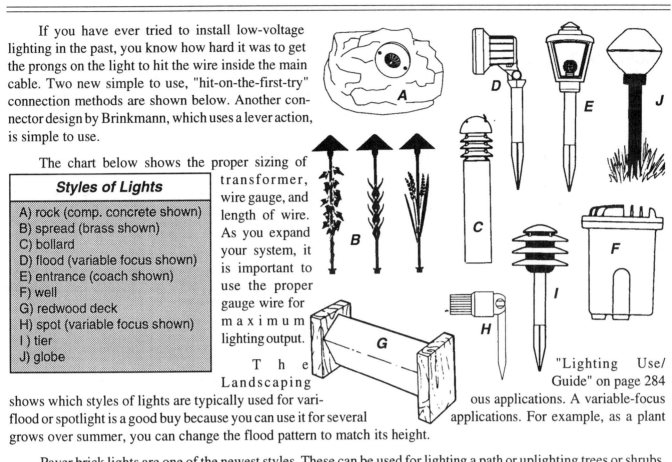

Styles of Lights

A) rock (comp. concrete shown)
B) spread (brass shown)
C) bollard
D) flood (variable focus shown)
E) entrance (coach shown)
F) well
G) redwood deck
H) spot (variable focus shown)
I) tier
J) globe

The Landscaping shows which styles of lights are typically used for various applications. A variable-focus flood or spotlight is a good buy because you can use it for several applications. For example, as a plant grows over summer, you can change the flood pattern to match its height.

"Lighting Use/Guide" on page 284

Paver brick lights are one of the newest styles. These can be used for lighting a path or uplighting trees or shrubs.

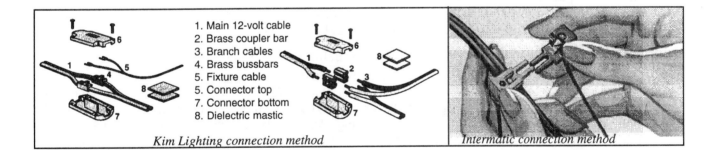

1. Main 12-volt cable
2. Brass coupler bar
3. Branch cables
4. Brass bussbars
5. Fixture cable
5. Connector top
7. Connector bottom
8. Dielectric mastic

Kim Lighting connection method

Intermatic connection method

System Selection Guide						
Total nominal wattage of transformer	16-gauge wire		14-gauge wire		12-gauge wire	
	max. total light watts	max. length	max. total light watts	max. length	max. total light watts	max. length
25 watts	25	100	25	125	25	150
44 watts	44	100	44	125	44	150
88 watts	88	100	88	125	88	150
121 watts	121	100	121	125	121	150
196 watts	150	100	196	125	196	150
300 watts	150	100	200	150	250	200

Manufacturers of High-Efficiency Low-Voltage Outdoor Lighting

ARGEE CORP., 9550 Pathway St., Santee, CA 92071 - (619) 449-5050

style - brick   material - plastic

special features - A strong, textured, natural looking brick manufactured out of heavy duty plastic with UV inhibitors. It is available with a green, amber, red or blue lens. The light bricks can be interspersed with other plastic brick edging.

BRINKMANN CORP., 4215 McEwen Rd., Dallas, TX 75244 - (214) 387-4939

style - entrance, flood, tier   material - plastic

special features - Easy installation with lever-action connection system. The bulb holder contains two brass points which pierce the cable to activate the light. Run the cable through the channel then pivot bulb holder down until it snaps and locks. Attach the head assembly over the bulb and ground stake.

BRONZELITE, PO Box 606, San Marcos, TX 78667 - (512) 392-5821

style - entrance, flood, tier, well   material - metal

special features - The fixtures have rounded contours and a textured dark bronze finish to blend into any landscape design. For added glare control, optional matching glare shields are offered.

HADCO, PO Box 128, Littlestown, PA 17340 - (717) 359-7131

style - entrance, flood, tier, spread, well, deck, bollard, brick   material - plastic - fiberglass reinforced

special features - The light fixtures are designed to withstand rugged coastal climates or conditions with highly acidic or heavily fertilized soils. Many decorative styles are available including composite concrete rock lights.

HANOVER LANTERN, 470 High St., Hanover, PA 17331 - (717) 632-6464

style - entrance, tier, spread, deck, bollard   material - metal

special features - The fixtures are constructed from heavy duty cast aluminum to withstand the abuses of nature. A low voltage conversion kit is available to convert any of their fixtures to 12 volts.

HUBBELL LIGHTING, 2000 Electric Way, Christiansburg, VA 24073 - (703) 382-6111

style - entrance, flood, tier, spread   material - plastic

special features - The system contains a photocontrol timer allowing the transformer to turn on the lights at dusk, when they are needed, providing safety illumination and saving energy.

INTERMATIC INC., Intermatic Plaza, Spring Grove, IL 60081 - (815) 675-2321

style - entrance, flood, tier, spread, well, globe, deck, bollard   material - plastic

special features - Available in a convertible light kit with interchangeable components that snap together quickly and easily. It is both a tier or a floodlight. The floodlight has zoom-focus capability which changes the light pattern from spot to flood with a turn of the wrist. A multi-angle lens distributes light evenly with the interchangeable prismatic lens. Special holiday decorations such as a Santa Claus or Halloween figurines are available. The wiring is simple two-piece snap together connectors.

KICHLER, 7711 E. Pleasant Valley Rd., Cleveland, OH 44131 - (800) 659-9000 (216) 573-1000

style - entrance, flood, tier, spread, well, deck   material - metal

special features - Available with unfinished copper shades painted white inside for greater reflectance to add beauty and security to your home. Solid brass post lights have ivy leaves or cattails cast into them with a natural verdigris (variegated green color) finish.

KIM LIGHTING, PO Box 1275, Industry, CA 91749 - (818) 968-5666

style - entrance, flood, tier, spread, well, deck   material - metal

special features - Fixtures are available in a subtle variegated green color that is mid-range between the lightest and darkest foliage or in black powder coat finish.

LITEFORM DESIGNS, PO Box 3316, Portland, OR 97208 - (800) 458-2505

style - entrance, tier, spread, globe, deck, bollard   material - metal and redwood

special features - Wooden fixtures are made from California redwood and treated with a water repellent preservative. Steel or aluminum fixtures are finished with gloss enamel. Price - $126 to $358 per unit.

PRESCOLITE, 1251 Doolittle Dr., San Leandro, CA 94577 - (510) 562-3500

style - well   material - metal

special features - The lens is available in clear, bronze or white with a lexan vandal resistant dome.

PRESTIGE LIGHTING, 1733 Kinglett Rd., San Marcos, CA 92069 - (619) 471-1813

style - brick   material - plastic

special features - A new in-ground architectural light fixture designed for use in driveways, sidewalks, concrete decks, entranceways, and steps. Made from specially compounded GE Plastics engineering resins capable of handling up to 10 tons.

TORO COMPANY, 8111 Lyndale Ave. S., Bloomington, MN 55420 - (612) 888-8801

style - entrance, flood, tier, spread, deck   material - plastic

special features - Varifocus feature changes light beam from horizontal to vertical, and adjusts the light beam from tight spotlight to broad floodlight.

Lighting Use/Landscaping Guide									
	Entrance	Flood	Tier	Spread	Well	Globe	Deck	Bollard	Brick
Art objects		X							
Boat docks	X		X	X		X	X	X	
Borders			X	X		X	X	X	X
Breezeways	X		X	X		X		X	X
Buildings				X		X		X	
Driveways	X	X	X			X		X	X
Eaves		X					X		
Entrances	X	X		X		X	X	X	X
Fences		X			X		X		
Flowering shrubs		X		X	X	X			
Foundations	X	X	X	X	X	X	X	X	X
Gardens		X	X	X	X	X		X	X
Gates			X	X		X		X	
Parking	X		X	X		X		X	X
Paths	X		X	X		X		X	X
Patios		X	X	X		X	X	X	X
Planters			X			X		X	
Ponds/Pools*			X	X		X		X	X
Porches	X		X	X		X		X	X
Rock Gardens		X	X	X		X		X	
Signs		X			X				
Silhouetting		X			X				
Steps	X		X	X		X	X		X
Tall trees		X			X				
Terraces			X	X		X			X
Trees		X			X				
Walks	X		X	X		X		X	X
Walls		X			X			X	

To be used around the perimeter of a pool or pond, not in the water.

Q: I'm considering a new cordless rechargeable lawn mower. I'm tired of the noise and hassle of starting my gas mower. Are cordless mowers powerful and how much will using one increase my electric bills?

A: I use a 24-volt cordless rechargeable mulching lawn mower on my own half-acre lot. Of all the products that I have tested over the past ten years, this is the only one that exceeds all the advertising claims. It uses only about 8 cents of electricity per cutting to recharge the battery.

Cordless lawn mowers run for 60 to 90 minutes on a single charge. This is generally long enough to cut most lawns. Since the blade rotates as fast as typical gasoline lawn mowers, cordless mowers cut and mulch as effectively.

Cordless mowers require no maintenance and always start on the first try. There is a one-lever cutting height adjustment that sets all four wheels simultaneously. A no-rust plastic housing and special blade are designed to mulch grass and drive the tiny clippings down to feed your lawn naturally.

These mowers run so quietly, you can still hear a telephone ring or talk to someone in your yard. This is ideal for me because I like to cut my grass very early in the morning or late in the evening, when it is cooler, without bothering neighbors.

To start the mower, you push a button on the side and lift the safety handle. There is a special "key" that you must push into the top of the mower to start it. This prevents children from accidentally starting it.

There are two basic designs of cordless mowers - 24-volt and 12-volt. The 24-volt models (with a built-in recharger) have a little more

Battery charge gauge

Control panel on back of mower

Control Panel

Safety key

No-rust deck and special blade mulches grass

Powerful 24-volt motor

Start button

Single all-wheel height adjuster

Larger rear wheels for easy rolling

Battery lasts 7 years

power and recharge in 16 hours. The 12-volt models have an external recharger and take about 24 hours for a complete recharge.

With the 24-volt model, when you are finished cutting, you pull out the key and plug a standard electric cord into it. You can store it on end indoors since it has no gasoline or oil. Fold up the collapsible handles and it takes up only 1-½ sq. ft. of floor space.

The 24-volt models have a power gauge to show how much battery charge is left. If it gets low and you are cutting a large lawn, just stop, put your feet up and relax. Recharge it for an hour or two, and finish the lawn. Batteries last seven years.

Cordless, like corded electric, and manual reel mowers, produce less pollution. A typical gasoline mower, running for 30 minutes, can produce more pollution than driving a car from Washington D.C. to Philadelphia.

Q: My furnace/air conditioner blower seems to run continuously, even when the thermostat is not calling for heat or cooling. What can cause this and is it wasting much electricity?

A: A malfunctioning blower that runs continuously pushes up your electric bills significantly. There are several possible causes. You may have the thermostat fan switch set to "on". The fan relay at the blower may be stuck in the on position. The thermostat may be faulty or wired improperly.

Some people do want the blower to run continuously. If you have a central air cleaner, it removes more dirt and allergens. If you want continuous air circulation, you should install a new efficient two-speed blower motor.

Non-gasoline powered lawn mowers (battery/cordless, electric, and manual-push) are inexpensive to operate, quiet, and produce much less pollution than gasoline mowers.

I have a half-acre wooded lot at my home and I use a 24-volt cordless electric mower. Mine has a battery charge status gauge and it has never run out of charge before finishing my lawn. 24-volt mowers have slightly more power and longer run time than 12-volt models, but they weigh a little more. The prices shown are suggested retail prices and the actual sale prices may vary.

I cut my lawn often (once a week or more) so mulching works well for me without bagging. This is best for the grass (see adjacent **Tips**). The clippings are cut so finely that I cannot even see them. If you cut your grass less often, then you might consider side or rear discharge with a bagging option.

When you cut very tall grass with a cordless mower, it draws more current and runs the batteries down faster. Therefore, it is best to cut often and mulch. As the chart shows below, it is very inexpensive to use a cordless mower. There is no maintenance other than regular blade sharpening. The single lever cutting height adjustment is quick and convenient.

For lawns without many trees, corded electric mowers are ideal. They are powerful, lightweight, and have mulch or bag options. Flip-over handles and cord systems improve convenience over old models.

For a small lot, a reel type push mower is good. These mowers are also the best for your grass. They cut with a scissors action that makes a smooth straight cut of the blades. This minimizes damage to the grass, diseases, and dryness problems. Some weigh less than 20 lbs.

Mulching Lawn Mowing Tips

To take full advantage of the benefits of your mulching mower, it is helpful to understand the mulching process that is taking place:

The grass is initially lifted and cut by the outboard cutting portion of the blade, then forced upward into the blade tunnel. Next, the clippings are recirculated into the inward mulching portion of the blade where they are recut to form smaller clippings. Finally, the downward deflector on the blade forces the clippings to the soil level of the lawn.

Since grass clippings are 80% to 95%, they decompose easily, leaving valuable nutrients in the soil. They also form a moisture saving layer of shade for the soil.

KEEP MOWER BLADE SHARP

A sharp blade provides a clean "just bagged" appearance without tearing the grass.

MOW REGULARLY AND ONLY THE TOP ONE-THIRD OF GRASS BLADES

Normal mowing height should remove only 1" to 1½" of the blades of grass.

ALTERNATE THE CUTTING PATTERN EACH TIME YOU MOW

Changing the cutting pattern avoids training the grass to grow in a certain direction ("graining") and avoids matting the grass by running the wheels in the same location each time you mow.

When mowing on a hill or slope, **ALWAYS** mow across the face of the slope. **DO NOT** mow up and down slopes. **DO NOT** mow excessively steep slopes.

KEEP UNDERSIDE OF MOWER DECK CLEAN

Keeping the underside of mower deck clean provides a clean smooth surface to channel the cut grass into the mulching portion of the blade.

DO NOT MOW YOUR LAWN WHEN THE GRASS IS WET

Wet grass will form clumps and stick to the underside of mower deck, interfering with the proper mulching action of grass clippings.

*Annual Electric Cost for Cordless Lawn Mower

electric rate	1 cut per week	2 cuts per week
$ per kwh	$	$
.06	1.87	3.21
.07	2.50	3.75
.08	2.68	4.28
.09	2.86	4.82
.10	3.12	5.35
.11	3.43	5.89
.12	3.74	6.42
.13	4.06	6.96
.14	4.37	7.49

* Based on mowing for 6 months and trickle charge for 12 months

Manufacturers of Efficient Non-Gasoline-Powered Lawn Mowers

AMERICAN LAWN MOWER, P.O. Box 369, Shelbyville, IN 46176 (800) 633-1501 (317) 392-3615

power source - manual: reel type	price - $60 to $100	cutting height - $1/2$ to $1 1/2$ in.
model no. - 1204-14	weight - 19 lbs.	cutting width - 14 in.
model no. - 1303-14	weight - 29 lbs.	cutting width - 14 in.
model no. - 1304-14	weight - 19 lbs.	cutting width - 14 in.
model no. - 1304-16	weight - 24 lbs.	cutting width - 14 in.

special features - scissors-cut action better for grass, 4 or 5 blades, ball bearings, zinc-plated handle

BLACK & DECKER, 701 E. Joppa Rd., Towson, MD 21286 - (800) 762-6672 (410) 716-3900

power source - battery/cordless	volts - 12	run/recharge time - 90 min./24 hrs.
cutting width - 18 in.	weight - 60 lbs.	cut height - $1 3/4$ to $3 1/2$ in - 6 positions
model no./price - CMM650/$350 or 750	warranty - two years	clippings - mulch or side discharge/bag

special features - single-lever height adjustment, easy switch from bag to mulch, model CMM750 ($25 more) is the same as CMM650 except it includes the bag and an adjustable handle.

power source - electric/corded	volts - 120	current draw - 9.1 amperes
cutting width - 18 in.	weight - 38 lbs.	cut height - $1 3/4$ to $3 1/2$ in. - 6 positions
model no./price - MM450/$200	warranty - two years	clippings - mulch or side discharge/bag

special features - has flip-over handle so you can cut in either direction without moving cord

MTD PRODUCTS, P.O. Box 368022, Cleveland, OH 44136 - (800) 800-7310 (216) 225-2600

power source - electric/corded	volts - 120	current draw - 12.0 amperes
cutting width - 19 in.	weight - 59 lbs.	cut height - $1 3/4$ to $3 1/2$ in - 9 positions
model no./price - 427/$160	warranty - two years	clippings - side discharge/bag

special features - 7" x 2" wheels, flip-over handle to cut in either direction, 1.6 bushel grass catcher bag

power source - electric/corded	volts - 120	current draw - 12.0 amperes
cutting width - 19 in.	weight - 60 lbs.	cut height - $1 3/4$ to $3 1/2$ in. - 9 positions
model no./price - 387/$220	warranty - two years	clippings - mulch or rear discharge/bag

special features - 8" x 2" ball bearing wheels, cord minder system to keep cord out of mowing path

power source - electric/corded	volts - 120	current draw - 12.0 amperes
cutting width - 20 in.	weight - 72 lbs.	cut height - $1 3/4$ to $3 1/2$ in. - 6 positions
model no./price - 107/$200	warranty - two years	clippings - mulch or side discharge/bag

special features - 8" x 2" ball bearing wheels, soft foam covered grip

RYOBI AMERICA CORP., P.O. Box 1207, Anderson, SC 29622 - (800) 525-2579

power source - battery/cordless	volts - 24	run/recharge time - 90 min./16 hrs.
cutting width - 18 in.	weight - 75 lbs.	cut height - 1 to 4 in. - 10 positions
model no./price - BMM2400/$400	warranty - two years	clippings - mulch only

special features - battery charge gauge, single-lever height adjustment, separate low/high cut height ranges

SEARS, 3333 Beverly Rd., Hoffman Estates, IL 60179 - (800) 359-2000 (708) 286-2500

power source - battery/cordless	volts - 24	run/recharge time - 90 min./16 hrs.
cutting width - 18 in.	weight - 75 lbs.	cut height - 1 to 4 in. - 10 positions
model no./price - 315.370270/$350	warranty - one year	

special features - one-touch height adjustment, battery status gauge, two cutting height ranges with five settings in each range for 10 settings, larger rear wheels for easy rolling

power source - electric/corded	volts - 120	current draw - 12.0 amperes
cutting width - 19 in.	weight - 60 lbs.	cut height - $1 3/4$ to $3 1/2$ in. - 9 positions
model no./price - 315.370025/$239	warranty - one year	clippings - mulch or rear discharge/bag

special features - 8" x 2" ball bearing wheels, cord minder system to keep cord out of mowing path

KNOW YOUR MULCHING MOWER

READ THIS OWNER'S MANUAL AND SAFETY RULES BEFORE OPERATING YOUR MOWER. Compare the illustrations with your lawn mower to familiarize yourself with the location of various controls and adjustments, operating features, and safety requirements. Save this manual for future reference.

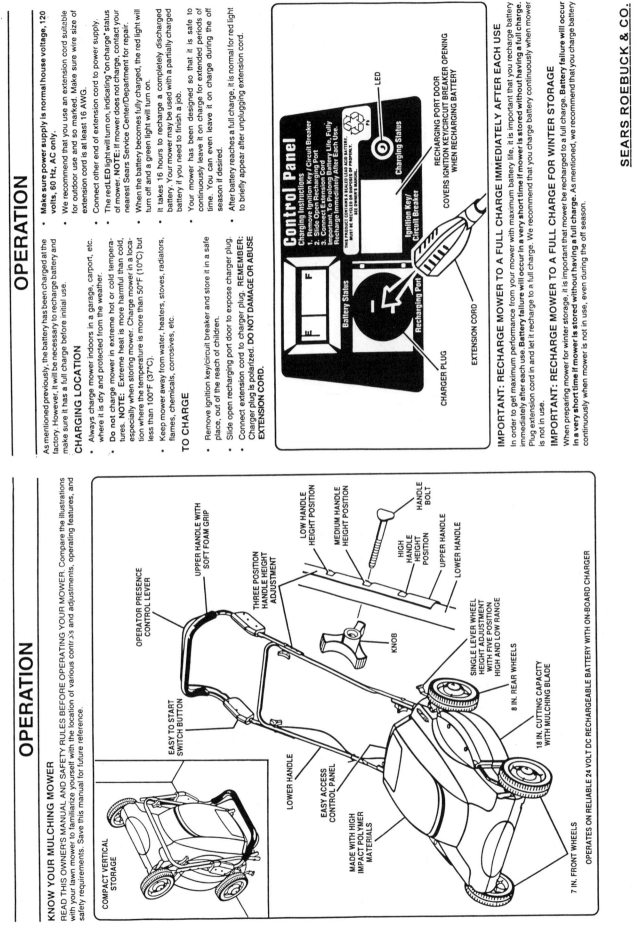

COMPACT VERTICAL STORAGE

OPERATOR PRESENCE CONTROL LEVER

UPPER HANDLE WITH SOFT FOAM GRIP

THREE POSITION HANDLE HEIGHT ADJUSTMENT

LOW HANDLE HEIGHT POSITION

MEDIUM HANDLE HEIGHT POSITION

HANDLE BOLT

HIGH HANDLE HEIGHT POSITION

UPPER HANDLE

LOWER HANDLE

KNOB

EASY TO START SWITCH BUTTON

LOWER HANDLE

EASY ACCESS CONTROL PANEL

MADE WITH HIGH IMPACT POLYMER MATERIALS

SINGLE LEVER WHEEL HEIGHT ADJUSTMENT WITH FIVE POSITION HIGH AND LOW RANGE

8 IN. REAR WHEELS

18 IN. CUTTING CAPACITY WITH MULCHING BLADE

7 IN. FRONT WHEELS

OPERATES ON RELIABLE 24 VOLT DC RECHARGEABLE BATTERY WITH ON-BOARD CHARGER

As mentioned previously, the battery has been charged at the factory. However, it will be necessary to recharge battery and make sure it has a full charge before initial use.

CHARGING LOCATION

• Always charge mower indoors in a garage, carport, etc. where it is dry and protected from the weather.

• Do not charge mower in extreme hot or cold temperatures. **NOTE:** Extreme heat is more harmful than cold, especially when storing mower. Charge mower in a location where the temperature is more than 50°F (10°C) but less than 100°F (37°C).

• Keep mower away from water, heaters, stoves, radiators, flames, chemicals, corrosives, etc.

TO CHARGE

• Remove ignition key/circuit breaker and store it in a safe place, out of the reach of children.

• Slide open recharging port door to expose charger plug.

• Connect extension cord to charger plug. **REMEMBER:** Charger plug is polarized. **DO NOT DAMAGE OR ABUSE EXTENSION CORD.**

• **Make sure power supply is normal house voltage, 120 volts, 60 Hz, AC only.**

• We recommend that you use an extension cord suitable for outdoor use and so marked. Make sure wire size of extension cord is at least 16 AWG.

• Connect other end of extension cord to power supply.

• The red **LED** light will turn on, indicating "on charge" status of mower. **NOTE:** If mower does not charge, contact your nearest Sears Service Center/Department for repair.

• When the battery becomes fully charged, the red light will turn off and a green light will turn on.

• It takes 16 hours to recharge a completely discharged battery. Your mower may be used with a partially charged battery if you need to finish a job.

• Your mower has been designed so that it is safe to continuously leave it on charge for extended periods of time. You can even leave it on charge during the off season if desired.

• After battery reaches a full charge, it is normal for red light to briefly appear after unplugging extension cord.

Control Panel

Charging Instructions
1. Remove Ignition Key / Circuit Breaker
2. Slide Open Recharging Port
3. Connect Extension Cord
Important. To Prolong Battery Life, Fully Recharge Immediately After Each Use.

THIS PRODUCT CONTAINS A SEALED LEAD ACID BATTERY. MUST BE RECYCLED OR DISPOSED OF PROPERLY. SEE OWNER'S MANUAL.

Battery Status

Ignition Key/ Circuit Breaker

Recharging Port

Charging Status

LED

RECHARGING PORT DOOR COVERS IGNITION KEY/CIRCUIT BREAKER OPENING WHEN RECHARGING BATTERY

CHARGER PLUG

EXTENSION CORD

IMPORTANT: RECHARGE MOWER TO A FULL CHARGE IMMEDIATELY AFTER EACH USE

In order to get maximum performance from your mower with maximum battery life, it is important that you recharge battery immediately after each use. **Battery failure will occur in a very short time if mower is stored without having a full charge.** Plug extension cord in and let it recharge to a full charge. We recommend that you charge battery continuously when mower is not in use.

IMPORTANT: RECHARGE MOWER TO A FULL CHARGE FOR WINTER STORAGE

When preparing mower for winter storage, it is important that mower be recharged to a full charge. **Battery failure will occur in a very short time if mower is stored without having a full charge.** As mentioned, we recommend that you charge battery continuously when mower is not in use, even during the off season.

Q: I have seen $10 do-it-yourself water-saver kits for old toilets that claim to cut water bills by $100 per year. Do they flush okay, are they easy to install and do they save that much water?

A: Flushing toilets account for about 40 percent of your water bills. By installing a simple water-saver kit, you can cut the toilet water usage by more than half and save tens of thousands of gallons per year. For a typical family, an annual savings of $100 is reasonable.

There are several basic designs of do-it-yourself toilet water saver kits that provide effective flushes. They range in price from $4 to $25. It takes about fifteen minutes to install even the most complicated kit.

Dual-flush kits are most effective. These provide a low water volume flush for liquid wastes and a full volume flush for solids. Ninety percent of flushes are for liquids only and do not require the full toilet tank volume.

With one dual flush kit, push the flush handle down for a water saving low volume flush. For a full tank volume flush for solids, lift up the handle. The handle does not have to be held continuously as the toilet flushes.

Other designs have two handles. Push a long handle down for a full volume flush. For a water saving flush, hold down a short handle while it flushes. These are effective, but less convenient than the above design.

Inexpensive rapid-closing flapper kits (about $10) are simple to install and effective. A flapper is the flexible seal that fits over the large drain hole inside the tank. It often attaches to the handle with a chain.

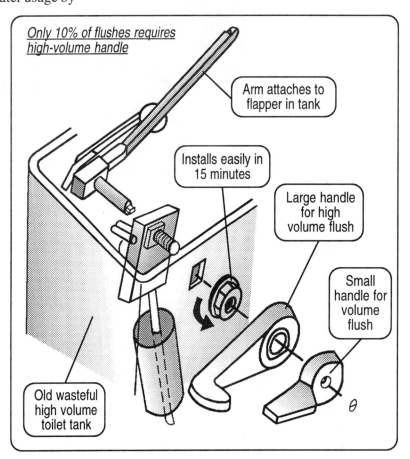

Only 10% of flushes requires high-volume handle

Arm attaches to flapper in tank

Installs easily in 15 minutes

Large handle for high volume flush

Small handle for volume flush

Old wasteful high volume toilet tank

The best rapid-closing flapper kits are adjustable because the amount of water needed for an effective flush varies with designs. When you first install a flapper, it takes several flushes to fine tune it.

One design has a simple adjustable knob in the flapper with various-size drain holes. Each size hole allows water to fill the flapper at different rates. This controls how fast the flapper closes and the amount of water savings.

Other types of inexpensive devices snap on or slip over the overflow tube in the tank. Some designs have a float that moves down the tube and forces the flapper to close earlier. Another inexpensive design (about $4) clips on the tube to limit how far the flapper opens. Both designs are adjustable.

Inexpensive water dam kits are better than just putting a brick in the tank. Bricks slowly disintegrate in the water and tiny granules can get under the flapper seal. This may cause a continuous leak. Good dams are made of springy sheet metal or plastic with foam or rubber seals around the edge. Simply bend them and fit them between the walls.

Q: I stretch plastic over my sliding patio screen door in the winter. The rollers are worn out and the door doesn't fit the track well. Can I repair it myself so it makes a better seal?

A: Putting clear plastic film over your screen door helps reduce air leaks from the wind. It also creates a dead air space which reduces heat loss.

The rollers are easy to replace yourself. You can purchase new rollers for about $5 a pair at your hardware store. Remove the screen door from the track. Unscrew each roller adjustment screw so the roller assembly hangs down. Replace the rollers and readjust the screws.

Operation of a Conventional Toilet

When the handle is pressed, the flapper valve rotates to the vertical position. Trapped air keeps it buoyant while it is submerged, *figure #1*. When the water level reaches the flapper valve, the flapper follows the water level down until the toilet tank is empty, *figure #2*. The weight of the water refilling the reservoir seals the flapper in the closed position thus preparing the toilet for the next cycle.

Operation of a Toilet Equipped with Frugal Flush®

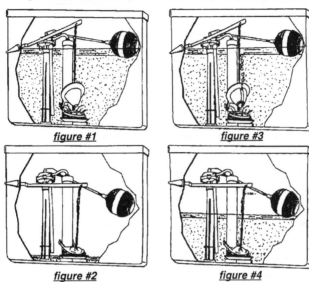

figure #1   figure #3

figure #2   figure #4

The Frugal Flush valve does not reduce the amount of water in the tank (water column). It re- lies on the toilet's original design to achieve the head pressure and scouring action necessary for ad- equate flushing. The tank's wa- ter level should be adjusted to the highest possible level to maxi- mize available head pressure. Fru- gal Flush simply conserves wa- ter by eliminating unnecessary re- sidual flow of water from the toilet tank.

When the handle is pulled, the flapper cavity is filled with air which causes the flapper valve to remain in the open position.

As the flapper rotates to the vertical position, water enters the preset gauged hole through the end cap on the bottom of the cone and causes air to exit through the small bleed hole, *figure #3*. The size of the bottom inlet hole se- lected determines the point at which the flapper becomes nonbuoyant and rotates closed, *figure #4*. The weight of the trapped water (ap- proximately half) firmly seals the flapper. The water in the cone runs into the bowl, thus preparing the toilet for the next cycle. With a 5 gallon reservoir, the end cap can be set so that rotation termi- nates flow after 1.5 to 3.5 gallons have exited the reservoir. With the new water conserving toilets, this point would occur after 1.5 to 2.7 gallons have exited.

The genius of the invention is that it utilizes the maximum head pressure available (the weight of 3.5 or 5 gallons of water); does not impede the scouring actions; and can start siphoning action with as little as 1.5 gallons of water. This is a major breakthrough in water conservation.

Converting a Toilet to a Water Saver with Water Saving Products							
Annual Savings of Water/Sewage Charges*							
Water/sewage rates per 1000 gallons	1/2 gal per flush	1 gal per flush	1 1/2 gal per flush	2 gal per flush	2 1/2 gal per flush	3 gal per flush	3 1/2 gal per flush
$1.00	$3.83	$7.66	$11.48	$15.31	$19.14	$22.97	$26.79
$1.25	$4.78	$9.57	$14.35	$19.14	$23.92	$28.71	$33.49
$1.50	$5.74	$11.48	$17.22	$22.97	$28.71	$34.45	$40.49
$1.75	$6.70	$13.40	$20.09	$26.79	$33.49	$40.19	$46.89
$2.00	$7.66	$15.31	$22.97	$30.62	$38.28	$45.93	$53.59
$2.25	$8.61	$17.22	$25.84	$34.45	$43.06	$51.67	$60.28
$2.50	$9.57	$19.14	$28.71	$38.28	$47.84	$57.41	$66.98
$2.75	$10.53	$21.05	$31.58	$42.10	$52.63	$63.15	$73.68
$3.00	$11.48	$22.97	$34.45	$45.93	$57.41	$68.90	$80.38
$4.00	$15.31	$30.62	$45.93	$61.24	$76.55	$91.86	$107.17
$5.00	$19.14	$38.28	$57.41	$76.55	$95.69	$114.83	$133.96
$6.00	$22.97	$45.93	$68.90	$91.86	$114.83	$137.79	$160.76
$7.00	$26.79	$53.59	$80.38	$107.17	$133.96	$160.76	$187.55
$8.00	$30.62	$61.24	$91.86	$122.48	$153.10	$183.72	$214.34
$9.00	$34.45	$68.90	$103.34	$137.79	$172.24	$206.69	$241.13
$10.00	$38.28	$76.55	$114.83	$153.10	$191.38	$229.65	$267.93

*Based on an average family of 4, flushing 21 times a day, 365 days a year

CREST/GOOD MFG. CO., 325 Underhill Blvd., Syosset, NY 11791 - (516) 921-7260

model - Big Ben

description - The flapper is made from a waterproofed silicone material which is resistant to minerals, chlorines and flourides. The design of the cup traps water for added weight and assures a tight seal.

installation instructions - It installs easily by hand by sliding the adapter ring and flapper around the overflow pipe. You seat the flapper firmly into place and attach the chain to the tank lever arm. It replaces old style tank balls and flappers and is ideal for slant and Douglas style flush valves.

water saved - Saves water because it eliminates small leaks.

ENERGY TECHNOLOGY LAB., 2351 Tenaya Dr., Modesto, CA 95351 - (800) 344-3242 (209) 529-3546

model - PopFlush

description - The PopFlush® is made of recycled ABS plastic and stainless steel which are both resistant to lime scale and toilet cleansers. The unique and adjustable cup offers a wide range of settings to get the most maximum water savings. The device forces the flapper to close earlier.

installation instructions - The unit is easy to install, it requires no plumber or tools and snaps onto 95% of all toilets. It includes adapters for American Standard and rod and ball type toilets.

water saved - 1.5 to 2 gallons per flush

FLUIDMASTER, INC., PO Box 4264, Anaheim, CA 92803 - (714) 774-1444

model - Bull's Eye Super Flapper

description - The flapper is made of thermoplastic and resists chlorine and other compounds found in household water.

installation instructions - The flapper is hinged to a rigid frame and snaps onto the overflow tube mounts. If mounts are not present, a self-adjusting adapter slides over the overflow tube where the flapper is snapped into place.

water saved - Saves water because it eliminates small leaks.

FRUGAL TECHNOLOGIES, 1209 E. Washington, Suite 4, Phoenix, AZ 85034 - (800) 626-8481

model - Frugal Flush Retroflapper and Frugal Flush Universal - Retroflapper installs on most 3.5, 5 and 7 gallon toilets, Universal installs on 1.6 gpf toilets

description - The chain assembly is stainless steel. The flapper is made of thermoplastic rubber and the cone is made of acetal resins to resist mineral buildup. It has a bleed hole to let air escape as water enters the cone. An end cap is made of flexible vinyl which allows adjustment with five gauged hole openings for optimum water savings.

installation instructions - No tools are required for installation. It fits standard flush valves with mounting ears. You slip the ears of the flapper valve over prongs at the bottom of overflow tube then fasten hook to lever and attach ball chain to hook. Adapters are available for easy installation to American Standard and Douglas flush valves.

water saved - 30% to 50% per flush - 1.5 to 2.3 gallons per flush

NIAGARA CONSERVATION, 230 Route 206, Flanders, NJ 07836 - (800) 831-8383 (201) 927-4545

model - Short Flush

description - An adjustable float controls the amount of water used with every flush. It is made of thermoplastic which resists fungus and chlorine. It stops existing leaks and prevents new leaks.

installation instructions - The flapper installs easily by hand simply by sliding the adapter ring and flapper down the overflow pipe. Attach the chain to the tank lever arm, seat the flapper and adjust the float by raising or lowering it.

water saved - 50% per flush - 2.5 gallons per flush

Manufacturers of Toilet Water Dams

MOON WATERSAVER, PO Box 642, Hillsboro, NC 27278 - (919) 732-3257

model - Water Bank

NIAGARA CONSERVATION, 230 Route 206, Flanders, NJ 07836 - (800) 831-8383 (201) 927-4545

model - Toilet Tank Dam R3130

RESOURCE CONSERVATION, PO Box 71, Greenwich, CT 06836 - (800) 243-2862

model - Incredible Superbowl

WHEDON PRODUCTS, INC., 21A Andover Dr., W. Hartford, CT 06110 - (800) 541-2184 (203) 953-7606

model - Saver Flush

description - Water dams consist of two corrosion-proof panels that fit inside vertical toilet tanks.

installation instructions -simply bend the flexible panels and install snugly between the walls of a standard toilet tank.

water saved - 40% to 50% per flush

Manufacturers of Other Toilet Water-Saving Devices

ECO PRODUCTS, 7748 Westlawn Ave., Los Angeles, CA 90045 - (310) 641-8649

model - Toilet Flush Control #106 and #107

description - The plastic attachments prevent the toilet flush valve from becoming buoyant. The device is clipped on the tube and limits how far the flapper opens. You have a choice of a short flush or a full flush depending on the time you hold down the handle.

installation instructions - #106 slides over the overflow pipe until it touches the top of flapper. You then tighten the screw to secure the control device. #107 is placed on ball lift rod and screwed into place.

water saved - 80% per flush

H & F INC., 2029 P St. NW, Washington, DC 20036 - (202) 467-4700

model - Aqua Saver

description - A small plastic divertor with four spouts.

installation instructions - Remove intake hose from overflow pipe and remove the hose clip. The divertor inserts into the end of the hose and at least one spout is inside the overflow pipe and the remaining spouts are outside the pipe.

water saved - .5 to 1.0 gallons per flush

NIAGARA CONSERVATION, 230 Route 206, Flanders, NJ 07836 - (800) 831-8383 (201) 927-4545

model - Diverter and Leak Detector (R3142)

description - A small plastic divertor with two spouts.

installation instructions - Remove intake hose from overflow pipe and remove the hose clip. The divertor inserts into the end of the hose and one spout is inside the overflow pipe and the remaining spout is outside the pipe.

water saved - 50% per flush

model - Toilet Tank Bank

description - This is a toilet tank displacement bag made of non-corrosive materials that resist fungus growth and microbes.

installation instructions - Simply fill the bag with water, snap it closed and place in the tank for water conservation.

water saved - .75 gallons per flush

– –

Manufacturers of Toilet Dual Flush Systems

JAWZ, INC., 501 Industrial Way, Fallbrook, CA 92028 - (619) 728-8380

model - Flush Wise

description - This device is made of plastic to withstand minerals and chemicals in the water. You slide it over the pipe and remove the existing flapper. It is versatile with the option of a full flush or a water saving flush without any adjustments. You just hold down the handle for a full flush.

installation instructions - No tools are needed, simply slip on and adjust in five minutes. It fits all standard flapper valve toilets.

water saved - 70% per flush

MILLER WATER SAVER ENTERPRISES, Box 743, Green Valley, AZ 85622 - (602) 625-6651

model - Fully Automatic Dual Flush II

description - The two piece constructed handle is made of durable and non corrosive plastics. It offers both a full flush for solid waste or a mini flush for liquids only. You simply choose which handle to flush. The mini flush lever regulates the flow of water from the tank automatically.

installation instructions - You simply replace the standard lever and lift arm, it fits most toilet tanks. You may need to use pliers to adjust it firmly into place. The kit includes handle, lift arm, flapper, chain and adjustable float.

water saved - average 67% per flush

SELECT-A-FLUSH CORP., PO Box 1725, Yakima, WA 98907 - (800) 545-0552 (509) 575-0239

model - Select-a-Flush

description - The Select-A-Flush® device is made of non-corrosive, wear resistant materials. It contains four moving parts. Push the handle down for an economy flush (no need to hold handle down) and lift the handle up for a full flush.

installation instructions - You replace the existing handle and lift arm with the device. The Select-A-Flush® device includes the handle, lift arm, valve and adjustable float. Replace the existing flapper, then adjust the float up or down until the minumum amount of water needed is released for the economy flush option.

water saved - 3 ½ gallons per flush for the economy flush

Q: I am on a limited budget, but I want to install a security (burglar) system in my home. I leave lights on now, but that pushes up electric bills. What type of easy-to-install systems are available?

A: Although security systems use some electricity, they consume less than keeping lights on. You can install a basic do-it-yourself security system for about $100 to $200. As your budget allows, expand the system with more window and door sensors and automatic police, fire, and emergency telephone dialers.

To protect only one door, like a back door, you can get inexpensive self-contained alarms. One loud alarm (about $40) is designed to fit a sliding glass patio door. Another is a small "electronic dog". If it senses vibration or noise at a door or window, its alarm sounds like a large barking dog.

Another unique system indicates, before you open the door to go in, if there was a break in while you were away from home. This eliminates the possibility of surprising an armed burglar inside.

The easiest-to-install security system, in an existing home, is a wireless remote design. You can install a complete system (window, door, motion sensors, and automatic dialer) in a couple of hours. If you ever move, you can remove the sensors and take them to your new home.

A wireless system uses small 9-volt battery-operated sensors that transmit signals to the main control unit. This unit is often located in a closet and has battery backup in case of a power outage. The batteries last about one year or you can use rechargeable ones and save.

An advantage of wireless systems is the small hand-held remote

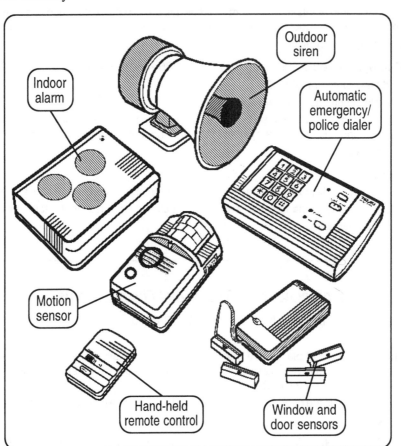

Indoor alarm

Outdoor siren

Automatic emergency/ police dialer

Motion sensor

Hand-held remote control

Window and door sensors

control. You can take it outdoors with you. If you get hurt, see smoke in your house, etc., you can hit either an "emergency", "fire", or "police" button to summon help immediately.

Sound or motion sensors in several rooms and a stairway are effective. If you have pets, select a motion sensor with a "pet alley". The scanning path is limited to above the height of your pet, so it won't set off the alarm.

One system senses a unique shock wave in the air when a door opens or a window is broken by a burglar. This allows you to arm the system and still move around your home without setting off motion sensors. If your small child opens a door and crawls out, the alarm signals you to get him.

A keyless combination door deadbolt is very effective. There is no key to lose and you can change the combination of the lock at anytime. With a keyless combination on the inside too, a burglar cannot get the door open to carry things out.

Q: I have made my house more airtight over the past several years and I am concerned about cancer-causing radon gas poisoning. Would you explain what the unit of measure, pCi/l, means and do I need more ventilation?

A: If you are concerned about radon gas poisoning, have your home tested before you make any changes. Increasing ventilation does help, but there are other more energy-efficient methods depending on the radon source.

The unit pCi/l, picocuriers per liter, is a measure of the concentration of radioactivity inside your home, not of the radon gas. Radon gas itself is not harmful. It is the radioactivity from its decay that is harmful.

ADEMCO, 165 Eileen Way, Syosset, NY 11791 - (800) 645-7568 (516) 921-6700

There are several security systems available with hardwire, wireless and multiplex capabilities which include many standard security features and they offer up to 64 zone capability. Many of these systems are customized just for your home, including extras like portable panic buttons and portable full-function keypads. You can expand the systems with motion and smoke detectors, glass guard sensors (sense broken glass), audio and shock sensors. Also available are nine designer colors for your security console to complement your residence.

Illustration shows how one wall-mounted, self-contained sensor can protect room, doors, and stairs.

AIPHONE CORP., 1700 130th Ave. NE, Bellevue, WA 98009 - (206) 455-0510

The basic video entry system uses a small door camera connected to an inside monitor. With the touch of a button you adjust the camera to any angle. The viewing angle range of 76° vertically and 122° horizontally. The camera uses infrared technology so you can see under any lighting conditions - whether it is the dead of night or in bright sunlight. If the monitor happens to be a long walk away from the door, there's an optional door release that automatically unlocks the door for your guests. The basic model is also available with a less expensive manually adjustable door camera. Six models are available. Also available are six different audio and video systems that have 2-stations and 2-wires.

CARLON, 25701 Science Park Dr., Cleveland, OH 44122 - (800) 321-1970 (516) 434-8080

The basic system, called "Homewatch 2000", is a self contained wireless security system that is easy to install (*figure #1*). You plug in the AC power transformer and all systems are ready to go . No further wiring is necessary. It is a single component unit with the motion sensors and alarm built into the control unit. It has built-in combination heat and motion sensors to minimize false alarms. Dual sensors produce a funnel shaped pattern that extends outward in an arc to protect up to 1,000 square feet of space. It includes a loud 90-decibel internal alarm and an emergency panic button. You can expand the system with wired perimeter loops and an external 125 decibel siren. You use a key to arm and disarm the unit.

DIMANGO PRODUCTS, 7258 Kensington Rd., Brighton, MI 48116 - (800) 654-9927 (313) 486-0770

The basic system, called "Safe & Sound Wireless Home Security System", includes a main control console with easy four button operation, two door/window sensors, remote power alarm, and a remote arm/disarm control transmitter. It offers an instant ear piercing alarm that sounds before an intruder gains entry. There is also an indicator that indicates, when you arrive home and disarm the system, whether or not there was a break in while you were gone. This can keep you from walking in and surprising a burglar. You can expand the system with glass break detector, external siren, and motion detector with special pet alley lens. You can also get an optional light flasher alarm and an interface to work with most automatic dialers when there is an alarm.

HOME AUTOMATION, PO Box 9310, Metairie, LA 70055 - (504) 833-7256

The basic system, called "Model 1503 Home Control and Security System", gives you security protection with lighting, appliance, and heating/cooling control integrated into the system. It also offers freeze protection when you're away from home. The system includes wall mounted keypad and remote control from any touch-tone phone. The system can be programmed to turn itself on and off automatically. The security features include motion, smoke, and temperature sensors (22 possible sensors - expandable up to 80 sensors). You can use a special "All Lights On" command from your bedside phone if you hear a strange sound at night.

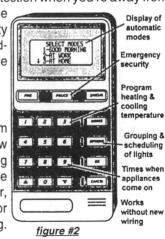

figure #2

HONEYWELL, 1985 Douglas N., Golden Valley, MN 55422 - (800) 468-1502

A self contained system to protect a window or sliding glass door, called the "Security Alarm and Lock Bar" ($40), is powered by four C-size batteries. Once it is armed in the window or door, if it is moved, a loud 90-decibel alarm sounds. It is available in a 20-3/4 inch-long window model and a 29-1/8 inch-long door model. "TotalHome" (*figure #2*), features home security, lighting, temperature and appliance control. The system includes window/door, motion, smoke and temperature sensors. It can be accessed by any touch-tone phone or touch panel with interactive voice. No wiring required, the system works with existing wiring.

INTELECTRON, 21021 Corsair Blvd., Hayward, CA 94545 - (510) 732-6790

The basic system includes an outdoor motion sensing device which switches on a light . They offer several decorative lantern styles with a hidden motion detector cleverly concealed with color matched lens. It instantly turns lights on when anyone approaches and the light stays on as long as motion is detected. There is a manual override that lets you use your indoor light switch to turn light on/off at any time. Allows light to stay on continuously when needed. Also available is a wireless infrared motion detector. It is powerful enough to scan the dark outside the home and signal receivers up to 75 feet away inside the home.

INTERACTIVE TECHNOLOGIES, 2266 N. 2nd St., N St. Paul, MN 55109 - (800) 777-4841 (612) 777-2690

Programmable Custom Zone Descriptions
Large Backlit Keys With Tactile Feedback Beep
Extra Large Backlit Super Twist LCD Display
Police Emergency Zone *figure #3*

The basic system, called "Caretaker Plus", is a 32-zone security system that can be hardwire, wireless or a combination of both. One model has 6 hardwire zones built-in. It can be controlled from any touch-tone phone, remote or a wall mount. It features a digitized voice for prompting for easy operation. In the event of an alarm, the system sounds a very loud siren and then yells a variety of messages such as FIRE or INTRUSION. Also available are door/window, motion, sound, shock, glass guard, temperature, and smoke sensors.

INTERMATIC, Intermatic Plaza, Spring Grove, IL 60081 - (815) 675-2321

The basic system is an indoor/outdoor sound activated light unit (*figure #4*). It has an adjustable sound sensitivity setting and sound turns the light on automatically. Also available is an automatic security light control, which turns on at dusk, off at dawn. They offer a variety of lighting and appliance timers to give an "at home" appearance.

MASTERVOICE, INC., 10523 Humbolt St., Los Alamitos, CA 90720 - (310) 594-6581

The system, called "Butler in a Box", is voice activated and is taught to recognize one to four different voices to accept verbal commands up to 20 feet from speaker. It controls heating/cooling, lighting appliances, and security systems. It has built in infra-red sensors for light and alarm system control. It uses existing household wiring to remotely control the devices and controls. Two other models available.

NAPCO SECURITY SYSTEMS, 333 Bayview Ave., Amityville, NY 11701 (516) 842-9400

These security systems are "Hardwire/Wireless Ready Control/Communicators", with advanced features, including time referenced history logs and add on flexibility in 9, 16 and 96 zones (*figure #3*). They control security, lighting,temperature and appliances. There are flexible options which include the partitioning of mutiple areas of your home into mini-systems for maximum convenience. Keypad controlled access to special areas. You can expand your system wilth door/window, smoke, temperature and motion sensors. Also offered are decorator custom color and designer keypads.

NOVI INTERNATIONAL, 9424 Abraham Way, Santee, CA 92071 - (619) 258-1500

The basic system, called "Video DoorPhone", uses a small television camera. It allows you to view your visitors by looking at the screen from the safety of your home regardless of lighting conditions. You then press the door release button to allow them to enter. Also available is the doorbell intercom security system which allows you to answer your doorbell from wherever you happen to be. It is easy to install and converts any doorbell into a complete in-home wireless intercom and security system.

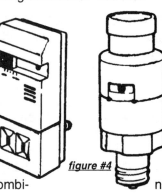

figure #4

PRESO-MATIC LOCK, 3048 Industrial 33rd St., Ft. Pierce, FL 34946 - (407) 465-7400

These are keyless entry locks which are all mechanical push button combination door locks (*figure #5*). They are guaranteed absolutely pickproof! There is no expensive electrical installation or batteries. The deadbolt or deadlatch bolts retract automatically, no knobs to turn. Also available are double combination locks which are operated on both sides of the door. Available in bright, satin, and antique brass, antique bronze, satin chrome, and black pebble finish. You can buy combination slides to easily change the combination.

QUORUM, 1550 W. Deer Valley Dr., Phoenix, AZ 85027 - (602) 780-5500

The basic system is a self contained unit that is easy to install. The system does not operate by detecting motion, so people and pets can move about the home freely while the system is armed. The security monitor detects sub-sonic air waves within an enclosed space. When a door or window is opened, a unique shock wave is detected and the system responds with a loud 103-decibel alarm. Since the unit is not hard-wired, it can be easily moved to another location if you should relocate. Two models are available.

RAB ELECTRIC, 170 Ludlow Ave., Northvale, NJ 07647 - (201) 784-8600

This is a basic outdoor motion-sensing light which switches on a light when motion is detected. Several types are available including double look down, animal alley and long range. There is a moveable knob allowing you to choose night only or 24-hour operation.

RADIONICS, 1800 Abbott St., Salinas, CA 93901 - (408) 757-8877

The basic system is hard wired, with a single control panel used to secure up to eight areas. This feature allows you to arm/disarm any area without affecting the security of others. This is ideal for rooms that need their own individual security control. You can expand your system with additional door/window and smoke sensors. There are several models available and are designed to meet your needs.

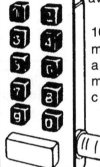

figure #5

RADIO SHACK, PO Box 1052, Ft. Worth, TX 76101 - (817) 390-3011

The basic system includes a main control center, a loud built-in siren/alarm, one window/door sensor, one lamp module to switch on a light, and a remote radio-controlled arm/disarm transmitter. Additional window/door sensors and motion sensor ($80) are available. This is a "supervised" system. This means that the main control cen-ter periodically checks with each sensor to check for proper operation and battery strength. If it senses a problem, a sensor indicator light on the main control center comes on.

STANLEY HOME AUTOMA-TION, 41700 Gardenbrook, Novi, MI 48050 - (313) 528-1400

The basic system uses two-channel window/door transmitters so that the control panel knows the status of each location before the system is armed. The built-in four channel receiver will monitor four wireless zones while four more zones can be hard wired. Other accessories available are a hand held transmitter, a remote keypad, door/window, light, and smoke sensor. Remote arm/disarm is also available through a miniature, keychain size transmitter.

TELKO, 26611 Cabot Ln., Laguna Hills, CA 92653 - (714) 367-1234

The battery-operated "barking dog" alarm is activated by vibration or light sensor which you can place on the table top or hang on the door (*figure #6*). Four models are available. Also available are battery operated sensor lights which are activated when a door or window are opened. Another basic system offered is a self contained motion sensing alarm for indoor use only. It runs off of batteries or AC operation and has 100 decibel siren alarm/chime. It has a 60 foot and 110° range of coverage. You can install one at each of several spots in your house.

TRANSCIENCE, 633 Hope St., Stamford, CT 06907 - (800) 243-3494 (203) 327-7810

The basic system, called "The Supervisor" is wire-less and comes complete with protection for two doors and interior motion sensor. It is a do-it yourself system that takes about two hours to install. It has eight functions, including 24 hour fire, medical, silent panic, audible panic, instant, delay, interior, and wireless remote arm. It is ex-pandable to 16 sensors for additional doors, motion detectors, portable panic but-tons, and medical alerts. Monitoring capibility for intrusion, fire, panic and medical and temperature alerts.

figure #6

UNITY SYSTEMS, 2606 Spring St., Redwood City, CA 94603 - (415) 369-3233

The basic system, "Home Manager", consists of standard security alarms and sensors, including passive infra-red, pressure, temperature sensors, and glass break detectors. It can protect up to 24 individual security zones, and limit access to spe-cific areas of the home. It sounds an alarm and turns on selected lights (steady or flashing) whenever any security zone is violated. It knows which doors and windows were left open. The system uses a computer and a wall mounted video touch screen, remote from touch-tone phone, or personal computer.

X-TRUDER SYSTEMS, 3200 Professional Pkwy., Atlanta, GA 30339 - (800) 987-8337 (404) 980-0708

These security systems consist of hardwire, wireless or both. The systems are customized because each home is different, the design can be the most basic or the most sophisticated.. The hardwire security systems secure each door and window with a magnetic contact to the alarm, while the wireless transmits radio signals from sensors to the alarm.

Q: I heard that new natural wood pellet barbecue grills make foods taste better and burn cleanly. Do they cost more to operate than gas or electric models and what else is new in efficient barbecues?

A: New wood pellet barbecues are convenient and efficient. By cooking over 100% real wood (renewable energy), you get an authentic "camp fire" flavor. The pellets are available in mesquite, cherry, hickory, and maple for unique flavors.

Pellet barbecues incorporate a small built-in auger and blower, but they look like typical gas barbecues. They use very little electricity and a small ten-pound bag of pellets should last for five cookouts.

A small hopper holds several pounds of ¼-inch diameter x 1-inch long wood pellets. The auger slowly feeds the pellets to the grill burner area. The auger speed is adjustable to control the barbecue temperature and smoke flavor.

The blower circulates air through the pellets for a hot pollution-free fire. This circulates air around the food for true smoked flavor. You only have to preheat it for about five minutes before grilling food.

There are new super-efficient futuristic-looking domed electric barbecues. These full-sized barbecues have a double wall insulated cover and use corrosion-resistant aluminized steel to retain heat using less electricity than a hair dryer.

Heating elements are built into a non-stick grill surface so there is less than a 25-degree temperature variation across it. This allows use of the entire grill surface and reduce

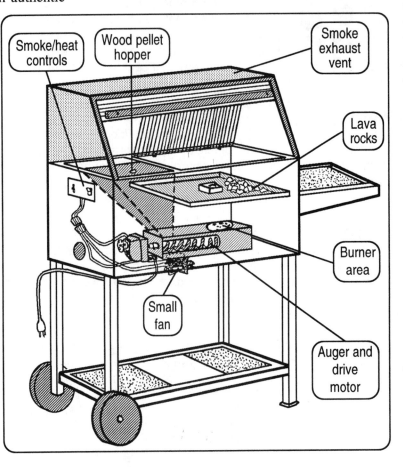

total cooking time. The circular domed top creates natural air flow inside to enhance flavor.

Other features to consider are an adjustable top vent that provides precise control over temperature and flavor. Smokers, with a water pan/steam heat feature, keep meat tender with more smoked flavor. An aluminized steel shell is efficient when used on gas barbecues.

A built-in drip vaporizer over the burners reduces flare-ups and improves the taste of the foods. A new "behind heat" (instead of under) rotisserie burner design roasts foods with less burnt taste and half as much gas.

There are new charcoal briquettes filled with real wood chunks. This provides the intense heat of charcoal with the flavor of real wood barbecuing. Keep in mind that burning charcoal produces more air pollution (100 times more CO gas) than using gas or electric barbecues.

Q: I want to make my old house more airtight by installing foam gaskets in my wall electric outlets. The package says that I should put them in all the wall outlets. Is this correct?

A: You should only put them behind the outlet faceplates on outdoor walls. Most builders do not seal around the conduit boxes during construction and this is one of the major areas for air leaks.

Little outdoor air, if any, should get into the interior walls of your home, so the draft sealers are not needed behind those outlet faceplates. Even though installing gaskets is a simple job, anytime you remove an electrical outlet faceplate, switch off the circuit breaker.

There have been several recent innovations in barbecue grills that improve the taste of grilled foods and cut energy usage and air pollution.

Typical open charcoal barbecues generate a lot of air pollution. As figure #1 shows, barbecuing one lb. of meat with charcoal produces as much CO (carbon monoxide) as barbecuing over 17,000 lbs. of meat on an electric grill. Several other common air pollutants are shown.

Pollution Comparison			
Type of Pollutant	Type of Barbecue Fuel		
	Electric	Gas	Charcoal
CO2 gas	18 lbs.	11 lbs.	1 lb.
NOx	24 lbs.	22 lbs.	1 lb.
CO	17,606 lbs.	130 lbs.	1 lb.
VOC*	359 lbs.	14 lbs.	1 lb.
*volatile organic compound			

Figure #1 - lbs. of meat you can grill to give off the same amount of these pollutants

Wood pellet barbecues, made by Traeger, produce much less air pollution than charcoal, but provide that real "campfire" smoked flavor to foods. They attain the efficient clean burn by forcing combustion air through and around the small pellets in the firepot. A 10-lbs. bag of pellets lasts for five cookouts. These pellets are available from Traeger in many types of wood for unique flavors - mesquite, cherry, hickory, alder, peach, apple, and maple. Manufacturers of combination charcoal/wood briquettes, for improved flavor, are listed below. I have listed manufacturers of efficient barbecues on pages 299 and 300 along with detailed information.

"Type" indicates the kind of fuel that the barbeque uses. If you have natural gas at your home and you don't move your barbecue, it is cheaper to use than propane gas. *"Maximum Btu (gas) or watts (electric)"* indicates the heat output. A higher maximum allows you to cook more food faster.

A greater *"total cooking area"* also indicates the quantity of food you can cook at one time. The *"grid finish"* is important for ease of cleaning and durability. Porcelain coated steel is fairly easy to clean. Stainless steel will handle scraping without damage and will not rust. Chrome-plated is similar to stainless steel.

I have listed several of the significant *"special features"* of each manufacturer to help you make a selection. Some of the most interesting ones are the "behind the food heat" rotisserie by Ducane. This reduces gas usage and improves the flavor of the foods. The Thermos electric barbecues use a double-walled domed top to save energy and cook quickly. This domed shape also improves flavor by creating natural air/smoke circulation inside the closed barbecue.

— —

Manufacturers of Hardwood Charcoal Briquettes

AMERICAN WOOD PRODUCTS, 9540 Riggs, Overland Park, KS - (800) 223-9046
Wood and hardwood lump charcoal products

BRINKMAN CORP., 4215 McEwen Rd., Dallas, TX 75244 - (214) 387-4939
Charcoal and wood smoking briquettes

HICKORY SPECIALTIES INC., PO Box 1669, Brentwood, TN 37027 - (800) 251-2076
Hardwood charcoal briquettes

MILAZZO IND. INC., 1609 River Rd., Pittston, PA 18640 - (717) 654-2433
Instant and lump charcoal, hardwood chunks and chips

NATURES OWN CHARWOODS, 453 S. Main St., Attleboro, MA 02703 - (800) 289-2427
Hardwood lump charcoal, herbwoods, chunk charwood and briquettes

WEBER-STEPHEN, 250 S. Hicks Rd., Palatine, IL 60067 - (800) 446-1071 (708) 705-8660
Hardwood charcoal briquettes and natural wood chunks

Manufacturers of Barbecues

BRINKMAN CORP., 4215 McEwen Rd., Dallas, TX 75244 - (214) 387-4939

type - gas   maximum Btu - 18,000
grid finish - chrome-plated   total cooking area - n/a - will handle 20 to 50 lbs. of food
special features - A unique hinged flip-top dome eliminates setting the dome on the ground or the table.

type - electric and charcoal smoker   watts - 850 to 1500
grid finish - chrome-plated   total cooking area - n/a - will handle 20 to 50 lbs. of food
special features - Equipped with a heat indicator and a hinged door for access to charcoal and water pans.

BROILMASTER, 301 E. Tennessee, Florence, AL 35631 - (205) 740-5115

type - gas   maximum Btu - 40,000
grid finish - porcelain coated cast iron   total cooking area in square inches - 393 to 1,009
special features - The Broilmonster is a double grill with a conversion kit to convert natural gas to propane.

CHAR-BROIL, PO Box 1300, Columbus, GA 31902 - (800) 252-8248

type - gas   maximum Btu - 40,000
grid finish - porcelain or cast iron   total cooking area in square inches - 454 to 1,033
special features - The Vaporiser® bar distibutes heat evenly and vaporizes food drippings on contact for a smoky barbecue flavor.

type - electric smoker   watts - 1,500
grid finish - porcelain or cast iron   total cooking area - n/a - will handle 40 to 50 lbs. of meat

type - charcoal grills and smokers
grid finish - porcelain or cast iron   total cooking area in square inches - 476 to 743

DUCANE, 2661 Metro Blvd, Maryland Heights, MD 63043 - (314) 291-5300

type - gas   maximum Btu - 60,000
grid finish - stainless steel   total cooking area in square inches - 384 to 575
special features - A special rotisserie grate rotisses from behind the meat instead of from below.

DYNASTY, 7355 E. Slauson Ave., City of Commerce, CA 90040 - (213) 728-5700

type - gas   maximum Btu - 164,000
grid finish - porcelain coated cast iron   total cooking area in square inches - 636 to 1,590
special features - Exclusive smoke-ejector system transfers the smoke flavoring through $1/2$ inch tubes.

GRILLMASTERS, 9112 NW 106th St., Medley, FL 33178 - (305) 882-8138

type - gas   maximum Btu - 32,000
grid finish - stainless steel   total cooking area in square inches - 434 to 1,375
special features - A special heat rack can be lowered or raised electrically and gives you control on heat intensity and flare ups.

JR ENTERPRISES, Rt. 1, Box 249A, DeWitt, AR 72042 - (501) 946-2780

type - charcoal grills and smokers
grid finish - expandable metal   total cooking area in square inches - 828 to 2,016
special features - Available with a 50º-500º thermometer for better cooking control.

KENMORE/SEARS, 3333 Beverly Rd., Hoffman Estates, IL 60179 - (800) 359-2000 (708) 286-2500

type - gas   maximum Btu - 44,000
grid finish - porcelain coated cast iron   total cooking area in square inches - 500 to 1,021
special features - A dual retracting warming rack is available.

KLOSE BAR-B-QUE PITS, 2214 $1/2$ W. 34th St., Houston, TX 77018 - (713) 686-8720

type - charcoal grills and smokers
grid finish - expandable metal   total cooking area - n/a - will handle 20 to 150 lbs. of food
special features - Over 100 different styles and models are available.

LAZY-MAN, PO Box 327, Belvidere, NJ 07823 - (908) 475-5315

<u>type</u> - gas
<u>grid finish</u> - stainless steel
<u>maximum Btu</u> - 72,000
<u>total cooking area in square inches</u> - 358 to 1,056
<u>special features</u> - The grills come equipped with stainless steel side and storage shelves.

MAGIKITCH'N, INC., 180 Penn Am Dr., Quakertown, PA 18951 - (800) 441-1492

<u>type</u> - gas or charcoal
<u>grid finish</u> - stainless steel
<u>maximum Btu</u> - 160,000
<u>total cooking area in square inches</u> - 350 to 1,075
<u>special features</u> - Options are easy to add in a few seconds without the use of tools such as a griddle, steamer, or rotisserie.

MODERN HOME PRODUCTS, 150 S. Ram Rd., Antioch, IL 60002 - (313) 545-4455

<u>type</u> - gas
<u>grid finish</u> - porcelain or aluminum
<u>maximum Btu</u> - 40,000
<u>total cooking area in square inches</u> - 126 to 625
<u>special features</u> - It has an easy to clean all weather simulated cultured marble shelf that will not warp, discolor or deteriorate.

SUNBEAM LEISURE PRODUCTS CO., 1600 Jones Rd., Paragould, AR 72450 - (501) 239-6215

<u>type</u> - gas
<u>grid finish</u> - porcelain or chrome
<u>maximum Btu</u> - 40,000
<u>total cooking area in square inches</u> - 187 to 901
<u>special features</u> - A steamer is available that is placed over a water reservoir.

<u>type</u> - charcoal grills and smokers
<u>grid finish</u> - chrome-plated
<u>total cooking area in square inches</u> - 185 to 575

THERMOS CO., PO Box 600, Freeport, IL 61032 - (800) 243-0745 (708) 240-3150

<u>type</u> - gas
<u>grid finish</u> - porcelain coated cast iron
<u>maximum Btu</u> - 44,000
<u>total cooking area in square inches</u> - 225 to 420
<u>special features</u> - Adjustable top vent controls smoke and air flow with the flip of your wrist.

<u>type</u> - electric
<u>grid finish</u> - non stick coated
<u>watts</u> - 1500
<u>total cooking area in square inches</u> - 225
<u>special features</u> - Consumes less electricity than a hair dryer and comes with an automatic shutoff after five hours of non-activity. The control panel features six pre-set temperature settings for easy cooking control.

TRAEGER INDUSTRIES, INC., PO Box 829, Mt. Angel, OR 97362 - (800) 872-3437 (503) 845-9234

<u>type</u> - pellet
<u>grid finish</u> - porcelain coated steel
<u>maximum Btu</u> - 36,000
<u>total cooking area in square inches</u> - 352 to 525
<u>special features</u> - Available with 3 speed control on the smoker model, side serving shelf and storage shelves are additional options. Real smoke flavor without the mess or fuss of adding wood chips.

ULTIMATE COOKER, 803 W. Fairbanks Ave., Winter Park, FL 32789 - (407) 644-6680

<u>type</u> - charcoal ceramic barbecue
<u>grid finish</u> - chrome plated
<u>total cooking area</u> - n/a - will handle 5 to 24 lbs. of food
<u>special features</u> - Cooks food quickly using a minimum of charcoal - able to cook a 20 lbs. turkey in 3 1/2 hours. Fires start easily with newspaper or electric starter.

WEBER-STEPHEN, 250 S. Hicks Rd., Palatine, IL 60067 - (800) 446-1071 (708) 705-8660

<u>type</u> - gas
<u>grid finish</u> - porcelain coated steel
<u>maximum Btu</u> - 36,000
<u>total cooking area in square inches</u> - 458 to 635
<u>special features</u> - The durable side and swing up tables are made of molded thermoplastic that resist stains.

<u>type</u> - charcoal kettle
<u>grid finish</u> - nickel plated steel
<u>total cooking area in square inches</u> - 150 to 397
<u>special features</u> - The lid stores away or serves as a wind shield when lighting the grill. Available in black, red, blue or brown.

Q: I am considering using an "activated oxygen" purifier instead of chlorine for my swimming pool and spa. Chemicals are expensive and irritate my eyes. How much electricity does a purifier use?

A: An activated oxygen (ozone) purifier is one of the most effective and environmentally-safe methods to purify your swimming pool or spa. It eliminates burning eyes, fading swim suits, and that "chemical" smell. In the 1984 Olympics in L.A., the swimming pool water was purified with ozone.

Using an ozone purifier can cut your chemical costs by up to 80%. The ozone actually improves the effectiveness of the low residual level of chlorine. Typical small ozone purifiers use about as much electricity as a 100-watt light bulb and high-output models use about 200 watts.

Ozone is a natural gas that is extremely effective for killing viruses and bacteria in water. After the ozone does its purifying job, it breaks down into pure oxygen within minutes as it goes back into the air. The actual concentration of ozone gas in the pool or spa water is extremely low.

Ozone gas is a natural flocculator, so it produces crystal clear water. Once it destroys the viruses, bacteria, and other contaminants, it causes the minute particles to coagulate into larger clumps. Al-

though still tiny, these clumps can now be trapped by your filtration system.

These purification systems use one of two methods to produce the ozone. In one design, air flows around a strong ultraviolet (UV) light. The UV rays convert the oxygen into ozone. This is same way the sun forms the protective ozone layer

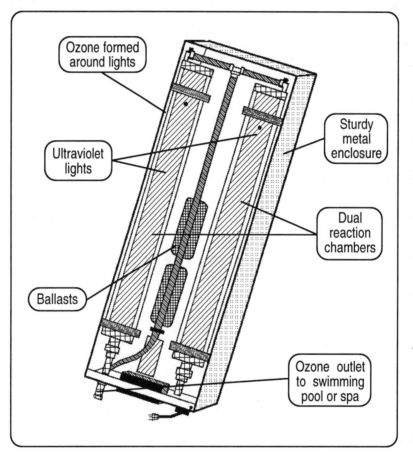

Ozone formed around lights

Ultraviolet lights

Ballasts

Sturdy metal enclosure

Dual reaction chambers

Ozone outlet to swimming pool or spa

around the earth. This is ideal for most pools and spas.

The UV lights look like fluorescent tubes and they are mounted inside a lightweight metal box. The lights are replaceable and should last for several swimming seasons. The ozone-rich air flows out a small tube into the water outlet from the filter.

For greater concentrations of ozone gas in large or heavily used

pools, a corona-discharge method is best and more energy-efficient. If you have ever noticed that distinctive "fresh" smell after a lightning storm or near a copier, you are smelling corona-discharge ozone. Your pool will also have a fresh clean, not a chemical, smell.

You should be able to easily install an ozone system yourself. It operates on standard house 110 voltage and draws in air to make the ozone (air is about 20% oxygen.) You just attach the ozone outlet tube to your pool. The venturi effect of the water flow naturally draws the ozone into it.

Q: I installed a skylight to cut my lighting costs, but it leaks. What is the best type of caulking to use to seal the leaky spots?

A: There is never one best type of caulking for every application. The proper selection depends on the exact place it is leaking, the materials to which it must adhere, and the amount of stress it must withstand. Skylights are particularly hard on caulking because of the tremendous temperature swings from sunny days to frigid nights.

One of the better types of caulking to try is a polyurethane base material. It tends to form a stronger bond to the materials than silicone, can be painted, and can be used underwater. It also has flexibility about equal to silicone.

Ozone gas is a strong oxidizing agent, like chlorine or bromine but more powerful. When it comes in contact with bacteria, virus, dirt, vegetable or animal waste, it literally reacts with it and destroys it. Since ozone is a natural flocculator, the fine debris coagulates into slightly larger particles. Although still very small, it is now big enough to be trapped by your pool or spa filter. Ozone purified pools have crystal clear water for this reason.

There are two methods of generating ozone gas for your pool. The least expensive method, which also produces the lowest ozone output, is the "ultraviolet" (UV) method. Air is circulated past a special fluorescent light tube which produces UV light. The other method is corona discharge. This produces ozone gas by passing an electrical spark through air or pure oxygen inside the unit. This produces higher concentrations of ozone gas at greater volume.

The manufacturers of ozone purification systems are listed below. After the model numbers, the type of ozone generation method is listed. **"UV"** stands for ultraviolet light and **"CD"** stands for corona discharge.

Manufacturers of Ozone Purification Systems

AQUAZONE PRODUCTS, 79 Bond St., Elk Grove Village, IL 60007 - (708) 439-4454

model - 100-V	type - UV	max. size - 20,000 gal
model - 200-VR	type - UV	max. size - 50,000 gal

CLEARWATER TECH, P.O. Box 15330, San Luis Obispo, CA 93406 - (800) 262-0203 (805) 549-9724

model - MZ-250	type - UV	max. size - 250 gal spa
model - UV-275	type - UV	max. size - 300 gal spa
model - S-1200	type - UV	max. size - 1,000 gal spa
model - PR-1300	type - UV	max. size - 1,000 gal spa
model - CS-1400	type - UV	max. size - 10,000 gal
model - UV-2800	type - UV	max. size - 20,000 gal
model - M-1500	type - CD	max. size - 50,000 gal
model - P-2000	type - CD	max. size - 100,000 gal

DEL INDUSTRIES, 3428 Bullock Ln., San Luis Obispo, CA 93401 - (800) 676-13357 (805) 541-1601

model - Z0-300	type - UV	max. size - 1,000 gal spa
model - Z0-151	type - UV	max. size - 1,000 gal spa
model - Z0-910*	type - UV	max. size - 25,000 gal
model - Z0-912*	type - UV	max. size - 50,000 gal
model - LK-2000	type - UV	max. size - 60,000 gal

* direct continuous input compressor available

GAS PURIFICATION SYSTEM, 700 W. Mississippi #C1, Denver, CO 80223 - (800) 722-9106 (303) 777-9106

model - 5V	type - UV	max. size - 600 gal spa
model - 7V	type - UV	max. size - 600 gal spa
model - 10V*	type - UV	max. size - 1,000 gal spa
model - 20V*	type - UV	max. size - 18,000 gal
model - 40V*	type - UV	max. size - 30,000 gal

* direct continuous input compressor available

HELIOTROPE GENERAL, 3733 Kenora Dr., Spring Valley, CA 91977 - (800) 552-8838 (619) 460-3930

model - SPA KING AUTO	type - UV	max. size - 1,200 gal spa
model - SPA KING MAXI	type - UV	max. size - 1,200 gal spa
model - BUBBLE GUN 2	type - UV	max. size - 350 gal spa
model - BUBBLE GUN	type - UV	max. size - 1,000 gal spa

LIFEGUARD PURIFICATION SYS., 4306 W. Osborne Ave., Tampa, FL 33614 - (813) 875-7777

model - 801	type - UV	max. size - 1,000 gal spa
model - 811	type - CD	max. size - 25,000 gal

OZOTECH INC., 2401 Oberlin Rd., Yreka, CA 96097 - (916) 842-4189

model - OZ1PCS	type - CD	max. size - 500 gal spa
model - OZ1BTU	type - CD	max. size - 25,000 gal

OXYGEN TECH., 8229 Melrose, Lenexa, KS 66214 - (913) 894-2828

model - 2000	type - CD	max. size - 20,000 gal
model - PWC111	type - CD	max. size - 25,000 gal
model - PWC6	type - CD	max. size - 50,000 gal

Manufacturers of Ionization Swimming Pool Purification Systems

CAREFREE CLEARWATER, 2307-A Browns Bridge Rd., #148, Gainesville, GA 30501 - (706) 778-9416
power - 120 volts

CARIBBEAN CLEAR, 101 Watersedge Shelter Cove, Hilton Head, SC 29928 - (803) 686-3424
power - 120 volts

CRYSTAL KING INC., P.O. Box 455, Middleville, MI 49333 - (800) 243-5464
power - 120 volts

ELECTRON PURE, 1300 Slaughter Rd., Madison, AL 35758 - (800) 525-7458 (205) 430-0841
power - 120 volts

ENVIRONMENTAL WATER PRODUCTS, 9316 Deering Ave., Chatsworth, CA 91311 - (818) 718-1795
power - 120 volts

FLOATRON, P.O. Box 51000, Phoenix, AZ 85076 - (602) 345-2222
power - solar

LIFEGUARD PURIFICATION SYS, 4806B N. Coolidge , Tampa, FL 33614 - (800) 678-7439 (813) 875-7777
power -120 volts

WITHERS MILLS CO., P.O. Box 347, Hannibal, MO 63401 - (800) 223-0858 (314) 221-4747
power - solar

OXY-TECH, 8229 Melrose Dr., Lenexa, KS 66214 - (913) 894-2828
power - 120 volts   note - this company also makes ozone purifiers for swimming pools

SUPERIOR AQUA ENTERPRISES, 7350 S. Tamiami Tr., Sarasota, FL 34231 - (813) 923-2304
power - 120 volts

LIQUITECH INC., 241 S. Frontage Rd. #40, Burr Ridge, IL 60521 - (800) 635-7873
power - 120 volts

VAK PAK, 9731 Beach Blvd., Jacksonville, FL 32246 - (800) 877-1824 (904) 642-2267
power - 120 volts

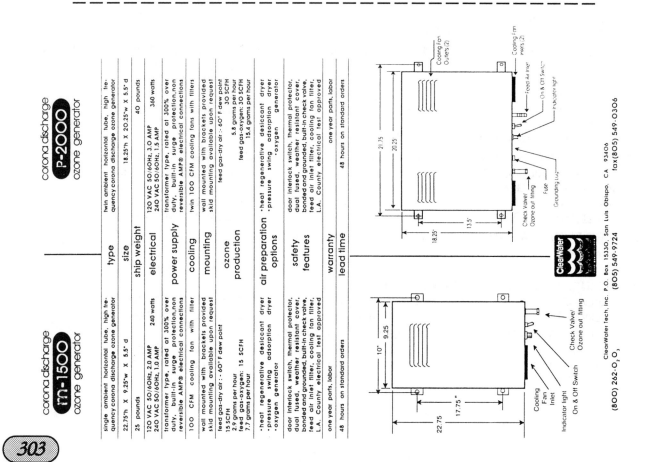

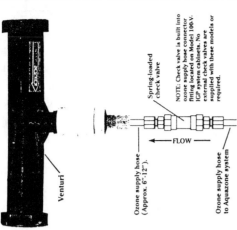

Ozone supply hose connections and spring-loaded check valve installation

Attach a short length of ozone supply hose to ozone supply hose connector fitting, located on venturi. Attach spring-loaded check valve to this hose, being sure to direct arrow on valve toward venturi and ozone flow. Connect remaining length of ozone supply hose to the suction side of check valve, and the other end of this hose to the connector fitting located on the Aquazone system. (See below.)

Spring-loaded check valve

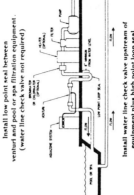

← FLOW

Ozone supply hose (Approx. 6"-12").

Ozone supply hose to Aquazone system

NOTE: Check valve is built into ozone supply hose connector fitting located on Model 100-V-IGP system cabinets. No external check valves are supplied with these models or required.

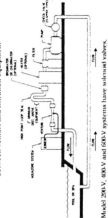

Important procedures for Model 100-V-IGP systems when venturi and pool equipment are above water level

To eliminate "drain down" of water pool's filtration equipment using 100-V-IGP systems, one of the following procedures must be followed when venturi and equipment are located above water level.

Install low point seal between venturi and pool or spa filtration equipment (water line check valve not required)

Install water line check valve upstream of equipment plus high point loop seal between venturi and filtration equipment

Model 200-V, 400-V and 600-V systems have solenoid valves, eliminating these procedures.

Venturi manifold installation

Venturi manifolds are installed in the return pipeline after all other equipment and pick-up point for an automatic pool cleaner, if used (e.g. Polaris). Direct arrow on the venturi to direction of water flow.

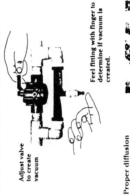

Venturi
Ozone Supply hose fitting
Adjustable by-pass valve
High-flow "C" Venturi Manifold

Cabinet mounting

Mount 100-V-IGP system cabinets in the vertical position on a wall, above water level if possible, or on stand which is provided. Place models 200-V, 400-V and 600-V systems on the equipment pad or near other filtration equipment. Place cabinets at least five (5) feet from the pool or spa for safety reasons, or the required distance as prescribed by local electrical codes.

Electrical (110 volts/60 Hz)

Hard wire 200-V, 400-V and 600-V systems to 110 volt systems, if used. If unit is to operate continuously, connect unit to an independent, GFI-protected power source. Model 100-V-IGP systems may be connected to a timer or GFI-protected electrical outlet, allowing the lamp to function by timer or continuously. (Ozone will be supplied only when the filter pump is operational, however.)

High-flow venturi start-up, valve adjustment

Once the venturi manifold has been installed and before the ozone supply hose connections are made, start-up water pump with gate valve completely open. Notice if venturi develops a vacuum. (You can feel it with your finger, hear it start to work and observe bubbles entering pool or spa through return fittings.) If no vacuum is observed, start to close gate valve slowly. Notice the point at which a vacuum is developed. When bubbles entering the pool are considered sufficient (small and highly diffused, not climbing up pool or spa wall), valve adjustment is complete and the ozone supply hose connections may be finalized. If ozone meter is used, flow rates of 15 to 30 SCFH are typical with high-flow venturis. (However, observing finely dispersed bubbles is adequate and use of flow meter is not essential.)

Adjust valve to create vacuum

Feel fitting with finger to determine if vacuum is created.

Proper diffusion essential!

Ozone must be finely dispersed when entering pool through return inlets (see photo). If no bubbles are observed, try removing eyeballs in return fittings. This will increase flow, reduce back pressures and possibly make the venturi operational

---

Vacuum pool systems

Vacuum pool systems are ideal for most swimming pool applications because they offer economy and provide excellent results by using highly effective venturies to properly diffuse ozone in pool water. High-flow "C" venturi manifolds come standard with all vacuum pool models and are effective in practically all pool installations using single speed pumps. However, it is the installer's responsibility to determine which venturi manifold is required for each vacuum pool system installation.

Although vacuum pool systems are ideal in most pool installations, these models are not recommended in the following circumstances.

- Installations with insufficient water flow.
- Installations with excessive back pressures.
  (Eyeballs in pool or spa returns may have to be removed.)
- Pools with in-floor cleaning systems. (Without a dedicated return to a standard pool inlet.)
- Pools and spas with two-speed pumps (without low-flow venturi).

Compressor models are recommended in the installations described above.

How water venturi manifolds work

High-flow venturi manifolds are designed to draw ozone from Aquazone systems to pool and spa water without using air compressors. By design, venturies restrict water passing through a small orifice. In turn, this restriction creates the necessary vacuum to supply ozone to the water. Because venturies are restrictive, high-flow venturi manifolds have a built-in by-pass to accommodate much of the water flow and minimize back pressures. A gate valve is also provided, which is an integral part of the venturi manifold. This valve is adjusted to direct some of the water to flow through the venturi (to create a vacuum) and some of the water to pass through the by-pass (to minimize back pressures).

High-flow "C" venturi manifolds standard with vacuum pool models

High-flow "C" venturi manifolds come standard with all vacuum pool models. (Packaged in separate cartons with 200-V, 400-V and 600-V systems.) These manifolds are appropriate in all typical swimming pool and spa installations when single speed pumps are employed (¾ H.P. or greater).

Venturi selection

Since the vacuum required to draw ozone to the water depends on flow and back pressure (from the point where the venturi manifold is to be located), it is necessary to estimate or calculate both factors before you proceed with the installation. In typical installations, you may estimate these factors and refer to the venturi operating charts shown in the following section and follow the procedures described below. If flow and back pressure can be calculated, follow the procedures described below.

Flow meter

To calculate flow, clean filters and install a flow meter in the return pipeline at the exact point where the venturi and by-pass are to be located. Restart water pump and calculate water flow. (Flow meter may be removed prior to venturi installation.)

Pressure gauge

To calculate back pressure, install a pressure gauge in the return pipeline where the flow meter was located and observe back pressure.

NOTE: If back pressure is excessive, remove eyeballs in pool returns to increase flow and reduce back pressure

Refer to the venturi operating charts and plot the "flow" and "back pressure" calculated or estimated on each chart. Select the venturi that will allow the maximum amount of water to flow through it, while working within the "operating range" shown on the chart

Flow meter

Pressure gauge

Venturi operating charts

Use the following charts to determine if "high-flow" or "medium-flow" venturi manifolds are appropriate using vacuum pool system and single speed pumps. Select the **Largest** venturi that will function within the venturi operating area.

High-flow "C" venturi

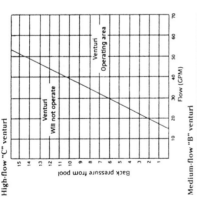

Back pressure from pool / Flow (GPM)
Venturi Will not operate — Venturi Operating area

Medium-flow "B" venturi

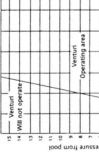

Back pressure from pool / Flow (GPM)
Venturi Will not operate — Venturi Operating area

Water venturi installations with two-speed water j umps using low-flow venturi manifolds

Low-flow water venturies are necessary for pools and swim spas using two speed pumps. Using this installation method, low-flow venturi manifolds are installed in the return pipeline after the pump, filter and heater. On low speed, the by-pass valve in the manifold is closed. This directs all of the water to pass through the venturi, supplying ozone to the water. On high speed, the by-pass valve opens to accommodate the high flow rate of the pump and provide for continued ozonation.

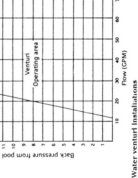

Spring-loaded by-pass valve
Ozone supply hose fitting
Venturi
Low-flow "A" Venturi Manifold

Q: I have heard that one of the new smart home total automation systems can cut my utility bills by 25%. What security and convenience features are included in these energy-efficient smart home systems?

A: New smart home automation systems offer you total control over lighting, security, heating, cooling, TV, stereo, cooking, appliances, etc. in your home. With precise room-by-room control over your furnace, air-conditioner and lighting, you can cut your utility bills by more than 30%.

In addition to saving money, an automated system (sometimes referred to as "smart house" technology) provides the ultimate convenience and security in your home. Some are so smart, that if you are vacuuming, they automatically switch off the vacuum cleaner when the telephone or doorbell rings.

When your alarm wakes you in the morning (with a "Good morning" message), the light and heater automatically come on in the bathroom. The coffee starts perking ten minutes later and your kitchen lights come on.

Twenty minutes later, your alarm system disarms and your outdoor lights come on so you can find the newspaper. Your morning TV news program is on when you get to the kitchen and the CD plays soft music. In the afternoon, if you leave

work early, just call your house and tell it to turn the air-conditioner on earlier and have another pot of coffee ready.

You have many options as to the sophistication and types of controls available. Most systems have several control methods - hand held TV-type remote, touch screens, and remote from a touch-tone telephone

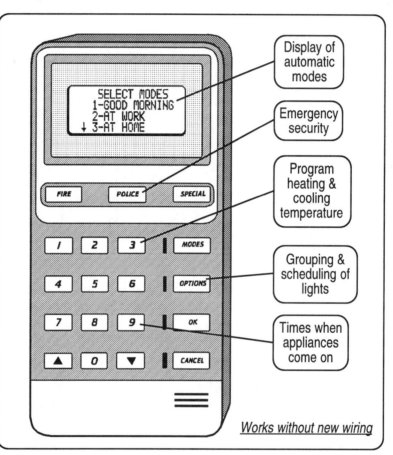

Display of automatic modes

Emergency security

Program heating & cooling temperature

Grouping & scheduling of lights

Times when appliances come on

Works without new wiring

when you're away. You can show the status of your house on your standard TV screen and control your house from your easy chair.

You can program one system to recognize the voices of two different family members. By saying "Party", the automated system switches on the CD player, adjusts the indoor lights for entertaining, sets the thermostat up, and switches on the outdoor lights for guests.

Most of the systems are designed so that the control signals flow over your existing electric wiring in your home. Each appliance or light simply plugs into a small control module that plugs into the standard wall outlet.

Smart systems provide complete energy-efficient home security. Instead of leaving several lights on when you leave, a smart system automatically switches different lights on and off after dark to simulate a person at home. The lights are on less and you save electricity. Also, you can telephone in and check the status to make sure you haven't left the iron on.

Q: Will it save much gas to shut off the pilot light in the oven of my range? I don't bake very often.

A: Although it saves gas, it is not a good idea to turn off the pilot light in your oven. If the valve is a little leaky and doesn't totally shut off, gas can collect in the oven. Then when you go to light it next time, you may end up roasting more than just the beef.

If your oven always feels warm, the pilot light may be burning too high. You may want to set it down a little, but not too low so it blows out when you open the oven door. After you reset it, open and close the oven door several times to make sure it stays lit.

A total home automation system not only provides great convenience, but it also can cut your utility bills. They give you precise control over your heating and air-conditioning. Also, with the precise and automatic control of your lighting, lights are never accidentally left on, so electricity is also saved.

Many also allow you to zone heat and cool your house (different rooms at different temperatures at different times of the day.) This is a great energy saver and comfort improver. You can set your bedroom temperature to come up when your alarm goes off. When you are done showering and dressing, the bedroom temperature drops again as your kitchen temperature goes up for breakfast. If you are gone during the day, the entire house is set cooler. In the evening, the dining room is warm for dinner and the family room warms up later when you watch TV. It works the same with your air-conditioning in the summer.

The prices for these home automation systems range from $1,500 to more than $10,000. The system that is best for you depends on your specific house and your family's needs. With this large an investment, you should contact each of the manufacturers that are listed to receive its comprehensive information packet. Once you select a general type of system, the manufacturer will customize the features and options for you and determine the exact price at that time.

Most of the retrofit systems for existing houses use the house 110-volt wiring for the communications between the control unit and the modules. The most common system uses what is called X-10 communications. This probably will become the industry standard. You can mix and match various X-10 accessories because they speak the same language.

The appliance and lighting modules plug into a standard electrical wall outlet where the appliance is now plugged. You just plug the appliance into the module. Each module receives its own set of on/off, dim, etc. signals from the automation control brain center.

All of the systems control lighting, HVAC (heating and air-conditioning), security (burglar alarms), and appliances to various degrees. The most expensive systems provide control over more items and more modes (programmed combinations) which you can select. Several of the systems use special fiber optic or coaxial cable for the best communications, but these can only be installed in new construction.

The touch screen interface (control method) is the most sophisticated. It is basically a computer TV screen mounted in the wall. The TV screen is sensitive to your touch. By touching the icons on it, you can control the system. On the most expensive systems, the entire floor plan of your house is programmed into the system. You can call up each room separately to control the lights, temperatures, or security devices. Figure 1 on this page shows a sample touch screen display of the temperature settings for a kitchen.

A standard keypad control is similar to most burglar alarm controls. Many have LCD readouts to indicate the current setting and changes. These are hardwired to your house's electrical wiring and usually mount on a wall. Most come with two keypads, but you can purchase additional ones. For a better display of the control options and your present settings, some of the systems status can be displayed on your standard television.

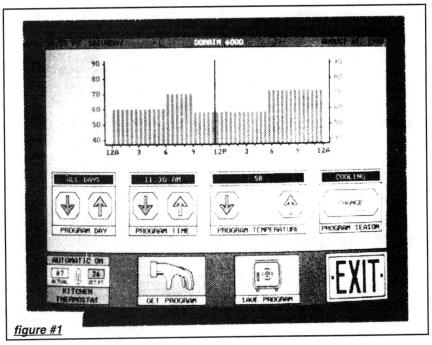

figure #1

Features and Details of Each Manufacturer's System

CSI/CARRIER, 2645 Snyder Court, Walnut Creek, CA 94598 - (510) 932-1346

model - "Maestro"

interface - Hand-held remote keypad and TV set, remote from touch-tone phone

features - Use the TV screen to monitor the status of systems, appliances, lights, and security. Controls HVAC, lighting, appliances. Use Carrier Corp. (furnaces & air conditioners) multi-zone residential control system. Capable of receiving messages and recording activities while no one is at home. These messages and reports can be played back later.

GROUP THREE TECHNOLOGIES INC., 2125-B Madera Road, Simi Valley, CA 93065 - (805) 582-4410

model - "Samantha" and "Samantha Gold"

interface - Wall-mounted keypad, remote from touch-tone phone

features - One of the less-sophisticated systems - limited control over appliances, lighting, security, does not handle HVAC zoning. Has excellent answering machine and intercom features. Works through telephone lines and house AC wiring.

HOME AUTOMATION INC., 2313 Metairie Road, Metairie, LA 70001 - (504) 833-7256

model - "1503"

interface - Wall-mounted keypad, remote from touch-tone phone

features - Controls lighting, HVAC, security, and appliances. Can handle HVAC zoning and has several built-in security sensors. System comes preprogrammed for three modes - Away, Asleep, and Home. You can reprogram the modes at your keypad. The motion sensor part of the security system can switch on lights and heat or cooling automatically when someone enters a room. When heat or smoke from a fire is detected, the furnace blower shuts off and the lights come on.

HONEYWELL INC., 1985 Douglas Drive North, Golden Valley, MN 55422 - (800) 345-6770 (612) 542-3339

model - "TotalHome"

interface - Wall-mounted keypad, remote from touch-tone phone

features - Controls lighting, HVAC, security, and appliances. Can be used for new construction or retrofit for existing homes. Honeywell technicians will program the system (up to 16 modes) at installation. They will make any future changes you request over the telephone. Sophisticated lighting controls for security and safety. Connected to Chronotherm computerized thermostat, zoning system, electronic air cleaner, and heat recovery fresh air ventilator.

INTELLIGENT SYSTEMS INC., 175 New Britain Ave., Plainville, CT 06062-2011 - (203) 793-9951

model - "Domain 6000"

interface - Wall-mounted touch screen, remote from touch-tone phone or computer modem.

features - The floor plan of your house is shown on the touch screen so you can control each room. Each system is completely customized for a specific house. Sophisticated HVAC controls from the programming mode or from motion sensors when a person enters a room. For new home installation, uses fiber optic lines for very fast reaction times and accuracy. The security system utilizes cameras and records the location and time that an intruder entered your house.

MASTERVOICE INC., 10523 Humbolt St., Los Alamitos, CA 90720 - (310) 594-6581

model - "E.C.U."

model - "Butler in a Box"

model - "Series II"

interface - Voice actuated, keypad, remote from touch-tone phone

features - Various models are "taught" to recognize from one to four different voices to accept verbal commands up to 20 feet from speaker. Controls HVAC, lighting, appliances, and security systems. Can program a built-in telephone to dial a specific number based on a verbal command. Uses existing household wiring to remotely control the devices and controls.

SMART HOUSE, 400 Pince Georges Rd., Upper Marlboro, MD 20772 - (301) 249-6000

model - "Smart House"

interface - keypad with LCD readout, remote from touch-tone phone

features - Uses its own coaxial cable system throughout house, so it's only for new construction. For security, it can use cameras and other standard security monitors. Can program wall light switches to preset lights and combinations of lights. Use gangs of switches to provide complete on-the-wall control in each room. Can use several types of zone dampers for room-by-room control of heating and cooling. Many modes for control of lights, appliances and security.

UNITY SYSTEMS INC., 2606 Spring St., Redwood City, CA 94063 - (415) 369-3233

model - "Home Manager"

interface - video touch screen, remote for touch-tone phone or personal computer.

features - House floor plan is shown on color touch screen. This allows you to control HVAC (zoning), appliances, lighting, security room by room. Can control both temperature and humidity levels and alarm sounds if preset levels are exceeded. Complete security system will sound alarm, switch on light, and telephone security station for help.

SERIES II

Manufacturer: Mastervoice, Inc.

Manufacturer's Suggested Retail Price: $3995.00

Manual Length: 80 Pages
Other aids: Audio. Video.

Description:

The Mastervoice Series II is a 4-user voice-activated home automation system with speech output that allows the user to operate (hands-free) all appliances, lights and telephones through 4-modes of operation: time, touch, voice, and situation. The system uses the existing household wiring to remotely active devices by using carrier current modules. The system recognizes any language or dialect, and operates (with the noise cancellation feature) in a room full of household noise from up to 20 feet away. It's both speaker dependent and independent. Once trained, the system recognizes specific words. The user trains certain categories of words in sections such as Commands, Devices, Phone, and Alarm. The system also has a built-in telephone that is totally hands-free that allows the user to remotely dial, answer, and speak on the phone. The system has 99 "smart" timers which allows any chosen appliance to be turned on or off at specific times during a day. Other timer features included: If...then logic, sunrise and sunset, X-10 receive, special holiday schedule, and wake-up. To allow for more flexibility, "macros" will allow several pre-programmed devices to complete several functions at one time. Macros can work by voice, time or through Remote Telephone Access. Remote Telephone Access allows (through a touch-tone phone) access to control devices from inside or outside the home. The system also has a built-in alarm system that can detect intruders by requesting that they identify themselves by giving the correct password. The system can operate ASCII codes, Infrared devices, X-10 Receive, and the telephone. The system also has voice output with pre-stored responses that can be changed with the use of an accessory called voice cartridge.

Accessories available: Infrared Control Interface (I.C.I.), RAM Pack 7000, Voice Mouse, Set-up Program, Voice Cartridge, Electronic Moisture Sensor and SPC-8 Sprinkler Controller.

Other models are: Butler-in-a-Box, Environmental Control Unit (E.C.U.), and Intelligent Home Controller (I.H.C.).

ENJOY THE ADVANTAGES OF TOTAL HOME TODAY

Integrated Home System. TotalHome is a breakthrough in home comfort and convenience that unites your temperature control, security, lights and appliances into an easy to use system.

Lifestyle Modes. Up to 16 lifestyle "modes" can be customized to meet your needs, and each "mode" includes specific instructions to tell your security, thermostat, lights and appliances exactly what to do.

Panel and Phone Access. Menus guide you when using the touch panel. It's as easy to use as an automated teller machine! Or use any touchtone phone to make changes. Interactive voice response guides you.

Programming. No need to learn. A Honeywell representative will customize your system to meet your needs, and we can make any changes you may want later, right over the phone.

Easy Installation. Designed for easy installation in new construction or existing homes.

Unbeatable Service. Honeywell will be there for you before, during, and after the sale with service and support you can count on—nationwide!

Security

Burglary Detection. Small discreetly located sensors protect doors and windows, and detect movement inside for added protection when asleep or away.

Fire. Smoke and heat sensors detect fire and high temperature early, when seconds count, and help is on the way, even if you're not home.

Medical. Help is called with a touch of a button, or small device you wear or carry.

Special Emergencies. 24 hour protection from the unexpected, such as flooding, frozen pipes, or hazardous gases.

Duress Signal. Enter a special code and a silent signal tells our Customer Service Center that you are being forced to disarm your system.

Temporary Codes. Grant entry to others, such as babysitters, without divulging your master code. Can be restricted in use for extra security.

Security Patterns. Modes may include points that are armed, disarmed, or on watch—all at the same time, for the ultimate in flexibility.

24 Hour U.L. Approved Monitoring. Ensures fast and reliable response.

Temperature Control

Programmable Heating and Cooling. With TotalHome's Chronotherm III thermostat, you schedule temperatures to maximize comfort and savings—up to 30%. Accurate control to within one degree of setting, with no temperature swings.

Adaptive Intelligent Recovery. "Learns" when the furnace/air conditioning should come on in *your climate*, to ensure a cost efficient and accurate return to normal temperature after an energy saving period.

Lighting/Appliances

Grouping and Scheduling. Sets or individual lights can turn on or off automatically, or at the touch of a button.

Security Lighting. Lights on during an alarm, light pathways in emergencies, outdoor lights on at night, or create a "lived in" look when you're away.

Appliance Control. Selected appliances come on when you want, while others, such as irons, shut off for added convenience and safety. Operates systems, such as pool pumps, and lawn sprinklers.

No Wiring Required. Our system works with existing wiring.

The TotalHome Panel

4-Line Visual Display. Tells you the status of your system, in words.

Mode Button. Displays a menu of modes that you have selected for your system. Use the up and down buttons to scroll through options.

Options Button. Displays menus that allow you to make individual changes to your Security, Thermostat, or Lighting and Appliances.

Fire, Police, & Special Buttons. One touch help, even when your system is disarmed.

O.K./Cancel. Confirm or cancel selection.

Alarm Sounder. Deters intruders and alerts or awakens you in an emergency.

Conveniently Located Instructions. Just flip the door down for quick and easy reference.

Partial Arming. Selectively bypass points from the panel, while arming the rest of your system.

Point Identification. Each protected point can be identified at the TotalHome panel. Point ID also allows our Customer Service Center to identify the exact door or window in an emergency.

Separate Interior Zones. Allow freedom of movement in one area, while arming others.

Entry/Exit Delays. Select short/long delays for different entrances, or no delay for instant alarm and added protection when you're at home.

On Watch. Tone tells you someone is entering or leaving when system is disarmed.

Back-up Power. In the event of power loss, it's automatic.

Financing options for qualified buyers.

SELECT MODES
1-GOOD MORNING
2-AT WORK
3-AT HOME

FIRE POLICE SPECIAL

1 2 3 MODES
4 5 6 OPTIONS
7 8 9 OK
◄ 0 ► CANCEL

Honeywell

Q: I'm remodeling my bathroom. What features should I look for in an efficient whirlpool bathtub. Are the new soft "cushioned" whirlpool bathtubs much more efficient than standard whirlpools?

A: Nearly one-third of all bathroom remodeling jobs includes a whirlpool bathtub. Several new features are multi-level waterfall inlets, built-in pillows, rotating massage jets, and underwater lighting.

The primary operating cost is heating the water. The small pump consumes only several cents worth of electricity per use.

There is a new soft whirlpool bathtub that looks like an ordinary hard tub. It is made of thick poly-foam molded over a fiberglass shell and frame. It is very comfortable to lay in and safe for the elderly and children.

This poly-foam acts as both a cushion and an insulator, so it keeps the water warmer longer without extra heaters. The foam is covered by a tough, puncture-resistant vinyl skin. If it gets cut, you can repair it for $10.

When selecting a whirlpool bathtub, there are several important features to consider - the tub material, the number, power, and control of water jets, and shape and size (gallons capacity) of the tub.

The basic hard tub materials are steel, gel-coat fiberglass, acrylic, and cast iron. Enameled steel tubs are usually the least expensive and enameled cast iron tubs are the most expensive. Being made of metal, the water tends to cool down faster.

Acrylic plastic, often reinforced with fiberglass, is most common for residential use. These are

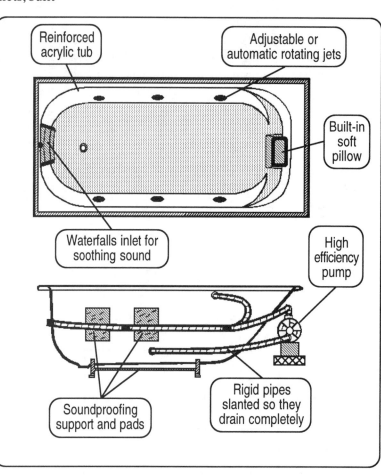

Reinforced acrylic tub

Adjustable or automatic rotating jets

Built-in soft pillow

Waterfalls inlet for soothing sound

High efficiency pump

Soundproofing support and pads

Rigid pipes slanted so they drain completely

good insulators, light-weight, and available in many shapes. The color goes completely through the acrylic material, so scratches and nicks are less apparent. Fiberglass tubs are easy to repair.

The water jets in the whirlpool tubs inject a mixture of water and air. Generally a larger tub has more jets, but more jets are not necessarily better. Fewer high-capacity jets

can provide a very soothing effect. The size of the pump (horsepower) and the jet flow rate are good indicators.

Check the amount of rotation of the water jets. You may want to change the direction and whirlpool action. By changing the water/air mixture ratio, you can vary the intensity of the whirlpool action too.

Some models offer an automatic rotating jet to massage a large area of your back.

You can install optional electric heaters to maintain the warm water temperature. These range from 1.5 to 6 kilowatts (costs about 2 to 8 cents of electricity per use). These are sized only to maintain the warm temperature, not heat up cold water. Your regular water heater does this.

Q: When I build an addition on to my home, I plan to use rigid foam insulated sheathing on the outside of the wall studs. Will it harm the efficiency to use more nails and fasteners for a stronger wall?

A: Adding more nails and metal fasteners than recommended by the manufacturer does not produce a better wall. In fact, it decreases the effectiveness of the rigid foam insulation. Tests show that using just the recommended number of nails and fasteners (on eight-inch centers) reduces the insulation value by 20%.

There are literally hundreds of whirlpool bathtubs to choose from. I have listed the manufacturers of the best and most efficient ones on the following pages along with general information about their models. This information will help you to select several manufacturers to contact for more detailed information and specifications on their whirlpools.

The chart below shows the cost to operate a whirlpool for one hour. The water heating costs are based on using an electric water heater. If you have a gas water heater, you can generally reduce the water heating cost figure by half. If you plan to use your whirlpool for longer than one hour, you will probably need an auxiliary electric heater in line with the pump. These can use from one to six kilowatts of electricity, depending on the size of your whirlpool.

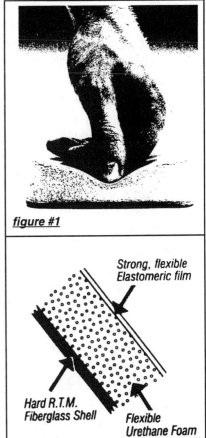

figure #1

The type of **_tub material_** is important for durability and energy efficiency. Acrylic is most popular and low maintenance. Cast iron is most expensive, but it is heavy and requires hotter water to start with. Enameled steel is usually the least expensive. The insulated flexible whirlpool is made by <u>International Cushioned Products</u>. Figure #1 shows how the wall flexes and how it is constructed. This type of tub is comfortable and it provides insulation to keep the water warmer longer.

Strong, flexible Elastomeric film

Hard R.T.M. Fiberglass Shell

Flexible Urethane Foam with "memory"

figure #2

Pump power is a good indicator of the forcefulness of the whirlpool action. You can generally adjust this with speed and air flow dials. The **_number of jets_** also affects the whirlpool action. Although larger tubs often have more jets, check the location of the jets too. You may want one with a jet positioned for a specific leg or back ailment.

Water Heating and Electricity (pump) Cost to Operate a Whirlpool - per hour		
electric rate - $/kwh	water heating - $	pump cost - $
0.04	0.35	0.029
0.05	0.43	0.037
0.06	0.52	0.048
0.07	0.61	0.054
0.08	0.69	0.060
0.09	0.78	0.067
0.10	0.86	0.075
0.11	0.95	0.082
0.12	1.04	0.089

I have tried to select a name of the **_Shape_** to describe the tub. Lay in a tub before you buy it. A shape may look attractive, but it may not fit your particular body. Keep in mind that the water provides buoyancy, so it feels somewhat different in actual use. **_Special features_**, like a built-in pillow and adjustable/rotating jets, are a plus. A hand-held jet allows you to concentrate the massaging on one particular spot.

Manufacturers of Whirlpools

ALMOST HEAVEN, Rt. 250, Renick, WV 24966 - (304) 497-3163
    <u>tub material</u> - acrylic or ceramic   <u>pump power</u> - 1 hp   <u>sizes</u> - 60 to 135 gal.
    <u>shapes</u> - rectangle, oval, round   <u># of jets</u> - 6 to 10
        <u>special features</u> - low water cutoff and an air switch inside the tub for complete user control.

AMERICAN STANDARD, 1 Centennial Plaza, Piscataway, NJ 08855 - (800) 821-7700 (908) 980-3000
    <u>tub material</u> - acrylic   <u>pump power</u> - 1/2 hp, 3/4 hp, 1 hp   <u>sizes</u> - 45 - 90 gal.
    <u>shapes</u> - rectangle, oval, hourglass, corner   <u># of jets</u> - 6 to 10
        <u>special features</u> - non-slip bottom and a complete freestanding tub.

AMERICAN WHIRLPOOL, 3050 N. 29th Ct, Hollywood, FL 33020 - (800) 327-1394 (305) 921-4400
    <u>tub material</u> - acrylic   <u>pump power</u> - 1 hp   <u>sizes</u> - 37 to 126 gal.
    <u>shapes</u> - rectangle, oval, round, hourglass, corner   <u># of jets</u> - 5 to 6
        <u>special features</u> - a dual opening hydromassage jet with a directional flow of 360 degrees.

AMERICH, 13222 Saticoy St. N. Hollywood, CA 91605 - (800) 453-1463 (818) 982-1711
    tub material - acrylic, polyester reinforced fiberglass   pump power - 1 hp   sizes - 46 to 90 gal.
    shapes - rectangle, oval, round, corner   # of jets - 6 to 10
    special features - some models available with pillows.

AQUA GLASS CORP, PO Box 412, Adamsville, TN 38310 - (800) 238-3940 (901) 632-0911
    tub material - acrylic   pump power - 3/4 hp   sizes - 45 to 100 gal.
    shapes - rectangle, oval, hourglass   # of jets - 4 to 8
    special features - a digital electronic control panel displays time and sets running time.

AQUATIC IND., PO Box 889, Leander, TX 78646 - (512) 259-2255
    tub material - acrylic   pump power - 1 hp   sizes - 37 to 125 gal.
    shapes - rectangle, oval, round, hourglass, corner   # of jets - 4 to 8
    special features - hand-held jet is available.

ARTESIAN, 201 E. 5th St., Mansfield, OH 44902 - (800) 877-6678 (419) 522-4211
    tub material - acrylic and fiberglass   pump power - 3/4 hp   sizes - 65 to 75 gal.
    shapes - rectangle, oval, hourglass   # of jets - 4 to 8
    special features - color-matched fully directional jets.

BAJA, 4065 N. Romero Rd., Tucson, AZ 85705 - (800) 845-2252 (602) 887-1154
    tub material - acrylic   pump power - 1 hp   sizes - 60 gal.
    shapes - heart   # of jets - 44 air jets
    special features - overflow and bottom drain furnished.

BRIGGS, 4350 W. Cypress St., Tampa, FL 33607 - (813) 878-0178
    tub material - porcelain enameled steel   pump power - 3/4 hp   sizes - 65 to 75 gal.
    shapes - rectangle, oval   # of jets - 4 to 6
    special features - slip resistant bottom.

CAMEO MARBLE, 540 Central Court, New Albany, IN 47150 - (812) 944-5055
    tub material - marble   pump power - 1/2 hp, 1 hp, 1-1/2 hp   sizes - 55 to 105 gal.
    shapes - rectangle, oval, round, corner   # of jets - 4 to 8
    special features - slip resistant bottom.

CLARKE PRODUCTS, 1202 Ave. J E., Grand Prairie, TX 75050 - (800) 426-8964 (214) 660-1992
    tub material - acrylic   pump power - 3/4 hp   sizes - 35 to 100 gal.
    shapes - rectangle, oval, corner   # of jets - 4 to 8
    special features - easy-touch on/off control and safety mood light.

ELJER, PO Box 879001, Dallas, TX 75287 - (214) 407-2600
    tub material - acrylic, cast iron , fiberglass   pump power - 3/4 hp   sizes - 38 to 83 gal.
    shapes - rectangle, oval, hourglass   # of jets - 4 to 8
    special features - two air controls so each side can be adjusted independently.

EPIC, PO Box 40980, Indianapolis, IN 46240 - (317) 848-1812
    tub material - acrylic   pump power - 3/4 hp, 1-1/2 hp   sizes - 60 gal.
    shapes - oval   # of jets - 6

HYDRO SYSTEMS, 50 Moreland Rd, Simi Valley, CA 93065 - (805) 584-9990
    tub material - acrylic, gel coat   pump power -1 hp, 1-1/2 hp   sizes - 40 to 140 gal.
    shapes - rectangle, oval, round, hourglass, corner   # of jets - 6 to 8
    special features - removable pillow head rest.

INTN'L CUSHIONED PROD., 202-8360 Bridgeport Rd., Richmond BC Can V6X 3C7 - (800) 882-7638
    tub material - urethane foam covered fiberglass and elastomeric film   pump power - 3/4 hp
    sizes - 39 to 85 gal.   shapes - rectangle, hourglass   # of jets - 4
    special features - the tub conforms to the contours of the body for comfort.

JACUZZI, PO Drawer J, Walnut Creek, CA 94596 - (800) 678-6889
    <u>tub material</u> - acrylic   <u>pump power</u> - 3/4 hp, 1-1/2 hp   <u>sizes</u> - 50 to 125 gal.
    <u>shapes</u> - rectangle, oval, round, hourglass, corner   <u># of jets</u> - 6 to 10
    <u>special features</u> - head and arm rests, mood lighting, fully adjustable jets.

KALLISTA, 1355 Market St., San Francisco, CA 94103 - (510) 895-6400
    <u>tub material</u> - acrylic   <u>pump power</u> - 3/4 hp   <u>sizes</u> - 55 to 100 gal.
    <u>shapes</u> - rectangle, oval,round, corner   <u># of jets</u> - 4 to 7
    <u>special features</u> - each tub is handmade and available in virtually any color.

KOHLER, Kohler, WI 53044 - (414) 457-4441
    <u>tub material</u> - acrylic, cast iron   <u>pump power</u> - 3/4 hp, 1 hp   <u>sizes</u> - 28 to 121 gal.
    <u>shapes</u> - rectangle, oval, hourglass, corner   <u># of jets</u> - 5 to 8
    <u>special features</u> - flexjet allows control and direction of the water flow.

LASCO BATHWARE, 3255 E. Miraloma Ave., Anaheim, CA 92806 - (800) 877-0464
    <u>tub material</u> - acrylic, gelcoat   <u>pump power</u> - 3/4 hp, 1 hp, 1-1/2 hp   <u>sizes</u> - 40 to 100 gal.
    <u>shapes</u> - rectangle, oval, hourglass, corner   <u># of jets</u> - 4 to 8
    <u>special features</u> - pulsating and variable lumbar jets, interchangeable mood lights.

LYONS, PO Box 88, Dowagiac, MI 49047 - (800) 458-9036 (616) 782-3404
    <u>tub material</u> - acrylic   <u>pump power</u> - 3/4 hp   <u>sizes</u> - 60 to75 gal.
    <u>shapes</u> - rectangle, oval, corner   <u># of jets</u> - 4 to 6
    <u>special features</u> - vinyl pillow with suction cups available.

PEARL BATHS, 9224 73rd Ave. N., Minneapolis, MN 55428 - (800) 328-2531 (612) 424-3335
    <u>tub material</u> - acrylic   <u>pump power</u> - 3/4 hp, 1 hp   <u>sizes</u> - 30 to 65 gal.
    <u>shapes</u> - rectangle, oval, corner   <u># of jets</u> - 2 to 3
    <u>special features</u> - the jets are located diagonally opposite to create a true whirlpool effect.

REGENCY NOVIAMERICAN, PO Box 44649, Atlanta, GA 30336 - (800) 726-6685 (404) 344-5600
    <u>tub material</u> - acrylic   <u>pump power</u> - 3/4 hp   <u>sizes</u> - 48 to 85 gal.
    <u>shapes</u> - rectangle, oval, corner   <u># of jets</u> - 4 to 6
    <u>special features</u> - jets with directional adjustment and flow.

ROYAL BATHS, PO Box 671666, Houston, TX 77267 - (800) 826-0074 (713) 442-3400
    <u>tub material</u> - acrylic, acrylic/marble   <u>pump power</u> - 3/4 hp   <u>sizes</u> - 45 to 90 gal.
    <u>shapes</u> - rectangle, oval, round, corner   <u># of jets</u> - 6
    <u>special features</u> - wall-mounted timer for safe operation.

SWIRL WAY, 1505 Industrial Dr., Henderson, TX 75653 - (800) 999-1459 (903) 657-1436
    <u>tub material</u> - acrylic   <u>pump power</u> - 1 hp   <u>sizes</u> - 45 to 100 gal.
    <u>shapes</u> - rectangle, oval, hourglass, corner   <u># of jets</u> - 6 to 8
    <u>special features</u> - a unique rotating jet produces a continuous circular massage.

UNIVERSAL RUNDLE, 217 N. Mill St., New Castle, PA 16101 - (800) 955-0316 (412) 658-6631
    <u>tub material</u> - acrylic and fiberglass   <u>pump power</u> - 3/4 hp   <u>sizes</u> - 25 to 100 gal.
    <u>shapes</u> - rectangle, oval, hourglass, corner   <u># of jets</u> - 4 to 7
    <u>special features</u> - soft curved back for comfort.

WATERTECH, 2507 Plymouth Rd., Johnson City, TN 37601 - (800) 289-8827 (615) 926-1470
    <u>tub material</u> - acrylic   <u>pump power</u> - 3/4 hp   <u>sizes</u> - 40 to 80 gal.
    <u>shapes</u> - rectangle, oval, round, corner   <u># of jets</u> - 4 to 6
    <u>special features</u> - each jet offers an on/off control.

Q: My yard looks terrible, but I don't have time to water the shrubs and flowers properly. Using the sprinkler wastes water and floods them. What is the most efficient (both water and my time) way to water my plants?

A: The most efficient and effective method to water your plants is micro-irrigation called "drip watering". It uses half the water of sprinklers, provides each plant with the proper amount directly above its roots, and is totally automatic requiring none of your time. The small pipes are buried several inches under the ground so they cannot be seen.

You can purchase complete drip watering kits or assemble your own system from many simple components. Some of the tiny drippers cost less than 50 cents each, and multiple drippers and mini-sprayers cost just a couple of dollars. The number of each you need depends on your individual landscaping designs and needs.

The drippers or individual mini-sprayers are color-coded, so you can quickly determine the water flow of each one. Different varieties and sizes of plants need different amounts of water for healthy foliage and flowers.

A typical watering systems may use a 12-outlet dripper for a larger shrub. Several mini-sprayers are effective for a small area with ground cover. A mini-sprayer for each large potted plant on a deck is effective. With the loose potting soil, standard drip watering just runs through too fast.

There are small battery-operated automatic watering controllers and timers available that mount outdoors. You program them very similar to a setback furnace wall thermostat. You can program watering schedules for several times a day and manually override them during extremely dry or wet periods.

If you water just a few shrubs or plants, there is a new flexible circular C-shaped dripper/sprinkler. It has holes around the top for mini-sprinkling and holes in the bottom for drip watering. It has a built-in adjustable water regulator where the garden hose screws in.

Because it is made of flexible plastic, you can spread the open ends apart and wrap it around the base of the plant. The two ends spring together again providing complete circular watering around the entire plant base. I use one around a small ornamental evergreen and my roses.

Porous soaker hoses provide slow watering of your plants. These are most effective in densely-planted flower or vegetable gardens. Sprinkler hoses, with larger holes on top, moisten a wider strip, but, because they are flat, they may be difficult to snake through a garden.

Q: My central air conditioner did not seem to be cooling the house well, so I replaced the old filter. I noticed ice on the cooling coils inside. Is this normal?

A: Air conditioner coils can get cold enough to freeze the moisture that they condense from the air inside your home. This accounts for the fact that it was not cooling your house adequately.

Your problem was most likely that old dirty filter that you replaced. A dirty filter reduces the air flow through the coils. The coils can not absorb enough heat from the slow moving air, so they get very cold and freeze. This further restricts the air and makes the problem worse.

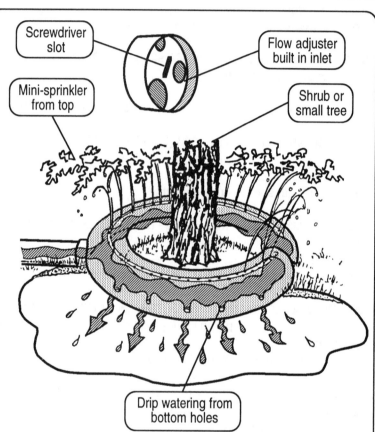

Screwdriver slot

Flow adjuster built in inlet

Mini-sprinkler from top

Shrub or small tree

Drip watering from bottom holes

Discuss your various plants with a landscaper to determine the best watering amount for each. You can adjust the amount of water by the drip emitter or sprayer you select and how many serve each plant. Then just layout your watering plan on paper, purchase the components, and put the system together. A sample layout on page 315 shows the various types of micro irrigation that are used for typical landscaping. You can buy the tubing and piping anywhere.

Manufacturers and Suppliers or Residential Irrigation Systems

ANSAN INDUSTRIES, 4704 American Rd., Rockford, IL 61109 - (800) 999-4133 then 26726 (815) 874-3541
> type - timers

AQUAPORE MOISTURE SYSTEMS, 610 S. 80th Ave., Phoenix, AZ 85043 - (800) 635-8379 (602) 936-8083
> type - drip irrigation, porous hose

COLORITE PLASTICS CO., 101 Railroad Ave., Ridgefield, NJ 07657 - (800) 631-1577
> type - porous hose

GALE GROUP, 111 N. Orlando Ave., Winter Park, FL 32789 - (800) 325-8790 (407) 621-4253
> type - drip irrigation, timers

GARDENER'S SUPPLY CO., 128 Intervale Rd., Burlington, VT 05401 - (802) 863-1700
> type - porous hose

HARDIE IRRIGATION, 27671 La Paz Rd., Laguna Niguel, CA 92656 - (800) 634-8873
> type - drip irrigation, timers

HEARTLAND PRODUCTS, P.O. Box 777, Valley City, ND 58072 - (800) 437-4780 (701) 845-1590
> type - flexible C-shape sprinkler

MELNOR, 1 Carol Pl, Moonachie, NJ 07074 - (800) 526-4631 (201) 641-5000
> type - drip irrigation, timers

NATURAL GARDENING CO., 217 San Anselmo Ave., San Anselmo, CA 94960 - (415) 456-5060
> type - drip irrigation

PRECISION POROUS PIPE, Rt. 2 Box 116C, McKenzie, TN 38201 - (901) 352-7981
> type - porous hose

RAIN BIRD, 145 N. Grand Ave., Glendora, CA 91740 - (800) 246-3782
> type - drip irrigation, timers

RAINDRIP INC., P.O. Box 2173, Chatsworth, CA 91313 - (818) 718-8004
> type - drip irrigation, timers

RAINMATIC CORP., 828 Crown Point Ave., Omaha, NE 68110 - (402) 453-5300
> type - timers

TORO, 5825 Jasmine St., Riverside, CA 92504 - (714) 688-9221
> type - drip irrigation, timers

WADE MFG., 3081 E. Hamilton Ave., Fresno, CA 93721 - (800) 695-7171 (209) 485-485-7171
> type - drip irrigation, timers

Plant Water Requirements

Maximum daily plant requirements can be quickly estimated using figure #1. This information should be used to establish the number and flow rate of emitters for individual plants. Minor differences in a localized condition can be solved by adjusting watering time.

Other sources of plant water requirements are landscape architects, designers, and the local plant supplier.

Examples

1. Mature plant, 10 ft. dia.
   avg. climate = 10 gal./day max.
2. Mature plant, 6 ft. dia.
   hot climate = 5 gal./day max.

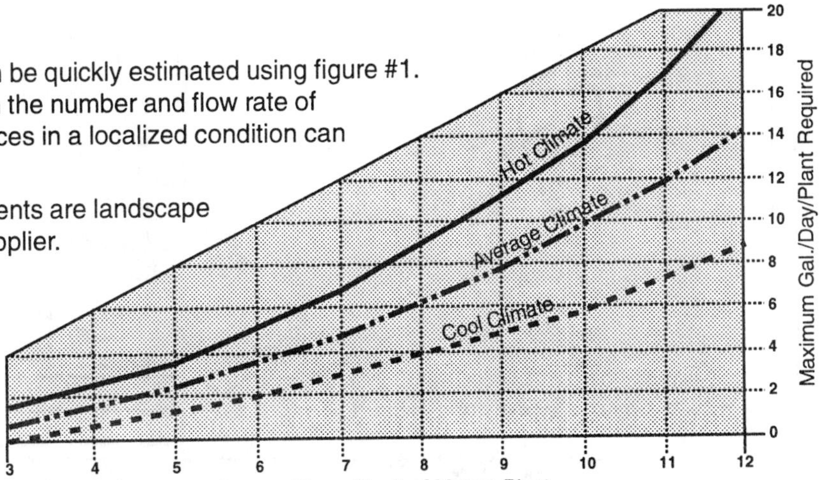

figure #1

Maximum Gal./Day/Plant Required

Canopy Diam. (Feet) of Mature Plant
Maximum Daily Plant Water Requirement

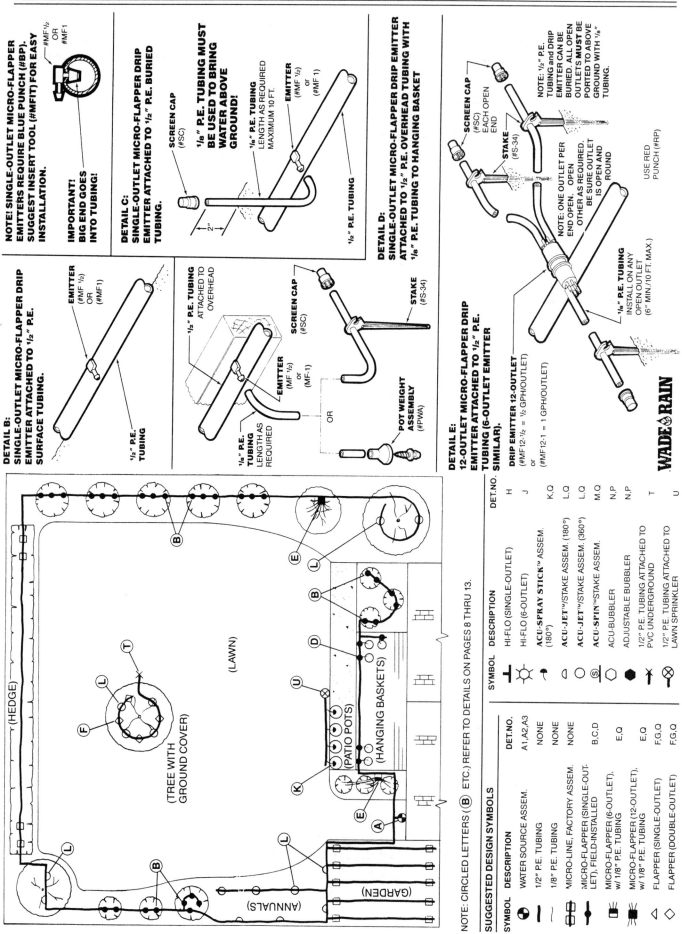

NOTE! SINGLE-OUTLET MICRO-FLAPPER EMITTERS REQUIRE BLUE PUNCH (#BP). SUGGEST INSERT TOOL (#MFIT) FOR EASY INSTALLATION.

IMPORTANT! BIG END GOES INTO TUBING!

#MF½ OR #MF1

DETAIL C:
SINGLE-OUTLET MICRO-FLAPPER DRIP EMITTER ATTACHED TO ½" P.E. BURIED TUBING.

SCREEN CAP (#SC)

⅛" P.E. TUBING MUST BE USED TO BRING WATER ABOVE GROUND!

⅛" P.E. TUBING LENGTH AS REQUIRED MAXIMUM 10 FT.

EMITTER (#MF ½) or (#MF 1)

2"

½" P.E. TUBING

DETAIL D:
SINGLE-OUTLET MICRO-FLAPPER DRIP EMITTER ATTACHED TO ½" P.E. OVERHEAD TUBING TO HANGING BASKET.

½" P.E. TUBING

⅛" P.E. TUBING TO HANGING BASKET

SCREEN CAP (#SC) EACH OPEN END

STAKE (#S-34)

NOTE: ONE OUTLET PER END OPEN. OPEN OTHER AS REQUIRED. BE SURE OUTLET IS OPEN AND ROUND

NOTE: ½" P.E. TUBING and DRIP EMITTER CAN BE BURIED. ALL OPEN OUTLETS **MUST** BE PORTED TO ABOVE GROUND WITH ⅛" TUBING.

⅛" P.E. TUBING INSTALL ON ANY OPEN OUTLET (6" MIN./10 FT. MAX.)

USE RED PUNCH (#RP)

DETAIL B:
SINGLE-OUTLET MICRO-FLAPPER DRIP EMITTER ATTACHED TO ½" P.E. SURFACE TUBING.

EMITTER (#MF ½) OR (#MF1)

½" P.E. TUBING

½" P.E. TUBING ATTACHED TO OVERHEAD

EMITTER (MF ½) or (MF-1)

⅛" P.E. TUBING LENGTH AS REQUIRED

SCREEN CAP (#SC)

STAKE (#S-34)

OR

POT WEIGHT ASSEMBLY (#PWA)

DETAIL E:
12-OUTLET MICRO-FLAPPER DRIP EMITTER ATTACHED TO ½" P.E. TUBING (6-OUTLET EMITTER SIMILAR).

DRIP EMITTER 12-OUTLET
(#MF12-½ = ½ GPH/OUTLET)
or
(#MF12-1 = 1 GPH/OUTLET)

WADE RAIN

(HEDGE)

(LAWN)

(TREE WITH GROUND COVER)

(ANNUALS)

(GARDEN)

(PATIO POTS)

(HANGING BASKETS)

NOTE: CIRCLED LETTERS (Ⓑ ETC.) REFER TO DETAILS ON PAGES 8 THRU 13.

SUGGESTED DESIGN SYMBOLS

SYMBOL	DESCRIPTION	DET.NO.
	WATER SOURCE ASSEM.	A1,A2,A3
	½" P.E. TUBING	NONE
	⅛" P.E. TUBING	NONE
	MICRO-LINE, FACTORY ASSEM.	NONE
	MICRO-FLAPPER (SINGLE-OUTLET), FIELD-INSTALLED	B,C,D
	MICRO-FLAPPER (6-OUTLET), w/ ⅛" P.E. TUBING	E,Q
	MICRO-FLAPPER (12-OUTLET), w/ ⅛" P.E. TUBING	E,Q
	FLAPPER (SINGLE-OUTLET)	F,G,Q
	FLAPPER (DOUBLE-OUTLET)	F,G,Q

SYMBOL	DESCRIPTION	DET.NO.
	HI-FLO (SINGLE-OUTLET)	H
	HI-FLO (6-OUTLET)	J
	ACU-SPRAY STICK™ ASSEM. (180°)	K,Q
	ACU-JET™/STAKE ASSEM. (180°)	L,Q
	ACU-JET™/STAKE ASSEM. (360°)	L,Q
Ⓢ	**ACU-SPIN**™ STAKE ASSEM.	M,Q
	ACU-BUBBLER	N,P
	ADJUSTABLE BUBBLER	N,P
	½" P.E. TUBING ATTACHED TO PVC UNDERGROUND	T
	½" P.E. TUBING ATTACHED TO LAWN SPRINKLER	U

315

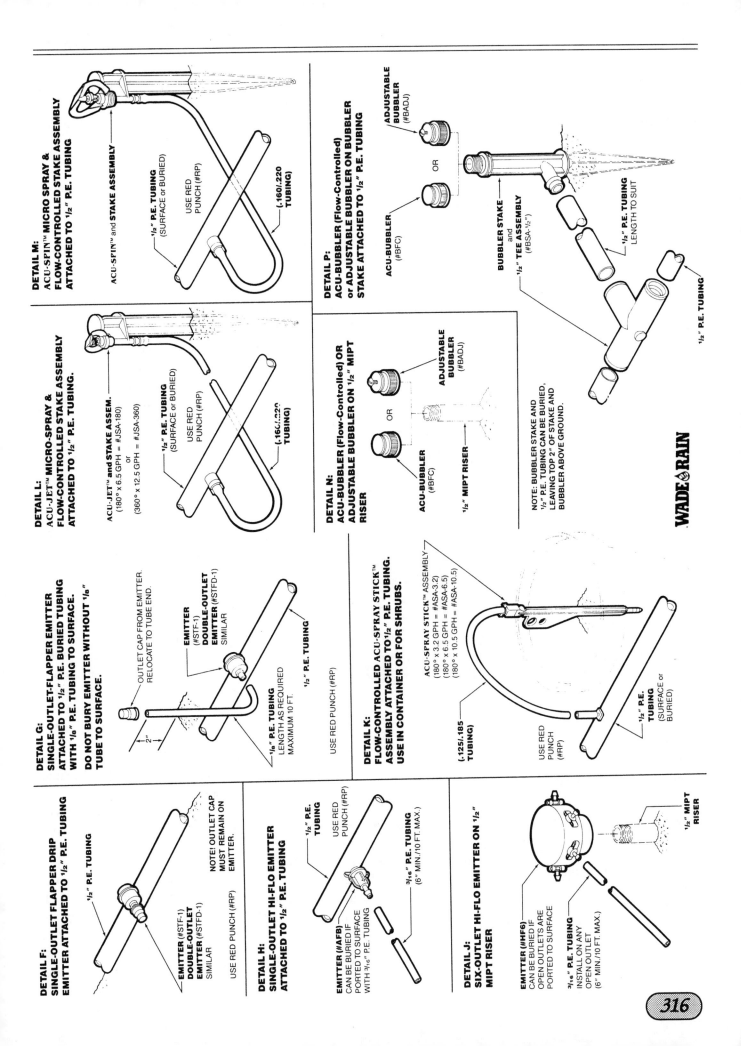

DETAIL M:
ACU-SPIN™ MICRO SPRAY & FLOW-CONTROLLED STAKE ASSEMBLY ATTACHED TO ¹/₂″ P.E. TUBING

ACU-SPIN™ and STAKE ASSEMBLY

¹/₂″ P.E. TUBING
(SURFACE or BURIED)

USE RED PUNCH (#RP)

(.160/.220 TUBING)

DETAIL L:
ACU-JET™ MICRO-SPRAY & FLOW-CONTROLLED STAKE ASSEMBLY ATTACHED TO ¹/₂″ P.E. TUBING.

ACU-JET™ and STAKE ASSEM.
(180° x 6.5 GPH = #JSA-180)
or
(360° x 12.5 GPH = #JSA-360)

¹/₂″ P.E. TUBING
(SURFACE or BURIED)

USE RED PUNCH (#RP)

(.160/.220 TUBING)

DETAIL P:
ACU-BUBBLER (Flow-Controlled) or ADJUSTABLE BUBBLER ON BUBBLER STAKE ATTACHED TO ¹/₂″ P.E. TUBING.

ADJUSTABLE BUBBLER (#BADJ)

OR

ACU-BUBBLER (#BFC)

BUBBLER STAKE and ¹/₂″ TEE ASSEMBLY (#BSA-¹/₂″)

¹/₂″ P.E. TUBING LENGTH TO SUIT

¹/₂″ P.E. TUBING

DETAIL N:
ACU-BUBBLER (Flow-Controlled) OR ADJUSTABLE BUBBLER ON ¹/₂″ MIPT RISER

ADJUSTABLE BUBBLER (#BADJ)

OR

ACU-BUBBLER (#BFC)

¹/₂″ MIPT RISER

NOTE: BUBBLER STAKE AND ¹/₂″ P.E. TUBING CAN BE BURIED, LEAVING TOP 2″ OF STAKE AND BUBBLER ABOVE GROUND.

WADE◆RAIN

DETAIL G:
SINGLE-OUTLET-FLAPPER EMITTER ATTACHED TO ¹/₂″ P.E. BURIED TUBING WITH ¹/₈″ P.E. TUBING TO SURFACE.

DO NOT BURY EMITTER WITHOUT ¹/₈″ TUBE TO SURFACE.

OUTLET CAP FROM EMITTER. RELOCATE TO TUBE END.

EMITTER (#STF-1) DOUBLE-OUTLET EMITTER (#STFD-1) SIMILAR

2″

¹/₈″ P.E. TUBING LENGTH AS REQUIRED MAXIMUM 10 FT.

¹/₂″ P.E. TUBING

USE RED PUNCH (#RP)

DETAIL K:
FLOW-CONTROLLED ACU-SPRAY STICK™ ASSEMBLY ATTACHED TO ¹/₂″ P.E. TUBING. USE IN CONTAINER OR FOR SHRUBS.

ACU-SPRAY STICK™ ASSEMBLY
(180° x 3.2 GPH = #ASA-3.2)
(180° x 6.5 GPH = #ASA-6.5)
(180° x 10.5 GPH = #ASA-10.5)

(.125/.185 TUBING)

USE RED PUNCH (#RP)

¹/₂″ P.E. TUBING (SURFACE or BURIED)

DETAIL F:
SINGLE-OUTLET FLAPPER DRIP EMITTER ATTACHED TO ¹/₂″ P.E. TUBING

¹/₂″ P.E. TUBING

EMITTER (#STF-1) DOUBLE-OUTLET EMITTER (#STFD-1) SIMILAR

NOTE! OUTLET CAP MUST REMAIN ON EMITTER.

USE RED PUNCH (#RP)

DETAIL H:
SINGLE-OUTLET HI-FLO EMITTER ATTACHED TO ¹/₂″ P.E. TUBING

¹/₂″ P.E. TUBING

USE RED PUNCH (#RP)

EMITTER (#AFB) CAN BE BURIED IF PORTED TO SURFACE WITH ³/₁₆″ P.E. TUBING.

³/₁₆″ P.E. TUBING (6″ MIN./10 FT. MAX.)

DETAIL J:
SIX-OUTLET HI-FLO EMITTER ON ¹/₂″ MIPT RISER

EMITTER (#HF6) CAN BE BURIED IF OPEN OUTLETS ARE PORTED TO SURFACE

¹/₂″ MIPT RISER

³/₁₆″ P.E. TUBING INSTALL ON ANY OPEN OUTLET (6″ MIN./10 FT. MAX.)

Q: I want to convert my car to run on natural gas too. Will operating a small natural gas compressor push up my utility much at home? Overall, is it less expensive to run my car on natural gas or gasoline?

A: Using a small gas compressor at home costs about 75 cents per gasoline gallon equivalent (GGE). Engine maintenance costs are reduced by two-thirds when running on compressed natural gas (CNG). A simple conversion kit can allow your car to run on either CNG or gasoline at the flip of a switch.

Running your car on CNG helps make the U.S. more energy independent and reduces smog. Ninety percent of the natural gas used is produced in the U.S. Running your car on CNG produces 90 percent less carbon monoxide, 85 percent less hydrocarbons and 39 percent less oxides of nitrogen (brown smog).

CNG is a safer fuel in many ways than gasoline. The ignition temperature of natural gas is 1200 degrees, twice as high as gasoline. The thick-walled gas cylinder, located under or in the trunk, is stronger and more impact resistant than a sheet metal gasoline tank. Leaks do not puddle like gasoline.

Engine maintenance costs are less with CNG. Spark plugs last 150,000 miles and it's not uncommon for engines to run for 500,000

miles without an overhaul. Cold weather start-up is improved. Octane of natural gas is 130 as compared to only about 90 for gasoline. Engine oil stays much cleaner.

Natural gas vehicle conversion kits are usually set up as bi-fuel. They automatically switch the fuel source, timing and other engine controls. The gasoline injection portion

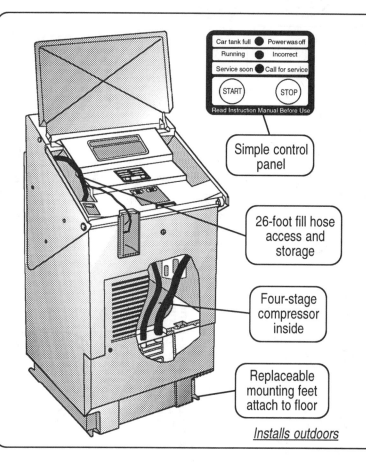

Car tank full　●　Power was off
Running　　　　Incorrect
Service soon　●　Call for service
(START)　(STOP)
Read Instruction Manual Before Use

Simple control panel

26-foot fill hose access and storage

Four-stage compressor inside

Replaceable mounting feet attach to floor

Installs outdoors

of the system is unchanged and functional.

New conversion kits have electronics to interface with the computer brain in most post 1985 fuel injected cars. They can be switched (on the dashboard) between gasoline and CNG while driving with no hesitation in performance.

Home-use compressors are simple to operate. Attach the fill nozzle to a small receptacle hidden

in the front grill. Turn on the compressor. It shuts off automatically when the gas cylinder is full to the proper pressure.

The small automatic gas compressor is connected to the natural gas line and runs on electricity like your air conditioner compressor. Also over 1,000 fast-fill (five minutes) public gas filling stations are open across the U.S.

Most passenger car conversions have one 12-inch diameter gas cylinder which holds about five GGE. This gives a daily range of 100 to 150 miles on natural gas alone. The compressor produces about one GGE per hour. A car is usually refilled at night when lower off-peak electric rates are often in effect.

Q: The beater bar brushes on my Hoover vacuum cleaner are worn down and it doesn't clean well. Is it worthwhile to have the brushes replaced?

A: It is worthwhile to repair your vacuum cleaner beater bar. Vacuum cleaners have fairly powerful motors that use much electricity. With worn brushes, you have to run it longer and this wastes electricity.

Beater bar brushes are easy to replace yourself. Remove the vacuum's bottom plate and release the agitator belt. Remove the agitator and slide out the old brushes. Slip in the new brushes and reassemble.

Cost per Gasoline Gallon Equivalent (¢ per gge) on Your Utility Bills

Electric Rate - ¢ per kilowatt-hour

Natural Gas Rate - ¢/therm	4.0¢	4.5¢	5.0¢	5.5¢	6.0¢	6.5¢	7.0¢	7.5¢	8.0¢	8.5¢	9.0¢	9.5¢	10.0¢	10.5¢	11.0¢	11.5¢	12.0¢
30¢	40.1	40.8	41.5	42.2	42.9	43.7	44.4	45.1	45.8	46.5	47.2	47.9	48.6	49.3	50.0	50.7	51.4
35¢	45.8	46.5	47.2	47.9	48.6	49.3	50.0	50.7	51.4	52.1	52.8	53.5	54.2	54.9	55.6	56.3	57.0
40¢	51.5	52.2	52.9	53.6	54.3	55.0	55.7	55.4	56.1	56.8	57.5	58.2	58.9	59.6	60.3	61.0	61.7
45¢	57.2	57.9	58.6	59.3	60.0	60.7	61.4	62.1	62.8	63.5	64.2	64.9	65.6	66.3	67.0	67.7	68.4
50¢	62.9	63.6	64.3	65.0	65.7	66.4	67.1	67.8	68.5	69.2	69.9	70.6	71.3	72.0	72.8	73.5	74.2
55¢	68.6	69.3	70.0	70.7	71.4	72.1	72.8	73.5	74.2	74.9	75.6	76.3	77.0	77.7	78.4	79.1	79.8
60¢	74.3	75.0	75.7	76.4	77.1	77.8	78.5	79.2	79.9	80.6	81.3	82.0	82.7	83.4	84.1	84.8	85.5
65¢	80.0	80.7	81.4	82.1	82.8	83.5	84.2	84.9	85.6	86.3	87.0	87.7	88.4	89.1	89.8	90.5	91.2
70¢	85.7	86.3	87.0	87.7	88.4	89.1	89.8	90.5	91.2	91.9	92.6	93.3	94.0	94.7	95.4	96.1	96.8
75¢	91.4	92.1	92.8	93.5	94.2	94.9	95.6	96.3	97.0	97.7	98.4	99.1	99.8	100.5	101.2	101.9	102.6
80¢	97.1	97.8	98.7	99.4	100.3	101.0	101.7	102.4	103.1	103.8	104.5	105.2	105.9	106.6	107.3	108.0	108.7

The chart shows the cost to operate your car on CNG by compressing the natural gas at home. The intersection of your local electric and gas rates shows the cost of a gasoline gallon equivalent (¢ per gge). A gge of CNG gives the same energy and range as one gallon of gasoline. The electric costs are based on using a FuelMaker compressor.

Computerized Electronic Bi-Fuel Compressed Natural Gas Conversion Kit

Solid State Closed Loop Electronic GFI (gaseous fuel injection) System - offers both fleet operators and individual vehicle owners a host of features and benefits that include -

• Computer based throttle body fuel injection -
• Above throttle fumigation
• Operates independently of OEM systems
• Self-adjusting spark angle or advance control to meet changing road conditions
• Manual control of choke (CNG or gasoline) and recalibration of fuel gauge for accurate measurement of either fuel
• Programmable idle speed and governing for maximum economy
• Expandable interfacing

Universal Application -

• Ideal for any gasoline engine from 50hp to 450hp in size
• Works with naturally aspirated or boosted engines
• Automatic altitude, temperature and fuel heating value compensation
• Applicable for systems with gas recirculation and catalytic converters
• Works with both distributor and distributorless ignition systems

Easy Installation and Calibration -

• System installation in less than 4 hours
• 65% fewer parts than mechanical systems
• Four air/fuel ratio and spark advance adjustments
• Rate and onset point EGR adjustment
• Stoichiometric air/fuel ration adjustment
• Adjustments for engine size and individual performance characteristics
• Can be totally recalibrated if moved to a new vehicle or if software is updated

Interfaces with -

Battery power
Switched power
Fuel Injector
Starter Solenoid
Coil Negative
Knock Sensor
TDC or tachometer
Intake air temp.
Manifold skin temp.
Selector switch
Oxygen sensor

Typical Conversion Kit Installation

High pressure gas line
Pressure regulator
Filter
Gas nozzles
MAP vacuum line tee
Engine coolant

"GFI System" by Stewart & Stevenson

Manufacturers of Small and Medium-size Natural Gas Compressors

BAUER COMPRESSORS INC., 1328 Azalea Garden Rd., Norfolk, VA 23502 - (804) 855-6006
  <u>output rate</u> - 2.0 gge   <u>size</u> - 24" long x 26" wide x 57" high   <u>pressure</u> - 3,000 or 3,600 psi
  <u>features</u> - single dispenser hose - allows for manual, timed, or fast fill with storage cylinders; optional extra fill hose; automatic final pressure shutdown, built-in timer
  <u>prices</u> - complete system - $14,000

FUELMAKER INC., 4745 Amelia Earhart Dr. #470, Salt Lake City, UT 84116 - (801) 328-0671
  <u>output rate</u> - .82 gge   <u>size</u> - 21" long x 20" wide x 39" high   <u>pressure</u> - 3,000 psi
  <u>features</u> - single dispenser hose - allows for manual, timed, or fast fill with storage cylinders; noise level - 45 dB at 16 feet; for fast fill - mounts on four storage cylinder cascade
  <u>prices</u> - complete system - $4,000

ILLINOIS INDUSTRIAL EQUIP., 16450 S. 104th Ave., Orland Park, IL 60462 - (708) 460-7070
  <u>output rate</u> - 2.0 gge   <u>size</u> - 48" long x 27" wide x 18" high   <u>pressure</u> - 3,000 or 3,600 psi
  <u>features</u> - single dispenser hose - allows for manual, timed, or fast fill with storage cylinders; noise level - 66 dB at 10 feet, 60 dB at 20 feet; for fast fill - mounts on four storage cylinder cascade
  <u>prices</u> - compressor assembly - $8,898; four-storage cylinder cascade - $5,428, safety breakaway hose and nozzle - $725; electrical components control box - $1,989; additional fill hose - $595

CNG Car Conversion Kit Suppliers and Conversion Facilities

ACCURATE FUEL SYSTEMS, INC., Oak & Astor Sts., Monee, IL 60449 - (800) 217-3001
AIR TESTING SERVICE, 200 W. 5th St., Lansdale, PA 19446 - (215) 362-1194
ALLSTAR COACHBUILDERS, 23010 Lake Forest, Ste. 339, Laguna Hills, CA 92653 - (714) 493-9700
ALTERNATE ENERGY CORP., 3 Brook St., Providence, RI 02903 - (401) 351-1232
ALTERNATE FUEL SPECIALISTS, 209 Alliance Blvd., Oklahoma City, OK 73128 - (405) 495-7240
ALTERNATIVE FUEL SYSTEMS INC., PO Box 373, Windham, NH 03087 - (603) 898-4686
ALTERNATIVE FUELS TECH. CORP.,111-30 Van Wyck Expwy, Jamaica, NY 11420 - (800) 264-7467
AMERICAN ECOFUEL, INC., 14290A Sullyfield Circle, Chantilly, VA 22021 - (703) 802-6302
AMERICAN GAS & TECHNOLOGY, 1695 S. Seventh St., San Jose, CA 95112 - (408) 292-6487
AMERICAN NATURAL GAS POWER, INC., 6601 Long Point Rd., Houston, TX 77055 - (713) 681-4700
ATLANTIC ADVANCED TECHOLOGIES, 330-2 Rte. 17 S., Lodi, NJ 07644 - (201) 779-5700
AUBURN CHEVROLET/GEO, 1600 Auburn Way N., Auburn, WA 98071 - (206) 833-2000
* AUTOMOTIVE NATURAL GAS INC., 265 N. Janesville St., Milton, WI 53563 - (608) 868-4626
BACHMAN NGV, 9650 Bluegrass Pkwy., Louisville, KY 40299 - (502) 499-6161
BAYTECH CORP., PO Box 1148, Los Altos, CA 94023 - (415) 949-1976
BOWGEN FUEL SYSTEMS, INC., 2745 W. Walnut Lawn, Springfield, MO 65807 - (417) 887-4773
BOYLE COMPRESSOR CO., INC., 1310 E. 49th St., Cleveland, OH 44114 - (216) 881-4747
CADY OIL CO., 5023 N. Galena Rd., Peoria Heights, IL 61614 - (309) 688-1264
CARBURETION LABS EAST, INC., 5728 Pendleton Lane, Warrenton, VA 22186 - (703) 347-5018
CARBURETION & TURBO SYSTEMS, 1897 Eagle Creek Blvd., Shakopee, MN 55379 - (612) 445-3910
CARDINAL AUTOMOTIVE INC., 7200 Fifteen Mile Rd., Sterling Heights, MI 48312 - (810) 268-3800
CARITRADE NGV SYSTEM INC., 1760 Fortin Blvd., Laval, PQ H7S 1N8 Canada - (514) 667-4700
CH 4 TECHNOLOGIES, INC., 679 Chaney, Collierville, TN 38017 - (901) 853-9125
CH 4 TECHNOLOGIES, INC., 24584 Gibson, Warren, MI 48089 - (810) 757-6281
CHAMPAGNE FUELS,1200 Spears Rd., Houston, TX 77067 - (713) 872-1618
CHESAPEAKE ALTERNATIVE FUELS CO., PO Box 18510, Baltimore, MD 21240 - (410) 768-1928
CITY FUEL SYSTEMS, INC., 3341 Scenic, Springfield, MO 65807 - (417) 889-9559
CLEAN AIR PARTNERS, INC., 5066 Santa Fe St., San Diego, CA 92109 - (619) 581-5600
CLEAN FUELS, 3125 W. Bolt, Ft. Worth, TX 76110 - (817) 924-2353
CLEAN VEHICLE SYSTEMS, 1160 Castleton Ave., Staten Island, NY 10310 - (718) 447-3038
CLEANAIRE CONVERSION CENTER, 1150 N. Peoria Ave., Tulsa, OK 74106 - (918) 836-1651
CNG AUTOMOTIVE, 4005 E. Jensen Ave., Fresno, CA 93725 - (209) 233-2711
CNG SERVICES OF PITTSBURGH, INC., 7125 Saltsburg Rd., Pittsburgh, PA 15235 - (412) 795-4698
COMBUSTION LABS INC., 4851 GA Hwy. 85, Ste. 210, Forest Park, GA 30050 - (404) 765-0425

COMPRESSED NATURAL GAS CORP., 2809 C Broadbent Pkwy., Albuquerque, NM 87107 - (505) 343-8808
COMPRESSED NATURAL GAS CORP., PO Box 557, Zephyr Cove, NV 89448 - (702) 588-7333
COMPRESSED NATURAL GAS CORP., 2441 N. Main Ste. 5, Sunset City, UT 84015 - (801) 774-5995
CONVERSIONS OF CT., 222 Pratt St., Southington, CT 06489 - (203) 238-3932
COVINGTON GAS COMPANY, 300 S. College, Covington, TN 38019 - (901) 476-9531
CRANE CARRIER CO., PO Box 582891, Tulsa, OK 74158 - (918) 836-1651
DIESEL EMISSIONS TECH. CO., Rt. 1, Box 1549, Hayes, VA 23072 - (804) 694-0865
ECOGAS CRYOGENICS, 5111 85th Ave., E. Bldg. C5, Puyallup, WA 98371 - (206) 926-7278
EDO CORP., PO Box 39, Milton, WI 53563 - (608) 868-4626
EFFICIENT FUELS, INC., 1002 McFarland Blvd., Ste. M, Northport, AL 35476 - (205) 339-9445
ENVIRONMENTAL CONVERSIONS INC., 944 W. 20th St., Ste. 2, Ogden, UT 84401 - (801) 629-0999
ENVIRONMENTAL FUELS TECH., LLC, 1442 S. Boston Ave., Tulsa, OK 74119 - (918) 599-9776
EQUITABLE GAS CO., Allegheny Center Mall Ste. 2000, Pittsburgh, PA 15212 - (412) 442-3119
EXPRO FUELS, 500 N. Loop 1604 E., Ste. 250, San Antonio, TX 78232 - (800) 831-9532 (210) 496-5300
FIVE FUELS CONVERSIONS, 300 Marshall St., Ste. 1101, Shreveport, TX 71101 - (318) 429-2525
GAS DEVELOPMENT RESOURCES, LLC, 8480 E. Valley Rd., Prescott Valley, AZ 86314 - (602) 772-6000
GAS EQUIPMENT SUPPLIES, 1467 Spitfire Pl., Port Coquitlam, BC V3C 5P1 Canada - (604) 942-3810
GASSWAGEN INC., PO Box 189, Annville, PA 17003 - (717) 867-1527
* GFI CONTROLS, 100 Hollinger Crescent, Kitchner, Ontario Canada N2K 2Z3 - (519) 576-4270
HAWTHORNE POWER SYSTEMS, 8050 Othello Ave., San Diego, CA 92111 - (619) 974-6822
* IMPCO TECHNOLOGIES, 16804 Gridley Pl., Cerritos, CA 90701 - (310) 860-6666
JL ASSOCIATES, INC., PO Box 467, Patuxent River, MD 20670 - (301) 863-9659
KING AUTOMOTIVE, 24588 Juban Rd., Denham Springs, LA 70726 - (504) 667-4771
KLEENAIR SYSTEMS, INC., PO Box 864, Martinsburg, WV 25401 - (304) 267-6441
LP GAS EQUIPMENT CORP., 29931 Beverly Rd., Romulus, MI 48174 - (313) 728-0300
LONE STAR ALTERNATIVE FUELS, 2804 Golfing Green, Dallas, TX 75234 - (214) 241-8729
* METROPANE INC., 2772 Sawbury Blvd., Columbus, OH 43235 - (800) 648-0233 (614) 792-7606
* MESA ENVIRONMENTAL, 3125 W. Bolt St., Ft. Worth, TX 76110 - (817) 924-2353
* MOGAS SALES, 4467 Juneau St., Burnaby, British Columbia, V5C 4C4 - (604) 294-3383 (604) 779-0478
MOTORFUELERS INC., 13790 B 49th St., N., Clearwater, FL 34622 - (813) 572-9762
MOUNTAIN FUEL SUPPLY CO., 180 E. 100 S., Salt Lake City, UT 84147 - (801) 534-5167
MULTI-FUEL CORP., 2384 Cedar Key, Lake Orion, MI 48360 - (810) 391-3524
NATIONAL FUEL SYSTEMS, INC., 636 Adams, Kansas City, MO 66105 - (913) 342-1328
* NATURAL FUELS CORP., 5855 Stapleton Dr. N., Denver, CO 80216 - (303) 322-4600
NATURAL GAS CONVERSIONS, INC., PO Box 6346, Chillicothe, OH 45601 - (614) 772-6231
NATURAL GAS VEHICLE TECH. CENTER, 6111 Hwy. 290 E., Austin, TX 78723 - (512) 452-1776
NATURAL GAS VEHICLES, INC., 41 S. Grant Ave., Columbus, OH 43215 - (614) 888-1099
NESC WILLIAMS INC., PO Box 31, Zanesville, OH 43702 - (614) 453-0375
NGV ECOTRANS TECH CENTER, 2424 E. Olympic Blvd., Los Angeles, CA 90021 - (213) 627-3333
NGV SYSTEMS INC., 2250 Cherry Industrial Cr., Long Beach, CA 90805 - (310) 630-5768
PARDEE ADVANCED FUELS, INC., PO Box 960, New Castle, DE 19720 - (302) 654-1098
PRO-STAFF FUELS LTD., PO Box 91016, W. Vancouver, BC V7V 3N3 Canada - (604) 992-8075
PROPANE EQUIPMENT CORP., 11 Apple St., Tinton Falls, NJ 07724 - (908) 747-3795
SOUTHERN UNION ECONOFUEL CO., 6111 E. Hwy. 290, Austin, TX 78723 - (512) 452-1776
STARGHILL ALTERNATIVE ENERGY CORP., 14411 Livernois, Detroit, MI 48238 - (313) 933-4141
STATE AVENUE GOODYEAR, 7908 State Ave., Kansas City, KS 66112 - (913) 788-7272
* STEWART & STEVENSON, P.O. Box 220, Commerce City, CO 80022 - (303) 287-7441
SYNCHRO-START PRODUCTS, INC., 6250 W. Howard St., Niles, IL 60714 - (708) 967-7730
TAR HEEL ENERGY CORP., 2708 Discovery Dr., Raleigh, NC 27604 - (919) 836-2370
TDM WORLD CONVERSION, LTD., PO Box 214587, Auburn Hills, MI 48321 - (810) 377-2288
TEECO PRODUCTS, 7471 Reese Rd., Sacramento, CA 95828 - (916) 688-3535
TRANSTAR TECHNOLOGIES, LC., 2415 Beatrice St., Dallas, TX 75208 - (214) 761-0143
TREN FUELS, 701 Brazos, Ste. 520, Austin, TX 78701 - (512) 320-1421
UNITED ENVIRONMENTAL, INC., 5555 W. Reno, Oklahoma City, OK 73127 - (405) 942-1676
WALLACE TESTING LABS, 2140 Wirtcrest, Houston, TX 77055 - (713) 956-7705
WILLIAMS DETROIT DIESEL - ALLISON, 2602 S. 19th Ave., Phoenix, AZ 85009 - (602) 257-0561
WINGO EQUIPMENT CO., INC., 25222 Glen Loch Dr., The Woodlands, TX 77380 - (713) 367-9000

*indicates complete kit manufacturer or assembler

Q: I'm tired of being a doorman for my cat and dog. Cold air comes in during winter and insects during summer. What types of inexpensive, easy-to-install automatic pet doors are available?

A: Frequently opening a door for your pets wastes a lot of energy year-round. Also, in the summer, you must battle mosquitoes and moths. If your pets are like mine, they are never in a hurry to get through the door.

There are many easy-to-install, energy efficient pet door designs to fit standard doors, sliding glass doors, windows and screens. Sizes range from a 6-inch by 6-inch opening for cats to a 15-inch by 27-inch opening for large dogs.

The most efficient ones use brush-type or other flexible weatherstripping to block air leaks. The swinging door often has molded-in magnets so it centers in the frame when it's closed. Other tight-sealing pet doors use combination in and out flexible flapper doors that seal against the frame.

Most pet doors have some design provision for locking, security is not generally a problem. Most thieves will not reach a hand through a large pet door knowing there may be a doberman or pit bull on the other side. A pet door indicates a barking dog and often deters a thief.

Four-way, battery-operated pet doors with an automatic lock keep unwanted animals from visiting. They can be set to in-only, out-only, both ways or locked. Most door flappers are made of clear plastic so your pet can see through it. Models with a built-in outdoor step make entry easier for your pet.

Your pet wears a small collar with a magnet or signaling device in it. A mechanism in the pet door senses the magnet or signal and allows only your pet to enter or exit. Without the collar, it will not open. Less expensive, manual four-way doors are available without the automatic sensors.

There are do-it-yourself pet door kits designed just for sliding glass patio doors. The pet door is built into the bottom of a one-foot wide glass door section. The height

is adjustable to fit most standard sliding door tracks. It is very secure and locks to your existing door when it's closed.

Two new designs of through-the-screen pet doors are simple to install. One design uses a channel that screws to the corner of the window screen frame. Just cut out the lower corner of the screen and screw on the channel.

Another simple snap-together design can be mounted anywhere in the screen. Use a template to cut a hole in the screen and snap the two frame halves together. The swinging pet door is attached to one of the halves.

Q: I cleaned and switched on my ceiling paddle fans to high speed to make sure they are working. One of them wobbled quite a lot. Last year it seemed fine. What would cause the wobble?

A: One of the blades probably came loose over winter. Since you generally run it on low speed (in reverse direction) in the winter, the wobble was not very noticeable.

Tighten all the screws that hold each blade on to the hub. If it still wobbles, the finish on one of the blades may have cracked and moisture has gotten in. This makes it heavier and out of balance. Replace that blade.

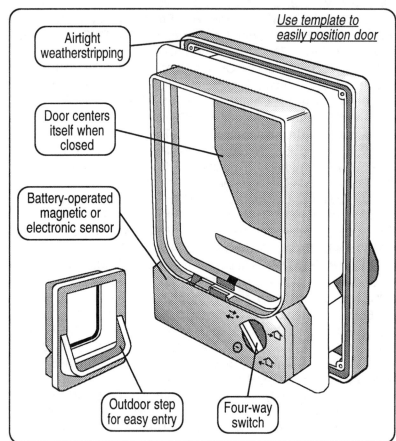

Airtight weatherstripping

Door centers itself when closed

Battery-operated magnetic or electronic sensor

Outdoor step for easy entry

Four-way switch

Use template to easily position door

Pet Doors for Sliding Glass Patio Doors

HALE SECURITY PET DOORS, 5622 N. 52nd Ave., Glendale, AZ 85301 - (800) 888-8914

pet opening area - 5½"w x 7½"h, 6½"w x 9½"h, 8½"w x 12½"h, 8½"w x 16"h, 11"w x 16"h, 11"w x 19½"h, 11"w x 23½"h, 11"w x 27½"h, 14"w x 19½"h, 14"w x 23½"h, 15½"w x 27½"h - all sizes come with standard 1" rise, optional 5" rise is available
door material - fully weatherstripped soft flexible flaps - lexan security cover - double flaps available in most models - $^3/_{16}$" thick tempered glass   adjustment range - 78½" - 80½" install in glass track only

IDEAL PET PRODUCTS, 24735 Ave. Rockefeller, Valencia, CA 91355 - (805) 294-2266

pet opening area - 5"w x 8"h 2" rise, 7"w x 11¼"h 2" rise, 9"w x 15"h 2" rise
door material - fully weatherstripped soft flexible flaps with a foam bumper - lock out security cover - safety glass
adjustment range - 78 $^5/_8$" - 80 $^7/_8$" install in glass track only   features - Fits right/left hand doors and has a security lock.

JOHNSON PET-DOR, 320 N. Graves Ave., Oxnard, CA 93030 - (800) 634-8666 (805) 988-4800

pet opening area - 5"w x 7½"h 3" rise, 8½"w x 12½"h 3" rise, 11½"w x 16½"h 10" rise
door material - weatherstipped around the soft two-way flexible vinyl flap - durable aluminum frame - shatter resistant tempered safety glass - magnetic closures to keep flap secure   adjustment range - 77½" - 82½" install in glass track only
features - It is available with a reversible door lock for left or right hand doors. It self-adjusts to any track size in adjustment range without cutting.

PATIO PACIFIC INC., 1931-C N. Gaffey St., San Pedro, CA 90731 - (800) 826-2871

pet opening area - 6"w x 9"h 1½" rise, 8"w x 12"h 1½" rise, 11"w x 20"h 6" rise
door material - weatherized flap with a magnetic wind catch - durable aluminum frame - shatterproof fiberglass panel, also available in clear plexiglass or screen   adjustment range - 77½" - 81" install in glass or outside screen track
features - The pet door can be ordered in a custom height for sliding window tracks.

PET-EZE, 13736 Saticoy St., Van Nuys, CA 91402 - (800) 843-7366 (818) 787-0041

pet opening area - 5½"w x 7½"h 2" rise, 8"w x 11"h 2" rise, 8"w x 15"h 5" rise, 10½"w x 15"h 5" rise, 10½"w x 15"h 9" rise
door material - all weather, soft and clear flap - heavy-duty aluminum frame - clear tempered safety glass - weatherstrip and adaptor included   adjustment range - 77½" - 81" install in glass track only
features - It has a reversible built-in security lock and it is also available with an outside keyed lock.

PRIDE PET DOOR, PO Box 4458, Glendale, CA 91202 - (213) 245-5185

pet opening area - 4½"w x 6½"h 4" rise, 8"w x 11"h 4" rise, 10½"w x 15"h 4" rise
door material - flexible dual-action rubber panel with imbedded magnets - heavy duty aluminum frame - clear or obscure tempered glass and full length weatherstripping - tempered hardboard security cover in a white laminate
adjustment range - 77½" - 81" install in glass or outside screen track
features - It fits left or right sliding doors and there is a security locking device.

Through-the-Door Pet Doors

ANI MATE INC., 1300 S. Frazier, Ste 303, Conroe, TX 77301 - (409) 760-4333

pet opening area - 5½"w x 5½"h, 8¾"w x 10¼"h, 11¾"h x 14$^1/_8$"h
door material - transparent flap - weatherproof brush and magnetic closure
features - Available in a special glass fitting cat flap for all single/double glazing windows or glass doors. One pet door is a 4-way locking door, you can set it out only, in only, unlocked or fully locked.

CONAGRA PET PRODUCTS (SERGEANTS), 2258 Darbytown Rd., Richmond, VA 23231 - (800) 228-9031

pet opening area - 5$^1/_6$"w x 7$^4/_{16}$"h, 8$^9/_{16}$"w x 12$^{11}/_{16}$"h, 11$^4/_{16}$"h x 17$^{14}/_{16}$"h
door material - smoky, magnetized, and heavy vinyl flap - aluminum frame - weather proof security lock out panel

GUN DOG HOUSE DOOR CO., Box 92B, RR 1, Sabin, MN 56580 - (218) 789-7128

pet opening area - one sits fits all 12½"w x 17½"h opening
door material - two -way door with ¼" clear plexiglass with adjustable spring hinges - welded aluminum frame

HALE SECURITY PET DOORS, 5622 N. 52nd Ave., Glendale, AZ 85301 - (800) 888-8914

pet opening area - 5½"w x 7½"h, 6½"w x 9½"h, 8½"w x 12½"h, 8½"w x 16"h, 11"w x 16"h, 11"w x 19½"h, 11"w x 23½"h, 11"w x 27½"h, 14"w x 19½"h, 14"w x 23½"h, 15½"w x 27½"h
door material - fully weatherstripped soft flexible flaps - lexan security cover - double flaps available in most models
features - The pet door may be custom built to fit french doors, special wall or window applications.

IDEAL PET PRODUCTS, 24735 Ave. Rockefeller, Valencia, CA 91355 - (805) 294-2266

pet opening area - 5"w x 8"h, 7"w x 11"h, 9"w x 15"h, 10½"w x 15"h, 15"w x 20"h
door material - clear flexible flap - high-impact thermoplastic - inner telescoping frame that adapts to hollow core and solid doors

JOHNSON PET-DOR, 320 N. Graves Ave., Oxnard, CA 93030 - (800) 634-8666 (805) 988-4800

pet opening area - 5$^1/_8$"w x 7½"h, 8$^5/_8$"w x 12½"h, 8$^5/_8$"w x 12$^5/_8$"h, 11½"w x 16½"h, 11½"w x 16$^7/_8$"h, 14¾"w x 19½"h
door material - weatherstipped around the soft two-way flexible vinyl flap - durable aluminum or plastic frame - magnetic closures to keep flap secure

PET-EZE, 13736 Saticoy St., Van Nuys, CA 91402 - (800) 843-7366 (818) 787-0041

   pet opening area - 5³/₈"w x 7"h, 8¼"w x 11"h, 10¼"w x 15"h, 14"w x 23"h
   door material - all weather, soft and clear flap - heavy-duty aluminum frame - flap magnets and an adjustable magnet bar can be raised or lowered to meet the flap magnets - heavy gauge steel security cover
   features - A spring loaded lock provides maximum security.

PLAZA ENTERPRISES INC., PO Box 307, Keosauqua, IA 52565 - (319) 293-7160

   pet opening area - 6"w x 8"h, 11"w x 13"h, 13"w x 19¾"h
   door material - durable high-impact styrene - permanent magnets on the door and frame - nylon lock security system

PRIDE PET DOOR, PO Box 4458, Glendale, CA 91202 - (213) 245-5185

   pet opening area - 4¼"w x 6½"h, 8"w x 11"h, 8½"w x 10"h, 10½"w x 15"h, 14½"w x 21¾"h
   door material - flexible dual-action rubber panel with imbedded magnets - heavy duty aluminum frame - tempered hardboard security cover in a white laminate

REILOR INC., 417 Caredean Dr., Horsham, PA 19044 - (800) 521-5294 (215) 956-0550

   pet opening area - 5⁷/₈"w x 6¼"h, 6¼"w x 5¼"h, 8½"w x 9¼"h, 11³/₈"w x 12¾"h
   door material - the magnetic and weatherproof flaps are available with a solid, clear or a soft flexible flap - interior security panel
   features - Available as a 4-way cat flap with a 4 position rotary security lock that has in only, out only, fully opened or fully locked. These pet doors are also available to fit on glass windows or doors.

Through-the-Wall Pet Doors

HALE SECURITY PET DOORS, 5622 N. 52nd Ave., Glendale, AZ 85301 - (800) 888-8914

   pet opening area - 5½"w x 7½"h, 6½"w x 9½"h, 8½"w x 12½"h, 8½"w x 16"h, 11"w x 16"h, 11"w x 19½"h, 11"w x 23½"h, 11"w x 27½"h, 14"w x 19½"h, 14"w x 23½"h, 15½"w x 27½"h
   door material - available in single or double flexible flaps -all aluminum self-framing, carpeted tunnel for walls up to 10" thick

Through-the-Window (sash or slider) Pet Doors

CLEAR THRU-CAT DOOR, 10147 Timbertrail Dr., Dallas, TX 75229 - (214) 353-9501

   pet opening area - 7"w x 7¼"h
   door material - clear, high impact panels and pet flap made of lexan® - swings both ways has weather seals, magnetic catch and lock pin
   adjustment range - 20" - 28", 20" - 36", 20" - 44", 20" - 52"
   features - The pet door is easy to install in windows that raise or slide. It is adjustable and if you relocate the doorand braces can be twisted from the old window with a screwdriver.

Through-the-Screen Pet Doors

IDEAL PET PRODUCTS, 24735 Ave. Rockefeller, Valencia, CA 91355 - (805) 294-2266

   pet opening area - 7¼"w X 14½"h

JOHNSON PET-DOR, 320 N. Graves Ave., Oxnard, CA 93030 - (800) 634-8666 (805) 988-4800

   pet opening area - 8"w x 10"h

PRIDE PET DOOR, PO Box 4458, Glendale, CA 91202 - (213) 245-5185

   pet opening area - 4¾"w x 7¹/₈"h, 8"w x 10"h, 8½"w x 12½"h, 11½"w x 16⁷/₈"h

Automatic Pet Doors - pet wears special collar

ANI MATE INC., 1300 S. Frazier, Ste 303, Conroe, TX 77301 - (409) 760-4333

   pet opening area - 5½"w x 5½"h
   door material - transparent flap - weatherproof brush and magnetic closure - 4-way lock setting
   features - An adaptor kit is available for glass windows or doors.

JOHNSON PET-DOR, 320 N. Graves Ave., Oxnard, CA 93030 - (800) 634-8666 (805) 988-4800

   pet opening area - 5½"w x 5½"h
   door material - clear flap with magnetic closure - 4-way lock setting

REILOR INC., 417 Caredean Dr., Horsham, PA 19044 - (800) 521-5294 (215) 956-0550

   pet opening area - 6½"w x 5"h
   door material - the magnetic and weatherproof flaps are available with a solid, clear or with a soft flexible flap - interior security panel - 4-way lock setting

SOLO INC., 970 W. 25th St., Upland, CA 91784 - (909) 989-9999

   pet opening area - 8"w x 10"h, 10"w x 12"h, 10"w x 15"h, 12"w x 15"h
   door material - bronzed, transparent lexan - dark bronzed aluminum frame - interior trim plate is textured acrylic
   features - Electrical motor raises and lowers door automatically. Door comes with a 6-foot extension cord but can also be hard wired inside the wall or connected to a home security system. The unit comes with an on/off switch.

Instructions for Making an Efficient Pet Door

1) First determine the size of the opening that you will need for your cat. An eight-inch square opening should be adequate for most cats. To be safe, cut a hole in a piece of cardboard to make sure your cat can fit through it.

2) Cut two rectangular openings through your wall that are level with your interior floor surface.. Based on your house construction, you will have to determine the best method to cut the wall openings.

3) Finish the sides of the opening with exterior grade plywood. Lay a piece of ½-inch plywood for the bottom of the opening. This will provide a lip for the door to rest against and a ridge to keep rain from leaking under the doors.

4) Using a piece of cardboard, cut a door piece to reach from the top of the interior wall to the bottom of the exterior wall. You will use this cardboard piece as a template for making the actual plastic doors.

5) Once you have made the cardboard template, cut four door pieces from either $^1/_{16}$ or $^1/_8$-inch clear acrylic (Plexiglass) plastic sheeting. $^1/_{16}$-inch material should be plenty strong and lighter for an old cat to push open. You will also need some acrylic plastic glue.

6) Cut ½-inch wide strips of the acrylic to use as spacers to form the air gap for the thermal doors. Glue a strip on edge around the perimeter of two of the doors. (See diagram.) Glue the other side of the door over the spacers to complete the plastic thermal doors. You can also use a single-panel acrylic door and attach thin foam insulation to the opposite side that your pet pushes against to go in or out.

7) Saw the piano hinge to the proper length and screw it near the top edge of each plastic door. You can drill the holes in the plastic very easily. Don't overtighten the screws in the plastic, or you will strip out the holes.

8) Stick ½-inch wide adhesive-backed foam weatherstripping around the edge of the door where it rests on the stops in the openings.

9) Screw the hinges to the interior and exterior of the openings in the walls and let the doors close against the wood finish piece at the bottom of the opening.

10) Cut the ¼ x ¼-inch wood stop strips long enough to reach from the bottom of the opening to the top at the same angle as the doors that are mounted. Position them on the sides of the opening so they just touch the foam weatherstripping on the doors and just slightly compress it. Don't push them so tight that they move the bottom of the door away from the finish piece at the bottom.

11) Nail the stops in that position. Put finishing trim around the interior edge of the opening. Paint the opening sides and trim with good-quality house paint.

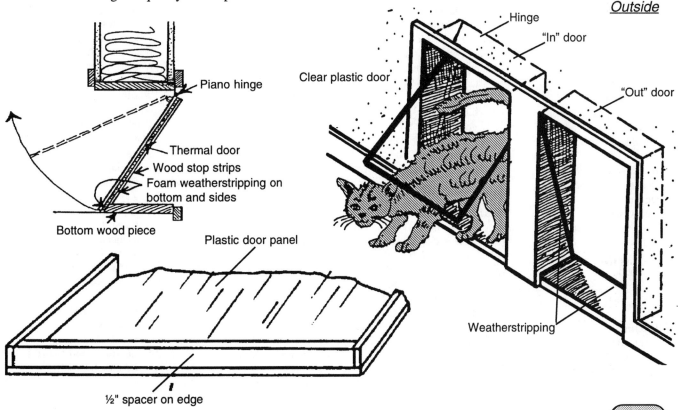

Piano hinge

Thermal door
Wood stop strips
Foam weatherstripping on bottom and sides

Bottom wood piece

Plastic door panel

½" spacer on edge

Outside

Hinge

"In" door

Clear plastic door

"Out" door

Weatherstripping

324

Index

A

Air barrier wrap, 69
Air cleaner
  central, 61
  room, 65
Air conditioner
  cover, 53, 137
  central, 9
  ductless, 5
  filter, 205, 313
  maintenance, 57
  room and window, 29
Appliances, 177-224
Attic
  cooling, 229
  foil, 231
  ventilation, 73
Automated house system, 305
Automobile - natural gas, 317
Awnings, 145

B

Barbecue grills, 297
Battery charger, 117
Bath fan, 89
Blower, 1, 285
Boiler, 33
Bookcase, 138, 268
Bread maker, 221
Brick veneer siding, 249
Burglar alarm systems, 293

C

Carbon dioxide gas, 17, 65, 101
Caulking, 301
Ceiling heat, 13
Ceiling paddle fan, 69
Central air conditioning, 9
Chimney flue, 73
Clothes
  dryer, 189
  dryer vent, 193
  washer, 185
Combustion, 193
Compressor, 5, 9, 17
Condensing heat exchanger, 1
Construction, 225-272
Crawl space, 261

D

Deadbolt lock, 29
Dehumidifying heat pipes, 156
Direct vent, 41
Dishwasher, 185
Door threshold, 261
Doors
  fiberglass, 121
  wood, 124
Dryer, 189
Dryer vent, 193

E-F

Electric
  radiant heat, 13, 273
  range, 201
  water heater, 161
Electronic air cleaner, 61, 65

Entry doors, 121, 124
Fan cooling, 69, 73
Fireplace
  gas, 49
  masonry - Finnish, 45
  wood-burning, 141, 257
Floor heating, 21
Flue liner, 241
Fluorescent lights, 25, 225, 273
Foam block/concrete walls, 237
Formeldehyde test, 49, 97
Furnace
  filter, 205
  gas, 1
  zone control, 25

G-H

Gas
  furnace, 1
  range, 205, 305
  space heater, 41
  water heater. 157
Glass block windows, 125
Heat pipe dehumidifier, 156
Heat pump, 7, 17
Heat recovery ventilator, 85
Heat trap fittings, 169
Heating & Cooling, 1-60
HID lighting, 277
Humidifiers, 93
Humidity, 153

I-J

Indoor air quality
  formaldehyde test, 49, 97
  heat recovery vent, 85
  room air cleaner, 65
  room humidifiers, 93
  whole-house air cleaner, 61
Indoor Environment, 61-100
Indoor ventilation, 85, 89
Indoor window shutters, 137
Induction cooking, 201
Instantaneous water heater, 149
Insulation
  blown-in, 213, 277
  non-settling, 257
  rigid foam, 97, 121
  wall exterior, 260
  wall interior, 253
  water heater, 171

K-L

Kitchen appliances
  dishwasher, 217
  electric range, 201
  gas range, 205
  microwave, 209
  self-cleaning oven, 237
  small appliances, 221
Landscaping, 313
Lawn mowers, 285
Leaky faucet, 129
Leaky toilet, 281
Lighting
  fluorescents, 25, 225, 273

low voltage, 281
outdoor, 277

M-N

Masonry fireplace, 45
Microwave oven, 209
Mini-split system, 585
Miscellaneous 273-320
Moisture sensor dryer, 189
Natural gas automobile, 317

O-P

Outdoor security lights, 277
Ozonator pool purifier, 301
Paint
  ceramic, 229
  low-emissivity, 230
Payback
  new furnace, 2
  new heat pump, 20
  from setback thermostat, 37
Pet doors, 321
Picture radiant heater, 13
Propane heater, 41
Purifier
  water, 77

Q-R

Radiant
  barrier, 229
  electric picture heater, 13
  warm water system, 21
Radon gas, 293
Refrigerator, 153, 213
Rolling shutter, 141
Roof vents, 201, 231
Roofing materials, 197, 245, 269
Room air-conditioning, 29
Room space heaters, 41

S

Scale reducer, 81
Screens, 129
Scroll, 9, 17
Security
  automated systems, 305
  home systems, 293
  outdoor lights, 277
Setback thermostat, 37
Shade air conditioner, 53
Shading, 269
Shower heads, 53, 165
Shutters, 137, 141
Siding materials, 249
Size ceiling fan, 72
Small cooking appliances, 221
Soapstone fireplaces, 47
Solar chimney, 232
Solar window heater, 185
Soundproofing
  floor, 81
  wall, 253
Space heater, 41
Storm windows
  exterior, 113
  interior, 109
Stucco coatings, 189

Stress-skin panels, 233
Sunroom, 221
Superinsulation, 241
Surge suppressor, 197
Swimming pool purifier, 301

T-V

Thermostat, 37
Toilet improvements, 289
Top-load washers, 185
Troubleshoot
  water heater, 173
Vacuum cleaner
  allergy, 177
  central, 181
  repairs, 317
Ventilation
  ceiling paddle fans, 69
  heat recovery ventilator, 85
  oscillating pedestal fan, 9
  quiet bath fans, 89
  whole-house fan, 73
Vestibule, 265
Vinyl siding, 249

W-Z

Warm water floor heat, 21
Washing machine, 185
Water
  dam, 289
  drip lawn system, 313
  saving devices, 168, 289
Water Heating, 153-176
Water heaters
  electric, 161
  gas, 157
  heat pump, 153
  insulation, 169
  tankless, 149
  troubleshoot, 173
Water irrigation, 313
Water purifier, 77
Water softener, 81
Waterbed, 77
Whirlpool baths, 309
Whole-house fan, 73
Wind screen - door, 269
Window air conditioner, 29
Window improvements
  awnings, 145
  film, 102, 129
  glass block, 125
  improvements, 101
  shade, 133
  shutters, 137, 141
  storm - exterior, 113
  storm - interior, 109
  tilt-in, 101
Windows
  fiberglass, 107
  vinyl, 105
  wood, 117
Windows & Doors, 101-152
Wood heat, 45, 113
Zone heat, 25